REVELATION

A MANUAL

of

SPIRITUAL WARFARE

REVELATION

A MANUAL
of
SPIRITUAL WARFARE

"These shall make war with the Lamb, and the Lamb shall overcome them: for he is Lord of lords, and King of kings: and they that are with him are called, and chosen, and faithful."

Revelation 17:14

EXPOSITORY SERMONS
ON THE BOOK OF REVELATION
~ VOL. 1 ~

Max Doner

REVELATION: A Manual of Spiritual Warfare
Expository Sermons on the Book of Revelation, Vol. 1

www.ReformedLighthousePress.com

ISBN: 979-8-9858473-0-7

Cover design: www.greatwriting.org
Book layout, design and preparation for publication:
www.greatwriting.org

Unless noted otherwise, Scripture quotations are taken from the King James (Authorized) Version

REFORMED
LIGHTHOUSE PRESS

About the Author

Max Doner graduated from Sacramento State University with a B.S. in Business Administration, and from Sacramento Bible Institute with a Diploma in Bible. He founded and pastored two Reformed Baptist Churches, one in Sacramento, California, and the other in Lebanon, Oregon. After thirty-four years of pastoral ministry, he retired and now devotes his time to writing, to the church he is a member of, and to his family. He has been married to his wife, Katherine, since 1975, and has four children.

Dedication

To my wife Katherine Doner, without whose loving and loyal companionship I could have never persevered in the work of the ministry,

and to my sister in Christ Barbara Wardlaw, without whose tremendous labors this book would have never come into existence.

Chapter Contents

To the Reader

By its very nature, the book of Revelation has a degree of complexity that is irreducible and which cannot be simplified. The famous scientist Albert Einstein once said, "Everything should be made as simple as possible, but no simpler." To simplify something further than the subject matter itself permits is to lose essential elements of it, and thereby to misrepresent it.

In writing this commentary on Revelation, I have sought to make it as simple as possible, but no simpler. Therefore, I have provided an explanation of every phrase in this book, because no part of it is dispensable or unimportant to our understanding. Every phrase contributes valuable information to the reader. This necessarily means that there is a lot of explanation and interpretation that requires much attention and thought. It also explains the size of the book.

This book is not light reading, but neither is it tedious, because I have striven to make it as clear and simple as possible. It is critical that the reader give attention to the first six chapters that comprise the introduction to the book. These chapters establish the foundation for the interpretation of the entire book and provide the justification for it. Without the principles set forth in these chapters, the interpretation of the book will be much more difficult to understand. Some assertions made in these introductory chapters will be proven later in the book.

In each chapter, I have provided an introduction containing a summary of the teaching of the previous chapter. If one were to read only the introduction to each chapter and nothing else, one would have a succinct summary of the teaching of the book but would lack the proof and support for it that is contained in the body of each chapter.

As the title indicates, these chapters are expository sermons I originally preached to my own congregation. This explains the structured nature of each chapter, which contains the sermon outline for that chapter. It also explains the applications and exhortations contained in this book that flow out of its teaching. Teaching that is not applied to the life is of little value, so I have sought to assist the reader in thinking through how the truth contained in Revelation should be worked out in his or her life.

I would encourage fathers to read this book out loud to their families for family worship in the evenings, and to use it as a springboard for discussion, instruction, and evangelism of their children. It is written to be easily read out loud to others, because it is sermonic in form.

If the reader is interested, I have over 3,000 sermons from thirty-four years of pastoral ministry on SermonAudio.com that can be accessed for free. Search by speaker, type in Max Doner, and hit enter. Click on my name. This will take you to my page. Click on the filter tab to search by series. This puts up a list of all the books and topics I have preached through.

I welcome feedback from the reader regarding any matter contained in this book. I may be reached at ramosw1714@gmail.com and I will do my best to respond in a timely fashion.

I would like to acknowledge the tremendous debt of gratitude I owe to Barbara Wardlaw for typing the transcripts of these sermons from the audio version. It was from them I composed this book. I would also like to acknowledge the debt of gratitude I owe to those who assisted in the proofreading of this book. To Katherine Doner, Barbara Wardlaw, Aric Wardian, Tim Barras, Linda Schmidt, and Jeff Black, thank you for your many hours of work in finding my numerous errors. Any remaining errors are my own. If the reader finds any further errors, please bring them to my attention.

Preface

The volume in your hands is based on an exposition of the book of Revelation I conducted at the conclusion of thirty-four years of ministry as a Reformed Baptist pastor. I wish I had understood the meaning and message of Revelation at the beginning of my pastoral ministry as well as I did at the end of it. It would have greatly helped me understand and process the spiritual warfare I was experiencing during all those years of ministry.

But regrettably, like so many others, I had been schooled in dispensational premillennial futurist eschatology, and coming to an understanding of covenantal amillennial idealist eschatology was a decades-long process of arduous labor in the text of the Scriptures that was only fully completed in the last several years of my ministry.

I wish I had been able to read a book like this to help me break through the confusion of the commonly taught dispensational eschatology that ensnares and misleads so many, and which directs them into a tremendous misunderstanding of the vast bulk of Revelation.

It is with the hope of assisting others in their understanding of the meaning and message of this book that I offer it to the Christian world, and especially to those who find themselves confused and mystified by a book whose primary purpose is to help them understand and fight the spiritual warfare that surrounds them every day.

It is critical for the church to understand that the book of Revelation is a manual of spiritual warfare. It is designed by God to equip us to understand the nature of the spiritual battle we face against Satan and his helpers, and to enable us to be overcomers in that conflict.

The failure of the church to understand and follow this manual of spiritual warfare has resulted in her inability to fight that warfare with the skill, understanding, and strength she ought to have possessed. Much confusion and defeat could have been avoided had she understood it.

The sad truth is that most Christians neglect the message of this book because they cannot make much sense out of the meaning of it. This is something I hope to remedy by offering these expositions, which explain the meaning of every verse in the book.

It is spiritually liberating and empowering to believers to have the mystery and confusion removed and to gain a clear and satisfying understanding of every passage. It is deeply satisfying to finally make sense out of what has been at best, a confusing book, or at worst, a closed book to the vast majority of Christians.

I would urge a careful perusal of the bibliography at the end of this book. These are the primary and most important resources I have used in gaining an understanding of Revelation, and they will richly repay anyone who spends the time to carefully read them. My gratitude to those who have been my teachers cannot be adequately expressed. I am indebted to each of them for helping me understand the meaning and message of this book.

I have carefully weighed their interpretation of Revelation, sometimes agreeing and sometimes disagreeing with them. I have added my own reflection and meditation, so that these resulting expositions provide a clarity and completeness that significantly advances the church's understanding of this book.

My hope is that Revelation will be understood as clearly and fully as every other book in the New Testament, and that it will be frequently used and applied to the everyday experience and walk of the believer just as much as any other book in the Bible.

It is past time we stop ignoring this book because we think we cannot understand it. Here the understanding of it is made both clear and compelling. My prayer is that this understanding will become universally held throughout the church until Christ returns, with the result that the church will overcome in the spiritual warfare she faces until the end of this age.

Max S. Doner

October 26, 2017

Foreword

The Importance and Simplicity of Biblical Eschatology

To study the book of Revelation is to study the subject of eschatology. God has revealed much of His plan for the future, and eschatology is the study of that plan. This plan enables us to know what the future will be and what we might expect to experience as we move into that future.

Jesus considered it important for His disciples to understand eschatology. He demonstrated this by spending entire chapters talking about it in the Gospels. He spoke of what would happen in the whole period of time between His first and second coming because it was important for His disciples to know that information. He did not want them to be surprised or dismayed or confused by what they were going to experience in the succeeding centuries.

Through the inspiration of the Holy Spirit, the apostles repeated and expanded the teachings of Jesus about the future plan of God, with the result that the entire New Testament is saturated with eschatological teaching.

It follows, then, that since the matter of eschatology was so important to Christ and the apostles that they devoted this kind of time to it and provided this volume of information about it, it should be important to us as well.

There are two foundational concepts we need to grasp in order to be able to successfully launch into a study of eschatology.

The Importance of Eschatology

There are many Christians who question the value and importance of eschatology. They are dismayed by all the controversy surrounding it. They are mystified by the seeming complexity and obscurity of many of the passages that address it. They are confused by the conflicts and contradictions among the people who teach and write about it. As a result, they adopt a reductionist mentality toward the whole subject which can be summarized by these statements: "I know Jesus is coming back to earth again. I know He is going to fix everything that is wrong. This is all I really need to know. Do not bother me with the details."

Their attitude is this: We need to focus on the present issues and the practical matters. We need to focus on evangelism; we need to learn about child-rearing; we need teaching about husband-wife relationships; and we need instruction on the struggle with remaining sin. We need practical teaching. Do not bother us with confusing and complex prophetic schemes. Just preach the gospel.

The rebuttal to this mindset is that the Christian gospel, which is at the very core of every single practical issue, is saturated with eschatology. This is because eschatology sets forth what the gospel promises and where the gospel will bring us in the end. God has a goal to achieve with the gospel, and that goal is described by eschatology.

The central purpose of the gospel is to destroy the work of the devil which was begun in the garden of Eden, to redeem us from the effects of sin that were introduced there, and to restore us to the paradise that was lost. This is the goal of Christ's saving work. Eschatology is the description of the achievement of that work, and where it will leave us in the end.

Eschatology has to do with God's central purpose in salvation. That purpose is to bring mankind back to his original, God-intended state of perfect righteousness before God and perfect fellowship with God in a perfect world designed by God, all for the purpose of bringing glory to God. This is the end and goal of the gospel. This is what eschatology addresses.

Eschatology is about the defeat of Satan's destructive purposes and the victory of God's redemptive purposes. Eschatology is about the final triumph of the cross over sin and Satan, and their utter defeat through the saving work of Christ. In short, eschatology is simply the conclusion and the outcome of the gospel in its final vindication and triumph.

There is nothing more practical and more important than the gospel and its final vindication and triumph. Therefore, when someone says: "Just give me the practical and the important teaching," the response must be: "There is nothing more practical than eschatology. There is nothing more important and basic to the gospel and its message."

We cannot separate the gospel from eschatology because eschatology is the end and the outcome of the gospel. If the gospel matters, eschatology matters as well. The second coming, the resurrection, the final judgment, and the eternal state of the saved and the lost matter to the gospel because they are the outcome of the gospel. They are essential elements of the Christian faith.

Several passages make this connection between the gospel and eschatology clear. One cannot talk about salvation without also talking about where it leads and what its outcomes are.

In Acts 3:19–21, we have the record of Peter healing a lame man at the gate of the temple. A crowd gathered and Peter preached the gospel. He said: "*Repent ye therefore, and be converted, that your sins may be blotted out, when the times of refreshing shall come from the presence of the Lord;* [20] *And he shall send Jesus Christ, which before was preached unto you:* [21] *Whom the heaven must receive until the times of restitution of all things, which God hath spoken by the mouth of all his holy prophets since the world began.*"

From the beginning of the world, God has been speaking about the end of the world. From the beginning in Genesis 3:15 when God first proclaimed the gospel message that the seed of the woman was going to crush the head of the serpent, God has been working out that plan. The prophets constantly spoke about how it was going to unfold and be accomplished.

The Old Testament prophets spoke about both the first and the second coming of Christ. The first coming of Christ was realized in the incarnation of Jesus. From the time of Jesus, the New Testament prophets have been speaking about the second coming of Christ.

Peter's preaching of the gospel leads into and concludes with eschatology. He sets forth the gospel: repent, believe, have your sins blotted out. Then he sets forth eschatology: Christ is coming back and is going to restore all things, including a refreshing, deliverance, and renewal of all that has been corrupted by sin. The gospel leads to and concludes with eschatology. They are inseparably connected. Peter did not preach one without preaching the other.

Furthermore, notice Matthew 19:16–29 in which Jesus preaches the gospel: "*And, behold, one came and said unto him, Good Master, what good thing shall I do, that I may have eternal life?* [17] *And he said unto him, Why callest thou me good? there is none good but one, that is, God: but if thou wilt enter into life, keep the commandments.* [18] *He saith unto him, Which? Jesus said, Thou shalt do no murder, Thou shalt not commit adultery, Thou shalt not steal, Thou shalt not bear false witness,* [19] *Honour thy father and thy mother: and, Thou shalt love thy neighbor as thyself.* [20] *The young man saith unto him, All these things have I kept from my youth up: what lack I yet?* [21] *Jesus said unto him, If thou wilt be perfect, go and sell that thou hast, and give to the poor, and thou shalt have treasure in heaven: and come and follow me.* [22] *But when the young man heard that saying, he went away sorrowful: for he had great possessions."*

Jesus is preaching the gospel and saying to this man: If you believe the gospel, you will have treasure in heaven. What is heaven, and what is this treasure, and when are we going to arrive there and possess it? The answer to those questions involves eschatology.

Jesus continues in verses 23–29: "*Then said Jesus unto his disciples, Verily I say unto you, That a rich man shall hardly enter into the kingdom of heaven.* [24] *And again I say unto you, It is easier for a camel to go through the eye of a needle, than for a rich man to enter into the kingdom of God.* [25] *When his disciples heard it, they were exceedingly amazed, saying, Who then can be saved?*" Notice, the subject is still salvation.

"[26] *But Jesus beheld them, and said unto them, With men this is impossible; but with God all things are possible.* [27] *Then answered Peter and said unto him, Behold, we have forsaken all, and followed thee; what shall we have therefore?* [28] *And Jesus said unto them, Verily I say unto you, That ye which have followed me, in the regeneration when the Son of man shall sit in the throne of his glory, ye also shall sit upon twelve thrones, judging the twelve tribes of Israel.* [29] *And every one that hath forsaken houses, or brethren, or sisters, or father, or mother, or wife, or children, or lands, for my name's sake, shall receive an hundredfold, and shall inherit everlasting life.*"

In this passage in which the gospel is preached, the sacrifice required of those who embrace the gospel is set forth. Eschatology is offered and declared to be the motive for embracing the gospel and the sacrifice it entails. Jesus said: If you are going to inherit eternal life, you have to follow me. That involves sacrifice. Peter asks: If we make that sacrifice, what are we going to have as a result? Jesus answers with eschatology: There is going to be a regeneration where everything will be made new. There will be a new heaven and a new earth, and you are going to sit on thrones as judges. The point is, without eschatology, there is no motivation to embrace the gospel and the sacrifices it calls us to.

The doctrine of hell and the doctrine of heaven is part of eschatology. If we are not teaching eschatology, we have removed the motivation for embracing the gospel. The gospel is not just about the here and now, it is also about the then and there. If there is no "then" or "there," or if our understanding of it is defective or minimal, then the gospel will not mean much and we will not be greatly motivated by it, whether to believe it, preach it, or live it.

However, when we tie the gospel to its outcomes, then the gospel becomes very precious precisely because of those outcomes. This is what Jesus is doing here. In His preaching, Jesus ties the gospel to eschatology, and eschatology is the whole foundation for saying to Peter: This is why you believe and why you make the sacrifices you do as a Christian.

Finally, notice 1 Thessalonians 1:9–10: *"For they themselves shew of us what manner of entering in we had unto you, and how ye turned to God from idols to serve the living and true God."* This is the "here" and "now." You turned away from idol worship and you started serving God. What was your motivation? Why did you do that? You did it because of what is said in verse 10: *"And to wait for his Son from heaven, whom he raised from the dead, even Jesus, which delivered us from the wrath to come."* This is the "then" and "there."

It was things to come in the future that motivated the Thessalonians in the present to turn to God from idols and to serve the true and living God. If we do not understand the things to come, then we cannot preach the gospel and provide people with proper motivation to give up their false gods and embrace the true God and start serving Him. The fruit of repentance and faith and service to God is the result of belief in the second coming and deliverance from the wrath to come. We must understand the second coming and its nature, the events that surround it, and the impact it has if we are to preach the gospel.

Examples could be multiplied, but the point is that the New Testament is saturated with extensive teaching on the subject of eschatology. The preaching of the gospel is always attended with teaching on eschatology, sometimes more, sometimes less, but it is always there. You cannot read the New Testament without constantly running into end-times teaching.

Indeed, there is one whole book of twenty-two chapters that is dedicated exclusively to the issue of eschatology. If eschatology were not important and we could simply dismiss it, why did God put the book of Revelation in the Bible? People say they cannot understand it so they do not bother with it. You need to do the work of trying to understand it because it can be understood, and this book is designed to enable you to do so.

If eschatology was important enough to Jesus Christ for Him to teach us about it constantly and extensively in the Gospels, then it ought to be important enough to us to do the work of learning about it. We may not treat eschatology with a dismissive attitude when Christ does not and the entire New Testament does not.

As Christians, we have the obligation to do the hard work of focusing on and figuring out what prophetic passages mean. When we do, the richness of the gospel will be seen in a clearer light than we have ever seen it before, and it will move us to worship and live better than we ever have in the past.

The Simplicity of Eschatology

One of the reasons why people shy away from the study of eschatology is that it seems so complicated and confusing. But, in reality, the eschatological system of the Bible is very simple. There is the age we are in now, and there is the age to come that will occur after the second coming of Christ.

It is really just that simple. The Bible teaches us about this age and it teaches us about the age to come, and that is all there is. There are not seven ages as dispensationalists teach. There are not three ages as post-millennialists teach. There are just two ages. There is this world, and there is the world to come.

These two ages are distinguished and divided from each other by the second coming and the Day of Judgment. There is the age from the creation to the second coming which is called this age or this world. The second coming and the final judgment occur, and then there is the age and the world to come, which is the eternal state of the new heavens and new earth. That is all there is. This world and the world to come are distinguished and divided from each other by the second coming of Christ and the Day of Judgment.

This simple two-step eschatology, which does not include any ages other than these two, is set forth numerous times in the Scriptures.

First, notice Matthew 12:31–32. Jesus is talking about the unpardonable sin, which is blasphemy against the Holy Spirit. "*Wherefore I say unto you, All manner of sin and blasphemy shall be forgiven unto men: but the blasphemy against the Holy Ghost shall not be forgiven unto men.* [32]*And whosoever speaketh a word against the Son of man, it shall be forgiven him: but whosoever speaketh against the Holy Ghost, it shall not be forgiven him, neither in this world, neither in the world to come.*"

This age and the age to come, this world and the world to come exhaust all of time. If you are not forgiven in this age or in the age to come, you will never have forgiveness, because there is no other time period in which to be forgiven. In the parallel passage in Mark 3:29, Jesus says, "*But he that shall blaspheme against the Holy Ghost hath never forgiveness, but is in danger of eternal damnation.*" Therefore, if you are not forgiven in this world, and if you are not forgiven in the world to come, then you will never be forgiven because this world and the world to come encompass all of time.

Second, notice Mark 10:29–30 which says, "*And Jesus answered and said, Verily I say unto you, There is no man that hath left house, or brethren, or sisters, or father, or mother, or wife, or children, or lands, for my sake, and the gospel's,* [30] *But he shall receive an hundredfold now in this time, houses, and brethren, and sisters, and mothers, and children, and lands, with persecutions; and in the world to come eternal life.*" There is just "*this time*" and "*the world to come.*" There is no other time period.

The parallel passage in Luke 18:29–30 says virtually the same thing. "*And [Jesus] said unto them, Verily I say unto you, There is no man that hath left house, or parents, or brethren, or wife, or children, for the kingdom of God's sake,* [30] *Who shall not receive manifold more in this present time, and in the world to come life everlasting.*" There is this present time, and there is the world to come. There is nothing beside that.

Third, notice Luke 20:34–36: "*And Jesus answering said unto them, The children of this world marry, and are given in marriage:* [35] *But they which shall be accounted worthy to obtain that world, and the resurrection from the dead, neither marry, nor are given in marriage:* [36] *Neither can they die any more: for they are equal unto the angels; and are the children of God, being the children of the resurrection.*"

Jesus is saying there are just two worlds. There is "*this world,*" and this world encompasses all the time that people marry and are given in marriage. Then there is *"that world,"* and that world contains people who are resurrected, who are all the children of God, and who never engage in marriage ever again.

This clearly encompasses all of time. Marriage and death began in Genesis 1–3. From creation until the second coming, people marry and are given in marriage, and people die. During that period there are saved and unsaved living together on the face of the earth. But from the second coming and into eternity on the new earth there is no marriage, there is no death, all the people there are resurrected to eternal life, and only the children of God are there. Jesus teaches that this world and the world to come encompass all of time.

Fourth, Romans 8:16–18 says: *"The Spirit itself beareth witness with our spirit, that we are the children of God:* [17] *And if children, then heirs; heirs of God, and joint-heirs with Christ; if so be that we suffer with him, that we may be also glorified together.* [18] *For I reckon that the sufferings of this present time are not worthy to be compared with the glory which shall be revealed in us."* We have the present time of suffering, and the future time of glorification in which there is no suffering, and that is all there is.

Fifth, Ephesians 1:20–21 says, speaking of the work of the Father in raising the Son from the dead: "*. . . he raised him from the dead, and set him at his own right hand in the heavenly places,* [21] *Far above all principality, and power, and might, and dominion, and every name that is named, not only in this world, but also in that which is to come."* This world and the world which is to come is all there is, and together they encompass all of time.

Sixth, Titus 2:11–13 says, *"For the grace of God that bringeth salvation hath appeared to all men,* [12] *Teaching us that, denying ungodliness and worldly lusts, we should live soberly, righteously, and godly, in this present world;* [13]*Looking for that blessed hope, and the glorious appearing of the great God and our Savior Jesus Christ,"* which is the end of this world, and the beginning of the world to come. The event of the second coming separates those two worlds and two ages.

Seventh, 1 Timothy 6:17–19 says, *"Charge them that are rich in this world, that they be not highminded, nor trust in uncertain riches, but in the living God,"* that they lay up in store for themselves "[19] *a good foundation against the time to come, that they may lay hold on eternal life."* There is *"this world,"* and there is *"the time to come,"* in which they obtain eternal life.

Repeatedly we see that there are just two ages. No others are mentioned or indicated.

The point is that this two-age terminology permeates the New Testament, and is foundational to it. People do not think of these passages as being prophetic, but in fact, they set forth the framework into which all prophecy must fit. All prophecy must fit either into this age or into the age to come, into this world, or into the world to come.

Therefore, the conclusion follows: the Millennium spoken of in Revelation 20 has to fit into one of these two ages. The Millennium is not a third age. The language of the Bible does not allow for a third age. The Millennium either fits into this age or into the age to come because these two ages encompass all of time.

The major framework of eschatology is clear. While we may wonder as to whether some details fit into this age or the age to come, the big picture is plain. In this world, we are going to have tribulation. In that world, we are not going to have any. This world is a present evil world. That world is going to be a perfect, sinless, and holy world. In this world, people marry and die. In that world, no one marries or dies. In this world, there are both the children of God and the children of the devil. In the world to come, there are only the children of God.

Complicated eschatology is unnecessary. It is unbiblical to say there are seven ages or there are three ages. There are just two, and everything fits into one or the other. When you understand this and start reading prophetic passages, asking the question where this fits, you will realize there is only one of two boxes to put it in. Understanding this dramatically improves your ability to understand the Bible's teaching on eschatology.

(There are a few passages in which the word "age" is used in the plural. They are Ephesians 2:7, 3:5, 3:21, and Colossians 1:26. When the word "ages" is used, it is simply referring to the passage of long, extended, indefinite periods of time. It has the same meaning as the expression "throughout the centuries," "across the millennia of time," or "down through the generations." When used in the plural, the word "ages" has no relationship to the two-age framework explained above.)

Having seen the importance of eschatology and the simplicity of eschatology, it should motivate you to say, "Eschatology is important.

I must strive to learn it." It should also motivate you to say, "Eschatology is simple. I can understand it."

You can put aside the false notions that have been taught in the Dispensational school of teaching, which is the most popular view in our day. There is just one coming and one Day of Judgment, which is the dividing line between this age and the age to come. The sequence of a secret rapture, and then a seven-year tribulation, and then a second coming, and then a millennium, and then a rebellion, and then a new heaven and a new earth is unbiblical.

Introduction to the Book of Revelation

1

The Name, Purpose, and Recipients of the Book

The book of Revelation is probably the most misunderstood book in the Bible. Leon Morris says in his commentary on the book of Revelation:

> The Revelation. . .is by common consent one of the most difficult of all the books of the Bible. It is full of strange symbolism. There are curious beasts with unusual numbers of heads and horns. There are extraordinary phenomena, like the turning of one-third of the sea into blood (8:8), which are impossible to envisage. Modern readers find it strange. They are, moreover, not usually attracted by the fantastic schemes of prophecy which some exegetes find in it, and whose ingenuity is matched only by their improbability. The result is that for many Revelation remains a closed book. Except for one or two passages, like the vision of the redeemed in chapter 7, or that of the heavenly Jerusalem in the final two chapters, it remains largely unread. We recognize that it is part of the canon of Scripture and therefore we accord it formal recognition. But we remain uneasy and do not make use of it.[1]

What he says is true, but what he says is also a great tragedy, because this book is intended to be a source of great comfort and encouragement to the church. Much of that comfort and encouragement is lost through misunderstanding its structure, its language, its symbolism, and its message.

This misunderstanding is largely due to an attempt to read first-century apocalyptic writing with a twenty-first-century mindset

1 Leon Morris. *Revelation* (Tyndale New Testament Commentaries). Downers Grove: InterVarsity, 1987, 17

and understanding. We cannot view the book of Revelation from a modern-day perspective. If we do, we will be utterly confused by it. We must understand the book of Revelation from two perspectives: from a first-century perspective, and from an Old Testament perspective.

What would John's first-century readers have understood as they read the book of Revelation? How would they have understood its structure, language, symbolism, and message? That is how we must seek to understand it. Modern-day dispensational schemes, current political events, and last-days speculations are not a basis for understanding the book of Revelation. The book of Revelation is firmly rooted in the first century, and in the Old Testament.

It is from those two perspectives—a first-century perspective and an Old Testament perspective—that we must approach this book and seek to gain an understanding of it. The book of Revelation was written to be understood. It can be understood if it is approached and interpreted with a proper methodology, a methodology that first-century Christians would have understood and used.

It says in Revelation 1:3, *"Blessed is he that readeth, and they that hear the words of this prophecy, and keep those things which are written therein: for the time is at hand."* The clear implication behind that verse is the expectation that the ordinary Christian would read this book, understand it, and obey the instructions that it provides.

The modern-day Christian is often baffled and confused by what it says and cannot comprehend what it means. This is entirely unnecessary. This book can be understood and will be understood as it is properly approached and interpreted. It does not need to be a mystery and a source of confusion and frustration as it is read.

It is fitting that the book of Revelation is the last book in the Bible because it tells us the end of the Bible's story and it concludes the message the Bible conveys. The Bible opens with the book of Genesis, otherwise known as the Book of Beginnings, where we see the original creation of the world and humanity. The book of Genesis describes the work of the devil in engineering the fall of humanity in the garden of Eden and the depravity and curse that fell upon creation and all mankind as a result. As we read the early chapters of Genesis, it seems that Satan has triumphed over God and has destroyed the work of God.

However, God will not be defeated. God promises in Genesis 3:15 that He will send the Seed of the woman who is Jesus Christ to crush the devil and his works. He will restore the paradise that has been lost, He will redeem the souls of fallen men, and the devil and his works will be destroyed.

Genesis 3:15 is God's declaration of war against Satan, and the rest of the Bible is a record of how that war develops and ends. As the Bible unfolds, we see the progressive defeat of Satan as the plan of God is slowly but surely developed over time. The book of Revelation records the conclusion of that plan, the ultimate triumph of Jesus Christ, and the final defeat of Satan.

Genesis tells us about the beginning of sin and paradise lost. Revelation tells us about the defeat of sin and paradise restored. Genesis tells us about the work of Satan established. Revelation tells us about the work of Satan destroyed. It is for this reason that the book of Revelation is such a great comfort and encouragement to the believer. It is a declaration of how everything is going to turn out in the end. It tells us that Jesus Christ wins and His people win, and that Satan and his followers, both demonic and human, suffer everlasting defeat and destruction in the lake of fire.

These then are the two goals we hope to accomplish as we study the book of Revelation together. Our first goal is to understand this book by understanding the structure, language, symbolism, and message of the book. We will do this by understanding it from a first-century perspective and from an Old Testament perspective. Our second goal is to see and rejoice in the triumph of Jesus Christ over Satan. It says in 1 John 3:8, *"For this purpose the Son of God was manifested, that he might destroy the works of the devil."* The book of Revelation is a declaration from start to finish that Jesus Christ has accomplished that purpose. Our goal is to see and rejoice in the triumph of Christ: to see His triumph in destroying the works of the devil, in restoring paradise lost, and in redeeming His people from sin and all its effects.

As we begin our introduction, there are several issues we need to consider, each of which has an important impact on our understanding and interpretation of the book. Some of these introductory issues might not seem too exciting at first, but each of these points is an important building block in understanding the book as a whole and in understanding its various parts. Without them, we cannot hope to achieve our two goals. Chapters 1–6, which form the introduction, are critical to understanding the exposition of the text in chapter 7 and following.

The Name of the Book

The title of this book in our English Bible is "The Revelation of St. John the Divine," and it is commonly called the "Book of Revelation." The word "revelation" is derived from Latin and simply means "unveiling." The basic idea here is of something being concealed behind a curtain and, when the curtain is removed, what is behind the curtain is revealed. There has been a revealing, or a revelation of what was formerly hidden.

When reading through the table of contents of some Bibles, the last book of the New Testament is listed as "Apocalypse." The word "apocalypse" is derived from the very first word of the Greek text of this book which is *"apokalupsis."* The Greek word *apokalupsis* is transliterated to apocalypse, which also means to uncover or to unveil things that were previously hidden.

Revelation unveils the plan of God for the future and what will unfold over the process of time. We are told what the church will do in the future and what will happen to it. We are told what the world will do in the future and what will happen to it. There is an unveiling of the things that will occur and characterize the age between the first and second coming of Christ. In the first century, believers did not know how God's plan was going to unfold over time. The book of Revelation pulls back the curtain and gives them an unveiling or revelation of how history is going to unfold and what spiritual warfare is going to look like from the first century until the second coming of Jesus.

Revelation 1:1 says this book is *"The Revelation of Jesus Christ, which God gave unto him. . ."* God the Father gave Jesus this revelation when He gave Him the book in Revelation 5 which was sealed with seven seals.

Contained in this book is the revelation describing the things that will occur and characterize the entire period from John's day on into eternity. What first-century Christians could see and what we can see today is the declaration by God of what history is going to look like and how it is going to unfold over the process of time.

This does not mean that this book foretells specific future events that have occurred over the last 2,000 years, like the rise of King Constantine, the French Revolution, the establishment of America, World War I, or World War II. When we say that Christ reveals future history, we are not saying that He reveals the specific events in the unfolding of that history so that this seal refers to the French Revolution, and that trumpet refers to World War I, or something similar. That is the historicist's view of the book of Revelation. We will be addressing that view in the next chapter. That is not the proper method for interpreting the book of Revelation.

When we say that Revelation gives us a view of what history is going to look like and how it is going to unfold over the process of time between the first and second coming of Christ, we mean that it foretells the general characteristics of the spiritual warfare that will take place in this age, it sets out the types of blessings that will be granted to the believers, and it describes the kinds of judgments that will fall on the wicked.

It tells us about the struggle between the church and the world, and what that will look like. It tells us about the conflict between God and Satan, and what that will consist of. It tells us about the second coming of Christ and the eternal state of the saved and the lost. And while it does deal with some very specific events that take place right at the end of this age, its primary thrust is to set out the characteristics of the spiritual warfare that is going to take place throughout this age between the first and second coming of Christ, and how that warfare will turn out.

In short, it reveals to us what we might expect to see and experience in the spiritual warfare that is going to go on until Christ returns, and the outcome His second coming will produce when He appears.

This is the reason for the name of the book. It unveils what the future will consist of between the first and second coming of Christ; and therefore, it is relevant to every generation until Christ returns.

Every section of this book has relevance to every generation of Christians. Every section describes each generation's spiritual conflict in fighting to establish the kingdom of God, in fighting against Satan and his forces, and in experiencing the protection and blessing of God as they fight.

The book of Revelation is a guidebook. It tells us what we are experiencing, why we are experiencing it, and how we should respond to it. During your lifetime, you have been undergoing spiritual warfare. What you have been undergoing is described in this book. It is described in the seven seals, in the seven trumpets, and in the seven vials. It is described in the conflict between the dragon and the beast and the false prophet on one side, and the people of God on the other side. It equips you to fight that spiritual warfare, as you rightly understand and apply its message and teaching.

Revelation is a field manual for our present spiritual warfare, for the spiritual warfare of all previous generations, and for the spiritual warfare of all subsequent generations until Christ returns. Since it is a field manual that explains what the spiritual warfare of the age in which we live looks like and how we might successfully fight and triumph in it, it is sad that this book is so badly misunderstood, misinterpreted, and misapplied.

It is especially sad that so many get frustrated with Revelation and throw up their hands in confusion over what it is saying and therefore ignore it and leave it unused. That is like a general giving his troops intelligence about the enemy, supplying them with a battle plan for defeating the enemy, telling them the proper tactics to employ, and promising them victory if they use them, and then for the soldiers to say, "We cannot understand all of this. We will just set it aside and figure out what to do on our own as we go along."

The failure of the church to properly understand and rightly use the book of Revelation is the reason for so much of the confusion and ineptitude Christians display in their methods of spiritual warfare. The modern-day church is largely characterized by ignorance as to how to conduct spiritual warfare and obtain victory in it.

My hope as we study this book is that we will say to ourselves as we go through it: "Of course! Now I see why things happen the way they do. Now I see why I experience the conflict I have. Jesus told us this is how it was going to be during this period. I can also see that if I patiently persevere, the triumph is mine and Christ will obtain the victory for Himself and for me. Therefore, I can fight these battles with confidence and with the knowledge that I am using proper tactics, and that I am assured of a triumphant outcome when I understand the battle as He describes it, and when I prosecute the battle as He instructs."

To summarize: what the book unveils to us is how history is going to unfold, the spiritual conflict that is going to characterize it, who the parties are, what the issues are, and how we are to fight that battle in our generation. How are we supposed to fight the battle in our generation? We must fight it the same way the first-century church fought it, and the same way the thirty-third-century church will fight it, if this world goes on that long.

This is not a book just about the past; this is not a book just about the future; this is a book about the spiritual warfare we are facing right now. To be sure, it covers issues regarding the past and regarding the future. But primarily, it is a revelation about how we fight spiritual warfare right now in our present lives and in our generation. It tells us how we may expect that battle to look, and how we should respond to it.

The Purpose of the Book

God never does anything without a reason and a purpose. We should expect that God has a definite reason for writing the book of Revelation and a definite purpose in placing it in our Bibles. We are not disappointed in that expectation. We are specifically told in Revelation 1:3 that the purpose of the book is to provide a blessing to all those who both hear and keep its teachings.

Revelation 1:3 says, "*Blessed is he that readeth, and they that hear the words of this prophecy, and keep those things which are written therein: for the time is at hand.*" God's purpose in giving us this book to read, hear, and obey is that we would be blessed by it.

At the end of the book in Revelation 22:7, Jesus says, "*Behold, I come quickly: blessed is he that keepeth the sayings of the prophecy of this book.*" He repeats in chapter 22 verse 7 what He said in chapter 1 verse 3. From the start of the book to the end of the book, the purpose is the same. The purpose is that the people of God would be blessed by understanding this prophetic revelation and by obeying the instructions it gives.

Many blessings accrue to those who read and obey the message of this book. Chief among those blessings is that of obtaining comfort and assurance as they struggle against the forces of evil. This whole book is about the struggle against the forces of evil. It opens with a description of this struggle.

Revelation 1:9 says, "*I John, who also am your brother, and companion in tribulation, and in the kingdom and patience of Jesus Christ.*" John is exiled on the island of Patmos because of persecution by the Roman Empire. Jesus comes and reveals the content of this book to John as he suffers because He wants John to be blessed. Among those blessings is the blessing of being comforted in the midst of persecution.

This book is full of help and comfort for persecuted and suffering Christians. Satan is a relentless foe of the people of God, and he stirs up his followers to persecute them mercilessly. The church is constantly struggling against the forces of evil. This has been going on for the last 2,000 years and will continue to go on for the next 2,000 years, if Christ delays His coming that long.

The purpose of this book is to comfort and strengthen and encourage believers, and to assure them of ultimate victory in their conflict against Satan and his people. This book opens with a glorious revelation of Christ in chapter 1. We see Him standing in the midst of His churches and saying to them, "Fear not. I am the First and the Last. I am He that lives and was dead and behold, I am alive forevermore. I have the keys to hell and death. Because I am all these things, you do not need to be afraid."

Revelation 17:14 states regarding the forces of evil: *"These shall make war with the Lamb, and the Lamb shall overcome them: for he is Lord of lords, and King of kings: and they that are with him are called, and chosen, and faithful."* It speaks of the fact that though the forces of evil are going to assault us, Christ is going to triumph over them, and we who are with Him will triumph too. Christ ensures our victory.

The book of Revelation declares in its closing chapters that Satan and the beast and the false prophet are all cast into the lake of fire, death and hell are cast into the lake of fire, and all those who served Satan and persecuted the church are cast into the lake of fire. But the people of God will have a totally different destiny. God will dwell with them, and they shall be His people, and God Himself will be their God. Revelation 21:4 says, *"And God shall wipe all tears from their eyes; and there shall be no more death, neither sorrow, nor crying, neither shall there be any more pain: for the former things are passed away."*

The theme of Revelation from start to finish is that Christ is with His church—His people—when they battle the forces of evil, and He will ensure their victory. Even though the battle is long and difficult and painful, and some Christians are martyred, the outcome is not in doubt. Christ wins, and His people win.

Knowing this is a tremendous comfort to a militant church that is fighting hard in every generation to establish and expand the kingdom of God throughout the earth. It encourages us as we are battered and beaten in spiritual warfare to remain faithful to Christ in spite of our sufferings, because faithfulness will be rewarded in the end. To those who overcome, the wonderful blessings of the new heavens and new earth are promised.

Revelation 21:7 says, *"He that overcometh shall inherit all things; and I will be his God, and he shall be my son."* The purpose of the book is to give Christians assurance of victory, comfort in their persecutions, and encouragement to remain faithful to death. It provides motivation to overcome the pressure put on them to compromise and apostatize, knowing that if they overcome and do not surrender, the promised outcome is of infinite worth, eternal duration, and an immeasurable blessing.

This book equips the believer to face the spiritual warfare he will experience with strength, confidence, and joy. That is the purpose of the book: to give you strength, confidence, and joy as you fight the spiritual warfare of your generation.

The Recipients of the Book

This book is directed to a very specific audience. It is specifically directed to the churches of Jesus Christ. This is stated repeatedly.

Three passages make this clear. Revelation 1:4 says, *"John to the seven churches which are in Asia."* In Revelation 1:11 Jesus says, *"I am Alpha and Omega, the first and the last: and, What thou seest, write in a book, and send it unto the seven churches."* John says, "I am writing to the seven churches." Jesus tells him to send the information to the seven churches in chapters 2 and 3. At the end of the book of Revelation in 22:16, Jesus says, *"I Jesus have sent mine angel to testify unto you these things in the churches."*

From beginning to end, this book is addressed to the churches. It speaks about what they will face in the first century, the second century, and every subsequent century until the second coming of Christ. The church is the sole institution Christ left on earth to do His work, build His kingdom, and represent His message. Christ expects every single believer to be committed to and involved in a local church. His teaching presupposes this.

For example, in Matthew 18:15–18, Christ says that if you have a problem with your brother, go to him alone. If he will not hear you, take two or three more. If he does not hear them, tell it to the church.

The clear expectation is that these brothers have a church they are involved in and there are elders in that church to whom this matter of church discipline can be taken.

Jesus said in Matthew 28:19–20, "*Go ye therefore, and teach all nations, baptizing them in the name of the Father, and of the Son, and of the Holy Ghost:* [20] *Teaching them to observe all things whatsoever I have commanded you: and, lo, I am with you alway, even unto the end of the world.*" We are to go out and witness and make disciples. We are to baptize them and teach them. The context in which baptism and teaching are done is in the context of the gathered assembly of the local church.

The New Testament knows nothing of lone-ranger Christianity or do-it-yourself spirituality. The New Testament everywhere expects and assumes that every Christian will be in a church, be committed to that church, and be participating in all the means of grace the church is entrusted with. It is as individual believers are involved in the life of the church that the church collectively and churches individually will be able to overcome the onslaught of Satan and his people.

Christ's work is always done through local churches. Revelation makes this clear. Local churches are the focus of His concern and the object of His care, because Christ is in the midst of His church. In Revelation 1:12–13 John says, "*And I turned to see the voice that spake with me. And being turned, I saw seven golden candlesticks;* [13] *And in the midst of the seven candlesticks one like unto the Son of man, clothed with a garment down to the foot, and girt about the [chest] with a golden girdle.*" What are these seven candlesticks? Revelation 1:20 says, ". . .*and the seven candlesticks which thou sawest are the seven churches.*"

When Christ reveals Himself to John, He is standing in the middle of the seven candlesticks which represent the seven churches. Christ is focused on His churches and Christ lives in the midst of His churches. In Matthew 18:20 it says, "*For where two or three are gathered together in my name, there am I in the midst of them.*" Christ is in the midst of His church because the local church is the New Covenant temple. It is made up of living stones with a universal priesthood that offers up spiritual sacrifices that are acceptable to God by Jesus Christ. Christ is in the midst of His church because the church is the habitation of His special personal presence on earth. If Christ is focused on His church and dwells in the midst of His church, where do you think we ought to place our focus and spend our time on the Lord's Day? Is it not in the midst of His church?

The local church is God's institution for getting His work done on earth in this age. It is through the local church that He builds His kingdom, proclaims His glory, and preaches His gospel. Therefore, we see that Christ's great concern in the book of Revelation is for the purity of His church, the doctrine of His church, the suffering of His church, the protection of His church, and the victory of His church. Christ is a church-centered Savior, and therefore we need to be church-centered Christians. To be church-centered is to be Christ-centered, because Christ dwells in the midst of His church.

In this book, we see the great concern Christ has for the purity, doctrine, persecution, protection, suffering, and victory of the church. We see His concern for these things in the letters He writes to the seven churches in chapters 2 and 3. There we see that Christ's heart is focused on His churches. There are seven of them, a number that is used forty-four times in the book of Revelation. The number seven symbolizes completeness. Therefore, these seven churches represent the church as a whole and the church throughout the centuries. These seven churches represent all the churches that exist, have existed, or shall exist between the first and second coming of Christ. They represent the complete church.

These seven churches represent the problems they struggle with, the virtues they possess, and the opposition they experience. In these seven churches we see the types of challenges, blessings, failings, and successes that churches have in this age. The afflictions the church was subjected to in the days of the apostle John are typical of the persecution churches must endure throughout the New Covenant period, and especially in the period after Satan is loosed shortly before the second coming of Christ.

Therefore, any church that hopes to please Christ, overcome the world, and triumph over persecution needs to understand and apply the lessons in Revelation. If there ever was a church epistle, the book of Revelation is it. Christ as the Head of His church gives instructions to His church, and the church needs to hear and heed the instructions and promises He provides.

Have you ever wondered: What should our church look like? The book of Revelation tells us what it should look like, as well as what it must not look like. It tells us how it can triumph. It tells us about the care and protection Christ provides for it. But it also tells us the work, labor, and faithfulness we must exercise if we are to be overcomers in the spiritual warfare we face. Christ made wonderful promises to every one of the churches, if they overcame in the spiritual warfare they were facing.

Overcoming implies that there is an obstacle in the way. The obstacle we face in our day is the same one John faced in his day, the obstacle of satanic opposition. Satan is fighting hard against the church and God's people, and we have to fight back and defeat him. If we follow Christ's instruction to His churches, we will overcome in this warfare. In the end, we will have been found to be faithful to Jesus, and Satan will be found to have failed in subverting us into apostasy. Those are the overcomers. They are not people who are perfect; they are people who persevere in spiritual warfare, and by the grace, strength, and blood of Christ overcome Satan. They send him away defeated in his purpose to pull them away from Christ and draw them to himself.

This is the name of the book, the purpose of the book, and the recipients of the book. In this book like nowhere else, we see the triumph of Christ over Satan, and we see God's sovereign control over the course of history as the seals are opened, the trumpets are sounded, and the vials are poured out.

Therefore, we should not be surprised at all by the way things are unfolding, by the things we experience, by the struggles we have, or by the fact that we actually do overcome! The Christ who chose us and called us is the same Christ who ensures by His grace that we remain faithful. Here we see the challenges that faced the church and the victory of the church over every opponent.

We have to understand that the church is not a place of ease and comfort. It is like a military base. It is an outpost in the war, and therefore people are going to come in bloodied and wounded. They need to have their wounds bound up and healed. They need to be equipped with spiritual weapons, and they need to go back out and fight some more. The church looks more like a field hospital than a retirement home, and we need to understand that.

People see conflict in their church and ask, "Why are people in the church fighting with each other? The church is to be a place of peace and harmony!" Sadly, there will always be conflict in churches because we are involved in a war. Satan is going to send his people into the church to try to subvert the church. Does the enemy ever try to infiltrate his opponent's military base? Satan does so as well. Paul himself said in Acts 20:29 that grievous wolves shall come into the church from without. He said that even from within the church, men would arise and speak perverse things and try to draw away disciples after them. It is no wonder there is conflict in the churches. There is a war going on, and often the battlefield is inside the church itself.

We have to understand that we are in a war. We need to have a war mentality and a war footing, and we need to be fighting the good fight of faith. The day of rest will come when Christ returns. Until then, we need to fight the good fight with all of our strength.

The book of Revelation is a field manual for the war. It is the General's plan. It is the unveiling of the tactics of the enemy. It tells us the tactics that Satan is going to use to try to defeat us, and it gives us instructions on how to respond in order to defeat him. Let us fight the good fight of faith. Christ is worthy of our most valiant efforts.

2

Four Interpretive Approaches to Revelation

Revelation is a book of victory. It declares the victory of Christ and His people over sin and Satan. It tells us this victory is both certain and total. Consequently, this book has been a great source of comfort to suffering saints in every century since it was written.

We live in a time of great spiritual warfare and conflict. Satan and his people relentlessly attack us. But the Lamb will overcome them, for He is Lord of lords and King of kings. He has the keys to hell and to death, and no one is able to defeat Him.

As we saw in chapter 1, the theme of Revelation from start to finish is that Christ is with His church as together they battle the forces of evil. Christ ensures their victory over those forces of evil even though the battle is long and difficult and painful.

One of our goals as we study Revelation is to understand its structure, its language, its symbolism, and most of all, its message. But understanding requires interpretation. If we are to rightly understand this book, we must properly interpret it. The question is, what principles should we employ to arrive at its proper meaning? This is supremely important, because if we do not employ a proper method of interpretation, we will fail to properly understand the message of the book, and fail to gain the benefit it has for us.

In this chapter, we will examine the four major approaches that have been taken to interpret Revelation. We will set forth the approach we will take, and explain why we believe it is correct. Here are the four major interpretations that historically have been applied to Revelation.

The Preterist View

The term Preterist comes from Latin, and it simply means "past." We could entitle this the "Past" view. The Preterist view of Revelation is that the prophecies it contains were either largely or else completely fulfilled in the fall of Jerusalem to the Roman army in AD 70. Everything, or almost everything that Revelation predicts, has been fulfilled for nearly 2,000 years.

There are two schools of thought in the Preterist movement. There are the extreme Preterists, who of course do not call themselves extreme Preterists. They prefer to call themselves "consistent" Preterists. They believe the prophecies contained in the book of Revelation were completely fulfilled in AD 70. They teach that the tribulation, wrath, and judgments described in Revelation were fulfilled in the fall of Jerusalem. They believe Jesus actually returned in AD 70, the resurrection occurred in AD 70, and we are now living in the new heaven and the new earth instituted in AD 70.

These positions can only be maintained by a very extreme spiritualizing of the nature of the second coming, the nature of the resurrection, and the nature of the new heaven and the new earth. Those who hold this view of extreme Preterism, or as they would prefer to call it, "consistent" Preterism, are in fact heretics. They fall under the condemnation of 2 Timothy 2:17–18 which says: *"And their word will eat as doth a [cancer]: of whom is Hymenæus and Philetus;* [18] *Who concerning the truth have erred, saying that the resurrection is past already; and overthrow the faith of some."* Maintaining that the final resurrection of the saints has already occurred is a malignant doctrine. Rather than establishing the faith of believers, it overthrows it.

The second and dominant school of Preterist thought is called "partial" Preterism. The partial Preterists hold that the vast majority of the prophecies in the book of Revelation were fulfilled in AD 70 with the fall of Jerusalem. However, they would say that the resurrection of the dead, the second coming of Christ, the final judgment, and the new heavens and the new earth are still in the future and remain yet to be fulfilled. They assert that the bulk of what is spoken of in Revelation did occur in AD 70, but that the final events of chapter 19 and chapters 21 and 22 will be fulfilled in the future, while chapter 20 is currently being fulfilled.

This view is usually associated with a post-millennial view of Revelation 20. Post-millennialism teaches that the kingdom of God will be physically manifested in the governments of the world in a millennial Christian golden age, in which Christianity dominates the world and its governments prior to the second coming of Jesus Christ.

Partial Preterists believe that the events of Matthew 24 and the events of Revelation 1–18 were fulfilled in the fall of Jerusalem in AD 70. The only thing that remains is for Christ to come back, the resurrection to occur, the final judgment to take place, and the new heaven and the new earth to be established. (See my interpretation of Matthew 24 in the appendix in volume 2 for a rebuttal of this view.)

There are several problems with the partial Preterist view of the book of Revelation. First of all, this view necessitates that Revelation had to be written very early, certainly before AD 70 when history informs us that Jerusalem fell. Therefore, proponents of this view posit that it was probably written sometime in the AD 60s. However, the vast majority of the evidence and the strongest consensus among scholars is that Revelation was written by the apostle John around AD 95 or 96 in the midst of the persecution that took place during the reign of Domitian, who was the Roman Caesar at that time. Therefore, the theory that Revelation is a prophecy of the fall of Jerusalem in AD 70 would not be possible if this book were written after that event.

The second problem with a Preterist interpretation of Revelation is that the judgment depicted in Revelation which constitutes God's final wrath is one that falls on all the nations of the earth, not just on Jerusalem. To consider the reference in Revelation to the fall of the city of Babylon as being a reference to the fall of Jerusalem is simply not tenable. Babylon is a term that symbolizes anti-Christian societies wherever they may be found across the world and down through time. It is not a term that is used in the Scriptures to refer to the city of Jerusalem, or to Israel itself.

The depictions in Revelation of God's wrath falling upon all the nations of the world are not compatible with the fall of a single city or nation like that of the fall of Israel and Jerusalem in AD 70. The wrath of God that will certainly fall on all the nations of the whole earth as described in Revelation will be infinitely greater than the destruction of Israel and Jerusalem in AD 70. The fall of Israel and Jerusalem in AD 70 is not a significant enough event to fulfill the descriptions of the worldwide pouring out of the wrath of God in the trumpets and the vials.

A third major problem with Preterism is that, if it is true, the book of Revelation largely ceased to have direct application to Christians after AD 70. If it had been fulfilled at that point, it would have had little relevance to those who lived after that time. Revelation would have been intensely relevant to Christians between AD 60 and 70, but after AD 70, the bulk of it would have become not a prophecy of the future but a history book of the past. Preterism confines the direct relevance of the vast majority of the book of Revelation to about a ten-year period and to a single generation, that of the first century.

This is the Preterist position of the interpretation of the book of Revelation. It is a position that says the vast majority of the book was fulfilled in AD 70 in the fall of Jerusalem. The only things that remain to be fulfilled are the second coming of Christ, the resurrection, the final judgment, and the new heavens and the new earth. Everything else has already been finished and fulfilled.

The Historicist View

You might imagine that this view has something to do with history since it is called the "Historicist view," and you would be correct. The Historicist interpreters of Revelation see the book as a calendar of historic events written in advance.

If someone were to look at the calendar in your home, they would see several events penciled in that you hope to participate in at some point in the future: birthdays, weddings, anniversaries, meetings, and chores. You have a calendar of future events you hope to accomplish. For the Historicist interpreters, this is what the book of Revelation consists of.

According to this view, Revelation predicts specific events that will occur during the time between the first and second coming of Christ. The seals, trumpets, and bowls picture successive stages of church history and events that are going to take place throughout that history. Historical events like the collapse of the Roman Empire, the rise of the corruption of the Roman Catholic Church, the Reformation, and various wars are described by the various pictures and symbols set forth in Revelation. For example, the swarm of locusts coming out of the bottomless pit in Revelation 9 is said by some to represent and predict the rise and spread of Islam and its destructive armies and actions.

Among Historicist interpreters, the historical events that are symbolically predicted in Revelation always seem to be those that occur in European Western civilization. This approach makes the book of little relevance to the world outside of Western Europe. It also makes it of little direct application to those who lived in the first century, since according to Historicists, most of what is addressed in the book of Revelation would occur centuries ahead of their time. Why would a first-century Christian even care or be impacted by a prophecy of a World War that was going to occur in the twentieth century?

The problem is that each Historicist interpreter views the book of Revelation differently, in order to make it fit the realities of the time in which he lives and the events he considers to be significant in his own historical frame of reference. For example, a Historicist interpreter writing in the 1400s would fit the statements in Revelation into the events that took place from the time of Christ until the 1400s. Someone else writing in the 1600s would fit the statements in Revelation into the events that took place from the time of Christ until the 1600s. Those writing today would engage in a similar methodology.

Some think they can now find the rise of America as a nation in Revelation 12:14 because it talks about the eagle with wings bearing the church into the wilderness. The national symbol of America is the eagle, so the eagle that bears the church on her wings into the wilderness represents the rise of America as a place to which persecuted Christians fled. Someone writing in the 1400s would have never thought of such a thing.

As the centuries unfold, Historicists continually reassess what these various symbols represent and which events they depict. The problem is that each Historicist interpreter conforms his interpretation to fit the realities and the historical events he considers significant.

Furthermore, there is little agreement among Historicists as to what the different symbols in Revelation have referred to over the last 2,000 years. There are nearly as many interpretations as there are Historicist commentators. Given that there is such a wide divergence among them as to which events are predicted by which symbols, it would appear that this approach cannot yield any real hope for ever properly understanding this book.

It is also telling that while insisting that all of history is set forth in this book under these various symbols, there has been no consensus among Historicists as to the events in history that these various visions symbolize. In 2,000 years, one would think that at least the main outline of human history would have emerged with some clarity, but this has not yet been the case. It seems that this Historicist approach in interpreting the book of Revelation can never yield any certainty as to its meaning.

Moreover, as we shall see in a subsequent chapter, the unfolding of the events in Revelation are not chronological, but cyclic. The seals, trumpets, and vials do not occur sequentially in time, but in parallel with one another. Therefore, the seals, trumpets, and vials cannot represent the chronological order of Western Civilization in history. Instead, the seals, the trumpets, and the vials represent the same time frame looked at from different perspectives.

The Historicists' view of the interpretation of Revelation was largely held by the Reformers. It is a perspective that figures prominently in their writings. They saw the Pope as the beast, the man of sin, and the Antichrist. They saw the Roman Catholic Church as the great whore, Babylon, whom Christ would destroy with His second coming. We see this in the major Reformed Confessions of Faith in which the Pope is identified as the Antichrist. This identification arose out of the Historicist view of the interpretation of Revelation.

The Futurist View

As the name suggests, the Futurist method of interpreting the book of Revelation holds that the vast majority of the book has yet to be fulfilled at some point in the future. This is the inverse of the Preterist view. The Preterist view says that the vast majority of the book has already been fulfilled, but the Futurist view says the vast majority of the book has yet to be fulfilled.

The Futurist view of the book of Revelation is the dominant view in our day among Evangelical Christendom. It has been widely popularized by dispensational premillennialism and by prolific end-times books and movies that have been produced for popular audiences.

According to the Futurists, the first three chapters of Revelation describe seven literal churches that existed in John's day during the first century, and these seven churches also represent seven periods of church history from John's day until the rapture.

Strangely enough, Futurists are therefore Historicists in their interpretation of chapters 1 to 3 of Revelation because they say that the churches of chapters 1 to 3 are prophetic of seven successive periods of church history as they chronologically unfold up until the rapture of the church. The characteristics of each of the seven churches are said to also characterize the period of church history that they represent.

For example, the church at Ephesus, the first church mentioned, represents the period of history from Pentecost to about AD 100, the apostolic era.

The second church mentioned, the suffering church Smyrna, represents the period from AD 100 to 300, when the church suffered under the great persecutions of the Caesars until Constantine ended that suffering with the Edict of Milan.

The third church mentioned, Pergamos, represents the period from AD 300 to 800, during which time great compromise occurred. This involved the integration of the church with the world through Constantine, the beginning of the Roman Catholic Church, and the union of church and state.

This scheme goes on in similar fashion with each of the remaining churches. The seventh church, the lukewarm church of Laodicea, represents the church that exists in the last days just before the rapture of the church.

Following the rapture of the church is a seven-year tribulation, the second coming of Christ, a thousand-year millennium, and finally, the creation of the new heavens and the new earth. Three different judgments occur during these events: one at the rapture, one at the second coming, and one at the end of the millennium.

Dispensational premillennialism is Historicist in its view of chapters 1 to 3, but then becomes Futurist with reference to the remainder of the book. Apart from the letters to the churches in chapters 1 to 3, the remainder of the book details the events that will immediately precede the second coming of Christ. The Futurist interpretation holds that chapters 4 to 19 have had no bearing on, or any fulfillment in, or any application to the last 2,000 years of church history.

According to this view, Revelation is not focused on the first-century Christians and neither is it focused on the last 2,000 years of church history. The Futurist view sees chapters 4 to 19 as focused on a very small and short period of time yet to come. In particular, chapters 4 to 19 refer only to a seven-year period of time called the Great Tribulation. They believe that the Great Tribulation will begin with the rapture of the church, which they say is described in Revelation 4:1. This Great Tribulation will last seven years, and it will end with the second coming of Christ in chapter 19. Chapter 4 to chapter 19 describes the seven-year Great Tribulation that will begin after the rapture and end at the second coming.

Futurists believe that chapter 20 details a millennium on this present earth that begins with the second coming of Christ, lasts a literal 1,000 years, concludes with the final judgment, and is followed by the new heavens and the new earth as described in chapters 21 and 22. Futurists see chapters 4 to 22 as not only future to our time, but they also see them as occurring chronologically. Chapters 4 to 22 are seen as representing the actual historical order of events as they unfold. The seals are followed by the trumpets which are followed by the bowls, and so on. The events of chapter 20 occur chronologically after the events of chapter 19.

Furthermore, Futurists not only see chapters 4 to 22 as an actual chronology, but they also literalize the symbolic language and imagery as much as possible. Literalism is a major characteristic of Futurism.

Thus, the mark of the beast is literally a physical mark in the forehead and hand, like a tattoo or an embedded computer chip. An actual one-third of all the creatures in the sea perish, and an actual one-third of all ships sink when the second trumpet is sounded, and so on. Language that is clearly symbolic is interpreted literally.

For Christians who live prior to the rapture, chapters 4 through 19 merely provide us with an exciting preview of what the Great Tribulation will be like, but they have no direct personal application to us, nor for the people of God who have lived during the last 2,000 years. It is not for them, but only for those who live during the Tribulation.

Chapters 4 to 19 are a mere curiosity to us, because even if we are alive when the Tribulation described in those chapters begins, we will completely miss it. We will have been raptured up into heaven before it begins, and we will come back with Christ after it is over. We are guaranteed to have zero participation in the events that occur on earth described in chapters 4 to 19.

This Futurist approach largely robs the book of any significance to the early Christians of John's day, and all subsequent generations as well. Chapters 4 to 19 apply only to those living during the seven-year Tribulation. Yet this is entirely contrary to the stated recipients of this book, which are the seven churches. These represent the church universal throughout this entire age. This book is meant for all believers in all periods of history, not just for those living during a brief seven years under the Great Tribulation.

The Idealist View

The Idealist view sees the entire book of Revelation as a symbolic presentation of the battle between Christ and Satan, between the followers of Christ and the followers of Satan, and between good and evil. In a word, the book of Revelation is a symbolic depiction of spiritual warfare. It depicts the participants in that warfare, the struggles of that warfare, and the outcome of that warfare. It depicts the warfare the church will experience in every generation between the first and second coming of Christ.

Key to understanding the book of Revelation is realizing that it is cyclic in its structure, not linear. It repeatedly takes us on a journey through the period between the first and the second coming of Christ, showing us in each of those journeys the nature and outcome of spiritual conflict from various perspectives.

In the imagery of the seven seals, John takes us on a journey through the time period between the first and second coming of Jesus and describes what spiritual warfare will look like from one perspective during that time period.

In the imagery of the seven trumpets, John takes us on a second journey through the same time period from the first coming to the second coming of Christ and describes from a second perspective what spiritual warfare will look like during that time period.

In the imagery of the seven vials, John takes us on a third journey through the same time period from the first coming to the second coming of Christ and describes from a third perspective what spiritual warfare will look like during that time period.

The seals, the trumpets, and the vials all run concurrently with one another from the first to the second coming. Each of them describes the spiritual warfare that takes place during that time from a different perspective and with reference to the various participants and their outcomes. Each of them describes the types of things we will experience and the wicked will experience as that time frame unfolds.

The seals, the trumpets, and the vials teach us about the spiritual conflict that exists in every generation, and the struggles every generation will experience between the first and second coming of Christ. They tell us about the faithfulness we must exercise in the face of persecution and the victory we shall obtain if we do.

This is not to say that every single thing in the book is merely a description of spiritual warfare. There are certainly predictive passages in the book that will be fulfilled during the end times.

The rise of the antichrist, the second coming of Christ, the final judgment, the disposition of the saved into the new heaven and the new earth, and the disposition of the lost into the lake of fire are all yet future, and they will occur in the end times. But the vast majority of the book is a description in symbolic language of the kind of spiritual warfare that will occur between the first and second coming of Christ before those specific end times events occur.

The second coming of Christ, the resurrection, the final judgment, the disposition of the saved and lost, and their respective eternal destinies are repeatedly, and with increasing clarity, set forth as we move from the beginning to the end of the book, and they will all be fulfilled in the future. Nevertheless, the vast majority of the book speaks of the nature of the spiritual warfare that each generation of Christians will have to fight until Christ returns.

What this means is that every generation must deal with the issues the seven churches in chapters 2 and 3 had to deal with. Every generation experiences the events described in the seals, the trumpets, and the vials. Every generation does battle with the dragon and the beast and the false prophet. Every generation must resist the seductions of the great whore Babylon. Every generation must refuse the mark of the beast. Every generation must obtain the seal of God in the forehead.

Therefore, this book and its message are of equally compelling relevance and value to all believers of all generations between the first and second coming of Christ. It is equally relevant to first-century Christians, to fifteenth-century Christians, and to twenty-first-century Christians.

Since Revelation is a depiction of the spiritual warfare we will engage in between the first and second coming of Christ, it is therefore designed to inspire persecuted, suffering, and battle-weary Christians of every generation to keep up the good fight of faith and to endure to the end, knowing that the kingdoms of this world will become the kingdoms of our God and of His Christ. He shall reign forever and ever, and we shall reign with Him.

To achieve this goal of depicting the spiritual warfare that is going to take place, symbolic language is employed. Symbolic language is used to depict the struggles believers will have and the triumph they will achieve through the power of Christ and His saving work. It is used to depict the wrath of God's judgments that will fall on the ungodly for their persecution of the saints. It is used to depict the work and the witness of the church in conveying the message of God to the world.

In vision after vision, with symbol after symbol, the truth is emphasized that God is sovereign and controls both people and events so that His purposes are always being achieved. This makes for a very thrilling book—one that comforts us, strengthens us, and fills us with joy and awe as we see God destroying His enemies, delivering His people, and advancing His cause and kingdom in every generation to the end of time.

The key to understanding these symbols and visions in Revelation is found in the Old Testament. There is not a symbol in the book of Revelation that is not contained in the Old Testament. As first-century Christians read this book they were saturated with a knowledge of the Old Testament, and as John referred to this symbol or that symbol, they immediately knew what that symbol represented from their knowledge of how it was used in the Old Testament.

The Idealist view is what we will be using as we interpret the book of Revelation. This view understands that the book of Revelation is a manual of spiritual warfare.

Therefore, as we interpret this book, we are not going to say it was largely fulfilled in AD 70, and it is mostly history. We are not going to say that when Columbus sailed across the ocean in 1492 to discover America, this was predicted in the first seal. We are not going to say you should not worry about what is in chapter 6 because that refers to the Great Tribulation, and you are going to be raptured out before it occurs. Such teaching does nothing to strengthen and sustain persecuted suffering saints throughout this age.

What we are going to say is that the book of Revelation describes the tribulation that all first-century Christians went through and all subsequent-century Christians go through until Christ returns. As we read Revelation and interpret these symbols and visions, you will see that these are the things you are experiencing in your own spiritual warfare. These are the things that are happening right now in your life. These are things that have happened to you in the last decade. These are the kinds of things you are going to struggle with in the next decade of your life. Every generation does.

What you have in Revelation is a description of the good fight of faith that you fight every day of your life. This is the fight every Christian has fought and will fight between the first and second coming of Christ. This battle will only end when Jesus returns. Revelation teaches us about the spiritual warfare we will experience until the second coming occurs and the battle is done. Then we go into the new heavens and the new earth, where we will never have to do battle again.

The Idealist view is the only view that makes proper sense out of the symbols and pictures set before us in the visions in Revelation, and this is the method of interpretation we will use.

In the next chapter, we are going to talk about specific principles of interpretation. These principles will be pursued within the framework of Idealism; that is, that the book of Revelation is a book that describes the spiritual warfare of every generation between the first and second coming of Christ. Revelation becomes increasingly clear about the end times and the second coming of Christ as it moves from the beginning to the end of the book. The book is progressive in its clarity regarding the end times, while being cyclic in its structure, as it teaches us from various perspectives about the spiritual warfare every generation will experience as we proceed toward the second coming.

3

Three Principles to Interpret Revelation

The purpose of the book of Revelation is to comfort and encourage the persecuted church in its battle to advance the kingdom of God. Encouragement and comfort arise from each section of this book.

First, we are comforted by seeing Christ in the midst of His churches in chapters 1 to 3. It is a great comfort to know that Christ loves His churches, and His letters show His heart toward them. They make it clear that His whole focus and affection are upon them. Christ is intensely concerned for the welfare of His churches, and He is determined that they will overcome in the conflict and persecution they are facing. We are comforted in these opening chapters by knowing that Jesus is with His church, Jesus is for His church, Jesus is in the midst of His church, Jesus is guiding and protecting His church, and Jesus is bringing His church to triumph and victory.

Second, we are comforted as we see God the Father seated on His throne in heaven in chapters 4 and 5. For believers to know that God the Father is sovereignly ruling over the world and all that occurs in it with infinite wisdom and power fills the churches with comfort and confidence. All of God's enemies are known to Him and are under His control and therefore we do not need to fear.

Third, we are comforted as we see the outcome of our warfare in chapters 6 and 7. Even though there are tremendous struggles and conflicts which we experience in this age, in the end, the wicked are crying out for the rocks to fall on them to protect them from the wrath of God, while the Christians are worshipping and rejoicing around the throne of God in heaven.

Fourth, we are comforted as we see God's wrath poured out on the persecutors of the church in chapters 8 through 11 when the seven trumpets are sounded. There we see that the wicked are severely dealt with by God in this life as well as in the next, and He does not relent in His punishment of them. We see that the wicked have it far harder than the righteous, because God is with us in our sufferings; but God is against them in theirs, and inflicts sufferings upon them as punishment for their persecution of His people.

Fifth, we are comforted as we see Christ victorious over the dragon, the beast, the false prophet, Babylon, and over those who have the mark of the beast in chapters 12 to 20. Christ defeats and destroys Satan and all of his helpers who afflict the people of God.

Sixth, we are comforted as we see in chapters 21 and 22 our ultimate destiny in the new heaven and the new earth, where we will dwell forever in the presence of God and under His blessing.

The book of Revelation from start to finish is designed to be one extended source of comfort and encouragement to the persecuted church.

Just a very simple survey of the book of Revelation gives us a tremendous sense of comfort; but in order to derive the full measure of comfort Revelation is designed to provide us, it is important to properly understand the full meaning of those chapters and the particular details they convey. We can only do this if we use the proper method and principles of interpretation in order to grasp not just the overall sweep of the book, but the full meaning of the details and descriptions it contains.

In the last chapter, we looked at the four major approaches people take in interpreting this book.

We saw the Preterist approach, the view that this book was largely fulfilled in the past in AD 70. The only things that remain to be fulfilled are the second coming of Christ, the final judgment, and the new heaven and the new earth. Everything else was fulfilled in AD 70. Interpreted from this point of view, the book of Revelation is largely a history book.

We looked at the Historicist approach, the view that the book is a calendar of historical events written in advance that covers the last 2,000 years of history. This view sees Revelation as a prediction of various particular events that would occur in Western European history.

We looked at the Futurist approach, the view that says, in contrast to the Preterists, that the vast majority of the book remains yet to be fulfilled in the future. For the last 2,000 years, the church is only seeing the fulfillment of the first three chapters. Chapters 4 to 19 will only be fulfilled during the seven years of the Great Tribulation, and chapters 20 to 22 will be fulfilled after that. From this point of view, chapters 4 to 22 are all future in their fulfillment.

Finally, we looked at the Idealist approach, which we will employ as we interpret this book. This is the view that this book is a symbolic depiction of the spiritual warfare that takes place in every generation until Christ returns. Revelation is a manual of spiritual warfare, and what is described in this book is what Christians of every century have experienced as they fight the good fight of faith.

The Idealist view certainly recognizes a future predictive element to the book. The Idealist position recognizes that Jesus has yet to come the second time and that He will come visibly, physically, and bodily to this earth. He will carry out the final judgment and He will bring in the new heavens and the new earth. But the vast majority of the book is a description of the spiritual warfare Christians will be going through in every generation until that event occurs.

In the historical book of Judges, Israel experienced repeated cycles of the same spiritual struggles over and over again for many generations. In the same way, the spiritual warfare that takes place in the book of Revelation occurs over and over again for many generations.

In order to properly interpret this book, we need to identify the specific principles that will enable us to understand the meaning and message of each of these chapters and the symbolic language they contain. Once those principles are identified and employed, then the book can be clearly understood and its teachings properly followed.

We are told in Revelation 1:3, *"Blessed is he that readeth, and they that hear the words of this prophecy, and keep those things which are written therein: for the time is at hand."* This verse tells us this book was written to ordinary Christians, and it was expected that ordinary Christians would be able to read, understand, and obey the teaching and commands it contains.

This is not a book that is intended to be mysterious, confusing, frustrating, or terrifying to the believer who reads it. Ordinary Christians will be able to understand this book when proper principles of interpretation are employed. There are three major principles of interpretation we must follow if we are going to rightly understand the meaning and message of this book.

We Must Understand the Literary Style of This Book

As we read the book of Revelation, we realize it is written in a completely different style than the vast majority of the books in the Bible;

in fact, it is unique in the genre of its content among all the books of the New Testament.

The vast majority of books in the Bible are written in ordinary prose—that is, in the normal language of everyday usage. We talk to one another in ordinary, normal language. When we write, we write in ordinary, normal language. This is called ordinary prose. This book you are reading is ordinary prose. However, the book of Revelation is not written in ordinary prose.

To be sure, there is some ordinary prose in this book. For example, we see ordinary, normal prose in Revelation 1:1–9. As we read the first nine verses, there is no mystery or difficulty there. It is straightforward, ordinary language. As we read chapters 2 and 3, we see the same thing: very ordinary prose and language which is quite easy to understand. However, the vast majority of the book of Revelation is not written in ordinary prose like Romans or Ephesians or Hebrews; rather, it is written in the form of highly symbolic visual imagery. That is, it is written like a picture book that uses symbolic images to convey its message rather than using ordinary, descriptive language to convey its message.

This highly symbolic visual imagery does represent various literal realities, but there is not a one-to-one correspondence between the symbols and the reality they represent. We cannot take symbolic language and literalize it.

For example, we read in Revelation 1:13–16 this description of Jesus Christ: *"And in the midst of the seven candlesticks one like unto the Son of man, clothed with a garment down to the foot, and girt about the [chest] with a golden girdle.* [14] *His head and his hairs were white like wool, as white as snow; and his eyes were as a flame of fire;* [15] *And his feet like unto fine brass, as if they burned in a furnace; and his voice as the sound of many waters.* [16] *And he had in his right hand seven stars: and out of his mouth went a sharp twoedged sword: and his countenance was as the sun shineth in his strength."*

It is obvious that Jesus does not literally have a sword coming out of His mouth, His feet are not literally made of burning brass, and He does not have literal flames coming out of His eye sockets. We cannot literalize this symbolic language. We must recognize that these are not actual descriptions of what is really there; rather, they are symbolic descriptions that indicate a truth about what is there.

Highly symbolic and dramatically figurative language characterizes the book of Revelation. Its message is couched in metaphors and symbolic imagery, and its message is to be understood and interpreted similar to the way parables are understood and interpreted.

When Jesus teaches in parables, He uses symbolic language. They are word pictures. Because we understand this, we do not literalize the parables. We recognize they are word pictures designed to describe and convey an idea. We recognize they convey those ideas by creating visual images in our minds.

The book of Revelation is written in the same kind of genre as a political cartoon. No one takes the drawing in a political cartoon literally; it is a visual symbol meant to convey a message. A political cartoon is a visually figurative way of conveying an observation on some current issue or about some individual's action; and although this cartoon conveys a literal message, the imagery the cartoon uses to convey that message is never meant to be taken literally. This is universally understood. It is a picture that conveys an idea in a highly symbolic form. The word pictures in Revelation are not meant to be taken literally either.

As we stated above, chapters 2 and 3 of Revelation are ordinary prose. Jesus dictated seven letters to John to convey to the seven churches. In each of them he said, *"He that hath an ear, let him hear what the Spirit saith to the churches."* Chapters 2 and 3 are verbally focused. They are directed to the ear (*"let him hear"*), and they are written in ordinary prose.

But beginning in chapter 4, the emphasis dramatically changes from a verbal focus that is directed to the ear, to a visual focus of word pictures that are directed to the eye. Fifty-two times in the book of Revelation John says, *"I saw," "I looked," "I beheld."* At this point, Revelation becomes a visual picture book, presenting picture after picture of the conflict between Christ and His people on the one side, and Satan and his people on the other side.

We must understand that, unlike any other book in the New Testament, Revelation is a picture book. Do not be obsessed with the details of the pictures, or the strangeness of them; instead, focus on the overall story and message those pictures represent.

Revelation gives us in pictorial form the same message the Gospels give us in spoken form. Both make it clear that Satan will not be able to prevent Jesus from building His church, and the gates of Hell will not be able to prevail against the church.

What do the Gospels present in verbal form? Christ's conflict with Satan and his people. What happens at the end of the Gospels? Christ triumphs over Satan and his people. Revelation conveys the same message in pictorial form. There is conflict between Christ and Satan, and between Christ's people and Satan's people. What happens at the end of Revelation? Christ and His people triumph over Satan and his people.

In the book of Revelation, we have the same spiritual conflict and triumph described in a pictorial form that is described in a verbal form in the Gospels. Both the Gospels and the book of Revelation make exactly the same message clear, and the message is this: Satan will not be able to stop Jesus from building His kingdom, and Satan will not be able to defeat Christ's kingdom. Christ and His people will triumph, and Satan and his people will go down to defeat. The difference is that this message is conveyed verbally in the Gospels, but it is conveyed by means of pictures in Revelation.

We must understand the literary style of this book and not literalize its symbolic language any more than we would literalize a parable or a political cartoon. Literature that contains large amounts of highly symbolic language is called apocalyptic literature. While it contains some ordinary prose, it has extensive passages that are made up of highly figurative language. We are supposed to interpret apocalyptic literature symbolically unless we are forced to interpret it literally. Examples of apocalyptic literature in the Bible are the books of Revelation, Ezekiel, and Daniel.

The Bible Itself Provides the Meaning of the Symbolic Language Revelation Contains

The London Baptist Confession of Faith of 1689 in chapter 1 paragraph 9 says this: "The infallible rule of interpretation of Scripture is the Scripture itself; and therefore, when there is a question about the true and full sense of any Scripture. . ., it must be searched by other places that speak more clearly."

The Confession of Faith is asserting that if you want to understand any passage of Scripture, understanding will be achieved by looking at other passages of Scripture that either speak more clearly or shed additional light on the passage you are studying. Scripture is self-interpreting; in other words, Scripture interprets Scripture. When you are struggling with an obscure or difficult passage, you do not need to go outside the Bible to find the proper understanding of that passage; rather, you look elsewhere within the Bible in order to find its meaning.

We do not look in the newspaper, we do not look at current world events, and we do not look back at the last 2,000 years of history in order to try to understand the Scriptures. The Scriptures are self-explanatory. We need to look in the Bible itself to gain an understanding of the symbolic language Revelation contains. When the meaning of a passage is uncertain, try to discover if the Bible addresses that issue, that statement, or that symbolic picture in some other place. As you find other passages that speak of them, you will find they cast light on the passage you are struggling with.

There are three points that are necessary to understand about interpreting symbolic language.

First of all, we must interpret symbolic language in light of clear prose passages elsewhere in the Bible that address the same issues. There are clear prose passages that address all the issues in the book of Revelation. For example, we have chapters like 1 Thessalonians 4 and 5, 2 Thessalonians 1 and 2, 2 Peter 3, and Matthew 24.

These chapters are not couched in symbolic, pictorial language. These passages are couched in ordinary prose. Therefore, if we want to understand the highly symbolic language of Revelation, we first go to ordinary prose passages that do not contain highly symbolic language and which speak about the same matters. We read and study them, and out of them draw an understanding and a framework of truth by which we interpret these highly symbolic passages. We must start with ordinary prose passages that address the same issue as the symbolic passage we are trying to understand in order to interpret the symbolic passage. We must not start with the symbolic passage and use it to try to interpret the ordinary prose passage.

Second, we must interpret symbolic language in light of the analogy of faith. What this means is that no interpretation of Revelation can contradict the teaching of the rest of Scripture; and whatever interpretation we make, it must conform to the teaching of the rest of Scripture.

In other words, we have a whole Bible, and the Bible teaches a system of theology. In particular, it teaches a system of eschatology—that is, the study of the end times. Whatever interpretation we arrive at as to the meaning of Revelation, it cannot contradict what the rest of the Bible says about the end times, and it has to conform to what the rest of the Bible says about the end times. One of the presuppositions with which we approach the Scripture is the principle of non-contradiction, which means one part of the Bible is not going to teach something that contradicts another part of the Bible. The Bible is a harmonious, unified, and coherent presentation of truth that is complementary, not contradictory.

Therefore, whatever interpretation we come up with in Revelation, it cannot contradict the teachings of the rest of the Scripture on the subject of eschatology, and it must conform to the teachings of the rest of Scripture on eschatology.

Third, we must interpret symbolic language in light of how this language is used elsewhere in the Bible.

This is really the key to the whole matter of interpreting Revelation. It is critical to understand that the book of Revelation cannot be understood without understanding all that was written before it, especially the Old Testament.

Revelation is chronologically the last book of the Bible that was ever written. Since that is the case, it must be understood in light of all that was written before it. In particular, it must be understood in light of what the Old Testament has to say, because the book of Revelation is saturated with references to the Old Testament.

According to G.K. Beale[2] in his commentary on Revelation, there are 404 verses in the book of Revelation in total, and 278 of those verses contain one or more references to Old Testament passages. Over two thirds of the verses in the book of Revelation contain allusions or references to Old Testament passages. In fact, in this one book, there are over 500 allusions to Old Testament passages, compared to fewer than 200 in the rest of the entire New Testament. Revelation is saturated with references to the Old Testament.

What is fascinating is that while the book of Revelation never once formally quotes the Old Testament, it alludes to it constantly by way of the imagery and symbolism it uses and the language it contains. These allusions and references show the unity of the Old Testament and the New Testament, and they demonstrate that a single Author is behind them both, and that a single narrative runs through them

2 G. K. Beale and David H. Campbell. *Revelation, a Shorter Commentary*. Grand Rapids: Eerdmans Publishing Company, 2015, 1

both. The single narrative that runs through the Old Testament and the book of Revelation is the outworking of Genesis 3:15.

In chapter 1, we said the book of Revelation tells the end of the story of the outworking of Genesis 3:15, where God declared that He would put enmity between the seed of the woman and the seed of the serpent. Christ and Satan are in this great battle; Christ's people and Satan's people are in this great battle; and the rest of the whole Bible is the outworking of that battle and the outcome of that battle. Therefore, when you see the book of Revelation saturated with references to the Old Testament, you should recognize that whatever the narrative of the Old Testament is, it is the narrative that is carried on and concluded in the book of Revelation.

The point is simply this: All these strange figures in the book of Revelation, all these symbolic creatures, and all these puzzling statements all find their meaning and interpretation in how they are used in the rest of the Bible. That is why first-century Christians did not have any problem understanding Revelation because their minds were saturated with the imagery and symbolism of the Old Testament. When they read Revelation, they immediately made the connection.

The better you know the Old Testament, the better you will understand the meaning of Revelation. All of the symbolism in Revelation is represented in one way or another in the Old Testament.

The Non-Consecutive Structure of the Book of Revelation

The book of Revelation is chronologically nonconsecutive in its structure. In other words, the book is not written as a linear chronology. Instead, it has a cyclical structure, in which the time period from the first to the second coming of Christ is traversed over and over again, each time from a different perspective and with a different emphasis.

For example, the seals, the trumpets, and the vials all cover the same time period from three different perspectives. Several other sections in the book of Revelation do so as well. In the next chapter we will describe each of those sections. Each of those sections starts out with the first coming of Christ and concludes with His second coming. The structure of Revelation is not that of a consecutive chronological prophecy of events as they follow one another; rather, what we see is a repeated repetition and recapitulation of the same time period.

This is clearly illustrated in Revelation 8 to 11, which contain the seven trumpet judgments. They announce the fall of the wrath of God on the wicked between the first and second coming of Christ. The seventh trumpet is a description of the final judgment.

Revelation 11:15 says, *"And the seventh angel sounded; and there were great voices in heaven, saying, The kingdoms of this world are become the kingdoms of our Lord, and of his Christ; and he shall reign for ever and ever."* Verse 18 goes on to say, *"And the nations were angry, and thy wrath is come, and the time of the dead, that they should be judged, and that thou shouldest give reward unto thy servants the prophets, and to the saints, and them that fear thy name, small and great; and shouldest destroy them which destroy the earth."* The time of the final judgment has come, the wicked are punished, the righteous are given their reward, and we have the end of the age.

At the end of Revelation 11, we have the second coming and the final judgment in the seventh trumpet. Then we come to chapter 12 which opens with these words: "[1] *And there appeared a great wonder in heaven; a woman clothed with the sun, and the moon under her feet, and upon her head a crown of twelve stars:* [2] *And she being with child cried, travailing in birth, and pained to be delivered.* [3] *And there appeared another wonder in heaven; and behold a great red dragon, having seven heads and ten horns, and seven crowns upon his heads.* [4] *And his tail drew the third part of the stars of heaven, and did cast them to the earth: and the dragon stood before the woman which was ready to be delivered, for to devour her child as soon as it was born.* [5] *And she brought forth a man child, who was to rule all nations with a rod of iron: and her child was caught up unto God, and to his throne.* [6] *And the woman fled into the wilderness, where she hath a place prepared of God, that they should feed her there a thousand two hundred and threescore days."*

Everyone agrees that these first six verses describe the birth of the Lord Jesus Christ. In chapter 11 we have a declaration of the end of time and the end of the New Covenant era. Then in chapter 12 we are brought back to the beginning of the New Covenant era. Revelation 11:15–18 speaks of the final judgment, while the passages immediately following take us back to the first coming of Christ in 12:1–6. Therefore, just because one chapter follows another, it does not necessarily mean that the events of the following chapter are subsequent in time to the events of the previous chapter.

We see this as well in Daniel 2 and Daniel 7. In Daniel 2, we see the prediction of future history in the symbolic visual image of a man who has a head of gold, chest of silver, legs of brass, lower legs of iron, and feet of iron and clay mixed together. A great stone representing Christ comes and shatters the image. Here is a declaration of history up to the coming of Christ. Then that same history is recapitulated in the symbolic visual imagery of the four beasts of chapter 7. The same four kingdoms are described by the four beasts, and then we have Christ coming and overwhelming them. The same time period is described twice, from two different perspectives. This is the same kind of pattern of repetition we see in the book of Revelation.

It is like repeatedly taking the same trip from one town to another some distance away. Each time you take ten photos along the way. One trip you take photographs of all the intersections, so you can tell the story of all the intersections from one town to the other. Then you take the same trip a second time and photograph all the bridges between the two towns to tell the story of the bridges that exist along that route. On a third trip, you photograph all the stores between the two towns, to tell the story about the stores in that area. We have the same journey described in three different ways, with three different themes.

That is how the book of Revelation is structured. We make the same trip each time from the same starting point to the same destination, beginning with the first coming of Christ and ending with the second coming of Christ, each time with parallel but different stories of the same journey. In the book of Revelation, there are seven journeys that are taken from the first coming of Christ to the second coming of Christ, each of them presenting that journey from a different perspective and with a different emphasis. We will explore this in detail in the next chapter.

Summary

If we are going to rightly understand the book of Revelation, we need to understand the literary style of this book. It uses highly symbolic visual imagery, and the message of the book is in the symbolic meaning of those pictures.

Furthermore, we have to look in the Bible itself, and especially in the Old Testament, to understand the meaning of the symbols, metaphors, and pictorial language that Revelation uses.

Finally, we have to grasp the non-consecutive, cyclical nature of the book of Revelation. It is full of repetition and recapitulation of the same time period again and again. It describes the nature of the spiritual warfare that takes place during that time period from various perspectives.

When we put together these seven journeys from the first to the second coming of Christ, we have an overall picture of the nature of the spiritual warfare that will take place during that time between Christ and Satan and between those who have the seal of God and those who have the mark of the beast. Each of those journeys concludes with the second coming of Christ at the end of the age.

We need to remember the overall theme of the book. The book is the revelation of Jesus Christ and His victory over Satan. It is a book of triumph in which Christ wins and His people win, and Satan loses and his people lose; therefore, even if we do not fully understand every one of these pictures as much as we might, the overall message is abundantly clear. The message is that God's blessing and deliverance is given to His people, and God's wrath and punishment falls upon all those who oppose Him and them.

Revelation is a book of triumph and a book of comfort, a book of victory and a book of encouragement, a book whose purpose is to keep us faithful in the spiritual warfare and persecution that we experience. Every generation has had to fight these same battles and endure these same persecutions, and therefore, Revelation is essential for every generation to understand and apply to their time and their struggles.

This means that, in our generation, we can fight our battles with confidence, not only looking back and seeing the triumph of our brethren, but also knowing that we too will triumph and overcome. It is those who have faith in Christ who do overcome and who will overcome. And how shall we overcome? We shall overcome by the blood of the Lamb, and by the word of our testimony of our faith in Him.

4

The Structure of the Book of Revelation

In chapter 3, we discussed three principles of interpretation we must follow if we are to rightly understand the meaning and message of the book of Revelation.

First of all, we need to understand the literary style of the book. It was primarily written in the form of highly symbolic visual imagery. It presents its message in symbolic pictures that are not meant to be taken literally, though these pictures do convey a specific and literal message.

The general rule of the interpretation of the rest of the New Testament is this: When the plain sense makes good sense, seek no other sense. Interpret what you read literally unless you are compelled to interpret it symbolically, because the literal sense makes no sense. But in the book of Revelation this rule is turned on its head. In Revelation 1:1, we are told that the message in this book is going to be communicated by means of signs. Therefore, the rule in the book of Revelation is this: Interpret what you read symbolically unless you are compelled to interpret it literally.

The main method of communication in this book is that of symbolism, and we need to start with the presupposition that what we are reading is symbolic. We start with the presupposition that we are expecting symbolism unless there are compelling reasons to say that it is not symbolic. This is a crucial principle to understand if we are going to properly interpret Revelation. We have to understand that it was primarily written in the form of highly symbolic visual imagery; therefore, we must interpret it symbolically unless we are compelled to interpret it literally.

The second principle of interpretation is that we need to look into the Bible itself to understand the meaning of the symbolic language Revelation contains. When we read about the beasts with their multiple heads and their multiple crowns and various other fantastic symbolic images, where will we gain an understanding of what those symbols mean? We will find that meaning in the rest of the Bible.

We are going to look in the New Testament at the non-symbolic passages that address these same issues—passages like 1 Thessalonians 4 and 5, 2 Thessalonians 1 and 2, 2 Peter 3, and Matthew 24. These passages do contain some symbolism, but they are not primarily symbolic; primarily, they are literal and are to be taken literally. We must interpret symbolic passages in light of literal passages.

We are also going to look in the Old Testament to see how these symbols are used there because there are hundreds of allusions to Old Testament stories, events, and symbols in the book of Revelation. In the Old Testament, we discover the meaning of the symbols that are contained in Revelation.

All we need to understand the Bible is the Bible itself. The Bible is a self-interpreting book. It will give us all the answers we need as to the meaning of the symbolic language in Revelation. If we understand the other sixty-five books of the Bible, understanding the sixty-sixth one will not be difficult. All these strange figures, symbolic creatures, puzzling statements, and this unusual numerology find their meaning and interpretation when we see how they are used elsewhere in the Bible.

The third principle of interpretation is that we need to understand the non-consecutive nature of the structure of the book of Revelation. This book has a cyclic structure, not a linear one. This book is not a consecutive chronological prophecy; instead, this book has a parallel structure in which the same period of time is traversed over and over again, each time from a different perspective. We are taken on seven journeys from the first coming of Christ to the second coming of Christ.

In this chapter, we are going to examine this cyclic structure of the book of Revelation. The following outline will help clarify that structure:

Outline of the Book of Revelation

1A THE PHYSICAL CONFLICT BETWEEN BELIEVERS AND UNBELIEVERS 1–11
- 1B The **first** parallel section of the book: 1:1–3:22
  - 1C The introduction to the book: 1:1–20
    - 1D The source of the revelation is God the Father: 1:1a
    - 2D The messenger of the revelation is John: 1:1b–3
    - 3D The recipients of the revelation are the seven churches: 1:4–9
    - 4D The focus of the revelation is the glorified Christ: 1:10–20
  - 2C The letters to the seven churches: 2:1–3:22
    - 1D To Ephesus: 2:1–7
    - 2D To Smyrna: 2:8–11
    - 3D To Pergamos: 2:12–17
    - 4D To Thyatira: 2:18–29
    - 5D To Sardis: 3:1–6
    - 6D To Philadelphia: 3:7–13
    - 7D To Laodicea: 3:14–22
- 2B The **second** parallel section of the book: 4:1–8:5
  - 1C The vision of the throne in heaven: 4:1–5:14
  - 2C The vision of the seven seals: 6:1–8:5
- 3B The **third** parallel section of the book: 8:6–11:19
  - 1C The first six trumpets: 8:6–9:21
  - 2C The vision of the little book: 10:1–11
  - 3C The vision of the two witnesses: 11:1–12
  - 4C The seventh trumpet: 11:13–19

2A THE SPIRITUAL CONFLICT BETWEEN CHRIST AND SATAN 12–22
- 1B The **fourth** parallel section of the book: 12:1–14:20
  - 1C The vision of the woman and the dragon: 12:1–17
  - 2C The vision of the two beasts: 13:1–18
  - 3C The vision of the victory of the Lamb: 14:1–20
- 2B The **fifth** parallel section of the book: 15:1–16:21
  - 1C The prologue to the seven vials: 15:1–4
  - 2C The presentation of the seven vials: 15:5–8
  - 3C The pouring out of the seven vials: 16:1–21
- 3B The **sixth** parallel section of the book: 17:1–19:21
  - 1C The vision of the judgment of Babylon: 17:1–19:6

2C The vision of the marriage supper of the Lamb: 19:7–10
3C The vision of the second coming: 19:11–21
4B The **seventh** parallel section of the book: 20:1–22:21
1C The vision of the binding and loosing of Satan: 20:1–10
2C The vision of the Great White Throne judgment: 20:11–15
3C The vision of the New Heaven and the New Earth: 21:1–22:7
4C The conclusion: 22:8–21
1D The exhortation of the angel: 22:8–11
2D The proclamation of Christ: 22:12–21

Each of these seven parallel sections of the book begins with the first coming of Christ and ends with the second coming of Christ. Each of these parallel sections describes from various perspectives the spiritual warfare that will take place during that time period. While all of these sections are parallel, they also progressively reveal, with increasing clarity, the nature of the second coming.

The theme of the book is that Christ will triumph over Satan and his people, and will bring deliverance and victory to His faithful suffering saints by His second coming and His establishment of the New Heaven and the New Earth.

The key verse of the book is Revelation 17:14. "*These shall make war with the Lamb, and the Lamb shall overcome them: for he is Lord of lords, and King of kings: and they that are with him are called, and chosen, and faithful.*"

The Two Major Divisions of the Book

The book of Revelation can be divided into two halves. The first half of the book consists of The Physical Conflict Between Believers and Unbelievers in chapters 1 through 11.

In this first group of John's visions, the world attacks the church and persecutes it. But in the end, God's wrath falls on the world, the church is avenged by God, and the church is made victorious over the world. Chapters 1 through 11 tell us what visible human history has looked like and what will take place on the earth between the first and second coming of Christ. For 2,000 years now, the church has gone out into the world and preached the gospel, and the world has pushed back against the church and tried to persecute her and crush her. Chapters 1 through 11 portray this visible, physical conflict between the church and the world.

The second half of the book consists of THE SPIRITUAL CONFLICT BETWEEN CHRIST AND SATAN in chapters 12 through 22.

In this second group of visions, we see that behind the visible struggle of the church against the world is the invisible, spiritual struggle between Christ and Satan. Beginning in chapter 12, we see Satan attacking Christ, and because Satan was repulsed and failed to destroy Christ, Satan then directs his fury against the church. What is described in chapters 1 through 11 where the world attacks the church is explained by what is described in chapter 12 when we see Satan attacking Christ. There are spiritual realities going on behind the scenes that explain why the physical realities we see with our eyes are taking place. The world is not attacking the church for no reason. It is doing it because, behind the scenes, Satan is attacking Christ, and this attack is manifested in the attack of Satan's people on Christ's people in the visible realm.

As the second half of Revelation develops, we learn that Satan, who is called "the dragon," employs four agents to assist him in his evil work: the beast that arises out of the sea; a second beast that arises out of the land, subsequently called the false prophet; the harlot Babylon; and all those who have the mark of the beast. All of these help the dragon in his assault upon Christ and His church. In the second half of Revelation, we see the development of Satan's arsenal and how he uses it in fighting Christ and His people. Satan recruits the beast, the false prophet, the harlot Babylon, and all the people who have the mark of the beast. Together, they all fight against Christ and His people.

However, we also see in this latter half of Revelation that each of these helpers of Satan is systematically destroyed by Christ. The church does not destroy them; Christ destroys them! Then at the last, in chapter 20, Satan himself is destroyed. The point is that we do not just fight against flesh and blood, as chapters 1 to 11 portray; we fight against principalities and powers and Satan himself, as chapters 12 to 22 reveal.

If you are living for Jesus, you have conflicts in your life with unsaved people. All those who live godly lives in Christ Jesus will suffer persecution. What is behind those persecutions? Is it just misunderstandings? Is it just personality conflicts? Not at all. There are spiritual forces behind these physical, visible conflicts. What is playing out in our lives is the behind-the-scenes battle between Christ and Satan himself.

The book of Revelation tells us that what we see is not all there is. We need to understand that in our conflicts, as the world assaults us because of our effort to bring the gospel to it, there is more to it than just that hostile person who resists our efforts. Satan is at work through that person, just as Christ is at work through us. In these earthly, visible conflicts, Satan is trying to devour Christ, and Christ is progressively crushing the head of Satan.

The Seven Parallel Sections in the Book

Notice the statement at the bottom of our outline: "Each of these seven parallel sections of the book begins with the first coming of Christ and ends with the second coming of Christ. Each of these parallel sections describes from various perspectives the spiritual warfare that will take place during that time period. And while each of these sections are parallel, they also progressively reveal with increasing clarity the nature of the second coming."

Look at the outline and notice all the "B" points: 1B, 2B, 3B, etc. Notice that the ordinal numbers are **bolded**. Under the first major heading 1A, we have: 1B, the **first** parallel section of the book; 2B, the **second** parallel section of the book; 3B the **third** parallel section of the book; and now under the second major heading 2A, we have: 1B, the **fourth** parallel section; 2B, the **fifth** parallel section; 3B, the **sixth** parallel section; and 4B, the **seventh** parallel section.

This **bolding** is to point out that even though we have two major divisions of the book, there is a continuity that flows through the entire book in these seven parallel sections. The reason these sections are parallel is that the first parallel section starts with the first coming of Christ, spiritual conflict takes place, and then the second coming of Christ occurs. The second parallel section starts with the first coming of Christ, spiritual conflict takes place, and then the second coming of Christ occurs, and so on with each of the remaining parallel sections.

Each of these sections takes us through the same time period. They tell us what spiritual warfare is going to look like between the first and the second coming of Christ from one perspective, and then from a second perspective, and then from a third perspective, and so on. This is why we say the book of Revelation is not a linear prophecy—that is, the things that happen in chapter 12 do not chronologically follow what happened in chapter 11, and what happens in chapter 20 does not chronologically follow what happened in chapter 19. How shall we know what marks the beginning and the ending of each of these parallel sections? What marks the beginning of each section is the first coming of Christ, and what marks the end of each section is the second coming of Christ.

In four of the seven parallel sections, the first coming of Christ is explicitly mentioned at the start of them. In all seven of them, the second coming of Christ is explicitly mentioned at the end of them. There are seven declarations of the second coming of Jesus in the book of Revelation, and they occur at the end of each of these sections. This is why we know that the next section goes back to the beginning again because once we have arrived at the second coming, we have arrived at the end of the age. If the narrative is to continue, John has to go back to the first coming and retrace that same journey to the second coming again, and this is what he does seven times. Thus, we see the cyclic nature of the book.

We will now briefly survey the book of Revelation and look at the start and finish of each of these seven parallel sections.

The first parallel section that covers chapters 1 to 3 opens with a mention of the first coming of Christ in 1:4–6, "*John to the seven churches which are in Asia: Grace be unto you, and peace, from him which is, and which was, and which is to come; and from the seven Spirits which are before his throne;* [5] *And from Jesus Christ. . .*" Now notice what it says: ". . .*who is the faithful witness, and the first begotten of the dead, and the prince of the kings of the earth. Unto him that loved us, and washed us from our sins in his own blood,* [6] *And hath made us kings and priests unto God and his Father; to him be glory and dominion for ever and ever. Amen.*"

Verse 5 describes the first coming of Jesus and the work He achieved on the cross. It speaks about Him washing us in His blood and rising from the dead. Notice 1:17–18, "*And when I saw him, I fell at his feet as dead. And he laid his right hand upon me, saying unto me, Fear not; I am the first and the last:* [18] *I am he that liveth, and was dead; and, behold, I am alive for evermore, Amen; and have the keys of hell and of death.*"

This chapter opens with a vision of Jesus and a description of His first coming and the work he achieved: His death, His burial, His resurrection, and the cleansing power of His blood shed on the cross.

Jesus then dictates seven letters to the seven churches in chapters 2 and 3, which are representative of all the churches that exist throughout this age. These seven churches portray the virtues, challenges, deficiencies, and blessings that all churches experience throughout the New Covenant era.

We see Jesus as the head of His church, standing in the midst of His church and giving directions to His churches. He commends them; He corrects them; He warns them; He issues challenges to them; He gives them wonderful promises; and He declares blessings upon them.

At the end of chapter 3, the final church spoken of is the church at Laodicea. Notice that in 3:20–21 the second coming is alluded to. *"Behold, I stand at the door, and knock: if any man hear my voice, and open the door, I will come in to him, and will sup with him, and he with me."*

The word *"sup"* is a very interesting word. It conveys the idea of sitting down to have supper with someone. It should remind us of the marriage supper of the Lamb spoken of in Revelation 19 which occurs after the second coming of Christ. Revelation 19:7–9 says, *"Let us be glad and rejoice, and give honour to him: for the marriage of the Lamb is come, and his wife hath made herself ready. . .[9]Blessed are they which are called unto the marriage supper of the Lamb."*

Jesus goes on to say in 3:21, *"To him that overcometh will I grant to sit with me in my throne, even as I also overcame, and am set down with my Father in his throne."*

When will we sit in Christ's throne with Him? We will do so at His second coming.

This first section opens with statements about Jesus' first coming: His death, burial, and resurrection. It closes with an allusion to the marriage supper of the Lamb that will occur after the second coming and a direct statement about sitting down with Him in His throne. This marriage supper and this sitting with Christ in His throne will occur when He returns.

The second parallel section of the book covers 4:1 through 8:5. Here we have the vision of the throne in heaven in chapters 4 and 5, and the vision of the seven seals in chapters 6 through 8:5.

Notice in this second parallel section the first coming of Christ. In chapter 4 we have the vision of the throne of God. It is a description of heaven and God sitting on the throne with the angels around it. In chapter 5 we have God the Father holding a book in His hand, and no one was found worthy to open the book until Jesus comes.

Notice 5:5–10: *"And one of the elders saith unto me, Weep not: behold, the Lion of the tribe of Judah, the Root of David, hath prevailed to open the book, and to loose the seven seals thereof.* 6 *And I beheld, and, lo, in the midst of the throne and of the four beasts, and in the midst of the elders, stood a Lamb as it had been slain, having seven horns and seven eyes, which are the seven Spirits of God sent forth into all the earth.* 7 *And he came and took the book out of the right hand of him that sat upon the throne.* 8 *And when he had taken the book, the four beasts and four and twenty elders fell down before the Lamb, having every one of them harps, and golden vials full of odours, which are the prayers of saints.* 9 *And they sung a new song, saying, Thou art worthy to take the book, and to open the seals thereof: for thou wast slain, and hast redeemed us to God by thy blood out of every kindred, and tongue, and people, and nation;* 10 *And hast made us unto our God kings and priests: and we shall reign on the earth."*

In chapter 5, the first coming of Jesus is described in verses 5, 6, and 9, where the slain Lamb of God is set forth who redeemed us to God by His blood. This second section opens with His work on the cross. Here is the throne and here is the Lamb viewed in His first coming.

The Lamb takes the book and opens these seven seals. In these seven seals is a symbolic description of the opposition to the building of the kingdom of God throughout this age and the evil unsaved humanity will carry out on the earth. The first five seals detail the wicked behavior of Satan's servants in this age. This also characterizes the entire age.

When the sixth seal is opened, we have the second coming. In 6:12–17 we read: *"And I beheld when he had opened the sixth seal, and, lo, there was a great earthquake; and the sun became black as sackcloth of hair, and the moon became as blood;* 13 *And the stars of heaven fell unto the earth, even as a fig tree casteth her untimely figs, when she is shaken of a mighty wind.* 14 *And the heaven departed as a scroll when it is rolled together; and every mountain and island were moved out of their places.* 15 *And the kings of the earth, and the great men, and the rich men, and the chief captains, and the mighty men, and every bondman, and every free man, hid themselves in the dens and in the rocks of the mountains;* [16] *And said to the mountains and rocks, Fall on us, and hide us from the face of him that sitteth on the throne, and from the wrath of the Lamb:* [17]*For the great day of his wrath is come; and who shall be able to stand?"* This is a description of the second coming and its effect on the lost.

Chapter 7 describes the second coming and its effect on the saved. Here we have the 144,000 sealed, 12,000 out of each of the 12 tribes, which are all symbolic numbers and terms that represent the totality of the saved. (We will prove this in chapter 25.) Where do we see these saved people residing?

Revelation 7:9–17 tells us, "*After this I beheld, and, lo, a great multitude, which no man could number, of all nations, and kindreds, and people, and tongues, stood before the throne, and before the Lamb, clothed with white robes, and palms in their hands. . .* [16]*They shall hunger no more, neither thirst any more; neither shall the sun light on them, nor any heat.* [17] *For the Lamb which is in the midst of the throne shall feed them, and shall lead them unto living fountains of waters: and God shall wipe away all tears from their eyes."* Here we have a vision of the New Earth (which is further expanded upon at length in Revelation 22) which the saved will inhabit after the second coming.

In chapter 5 is the first coming of Jesus. At His ascension, based upon His recently completed redemptive work on the cross, He receives the book, and He begins to open the seven seals. In them, we see the work of the wicked throughout this age. At the opening of the sixth seal at the end of this age, we see the wicked under the wrath of God and the righteous in the heaven of God. This concludes the second parallel section of the book. Just as the first parallel section opened with the first coming and closed with the second coming, the second parallel section opened with the first coming and closes with the second coming.

The third parallel section covers 8:6 through 11:19. Chapter 8 opens with these words, "[1] *And when he had opened the seventh seal, there was silence in heaven about the space of half an hour.* [2] *And I saw the seven angels which stood before God; and to them were given seven trumpets."* Out of the seventh seal come the seven trumpets. The seventh seal begins a new vision and a new parallel section.

In this third parallel section of the book, we see tremendous judgments poured out on the unsaved which are symbolized by these seven trumpets. These seven trumpets describe what God does to the wicked to punish them for their evil deeds described in the first five seals of chapter 6.

These seven trumpets are Christ's warnings to the wicked to repent. The reason He makes things so hard and difficult for them is to give them powerful incentives to stop rebelling against Him and to move them to repent and submit themselves to Him. The purpose of these trumpets is to say to the wicked, "The way of the transgressor is hard. You need to repent. You need to humble yourself before God."

In this third parallel section, the seven trumpets sound, beginning with chapter 8, "[7] *The first angel sounded. . .* [8] *And the second angel sounded. . .* [10] *And the third angel sounded. . .* [12] *And the fourth angel sounded. . .*" Chapter 8 ends by telling us there are three more trumpets to go. In chapter 9:1–13 it says, "[1] *And the fifth angel sounded. . .* [13] *And the sixth angel sounded.*"

What is the conclusion? Notice chapter 9:20–21, "*And the rest of the men which were not killed by these plagues yet repented not of the works of their hands, that they should not worship devils, and idols of gold, and silver, and brass, and stone, and of wood: which neither can see, nor hear, nor walk:* [21] *Neither repented they of their murders, nor of their sorceries, nor of their fornication, nor of their thefts.*" Sadly, these judgments did not bring them to repentance. Any rational person would recognize the advantage and wisdom of repentance, but fallen sinners are not rational. They are darkened, blinded, and hardened by sin and Satan.

The seventh and final trumpet is spoken of in chapter 10:7; and there we are told that when it sounds, it will bring us to the end of this age: "*But in the days of the voice of the seventh angel, when he shall begin to sound, the mystery of God should be finished. . .*" That is, when the seventh trumpet sounds, it will bring us to the conclusion of God's plan for this world.

But before the seventh angel sounds, in chapter 11, we have the two witnesses who travel about and preach the gospel. They are invincible. They are unstoppable. No one can successfully oppose them. These two witnesses represent the church preaching the gospel to the world throughout the entire period of time between the first and second coming of Christ. (See chapter 33.) When Jesus sent out His apostles, how did He send them out? They are sent out two by two, for example, in Matthew 10. These two witnesses represent the people God has sent into the world to preach the gospel and spread it to all the nations of the earth, and the witness of believers cannot be stopped until the end.

Notice it states in chapter 11:7: *"And when they shall have finished their testimony, the beast that ascendeth out of the bottomless pit shall make war against them, and shall overcome them, and kill them."* Only when all of God's elect are saved, and therefore the testimony of the church is completed, can the Antichrist arise and end the public and visible testimony of the church on the earth. (See chapter 34.)

Verse 7 speaks of the great tribulation that occurs at the end of the age when the voice of the church is going to be silenced. The transnational persecution that takes place against the church is going to be so great during the reign of the Antichrist that only a small remnant of believers is going to be left alive. The voice of the church will be silenced. However, this silencing is only going to last a little time, a symbolic three and a half days.

When we deal with numerology in the next two chapters, we will explain the symbolic meaning of these numbers. In this chapter, we see time periods of three and a half years, a longer time, and then three and a half days, a very short time. Three and a half years symbolically describes the whole time frame between the first and the second coming, but three and a half days symbolically describes the short time period of the great tribulation, at the end of which, the resurrection of believers and the return of Christ occurs. Those who thought they had killed the church and wiped it off the face of the earth are devastated to see the church resurrected back to life again, and now they are in the worst possible trouble.

Notice chapter 11:11–18: *"And after three days and an half the Spirit of life from God entered into them, and they stood upon their feet; and great fear fell upon them which saw them.* [12] *And they heard a great voice from heaven saying unto them, Come up hither"* (this is the rapture spoken of in 1 Thessalonians 4:13–18). *"And they ascended up to heaven in a cloud; and their enemies beheld them.* [13] *And the same hour was there a great earthquake, and the tenth part of the city fell, and in the earthquake were slain of men seven thousand and the remnant were affrighted, and gave glory to the God of heaven.* [14] *The second woe is past; and, behold, the third woe cometh quickly."* This third woe is the final trumpet spoken of in the following verse.

"[15] *And the seventh angel sounded; and there were great voices in heaven, saying, The kingdoms of this world are become the kingdoms of our Lord, and of his Christ; and he shall reign for ever and ever."* This describes the second coming. "[16] *And the four and twenty elders, which sat before God on their seats, fell upon their faces, and worshipped God,* [17] *Saying, We give thee thanks, O Lord God Almighty, which art, and wast, and art to come; because thou hast taken to thee thy great power, and hast reigned.* [18] *And the nations were angry, and thy wrath is come, and the time of the dead, that they should be judged, and that thou shouldest give reward unto thy servants the prophets, and to the saints, and them that fear thy name, small and great; and shouldest destroy them which destroy the earth."* Once again, at the end of this third section, we are brought to the second coming and final judgment.

In this third parallel section of the book, we do not have a distinct mention of the first coming of Christ. But we do have a very clear mention of the unstoppable gospel preaching that was commissioned by Christ at His first coming in Acts 1:8, which will go on until the end of this age when the second coming occurs. When did the testimony of the two witnesses begin—that is, when did the witness of the church to the gospel begin? It began at the first coming of Christ. It seems very plain that this section of the seven trumpets spans the entire gospel age from when the great commission was given until that great commission is finally completed and finished.

That brings us to the fourth parallel section of the book which covers chapters 12–14. This begins the second half of the book where there is a shift in emphasis to the spiritual conflict between Christ and Satan that lies behind the conflict between the people of Satan and the people of God. In chapter 12, we have the vision of the woman and the dragon; in chapter 13, we have the vision of the two beasts, one that arises out of the sea and one out of the land; and then in chapter 14, we have the vision of the victory of the Lamb.

Since this is a new parallel section, we would expect that it would begin with a reference to the first coming of Christ, and this is exactly what we find. Revelation 12:1–5 says: *"And there appeared a great wonder in heaven; a woman clothed with the sun, and the moon under her feet, and upon her head a crown of twelve stars:* [2] *And she being with child cried, travailing in birth, and pained to be delivered."*

This woman represents Israel bringing forth Jesus. "[3] *And there appeared another wonder in heaven; and behold a great red dragon"* (the dragon represents Satan), "*having seven heads and ten horns, and seven crowns upon his heads.* [4] *And his tail drew the third part of the stars of heaven, and did cast them to the earth: and the dragon stood before the woman which was ready to be delivered, for to devour her child as soon as it was born.*"

How was Satan going to accomplish this devouring of Christ? Satan would use his servant Herod to kill Christ, and this is why Herod killed all the children two years and under in Bethlehem. Verse 5: "*And she brought forth a man child* (Jesus) *who was to rule all nations with a rod of iron: and her child was caught up unto God, and to his throne.*"

In verse 5, we have the birth, life, death, resurrection, and ascension of Jesus. It is a description of His first coming. As a result of the ascension of Jesus, the dragon is cast out of heaven. And because he knows he has lost the battle, he is violently angry. As a result, he goes out to persecute the church. Notice chapter 12:9: "*And the great dragon was cast out, that old serpent, called the Devil, and Satan.*" Verse 17: "*And the dragon was wroth with the woman, and went to make war with the remnant of her seed, which keep the commandments of God, and have the testimony of Jesus Christ.*"

Now that Satan has been defeated at the cross and cast out of heaven, what is he doing? For the last 2,000 years he has been persecuting the church, but not all by himself. He uses his helpers, which are described in chapter 13. His first helper is the beast out of the sea in 13:1, "*And I stood upon the sand of the sea, and saw a beast rise up out of the sea.*" His second helper is the beast that arises out of the earth, verse 11, "*And I beheld another beast coming up out of the earth; and he had two horns like a lamb, and he spake as a dragon.*"

The beast out of the sea represents anti-Christian civil government, and the beast out of the land represents anti-Christian false religion, in whatever time and place and form they may manifest themselves. We will prove these designations in chapters 41 and 42; but for now, it is necessary to understand that, inspired and empowered by the dragon, they both fight against the people of God. They deceive the people who dwell on the earth, and they cause the people that dwell on the earth to worship the dragon and the beast out of the sea. They impose the mark of the beast on all who serve them.

Now if all this is describing what happens between the first and the second coming, what does it tell you? It tells you that the mark of the beast has been in existence since the day of Pentecost. It is here now. It will always be here. The mark of the beast is not a literal tattoo on your forehead or on the back of your hand or an implanted computer chip. Recall that we are supposed to interpret apocalyptic literature symbolically unless we are forced to interpret it literally.

Therefore, when it says the mark of the beast is in the forehead and in the hand, we must look for a symbolic meaning, not a literal one. And what is that symbolic meaning? The mark on your forehead is symbolic of how you think. The mark on your hand is symbolic of how you behave. So, when Satan is guiding your thinking and your behavior, you have the mark of the beast in your thinking and in your actions.

When you look at the unsaved, you can see Satan's mark on them by the way they think and the way they act. If you have the mark of the beast on you while you live—that is, if your thinking and actions are guided by Satan while you live—then when you die, you will go to hell. The mark of the beast is not something that is going to appear at some point in the future. It is something that people have had since the first coming of Christ and it is something people have now. But if you do not think like the world and you do not act like the world, the world does not want to do business with you. Its people do not want to have interactions with you. They reject you. We will explain and apply those principles in detail in chapter 42.

Having seen the persecution that the dragon and the two beasts bring to bear on us throughout this age, we are then brought to the second coming in chapter 14. Revelation 14:1 says, "*And I looked, and, lo, a Lamb stood on the mount Zion, and with him an hundred forty and four thousand*" (who represent all of God's elect), "*having his Father's name written in their foreheads.*" Notice, the people of God have His mark in their foreheads, and the wicked have the mark of the beast in their foreheads. Both are symbolic of how the respective parties think, and, therefore, how they act. Verse 14: "*And I looked, and behold a white cloud, and upon the cloud one sat like unto the Son of man, having on his head a golden crown, and in his hand a sharp sickle.* [15] *And another angel came out of the temple, crying with a loud voice to him that sat on the cloud, Thrust in thy sickle, and reap: for the time is come for thee to reap; for the harvest of the earth is ripe.*[16] *And he that sat on the cloud thrust in his sickle on the earth; and the earth was reaped."*

Here the second coming is described when all the earth is gathered together for the final judgment. This fourth parallel section of the book opens with the first coming of Christ as the woman brings Jesus to birth in 12:1–5. It closes with the second coming of Jesus when He reaps the earth on the day of judgment in 14:14–16 when the wheat and the tares that grew up together are separated from one another in the harvest at the end of the world.

This fourth parallel section begins at chapter 12 and runs through chapter 14. We have the first coming of Christ, all the spiritual warfare with Satan and his helpers all throughout the age, and then the second coming.

The fifth parallel section of the book covers chapters 15 and 16, which contain the vision of the seven vials.

Seven vials of wrath are being poured out which represent God's final punishment for the unrepentant. We were told in 9:20–21 that the purpose of the seven trumpets was to awaken the unsaved to their danger and to provoke them to repentance. They had a merciful purpose, but in the end, the unsaved did not repent. When God's invitations of mercy are spurned, only judgment awaits. From these seven vials God's wrath is poured out on the unrepentant. The purpose of these seven vials is not to bring people to repentance; instead, it is to punish them.

In this fifth parallel section, we have no mention of the first coming of Christ at the start of it, but we do have a very clear mention of the second coming of Christ at the end of it. This leads us to believe that these seven vials of wrath span the same time period that the previous parallel sections cover, which also concluded with the second coming of Christ.

We have these vials of wrath introduced to us in chapter 15 in verses 1, 6, and 7. Notice verse 1, *"And I saw another sign in heaven, great and marvellous, seven angels having the seven last plagues; for in them is filled up the wrath of God.* Verse 6, *"And the seven angels came out of the temple, having the seven plagues."* Verse 7, *"And one of the four beasts gave unto the seven angels seven golden vials full of the wrath of God."*

These vials of wrath are then described in chapter 16. Verse 2: *"And the first went, and poured out his vial upon the earth;"* Verse 3: *"And the second angel poured out his vial upon the sea;"* Verse 4: *"And the third angel poured out his vial upon the rivers and fountains of waters;"* Verse 8: *"And the fourth angel poured out his vial upon the sun;"* Verse 10: *"And the fifth angel poured out his vial upon the seat of the beast;"* Verse 12: *"And the sixth angel poured out his vial upon the great river Euphrates;"* Verse 13: *"And I saw three unclean spirits like frogs come out of "* (notice the unholy trinity here) *"the dragon"* (Satan), *"out of the mouth of the beast"* (the beast that rises out of the sea), *"and out of the mouth of the false prophet,"* (the beast that rises out of the land). Jesus is at war with this unholy trinity, and they are at war with Him. "[14] *For they are the spirits of devils, working miracles, which go forth unto the kings of the earth and of the whole world, to gather them to the battle of that great day of God Almighty."* This sixth vial brings us up to the Battle of Armageddon.

Verse 15: *"Behold, I come as a thief."* Christ's second coming is said to come as a thief in the night in 1 Thessalonians 5:2–4. "*Blessed is he that watcheth, and keepeth his garments, lest he walk naked, and they see his shame.* [16] *And he gathered them together into a place called in the Hebrew tongue Armageddon."*

Once again at the end of this section we are brought to the second coming of Christ. Verse 17: *"The seventh angel poured out his vial into the air;" Verse* 20: *"And every island fled away, and the mountains were not found."* These verses describe the destruction of the world at Christ's second coming in the same way it is described in Revelation 6:12–14 and in 2 Peter 3:10–13. We see then that this fifth parallel section concludes with the second coming of Christ.

The sixth parallel section of the book covers chapters 17 to 19. Here we see the nature and function and identity of Babylon the harlot. Revelation 17:1: *"And there came one of the seven angels which had the seven vials, and talked with me, saying unto me, Come hither; I will shew unto thee the judgment of the great whore that sitteth upon many waters;"* Verse 5: *"And upon her forehead was a name written, Mystery, Babylon the great, the mother of harlots and abominations of the earth."*

Chapter 17 describes the nature of Babylon the harlot. She is another of Satan's helpers. Babylon represents anti-Christian society, with all of its entertainments, honors, pleasures, and wealth. (See chapter 44.) Babylon represents worldliness and the seduction of the world. When John says, *"Love not the world, neither the things that are in the world,"* he is speaking of Babylon.

Chapter 18 describes the destruction of Babylon the harlot. Notice verse 2, *"And he cried mightily with a strong voice, saying, Babylon the great is fallen, is fallen."* Notice 19:2, *"For true and righteous are his judgments: for he hath judged the great whore, which did corrupt the earth with her fornication, and hath avenged the blood of his servants at her hand."*

After the destruction of Babylon, the second coming of Christ and the marriage supper of the Lamb immediately occurs in chapter 19. Verses 7–9 say, *"Let us be glad and rejoice, and give honour to him: for the marriage of the Lamb is come, and his wife hath made herself ready. [8]And to her was granted that she should be arrayed in fine linen, clean and white: for the fine linen is the righteousness of saints. [9]And he saith unto me, Write, Blessed are they which are called unto the marriage supper of the Lamb. And he saith unto me, These are the true sayings of God."*

This marriage supper of the Lamb is the supping that Jesus promised in Revelation 3:20.

Verse 11: *"And I saw heaven opened, and behold a white horse; and he that sat upon him was called Faithful and True, and in righteousness he doth judge and make war."* This is Jesus. Verse 14: *"And the armies which were in heaven followed him upon white horses, clothed in fine linen, white and clean."* These are the saints that accompany Jesus from heaven at His second coming as promised in 1 Thessalonians 4:14. At His second coming, Jesus will be revealed to the whole world as *"[16]KING OF KINGS AND LORD OF LORDS."*

Verse 19: *"And I saw the beast, and the kings of the earth, and their armies, gathered together to make war against him that sat on the horse, and against his army."* Here we see the Battle of Armageddon set forth once again. Verse 20: *"And the beast was taken, and with him the false prophet that wrought miracles before him, with which he deceived them that had received the mark of the beast, and them that worshipped his image. These both were cast alive into a lake of fire burning with brimstone."*

Once again, we are brought to the second coming and final judgment. In this sixth parallel section, we see no specific mention of the first coming in particular, but we do see a very clear description of the second coming at the end of this section, just as we see Christ's second coming at the end of every one of these sections.

The seventh parallel section of the book covers chapters 20 to 22.

Once again, we see the first coming of Christ. Chapter 20:1–3, *"And I saw an angel come down from heaven, having the key of the bottomless pit and a great chain in his hand.* [2] *And he laid hold on the dragon, that old serpent, which is the Devil, and Satan, and bound him a thousand years,* [3] *And cast him into the bottomless pit, and shut him up, and set a seal upon him, that he should deceive the nations no more, till the thousand years should be fulfilled: and after that he must be loosed a little season."*

We see the first coming of Christ in 20:1–3 when Satan was bound. Satan was bound at the cross, at the first coming of Jesus. (See chapter 57.) In Matthew 12:29, Jesus said: You cannot spoil the strong man's house unless you first bind the strong man, and then you can spoil his house. He told how His casting out of demons was proof that He was victorious over Satan and his people. By His work at his first coming, He was going to bind the strong man Satan, and He bound him.

Why do you suppose, from Genesis to the first coming of Christ, the kingdom of God was comprised of a tiny little nation confined to a tiny piece of real estate? It is because Satan was deceiving the whole rest of the world. But when Satan is bound at the cross, what happens to the kingdom of God? It explodes in size and scope so it now covers the whole earth. The reason it did not cover the whole earth for the first 4,000 years is because Satan was loose and had all the rest of the world held in bondage and darkness.

Satan became bound at the cross; and as a result, he could deceive the nations no longer. The nations heard the gospel, the nations received the gospel, and the gospel spread throughout the whole world. But at the end, Satan is going to be loosed, and he will deceive the nations once again. He will gather them all together under the Antichrist into a transnational coalition that will have as its goal the destruction of the church. This was symbolically represented by the killing of the two witnesses of Revelation 11. Satan and his helpers will succeed for three and a half days—a symbolic term for a very short period of time. However, Satan and his helpers will be destroyed at the second coming.

Notice Revelation 20:7–15. The thousand years are expired. The thousand years symbolically describes the time between the first and second coming of Christ, which we will prove in chapter 57. *"And when the thousand years are expired, Satan shall be loosed out of his prison,* [8] *And shall go out to deceive the nations which are in the four quarters of the earth."* Notice, Satan can now deceive nations. He could not do it before, but he is going to do it now. The "four quarters" refer to north, south, east, and west. He is going to *"gather them together to battle:"* (which is the battle of Armageddon) *"the number of whom is as the sand of the sea. [9] And they went up on the breadth of the earth, and compassed the camp of the saints about, and the beloved city."* The church is just about to be destroyed from the face of the earth. But Christ intervenes: *"and fire came down from God out of heaven, and devoured them. [10] And the devil that deceived them was cast into the lake of fire and brimstone, where the beast and the false prophet are, and shall be tormented day and night for ever and ever. [11] And I saw a great white throne, and him that sat on it. . ."* Now we have come to the last judgment—verse 14: *"And death and hell were cast into the lake of fire. This is the second death. [15] And whosoever was not found written in the book of life was cast into the lake of fire."*

Chapter 20 opens with the first coming of Christ when He bound Satan at the cross, and it closes with the final destruction of Satan at His second coming after this intervening millennial period in which the church is severely persecuted. Notice 20:4, *"And I saw thrones, and they sat upon them, and judgment was given unto them: and I saw the souls of them that were beheaded for the witness of Jesus, and for the word of God, and which had not worshipped the beast, neither his image, neither had received his mark upon their foreheads, or in their hands; and they lived and reigned with Christ a thousand years."*

During this symbolic thousand-year period while Satan is bound from deceiving the nations, Christians are being martyred. Christians are refusing to receive the mark of the beast. Christians are saying: "I will not follow and submit to persecuting governments, perverse religious systems, or Babylonian worldliness. Those who do are those who have the mark of the beast on them. They think like the beast and the false religions and the world, and they act in accordance with them; but those are not my people, and I am not one of them. I belong to Christ, and I will serve Him alone!" Such attitudes and choices will cost Christians their lives all throughout this age.

What we see is Satan bound at the cross, and tremendous persecutions and beheadings of individual Christians during this age. At the end of the age, Satan is loosed to deceive the nations once again; but Jesus comes back when the persecutors are just about to destroy the last of the believers, and Jesus conquers Satan and all his helpers who are then cast into the Lake of Fire. We then have the great white throne of judgment, and the new heavens and the new earth are brought forth in 21:1. *"And I saw a new heaven and a new earth: for the first heaven and the first earth were passed away."*

In chapter 6, the wicked were crying out for the rocks and mountains to fall on them to hide them from the wrath of the final judgment. In chapter 7, we saw the saints in the New Earth. We see the same pattern here. In chapter 20, the wrath of the final judgment falls and the wicked are cast into the lake of fire. Then in chapters 21–22, we see the saints in the New Earth. There is a great deal of parallelism and recapitulation in this book.

The third, fifth, and sixth parallel sections did not open with a direct mention of the first coming of Christ, but the other four parallel sections did, indicating that the first coming begins the time frame during which all these parallel sections unfold. However, all seven sections do explicitly close with the second coming of Christ. The implication is that they all occur over the same time frame between the first and second coming, because they all close with the second coming.

Each of these seven sections closes with the second coming of Christ; and that second coming is progressively revealed in more and more detail and with greater and greater precision and clarity until it is revealed in all of its fullness in the final chapters. The second coming is not revealed in much detail at the start of the book; but as we proceed through the book, we are provided with more detail until finally, in chapters 20, 21, and 22, we are given the full revelation of the second coming and all the results that are going to flow out of it both for the wicked and for the righteous.

Summary

This is the structure of the book. Each of these seven parallel sections takes us from the first coming of Christ to the second coming of Christ—revealing the nature of that time period, and revealing the spiritual warfare that goes on during it, first from one perspective, then from another. We have seven pictures in these seven parallel sections of what the time period between the first and second coming of Christ is going to look like in every generation, and what we can expect to experience during the time period of our own generation.

Revelation is not primarily about what happened in the past, and it is not primarily about what happens in the future. It is primarily about the spiritual warfare we are going through right now. This helps us understand the spiritual battles we are fighting today in our Christian lives. We are living these things described in these seven parallel cycles, and the book of Revelation helps us make sense of them.

Recall the theme of the book stated at the end of our outline above: Christ will triumph over Satan and his people, and will bring deliverance and victory to His faithful suffering saints by His second coming and His establishment of the New Heavens and the New Earth.

What is this book about? It is about the fact that Christ is going to triumph over Satan and his people. Christ will bring deliverance and victory to His faithful, suffering saints. How is He going to do it? By sustaining them in the battle and by delivering them at the end of the battle so they are able to overcome Satan and his helpers. It is those who are the overcomers, who are faithful unto death, who will have a crown of life in the New Earth. They will not go apostate and join the other side and take the mark of the beast.

How many people have you known that started out being Christians, who went along with a Christian profession for a while, but the world and the flesh and the devil relentlessly attacked them and they finally caved in? The book of Revelation is saying this to every one of you: Do not give in to the temptations and the persecutions that Satan and his helpers bring to bear on you. What you are going through is normal. Jesus is saying: Trust Me. I will give you victory. You may even be beheaded. Christ does not have a problem with His people being beheaded. You notice both in chapter 6 and chapter 20 that there are very many people in heaven who were once heheaded. Could God have stopped that? Sure. But He says to us: Be faithful to death. I will give you a crown of life. I will fix your martyrdom. I will resurrect you back to life. Death is an easily solved problem for God.

In God's mind, for us to be killed is not a problem, and it should not be a problem for us either. If you are killed financially, if you are killed socially, if you are killed reputationally, or if you are killed physically, it is not a problem because God will remedy all of those things at the second coming. You are going to wind up in heaven with the rewards and riches and blessing of God, and God will say to you, "Well done, you good and faithful servant." The sorrows of this present time are not worthy to be compared with the glory that shall be revealed in us.

Notice the key verse of the book is Revelation 17:14: "*These*" (speaking of the Antichrist, the beast, the false prophet, the dragon, those with the mark of the beast, and Babylon) "*shall make war with the Lamb, and the Lamb shall overcome them: for he is Lord of lords, and King of kings: and they that are with him*" (the believers) "*are called, and chosen, and faithful.*"

There are two sides to this battle. There are those that are with the Lamb, and those that are against Him. We who are with the Lamb are those who have been effectually called because we were divinely and sovereignly elected. The result of that election and calling is that we are the faithful ones who endure to the end, who go through tribulation, and who stay faithful. Even if we are martyred, we do not change sides.

This all becomes increasingly relevant to you as you experience increasing persecution here in America. You see the Muslim hoards coming. Does that make you afraid? This book will tell you how to handle that. It will also tell you the outcome of it. The Muslims think they are very powerful as they behead the Christians. There is going to come a day when Jesus returns and raises all the Christians they beheaded from the dead, and then they are going to be absolutely terrified and cast into the lake of fire.

When we read in chapter 11 about the resurrection of the two witnesses, it says in verse 11, "*And after three days and a half the Spirit of life from God entered into them, and they stood upon their feet; and great fear fell upon them which saw them.*" When the Muslims see their beheaded victims rise up and be taken up to God, they are going to realize they were on the wrong side in the battle. We do not have anything to be afraid of because Christ wins and His people win, even though we go through terrible things in getting to that point of victory.

Mark it down: we are going to go through terrible things, but the sufferings of this present time are not worthy to be compared with the glory that shall be revealed in us. Do not quit because you are suffering. Just keep on persevering. In the end, we will be with Him in the new heavens and the new earth, and then everything that happened here will not matter. Let us keep that perspective as we suffer so that we keep on being faithful in our suffering. That is what the book was designed to encourage the first-century Christians to do, and Christians in every century afterward as well.

5

Biblical Numerology, Part 1

In the previous chapter, we saw that the structure of the book of Revelation was cyclic and not linear. The book of Revelation is not a consecutive chronological prophecy in which each event spoken of follows the one before it and precedes the one after it. The book of Revelation has a parallel structure in which the same period of time is traversed over and over again, but in each instance from a different perspective.

It repeatedly takes us on a journey from the first coming of Christ to the second coming of Christ, and each of these journeys describes from a different perspective the spiritual warfare that will occur during that time. Each makes it clear that even though this spiritual warfare will be difficult and painful, Christ will triumph over His enemies, and the people of God will triumph over them, too.

As we examined these parallel sections, we said there were seven of them. We saw the number seven has a prominent role in the book of Revelation, occurring forty-four times. We briefly discussed the meaning of the number seven.

Furthermore, as we surveyed the entire book of Revelation in the previous chapter, we alluded to the meanings of various other numbers in the book as we came to them. We did not spend any time developing those meanings; we just took note of them in passing. As you read Revelation, you recognize that it is filled with numbers, and they occur with great frequency.

We must remember that this book is primarily written in symbolic form, not literal form; therefore, these numbers we observe must be taken symbolically and not literally. The rule for the interpretation of the book of Revelation is this: we are to interpret it symbolically unless there are compelling reasons to interpret it literally, and this rule applies to the numbers it mentions as well. Numbers are to be taken symbolically unless there are sound reasons to take them literally.

The question then arises: what is the symbolic meaning of the various numbers that are used in Revelation? It is this question we want to turn our attention to in the next two chapters. This is a really important matter to get right. If we do not properly understand the symbolic meaning of the numbers in the book of Revelation, and if we literalize them, we wind up participating in and promoting all kinds of heresies.

One such heresy would be that God is not a Trinity but a "Nineity" because Revelation speaks of the seven Spirits of God in 1:4-5 as well as the Father and the Son. We read about the seven Spirits of God repeatedly as we proceed through the book of Revelation. If we have seven Spirits of God, plus the Father, plus the Son, then there are nine members in the Godhead. This cannot possibly be true. The Godhead always and only consists of three Persons: the Father, the Son, and the Holy Spirit. If we literalize these numbers, we fall into grave heresies.

If we literalize these numbers, the doctrine that only 144,000 people are going to be saved, as the Jehovah's Witnesses taught in the 1800s, becomes compelling.

If we literalize these numbers, we will try to start setting dates for the second coming of Christ like so many have throughout history. For example, the number 1,000 is used in Revelation chapter 20. After the 1,000 years are expired, Jesus returns. Some therefore thought that around AD 1000, Jesus was coming. When He did not come in AD 1000, they thought that it is not 1,000 years from His birth, but 1,000 years from His death. The date for the second coming was reset to AD 1033. But here we are a thousand years after that, and He still has not come back.

If you literalize these numbers, you can arrive at other erroneous conclusions, such as a three-and-a-half-year tribulation, a 1,000-year golden age, and the number "666" literally implanted into the forehead and the hand.

All these errors arise out of the inappropriate literalization of numbers that are meant to be taken symbolically. It is time to reconsider the way numbers are utilized in a symbolic book like Revelation. We must realize that while numbers are largely used literally in the rest of the Bible, in Revelation, numbers are seldom used literally and are virtually always used symbolically.

Let us then examine the symbolic meaning of the numbers used in the book of Revelation.

The General Nature of Numerology

While it is clear that symbolic numerology is used in the book of Revelation, it is very important that we separate biblical numerology from mystical and non-biblical numerology.

First of all, consider what numerology is not.

Some of the non-biblical numerology that is in use today is the so-called "Bible code," also known as the "Torah code." This was popularized by Michael Drosnin in his book entitled *The Bible Code* which was published in 1997. It was also popularized by a movie named *The Omega Code* which was produced in 1999.

This form of Bible code uses as a starting point some Hebrew letter, then combines with it the next 33rd letter, or the next 50th letter, or some other number of letters after that, to find patterns and hidden meanings supposedly appearing in the text, usually some kind of a prophecy. So they take the Hebrew text and start with a letter, then pick every fourth letter after that, (or tenth or thirty-third or whatever number they choose) and then put all those letters together, and those letters will form words that will say something, and that will be the coded message.

Another form of non-biblical numerology is the numerology used in the Kabbalah. The Kabbalah is a Jewish Gnostic mystical tradition in which numerical values are assigned to the letters of the Hebrew alphabet. The first letter "aleph" gets the number "1," the second letter "beth" gets the number "2," and so on. Then they take words in the Bible and look at the numerical values of them and add and subtract and multiply them in various ways, and then come up with hidden meanings in the Bible. This is called "gematria."

The numerical values of the Hebrew letters that result supposedly convey some deeper understanding of the Old Testament and reveal hidden meanings. This is often used by Christians to try to determine the name of the Antichrist. They will add up the numbers of the letters of someone's name, come up with "666" in some way, and conclude that he is the Antichrist.

Still others employ computer codes and programs to troll through the Bible, looking for hidden messages that are encoded in the text, based on some algorithm or numerical pattern.

None of this, or anything even similar to this, is biblical numerology. Biblical numerology has nothing to do with secret codes.

Secondly, consider what biblical numerology is.

Biblical numerology has to do with the Bible's use of numbers that are plainly stated in the text itself, numbers like "forty" or "twelve" or "seven" or "four." Most of the numbers plainly stated in the text of the Bible are used literally. They are associated with events or objects that literally occurred in history, and numbers are used to describe those events or those objects in a literal way.

If somebody has seventy camels, that is how many camels there were. If you counted them, there would be seventy of them. It is the literal use of numbers in history, numbers that are plainly stated in the text of Scripture, which provide us with a basis for understanding their symbolic significance. They provide us with an understanding of their symbolic significance when it is apparent that these numbers are used in a symbolic way in symbolic writings such as the book of Revelation.

For example, we know that the number seven was used literally in the creation account. God made the world in six literal days, and rested on the seventh. The week is seven days long; six days we do all our labor, and the seventh day is the Sabbath. Those are real numbers, describing actual days. But when we come to Revelation, we are immediately told there are seven spirits of God. We know from the teaching of the rest of the Bible there is only one Holy Spirit. Therefore, we conclude there must be a symbolic meaning to the number seven as well as a literal meaning, and the literal usage of the number gives us an indication as to what the symbolic meaning is.

This is biblical numerology. We look at how Bible numbers are used when plainly stated in Bible texts, and from that usage, we derive an understanding of their meaning when they are used symbolically.

The Meaning of Numbers Used in Revelation.

To any observant reader of the Bible, it is clear that the Bible uses certain numbers over and over again—numbers like seventy and forty and twelve and seven. Furthermore, many other numbers occur repeatedly in the Bible in both the Old and the New Testament.

Not only do these numbers occur repeatedly; they are also used in a consistent pattern and in a consistent way. It is this repeated and consistent usage of these numbers that provides us with an understanding of their meaning and significance.

Furthermore, there are many different numbers that are used in the book of Revelation—and the vast majority of the time, indeed almost exclusively, these numbers are used symbolically. Understanding those symbolic meanings is critical to the proper interpretation of the passage.

In learning the meanings of biblical numbers, not every passage where a number is used in the Bible will give us an indication of its symbolic meaning. For example, every time you see the number seven or the number four, it does not necessarily convey anything about its symbolic meaning. Usually, when you read a number in the Bible, it is just a number, and the passage it occurs in really tells us nothing about the symbolic meaning of that number. It is usually the case that an ordinary prose passage is neutral in terms of conveying the symbolic meaning of the numbers it contains.

For example, consider the number four. It is used over 300 times in the Bible. Numbers like seven occur over 500 times in the Bible. The vast majority of the passages do not tell you anything about the meaning of that number, but a few of them do.

The vast majority of the time when you come across one of these numbers, it is just a number and that is all it is. Trying to discover the symbolic meaning of a number used in an ordinary prose passage seldom bears fruit simply because there generally is not one. The symbolic meaning of a number is actually derived from a relatively small minority of the passages where it appears, in which the symbolic meaning is made clear by the way it is used in those passages.

The ordinary use of numbers in ordinary prose passages usually conveys ordinary information about quantities of people and things, and that is all that is there. Therefore, we do not make a big deal out of the number seven every time it appears in the Bible. We do not try to develop the symbolic meaning of numbers in the vast majority of passages in which they occur because the vast majority of passages in which they occur are neutral as to the meaning of that number. It is just a number that describes a quantity of something.

However, when numbers are used in symbolic literature like Daniel or Ezekiel or Revelation, we need to pay much more attention to the use of numbers and their symbolic meaning, and recognize that their symbolic meaning is part of the message the passage conveys to us. In apocalyptic passages, we must pay a lot of attention to the symbolic meaning of numbers, but in ordinary prose passages, we must pay very little.

In this chapter and the next, we will not be looking at certain biblical numbers like seventy and forty because they do not appear in the book of Revelation. Instead, we will be looking at eighteen different numbers that do appear there. We are limiting the scope of our investigation of numerology to only the numbers used in Revelation.

The Primary Numbers Used in Revelation

Primary numbers are uncompounded numbers. The number one, two, three, four, six, seven, eight, ten, and twelve are all primary uncompounded numbers.

The number ONE conveys the concept of unity. Here are some passages that convey that concept:

- Deuteronomy 6:4 *"Hear, O Israel: The LORD our God is one LORD."* There is a unity in the Godhead.
- Acts 17:26 God *"hath made of one blood all nations of men for to dwell on all the face of the earth." "One blood"* conveys the idea of unity among all people.
- Romans 5:12 *"Wherefore, as by one man sin entered into the world, and death by sin; and so death passed upon all men, for that all have sinned."* One man, Adam, unites us all together in sin.
- John 10:30 Jesus says, *"I and my Father are one."* There is a unity between the Father and the Son both in essence and in purpose.
- John 17:21 *"that they all may be one; as thou, Father, art in me, and I in thee, that they also may be one in us: that the world may believe that thou hast sent me." "That they all may be one"* describes the unity of all the believers.

These are just a sampling of passages, and we could cite many more. These will give you enough information so you can pick up the idea that the symbolic meaning of "one" is the idea of unity. Sometimes "one" just means one. If I say that I have one hymnal in my hand, "one" means literally one. But if I wanted to convey the idea of unity, I might also use "one" in a nonliteral way. For example, if I said: "We are all of one mind on this issue," you would draw the conclusion that we were united in our attitudes about the subject being addressed.

The number TWO conveys the concept of a complementary and interdependent union. The classic example is marriage. Matthew 19:5 says, "*For this cause shall a man leave his father and mother and shall cleave to his wife, and they two shall be one flesh.*" As used here, "two" is the idea of a complementary and interdependent union.

- Genesis 7:9 "*There went in two and two unto Noah into the ark, the male and the female, as God had commanded Noah.*" There had to be a male and a female among animals in order to have offspring after the flood.
- Joshua 2:1 "*And Joshua the son of Nun sent out of Shittim two men to spy secretly, saying, Go view the land, even Jericho.*" We see that when spies were sent out, they were sent out two at a time. Jesus did the same thing when He sent out His disciples.
- Mark 6:7 "*And he called unto him the twelve, and began to send them forth by two and two; and gave them power over unclean spirits.*"
- Luke 10:1 "*After these things the Lord appointed other seventy also, and sent them two and two before his face into every city and place, whither he himself would come.*"

When Jesus sent out his disciples as missionaries, they went out in pairs because they needed each other. There was a complementary and interdependent union of two people working together, either in marriage (or in procreation in the case of animals), or in the case of disciples, in sharing the gospel. Therefore, when we read about the two witnesses in Revelation 11, we realize these two witnesses represent the gospel going out to the world through God's servants as they work together in a complementary and interdependent fashion.

The number THREE conveys the concept of perfection, completion, and finality. The ultimate expression of that concept is the Trinity.

- Matthew 28:19 "*Go ye therefore, and teach all nations, baptizing them in the name of the Father, and of the Son, and of the Holy Ghost.*" There are three persons in the Godhead, and these three persons make up a perfect, complete, and final unity of the Godhead.
- Matthew 12:40 "*For as Jonah was three days and three nights*

in the whale's belly; so shall the Son of man be three days and three nights in the heart of the earth." Three was the number of completion for the time that Jesus had to be in the grave. For Him to be in the grave three days marked the complete, final, and perfect time that was necessary to pass before His resurrection.

- Ecclesiastes 4:12 *"And if one prevail against him, two shall withstand him; and a threefold cord is not quickly broken."* It is the threefold cord that is perfect and complete and final in terms of its strength.
- 1 Corinthians 13:13 *"And now abideth faith, hope, charity, these three; but the greatest of these is charity."*

Whenever we see these groupings of three or this idea of three, it conveys the message that this is the totality of a matter; we have the beginning, the middle, and the end. It is complete, it is finished, it is final. Nothing can be or needs to be added to it. Romans 11:36 says, *"For of him, and through him, and to him, are all things: to whom be glory for ever."*

The number FOUR conveys the concept of the entire world—that is, the created world, the physical earth.

- Genesis 2:10 *"And a river went out of Eden to water the garden; and from thence it was parted, and became into four heads."* There were four rivers that watered the whole earth, which all came out of Eden. These four rivers covered the earth. Obviously, they were all rerouted or ruined in the flood so they do not exist anymore, except the River Euphrates. The other three were lost in the geographical changes that occurred during the worldwide flood.
- Jeremiah 49:36 *"And upon Elam will I bring the four winds from the four quarters of heaven, and will scatter them toward all those winds; and there shall be no nation whither the outcasts of Elam shall not come."* God is going to scatter the people of Elam to the four winds and the four corners of the earth. The reason the Bible talks about four winds and four quarters of the earth is because there is north, south, east, and west, which are the four corners of the earth and the four cardinal directions of the compass. He is going to bring these four winds from the four quarters of

heaven—that is, from every direction—and scatter them toward all those winds. The result is that there shall be no nation of the earth where the outcasts of Elam shall not come. These four quarters represent the whole earth because this wind is going to scatter these people of Elam over every single nation there is, and there is not going to be any nation where these people are not.

- Revelation 7:1 *"And after these things I saw four angels standing on the four corners of the earth, holding the four winds of the earth that the wind should not blow on the earth, nor on the sea, nor on any tree."* Notice how the word "earth" is used repeatedly in relation to the number four. The four corners and the four winds are talking about the four cardinal directions: north, south, east, and west. The idea is that what is being described is going to be a worldwide phenomenon.
- Revelation 20:8 *"And shall go out to deceive the nations which are in the four quarters of the earth"*; that is, in every part of the earth, *"Gog and Magog, to gather them together to battle: the number of whom is as the sand of the sea."* The idea is that the whole population of the entire world will be deceived to participate in the final persecution of the Christians.

The number SIX conveys the concept of man because man was created on the sixth day.

- Genesis 1:27 *"So God created man in his own image, in the image of God created he him; male and female created he them."* Verse 31 goes on to say, *"And the evening and the morning were the sixth day."* Man was created on the sixth day, and that is why the number "six" represents man.
- Exodus 20:9–10 *"Six days shalt thou labour, and do all thy work: [10] But the seventh day is the sabbath of the Lord thy God."* The point is that the number "six" pertains to man. Man gets six days; the number "seven" pertains to God; He gets the seventh day.
- Revelation 13:18 is the key passage. *"Here is wisdom. Let him that hath understanding count the number of the beast: for it is the number of a man; and his number is Six hundred three score and six"*; that is, 666. We are clearly told the number "6" represents man, so there can be no question about its meaning.

The number SEVEN conveys the concept of completeness—that of something being finished or done.

- Genesis 2:1, 3 "*Thus the heavens and the earth were finished, and all the host of them. . .* [3] *And God blessed the seventh day, and sanctified it: because that in it he had rested from all his work which God created and made.*" The seventh day marked the completion of the creation. It was finished and done.
- Genesis 29:18 "*And Jacob loved Rachel; and said, I will serve thee seven years for Rachel thy younger daughter.*" Seven years would be his complete service in order to obtain Rachel as his wife. It would finish his obligation to Laban.
- Leviticus 25:3–4 "*Six years thou shalt sow thy field, and six years thou shalt prune thy vineyard, and gather in the fruit thereof;* [4] *But in the seventh year shall be a sabbath of rest unto the land, a sabbath for the Lord: thou shalt neither sow thy field, nor prune thy vineyard.*" This cycle was completed in the seventh year. Six years, they sowed the land; the seventh year, that cycle was completed and they did not sow the land in that year. It was then expanded; notice verse 8:
- Leviticus 25:8, 10 "*And thou shalt number seven sabbaths of years unto thee, seven times seven years;*" (notice the multiplication) "*and the space of the seven sabbaths of years shall be unto thee forty and nine years*"; seven times seven is forty-nine. Verse 10: "*And ye shall hallow the fiftieth year, and proclaim liberty throughout all the land unto all the inhabitants thereof: it shall be a jubilee unto you; and ye shall return every man unto his possession, and ye shall return every man unto his family.*" Here we have seven times seven being the completion of an important period of time.
- Joshua 6:2, 4–5 "*And the* LORD *said unto Joshua, See, I have given into thine hand Jericho, and the king thereof, and the mighty men of valour. . .* [4] *And seven priests shall bear before the ark seven trumpets of rams' horns: and the seventh day ye shall compass the city seven times, and the priests shall blow with the trumpets.* [5] *And it shall come to pass. . .the wall of the city shall fall down flat, and the people shall ascend up every man straight before him.*" The completion of the siege of Jericho was marked by this multiplied use of sevens.

Seven is the number of completion. Seven is a very prominent number in the Bible, occurring over 500 times.

The number EIGHT conveys the concept of salvation.

- 1 Peter 3:20, speaking of the flood says, "*Which sometime were disobedient, when once the longsuffering of God waited in the days of Noah, while the ark was a preparing, wherein few, that is, eight souls were saved by water.*" It is interesting that God saved eight; he did not save seven, he did not save nine. He saved eight. Peter repeats the concept of eight in 2 Peter as well.
- 2 Peter 2:5 "*And spared not the old world, but saved Noah the eighth person.*" Why did he need to indicate that Noah was the eighth one? There is a reason for that. Eight is the number of salvation. Noah was "*a preacher of righteousness, bringing in the flood upon the world of the ungodly.*"
- Genesis 17:11–12 "*And ye shall circumcise the flesh of your foreskin; and it shall be a token of the covenant betwixt me and you.* [12] *And he that is eight days old shall be circumcised among you, every man child in your generations.*" Circumcision was a sign of salvation. When it was performed, the child was brought into the covenant community of the people of God. It was an external, visible placing of that child into the covenant community of God's people—thus, a picture of salvation. Circumcision of the body pictures circumcision of the heart (which is regeneration), which produces salvation.
- Acts 9:33–34 "*And there he found a certain man named Æneas, which had kept his bed eight years, and was sick of the palsy.* [34] *And Peter said unto him, Æneas, Jesus Christ maketh thee whole: arise, and make thy bed. And he arose immediately.*" Salvation came to him after eight years.
- Judges 3:8–9 "*Therefore the anger of the LORD was hot against Israel, and he sold them into the hand of Chushan-rishathaim king of Mesopotamia: and the children of Israel served Chushan-rishathaim eight years.* [9] *And when the children of Israel cried unto the LORD, the LORD raised up a deliverer to the children of Israel, who delivered them, even Othniel the son of Kenaz, Caleb's younger brother.*" We see people struggling under oppression for eight years, and at the end of eight years, they

receive salvation and deliverance. The meaning of the number eight is that of deliverance or salvation.

The number TEN conveys the concept of perfection and totality.

- Deuteronomy 4:13 *"And he declared unto you his covenant, which he commanded you to perform, even ten commandments; and he wrote them upon two tables of stone."* Two is the number of interdependence. The two parts of the Ten Commandments, to love God and love our neighbor, are interdependent and inseparable. Ten is the number of perfection. There are not nine commandments; there are not eleven commandments; there are Ten Commandments that perfectly and totally comprehend God's moral will for humanity.
- Psalm 19:7 *"The law of the LORD is perfect, converting the soul. . ."* Here, the Ten Commandments are said to be the manifestation of perfection. Ten represents perfection.
- Matthew 25:1–2 *"Then shall the kingdom of heaven be likened unto ten virgins, which took their lamps, and went forth to meet the bridegroom. 2 And five of them were wise, and five were foolish."* We will address the meaning of the number five in the next chapter; however, the number ten represents the totality of those who are perceived to be in the kingdom of God, or that externally profess to be in the kingdom of God.
- Deuteronomy 23:3 *"An Ammonite or Moabite shall not enter into the congregation of the LORD; even to their tenth generation shall they not enter into the congregation of the LORD forever."* "Ten" conveyed the idea of perfection; it was the idea that those who are of the Ammonite and the Moabite tribe will never enter the kingdom of God. Ten was the number to describe the perfection of that prohibition that lasts forever.
- 1 Samuel 1:8 *"Then said Elkanah her husband to her, Hannah, why weepest thou? and why eatest thou not? and why is thy heart grieved? am not I better to thee than ten sons?"* He is saying: If you had all the sons you ever wanted, the perfect number of sons, I would be better to you than they.

There were also ten plagues brought upon Egypt by Moses. The number ten is never used to describe them so I could not quote a passage containing that number, but there were ten plagues. These plagues were the perfect expression of God's wrath on Egypt.

Ten Commandments, ten virgins, ten generations, ten sons, ten plagues—these things convey the idea of perfection and totality.

The number TWELVE conveys the concept of the chosen people of God.

- Genesis 49:28 *"All these are the twelve tribes of Israel: and this is it that their father spake unto them, and blessed them; every one according to his blessing he blessed them."* How many tribes did God choose to make up His chosen people? He chose twelve. Therefore, twelve is the number of election, the number of the chosen people of God.
- Acts 7:8, (Stephen speaking here): *"And he gave him the covenant of circumcision: and so Abraham begat Isaac, and circumcised him the eighth day; and Isaac begat Jacob; and Jacob begat the twelve patriarchs."* These twelve patriarchs are the twelve men from whom God produced the twelve tribes of Israel, who are the chosen people of God.
- Luke 6:13 *"And when it was day, [Jesus] called unto him his disciples: and of them he chose twelve, whom also he named apostles."* It is interesting that not only were there twelve tribes in the Old Testament, but that there were also twelve apostles in the New Testament, and both groups of twelve were the heads of the chosen covenant community of the people of God.
- Matthew 19:28 *"And Jesus said unto them, Verily I say unto you, That ye which have followed me, in the regeneration when the Son of man shall sit in the throne of his glory, ye also shall sit upon twelve thrones, judging the twelve tribes of Israel."* In glory, there will be the twelve apostles and the twelve tribes. What do we see in Revelation? We see the twenty-four elders who represent the combined chosen Old and New Testament people of God.

In the next chapter, we will cover multiples and divisions of the primary numbers in Revelation.

The multiplication or addition or repetition of primary numbers—that is, the numbers we just talked about—represent increased degrees of the intensification of the meaning of those numbers.

For example, when Peter asked if he should forgive someone up to seven times for sinning against him, Jesus replies: No, you must forgive him seventy times seven; that is, to a much higher level than that represented by seven.

On the other hand, the division of a primary number represents a partial or diminished level of the meaning of those numbers. We will see in the next chapter that multiples and divisions of primary numbers represent an intensification or a diminishing of the meaning of those primary numbers.

6

Biblical Numerology, Part 2

In the last chapter, we began to explore the issue of biblical numerology and we saw that Revelation is saturated with numbers. We discovered these numbers are to be understood symbolically, not literally, because the book of Revelation itself is a symbolic book written in symbolic language. It is not ordinary prose; it is a book of verbal pictures. These verbal pictures are symbolic in their nature. Though they convey a very specific message, they convey it in symbolic form rather than in a literal form.

We said in a previous chapter that the rule for the interpretation of Revelation is that we are to interpret it symbolically unless there are compelling reasons to interpret it literally. We saw this rule applies to numbers as well. Numbers are to be taken symbolically unless there are sound reasons to take them literally.

What is the symbolic meaning of the numbers used in the book of Revelation? It is really important to get the answer to that question right because if we do not properly understand the symbolic meaning of the numbers in Revelation, or if we literalize those numbers, we can fall into heresies.

In the previous chapter, we looked at the general nature of numerology and began by discussing what numerology is not. Biblical numerology does not consist of some kind of hidden code in the Scriptures (in particular in the Hebrew Scriptures) where meanings are discovered by some kind of mathematical formulation or sequence or algorithm. Biblical numerology has nothing to do with secret codes in the Bible based on a numerical pattern that looks for some kind of hidden meaning, especially prophetic meanings.

We then discussed what biblical numerology is. We said that biblical numerology has to do with the Bible's use of numbers that are plainly stated in the text itself, numbers like forty or twelve or seven or four.

Most of the numbers plainly stated in the text of Scripture are used literally. They are just numbers that describe quantities of things or people. However, in a few of these passages where numbers are used literally, we are also given an indication as to the symbolic meaning of those numbers. Therefore, by a careful examination of how the Bible itself uses the numbers it plainly states in the text, we can gain an understanding of their symbolic meaning as well, and then apply that symbolic meaning in passages where numbers are used symbolically.

Numbers have a literal meaning and they have a symbolic meaning. The vast majority of time in the Bible they are used literally. But in books that are written in symbolic form, like Ezekiel, Daniel, and Revelation, numbers are frequently used symbolically.

In the previous chapter, we looked at primary numbers used in the book of Revelation. Primary numbers are uncompounded numbers.

We saw that the numbers one, two, three, four, six, seven, eight, ten, and twelve were all primary uncompounded numbers.

In this chapter, we want to look at multiples and divisions and repetitions of these primary numbers. In Revelation, primary numbers are sometimes multiplied either by themselves or by some other primary number. Sometimes those primary numbers are divided, and sometimes they are repeated. This use of these primary numbers conveys information to us.

The multiplication or addition or repetition of primary numbers in various passages represents an intensification of the meaning of those numbers. For example, when Peter asked if he should forgive someone up to seven times for sinning against him, Jesus replied: No, you must forgive him seventy times seven—that is, to a much higher level than represented by seven. We see Jesus doing multiplication of numbers; seven times seventy.

The idea that the Bible would take numbers and multiply them, add them, divide them, or repeat them is established in many passages in which numbers are handled in precisely that fashion.

When the Bible multiplies primary numbers, adds them together, or repeats them in a series, it represents an intensification of the idea and concept that the primary number conveys.

Conversely, the division of a primary number represents a diminished level of the meaning of that number. For example, if seven, which is the number of completeness is divided in half, it indicates something less than what is complete.

Multiples and divisions of primary numbers represents either an intensification or a diminishing of the meaning of the primary number. We do not have to come up with new meanings for numbers like one hundred forty-four thousand, twelve thousand, or twenty-four. Those numbers are simply multiplications of primary numbers. In the same way, we do not have to come up with new meanings for numbers such as five or one-third, which are simply divisions of a primary number.

As long as we get the meaning of the primary numbers right, when we see the multiplication or division of those numbers, we only have to understand that there is an intensification or a diminishing of the idea indicated by the primary number. Once we get the primary numbers right, all the rest of the numbers are easy.

Let us proceed to consider this second class of numbers in the book of Revelation.

Numbers derived from TWO: The number two conveys the idea of a complementary and interdependent union. We find in Revelation 9:16 the number "two hundred thousand thousand."

Revelation 9:15–16, *"And the four angels were loosed, which were prepared for an hour, and a day, and a month, and a year, for to slay the third part of men.* [16] *And the number of the army of the horsemen were two hundred thousand thousand: and I heard the number of them."*

If you do the math, that is two hundred million. The number is two times a hundred times a thousand times a thousand. One hundred is ten times ten. One thousand is ten times ten times ten. What we have is the multiplication of these numbers: the number two intensified dramatically by the repeated multiplication of the number ten, which conveys the idea of perfection. This symbolic number represents the perfect interdependent union of the vast armies that will gather together to war with each other throughout this age, and to persecute the people of God when Satan is loosed to deceive the nations at the end of this age. (See chapter 30.)

We read in Matthew 24:9 that *"ye shall be hated of all nations for my name's sake,"* which predicts the coming transnational persecution of believers that is going to take place in the Great Tribulation. This will be the result of Satan being loosed so he can go out and deceive the nations. This is expanded in Revelation 20:7–9.

We stated earlier that from the time of Genesis until the time of

Jesus, the gospel was confined to a very small part of the earth, basically to Israel. Then Jesus bound Satan at the cross, and the gospel spread over the whole world. Why was it able to spread over the whole world, when before it was confined? Because when Satan was loose, he was able to deceive the nations and keep the gospel from spreading; but when he was bound, he could no longer deceive the nations. The result is that the gospel spread throughout the whole world. But at the end of the age, Satan is going to be loosed again, and he is going to deceive the nations and lead them to form a transnational coalition to persecute the believers and virtually wipe them from the face of the earth.

The number 200,000,000 represents the vast number of people involved in the complementary and interdependent union of the nations of the earth as they war with each other throughout this age, and it represents the interdependent transnational coalition under the leadership of the released Satan to try to destroy Christianity and Christians from off the face of the earth at the end of this age. Therefore, we are not looking for a giant army from China of exactly 200,000,000 people to attack Israel as some dispensationalists assert. Instead, we are recognizing this is a complementary and interdependent union of all those who have the mark of the beast, who are gathered together under the deception of a released Satan at the end of this age, in order to attack and assault the kingdom of God. This number symbolically represents the size and perfect interdependent union of the army of the antichrist.

Numbers derived from THREE: The number three is the number of perfection, completion, and finality. We find this number divided to one-third repeatedly in the book of Revelation.

Notice Revelation 8:7–12: "*The first angel sounded, and there followed hail and fire mingled with blood, and they were cast upon the earth: and the third part of trees was burnt up, and all green grass was burnt up.* [8] *And the second angel sounded, and as it were a great mountain burning with fire was cast into the sea: and the third part of the sea became blood;* [9] *And the third part of the creatures which were in the sea, and had life, died; and the third part of the ships were destroyed.* [10] *And the third angel sounded, and there fell a great star from heaven, burning as it were a lamp, and it fell upon the third part of the rivers, and upon the fountains of waters;* [11] *And the name of the star is called Wormwood: and the third part of the waters. . .*" and it goes on further in verse 12 with "the third part" of this and "the third part" of that and "the third part" of the next thing. We see this throughout the book of Revelation.

What does this "one-third" represent? It represents a diminishing of the meaning of the primary number because it is the division of a primary number. The number three represents perfection, completion, and finality. Therefore, one-third represents a diminishing of that concept because it is a division of it.

One-third represents God's partial, incomplete, and temporal judgment on the wicked—not His perfect, complete, and final judgment on them. The wicked will be punished for their evil works on this earth, but only in an incomplete fashion. Perfect, complete, and final judgment will only occur at the end of the world.

As John describes what is happening between the first and the second coming of Christ and the judgments of God that fall on the wicked during that time frame, he tells us they are only partial judgments. For example, when you look at the tsunami that took place in the Indian Ocean in 2004 in which over 200,000 people were killed, not everybody in the whole world was killed. The tsunami was a partial judgment. We have partial judgments of God that fall on various areas of the earth described in Revelation 8. He speaks about the sea and the land and the sky, which are all different areas which men inhabit, and judgments fall on each of them. There is no place to go to escape these partial judgments of God.

Not only is there going to be complete, perfect, and final judgment at the end; but along the way, God is going to bring His limited judgments on the wicked. Those judgments are going to be imperfect, incomplete, and temporary. This is what is conveyed by the use of the number "one-third."

Numbers derived from FOUR, which refers to the entire world: In Revelation 14:20 we have the number one thousand six hundred. "*And the winepress was trodden without*" (or, outside) "*the city, and blood came out of the winepress, even unto the horse bridles, by the space of a thousand and six hundred furlongs.*" The word translated furlong is "*stadion*" in the Greek. It is about 660 feet, or about an eighth of a mile. One thousand six hundred stadia is about 200 miles (and assuming that number also represents its breadth) and as deep as a horse's bridle. It is about four feet to a horse's bridle. That is over 30 cubic miles of blood. There is over a trillion gallons in a cubic mile. That is over 30 trillion gallons of blood. That is tremendously more blood than all the humans in the world put together have. This is clearly not a literal number.

Revelation 14 sets forth the second coming of Christ. It declares the final outpouring of the wrath of God on the wicked, and it describes the treading of this winepress and the vast volume of blood that comes out.

One thousand six hundred is four times four times one hundred. One hundred is ten times ten, the number of perfection. What is symbolically represented by this number is that God's judgment is perfect (ten times ten) and covers the whole world (four times four).

This number signifies that the wrath of God will extend to every corner of the earth: north, south, east, and west. No place will be exempt from His judgment. What is symbolized is the world perfectly covered with the wrath and the judgment of God. In other words, when Jesus comes back, there is not going to be any place on the earth where people can go to hide from the wrath of God. There is no place where God's wrath can be escaped.

Numbers derived from SIX: Six is the number of man. Man was created on the sixth day of creation. He has six days to labor. Notice the well-known passage in Revelation 13:18. Here we have the number six hundred sixty-six—the infamous mark of the beast. It says, *"Here is wisdom. Let him that hath understanding count the number of the beast: for it is the number of a man; and his number is six hundred threescore and six"* A score is twenty, so threescore is three times twenty, which is sixty: *"six hundred [sixty] and six."*

Six hundred sixty-six represents perfection because the six is repeated three times. Furthermore, the number six itself represents mankind or humanity. Three is the number of perfection, and six is the number of mankind or humanity. Therefore, the three sixes represent perfect humanism.

These people with the mark of perfect humanism both think and act. There is a mark in their forehead. Symbolically, the forehead represents what you think. There is a mark in the hand. Symbolically, the hand represents what you do. There is a positive example of this in Deuteronomy 6:6, 8 where God said to the children of Israel, *"And these words, which I command thee this day, shall be in thine heart:* [8]*And thou shalt bind them for a sign upon thine hand, and they shall be as frontlets between thine eyes."* The idea is not that you would make little boxes with Scripture portions in them and tie them to your forehead and tie them to the back of your hand; rather, the idea is that Scripture would guide all your thinking and all your actions because you think with your head and you act with your hand.

The idea in Revelation 13:18 is that these people with the mark of the beast—that is, with the mark of perfect humanism—both think and act according to the will of sinful rebellious man personified in the beast. The mark of the beast is not a computer code that is going to be tattooed into your forehead or into your hand. It is not something that has yet to come. It has been around for thousands of years. All unsaved people have the mark of the beast because they think as Satan would have them think, and they act as Satan would have them act. They think like unsaved men, and they act like unsaved men.

The notion that a computer chip will be implanted into the forehead or hand is not what this passage is teaching. In the same context in which the concept of the mark of the beast in the forehead occurs (indeed, in the very next verse), we have the parallel teaching about the people who have the seal of God in their foreheads. Revelation 14:1 says, *"And I looked, and, lo, a Lamb stood on the mount Zion, and with him a hundred forty-four thousand, having his Father's name written in their foreheads."*

Believers have the seal of God in their forehead, and unbelievers have the seal of the beast in their forehead. We think according to God's mind and Word, and the ungodly think according to Satan's mind and word. Therefore, when we get to this "666" in our exposition (see chapter 42), we are going to see that this is not something that has yet to come; this is something that has been around since the time of Jesus. You either have the mark of the beast or you have the mark of God. Everyone has one or the other. How do you tell who has the seal of God and who has the mark of the beast? You can tell by how they think and how they act. Just as the seal of God in the forehead is not a computer chip, neither is the seal of the beast in the forehead a computer chip.

Numbers derived from SEVEN: Seven is the number of completeness. In Revelation, we repeatedly find the number three and a half years, which is referred to as a time and times and half a time. Furthermore, forty-two months and one thousand two hundred sixty days are also spoken of. Since a Jewish year is three hundred sixty days (twelve months of thirty days each because they operate on a lunar calendar), these numbers are all equal to each other. Three and a half years, forty-two months, and one thousand two hundred and sixty days are all precisely the same length of time. They are exactly equivalent.

Notice Revelation 11:1–3: *"And there was given me a reed like unto a rod: and the angel stood, saying, Rise, and measure the temple of God, and the altar, and them that worship therein.* [2] *But the court which is without the temple leave out, and measure it not; for it is given unto the Gentiles: and the holy city shall they tread under foot forty and two months"* (one thousand two hundred sixty days, or three and a half years). "[3] *And I will give power unto my two witnesses, and they shall prophesy a thousand two hundred and threescore days, clothed in sackcloth,"* which is forty-two months, or three and a half years.

Notice 12:6: *"And the woman fled into the wilderness, where she hath a place prepared of God, that they should feed her there a thousand two hundred and threescore days."* Notice 12:14: "*And to the woman were given two wings of a great eagle, that she might fly into the wilderness, into her place, where she is nourished for a time,"* (singular) *"and times,"* (plural) *"and half a time, from the face of the serpent."* This is three and a half years.

As we examine these passages, it is clear that these numbers of time, times, and half a time (which is three and a half years), forty-two months, and one thousand two hundred and sixty days, all refer to the exact same span of time: three and a half years.

If you were to choose a number to represent the complete time of human history, it only makes sense to choose the number of completeness, which is seven. Seven is the number of completeness; so what is three and a half, but half of completeness?

If human history is divided into equal symbolic halves, the old and the new dispensation, the time before and the time after the coming of Christ, then the last half of human history would be half of seven, which is three and a half. Thus, three and a half years, forty-two months, and one thousand two hundred and sixty days all represent the time after the coming of Christ. We divide all of time into two halves, BC and AD. BC is all the time before Christ's first coming; AD is all the time after Christ's first coming. So three and a half represents the second half of time, the AD period, the church age, the time from the first to the second coming of Christ.

Dispensational interpreters say this number three and a half refers to the last half of the seven-year tribulation; whereas, in fact, it refers to the last half of God's history, the time between the first and the second coming of Christ. There are only two periods of human history: there is creation to Christ, and there is Christ to the consummation. If seven represents complete history, then three and a half would represent half of that history. These "three and a half" numbers do not have anything to do with the timeline for the great tribulation. In fact, we do not know how long the great tribulation is going to be. All we know is that it is going to be less than a generation, based on Matthew 24:34.

Notice Revelation 11. We have seen the meaning of three and a half years; now we are going to see the meaning of three and a half days. In Revelation 11:9–12, after the two witnesses have finished their testimony and have been killed, it says:

"And they of the people and kindreds and tongues and nations shall see their dead bodies three days and an half, and shall not suffer their dead bodies to be put in graves. [10] *And they that dwell upon the earth shall rejoice over them, and make merry, and shall send gifts one to another; because these two prophets tormented them that dwelt on the earth.* [11] *And after three days and an half the Spirit of life from God entered into them, and they stood upon their feet; and great fear fell upon them which saw them.* [12] *And they heard a great voice from heaven saying unto them, Come up hither. And they ascended up to heaven in a cloud; and their enemies beheld them."*

Verses 11–12 are describing the resurrection and the rapture into heaven, all of which occur at the second coming. The resurrection, the rapture, and the second coming occur together, as verses 13–19 which immediately follows make clear. There is not a seven-year gap between the rapture and the second coming as the dispensationalists teach.

Three and a half days represents the very short period of time the great tribulation will last, compared to the long period of time of one thousand two hundred sixty days between the first and second coming of Christ. Three and a half days, compared to one thousand two hundred and sixty days, is less than one-third of one percent of that time. When we look at the length of time between the first and second coming of Christ, and the length of time the great tribulation lasts, we see that in proportion to the time between the first and second coming of Christ, the great tribulation is very short.

The point is this: in proportion to the time between the first and second coming of Christ, the time the great tribulation lasts is going to be very short.

Instead of trying to literalize these numbers and say they must refer to exactly three and a half years, we need to understand these numbers are used symbolically and are not to be viewed as literal or taken as literal representations of time.

Numbers derived from TEN: Ten is the number of perfection and totality. Most prominent in the minds of those who study Revelation is the number one thousand, the number that represents the millennium.

In Revelation 20:1–7, the number one thousand is used six times:
"And I saw an angel come down from heaven, having the key of the bottomless pit and a great chain in his hand.
2 *And he laid hold on the dragon, that old serpent, which is the Devil, and Satan, and bound him a thousand years,*
3 *And cast him into the bottomless pit, and shut him up, and set a seal upon him, that he should deceive the nations no more, till the thousand years should be fulfilled: and after that he must be loosed a little season.*
4 *And I saw thrones, and they sat upon them, and judgment was given unto them: and I saw the souls of them that were beheaded for the witness of Jesus, and for the word of God, and which had not worshipped the beast, neither his image, neither had received his mark upon their foreheads, or in their hands; and they lived and reigned with Christ a thousand years.*
5 *But the rest of the dead lived not again until the thousand years were finished. This is the first resurrection.*
6 *Blessed and holy is he that hath part in the first resurrection: on such the second death hath no power, but they shall be priests of God and of Christ, and shall reign with him a thousand years.*
7 *And when the thousand years are expired, Satan shall be loosed. . ."*

The number one thousand is ten times ten times ten. The number is perfection cubed—perfection raised to the third power. The number three is the number of perfection, and the number ten is the number of perfection. We have perfection times perfection times perfection—perfection multiplied by itself the perfect number of times. This represents the perfect duration of the time allotted by God between the first coming of Christ and the loosing of Satan.

We are in the millennium right now. That statement might surprise you. But let me ask a simple question: when was Satan bound for a thousand years? He was bound at the cross. In Matthew 12:22–29 Jesus, after casting out a demon and hearing His critics say He was doing it by the power of Satan, asked a penetrating question: How can Satan be divided against Satan? If you are going to spoil a strong man's house, you first have to go in and bind the strong man, and then you can spoil his house.

Satan's house was the world. He is the god of this world. Jesus bound him at His first coming, and for the last two thousand years He has been spoiling his house, taking his people captive, and bringing them into His own kingdom. Satan's kingdom has been ravaged by many hundreds of millions of his people being brought out of his kingdom and into the kingdom of Jesus. When did the millennium begin? It began when Satan was bound. When was Satan bound? He was bound at the cross. (See chapter 57.)

When is Satan going to be loosed? He is loosed at the end of this age when it is time to bring things to the consummation. Once again, he is going to deceive the nations, and they are all going to gather together into a transnational coalition to persecute the believers as Matthew 24:9 says: *"Then ye shall be hated of all nations for my name's sake."* This number one thousand represents the perfect duration of the time allotted by God between the first coming of Christ and the loosing of Satan, which inaugurates the very short great tribulation, and concludes with the second coming of Christ.

We have another interesting number derived from ten—ten thousand times ten thousand. That is one hundred million. Notice Revelation 5:11. This is a picture in heaven, and it says, *"And I beheld, and I heard the voice of many angels round about the throne and the beasts and the elders: and the number of them"* (the number of the angels) *"was ten thousand times ten thousand, and thousands of thousands."*

The idea here is that of thousands and thousands and lots more thousands. These are not literal numbers. John is not counting here. This represents the perfect number of angels in heaven. Just like a thousand represents the perfect duration of time allotted by God between the first coming of Christ and the loosing of Satan, ten thousand times ten thousand represents the perfect number of angels in heaven. However many angels there were, it was all there was supposed to be. What we have is perfection times perfection. Perfection intensified is the idea in these multiples of tens, whether it is a thousand, a million, or millions of millions. They are all intensifications of the idea of the number ten.

We also have the number five in Revelation. Five is one half of ten. Revelation 9 talks about locusts that come out of the pit, and they hurt the men who do not have the seal of God in their foreheads. Revelation 9:3–4 says, *"And there came out of the smoke locusts upon the earth: and unto them was given power, as the scorpions of the earth have power.* [4] *And it was commanded them that they should not hurt the grass of the earth, neither any green thing, neither any tree; but only those men which have not the seal of God in their foreheads."*

It is interesting that everybody talks about the mark of the beast, but nobody talks about the mark of God, which is the seal of God in the forehead. The mark of God is just as prevalent in the book of Revelation as the mark of the beast. They are parallel concepts.

Revelation 9:5, 10 says, *"And to them it was given that they should not kill them, but that they should be tormented five months: and their torment was as the torment of a scorpion, when he striketh a man. . .* "[10] *And they had tails like unto scorpions, and there were stings in their tails: and their power was to hurt men five months."*

Here the number five is used in the same way the number one third is used—that is, it is used as a partial torment, as opposed to a perfect torment. If the number ten is the number of perfection, then half of ten is something less than perfection. It is a diminution of the symbolic meaning of the number ten because it is ten divided in half. It is a partial torment, as opposed to a perfect torment. This represents something less than the worst possible suffering, a partial suffering, not a complete or a perfect one. God is not executing a perfect judgment, but a partial judgment.

We also have the number one-tenth in Revelation 11:13 ". . .*and a tenth part of the city fell. . .*" Here is a partial as opposed to a total destruction of the city by an earthquake.

Numbers derived from TWELVE: The number twelve represents the chosen people of God because there were twelve tribes and twelve apostles. They represent the Old Testament church and the New Testament church, Old Testament believers and New Testament believers.

In Revelation, the number twenty-four occurs repeatedly. Notice Revelation 4:4. This is the vision of the throne of God. It says, *"And round about the throne were four and twenty seats: and upon the seats I saw four and twenty elders sitting, clothed in white raiment; and they had on their heads crowns of gold."* This vision of twenty-four elders sitting around the throne occurs several other times in Revelation.

This number twenty-four represents the church of God of the old and the new dispensations combined—the twelve tribes plus the twelve apostles. The number twelve is the number of God's chosen people.

These twenty-four elders represent the chosen people of God. This is why the New Jerusalem in Revelation 21 has all of its dimensions as multiples of twelve—a perfect cube of twelve thousand furlongs in each direction, representing the perfection of the number of people of God. It represents all of the church of God of the old and new dispensation combined, the twelve tribes plus the twelve apostles.

We have the number twelve thousand in Revelation 7:5–8 which says: *"Of the tribe of Judah were sealed twelve thousand. Of the tribe of Reuben were sealed twelve thousand. Of the tribe of Gad were sealed twelve thousand. [6] Of the tribe of Asher were sealed twelve thousand,"* and it goes on and lists other tribes, in which each had twelve thousand sealed.

Twelve thousand is twelve times ten times ten times ten, which is twelve multiplied by the number ten repeatedly. This represents the perfect or whole number of the chosen people of God who are saved, who are in various locations and in various identity groups.

Some try to literalize this and say there are exactly twelve thousand in the tribe of Judah who are saved. Therefore, if you are not of the tribe of Judah and you are not of that twelve thousand (or one of the other tribes mentioned), then you cannot be sealed with the seal of God. Remember, however, it is only the people with the seal of God that appear in heaven! When you literalize this number, you have to say: "I am not a Jew that is a member of any one of those tribes, and there have certainly been one hundred and forty-four thousand people saved long before I ever came along; therefore, I have no hope of salvation!"

The tribes in Israel were located in different regions of the Promised Land: up north, down south, and in the middle. They represented various regional areas. This listing of various tribes that were in various locations represents the large number of the chosen people of God in various locations and in various identity groups that are saved. Judah was an identity group; Asher was an identity group. If someone was of the tribe of Asher, that person was not of the tribe of Judah.

Across the world, there are various identity groups: races, nationalities, language groups, and cultures located in various places. The idea is that God is going to save the perfect number of people out of every one of those groups, in every one of those locations, of every one of those diverse identities. He is going to save the perfect number of people out of all places and regions and peoples and identity groups. They will all be spiritual Jews because they will all be born of Christ, as Galatians 3:29 says. (See chapter 25.)

The number one hundred forty-four thousand is used—twelve times twelve times a thousand, which is ten times ten times ten. Notice Revelation 7:4, *"And I heard the number of them which were sealed: and there were sealed an hundred and forty and four thousand of all the tribes of the children of Israel."*

This number appears once again in Revelation 14:1, *"And I looked, and, lo, a Lamb stood on the mount Zion, and with him an hundred forty and four thousand, having his Father's name written in their foreheads."* Notice verse 3, *"And they sung as it were a new song before the throne, and before the four beasts, and the elders: and no man could learn that song but the hundred and forty and four thousand, which were redeemed from the earth."*

Previously we had twelve thousand from each group. Now we have one hundred and forty-four thousand, representing all of them. That number is twelve intensified—the chosen people of God intensified. Twelve times twelve, and then intensified by perfection, ten times ten times ten, which equals one hundred and forty-four thousand. This represents the full number of the chosen people of God—that is, all of God's elect of all the ages.

Conclusion

This chapter and the previous one cover all the numbers used in the book of Revelation. We have to get this right. If we do not, we wind up making a mess out of the interpretation of the book because it is saturated with numbers.

What is being taught here is not something new or unique. This is how reformed orthodoxy has interpreted and understood numerology in the Bible for centuries. Every time interpreters start literalizing these numbers, they come up with false date setting, with heresies, and with various aberrant concepts Revelation does not contain. This book is a book of symbolic pictures; and when you understand the meaning of the symbolism, then the proper message comes through. The proper meaning of symbolic numbers does not arise from literalizing them.

As previously stated, interpreting Revelation is like interpreting a political cartoon. When you look at the illustrations, you immediately recognize that what they portray is not literal, even though they convey an idea that is literal and genuine.

I once saw a political cartoon of a child sitting in front of a television. The television is on, and there is a person leaping out of the television. His feet are still inside the screen, but he is leaping out and has garbage in one of his hands. He has opened the top of the child's head with his other hand, and he is pouring the garbage into the child's head.

Is it literally true? No. It is a symbolic picture of how television pours immoral garbage into children's minds with their programming; and when you look at the picture, you instantly understand it. You never for one second think that a guy really does come out of the TV and he really does take the tops of children's heads off and he really does pour literal garbage into their heads. It never crosses your mind to take the picture literally.

We have to read the book of Revelation this way. You must not look at the pictures presented by verbal description in Revelation and instantly go to the literal. You start with the symbolic and ask: "What is this a symbol of?" When you understand how the Bible itself explains the symbols that are contained in the book, then you understand the meaning.

The problem is that many people try to read modern technology or news headlines or political developments into the book of Revelation to try to understand it, instead of reading the Old Testament and seeing what it has to say about the meaning of these symbols. When you look in the Old Testament and see how it uses these symbols, then you understand what John is doing as he uses these same symbols to convey these ideas. Revelation is a symbolic picture book; it is not meant to be taken literally, though it does convey very literal truths.

The Exposition of the Book of Revelation

7

The Prologue to Revelation, Revelation 1:1–3

> "[1] *The Revelation of Jesus Christ, which God gave unto him, to shew unto his servants things which must shortly come to pass; and he sent and signified it by his angel unto his servant John:* [2] *Who bare record of the word of God, and of the testimony of Jesus Christ, and of all things that he saw.* [3] *Blessed is he that readeth, and they that hear the words of this prophecy, and keep those things which are written therein: for the time is at hand.*"

It is important to understand that the book of Revelation takes up where the book of Daniel leaves off.

In Daniel 2, Daniel has the vision of a great image of a man. The head is of gold, the arms and the chest are of silver, the waist and the thighs are of brass, and the legs are of iron. These represent four kingdoms which were world empires. The head of gold represented Babylon, which was then extant; the arms of silver, the Medo-Persian Empire; the thighs of brass, the Greek Empire under Alexander the Great; and finally, the iron legs representing the Roman Empire, the empire in existence when Jesus came into the world.

Daniel then saw in his vision a stone that was cut out without hands. It was cast at the image and completely crushed and destroyed it so it was turned into powder. The stone then grew and became a great mountain that filled the whole earth. This stone is Christ and His kingdom which overcame the Roman Empire, and the kingdom of God then spread to fill the entire earth.

When Jesus came, the kingdom of God started out very small, but that kingdom has grown to fill the entire earth. Every nation on earth has a Christian witness and a Christian church and a Christian community.

The last days have arrived. The last days are the days between the

first and the second coming of Christ, which is the last covenantal period before the end of the world. Many people think that the last days have yet to come, but we have been in the last days for the last 2,000 years. It says in Hebrews 1:1–2, *"God, who at sundry times and in divers manners spake in time past unto the fathers by the prophets,*
2 *Hath in these last days spoken unto us by his Son. . ."*

The reason why the last 2,000 years have been the *"last days"* is that they comprise the last covenantal period before the consummation of all things. The first covenant was the Noahic Covenant, followed by the Abrahamic Covenant, the Old Covenant, the Davidic Covenant, and now the New Covenant, which Jesus established at the Last Supper when He said, *"This cup is the new covenant in my blood."*

We are in the last covenantal period before the consummation of all things, and that makes this covenantal period the "last days"—that is, the last covenantal period that will ever be on this present earth.

What Daniel said was going to occur in the latter days is now present as John writes; and therefore, John says regarding what he writes that it *"must shortly come to pass,"* and that *"the time is at hand."* What Daniel spoke regarding the coming of the stone *"cut out without hands"* had just happened. Now it is going to overcome the Roman Empire and grow to fill the whole earth. The great stone Jesus Christ has now appeared to build His kingdom that is going to transcend and destroy all the kingdoms of this world. Revelation records the conflict involved in the growth of that stone and the building of that kingdom so that ultimately *"the kingdoms of this world are become the kingdoms of our Lord and of his Christ; and he shall reign for ever and ever."*

This is where we are in the eschatological timetable. We are in the last days. The stone has smitten the kingdoms of the world, it is now growing and filling the whole earth; and ultimately, all the kingdoms of the world will become the kingdoms of our Lord and of His Christ. However, that is not going to happen without a lot of conflict and spiritual warfare. The book of Revelation teaches us about this warfare. It tells us the parties who are involved, the battles that must be fought, and the ultimate outcome that will occur.

John opens the book of Revelation with a prologue in verses 1–3 in which he tells us where this book came from, what it contains, and why it is important that we take heed to its message and obey its precepts. This prologue provides us with a background and framework for the remainder of the book.

The Source of the Book of Revelation

The source of the book of Revelation is stated in the first part of verse 1 when it says, *"The Revelation of Jesus Christ, which God gave unto him."* The very first word in the original language of this book is the word *apokalupsis*, which means to unveil or to reveal, and from it we derive the word *revelation*. It means to unveil. The word means to uncover something that is hidden so we might see that which we could never perceive on our own.

In this book, God reveals what we could never know unless He told us about it. This is why it is a revelation; it is a revealing of things we could not know without it. Specifically, we are told this is the revelation of Jesus Christ; that is, it is the revelation that belongs to Him which He provides to us. Jesus Christ has a revelation to give us.

Where did this revelation that Jesus has to give us come from? Verse 1 specifically says that God the Father gave this revelation to Jesus. Notice, *"The Revelation of Jesus Christ, which God gave unto him."* We see this gift of God the Father being transferred to God the Son in Revelation 5:1–10. *"And I saw in the right hand of him that sat on the throne a book"* (the book of Revelation) *"written within and on the backside, sealed with seven seals. [2] And I saw a strong angel proclaiming with a loud voice, Who is worthy to open the book, and to loose the seals thereof? [3] And no man in heaven, nor in earth, neither under the earth, was able to open the book, neither to look thereon. [4] And I wept much, because no man was found worthy to open and to read the book, neither to look thereon.[5] And one of the elders saith unto me, Weep not: behold, the Lion of the tribe of Judah, the Root of David, hath prevailed to open the book, and to loose the seven seals thereof. [6] And I beheld, and, lo, in the midst of the throne and of the four beasts, and in the midst of the elders, stood a Lamb as it had been slain, having seven horns and seven eyes, which are the seven Spirits of God sent forth into all the earth. [7] And he came and took the book out of the right hand of him that sat upon the throne. [8] And when he had taken the book, the four beasts and four and twenty elders fell down before the Lamb, having every one of them harps, and golden vials full of odours, which are the prayers of saints. [9] And they sung a new song, saying, Thou art worthy to take the book, and to open the seals thereof: for thou wast slain, and hast redeemed us to God by thy blood out of every kindred, and tongue, and people, and nation;* [10] *And hast made us unto our God kings and priests: and we shall reign on the earth."*

Here is the transfer of the book of Revelation from God the Father to God the Son. This book was in the form of a scroll. God the Son starts opening the seals of the book, and as He opens them each in turn, new information is revealed and the revelation progressively unfolds. Scrolls were long strips of paper several inches wide and several feet long that were rolled around a rod. The way these scrolls functioned is that words would be written, then the section written on would be rolled up, a little bit of wax would be placed there, and this would seal that section of the book. Then more would be written, this newly written section would be rolled up, wax would be placed there, and this would seal that section. In this manner the book was rolled up and written on the inside and outside. When the scroll was read, these progressive seals were broken to reveal the next section of content in the book.

As the seals of this book are opened, there is the unveiling and revealing of the things that will occur and characterize the future from the time of John until the final consummation of all things. The Revelation of Jesus Christ which God the Father gave Him is this book sealed with seven seals; which when they are opened, reveal the things that will characterize these last days in which we are living. The source of this book is that it is a gift of the Father to the Son.

The Recipients of the Book of Revelation

It says in verse 1, *"The Revelation of Jesus Christ, which God gave unto him, to shew unto his servants"* (the recipients) *"things which must shortly come to pass."*

When God the Father gave this revelation to God the Son, He did not keep it to Himself. We are specifically told that God gave this revelation to Jesus so that He might show these things to His servants. The servants of Jesus Christ are the recipients of the book. This is a book for the people of God. It is for the ordinary Christian.

Are you a servant of Jesus Christ? If you are, then this book was written to you and for you. It is Christ's intention that you read it, understand it, obey it, and draw great comfort from it.

This book was not made for the scholar. It was not written for the highly advanced Christian who has multiple degrees in biblical studies. It was made for and given to those who serve Jesus Christ every day according to their calling and station in life. This means that this book is not over your head or beyond your grasp. That is not to say that it is easy to understand. You have to do some work to grasp its meaning and message. But if you do that work, if you pay attention to this exposition of the book, you can understand and apply the message it contains with the confidence you are on the right track as you do so.

Furthermore, this book is not primarily for those who live at some distant point in the future when the Great Tribulation finally comes. The purpose of this revelation which the Father gave the Son was *"to shew unto His servants things which must shortly come to pass."* Notice: *"the things which must shortly come to pass."* In other words, the events prophesied in this book were to begin in John's day and in John's lifetime. Those who obtained this book and read it would say: "These things are starting right now. They are happening right now."

Notice verse 3: *"Blessed is he that readeth, and they that hear the words of this prophecy, and keep those things which are written therein: for the time is at hand."* We are told twice in the prologue that what John is writing is starting to be experienced and seen and fulfilled right now. The time for these things to begin is *"shortly. . . for the time is at hand."* What John describes was to start in his own lifetime and was therefore immediately relevant to first-century believers.

But even though what John prophesies will begin in his lifetime, it will not end in his lifetime. What Revelation reveals is inaugurated as John writes, but it will continue to be carried out until the second coming of Christ. The spiritual warfare that accompanies the establishment and expansion and the final victory of the kingdom of God is beginning in John's day and will be carried out in every subsequent generation until it concludes with the second coming of Christ. This revelation given by Jesus Christ is relevant to John in his generation, and it is relevant to every subsequent generation until Jesus returns.

Revelation was not primarily for first-century Christians, nor primarily for those who live a few years before the second coming. It has equal application to every generation throughout the time period between the first and second coming. The recipients are equally the servants of God in every generation.

The Messengers of the Book of Revelation

It says in verse 1, "*The Revelation of Jesus Christ, which God gave unto him, to shew unto his servants things which must shortly come to pass; and he sent and signified it by his angel unto his servant John.*"

It is important for us to understand that the message of the book of Revelation is transmitted through five parties. It begins with and finds its origin in (1) God the Father. Then, (2), He gives it to God the Son, Jesus Christ. The message now belongs to Him. It is the revelation of Jesus Christ. Jesus then sent this message by means of signs and symbols to (3) His angel. The angel then shows it to (4) John. Then John, through the writing of this book, shows it to (5) His servants, who are all those who believe in Christ as Lord and Savior in this age.

When it says "*he sent and signified it,*" the word "signify" is a very interesting and important word. It means to communicate by means of symbols or signs. Ordinarily, we communicate with words. Such ordinary communication is called prose. In our introduction to this book, we said the book of Revelation is not primarily ordinary prose, but it is primarily a series of symbolically illustrated pictures. For example, we have beasts with seven heads and ten horns, and many other very strange word pictures. Those symbolic images are the signs by which the message of this book is communicated.

God gave His Son the revelation, the Son gave it to the angel, and the angel then gave it to John. We see several examples of this occurring in this book. Revelation 17:1, "*And there came one of the seven angels which had the seven vials, and talked with me, saying unto me, Come hither; I will shew unto thee the judgment of the great whore that sitteth upon many waters.*" Here is a clear example of what is stated in 1:1. The angel says to John: "Come here, I am going to show you a picture," and he shows him a picture of a whorish woman sitting on the back of a beast.

Notice further Revelation 22:8, which is looking back over the book and summarizing what it has to say and how it was transmitted: "*And I John saw these things, and heard them. And when I had heard and seen, I fell down to worship before the feet of the angel which shewed me these things.*"

In Revelation 1:1, John says the angel showed him this revelation, and at the end of the book John says the angel showed him this revelation. This is how these visual images were transmitted to John. They were transmitted to him by an angel.

God the Father gives the book to God the Son; God the Son gives it to the angel; the angel gives it to John, and John finally communicates this revelation to all of Christ's servants by means of this book which he wrote.

In Revelation 1:11, Jesus is saying to John, ". . .*I am Alpha and Omega, the first and the last: and, What thou seest, write in a book, and send it unto the seven churches which are in Asia.*" In the beginning, John had no book. Jesus said: "You are going to be shown some things; write it all down." At the end of the book, Jesus says in 22:18–19 that it has now been written and that John is not to add to the book that he has written, and not to take away from it. This is the revelation. He was told to write, and he wrote.

These, then, are the five stages of transmission, and in them, the stress is upon the divine origin of this revelation. People have all kinds of wrong ideas about where the book came from and what its source was. Therefore, it is important to emphasize that this is a book of divine origin, and the reason it is written in this fashion is because it is intended to be a picture book. As you look at each of the pictures, you draw from them the meaning they were intended to convey.

This book is not something John fabricated out of an overwrought imagination. Its source is God the Father—and therefore, it is inerrant, infallible, and authoritative. It is not of mere human origin. Therefore, it can be trusted as a safe guide as to the spiritual warfare we will face and the outcomes we may expect as we participate in the worldwide expansion of the kingdom of God until the end of time.

The Content of the Book of Revelation

Notice verse 2: "*Who bare record of the word of God, and of the testimony of Jesus Christ, and of all things that he saw.*"

When John wrote this book, he was fully aware of what he was writing, and that what he wrote was no ordinary communication. He was bearing record on behalf of God; and therefore, he was careful to omit nothing given to him nor to add anything to it.

First of all, John bore record "*of the word of God.*" In other words, he explicitly says right up front: "These are not my words. This is the word of God. These are not the words of men." These words John wrote proceeded out of the mind of the Father and came with all the majesty and authority of God the Father Himself.

Furthermore, when it says that he bore record of the word of God, this is also a reference to all the Old Testament allusions that he brings out as he writes the book of Revelation. There are more allusions to the Old Testament in the book of Revelation than there is in all the rest of the New Testament books combined. The book of Revelation is saturated with references to the Old Testament. So, when John says he bears testimony to the word of God, he is not only talking about the word that proceeds from God, but he is also talking about all the words of God that have already been given in the Old Testament.

Secondly, he says he bore record *"of the testimony of Jesus Christ,"* in verse 2. This can mean both the testimony that proceeds from Christ and also the testimony regarding Christ.

Revelation 1:1 says that this book is *"The Revelation of Jesus Christ."* Here is the testimony that proceeds from Christ. It is His; He gave it. Therefore, as John is writing, he is saying: "I am writing the testimony of Jesus. These are Jesus' words. This is what Jesus is telling me." Jesus says to John in Revelation 1:11, "*What thou seest, write in a book.*" John wrote the testimony Jesus Christ gave to him.

But John also testified regarding Christ Himself, especially regarding His authority and identity. John testified of Christ's authority in Revelation 1:18 where Jesus says, *"I am he that liveth, and was dead; and, behold, I am alive for evermore, Amen; and have the keys of hell and of death."* This speaks of His triumphant, transcendent, and exalted authority over all things. If someone has authority over hell and over death, that person has ultimate authority. John also testified regarding Christ's identity in Revelation 1:8, where he records that Jesus is *"the Alpha and the Omega, the beginning and the ending. . .which is, and which was, and which is to come, the Almighty."* Jesus is none other than the God of the Bible.

In Revelation 22:16, 18, and 20, Jesus says this book of Revelation is His testimony. It is truly the Revelation of Jesus Christ.

Thirdly, John says that he bore record *"of all things that he saw."* Notice, this is not a reference to what *he heard*, though he did hear a lot of things, but to what *he saw*. This is a reminder to us from the beginning of the book that this is primarily a book of visual imagery. The message is in the rich visual imagery the book contains, and as you understand the meaning of the symbolic pictures, you understand the message of the book.

We are specifically told that John *saw* these things. Notice once again Revelation 1:11 where Jesus says, "*I am Alpha and Omega, the first and the last: and, What thou seest, write in a book.*" It is a book about what John saw with his eyes.

In our introduction to the book, we said that this is a book of visions. It is a book of symbolic visual images that represent what is going to occur throughout the future between the first and second coming of Christ while the stone is growing to fill the earth. These visions had their source in God the Father, and they were shown to John by God's angel while John was on the Island of Patmos.

The Blessing of the Book of Revelation

Notice Revelation 1:3. Here is the blessing of the book. "*Blessed is he that readeth, and they that hear the words of this prophecy, and keep those things which are written therein: for the time is at hand.*"

Verse 3 is a beatitude, much like the beatitudes in the Sermon on the Mount. The book of Revelation contains seven beatitudes. Seven is the number of completeness, and those who follow Christ faithfully and who do not abandon Him under the persecution of the world are completely blessed in every respect, in every way, for all eternity.

Here are the seven beatitudes in the book of Revelation:

- Revelation 1:3 "*Blessed is he that readeth, and they that hear the words of this prophecy, and keep those things which are written therein: for the time is at hand.*"
- Revelation 14:13 "*And I heard a voice from heaven saying unto me, Write, Blessed are the dead which die in the Lord from henceforth: Yea, saith the Spirit, that they may rest from their labours; and their works do follow them.*"
- Revelation 16:15 "*Behold, I come as a thief. Blessed is he that watcheth, and keepeth his garments, lest he walk naked, and they see his shame.*"
- Revelation 19:9 "*And he saith unto me, Write, Blessed are they which are called unto the marriage supper of the Lamb.*"
- Revelation 20:6 "*Blessed and holy is he that hath part in the first resurrection: on such the second death hath no power.*"
- Revelation 22:7 "*Behold, I come quickly: blessed is he that keepeth the sayings of the prophecy of this book.*"

- Revelation 22:14 *"Blessed are they that do his commandments, that they may have right to the tree of life, and may enter in through the gates into the city."*

Revelation encourages us to be faithful in spiritual warfare and not give up when the wicked persecute us, imprison us, and put us to death. It does so by setting before us the blessing we will have if we are faithful to Christ. God says, in effect, "Serve Me, and I will reciprocate in a manner and to a degree that will make the present sufferings not worthy to be compared with the pleasures, the joys, and the blessings that I will bestow on you."

The blessing of Revelation 1:3 consists in three particulars. First it says, *"Blessed is he that readeth."* That might strike you as a little strange, but we have to understand that in biblical times not everyone had a copy of the Bible. Furthermore, not everyone could read.

Therefore, this book—like all Bible books—was read aloud in the assembly of the church. The one who did the reading aloud was called a lector. The lector could read and write, and he would take the single copy of the book the church had, and he would read it to the congregation. He was declared to be blessed by God for doing that public reading because he was setting forth the word of God to the people of God just by reading the Bible out loud to them.

Secondly, there were also those who gathered together to hear the reading. Notice verse 3, *"Blessed is he that readeth"* (the public lector), *"and they that hear the words of this prophecy,"* who were the believers who gave their full attention to the hearing of the book as it was read aloud. They listened intently as it was read so they might not miss anything it said and so they could remember its content.

Thirdly, verse 3 says, *"Blessed is he that readeth, and they that hear the words of this prophecy, and keep those things which are written therein."* It is not enough to merely read the book or hear it read. Those things alone do not result in the blessedness that is pronounced. Both the readers and the hearers must *"keep those things"* that are written in this book. We have to obey the instructions and commands it conveys if we would have the outcome and the blessedness that it promises.

The time for obedience to this book is not at some point in the distant future. Notice the last phrase of verse 3: *"for the time is at hand."* John is saying that the time for the things written in this book to occur is at hand; and therefore, the time to obey these instructions is now.

Revelation 22:6–7, 10, and 14 further clarify this point. *"And he said unto me, These sayings are faithful and true: and the Lord God of the holy prophets sent his angel to shew unto his servants the things which must shortly be done.* [7] *Behold, I come quickly: blessed is he that keepeth the sayings of the prophecy of this book.* [10] *And he saith unto me, Seal not the sayings of the prophecy of this book: for the time is at hand,* [14] *Blessed are they that do his commandments, that they may have right to the tree of life."*

It has never been those who are merely professing believers who have made it to heaven. It is the professing believers who actually did what the Lord Jesus commanded them to do that gained the right to the tree of life. This is not salvation by works; rather, it is saying that true salvation results in a desire to obey and a lifelong pursuit of obedience to Jesus Christ. Do we fail? Yes. Do we sin? Yes. But for the true believer, the dominating characteristic of his life is that he does keep the commandments of Christ. Believers *"keep those things which are written therein."*

Blessed are they who *"keep those things which are written therein: for the time is at hand."* Because the time is at hand, we need to have a sense of urgency about this obedience spoken of here. The time to obey the instruction given in the book of Revelation is right now. Revelation is not a book about events in the far distant future that we learn about just for curiosity's sake.

Revelation is about the spiritual warfare we must engage in right now, and the vast majority of the book talks about the spiritual warfare that every generation faces. It is certainly true that the second coming of Christ and the establishment of the new heavens and the new earth may be in the far distant future. But the battle to build the kingdom of Christ is going on right now, and this is the battle Revelation describes, and the battle we must fight every day. It is this present spiritual warfare and how we are to understand it and fight it that comprises the vast bulk of the book.

We must recognize that Revelation is not written to satisfy our curiosity. It is a book of commandments and a book of comforts, and the comforts encourage us to keep the commandments until the day that the second coming of Christ does occur.

8

The Opening Perspective of Revelation, Revelation 1:4–6

> *"4 John to the seven churches which are in Asia: Grace be unto*
> *you, and peace, from him which is, and which was, and which*
> *is to come; and from the seven Spirits which are before his*
> *throne; 5 And from Jesus Christ, who is the faithful witness,*
> *and the first begotten of the dead, and the prince of the kings*
> *of the earth. Unto him that loved us, and washed us from our*
> *sins in his own blood, 6 And hath made us kings and priests*
> *unto God and his Father; to him be glory and dominion for*
> *ever and ever. Amen."*

In our last chapter, we looked at the prologue to Revelation in verses 1 through 3. First of all, we saw the source of the book of Revelation. John informed us that it is of divine origin. It is the revelation that comes from Jesus Christ, which was given to Him by God the Father. What John wrote came from God the Father and God the Son. Clearly, this book is not of human origin.

Secondly, we saw the recipients of the book of Revelation. This book was written to the servants of Christ. That is, it was written to ordinary Christians. It was meant to be read and understood by all believers, and all believers can understand it when they grasp the symbolic method it uses to convey its message. It was not written to highly advanced Christians or to great scholars. It was written to the ordinary servants of Jesus Christ.

The recipients of this book are not only the ordinary believers of John's generation, but they are also the ordinary believers of every generation until Christ returns. The things in this book are things that must shortly come to pass. The time is at hand for these things to occur. The time for the beginning of the fulfillment of the things of this book was starting in John's day, it has continued to this very day, and will continue until the end of time. Wherever you find servants of Jesus Christ, this book is written to them, it applies to them, and it is fulfilled for them in their lifetimes.

Thirdly, we saw the messengers of the book of Revelation. We saw that God the Father gave this revelation to God the Son, who then sent it by an angel to the apostle John, who then wrote it down in a book. Therefore, as we read this book, we see all four of these persons involved in transmitting this book to us.

Fourthly, we saw the content of the book of Revelation. We saw that it contained a record of the word of God the Father, a record of the testimony of Jesus Christ, and a record of the witness of John of all that he saw.

The entire book is divine revelation, filled with divine content, and marked by divine infallibility. This book has no content that arises out of men's ideas or imaginations. Instead, it is a revelation of symbolic visions that have been given to John by the Father and the Son through the agency of an angel.

Fifthly, we saw the blessing of the book of Revelation. Those who read and hear and keep the instructions and commands it contains will obtain the comforts and rewards and promises Jesus made to those who endure to the end. Those who follow Christ faithfully and do not deny and forsake Christ because of the persecution of the world are completely blessed in every respect and in every way for all of eternity. Blessed are they that read, and hear, and keep the sayings of this book.

Having completed the examination of the prologue of this book in verses 1 to 3, we now come to the main body of the book which begins at verse 4 and extends to chapter 22. It is addressed to the churches in particular. Notice verse 4: "*John to the seven churches.*" The first three chapters directly address the seven churches in Asia.

It is important to understand that it is not just the first three chapters that are directed to the church. The entire rest of the book is written to the church as well. We are told by Jesus at the end of this book that the whole book is a testimony from Him to the churches when He says in 22:16, "*I Jesus have sent mine angel to testify unto you these things in the churches.*"

Everything this book contains was sent to the churches in particular. Jesus makes it clear that from start to finish Revelation is a church epistle that is specifically for the churches. Let each church give careful heed to its message and consider what the Head of the church has to say to His church in this wonderful and encouraging book.

The Parties Addressed

The parties addressed are revealed to us in verse 4 when it says, "*John to the seven churches which are in Asia.*" Asia in the Bible is modern-day Turkey. There were seven churches in that geographical region. They were literal churches that actually existed there.

In our previous chapter, we said that the recipients of this letter were the servants of Jesus Christ. In verse 1 it says, "*The Revelation of Jesus Christ, which God gave unto him, to shew unto his servants things which must shortly come to pass.*" We said the recipients of the letter were ordinary Christians. However, John now says he is writing to the seven churches. So which is it? Is he writing to His servants, or is he writing to His seven churches? The answer is simply this: The servants of Christ are those who are committed members of local churches.

In other words, when he is writing to the servants of Christ, he is writing to them in the expectation that they will be committed to and involved in a local church. To write to the churches is to write to the servants of Christ, and to write to the servants of Christ is to write to the churches, because all servants of Christ are in churches. The New Testament knows nothing of Christians who think involvement in a local church is unnecessary or optional.

Christ expects every one of His servants to be involved in a biblically functioning local church. As individual believers are joined together in a biblical church, they obtain the strength and the resources to overcome the onslaught of Satan and his people. This onslaught is described in the remainder of this book. Involvement in a local church is critical to triumph in this onslaught because it is in the church that most of the means of grace are deposited and function. Through these collective means of grace deposited in the local church, we obtain the strength we need to be victorious overcomers in the battles we face.

When John speaks of showing these things to the servants of Christ in verse 1, he views those servants as those who are gathered together into individual local churches in verse 4. This is critical to understand: The New Testament knows nothing of unchurched Christians. Every Christian in the New Testament is fully involved in a local church.

Therefore, unless you are providentially hindered by illness or distance from meeting with other believers, then you need to be part of a biblically functioning local church. John and Jesus expect you, as a servant of Christ, to be in a church of Christ. Do not forsake the assembling of yourselves together with the believers and still expect to triumph in spiritual warfare.

We notice here that John writes to the seven churches which are in Asia. Although there were more than seven churches in Asia (there was a church in Colossae and in Hierapolis), John was instructed by Christ in verse 11 to write to only seven of them.

Notice Revelation 1:11 where Jesus is saying, *"I am Alpha and Omega, the first and the last: and, What thou seest, write in a book, and send it unto the seven churches which are in Asia,"* and then he lists them by name in the remainder of the verse. The church at Hierapolis is not mentioned there, nor the church at Colossae, nor other churches which we know existed because we are told about them elsewhere in the book of Acts and in the epistles.

John was instructed by Christ to write to only seven of them because the number seven is used symbolically to indicate completeness. These seven churches represent the complete church of Jesus Christ.

These seven churches are representative of the whole church throughout the entire time between the first and the second coming of Jesus Christ. As Christ addresses each individual church, He closes His exhortation to each of them with these words: *"He that hath an ear, let him hear what the Spirit saith unto the churches."* Notice the plural "*churches*."

For example, when He writes to the church (singular) at Ephesus and conveys His message to them, He then says, *"He that hath an ear, let him hear what the Spirit saith unto the churches"* (plural). Jesus is not just addressing these seven churches that literally existed in this day on this literal piece of real estate. He is saying the message to each individual church is a message for all of the churches throughout the world and throughout time. These seven individual churches represent the complete church of Jesus Christ.

These letters are for all churches. They address the problems they struggle with, the virtues they possess, and the opposition they experience. These seven churches, and by extension all churches, are the parties the book of Revelation is addressed to. This book is addressed to the local church that you attend.

The Prayer Offered

The prayer offered is in verse 4: *"Grace be unto you, and peace."* This prayer for grace and peace is for these churches in particular and all the churches they symbolize. This prayer John offered is found in nearly all of the New Testament epistles.

For example, we see that Paul opens every one of his letters with a prayer for grace and peace to those to whom he is writing. This prayer is not a mere throwaway line like we use when we say, "Hello" to people. We do not really mean anything by the word "hello"; it is just a way of saying, "I am paying attention to you, and you need to pay attention to me." When you greeted someone with "grace and peace," that was not a throwaway line—it meant something; indeed, it meant a great deal. Here, it is a prayer that God's grace and God's peace would be given to those to whom John is writing.

The first request is that God's grace would be upon his readers. He says, *"Grace be unto you."* Grace is God's unmerited saving favor that is given to undeserving sinners. Through God's grace, all the saving benefits of Christ's saving work are conveyed to God's elect.

Grace is always salvific; that is, it always conveys salvation to those who are the objects of it. God's goodness is not necessarily saving, and God's mercy is not necessarily saving. Goodness and mercy are shown by God to all people without exception. But God's grace is shown in particular to God's elect. Initially, grace conveys regeneration and justification to us. Subsequently, grace conveys sanctification and preservation to us. Ultimately, grace conveys resurrection and glorification to us.

All we have of salvation we have through God's grace. Whether it is the initial reception of salvation, the ongoing outworking of salvation, or the ultimate consummation of salvation—from start to finish salvation is conveyed by God's grace. We need grace to be saved, we need grace to live out that salvation until the end, and we especially need grace to persevere under the persecution and temptation Satan and his helpers assault us with that is described in this book.

Great grace is needed to enable us to be overcomers in our spiritual warfare. You received grace when you became saved, but you need ongoing supplies of grace in order to be an overcomer when assaulted by Satan and his helpers. Therefore, John prays for further applications of Christ's saving work to His people when he prays that God would extend grace to them.

The second request is that God's peace would be upon his readers. He says, "*Grace be unto you, and peace.*" Peace is first obtained when we become saved. Romans 5:1 says, "*Therefore being justified by faith, we have peace with God through our Lord Jesus Christ.*" Not only did the enmity and conflict between our souls and God cease when we were saved, but we also became fully reconciled to God. God is now at peace with us and we are at peace with Him.

But there is much turmoil in the Christian life and there are many anxieties that arise in the course of spiritual warfare. In John 16:33 Jesus says, "*These things I have spoken unto you, that in me ye might have peace. In the world ye shall have tribulation: but be of good cheer; I have overcome the world.*" While the conflict between our souls and God ends when we become saved, the conflict between our souls and the world begins when we become saved. Jesus tells us in plain language that we will have tribulation in this world and from this world. We have no fellowship with the world; and therefore, the world hates us and persecutes us.

In John 14:2 Jesus says, "*Peace I leave with you, my peace I give unto you: not as the world giveth, give I unto you. Let not your heart be troubled, neither let it be afraid.*" Jesus is well aware that even though we are at peace with Him, there are still many things in this world that trouble our hearts and create fear in us, and we need additional ongoing supplies of peace in our conflict with the world and the flesh and the devil.

We are told in Philippians 4:6–7 to be anxious for nothing, but in everything by prayer and supplication with thanksgiving to let our requests be made known unto God, and the peace of God, which passes all understanding, will guard our hearts and our minds. There is a great deal to be anxious about because Satan and his people are at war with us and we with them. Peace comes from knowing that all things are under the control of God, and are working together for our good and God's glory and the accomplishment of His purposes. Believers need ongoing supplies of a felt sense of peace from God because their peace is disturbed by their warfare with Satan and his helpers.

Grace is God's saving favor given to those who do not deserve it, pardoning their sins and bestowing on them the gift of eternal life. Peace is the rest in our spirit we experience when we know that God's smile is on us and He is reconciled to us. Having them both gives us great strength and courage in the midst of the tremendous spiritual warfare we face.

This prayer for grace and for peace really sums up all the benefits and blessings of the gospel. What he means when he says *"Grace be unto you and peace"* is this: "May all of the benefits and blessings of Christ's saving work be applied to your lives in the midst of the conflict you are facing." God's grace and peace give us strength that enables us to overcome in this conflict.

The Persons Described

We do not generate either grace or peace. These things are given to us from outside of us. John tells us they arise from the divine Trinity. They arise from the Father, from the Spirit, and from the Son.

Notice the description that God gives for each member of the Trinity. Verse 4: *"John to the seven churches which are in Asia: Grace be unto you, and peace"* (now notice the source) *"from him which is, and which was, and which is to come."*

Here we have a description of the Father. In this description is a declaration of the eternality of God as the One who has always existed from eternity past, as the One who presently exists to be with us and to give us grace and peace, and as the One who will always exist in the future to continue to supply grace and peace into eternity. God's eternal self-existence is a profound source of comfort to the believer.

God will always be there for us. He always has been, He is now, and He always will be, and no kind of enemy and no length of time will ever be able to erase His life or power or presence from us. Because God is eternal, the grace and the peace He gives us will never end.

Having seen the description of the Father, notice the description of the Spirit. It says that this grace and peace also comes *"from the seven Spirits which are before his throne."* Here is a second symbolic use of the number seven.

Notice the word *"Spirits"* is capitalized. It is clearly a reference to the Holy Spirit, and the question we have to ask is whether there are seven different and distinct holy spirits. The answer is clearly, loudly, and resoundingly, No! In Ephesians 4:4, we are plainly told, *"There is one body, and one Spirit."* Never in the rest of the Bible is the Holy

Spirit, the third Member of the Trinity, ever referred to in the plural. He is always referred to in the singular. He is always "the Spirit," or "the Holy Spirit," or "the Spirit of God."

Why, then, does it speak here of *"the seven Spirits"*? The symbolic meaning of the number seven is completeness. Here the Holy Spirit is set before our eyes in all the fullness and completeness of His many-faceted works—works that execute the will of the enthroned God both in the world and in the church.

Jesus said in John chapters 14 through 16, to summarize His key points, "When I leave, I and the Father are going to send the Comforter, who is the Holy Spirit. He will do work in the world. He will convict the world of sin and righteousness and judgment. He will do work in the church. He will bring comfort, teaching, and illumination. He will bring all things to your remembrance that I have said to you." The Spirit of God is before the throne of God, ready to completely and fully execute the will of God in building the kingdom of God.

The lampstand in the temple had seven lights, and these seven lights represented the perfect illumination that the Holy Spirit provided to make us able to see and understand the person of God and the will of God.

This term "the seven Spirits" draws its number from the candelabra with its seven lights. This term "seven Spirits" refers to the Holy Spirit in the completeness and fullness of His operations and influences in the world and in the church, as He brings the light of God's revelation to humanity. He is ever before the throne of God, ready to be sent to execute the will of God.

This brings us to the description of the Son, Jesus Christ. Grace and peace also come from Jesus Christ; notice verses 5–6: *"And from Jesus Christ, who is the faithful witness, and the first begotten of the dead, and the prince of the kings of the earth. Unto him that loved us, and washed us from our sins in his own blood,* [6] *And hath made us kings and priests unto God and his Father; to him be glory and dominion for ever and ever."*

You may wonder about the unusual order of the presentation of the Persons of the Trinity. Ordinarily when the Bible speaks about the Trinity, it speaks of the Father, the Son, and the Holy Spirit, in that order. We see this order in Matthew 28:19. But here we have the Father, the Spirit, and the Son. Why are they presented in that order? Once again, this has its roots in the Old Testament tabernacle. Hebrews 9:24 says that the earthly tabernacle is a picture of the true tabernacle which is in heaven. At the rear of the earthly tabernacle was the Holy of Holies, containing the ark of the covenant. The Shekinah glory of God dwelt over the mercy seat between the cherubim, and only the high priest could go into it, and only once a year. It was very remote, hidden, and closed off.

Then as we proceed toward the front of the tabernacle, we come into the Holy Place, and there we have the menorah consisting of seven lamps. All the priests entered and ministered there continuously. The common people were never allowed to enter the Holy Place.

Then as we move further outward, we emerge outside the tabernacle, and in front of the tabernacle is the brazen altar. This is where the sacrificial lambs were offered. There the people could come right up to the altar, give their lamb to the priest, and watch it slain in front of their eyes. The priest would take the blood into the Holy Place and sprinkle it on the altar of incense.

Once a year on the Day of Atonement, the high priest would go into the Holy of Holies. The Holy of Holies represents the Father in His infinite holiness and unapproachable majesty. Only the high priest could see the Father's dwelling place and glory. The seven lights of the menorah represent the Holy Spirit. All the priests could see the menorah. Then there was the brazen altar before the tabernacle which represents the slain Lamb of God who takes away the sins of the world—and all the people could see that.

As we look at the structure of the tabernacle, it goes from the distant and hidden to the near and visible. The distant and the hidden was the Holy of Holies; then to something a little closer and a little more visible, the Holy Place; and then to something that is very close and highly visible, the brazen altar. Because Jesus is the nearest to us and the most visible to us, we have the fullest description of Him given to us. Thus, the order: the Father, the Spirit, and the Son; the Holy of Holies, the Holy Place, and the brazen altar.

Notice this extended description of Jesus in 1:5–6. It says of Him that He is "*the faithful witness, and the first begotten of the dead, and the prince of the kings of the earth. . .that loved us, and washed us from our sins in his own blood,* [6] *And hath made us kings and priests unto God and his Father; to him be glory and dominion for ever and ever. Amen.*"

The glorious nature and the authoritative position of Christ is set forth in six terms used to describe Christ in who He is, and in what He has done.

First of all, Christ is glorious in who He is.

Christ is *"the faithful witness."* That is, He always told the truth about everything He described. His witness is infallible and completely faithful to the truth.

Many times, people tell you things, but you find out later they were false witnesses. They did not tell you the truth. But you can count on the fact that everything Jesus says is a faithful, infallible, and inerrant representation of the truth. Jesus always and exclusively told the truth and nothing but the truth.

Christ is *"the first begotten of the dead."* He is the resurrected Savior who conquered death. Not only did He conquer death for Himself, but for all those who are begotten of Him. He is the first begotten, and there are many more after Him who will be begotten from the dead. He leads the way, He opens the tomb, He goes forth first to show that not only has He defeated death, but that there are going to be many more after Him who will also experience victory over death.

Christ is *"the prince of the kings of the earth."* This means that Jesus is Lord of lords and King of kings. We do not need to fear any prince or king because the heart of each one is in the hand of the Lord, and He turns it wherever He wills.

John is writing to believers facing persecution, and he tells them three truths about Jesus. He tells them the faithful witness of Jesus will overcome the lies of Satan and his people. He tells them the resurrection of Jesus will overcome their efforts to put them to death. He tells them the kingship of Jesus will subdue all of these kings and bring them beneath His feet. In effect, he says, "Therefore, you can have peace when they lie to you, when they try to kill you, and when they exercise cruel dominion over you. You recognize there is One who triumphs over them in all of those things because of who He is."

Secondly, Christ is glorious in what He does.

Jesus is the one who *"loved us."* We are the objects of the infinite love and care of Jesus to the point that nothing can ever separate us from His love, either in time or in eternity. He will forever draw us to Himself, He will forever keep us near Himself, He will forever give Himself to us, and He will never leave us or forsake us.

Jesus is the one who *"washed us from our sins in his own blood."*

The greatest manifestation of His love for us is that He laid down His life for us. He has cleansed us from the guilt and penalty of our sins, and He presents us holy and unblameable and unreproveable before His Father. We have redemption through His blood, the forgiveness of sins, according to the riches of His grace, so that He presents us faultless before God's throne, and does so with exceeding joy.

Jesus is the one who *"hath made us kings and priests unto God and his Father."* He allows us to share in His rule, we sit in His throne with Him, and He enables us to serve in His kingdom. He gives us access as priests to bring before God the Father the spiritual sacrifices of praise and thanksgiving in the New Covenant temple, which is the church.

We see that this grace and peace come from God the Father, who is always there; from God the Spirit, who is working to implement and accomplish the will of the Father and the Son; and from God the Son, who is glorious in who He is and is glorious in what He has done. What is the conclusion of all of this? Verse 6: *"to him be glory and dominion for ever and ever."*

What should our response be when we see that Jesus is the faithful witness, the first begotten from the dead, and the Lord of the kings of the earth? What should our response be when we see that Jesus has loved us, washed us from our sins in His own blood, and made us kings and priests? We should say: "To Him be the glory!" We should give Him worship and praise. We should yield dominion to Him; that is, we should render submission and service to Him because He has dominion over our lives. How long should we give Him glory and dominion? We should do it forever and ever.

We give Him worship and thanksgiving, we give Him submission and service, we do it all without limit, and we do it all without end. We do it because He is the faithful witness; He is the first begotten from the dead; He is the Lord of the kings of the earth; He loved us; He washed us from our sins in His blood; and He elevated us to be kings and priests. Who would not want to worship and thank and obey and serve forever a Savior like that?

This book is going to describe the conflict we have with Satan and his helpers. But we need to remember as we are dealing with that conflict and going through that warfare that we will have grace from God and peace from God. It is this triune God who is on our side, who is for us, and who is employing all His resources on our behalf to ensure that we will be overcomers.

Let us fight the good fight of faith with the confidence that the triune God is with us, is for us, and is fighting our battles. He will triumph, and in His triumph is our triumph. May we recognize that and rejoice in it and find our confidence in Him, and not dwell on the human resources and the human numbers we have. Instead, let us look above and see the divine God that we have, and with our focus on Him, move forward in triumph and victory in the conflict we will face until the end of our lives.

Thank God for such an elevated picture of the position we are in and the blessings we have as we fight this good fight of faith. John is saying: "Churches, look up! See the Father, see the Spirit, and see the Son. As you are looking up at God, you will have strength and grace to fight the spiritual battles down here."

The book opens on a grand note of victory. Because of Jesus Christ and who He is and what He has done, the victory has already been secured. It is just a matter of implementing it through the process of spiritual warfare. Therefore, settle down and fight, but fight with the confidence that the victory is certain.

9

Christ Returning to Judge the Wicked, Revelation 1:7–8

> "[7] *Behold, he cometh with clouds; and every eye shall see him, and they also which pierced him: and all kindreds of the earth shall wail because of him. Even so, Amen.* [8] *I am Alpha and Omega, the beginning and the ending, saith the Lord, which is, and which was, and which is to come, the Almighty.*"

In the last chapter, we examined the introduction to the book contained in verses 4 to 6. But the introduction of the book does not end at verse 6, though our last chapter ended there. The introduction to the book continues on to include verses 7 and 8.

John addressed this book to all Christian local churches, represented by these seven churches in Asia. He asks that grace and peace be given to them. This grace and peace does not arise out of a vacuum. It is provided to the churches by the Holy Trinity.

John gives us a description of this Holy Trinity. He speaks of the Father and of the Holy Spirit. But primarily, John tells us about Jesus Christ. Jesus Christ and His victory over Satan is the theme of this book, and therefore it is fitting that John should focus the vast bulk of what he has to say on Him.

In light of who Jesus is to us, and in light of what Jesus has done for us, it is no wonder that we love to give Him glory and submit to His rule. But as wonderful as this description of Christ was, John is not finished describing Him. In verses 5 and 6, we see that Christ is a glorious Lord. In verses 7 and 8, we see that Christ is a returning Lord.

In verse 7, John tells us about the second coming of Jesus and His triumph over all those who oppose Him. In verse 8, Jesus speaks of His own eternity and sovereignty. Foolish people think they can triumph over Christ, escape Christ, and thwart Christ. Foolish people are wrong. Verses 7 and 8 summarize why the wicked will utterly fail in their war against Christ.

John represents Jesus Christ as a tremendous source of joy and comfort to the believer in verses 5 and 6. But John presents Jesus Christ as a tremendous source of terror and dread to the wicked in verses 7 and 8. Wicked people fail in their war against Christ because He is coming back in wrath and judgment, and the wrath He brings is inescapable because it is the wrath of the almighty, eternal God.

Let us examine John's teaching as he turns from comforting the believers in verses 5 and 6, to declaring the doom of the unbelievers in verses 7 and 8.

Jesus Is the Returning Judge

Verse 7, *"Behold, he cometh with clouds; and every eye shall see him, and they also which pierced him: and all kindreds of the earth shall wail because of him. Even so, Amen."*

When it says, "*Behold, he. . .*" the antecedent of *"he"* is *Jesus Christ* of verse 5.

We have pointed out that the book of Revelation is rooted in the Old Testament and is saturated with references to it. Verse 7 demonstrates this point. It is made up of two Old Testament passages—Daniel 7:13 and Zechariah 12:10.

Verse 7 says, *"Behold, he cometh with clouds."* In Daniel 7, God gives Daniel a vision, and in this vision, he sees four great beasts. These four beasts represent four successive kingdoms that are going to arise: the Babylonian, Medo-Persian, Grecian, and Roman empires. At the conclusion of the rise of these human kingdoms, we see the final judgment in verse 9: *"I beheld till the thrones were cast down."* All these human kingdoms have now been defeated.

Daniel 7:9–10 says, *"I beheld till the thrones were cast down, and the Ancient of days did sit, whose garment was white as snow, and the hair of his head like the pure wool: his throne was like the fiery flame, and his wheels as burning fire.* [10] *A fiery stream issued and came forth from before him: thousand thousands ministered unto him, and ten thousand times ten thousand stood before him: the judgment was set, and the books were opened."*

Here is a vision of God sitting on His throne at the final judgment. Verse 11 goes on to say, *"I beheld then because of the voice of the great words which the horn spake: I beheld even till the beast was slain, and his body destroyed, and given to the burning flame."* This is a reference to Revelation 19:20 when Jesus returns and takes the beast and the false prophet and casts them into the lake of fire.

Verse 12: *"As concerning the rest of the beasts, they had their dominion taken away: yet their lives were prolonged for a season and time."* When the Babylonian and the Medo-Persian and the Grecian kingdoms were destroyed, the people that made them up were not annihilated; their generations were prolonged until the time of the end. Their dominion was taken away, but the people that were in those kingdoms continued to live on in their successive generations.

Verses 13–14: *"I saw in the night visions, and, behold, one like the Son of man came with the clouds of heaven, and came to the Ancient of days, and they brought him near before him.* [14] *And there was given him dominion, and glory, and a kingdom, that all people, nations, and languages, should serve him: his dominion is an everlasting dominion, which shall not pass away, and his kingdom that which shall not be destroyed."*

Notice in verse 13, Daniel says the Son of man came with the clouds of heaven. Revelation 1:7 says, *"Behold, he cometh with clouds."* Revelation 1:7 draws on the imagery of Daniel 7:13; and clearly, Daniel 7:13–14 describes the second coming of our Lord Jesus Christ.

In Revelation 1:7, John alludes to Daniel 7:13, which gives us the context and meaning of Revelation 1:7. When it says *"he cometh with clouds,"* it is not talking about Him coming in some sort of a judgment at various times and circumstances throughout the age; rather, it is talking about His second coming at the end of the age, when the final judgment has been set and the books have been opened.

Therefore, we know that Revelation 1:7, based on Daniel 7:13, is a reference to the final, visible, physical second coming of the Lord Jesus Christ at the end of this age to carry out the final judgment.

In Revelation 1:7, John goes on to say not only, *"Behold He cometh with clouds"*; but also, *"and every eye shall see him, and they also which pierced him: and all kindreds of the earth shall wail because of him."* Verse 7a talks about the fact of His coming; verse 7b talks about the response to His coming.

What is the response to His coming? The people who see Him coming are really unhappy and upset about His coming. Not only are they not welcoming Him, but they are weeping and wailing over the fact that He is coming back. Why? Because they are of the class and category of people who pierced Him.

Once again, this passage is rooted in the Old Testament, this time in Zechariah 12:8–11, in particular in verse 10. *"And in that day shall the LORD defend the inhabitants of Jerusalem. . .* [9] *And it shall come to pass in that day, that I will seek to destroy all the nations that come against Jerusalem.* [10] *And I will pour upon the house of David, and upon the inhabitants of Jerusalem, the spirit of grace and of supplications: and they shall look upon me whom they have pierced, and they shall mourn for him, as one mourneth for his only son, and shall be in bitterness for him, as one that is in bitterness for his firstborn.* [11] *In that day shall there be a great mourning in Jerusalem. . ."*

There was a favorable fulfillment of this passage at the first coming of Jesus. It says in verse 10 that *"they shall look upon me whom they have pierced."* We know from verse 8 that Jehovah is speaking and He is the one saying, *"they shall look upon me whom they have pierced."* Who is that person on the cross that was pierced? It was no one less than Jehovah God. The conclusion is inescapable: Jesus is God in human flesh.

In John 19:18, 34, 37, they crucified Jesus, pierced His hands and His feet, and the soldier took his spear and pierced Jesus' side. Under the inspiration of the Holy Spirit, in verse 37 John quotes this passage in Zechariah 12:10, *"they shall look upon me whom they have pierced,"* and applied to the Lord Jesus Christ when He died on the cross. It says, regarding the house of Israel, that *"they shall look upon me whom they have pierced, and they shall mourn for him."*

Israel pierced Christ, and after piercing Him, they started mourning over having done this. This mourning happened on the day of Pentecost. Peter preached a sermon in Acts 2:23 where he said: "This same Christ that God promised, you have taken and with wicked hands have crucified and slain." In verse 37, it says that they were pricked in their hearts, and said: "Men and brethren, what must we do?" Peter replied: "Repent, believe in Christ, be saved, and be baptized." We see in Acts 2:36–37 Peter indicting them for crucifying the Lord Jesus Christ, their mourning over having done such a wicked deed, and their being saved.

However, there is also an unfavorable fulfillment of this passage that takes place at the second coming. John also applies the passage in Zechariah 12:10b to the second coming of Christ in Revelation 1:7.

Look at it from the point of view of the second coming of Christ:

Zechariah 12:10 states, *"and they shall look upon me whom they have pierced, and they shall mourn for him, as one mourneth for his only son, and shall be in bitterness for him, as one that is in bitterness for his firstborn."*

Verse 10b is referring to the Jews who crucified Jesus. What applied to Israel as a nation when she mourned over the fact that she crucified her Messiah is now universalized and applied by John to all the peoples of the earth. John is saying in Revelation 1:7 that those who crucified Jesus, and all the people of the earth that join them in spirit by their hostility and hatred to Jesus through the ages, will respond in terror and anguish when they see Jesus coming back.

Notice Revelation 1:7 says, *"Behold, he cometh with clouds"* (this is the second coming); *"and every eye shall see him, and they also which pierced him: and all kindreds of the earth shall wail because of him. Even so, Amen."*

When Jesus comes and sits on the throne of judgment, every eye is going to see Him. He will be visible to all humanity when it is gathered before Him. Those who hated Him and sought to destroy Him, who stood in union with His crucifiers, who realize too late they have hated and rejected the King of Glory, will wail and mourn over their fate. This is not a mourning of repentance, but a mourning of hopelessness.

What Daniel and Zechariah spoke of, Jesus spoke of also. Notice Matthew 24:30. Jesus is giving the Olivet Discourse in which He is describing His second coming. Jesus speaks of His second coming and says, *"And then shall appear the sign of the Son of man in heaven: and then shall all the tribes of the earth mourn, and they shall see the Son of man coming in the clouds of heaven with power and great glory."*

What Jesus said in Matthew 24:30 is a very close parallel to what John said in Revelation 1:7.

To come in the clouds or to come with clouds is a frequent metaphor in the Bible. Coming with clouds often refers to God coming in judgment. For example, in Isaiah 19:1 it says, *"Behold, the* L*ORD* *rideth upon a swift cloud, and shall come into Egypt: and the idols of Egypt shall be moved at his presence, and the heart of Egypt shall melt in the midst of it."* It says in Zephaniah 1:15, *"That day is a day of wrath, a day of trouble and distress, a day of wasteness and desolation, a day of darkness and gloominess, a day of clouds and thick darkness."*

Often when the metaphor of clouds is used, it is used of God coming in wrath and judgment. The clouds are like the chariot in which He rides to come and defeat His enemies. The whole point of Revelation 1:7 is simply this: those who rejected Christ are going to bewail their hatred of Christ, bewail standing in continuity with the piercers of Christ, and bewail their lost opportunity for salvation through Christ. They are going to cry out in terror when Jesus returns in the clouds of judgment to this earth at the end of the age.

This terror of the lost at the second coming is further pictured in Revelation 6:15–17: "*And the kings of the earth, and the great men, and the rich men, and the chief captains, and the mighty men, and every bondman, and every free man, hid themselves in the dens and in the rocks of the mountains;* [16] *And said to the mountains and rocks, Fall on us, and hide us from the face of him that sitteth on the throne, and from the wrath of the Lamb:* [17] *For the great day of his wrath is come; and who shall be able to stand?*"

Revelation 1:7 is saying that Jesus is coming back and is going to bring His wrath and judgment to bear upon those who pierced Him; that is, upon His crucifiers and haters. It is not just those who actually nailed Jesus to the cross, or who moved the Roman government to do it by crying out: "*Crucify him, crucify him*" (Luke 32:21) that He will judge in His wrath. Christ will judge and cast into hell every voice in every century who has rejected Him as Lord and Savior, who has dismissed Him as being the incarnate God, and who has said, "Away with Him, I do not want Him in my life!" The rejectors of Christ in every age are in the class and the category of those who persecuted Him and pierced Him. The one whom they thought they had dismissed is now coming to be their judge.

What is John's response to this weeping and wailing and terror that the rejecters of Christ are going to have at the second coming? He says, "*Even so. Amen.*" He says: "So be it." That is an affirmation of the righteousness of God's judgment on the wicked haters of Jesus Christ.

The overthrow of the wicked at the second coming is the triumph of Christ over those who pierced Him, and it is the vindication of the Christians who suffered so much at their hands. When Jesus met Saul on the road to Damascus, He said, "*Saul, Saul, why persecutest thou me?*" Jesus was in effect saying: "I take your persecutions of My people as your persecution of Me." Saul never persecuted Christ, but he did persecute Stephen. Saul was a Christ-piercer. But he was also redeemed. Those who crucified Christ can be forgiven if they will repent and say, along with the centurion who actually crucified Christ, *"Truly, this man was the Son of God!"*

But for those who persist in their hatred of Christ, the second coming of Christ will be a time of terror and dread and weeping and wailing and gnashing of teeth. When we see them in that condition, we are not going to be saying to them, "Oh, I am really so sorry for you!" We are going to be saying, *"Even so. Amen."* The righteous wrath of God upon the wicked will be seen as entirely and completely just, and we will have nothing but affirmation for God when He casts the wicked into hell.

Jesus Is the Inescapable God

Notice verse 8, *"I am Alpha and Omega, the beginning and the ending, saith the Lord, which is, and which was, and which is to come, the Almighty."*

In verse 7, we have seen Jesus returning in all of His glory to exercise His judgment on those who hated Him. Those who hated and persecuted Christ are now standing before Him. They are weeping and wailing because of Him and because of their impending doom. As they are gathered before Him and are weeping and wailing, Jesus now speaks to them, and identifies Himself to them.

When Jesus came the first time, they dismissed Him as a deceiver, they called Him a glutton and a winebibber, they claimed He was born of fornication, they derided Him as a friend of sinners, they accused Him of being a traitor to Rome, and they said that He was demon possessed. They applied these and many more derogatory labels to Jesus, and billions more people throughout the ages have called Him all of these things and worse. Others have been more diplomatic. They have condescendingly called Him a great man. They have said He was a great teacher, or that He was a man of peace.

But all of them, whether they were derogatory or whether they were condescending, thought they could dismiss Jesus and His claims out of their lives by reducing Him to an object of contempt or by reducing Him to being merely another man, one among many historical religious figures. Jesus was someone to give a tip of the hat to or someone to contemptuously sneer at; but however the wicked expressed their scorn of Christ and His teaching and claims, they ultimately were identifying themselves with those who crucified Christ and pierced His hands and feet and side.

In the face of all of these lesser, lower, and despicable things they identified Christ as being, Jesus now tells them who He really is, who He has been all along, and who He will forever be. He is God. He is the eternal God. He is the almighty God. He is the inescapable God, from whom they can no longer hide and with whom they must now have dealings as their final judge.

Notice what Jesus proclaims about Himself as they tremble before Him. The first thing Jesus tells them is that He is eternal and inescapable. He says in verse 8a, *"I am Alpha and Omega, the beginning and the ending, saith the Lord, which is, and which was, and which is to come."* He is the Alpha and Omega, the start and the finish of all things. He is the beginning of everything that exists, and the ending toward which everything moves. Everything begins with Him and concludes with Him. Everything starts with Him and finishes with Him. He is the first and He is the last.

This means that, from start to finish, Christ was always there, He is there now, and He will always be there. He is, He was, and He is to come. The multiplication of these terms, the Alpha, the Omega, the beginning and the ending, and He which was and is and is to come, all say this: "No matter how far you go back, I was there; no matter how far you go forward, I will always be there; and I have always been present at every point in between." His presence is inescapable. There is no time and place where He is not. He is the eternal and inescapable God.

This is what David was declaring in Psalm 139:7–12 when the question was asked: *"Whither shall I go from thy spirit? or whither shall I flee from thy presence?* [8] *If I ascend up into heaven, thou art there: if I make my bed in hell, behold, thou art there.* [9] *If I take the wings of the morning, and dwell in the uttermost parts of the sea;* [10] *Even there shall thy hand lead me, and thy right hand shall hold me.* [11] *If I say, Surely the darkness shall cover me; even the night shall be light about me.* [12] *Yea, the darkness hideth not from thee; but the night shineth as the day: the darkness and the light are both alike to thee."*

Jesus tells these weeping and wailing people who are assembled before Him they must now face and understand who He really is. He is the eternal and inescapable God.

The second thing Jesus tells them is that He sovereignly rules over all of history. In the last phrase of verse 8, Jesus says: "I am the Almighty." This does not just mean that He is all-powerful, though it does mean that. It also means that nothing lies outside the scope of His sovereignty in the exercise of that power. Jesus is not just strong; there is also nothing outside the reach of the exercise of that strength.

Jesus is not only all-present throughout all of history from start to finish, but Jesus is also all-powerful throughout all of history from start to finish. It does not matter if someone is there if that person does not have either authority or strength. But if someone is always there and has both universal authority and infinite strength, then that person looms infinitely large in significance to those over whom He rules.

Who are these wicked men facing on the Day of Judgment? Who is this person they are being judged by? They are facing the all-present, all-powerful Lord of Glory, whose presence and power is inescapable. The reason they are weeping and wailing is that they have no place to go to escape from this person who has sovereign authority and power over them. Where will they flee and where will they hide from this all-present and all-powerful Christ? There is nowhere to go, and they have no ability to escape for all of eternity.

This proclamation of His identity both seals the doom of His enemies and secures the deliverance and vindication of His persecuted servants. As we look at the scene John unfolds before us, we rejoice in the fact that Jesus is eternal and inescapable, and that Jesus always has ruled and always will sovereignly rule over all of us for all of eternity. We rejoice that His almighty power is employed to provide for all of our needs forever.

The book of Revelation might have just ended here, because here the story of the book is fully summarized. Here is who Jesus is to us: He is a glorious Lord (verses 4 to 6). He is glorious in who He is to us, and He is glorious in what He has done for us. We will give Him glory forever. Here is who Jesus is to the wicked: He is a terrifying judge (verses 7 and 8). He is the inescapable, almighty, avenging God who will damn to hell all those who pierced Him with their words, their lives, and their actions. They will wail and mourn forever.

In this introduction, we have a summary of how it is all going to turn out. When you listen to a properly constructed sermon, you should be able to listen to the introduction and understand the essence of the message, because the message would be summarized in the introduction. The body of the sermon only develops and proves and expands and applies the message the introduction summarizes.

That is what John has done here. Like a good homiletician, he has summarized the entire message of the rest of the book in his introduction. He said: "Here is who Jesus is to the believers. Have comfort, rejoice always, have peace, be confident, and persevere. Here is who Jesus is to the wicked: Let them tremble and wail. Let them feel dread and terror at the fact that they have resisted the eternal, inescapable, almighty, sovereign God."

We look at how Jesus deals with us and we look at how He deals with them, and we say: *"Even so. Amen."* How many times have you longed for justice to be done and it was not done? On this great day, you will see it done, and you will say, "Amen! The piercers of Christ got what they deserved." The rest of the book of Revelation is just a development and expansion of that message.

We have a wonderful message of comfort, and we have a sobering message of warning. Flee to Christ and find in Him a faithful witness, a first begotten from the dead, and a prince of the kings of the earth. Find in Him someone who loves you and washes you from your sins in His blood and elevates you to be a king and a priest. Or, fight against Him, resist Him, and attack His people, and find yourself weeping and wailing when He returns and sits on His throne and reveals Himself to be the eternal, inescapable, sovereign, almighty judge who will damn to hell the souls of all of those who crucified Him in their hearts and in their minds, and with their lives and by their words.

This is the message of the book. It is all summarized in the introduction. At the end of this book, we see Jesus doing what is said in verses 6 to 8. We are brought into this glorious new heaven and new earth, and the wicked are cast into the eternal lake of fire. Knowing all of this, why would we ever switch to their side, no matter how much they persecute us, shame us, or slander us, and no matter what enticements they offer us or what incentives they provide us with?

When you look at the piercers of Jesus versus the believers in Jesus, there is no question on whose side you belong. Choose Jesus as your Lord and Savior, so that when He returns, you will not be among those on His left hand who are weeping and wailing, but among those on His right hand to whom He says: *"Come ye blessed into the kingdom prepared for you by my Father from the foundation of the world."*

10

The Setting and Substance of the Vision, Revelation 1:9–11

> *"[9] I John, who also am your brother, and companion in tribulation, and in the kingdom and patience of Jesus Christ, was in the isle that is called Patmos, for the word of God, and for the testimony of Jesus Christ. [10] I was in the Spirit on the Lord's day, and heard behind me a great voice, as of a trumpet,*
> *[11] Saying, I am Alpha and Omega, the first and the last: and, What thou seest, write in a book, and send it unto the seven churches which are in Asia; unto Ephesus, and unto Smyrna, and unto Pergamos, and unto Thyatira, and unto Sardis, and unto Philadelphia, and unto Laodicea."*

Having completed our study of the prologue in verses 1 to 3, and the introduction to Revelation in verses 4 to 8, we now come to the body of Revelation which begins with verse 9 and continues to chapter 22.

John the apostle, who is the author of this book, was barely mentioned in verse 1, but now in verses 9 and 10 John gives us significantly more information about himself. We see in verses 9 and 10 that John was suffering severe persecution from the Roman government because of his work for Christ and his witness for Christ.

It has always been the case that believers are persecuted by Satan and his helpers, and the book of Revelation describes and documents that persecution in a powerfully descriptive way. It tells us that we must through much tribulation enter into the kingdom of God. The world hates the church and relentlessly persecutes it. We must expect that all who live godly in Christ Jesus will suffer persecution.

The good news about this persecution is that we do not face it alone and we do not fight it alone. From verse 11 to verse 20, Jesus Christ is set forth as the glorified exalted King of kings and Lord of lords, as the Almighty God who has conquered death, and as the One who has the keys to hell and death. He will assist us in fighting these battles; and indeed, He will fight these battles for us. Jesus will give us victory over all those who fight against us.

It says in Revelation 17:14, *"These shall make war with the Lamb, and the Lamb shall overcome them: for he is Lord of lords, and King of kings: and they that are with him are called, and chosen, and faithful."* Our job is to faithfully bear witness to the word of God and to the Son of God. His job is to defeat and destroy all our enemies and secure our victory over Satan and his servants. The Lamb will overcome them, and He will lead us into triumph. In this fact lies our peace and our perseverance in the spiritual warfare that lies ahead of us. Therefore, when you begin to become discouraged with the unrelenting intensity of spiritual warfare, meditate on the Christ John portrays before us in this vision, and you will renew your confidence and strength.

As John is engaged in spiritual battle on the Island of Patmos, he is given this wonderful vision of the Lord Jesus, and it is this vision of the Lord Jesus that strengthens his hand for the battle that lies ahead of him, and gives him the encouragement and hope that he will prevail in it. The sight of Christ strengthens us for the battle because we know that through Him, we will prevail. Here in this chapter we have John's suffering described, we have Christ's power revealed, and as a result, we have our confidence strengthened.

The Setting of the Vision

The setting for the vision of the rest of the book of Revelation is described in verses 9 through 10a. *"I John, who also am your brother, and companion in tribulation, and in the kingdom and patience of Jesus Christ, was in the isle that is called Patmos, for the word of God, and for the testimony of Jesus Christ.* [10] *I was in the Spirit on the Lord's day."*

In verse 9, John tells us several things about himself. It is interesting to note that he does not call himself, "John the Apostle." Instead, he calls himself *"your brother and companion."* In other words, he places himself on the same level as his fellow believers, and states that he stands on common ground with them. He reveals his humility and his sense of unity with all of his Christian brethren by the terminology he uses.

He does possess a higher office than his Christian brethren. Make no mistake; he is an apostle. But though he possesses a higher office than his Christian brethren, at the same time he also stands on equal ground with them, especially with regard to being fellow citizens in the kingdom of God and being fellow sufferers for the kingdom of God.

All believers have equality between themselves, as well as a hierarchy among themselves. There are those who possess office, and those who do not. That is a very real distinction. But all of God's people are equally children of God, and they all equally share in suffering for the kingdom of God. Notice that he not only says *"I John who also am your brother,"* he also says I am *"a companion"* of yours *"in tribulation."*

John was undergoing great tribulation at this point in time. He had been exiled to the Island of Patmos for the word of God and for the testimony of Jesus Christ. Tribulation is something that is a common experience of all believers; and no believers are exempt from it no matter their giftedness, their maturity, or their office. John was highly gifted, highly mature, and in the highest office that the church has ever provided. Nevertheless, he was not exempt from suffering and tribulation. We are all fellow citizens in the kingdom of God, we all suffer for the cause of the kingdom of God, and we all must exercise patience in suffering for that kingdom.

He says in verse 9, *"I John, who also am your brother, and companion in tribulation, and in the kingdom and patience of Jesus Christ. . ."* John was not only in a state of suffering and tribulation; he was also saying: "I am being patient in suffering just like you have to be patient in suffering for the sake of the kingdom." Being patient under suffering is something that is extremely difficult. *"How long, O Lord?"* is a question that frequently arises in our thoughts. As we do spiritual battle, we suffer spiritual persecution, and it seems there is no end to it. Decade after decade rolls past, and the Evil One and his human agents still viciously assault the people of God. We patiently endure, but it seems that relief never comes.

John understood this. He, as a very young man, began to follow Jesus. The Bible specifically describes him in the garden of Gethsemane as being a young man. Here he is as a very old man, and yet he is still in a state of tribulation. He never moved past it or escaped it. When he was in the garden of Gethsemane, they sought to arrest him and laid hands on him, and he left his garment in their hands and fled away. They wanted to arrest him at the same time they arrested Jesus. And now here he is in his old age, under arrest by the Roman authorities.

John tells us in verse 9 that he has been exiled to the Island of Patmos by the Roman authorities. This island is off the southwest coast of what is modern-day Turkey. It was an island where there were mines, and slaves were sent there by the Roman government to labor in the mines. It may very well have been the case that when John was exiled to Patmos, he was not just sitting around writing books. He may very well have been forced into labor in the mines.

John tells us he has been exiled to the Island of Patmos by the Roman authorities because of his faithful teaching of the word of God and the consistent testimony of his faith in Jesus Christ. He refused to worship Caesar as his lord, and the Roman government was persecuting him for his fidelity to Christ as his Lord.

Notice what he says: *"I John, who also am your brother, and companion in tribulation, and in the kingdom and patience of Jesus Christ, was in the isle that is called Patmos,"* He was not there for a vacation. He says he was on that island *"for"* (or because of) *"the word of God, and* (because of) *the testimony of Jesus Christ."* John preached the word of God, and John bore faithful testimony to Jesus Christ, and that is why he was on this island.

It is always the case that when you do not worship what the world worships, the world will hate you, persecute you, and exile you out of their company. The Romans threw John out of their society and out of their company, and people will throw you out of their society and out of their company as well when you do not bow to their gods of pride and self-will and materialism and immorality. These are all the things the world worships. They say to you: "Come along and party with us! Worship the things we worship!" But when you say, "No, I am not going to worship what you worship," what do they do? They exile you out of their lives. You are no longer welcome in their company.

Believers who proclaim the word of God in their speech and who give testimony to the saving work of Jesus Christ in their lives will wind up living in social exile from the world. Just count on it. You cannot be everyone's friend and the friend of Christ at the same time. Your faithfulness to Him will cause you to be rejected by those who are His enemies. Therefore, there is a sense in which we all live on our own Isle of Patmos, that place of rejection and reviling, for simply preaching the Scriptures and living for Christ.

Notice what John was doing during his exile. He was not indulging in self-pity. He was not bemoaning how poorly others had treated him. Instead, it says he was observing the Lord's worship on the Lord's Day. John says in verse 10, *"I was in the Spirit on the Lord's day."* Though John was persecuted, John was persevering. He was persevering in particular in observing the Fourth Commandment to remember the Sabbath Day to keep it holy.

The Christian Sabbath is on Sunday. Jesus said in Mark 2:28, *"the Son of man is Lord also of the sabbath."* When Jesus says He is Lord of the Sabbath, He is saying that the Sabbath is His day. It belongs to Him, and we must conduct ourselves on it as He sees fit. When we say that Sunday is the Lord's Day, we are saying that it is a day that belongs to the Lord. The Sabbath was therefore the Lord's Sabbath; that is, the Lord's Day. When John says, *"I was in the Spirit on the Lord's day,"* he is speaking of that one day out of seven that belongs to God and not to us, in which we spend the whole day in the worship and service of God.

Under the fourth commandment in the Old Covenant, this one day out of seven was appointed to be Saturday, the last day of creation. But now under the New Covenant, this day has been appointed to be Sunday, the first day of creation. The permanent moral principle in the fourth commandment is that we worship God one day out of seven, but it is a positive command as to which day that is. We are not free to decide for ourselves. God decided it would be the last day of the week from Creation until Christ; then He decided it would be the first day of the week from Christ until the Consummation.

The Lord's Day was changed from Saturday to Sunday because it was on Sunday that Jesus rose from the grave, and it was on Sunday that Jesus appeared to His disciples after His resurrection, and it was on Sunday that the day of Pentecost occurred when the Holy Spirit was poured out on the church in Acts 2.

What do we see the church doing in Acts 20:7? We see them gathering for worship on the first day of the week, which is Sunday. In 1 Corinthians 16:2, we see them gathering as a church on the first day of the week, which is Sunday. This is the reason why we worship on Sunday, which we call "the Lord's Day."

It is unlikely there were other believers on Patmos when John was there. We read of none. And yet, John still observed the Lord's Day. He certainly seems to be alone when he received these visions.

The point is simply this: If you are traveling, if you cannot be in church, even if you are out in the wilderness all alone by yourself, still observe the Lord's Day. Set that day apart for reading, for prayer, for meditation, for worship, and for singing and making melody in your heart to the Lord. This is what John did when he was exiled away from the church. When he was in the midst of his persecution, he worshiped. He observed Sunday as the Lord's Day, giving himself over to the worship of God. As he worshiped in the midst of his persecution, God came to him and ministered to him in a way He did not on any other day of the week. As he worshiped in the midst of his persecutions, he received tremendous comfort in the form of this revelation and this book and the promises it contained.

Do you suppose that because John was observing the Lord's Day, spending that day in private worship because there was no public worship available to him, that he was comforted by it? How many times when we are suffering persecution do we go to church on the Lord's Day, and in the worship of God receive a word from God that greatly encourages and strengthens us for the battles we are in?

We all have tribulation because of our preaching of the word of God and because of our testimony for Jesus Christ. We have to be patient in that tribulation. It is part of what happens in the kingdom. Observing the Lord's Day and spending time with God on His day is the surest way to obtain the patience and strength we need to keep persevering through the persecution we are experiencing.

It was as John was worshiping the Lord on the Lord's Day that he received this wonderful revelation of Christ. As you go to church, and as you sing and pray and hear the Scriptures read and preached, you gain a sight of Christ that you never have during the week. Christ comes and meets with you and ministers to you and reveals Himself in the public means of grace in a profound way. That is what He did for John. That is what He does for us when we respect and honor His day and give ourselves wholly to focusing on Him and worshiping Him on it. John was in the Spirit on the Lord's Day.

The Substance of the Vision

The substance of the vision is found in verses 10b to 20, but we are not going to proceed all the way to verse 20 in this chapter. We are only going to look at verse 10b to 11; however, we will look at the larger context in which verses 10b to 11 appear.

John tells us in verse 10 that he was in the Spirit on the Lord's Day. Notice verse 10, *"I was in the Spirit on the Lord's day, and heard behind me a great voice, as of a trumpet,* [11] *Saying, I am Alpha and Omega, the first and the last: and, What thou seest, write in a book, and send it unto the seven churches which are in Asia; unto Ephesus, and unto Smyrna, and unto Pergamos, and unto Thyatira, and unto Sardis, and unto Philadelphia, and unto Laodicea."*

When it says, *"I was in the Spirit on the Lord's day,"* this means that John began to enter into a prophetic trance in which the reality of the world around him faded into oblivion and his eyes and ears were opened to see and hear the spiritual world that is ordinarily invisible and inaudible to us.

When was the last time you heard a conversation between a couple of angels? When was the last time you saw the throne of God with God sitting on it? These things are realities. There are angels and they do talk to each other. There is a God, and He does sit on a throne. You cannot see it and hear it with the ordinary human senses. But because John was *"in the Spirit"*—that is, because he entered into a prophetic trance enabled and empowered by the Holy Spirit—his eyes were opened to see the spiritual world, and his ears were opened to hear the spiritual world which is ordinarily invisible and inaudible. In a word, he began to have a vision.

This vision he was having is something far sharper and clearer than the things people see when they dream. When you are asleep, the visible and audible world fades away, you start dreaming, and you see and hear things. They are not really there, are they? The dream is kind of hazy and foggy and it jumps around and does not make much sense, and is often weird and crazy. Sometimes it is terrifying; other times you do impossible things, like flying.

This is not what John was experiencing. This was not a dream; this was a vision. This vision is as clear and as sharp to him as the reality you are now seeing as you sit and read this book. Can you see and hear all that is around you? Is it sharp and clear? That is how sharp and clear it was for John in this vision that he had as a result of being *"in the Spirit."*

What John experienced is the same thing Peter experienced in Acts 10:10–17. It says Peter went up to the rooftop to pray, that he fell into a trance, and he began to see things. There was a sheet knitted at the four corners, it was let down, God opened it up, and it was full of all manner of animals. God said to Peter, "[13]*Rise, Peter; kill, and eat."* He replied that he could not eat those animals because they were unclean. God said, "[15] . . .*What God hath cleansed, that call not thou common."*

This happened three times and then it was all taken up. Peter came back to his senses and his awareness of the normal world around him, and we are told that he wondered what the vision meant. Then some Gentiles came and said to Peter that Cornelius wanted him to come to his home and preach to him. Then Peter realized: "So that is what it means! The Gentiles are no longer unclean. I can go preach the gospel to them. I can enter into their house."

Peter had a vision in a very similar manner to what John is having here, though much briefer, with different content and substance, but with the same dynamic in which they both saw things and heard things in a crystal-clear fashion as though they were actually there, while being, as it were, transported out of the world they were ordinarily functioning in.

This also happened to Old Testament prophets. Notice Ezekiel 1:1 where it says, *"Now it came to pass in the thirtieth year, in the fourth month, in the fifth day of the month, as I was among the captives by the river of Chebar, that the heavens were opened, and I saw visions of God."* This is the same thing. Ezekiel was sitting by a riverbank, but suddenly it was like the riverbank was not even there anymore and now he was seeing a whole new world. He then described this vision of God in heaven, and it was an amazing description. This was all the result of the revelation of the Holy Spirit.

We see the same thing in Daniel. Daniel 8:1–3 says, *"In the third year of the reign of king Belshazzar a vision appeared unto me, even unto me Daniel, after that which appeared unto me at the first. [2] And I saw in a vision; and it came to pass, when I saw, that I was at Shushan in the palace, which is in the province of Elam; and I saw in a vision, and I was by the river of Ulai. [3] Then I lifted up mine eyes, and saw, and, behold, there stood before the river a ram which had two horns."*

Physically he is in a particular geographical location, but in his vision, he has moved to a different geographical location. He was physically in the palace, but now he sees himself out by a river, and he sees a ram, and the vision goes on revealing further details.

What was happening to John in the book of Revelation is exactly the same thing that happened to the prophets in the Old Testament. It was no different. This idea of seeing visions is something that is pervasive throughout the Scripture and occurred to the prophets. It did not occur to all of them, but it did occur to many of them.

John falls into this prophetic trance and has a vision in which he hears Jesus speaking and sees Jesus standing, and the remainder of Revelation 1 tells us the substance of this vision of Christ.

First of all, notice the voice John heard. This is all we are going to look at in this chapter, but in the next chapter we will look at, secondly, the sight John beheld; thirdly, the response John gave; and fourthly, the comfort John received. This will take us to the end of Revelation 1.

The voice John heard is in verse 10b and 11. It says, *"and [I] heard behind me a great voice, as of a trumpet, [11] Saying, I am Alpha and Omega, the first and the last: and, What thou seest, write in a book, and send it unto the seven churches which are in Asia,"* and he identifies them all by name.

It specifically says that John heard behind him a great voice like a trumpet. Trumpets are very often associated with the appearance of God to people. In particular, they are associated with the appearance of God to His people when He is giving them a new revelation of Himself.

In Exodus 19, Israel has come out of Egypt. They have now come to Mount Sinai and there God appears to them and makes the Old Covenant with them. Exodus 19:9–21: *"And the LORD said unto Moses, Lo, I come unto thee in a thick cloud, that the people may hear when I speak with thee, and believe thee for ever. And Moses told the words of the people unto the LORD. [10] And the LORD said unto Moses, Go unto the people, and sanctify them today and tomorrow, and let them wash their clothes, [11] And be ready against the third day: for the third day the LORD will come down in the sight of all the people upon mount Sinai. [12] And thou shalt set bounds unto the people round about, saying, Take heed to yourselves, that ye go not up into the mount, or touch the border of it: whosoever toucheth the mount shall be surely put to death:* [13] *There shall not an hand touch it, but he shall surely be stoned, or shot through; whether it be beast or man, it shall not live: when the trumpet soundeth long, they shall come up to the mount"* (to the edge of the mount). "[14] *And Moses went down from the mount unto the people, and sanctified the people; and they washed their clothes.* [15] *And he said unto the people, Be ready against the third day: come not at your wives.* [16] *And it came to pass on the third day in the morning, that there were thunders and lightnings, and a thick cloud upon the mount, and the voice of the trumpet exceeding loud, so that all the people that was in the camp trembled.* [17] *And Moses brought forth the people out of the camp to meet with God; and they stood at the nether part of the mount"* (at the edge of the mount). "[18] *And mount Sinai was altogether on a smoke, because the* LORD *descended upon it in fire: and the smoke thereof ascended as the smoke of a furnace, and the whole mount quaked greatly.* [19] *And when the voice of the trumpet sounded long, and waxed louder and louder, Moses spake, and God answered him by a voice.* [20] *And the* LORD *came down upon mount Sinai, on the top of the mount: and the* LORD *called Moses up to the top of the mount; and Moses went up.* [21] *And the* LORD *said unto Moses," etc.*

We see this trumpet sounding very loudly, announcing the presence and revelation of God Himself. When John said he heard a voice like a trumpet, this voice was announcing that God was showing up to speak to His people. When Jesus returns, it will be with a voice of the archangel and *"the trump of God,"* (1 Thessalonians 4:16). When John heard the great voice like the sound of a trumpet behind him, he knew this was no ordinary voice. This was an appearance of God, just as He appeared at Mount Sinai when the trumpet sounded there.

We will see the trumpet being sounded on several occasions in the book of Revelation as we proceed through it. In fact, the trumpet is spoken of far more in the book of Revelation than it is in the rest of the New Testament. The sounding of the trumpet is an announcement that God has shown up. God is revealing Himself.

The person speaking to John in verse 10 leaves him with no doubt as to who He is. He identifies Himself in verse 11 as God. Notice the terminology that he uses to identify Himself in verse 11: *"Saying, I am Alpha and Omega, the first and the last."* We would expect that it would be God who was speaking because there is the sounding of this great trumpet. The person who shows up and speaks says in essence,

"I am God," and He does so by taking to Himself the names of God.

First of all, He calls Himself the Alpha and Omega. Alpha is the first letter of the Greek alphabet and Omega is the last letter, like our A and Z, and all other letters exist between them. God is the one who is the beginning of all things, and He is the end of all things. He is the one who manages and controls everything between the beginning and the end. What is interesting is that these terms, Alpha and Omega, occur only in the book of Revelation, and nowhere else in the Bible—but they occur in this book in four places.

First it occurs in Revelation 1:8, *"I am Alpha and Omega, the beginning and the ending, saith the Lord, which is, and which was, and which is to come, the Almighty."* What we see is that the Alpha and Omega is the eternal almighty Lord. The Lord is speaking, and He says: "I am eternal, and I am Almighty. This is who the Alpha and Omega is."

Secondly, it occurs in Revelation 21:5–7. It is interesting how much of the content of chapter 1 is also stated in chapters 21 and 22. *"And he that sat upon the throne said, Behold, I make all things new. And he said unto me, Write: for these words are true and faithful. [6] And he said unto me, It is done. I am Alpha and Omega, the beginning and the end. I will give unto him that is athirst of the fountain of the water of life freely. [7] He that overcometh shall inherit all things; and I will be his God."* Clearly, whoever this Alpha and Omega is, He is God. He is speaking in the first person. He says in verse 6, "I am the Alpha and Omega," and He says in verse 7, "I am God."

The third place it occurs is in Revelation 22:12–13, *"And, behold, I come quickly."* Who is coming back? It is Jesus. The *"I"* is clearly a reference to Jesus. It is speaking of His second coming. He says, *"I come quickly; and my reward is with me, to give every man according as his work shall be."* There is His judging work. *"[13] I am Alpha and Omega, the beginning and the end, the first and the last."* Jesus takes all of these titles to Himself. He says: "I am Alpha and Omega. I am the beginning and the end. I am the first and the last."

What do we know about the Alpha and Omega from Revelation 21:6–7? We know that the Alpha and Omega sits on the throne, and is God. The Alpha and Omega in Revelation 1:8 is the eternal Almighty Lord. In Revelation 22:13, He is Jesus Christ the coming Lord. There is no clearer or more powerful declaration of the deity of Jesus Christ than this title of the Alpha and Omega that is given to Him.

Therefore, in this fourth occurrence in Revelation 1:11 when He says, *"I am Alpha and Omega,"* He is saying: "I am Jesus Christ, the Almighty God," because that is how the title Alpha and Omega is used in these other three passages.

Furthermore, a second term is used in Revelation 1:11. Not only does He say, "I am Alpha and Omega," but He also says: I am *"the first and the last."* This term, unlike the term Alpha and Omega, is drawn out of the Old Testament, and is used repeatedly as a title and name for Jehovah, the covenant-keeping God of the Old Testament.

In Isaiah 41:4, God is speaking and He says, *"Who hath wrought and done it, calling the generations from the beginning?"* Now here it is: *"I the Lord,"* notice Lord is all in small capital letters. It is a translation of "Jehovah," which is God's special personal name for the God of Israel. He says He is Jehovah, *"the first, and with the last; I am he."* Jehovah applied the title of the first and the last to Himself.

In Isaiah 44:6 when it says, *"Thus saith the Lord,"* notice it is all caps. *"Thus saith the Lord, the King of Israel, and his redeemer"* (that is, Israel's redeemer) *"the Lord"* (notice all caps again) *"of hosts; I am the first, and I am the last; and beside me there is no God."* How many firsts and lasts are there? Just one. He is the only God; He is Jehovah.

Then notice Isaiah 48:12. It says, *"Hearken unto me, O Jacob and Israel, my called; I am he; I am the first, I also am the last."* In the context it is clear once again that Jehovah is speaking.

Three times in Isaiah, Jehovah says of Himself: "I am the first and the last. I am the only first and last. There is no other first and last except Me. There is no God beside Me."

In Revelation 1:8, this voice that John hears identifies Himself by the title that Jehovah uses of Himself in the Old Testament. It is also a title that Jesus uses to identify Himself. Notice Revelation 1:17: John says, *"And when I saw him, I fell at his feet as dead. And he laid his right hand upon me, saying unto me, Fear not; I am the first and the last:* [18] *I am he that liveth, and was dead; and, behold, I am alive for evermore, Amen; and have the keys of hell and of death."*

Who is it who is alive and died and came to life but Jesus Christ? This Jesus Christ says of Himself: "I am the first and the last. I take to Myself the title of Jehovah God." He does this in Revelation 1:17 and He does it in Revelation 2:8: *"And unto the angel of the church in Smyrna write; These things saith the first and the last, which was dead, and is alive.*" He says it in Revelation 22:13 when He says, "*I am Alpha and Omega, the beginning and the end, the first and the last.*" As we tie these verses together, it becomes undeniable that Jesus Christ is God, and that He is the God of the Old Testament as well as the God of the New Testament. He is the God of the past and He is the God of the future. He is the God who always has been here, who is here now, and who always shall be here.

Jesus identifies Himself as God, as equal with Jehovah of the Old Testament and as equal with God the Father in the New Testament as to His attributes. This does not mean that Jesus is the Father; it simply means that Jesus is completely equal to the Father. He shares all the attributes and essence of the Trinity. No clearer claim to Deity could be made by Christ, and no clearer ascription of Deity to Christ could be made by John, than to use and record these titles of Him.

This person speaking to John, who is clearly none other than the Son of God, tells him twice in Revelation 1:11 and 19 to write all he sees in his visions in a book. What he wrote was the book of Revelation which you have in your Bibles. It was to be sent to the seven churches in Asia, who represent the whole church and all the churches that are called into existence between the first and second coming of Christ.

We need to take away two points by way of application. The first point is this: We will suffer for the cause of the kingdom of God. When you bear witness to the word of God and what it says, and when you bear testimony to the Son of God and what He has done for you, you will be exiled by the world, you will be rejected, and you will suffer persecution and tribulation. You have to be patient with that, and the way you are able to be patient is by observing the Lord's Day, and by staying in close contact with Jesus Christ through His appointed means of grace. By worship and through the means of grace you derive strength and grace to persevere with joy in the face of the evil that is done to you.

The second point is this: You have God the Son speaking to you, revealing Himself to you, and saying to you, "Fear not. I have the keys of hell and death. I will fight your battles for you. You will overcome, because I am King of kings and Lord of lords, and no one can stand against Me and ever win or succeed."

We have this wonderful Person showing up when we are on our Patmos, saying to us: "Fear not. I am here." Do not ever forget that.

When you feel like you do not have a friend in the world and you have been exiled out of everybody's life because you have stood for Jesus Christ, remember that Jesus is standing with you, He is standing near you, He is standing for you, and He is fighting on your behalf. He is saying to you, "Do not worry. I will take care of it. You just be patient until I do."

This is the voice John heard. We have not yet gotten to the sight John beheld. What happens when he turns around and sees the glorified Christ? He falls on his face. Jesus gives him some instructions: "I want you to write to My churches. Here is what I want you to say to them."

Where is Christ's heart and concern? It is with His suffering saints. It is with His churches. He is determined they will overcome, and He provides them with His presence and His teaching that will enable them to do so. Do not be discouraged in the midst of the spiritual battles you are fighting. You have the exalted, glorified, resurrected Son of God speaking to you, standing with you, and fighting for you. He will triumph.

11

The Vision of the Resurrected Christ, Revelation 1:12–20

"12 *And I turned to see the voice that spake with me. And being turned, I saw seven golden candlesticks;* 13 *And in the midst of the seven candlesticks one like unto the Son of man, clothed with a garment down to the foot, and girt about the [chest] with a golden [belt].* 14 *His head and his hairs were white like wool, as white as snow; and his eyes were as a flame of fire;*
15 *And his feet like unto fine brass, as if they burned in a furnace; and his voice as the sound of many waters.* 16 *And he had in his right hand seven stars: and out of his mouth went a sharp two-edged sword: and his countenance was as the sun shineth in his strength.* 17 *And when I saw him, I fell at his feet as dead. And he laid his right hand upon me, saying unto me, Fear not; I am the first and the last:* 18 *I am he that liveth, and was dead; and, behold, I am alive for evermore, Amen; and have the keys of hell and of death.* 19 *Write the things which thou hast seen, and the things which are, and the things which shall be hereafter;* 20 *The mystery of the seven stars which thou sawest in my right hand, and the seven golden candlesticks. The seven stars are the angels of the seven churches: and the seven candlesticks which thou sawest are the seven churches.*"

In the previous chapter, we saw that the apostle John was suffering severe persecution at the hands of the Roman government. They had sent him into exile on the Island of Patmos because he was preaching the word of God, and because he was bearing testimony to the saving work of Jesus Christ.

What John was experiencing individually, the church at large experiences universally. Satan hates Christ and His people, and Satan uses those who serve him to severely persecute them. The world would like nothing better than to exile Christians from their presence and destroy their influence, their message, and their very existence.

Christ did not leave John to suffer his persecution alone, and He does not leave us to suffer ours alone either. Jesus comes to us and fights for us and comforts us with His presence and power. When John was in the midst of his persecution by the world, Jesus came and revealed Himself to John and reassured him that sin and Satan and death would not triumph over him. The story of the book of Revelation is the story of spiritual warfare, in which Jesus and His people triumph over Satan and his people.

In the passage before us, the resurrected, glorified, and triumphant Christ appears to John. He reveals Himself and says to John: "Do not fear the exile, the persecution, and the hatred of Satan and the world. I am here. I am with you. I will give you victory." This vision John has of the resurrected Christ is spoken of in verses 10 to 20, which begins with Christ audibly identifying Himself. John says, *"I was in the Spirit on the Lord's day, and heard behind me a great voice, as of a trumpet,* [11] *Saying, I am Alpha and Omega, the first and the last: and, What thou seest, write in a book, and send it unto the seven churches which are in Asia. . ."*

The voice John heard was like that of a trumpet. Trumpets are often used in the Bible to announce the appearance of God to people, and that is what occurs here. So there would be no doubt as to the identity of the person speaking, the person speaking declares that He is the Alpha and Omega, and the first and the last. Since these two titles are used by God to describe Himself elsewhere in the Bible, by using these titles, the person speaking is declaring Himself to be God. By the sound of His voice and by the titles He uses, it is clear that this person speaking is none other than God.

After revealing His presence to John and identifying Himself to John, He tells John to write to these seven churches in Asia all that he sees in the visions he is going to receive. That book is the book of Revelation. This is the voice John heard when he was in the Spirit on the Lord's Day.

As we considered the substance of John's vision in the previous chapter, we only gave attention to the voice John heard. In this chapter, we want to consider the sight John beheld, the response John gave, and the comfort John received. These four points make up the substance of John's vision in chapter 1. Having seen the voice John heard in the previous chapter, notice secondly,

The Sight John Beheld

The sight that John beheld is in verses 12 to 16. As John was on the Island of Patmos worshipping on the Lord's Day, he not only heard a voice behind him speaking, but he also turned around to see who it was. Verses 12 to 16 tell us what he saw. Notice verse 12: *"And I turned to see the voice that spake with me. And being turned, I saw seven golden candlesticks."* Verse 12 tells us he saw seven individual candlesticks made out of gold, apparently arranged in a circle, because later he tells us that Jesus is in the middle of them.

We are told in verse 20 what these candlesticks represent. Jesus says: *"The mystery of the seven stars which thou sawest in my right hand, and the seven golden candlesticks. The seven stars are the angels of the seven churches: and the seven candlesticks which thou sawest are the seven churches."* These candlesticks are symbolic imagery designed to represent an actual reality, and the actual reality they represent is the seven churches listed in verse 11. These candlesticks represent the seven churches John is writing to.

Throughout the New Testament, the church is described as being the light of the world. The church casts God's light upon the sin-darkened world, a world darkened by lies and evil. We read passages like Matthew 5:14–16 where Jesus says, *"Ye are the light of the world. A city that is set on an hill cannot be hid. [15] Neither do men light a candle, and put it under a bushel, but on a candlestick; and it giveth light unto all that are in the house. [16] Let your light so shine before men, that they may see your good works, and glorify your Father which is in heaven."* It is entirely fitting for candlesticks to be symbols of the churches, because the churches are a source of light to the world, and they shed that light by doing good works.

Paul tells the Philippians in Philippians 2:14–16 to *"Do all things without murmurings and disputing: [15] That ye may be blameless and harmless, the sons of God, without rebuke, in the midst of a crooked and perverse nation, among whom ye shine as lights in the world; [16] Holding forth the word of life; that I may rejoice in the day of Christ, that I have not run in vain, neither laboured in vain."* Paul tells the Philippian church that they are to shine as lights in the world. How do they shine this light? By holding forth the word of life.

The church provides illumination to the dark world by the proclamation of the truth—that is, by *"holding forth the word of life,"* and by the performance of good deeds: *"let your light so shine. . . that they may see your good works."* By holding forth the word of life and by exercising good works toward others, the church illuminates the world with truth and goodness, in contradiction to the lies and evil that characterize the darkness of the world.

These candlesticks not only shed light, which is their primary function, but it also says of them that they are made of gold. That these candlesticks are made of gold shows the value and the preciousness of the witness the church has to the world through its proclamation of the truth and its performance of good works. It shows the value of the church not only to the world, but to Christ Himself. Jesus places a very high value on His church, and that is why the candlesticks are made of gold. Jesus loves the church. Jesus died for the church. Jesus is building His church. Jesus indwells His church. Jesus is married to His church—it is His bride. Is it any wonder that Jesus views the church as golden light-bearers?

John sees seven candlesticks, each representing one of these seven churches that are mentioned in verse 11. Since seven is also the number that symbolizes completeness, these seven candlesticks completely represent all the churches of all the centuries between the first and second coming of Christ. The lamp and the light of each individual church scattered across the world and throughout the ages bears a collective witness to the same message by preaching the truth and by the performance of good works. All true churches of all time in all places shed the same light of the gospel of Jesus Christ wherever they are and whenever they exist.

So the first thing that John sees when he turns around is these seven candlesticks, which represent the seven churches and the light they shed in the world. They shed this light by their preaching of the gospel and by their performance of good works. They have tremendous value to the world and to Christ as they do these things.

Verse 13 says that *"in the midst of the seven candlesticks one like unto the Son of man, clothed with a garment down to the foot, and girt about the paps,"* literally, the breasts or nipples, *"with a golden girdle,"* or belt, which goes all the way around something. He has a golden belt around his chest, and he has a long robe that goes all the way down to his feet.

These seven churches represented by these seven candlesticks John sees in verse 12 are not alone. Verse 13 tells us Christ is in the midst of His churches. Notice it says that in the middle of the seven candlesticks stands the Son of man. Christ is not in one place and His churches somewhere else. The passage makes it clear that Christ is in the midst of His churches, to lead them, to protect them, and to empower them as they worship and serve Him and proclaim His gospel.

In Matthew 18:15–20, Jesus concludes His instruction about the function of the local church by saying regarding it: *"For where two or three are gathered together in my name, there am I in the midst of them."* Where is Jesus on Sunday? He is right in the middle of His churches. His spiritual presence is manifested in each local church in a special way in which it is not manifested anywhere else in the world. Christ saved His church, Christ sanctifies His church, and Christ indwells His church with His special personal presence. The church is the sole institution through which Jesus accomplishes His work in this world. It is His temple on this earth, and believers are the kingdom of priests who serve within that temple.

The position of Christ in the midst of the churches and the special concern He exercises toward those churches, both in this chapter and in the following two chapters, show us the centrality and importance of the church to Christ in His work of destroying the works of the devil, and in establishing the kingdom of Light.

Christ accomplishes all of His work through His churches. This is why it is so important to be involved in a biblically functioning local church. It is the place of Christ's special presence. It is the spiritual temple which He indwells and in which He receives worship. It is the place from which the light goes out to the world. Through the church, the proclamation of the gospel is accomplished, spiritual warfare is carried out, and spiritual victory is achieved, both collectively and individually.

Notice the description of this resurrected, reigning, and returning Christ in verses 13 to 16. It says in verse 13 that John saw *"one like unto the Son of man."* The Son of man is a title that Jesus took to Himself many times when He was on earth. He frequently called Himself the Son of man. He appeared to be a man because He was a man. But He was also more than a man; He was the God-man. He was God incarnate in human flesh so that He was fully divine and fully human in one person.

When our passage says He is *"like unto the Son of man,"* this phrase is taken directly out of Daniel 7:13, *"I saw in the night visions, and, behold, one like the Son of man came with the clouds of heaven, and came to the Ancient of days, and they brought him near before him."* This is when Jesus triumphed over the kingdoms of this world, and the kingdoms of this world became the kingdoms of Christ.

In this prophetic passage in Daniel 7:13, Jesus is identified as one like the Son of man. He is like us, but He is only partly like us, because unlike us, He has Deity, and we do not. He is like us, but He is also not like us. He is like us in His humanity, but He is not like us in his Deity. This is the explanation for the phrase, *"one like unto the Son of man."*

John had a vision similar to the one recorded in Revelation 1 earlier in his life on the Mount of Transfiguration. In Matthew 17:2, it says Christ's *"face did shine as the sun, and His [clothing] was white as the light."* In verse 13, John sees Jesus in the same majestic royal attire, the attire of a king, wearing a robe that reaches to His feet with a band of gold around His chest. Only kings were arrayed in such apparel.

Verse 14 goes on to describe His head: *"His head and his hairs were white like wool, as white as snow; and his eyes were as a flame of fire."* John describes Jesus' hair as being pure white, symbolizing His eternality, His purity, and His wisdom. In Daniel 7:9, the Ancient of days is said to have *"the hair of his head like the pure wool."* The same thing is said of the hair of the Lord Jesus, indicating that He, too, is the Ancient of days—that is, He is God from eternity past. He possesses the divine attributes of purity and wisdom.

In most cultures, someone with white hair is considered to be experienced and have a lifetime of learning, and as a result, is marked out as someone who has wisdom. White hair is associated with the old and the wise, and Jesus is infinitely old and infinitely wise. White hair, that is as white as snow or wool, is also associated with purity. In Isaiah chapter 1:18 it says, *"Come now, and let us reason together, saith the Lord: though your sins be as scarlet, they shall be as white as snow; though they be red like crimson, they shall be as wool."*

The white hair Jesus has identifies Him as the Ancient of days. It identifies Him as being the eternal one, the infinitely pure one, and the infinitely wise one. Verse 14 goes on to say that *"his eyes were as a flame of fire."* This echoes the imagery contained in Daniel 10:6 when it says, *"His body also was like the beryl, and his face as the appearance of lightning, and his eyes as lamps of fire, and his arms and his feet like in colour to polished brass, and the voice of his words like the voice of a multitude."* What Daniel was seeing in the heavenly messenger who spoke to him, John is also seeing in Christ. So this is not something new. This is something set forth previously in the Old Testament.

When it says His eyes were as a flame of fire, this means that His eyes burned down through every layer of deceit to lay bare the truth. It also means His eyes burned with indignation at the wickedness of Satan and evil men which he sees. His eyes being like a flame of fire symbolizes not only the omniscient, penetrating perception of the Son of man, but it also expresses His anger and indignation at the sin which His divine insight observes.

But this is not all. Verse 15 goes on and says, *"And his feet [were] like unto fine brass, as if they burned in a furnace."* This continues to echo the words of Daniel 10:6, where it says of the heavenly messenger that his feet are *"like in colour to polished brass."* Here, the brass is seen as almost molten. It is glowing like it has been heated in a furnace. The appearance of Christ's feet was like that of metal glowing in a furnace, signifying the consuming fire of His coming judgment in which He will trample His enemies under His feet in the heat of His anger. He will come, the Bible says in 2 Thessalonians 1:8, *"In flaming fire taking vengeance on them that know not God, and that obey not the gospel of our Lord Jesus Christ."*

These two attributes of Christ—His flaming eyes, and His feet that glow like metal heated in a furnace—are emphasized in Revelation 2:18. In one of the letters to the seven churches it says, *"And unto the angel of the church in Thyatira write; These things saith the Son of God,"* (notice the attributes emphasized) *"who hath his eyes like unto a flame of fire, and his feet are like fine brass."* Why is Jesus pointing that out about Himself to this particular church?

Here is why—verse 19: *"I know thy works, and charity, and service, and faith, and thy patience, and thy works; and the last to be more than the first."* So far, so good. But here is the problem—verse 20: *"Notwithstanding I have a few things against thee, because thou sufferest that woman Jezebel, which calleth herself a prophetess, to teach and to seduce my servants to commit fornication, and to eat things sacrificed unto idols.* [21] *And I gave her space to repent of her fornication; and she repented not.* [22] *Behold, I will cast her into a bed, and them that commit adultery with her into great tribulation, except they repent of their deeds.* [23] *And I will kill her children with death;*

and all the churches shall know that I am he which searcheth the reins and hearts: and I will give unto every one of you according to your works."

The idea of the fiery eyes is that Jesus sees the sin and hypocrisy in this woman and her followers' lives; and the burning feet say, "I am coming in judgment! Repent before I arrive!" Therefore, His flaming feet and His fiery eyes speak of His fearful judgment.

Verse 15 goes on to say, not only that His feet are like unto fine brass as if they burned in a furnace, but that *"his voice [is] as the sound of many waters."* The allusion here is to the roar of a massive waterfall. If you have been to a major waterfall like Niagara Falls, you know it roars so loudly it is difficult to hear people talk. It could also be an allusion to the mighty waves of a monster storm that smash on the shore and explode like bombs. If you have spent any time at the ocean's side, you have seen and heard them. John is on an island, and Patmos was not a very big island either. When the storms came across the Aegean Sea, he heard the waves pounding on the shore.

The allusion is to the roar of a massive waterfall or the mighty waves smashing on the shore. It says in Ezekiel 43:2, *"behold, the glory of the God of Israel came from the way of the east: and his voice was like a noise of many waters: and the earth shined with his glory."* This metaphor of the voice of God being like the power of the smashing wave or the crashing waterfall is one that occurs frequently in the Scriptures. The point being made is this: The God of Israel has a voice that is overwhelming in its power; and when Jesus speaks, no one can resist the power of His voice.

Have you ever tried to stand under a waterfall that is dropping tons of water every second, or tried to stand up on the shore to a fifteen-foot wave that is coming toward you? That is the power of the voice of God as He speaks. When Jesus speaks, no one can resist the power of His voice.

Verse 16 says, *"And he had in his right hand seven stars."* We are not left to doubt what these stars represent, because in verse 20 we are told what they represent: *"The mystery of the seven stars which thou sawest in my right hand, and the seven golden candlesticks. The seven stars are the angels of the seven churches: and the seven candlesticks which thou sawest are the seven churches."*

The seven stars represent the angels of the seven churches. There are those who assert these angels are literal angels, and that every local church has a guardian angel watching over it. The Bible nowhere teaches that concept. The Bible does teach that as individuals we have guardian angels that watch over us. But it does not teach that collective bodies of people have an angel watching over them. It helps us to understand the meaning of verse 20 when we understand that the word "angel" literally means "messenger."

These stars in Jesus' right hand are messengers. He says in verse 20 that they are the messengers of the seven churches. A messenger is someone who bears and conveys a message. These messengers in Christ's hand are the ones who represent Christ's message to the seven churches. He declares that plainly in verse 20. And who are the ones who bring Christ's message to the churches but the pastors of those churches?

We read in Daniel 12:3 about these messengers when it says, *"And they that be wise shall shine as the brightness of the firmament; and they that turn many to righteousness as the stars for ever and ever."* We are told in Daniel 12:3 that those who turn others to righteousness are to be likened to stars. They will shine like stars. Individuals who convey Christ's message to the people of God are likened unto stars in both Daniel 12:3 and Revelation 1:20.

We read in Revelation 2:1, *"Unto the angel of the church of Ephesus write"*; that is, *"Unto the [messenger or pastor] of the church of Ephesus write. . ."* These letters are to be given to the pastors, who are the messengers of Christ's word to the churches, and who turn the churches to righteousness by that word. Pastors receive Christ's words, and then read and preach them to the congregation.

Verse 16 says Christ holds the pastors of His churches in His right hand. This means that He upholds them, He protects them, He sustains them, and He empowers them. He puts them in a place of honor in His kingdom and in His presence. He walks in the midst of the churches. He holds their pastors in His right hand. He gives them the message He wants them to deliver to His churches, and this is what we see Him doing in chapters 2 and 3.

Christ has a special care for the pastors of His churches. He holds them in His right hand, and that is the only reason they are able to persevere in their work and accomplish it, because without Him, they would have no message, no power, and no protection from the ravages of Satan.

The blessed Christ gives pastors who are teachers as a gift to His church. It says in Ephesians 4:11–12, *"And he* (Jesus) *gave some, apos-*

tles; and some, prophets; and some, evangelists; and some, pastors and teachers; [12] *For the perfecting of the saints, for the work of the ministry, for the edifying of the body of Christ."* Just as Jesus gave the apostles to His church, and just as Jesus gave prophets to His church, and just as Jesus gave great evangelists to His church, Jesus gives pastor-teachers to His churches. He gives them a special understanding of His message, and a special authority and power and protection in the proclamation of it.

Revelation 1:16 goes on to say that "*out of his mouth went a sharp two-edged sword.*" This is a symbolic reference to the word of God. This point is evident from passages such as Ephesians 6:17 which says, "*And take. . . the sword of the Spirit, which is the word of God*" and Hebrews 4:12 when it says, "*the word of God is [living], and powerful, and sharper than any two-edged sword.*"

It is interesting to note that this sword is said to be two-edged. There were swords that had only one edge, but this one has two edges. The number two conveys the idea of complementary and interdependent union. The two edges of this sword represent the Old and the New Testaments, which are the two complementary and interdependent parts of the Bible, whose union comprises the totality of the sword of the Spirit which is the word of God.

People who throw away the Old Testament as irrelevant and just claim to follow the New Testament have a one-edged sword. It is imperative that we understand and preach both Testaments because they are inextricably intertwined and joined together in as much of an inseparable union as a sword with two edges has those two edges joined together into one sword.

A sword is used to slay. You kill people with swords. It is all they are good for. You do not do anything else with them. You do not use them to do surgery or serve cake. A sword is used to slay, and by the power of Christ's word spoken in this world, the powers of darkness are slain and defeated, and the prince of darkness is slain and destroyed. We see this clearly set forth in Revelation 19:15: "*And out of his mouth goeth a sharp sword, that with it he should smite the nations.*"

This imagery is once again rooted in the Old Testament. In Isaiah 49:2, it speaks of Christ in His role as judge. Jesus speaking of His Father says, "*And he,*" (my Father) "*hath made my mouth like a sharp sword; in the shadow of his hand hath he hid me, and made me a polished shaft; in his quiver hath he hid me.*" Isaiah continues this imagery of Jesus as the sword of God and Jesus as the arrow of God bringing God's judgment on a wicked world. Ephesians 6:17 says we are to use the word of God as Jesus does, to do spiritual warfare with the forces of darkness.

Verse 16 closes with a declaration that Christ's face shone like the sun at its brightest: "*and his countenance was as the sun shineth in his strength.*" When the sun shines, it shines very strongly. Have you ever tried to stare at the sun? How long does that last? That is how long those who stand against Christ will last when He looks on them with that burning countenance like the shining of the sun, and that burning eye of flaming fire. People think when they get to heaven they are going to walk up to God and have a chat. People will wither like a spider in a fire when they stand before God. It is a fearful thing to fall into the hands of the living God. "*For our God is a consuming fire.*"

It says in 2 Thessalonians 2:8, "*And then shall that Wicked [one] be revealed,*" speaking of Antichrist, "*whom the Lord shall consume with the spirit of his mouth,*" (that is the sword) "*and shall destroy with the brightness of his coming.*" That brightness is His face shining like the sun. On the Mount of Transfiguration, Jesus' face began to shine like the sun. What happened to the apostles? They fell down on their faces before Him. They could not look on the face of the glorified Christ for even a moment.

Christ is going to exercise instantaneous, overwhelming power against His enemies, and they will wither in an instant before it and be completely unable to stand against it. Those who think they can stand against Christ need to go out and have a look at the sun and learn a lesson about how well they will be able to stand against Christ when He returns.

This is the sight John beheld. We have seen the voice John heard in verses 10 and 11 in the last chapter. We have just now seen the sight John beheld in verses 12 to 16. Notice, thirdly, the response John gave.

The Response John Gave

The response John gave is in verse 17. He says, "*And when I saw him, I fell at his feet as dead.*"

I want to summarize what we just talked about, and there is no better way to summarize it than to read the description that William Hendriksen gave in his book, *More than Conquerors*.

> The Son of Man is here pictured as clothed with power and majesty and with awe and terror. That long royal robe; that golden belt buckled at the breast; that hair so glistening white that like snow on which the sun is shining it hurts the eyes; those eyes flashing fire, eyes that read every heart and penetrate every hidden corner; those feet glowing in order to trample down the wicked; that loud, reverberating voice, like the mighty breakers booming against the rocky shore of Patmos; that sharp, long, heavy great-sword with two biting edges; that entire appearance "as the sun shines in its power," too intense for human eyes to stare at—the entire picture, taken as a whole, is symbolic of Christ, the Holy One, coming to purge His churches, and to punish those who are persecuting His elect.[3]

That is what John saw. Is it any wonder John fell on his face? This is not the sweet, comforting, limp-wristed Jesus of our modern cultural understanding. This is the awesome, almighty, majestic, all-powerful, returning judge. John sees this terrifying vision of the risen Christ standing before him as the overwhelmingly powerful judge who is inescapable and irresistible and dreadful in His wrath and terrible in His judgments. Is it any wonder this sight should cause John to collapse on his face in fear and terror?

Like all of the prophets before him, he felt utterly unfit to be in the presence of God. Whether it was Isaiah or Ezekiel or Daniel, all had the same response when brought into the divine presence. They said: "I am unfit to be in the presence of God! Woe is me! I am overwhelmed by the majesty of God! I lose all my strength! I fall on my face in reverence and awe and worship and dread!"

If this is how believers react in the presence of God, what will be the state of the unsaved when they come into His presence? We read previously in Revelation 1:7, *"Behold, he cometh with clouds; and every eye shall see him, and they also which pierced him: and all kindreds of the earth shall wail because of him."* The unsaved will be utterly terrified.

Having considered the voice John heard in verses 10 and 11, having seen the sight John beheld in verses 12 to 16, and having

3 William Hendriksen. *More Than Conquerors: An Interpretation of the Book of Revelation*. Grand Rapids: Baker, 1962. 56, 57.

seen the response John gave in verse 17a, notice fourthly, the comfort John received.

The Comfort John Received

The comfort John received is in verses 17b to 20. *"And he laid his right hand upon me, saying unto me, Fear not; I am the first and the last:* [18] *I am he that liveth, and was dead; and, behold, I am alive for evermore, Amen; and have the keys of hell and of death."*

No more comforting words were ever spoken than those words. With a comforting touch, and with a reassuring word, and with a wonderful promise, Jesus strengthens John and raises him up again. The purpose of this vision for John was not to terrify him; the purpose of this vision both for John and all believers is to comfort them. Even though Jesus is this awe-inspiring, terrifying, overwhelming God, yet He employs all of that power for the blessing and comfort and upholding of His precious children whom He loves with all His heart and for whom He laid down his life.

We see the comforting touch: "*He laid His right hand upon me.*" We see the reassuring word: "*Fear not.*" "John, you have nothing to fear from Me. I am for you, not against you." *"I am the first and the last."* "I am God, yes, but My divine power will be used to protect you, not to harm you. I will protect you from death, and in the protection from death come all the other protections."

We see the wonderful promise: Jesus says in verse 18, *"I am he that liveth, and was dead; and, behold, I am alive for evermore, Amen; and have the keys of hell and of death."* He is saying, "I am alive. I was dead. But behold, I am alive forevermore. I have defeated death. It has no more power over Me. I have eternal life. I am alive forevermore, and I have the keys; that is, I have the authority and the control over hell and over death."

If someone gives you the key to a building, that person is giving you authority over the building and its use. When Jesus has the keys to death and to hell, He has authority and control over death, and He has authority and control over hell. He is saying to John, "You do not need to fear sin and its consequence, death. I have defeated them both, I control them both, and therefore death cannot hurt you and hell cannot threaten you. Therefore, do not fear your persecutors. I will cast them into death and into hell, but I will sustain you in life, and I will bring you into heaven. John, fear not."

Here is a man who had many reasons to fear. He was the object of persecution by the Roman government and he was on this Isle of Patmos in exile, not knowing if or when he was going to be summoned and executed. Jesus said, "John, I am here. You are never going to die unless I turn the key. The key is in the hand of the infinite, almighty God, who is angry with your enemies, and who loves you with all of His heart and strength. John, how can you be afraid? John, fear not."

That is what Jesus is saying to all of us who are trusting in Him: Do not be afraid of the spiritual warfare you are facing. Understand that this Christ pictured in this passage in the glory of all of His attributes is fighting for you. Do not pity yourself. Pity your enemies who set themselves against Jesus Christ. They shall all be cast into the Lake of Fire, while those who serve this exalted Christ will be conducted into the new heavens and the new earth.

Having assuaged John's fears with a reassuring touch and a wonderful promise, Jesus now gives him a mission. Notice verse 19: *"Write the things which thou hast seen, and the things which are, and the things which shall be hereafter."* In other words, "Write everything you have seen up to this point. Write everything that you are seeing now. Write all the things you are going to see after this point. Omit nothing. Include everything." He did, and this is why we have the book of Revelation.

In verse 20, Jesus gives John the meaning of the two symbols that are necessary to be given, namely, the stars and the candlesticks. One represents the pastors, and the other the churches. The rest of the symbols in this chapter are self-explanatory, as we have seen. Jesus then begins to dictate His letters to the churches which are to be given to the pastors to be read to the people and expounded to them. He gives these letters to the local churches to be preached to them and possessed by them as His special message to them, and to churches all throughout this age.

God has raised up ministers of the gospel to preach His word to His people. What is the message that the minister of the gospel who is held in Christ's right hand supposed to be conveying to their people? It is the message Jesus sets forth in these seven letters.

When you show up to church, you expect a message from your pastor. He is supposed to be a messenger of Christ, and convey Christ's message to you. The question is: What is that message? It is the message in these seven letters. Pastors do not get to make up the message. This is why faithful pastors expound the Bible verse by verse and explain it phrase by phrase, because it is Christ's message. A faithful pastor is required to be a messenger of Christ and to take the word of Christ, and as Paul says to Timothy, *"preach the word."* Preach it when it is popular, preach it when it is not, and keep on preaching it patiently. The time will come when they will not even want to hear it. But Jesus says, "You just keep on preaching it and you will be my faithful servant, and I will hold you in My hand and I will protect you. On that great day, you will shine as the stars of heaven."

There is a special reward for faithful pastors. There is also a special wrath and judgment for unfaithful pastors. 1 Corinthians 3:17 says, *"If any man defile the temple of God, him will God destroy."* He is speaking specifically to pastors there. That is why James says in James 3:1, "Let not many of you be teachers, knowing we will receive the greater judgment." That is why preaching in the pulpit is at once the most wonderful and the most terrifying activity that a man can ever engage in. Wonderful, because you feel the power and enablement of Christ, and terrifying, because if you misrepresent His message, then you have just defiled His bride, and Christ does not take it kindly when someone abuses His wife.

As we proceed through this book, we are going to be reading the message the messenger is charged to give, and that is the message of Christ to His churches. May we have ears to hear, to respond, and to overcome. This is a serious business because we are involved in serious spiritual warfare. Let us listen seriously to the voice of Christ because this person pictured in this passage is the judge we are going to face, and He is either going to say to you on the day of judgment, *"fear not;"* or He is going to say to you, *"depart from me."* The difference between those two outcomes depends on whether we embraced and followed the message He gave in this book, or whether we did not.

We need to take this message seriously, we need to study it diligently, and we need to obey it comprehensively. Let us live by every word that proceeds out of the mouth of God. Nothing less will give us a good outcome on the Day of Judgment.

12

The Letter to the Church at Ephesus, Revelation 2:1–7

> "[1] *Unto the angel of the church of Ephesus write; These things saith he that holdeth the seven stars in his right hand, who walketh in the midst of the seven golden candlesticks;* [2] *I know thy works, and thy labour, and thy patience, and how thou canst not bear them which are evil: and thou hast tried them which say they are apostles, and are not, and hast found them liars:* [3] *And hast borne, and hast patience, and for my name's sake hast laboured, and hast not fainted.* [4] *Neverthe-less I have somewhat against thee, because thou hast left thy first love.* [5] *Remember therefore from whence thou art fallen, and repent, and do the first works; or else I will come unto thee quickly, and will remove thy candlestick out of his place, except thou repent.* [6] *But this thou hast, that thou hatest the deeds of the Nicolaitans, which I also hate.* [7] *He that hath an ear, let him hear what the Spirit saith unto the churches; To him that overcometh will I give to eat of the tree of life, which is in the midst of the paradise of God.*"

We must never forget that the book of Revelation is a church epistle. It is a letter written to these seven local churches, and by extension, to every local church that will exist after them. This book is Christ's letter to your local church.

It is evident from these opening chapters that Christ's focus is on His church. The goal of Christ is to encourage, strengthen, purify, comfort, and challenge His churches. These churches are engaged in intense spiritual warfare, and if they are to overcome and triumph in that warfare, they must heed the message of these letters.

These letters tell us what Christ thinks of His churches and expects from His churches. We know that Christ loves His church and gave Himself for it on the cross. Therefore, He cannot be indifferent toward the church or unconcerned with it. If Jesus loved the church to the point He laid down His life for it, then He cannot possibly abandon it now. That is why no Christian is ever indifferent toward the church. He has the same heart for it and attitude toward it that Christ does. A Christian would never abandon involvement with his local church.

The Bible tells us that the church is Christ's body, Christ's bride, Christ's temple, and Christ's kingdom. Do you suppose that Jesus is concerned with His own body? Is He concerned with His own bride? Is He concerned with the temple in which He dwells? Is He concerned with the kingdom over which He rules? If so, then Christ has the most intense and focused concern conceivable for the church. The church is at the center of Christ's heart, and it is the focus of Christ's affection.

Knowing that Christ has an intense focus, concern, and affection for His church should cause us to listen very carefully to what Christ has to say, and to gladly respond to the directions He gives. These letters are, if you will, love letters. They express Christ's love for His church. They are an extension and outflow of Christ's heart to His people.

These letters are also an extension and outflow of John's vision of the Lord Jesus Christ in chapter 1. We must understand chapters 2 and 3 in the context of chapter 1. In chapter 1, we saw a glorious revelation of the person of Jesus Christ, and it is the person revealed in chapter 1 who speaks the things contained in chapters 2 and 3.

In these seven letters, Christ identifies Himself to each church by some characteristic that was revealed about Him in chapter 1. The particular aspect of Christ selected by Him to identify Himself to each individual church is that which is particularly suited to address the unique needs of that church. In each letter He says, *"Unto the angel of the church of. . .,"* (and then names the church) *"write, These things saith he that. . ."* and then He identifies Himself by one or more of the attributes revealed about Him in chapter 1.

Each of these seven letters follows a similar structure that consists of seven elements.

First of all, there is an address to the pastor of each church. Each opens with: ". . . unto the angel, (messenger) of Ephesus or Smyrna or Pergamos, etc., write. . . ." The Greek word *"angelos"* is often translated "messenger" because that is what it means. It is repeatedly used of humans. For example, in Matthew 11:10, Mark 1:2, and Luke 7:24, the word *"angelos"* is used of human messengers. These seven stars in the hand of Jesus are the seven angels of the churches; that is, they are Christ's messengers, who are the pastors who bring the message of Christ to the churches.

Secondly, there is a description of Christ in each letter. They go on to say, *"These things saith he that. . ."* and then He describes Himself. He describes Himself as He that has the seven stars and walks in the midst of the seven golden candlesticks in His letter to Ephesus. In His letter to Smyrna, He identifies Himself as the first and the last, the one who was dead and is now alive. In the letter to Pergamos, He identifies Himself as the one who has the sharp sword with two edges. In the letter to Thyatira, He identifies Himself as the one who has eyes like a flame of fire and feet like fine brass. To the church at Sardis, He identifies Himself as the one who has the seven Spirits and the seven stars. To the church at Philadelphia, He identifies Himself as the one who has the key. Finally, to the church at Laodicea, He identifies Himself as the one who is the faithful witness. All of these descriptors are taken directly out of chapter 1.

Thirdly, there is a commendation of their good works and character. Jesus finds something to praise about every single one of these churches, with the exception of Laodicea. He speaks of their charity, their faith, their labor, their patience, their faithfulness, their rejection of false teachers, and various other virtues that they possess. Jesus looks at His churches and He says, in effect, "There are some very good things in this church." He identifies them and He expresses approval and gratitude for them with the exception of the church at Laodicea, for which He has nothing good to say.

Fourthly, each letter has a correction of their sins and defects. He condemns their failure to obey and He criticizes their departure from godliness and truth in various areas. He condemns things like tolerating false doctrine and false teachers, immoral behavior, worldliness and materialism, and loss of love for Christ. There are two churches He does not criticize. He has no criticism for the church at Smyrna and the church at Philadelphia. Smyrna was a suffering church; its people were suffering martyrdom. The church at Philadelphia was a weak church; it had small resources. The point is that the churches that were suffering and struggling the most were the ones for which He had no criticism.

The question is, what does Christ think of your church? For one church He may say: "I do not have anything bad to say about it. I only have praise for it." For another church He may say: "I do not have one good thing to say about it. I only have criticism of it." For still other churches He may say: "You are a mixed bag. There are some very good things here, but there are also some things that are seriously wrong." Churches are not homogeneous, even within the same denomination or affiliation. Therefore, it is imperative for us to ask: "What does Jesus say about these churches that is true of my church, whether for good or bad?"

Fifthly, He issues a warning to each church. These warnings are mainly calls to repent of the sins He identified and to reform their behavior. That is true with five of the seven churches. He identifies things that are wrong and says: "You need to repent of those things." There are two churches for which He has no criticisms, and therefore no rebukes. Nevertheless, He still issues warnings to them. Just because He did not have anything negative to say about them did not mean they could coast along or be complacent. They need to remain faithful even to the point of death. They must be diligent to remember His teaching and develop their faith so they do not fall away. Just because a church has nothing in particular wrong with it and has a lot of things right with it in the present does not mean it is going to be permanently virtuous forever. It may fall away in the future.

We have to watch and pray lest we enter into temptation. We may not have fallen into it yet, but we certainly can, and therefore we need to always be watching and praying. Jesus is saying that every church has work to do, either by way of repentance of what is wrong, or by way of reinforcement of what is right. Every church is warned to either repent or reinforce.

Sixthly, each of these letters has an exhortation to hear and to heed what the Spirit is saying to the churches. Every letter has this phrase in it: *"He that hath an ear, let him hear what the Spirit saith unto the churches."* It is as if He is saying, "Pay attention! Ponder the true meaning and application of these things." In other words, Jesus is not talking so that we can let it go in one ear and out the other. He is saying: "When I speak, I am not wasting My time or yours. You need to carefully listen, you need to thoughtfully consider, and you need to diligently apply what I am telling you. Do not let this pass out of your mind."

Seventh, every letter has a promise of comfort and consolation to the overcomer. To those who overcome—that is, to those who persevere in faithfulness to Christ in the midst of a persecuting world—wonderful things are promised: things like the opportunity to eat of the tree of life, to have a crown of life, to escape the second death, to have power over the nations, and to sit with Christ in His throne. These and many other promises are given to those who have an ear to hear what the Spirit is saying to the churches.

These are the seven elements of these letters. There is an address to the pastor of each church; there is a description of Christ; there is a commendation of their good works and character; there is a correction of their sins and defects; there is a warning given; there is an exhortation to hear and heed what the Spirit is saying to the churches; and there is a promise of comfort and consolation.

As we survey these seven letters to these seven churches, we see there is not one of them that is without severe struggles and challenges. Not one of these churches is on Easy Street. Five of the seven churches have serious sins to repent of. One of them is experiencing martyrdom. Another one of them is very weak. The rest of them either have false teachers, spiritual deadness, spiritual indifference, cold-heartedness, or materialism. Every church is severely tested and tried in the crucible of the spiritual warfare it is engaged in.

Therefore, we should not be surprised that our own churches have gone through great conflicts and great difficulties. We have experienced great pressures to compromise the truth and the will of Christ. Churches still have to do battle with the world's seductions and the world's persecutions, just like these churches did. Churches today still struggle with sins in their midst and with hostility from the world.

The things that characterize these seven churches are the things that characterize the churches in every age and in every land. What we see in these seven letters we see reflected in our own assemblies, and they are the things churches in the future will continue to struggle with.

We need to understand that these seven letters are not a chronology of church history; they are a chronicle of church struggles throughout history as the churches have battled the wiles of the devil and his helpers. There is the theory addressed in the introduction to this book that each of these seven churches represents seven periods of church history, but there is no biblical basis for such a conjecture.

These seven churches do not represent seven successive ages of church history; they represent the kind of struggles that exist in every age, among all of the churches, throughout history. There are churches like the church at Ephesus today, there are churches like the church at Smyrna today, and there are churches like the church at Pergamos today. We can find represented among churches in our own day what each of these churches were in John's day.

These introductory thoughts on the seven letters to these seven churches now brings us to the consideration of the first of those letters, and that is Christ's letter to the Ephesians in 2:1–7.

The Introduction to the Letter

The introduction to this letter is in verse 1 which says, *"Unto the angel of the church of Ephesus write; These things saith he that holdeth the seven stars in his right hand, who walketh in the midst of the seven golden candlesticks."* Each of these letters is introduced by a statement about who the recipient and author of the letter is.

The recipient of this letter is the pastor and the church at Ephesus. We do not know who the pastor of the church was at this point in time, but we do know that Ephesus was a wealthy and prosperous city of about a quarter of a million people. It was a seaport city, it was a great center of commerce and trade, and it was most noted for the great temple of Diana which was one of the Seven Wonders of the World at that time in history.

Paul established the church at Ephesus as recorded in Acts 18–19, and he gave it his final exhortation in Acts 20. Paul began the church about AD 52. He ministered there for a couple of years as its pastor. The work at Ephesus was so successful that the worship in the temple of Diana fell off sharply, and all they that dwelt in Asia heard the word of the Lord Jesus. From Ephesus, the gospel went out powerfully into the surrounding regions and towns.

However, it is now forty years later as John writes this letter to the Ephesians, and during this time, while their love for the truth and their defense of the truth has not lessened, their love for Christ and for one another and for the lost has diminished greatly, and therein lies the problem.

The author of the letter is Christ, who designates Himself in verse 1 as the one who holds *"the seven stars in His right hand"* and who walks "*in the midst of the seven golden candlesticks.*" We saw that these seven stars represent the pastors of the churches, who are Christ's true messengers. These seven stars are commissioned by Christ, they are illuminated by Christ, and they are taught by Christ. They preach the light of truth, and they stand against the heresy that was assaulting the churches and the deceivers who taught it. By identifying Himself as the one who holds "*the seven stars in His right hand,*" Christ is encouraging the true pastors at Ephesus. He is protecting them, upholding them, and strengthening them in the face of these false apostles who are seeking to assault and undermine them. Christ identifies Himself as the one who holds the pastors of the church in His right hand.

To know that Christ holds His true ministers in His right hand is a great comfort and encouragement, both to the pastors themselves as well as to the congregations they serve. It is the case that "as goes the pastor, so goes the church." The future of the church is secured as Christ upholds the pastors of the churches.

But Christ is not only the one who holds the seven stars in His right hand; He further identifies Himself as the one who walks "*in the midst of the golden candlesticks*" in verse 1. We saw that these golden candlesticks represent the churches. Christ is saying by this language and imagery that He is active in His churches. He walks among them, lives in the midst of them, observes all that goes on in them, ministers to them, receives worship from them, and directs and guides them.

The point is this: the church is not alone. Christ is with her, He is in the midst of her, and He is filling her with His power and His presence. Each local church is under His constant oversight. Christ is present where two or three are gathered together in His name. He dwells in the midst of His churches, showing that He is intimately involved with them and that He personally cares for each of them.

The Message of the Letter

The message of the letter consists of three things: His commendation, His correction, and His warning.

First, notice His commendation. His commendation is in verses 2, 3, and 6. "*I know thy works, and thy labour, and thy patience, and how thou canst not bear them which are evil: and thou hast tried them which say they are apostles, and are not, and hast found them liars:* [3] *And hast borne, and hast patience, and for my name's sake hast laboured, and hast not fainted.* [6] *But this thou hast, that thou hatest the deeds of the Nicolaitans, which I also hate."*

Jesus starts in verse 2 with a declaration of His omniscience. He says, *"I know."* These words *"I know"* precede each message to each church. Christ knows what each church is experiencing. He knows their virtues and He knows their weaknesses, and He is saying He is intimately acquainted with every detail of their life. He knows their works. There is no hiding what they have done, either good or bad. He is fully aware of all that they face and experience and accomplish. Therefore He says, *"I know."*

Now regarding what He knows, He says: "I know your works; that is, the deeds you have undertaken to accomplish. I know your labor; that is, the intense effort that went into the accomplishment of those deeds, even in the face of grievous opposition. I know your patience; that is, the steadfastness over the long periods of time in engaging in intense effort in the works you have done." They had been steadfast over long periods of time, even when few results seemed to appear from their efforts.

Then He says, in effect, "Not only do I know your works, but I also know how you cannot bear them which are evil. Not only did you work hard for Me with intense effort over a long period of time even when there were few results, but you also rejected heretics. When evil people came into the congregation, you did not say: 'Great! We are building the numbers!' Instead, you ran them out. You could not bear those who were evil or those who defended their moral impurity. You did not tolerate such people or their moral corruption in your midst."

It is important to understand that we do welcome morally corrupt people to come to church; we welcome morally corrupt people to hear the gospel; we welcome morally corrupt people who struggle with their sin and despise it and are seeking deliverance from it. But we do not welcome people who glory in their sin, who defend their sin, and who seek to publicly justify it and involve others in it. That is not to be tolerated for a moment.

It says further in verse 2 that they tried them which said they were apostles but were not, and found them to be liars. These people claiming to be apostles were probably saying they were the successors of the apostles. It is unlikely they were saying they were one of the twelve, because everybody knew who the twelve were. They were claiming to be the leading teachers among the churches—the high profile, widely known, and broadly promoted teachers of the Bible.

Jesus says: "You put to the test those who claim to be leading teachers in the church. You put to the test those who claim to have special power and anointing from Jesus Christ." Their teaching was examined in the light of Scripture, and it was exposed as being false. The Ephesians did not mince any words. They publicly said: "These men are liars. They are lying when they say this or that doctrine is the truth of God." They called a liar a liar, and they called a heretic a heretic, and they called the wicked man a wicked man, and Christ approves of the use of these labels and commends them for using them. If someone is publicly teaching lies, then you need to publicly say: "That person is a liar."

The Bible has no problem with saying things like: "[14]*Alexander the coppersmith did me much evil: the Lord reward him according to his works:* [15] *Of whom be thou ware also; for he hath greatly withstood our words"* in 2 Timothy 4:14–15. Paul named him, called him out, and said who he was and what he did. Here Jesus is saying: "You found these people to be liars, and you publicly marked them out as such, because liars are what they are."

The Ephesians did not speak words like these: "We are all on our own individual spiritual journey. We need to be broadminded and latitudinarian, and we need to have a big tent and embrace all who claim to be Christians, and affirm everyone's beliefs." This is the voice of compromised evangelicalism; it is not the voice of churches that are faithful to Christ.

If they are teaching a false gospel, they are liars. They are not of us. They are not in the kingdom. They are servants of Satan, because Satan is a liar from the beginning. We need to understand false teachers are not harmless people who are just misguided. These are people who are active in the service of Satan and are spreading a false gospel in order to damn people to hell and turn them away from Christ.

These Ephesian elders heeded Paul's warning in Acts 20:28–31. When Paul was giving his final charge to the Ephesian elders, he said to them, "*Take heed therefore unto yourselves, and to all the flock, over the which the Holy Ghost hath made you overseers, to feed the church of God, which he hath purchased with his own blood.* [29] *For I know this, that after my departing shall grievous wolves enter in among you, not sparing the flock.* [30] *Also of your own selves shall men*

arise, speaking perverse things, to draw away disciples after them.
31 *Therefore watch, and remember, that by the space of three years I*
ceased not to warn every one night and day with tears."

In his final admonition to the Ephesian elders in about AD 54 or 55, Paul said, "Take heed." Here they are forty years later, and they are still taking heed. They are protecting the flock from false teachers from without and from within. They are working diligently against great opposition and with tremendous patience in marking out and naming these evil men who would promote immorality in the congregation and these lying men who would promote false theology in the congregation. They have stood like a rock against their immoral behavior and their unbiblical teaching. They said to them on the one hand, "You are evil," and on the other hand, "You are liars." They kept the congregation morally and theologically pure. These were good men. Would to God we had many more like them.

Furthermore, Jesus says in Revelation 2:3, I know thou *"hast borne, and hast patience, and for my name's sake hast laboured, and hast not fainted."* This word *"borne"* means they carried the burden of the battle for the truth. They did the heavy lifting and the hard work of defending the truth.

He says: "You had patience." This is the second time He commends them for their patience. He commended them in verse 2: *"I know thy works, and thy labour, and thy patience,"* and now in verse 3 He says: "You have borne and have had *'patience,'"* exactly the same Greek word. For the second time, He commends them for the steadfastness and endurance they had in their unwavering battle for truth.

Then He says that they had pure motives because it was *"for my name's sake [you have] laboured."* "You did not labor for the sake of your own glory, but for My glory and My name. For My name's sake, you have *"laboured."* This word "labor" is a verbal form of the noun form in verse 2, *"I know thy works, and thy labour."* Verse 3, thou *"hast borne, and hast patience, and for my name's sake hast laboured."* In all that labor and laboring, they did not faint.

This rejection of moral and theological pollution and corruption that tried to assault and enter the church, and that was so successfully resisted and driven out of the church, of all this Jesus said: "You did that for My name's sake." It was not stubbornness or self-glorification that was driving these men. Rather, their motive was the glory of Christ and the honor of His name and the upholding of His truth. It was these things that motivated them to work so hard to uphold the truth for so long in the face of so much opposition. The honor of Christ's name and the honor of Christ's truth is what kept them going and kept them from fainting and giving up the battle for the truth and doctrinal purity.

In a word, they earnestly contended for the faith that was once delivered to the saints, and they did not give up or say, "This is too hard! We will just compromise the truth a little here and little there, and we will keep the people happy." They would not do it. The point is that fighting for moral and doctrinal purity in the church is hard. The language he uses here of laboring and patience and bearing of burdens and not fainting is the language of very exhausting work.

Finally, in verse 6 he says, "*But this thou hast, that thou hatest the deeds of the Nicolaitans, which I also hate.*" God hates, and His people need to hate as well. In this case, the hatred is directed toward the deeds of the Nicolaitans.

The Nicolaitans were an early Gnostic sect who advocated sinful license in the name of Christian liberty, or they advocated sinful license on the ground that spiritual perfection could not be impaired by sensual indulgence. In other words, they said that what you did with your body had no impact on your soul, because Gnostics saw the material as being completely separate and entirely irrelevant to the spiritual. Gnostics believed that there was a dichotomy between the spiritual and the material; they had a dualistic philosophy in which the material was viewed as wholly evil and entirely irrelevant, and the spiritual as wholly good and entirely separate. Therefore, you could fornicate all you wanted with your body and still be holy and pure in your soul because there was no real connection between them. God hates such teaching. The Ephesian Christians hated it as well, and they fought hard against it and would not tolerate those who taught it.

This was the city of Ephesus where the temple of Diana was. Diana worship was a fertility cult and the temple was filled with prostitutes. Devotees worshiped by having intimate relations with the prostitutes before Diana, hoping to provoke her to bring fertility to the earth by bringing rain and crops in abundance. The Nicolaitans were teaching that Christians could go to church and worship God on Sunday and go to the temple and participate with the prostitutes on Monday, because what they did with their bodies did not have any impact on their souls.

The teaching today sounds like this: You can be a practicing homosexual and a good Christian at the same time. A heterosexual couple can live together without being married and be good Christians. Premarital sex is not sin. Adulterous affairs are to be expected and open marriages are just a lifestyle choice.

God hates that teaching. God will have no sexual impurity in His churches. It is important to understand that God does not hate sex. He invented it. He thinks it is very good. He commanded it to be engaged in. He provided the circumstances to engage in it when He created the institution of marriage and brought one man and one woman together in marriage and said to them, "Be fruitful and multiply and fill the earth." But outside of the heterosexual covenant commitment of marriage, sex with another person is sin and it is to be abstained from.

We have seen that the church at Ephesus was morally pure and doctrinally pure. We would think this was a great church. But Jesus said to them, in effect, "Something is missing here. Your doctrine and practice are as straight as a gun barrel, but sadly, they are just as empty." This brings us to our next point under the message of the letter.

Secondly, notice His correction. His correction is in verses 4 and 5. Verse 4, *"Nevertheless I have somewhat against thee, because thou hast left thy first love."* Notice first, the charge that is made in verse 4. The charge is that they have left their first love. They had focused on the truth of Christ, but they had forgotten the Christ of the truth. They had become more concerned with the doctrine than with the Christ this doctrine revealed and defined.

Jude told those to whom he was writing in Jude 1:21 that they were to *"keep [themselves] in the love of God."* That is, they were to keep themselves in a state of warmhearted love toward God. Jude was telling them to keep on loving God with all of their heart and soul and mind and strength. This is what the Ephesians were failing to do. They were so concerned with moral purity and doctrinal purity they had forgotten why they must be morally pure and doctrinally pure. Yes, they were doing it for His name's sake, but He almost became an abstraction and a footnote to what they were giving the focus of their attention to, which was fighting this tremendous battle for moral and doctrinal purity in an age where immorality and lies were rampant and constantly assaulting them.

To put it another way, He is saying to them: "You have forgotten to love Me! Your love for Me has grown cold. All of your focus and efforts and energy in the church are horizontal, and in that horizontal focus you are doing extremely well, but the vertical dimension of your church is missing. You are so focused on people and what they are doing and what they are teaching, you have forgotten to focus on Christ and who He is to you and what He has done for you."

Notice secondly, the remedy prescribed in verse 5. He says to them, *"Remember therefore from whence thou art fallen, and repent, and do the first works."* In other words: Remember how you used to love Jesus when you were first saved? Go back to that degree of focus and intensity and attachment and affection. Stir up your love for Him.

How do we go about doing that? We all struggle with keeping up warmheartedness toward the Lord Jesus in the midst of all the struggles and battles we have to fight. Loving God does not come automatically to the soul of even the most experienced believer. Loving God is something you have to work at stirring up.

Just like you have to stir up and work at maintaining your love for your husband or wife, you have to work at stirring up and maintaining your love for Christ. Remember when you and your spouse first met? All the infatuation and excitement of just being in their presence made you feel electrified! Then a few years pass after marriage, and it can easily descend into the ordinary and mundane. What do you have to do? You have to start dating that person again. You have to start working up romance and love for that person and continue to do it all of your life. When the infatuation phase is over, the work of constantly renewing love begins. It is not automatic; you have to plan for it, you have to work on it, and you have to keep stirring it up. What is true with your spouse is also true with Christ.

Here are some suggestions as to how you can stir up that coldheartedness and transform it into warmheartedness toward the Lord Jesus Christ.

First of all, meditate on the love that Christ has for you. When you do, your love for Him will grow. It says in 1 John 4:19, *"We love him, because he first loved us."* If you do not love Him very much, it is because you are not thinking about how much He has done to show His love for you.

Secondly, we can increase our love for Christ by rejecting and hating all sin. It says in Matthew 24:12, that *"because iniquity shall abound, the love of many shall wax cold."* Love for Christ and participation in sin are mutually exclusive. The more you sin, the less you love Jesus. The more you love Jesus, the less you sin.

Thirdly, we need to reflect on the love Christ has for us in particular in laying down His life for us. In other words, focus on the cross. John 15:13 says, *"Greater love hath no man than this, that a man lay down his life for his friends."* In 2 Corinthians 5:14 it says, *"For the love of Christ constraineth [controls] us; because we thus judge, that if one died for all, then were all dead:* [15] *And that he died for all, that they which live should not henceforth live unto themselves, but unto him which died for them, and rose again."*

The Bible does not just point us to the works God has done for us in general as a reason why we should love Him; it specifically points to the cross as the reason why we should love Him. Do we love God because He first loved us by creating us, putting us in this wonderful world, and providing us with all the material comforts and blessings we have? Do we love Him for giving us friends and family, and giving us a beautiful place in which to live? Yes. But we love Him even more as we focus on what He did for us on the cross.

As we sing hymns about Christ and His sacrifice for us; as we read books about Christ and His redemption of us; as we read the Gospels over and over again, these things powerfully provoke our love for God. The Bible says in Romans 10:17 that *"faith cometh by hearing, and hearing by the word of God."* We could also say: Love comes by hearing, and hearing by the Word of God. I cannot cite a chapter and verse for that, but all I know is, as I read my Bible, I find my heart warming toward God. If I do not read my Bible for several days on end, I find myself growing cold in my love for God. The more I think about Jesus saving me from my sins, the more I love Him.

Fourthly, pray and ask the Spirit to increase your love for God. In Galatians 5:22, the first fruit the Spirit produces in us is love. If the fruit of the Spirit is love, then ask the Spirit to generate that fruit in you. Pray and lament over your coldheartedness toward Christ, and ask the Holy Spirit to work a love for Jesus in you. Apply yourself to the means by which He would achieve the growth of that love. Read about Christ. Repent of your sins. Reflect on the love of God for you. This is how the Spirit works the fruit of love in your life.

Fifthly, keep company with those who love God. Hebrews 10:24 says, *"Let us consider one another to provoke unto love and to good works."* When I am around people who love God, it helps me love

God. When I am around people who are in love with Jesus and it flows out of them in their speech and actions, it makes me love Jesus too!

Sixthly, attend the Lord's Supper. You can increase your love for Jesus by participating in the Lord's Supper. Here, our love for Him is enflamed as we remember His past work of saving us from our sins, His present work of preserving us in grace, and His future work when He comes again to glorify us and deliver us from sin forever. The Lord's Supper is a place where our love for the Lord is renewed and refreshed and reignited.

Seventhly, we can increase our love for Christ by loving our brethren. Matthew 25:40 says, *"Inasmuch as ye have done it unto the least of these my brethren, ye have done it unto me."* When I love you and you love me, we are loving Jesus. As you engage in acts of love, the feelings of love follow.

This, then, is the correction Jesus gives. The charge is this: "You have grown cold in your love toward Me." The remedy is this: "Heed this warning to remember from whence you were fallen, and repent and do the first works." If you do those seven things just mentioned, it will reignite your love for the Lord Jesus, and it will enable you to do those first works of affection that you had toward Him, before you got so wrapped up in the battle for moral and doctrinal purity that you forgot the person you were doing it for.

It is like the married man who goes to work and finds it miserable and hard; he has nasty customers to deal with, he has an obnoxious boss, and he has annoying coworkers. He inwardly asks Himself: "Why am I doing this?" And then he thinks of his wife: "I am doing it for her. That makes it all worthwhile." Why do we strive for moral purity in the church? Why do we strive for doctrinal purity in the church? It is for Him. And if we ever let the "Him" diminish, and just get involved with the activities, we run into the danger of heartless dead orthodoxy.

Thirdly, notice the warning. The warning is in verse 5b: *"or else I will come unto thee quickly, and will remove thy candlestick out of its place, [unless you] repent."*

The candlestick represents the church because the church is intended by Christ to be the light of the world. By the way we live and teach we shed light on the world.

But if the central focus of the church is not love for Jesus Christ, then it has ceased to shed light. No matter how morally pure you are, no matter how doctrinally straight you are, if people walk in the door and do not see Jesus Christ and a love for Him, then the church is really not shedding any light. A tree that does not bear fruit gets chopped down. A church that does not have a love for Christ is a church that has ceased to bear light. The warning Jesus gives to the church is this: Your witness will be extinguished. The church will cease to exist.

Sound doctrine without a sincere love for Christ is an empty intellectualism and a dead orthodoxy and a useless witness. What good is doctrine if it doesn't lead us to love Christ? Without loving Christ and His people, all we have is a vain formalism. All we have is a dead orthodoxy. Doing the work of God, upholding the truth of God, maintaining the morality of God while devoid of loving affection for God is like sounding brass and a tinkling cymbal—much noise about nothing. If I understand all mysteries and have all knowledge and have not love, I am nothing. We have to speak the truth, but we had better speak it in love, or it is worthless.

The Conclusion of the Letter

The conclusion of the letter is in verse 7: *"He that hath an ear, let him hear what the Spirit saith unto the churches; To him that overcometh will I give to eat of the tree of life, which is in the midst of the paradise of God."*

There are two elements to this conclusion. First of all, there is the exhortation given in verse 7a: *"He that hath an ear, let him hear what the Spirit saith unto the churches."* God is speaking here. The question is, are we listening?

Sometimes when my mind is on something else and my wife says something to me, it just goes in one ear and out the other. I heard the sounds and I knew she was talking to me, but I ignored her because I was focused on what I was doing, and I did not want to turn my attention away from it to hear what she had to say. When I was done, I asked, "Now what did you say?" I was not actually listening when she had spoken.

We do that to people all the time. We must never do it to Christ. When we read His Word, we need to give it focused and undivided attention. When we hear His Word preached in church, we need to give it focused and undivided attention. It does no good to hear the sound of good preaching if we are inattentive. It does no good to spend time reading the words of Scripture if our mind is off somewhere else.

This is a personal challenge from Christ to each of us, for every one of us to take heed how we hear. To him that has a hearing ear, more shall be given. But to him that does not, it shall be taken away, even that which he seems to have. It is amazing to me how people who really do not listen, even though they are exposed to the truth, wind up knowing less of it and following less of it as the years go by. They can sit under the best preaching and they can read the Bible every day, but if they are not hearing it does them no good. In fact, it just hardens them in sin because their very familiarity with the truth breeds contempt for it.

The question is this: When the Word is brought to us, will we listen to it carefully? Will we meditate on it thoughtfully? Will we act upon it zealously? Will we remember it faithfully? The Spirit speaks to the heart through the Word and the preaching and the message of Jesus. Let us not quench Him, and let us not grieve Him.

Take note of one very important thing. Verse 7 says, *"He that hath an ear, let him hear what the Spirit says."* But in verse 1, it is Jesus who is speaking. The point is, the words of the Spirit and the words of Jesus are made equivalent. This is because Their persons are equivalent in terms of Their deity. They share the same divine essence. Jesus is the word, but the Spirit is the one who inspires the word so it can be written down, illuminates the word so it can be understood, and brings the word to remembrance so it can be applied. The Spirit plays a huge role in conveying the words of the Lord Jesus to us. When Jesus speaks, the Spirit is speaking also.

But notice further what it says: *"He that has an ear, let him hear what the Spirit saith unto the churches,"* plural. In other words, this letter is not meant for just this church; it is meant for the other six churches of Asia, and their letters are meant for the church at Ephesus, because every one of these letters uses the plural *"churches"* in the conclusion. This letter is not just for this assembly and nobody else; this letter is also for all the churches of all the centuries between the first and second coming of Jesus.

Secondly, notice the promise made, verse 7b. Here is the promise: *"To him that overcometh will I give to eat of the tree of life, which is in the midst of the paradise of God."* Notice, *"To him"* that overcomes. Here is the person who did not give in to the forces of evil; he overcame them. This does not mean he did not ever sin again or that he was perfect. What it means is that all the days of his life, he fought the good fight of faith and remained faithful to Christ to the end, pursuing the work of loving Jesus, learning about Jesus, and living for Jesus by the grace and mercy of God. In other words, he kept the faith. The overcomer is the conqueror. He fights against sin and the devil and the world, and he perseveres in the battle to the end. He never quits, he never changes sides, and he never goes apostate.

How many people have you known who made a public profession of faith in Christ who were baptized, went to church, learned the doctrine, lived the life, and then grew cold and indifferent? Over the years they quit going to church, they quit reading their Bibles, and they became indistinguishable from the world in the way in which they lived; and, when challenged about this, say things like: "Well, that was my old life, but now I am living the way I think best."

Those people did not overcome; instead, they were overcome. Some people say: "Once saved always saved." They made a profession of faith in Christ, and therefore it does not matter how they live; they are going to heaven. But the Bible knows nothing of such teaching. The Bible says you have to be an overcomer if you are going to make it to heaven. And what do you have to overcome? You have to overcome the temptation to abandon Christ and apostatize from Christ under the pressure of the seductions and persecutions of the world. You have to persevere in loving Christ. That is what it means to be an overcomer. It means you never stop following Christ, loving Christ, serving Christ, and witnessing for Christ. You never stop seeking to learn more of Christ and how to follow Him better and love Him more. Those are the overcomers.

What is this book about? It is about the battle between Christ and Satan, and between Satan's people and Christ's people. The question is, are you going to take the mark of the beast? Are you going to start thinking like the world and acting like the world? Those people were overcome. But those who think like God and act like God and seek to serve God are the overcomers. They overcome the pressure from the world to apostatize from Christ, to move out of the kingdom of light, and move into the kingdom of darkness.

That is the temptation and pressure we have to overcome. If we do, we will get *"to eat of the tree of life, which is in the midst of the paradise of God."* This tree of life is described in Revelation 22:1–2, 14. It is in the new heavens and the new earth.

"And he shewed me a pure river of water of life, clear as crystal, proceeding out of the throne of God and of the Lamb. [2] *In the midst of the street of it, and on either side of the river, was there the tree of life, which bare twelve manner of fruits, and yielded her fruit every month: and the leaves of the tree were for the healing of the nations."* Verse 14: *"Blessed are they that do his commandments, that they may have right to the tree of life, and may enter in through the gates into the city."*

This tree of life is a metaphor for entrance into heaven and the blessings it contains. When He says in Revelation 2:7b, *"To him that overcometh will I give to eat of the tree of life, which is in the midst of the paradise of God,"* He is saying that the one who overcomes gets to enter heaven. That person lives forever in the paradise of God. He is offering them eternal salvation if they overcome the temptation to treat Christianity as dispensable or to make it something they only do from time to time.

Overcoming is something we must fight hard for, labor for, have patience in, persevere in, and do for Jesus' name's sake; all the while loving Him with all our heart and soul and mind and strength. Such a person has genuine faith, and such a person will wind up in the paradise of God. That is the conclusion of the letter. Be an overcomer. Paradise will be your destiny if you are.

The Bible teaches us the doctrine of the perseverance of the saints. It is those who endure to the end that are saved; not those who endure as long as it is easy, but when seduction comes or persecution comes, they throw it overboard for the pleasures of the world or the favor of the world, and thereby deny Christ. Do not go there. That is the message of Revelation.

You are going to read this message repeatedly as we go through this book: Be an overcomer. You are in a spiritual war. You are getting clobbered. But in spite of that, fight the good fight. Keep focused on Christ. Keep loving Him. Stay faithful to Him. Overcome. Heaven will be your reward.

13

The Letter to the Church at Smyrna, Revelation 2:8–11

> "[8] *And unto the angel of the church in Smyrna write; These things saith the first and the last, which was dead, and is alive;*
> [9] *I know thy works, and tribulation, and poverty, (but thou art rich) and I know the blasphemy of them which say they are Jews, and are not, but are the synagogue of Satan.* [10] *Fear none of those things which thou shalt suffer: behold, the devil shall cast some of you into prison, that ye may be tried; and ye shall have tribulation ten days: be thou faithful unto death, and I will give thee a crown of life.* [11] *He that hath an ear, let him hear what the Spirit saith unto the churches; He that overcometh shall not be hurt of the second death.*"

The book of Revelation opens with Christ and His church. In chapter 1, we have the revelation of Jesus Christ as the majestic sovereign over His people, and the victorious Savior of His people. He is portrayed as the powerful ruler and merciful deliverer of all who trust in Him. He is the faithful witness who always speaks the truth. He is the Prince of the kings of the earth who always defeats His enemies. It is this Christ revealed in chapter 1 who speaks to His churches in chapters 2 and 3.

We see in chapters 2 and 3 that Jesus is focused on His churches. He is focused on how they are doing, the struggles they have, the persecutions they endure, the sins they have fallen into, and the virtues they practice. These things are of the most intense concern to Jesus Christ. The church is the kingdom of God on earth. The church represents Christ and His message to the world. The church is Christ's body. The church is Christ's bride. Therefore, the church is at the forefront of Christ's attention and at the center of Christ's affection. Everything Christ is doing in this world revolves around the church; and through it, He is destroying the works of the devil on earth. Therefore, it is no wonder that the churches' condition and conduct are the first thing Christ addresses as He opens this manual of spiritual warfare.

In the last chapter, we said that each of these letters that Christ writes to His churches follows a similar seven-point structure, with a few exceptions:

- first, there is an address to the pastor of each church;
- second, there is a description given of Christ;
- third, there is a commendation of their good works and character, with the exception of the church at Laodicea of whom Jesus has nothing good to say;
- fourth, there is a correction of their sins and defects, except for the churches of Smyrna and Philadelphia about which He has nothing negative to say;
- fifth, there is a warning given to each church, either of the need to repent or the need to reinforce what the people are already doing right and to remain faithful to it;
- sixth, there is an exhortation to hear and heed what the Spirit is saying to the churches;
- seventh, there is a promise of comfort and consolation given to those who overcome the temptation to apostasy.

Therefore, each of these letters has the same outline. First, there is the introduction, consisting of the recipient of the letter and the author of the letter. Second, there is the message, which contains the commendation if any, the correction if any, and the warning to repent or endure or remain faithful. Third, there is the conclusion, which consists of an exhortation and a promise.

This is the outline that we used as we expounded the letter to the church at Ephesus, and it is the same outline we will be using as we proceed through each of these seven letters.

It is useful to note that each of these churches has a unique characteristic. No two of them are the same. Ephesus is the orthodox but coldhearted church. The people had left their first love. Smyrna is the suffering church. Pergamos is the morally compromised church. Thyatira is a church with corrupt leadership. Sardis is the dying church. Philadelphia is the weak church. Laodicea is the lukewarm church.

When we look at these churches, we see they are a mixture of good and bad. As a whole, these churches seem to be in poor spiritual health. They are very much like the churches we see in our day. We look across America, and what condition do we see the churches in? We see that, overall, the Christian churches are compromised in many ways, and, in general, they are in poor spiritual health.

Never were the letters to these seven churches more relevant than they are right now. All of the defects and weaknesses and problems we see in these seven churches we see in the churches in America. These letters are not only relevant to the churches of our day; they are relevant to the particular church we personally attend.

We want to carefully read and listen to the message Christ has to these churches because that is His message to our church. It is our job as a church to ask these questions: Do we have these virtues? Do we have these weaknesses? Are we heeding these warnings? Are we following these exhortations? Do we see Christ in the same way He reveals Himself to be to His churches?

It is important to understand how this book begins and what its frame of reference is. Chapter 1 opens with Christ, chapters 2 and 3 present His church, and in chapters 4 and 5 we see God enthroned in heaven. Only after that are we going to look out and see what is happening in the world in chapter 6 and following. These first five chapters set the stage and provide the framework from which all that happens in the world is to be viewed. Christ, His church, and the enthroned God are the starting point and the ending point of all that occurs in this book. All that Satan and his helpers do is merely a subtext and a failure as Christ and His people triumph over them.

Let us now examine the letter to the church at Smyrna, a suffering church, and a church for which Christ has no criticism to offer; rather, there is only an encouragement, a warning, an exhortation, and a wonderful promise.

The Introduction to the Letter

The introduction to the letter of Smyrna is in verse 8: *"And unto the angel of the church in Smyrna write; These things saith the first and the last, which was dead, and is alive."* In verse 8, we are told who the recipient and author of this letter is.

First of all, the recipient of this letter is the pastor and the church in Smyrna. It says, *"And unto the angel* (the pastor) *of the church in Smyrna write."*

Smyrna was a town a little north of Ephesus on the west coast of Asia, which is modern-day Turkey. Like Ephesus, Smyrna was a port city. It was noted for its beauty and its pleasant climate. It was especially noted for being a city that was incredibly loyal and faithful to Rome, and it was very zealous in serving the Roman government. They had temples to Roma, which was the spirit of the kingdom of Rome. It was a city that was very much in favor of the Roman Empire.

We do not know for sure because we are not explicitly told, but it is highly probable that the church at Smyrna was founded by Paul during his third missionary journey sometime between AD 53 and 56, while he was at Ephesus. Acts 19 describes the two-year ministry of Paul in Ephesus, and we are told in Acts 19:10 that during that time *"all they which dwelt in Asia heard the word of the Lord Jesus, both Jews and Greeks."*

These two cities of Ephesus and Smyrna were only about thirty miles apart. Therefore, during the two years Paul was there, in which it says *"all they which dwelt in Asia heard the word of the Lord,"* Paul may very well have led missionary efforts to reach Smyrna for Christ.

It is also highly probable that, at the time this letter was written to Smyrna, Polycarp was the pastor of the church. We know that Polycarp was a disciple of the apostle John. We know that John was an elder in the church at Ephesus after his exile in Patmos ended. Therefore, we can learn something about the conditions in Smyrna by reading the early church fathers' writings about this man Polycarp. Polycarp was burned at the stake by the Roman government in AD 155.

William Hendrickson in his book *More Than Conquerors* relates this record of Polycarp's martyrdom:

> He had been asked to say, "Caesar is Lord," but he refused. Brought to the stadium, the proconsul urged him, saying, "Swear, and I will set thee at liberty, reproach Christ." Polycarp answered, "Eighty and six years have I served Him, and He never did me any injury: how then can I blaspheme my King and my Savior?" When the proconsul again pressed him, the old man answered, "Since thou art vainly urgent that. . . I should swear by the fortune of Caesar, and pretendest not to know who and what I am, hear me declare with boldness,

> I am a Christian. . ." A little later, the proconsul answered, "I have wild beasts at hand; to these will I cast thee, except thou repent. I will cause thee to be consumed by fire, seeing that thou despisest the wild beasts if thou will not repent." But Polycarp said, "Thou threatenest me with fire which burneth for an hour, and after a little is extinguished, but art ignorant of the fire of the coming judgment and of eternal punishment, reserved for the ungodly. But why tarriest thou? Bring forth what thou wilt." Soon afterwards, the people began to gather wood and faggots; the Jews especially, according to custom, eagerly assisting them. Thus Polycarp was burned at the stake.[4]

Polycarp says he was eighty-six years old. We know he was burned in AD 155, which means that he would have been about twenty-five or twenty-six years of age when Revelation was written in the mid-90s. This tells us what conditions were like among the cities and provinces that were zealously loyal to Rome, and who desired to make it known to Caesar they were loyal to Rome by compelling every citizen to acknowledge that Caesar was lord.

Persecution against Christians was not uniform across every area and every city; but in Smyrna, the people were zealous for Rome and therefore they were zealous in persecuting Christians in order to show their loyalty to Caesar. They wanted every citizen to acknowledge Caesar as lord. The Christians' refusal to do this resulted in their being severely persecuted by the Roman authorities in Smyrna.

Notice secondly, the author of the letter. The author of the letter is Christ, who identifies Himself with two titles in verse 8. He says He is the first and the last, and He is the one who was dead and is now alive.

These descriptions Christ gives of Himself to each church are especially suited to the needs of that particular church, and to any other church that is in the same situation as that church was. Jesus identified Himself by one set of titles to the church at Ephesus, another set of titles to the church at Smyrna, yet another set of titles to the church at Pergamos, and so on. We need to pay attention to what Jesus says of Himself in verse 8 when He says, "*These things saith the first and the last, which was dead, and is alive.*" Those titles have relevance to

4 William Hendriksen. *More Than Conquerors: An Interpretation of the Book of Revelation*. Grand Rapids: Baker, 1962. 64.

what was going on in the church at Smyrna.

First of all, He identifies Himself as the first and the last. When this term was first introduced to us as applying to Christ in Revelation 1:11, we saw that this term *"first and last"* was drawn out of the Old Testament and is used repeatedly as a title and name for Jehovah in the book of Isaiah. We saw that Jesus is Jehovah, the God of the Old Testament.

It is Christ, not Rome, who is the supreme authority over the world and the nations and all the people within them. Rome is not the first to come, and Rome will not be the last to go. Rome began in time, and Rome will end in time. But Christ is before all time, and Christ outlasts all time. He is truly the first that has ever been, and He is the last that will ever be, and He has all authority over all things that occur between the first and the last.

The first thing Jesus reminds the church at Smyrna of is that He is greater than Rome, He is sovereign over Rome, He was before Rome, and He will outlast Rome. He is the God of the Old Testament. As a result, He gave Rome its beginning and he will determine Rome's end; and then it will be gone, but He will remain forever. Therefore, the believers at Smyrna should not fear what Rome would do to them; but instead, have faith in what Christ would do for them. It is not Rome but Christ they should reverence and rejoice in and worship as God.

This is the first title by which Jesus identifies Himself: He identifies Himself as the first and the last, and therefore as the sovereign God over all kingdoms and all persecutors.

Secondly, He identifies Himself as He *"which was dead, and is alive."* This phrase was also taken out of Revelation 1. Notice verses 17b and 18: *"Fear not; I am the first and the last: [18]I am he that liveth, and was dead; and, behold, I am alive for evermore, Amen; and have the keys of hell and of death."*

Once again, we see Jesus going back to chapter 1 and drawing on the attributes that were revealed of Him and then using them to bring comfort and guidance and instruction to His churches. Jesus is reminding this suffering church that is experiencing martyrdom at the hands of Rome that they do not need to fear being put to death for their refusal to acknowledge Caesar as lord.

Death is not a problem for the believer because it is a condition that is easily remedied by Jesus Christ. He has defeated death, He has raised Himself from the grave; and therefore, He will defeat our death and He will raise every believer from the grave as well. Let the wicked threaten us with death. Let them put us to death. It is not a problem because Christ will simply raise us from the dead!

We are told by Jesus in Luke 12:4, *"And I say unto you my friends, Be not afraid of them that kill the body, and after that have no more that they can do."* They can kill you? No problem. Do not be afraid of that.

It is as if somebody issued this threat to you: "I am going to come over to your house and go out in your yard and grab some stems of your grass and snap them off!" That is not a problem, is it? You can grow more grass. You would not worry about that kind of a threat. Therefore, if the wicked come and say, "I am going to come and snap your life out of existence," it is as if Jesus is saying, "No problem. I will just bring your life back. Do not be concerned about their threats."

Jesus says in John 11:25, *"I am the resurrection, and the life: he that believeth in me, though he were dead, yet shall he live."* So yes, you are going to die. But that is a temporary, solvable problem. You are going to be brought back to life. Rome does not have the final authority over your person. Rome does not have the final authority over your life. Jesus says, in effect, "I am the first and the last. I am He who was dead and am alive. I am sovereign over Rome and I am sovereign over death; and therefore, fear neither Rome nor death when you see who I am. Rome is not a problem. Death is not a problem."

Whatever suffering Christ ordains for believers to endure at the hands of wicked men, whether imprisonment or death, it will always end in victory and triumph over their persecutors because He is the one who opens the prison and He is the one who raises the dead.

The Message of the Letter

The message of the letter is in verses 9 and 10: *"I know thy works, and tribulation, and poverty, (but thou art rich) and I know the blasphemy of them which say they are Jews, and are not, but are the synagogue of Satan.* [10] *Fear none of those things which thou shalt suffer: behold, the devil shall cast some of you into prison, that ye may be tried; and ye shall have tribulation ten days: be thou faithful unto death, and I will give thee a crown of life."*

First of all, notice the commendation. Jesus says in verse 9, *"I know."* Jesus is saying, "I am completely aware and fully acquainted with everything that goes on in the church at Smyrna, and indeed, in every church. Nothing escapes My notice or knowledge."

He goes on to say in verse 9, *"I know thy works"*; that is, the good deeds in obedience to my commands that you have carried out. "You have sought to observe and carry out all I instructed you to do. I have seen your service and obedience to Me and I approve of all you have accomplished. I know the hard work you have done, and that you have done it for My name's sake."

He also knows their *"tribulation."* He says, "I know the oppression and afflictions and distress and persecutions you have endured. I understand the trouble and anguish you are experiencing. I know the pressures you face and the crushing burdens that you bear. I am fully acquainted with every one of them in every detail."

He also knows their *"poverty."* He knew that these people were very poor and destitute regarding material things. Why were they so poor in a very wealthy, rich, and economically vibrant city? Smyrna was a rival to Ephesus in terms of economic prosperity and activity. Perhaps they were poor because of their refusal to join the pagan trade guilds that required the worship of pagan gods in order to be members. If you were not part of the guild, you could not do business in that trade. Perhaps they were poor because their persecutors had robbed them of their goods or seized those goods through force, fraud, or fines.

In Hebrews 10:34, the writer says regarding the Hebrew Christians that they *"took joyfully the spoiling of your goods, knowing in yourselves that ye have in heaven a better and an enduring substance."* These people were poor, but it was not because they did not work or were not frugal or did not strive to accumulate something, but because the persecution was robbing them of their wealth.

But notice what is said in parenthesis in Revelation 2:9. Jesus says: "I know your poverty," *"(but thou art rich.)"* Christ saw they had immense treasure laid up in heaven as a result of their good works. They also possessed the unsearchable riches of Christ Himself. They had the true riches of salvation, and they had a reward that would last for eternity. Therefore, it mattered not if they had little of the temporary riches that are soon going to pass away, and which will certainly be left behind at death. Though they were poverty-stricken materially, they were wealthy spiritually.

Recall the story of the rich man and Lazarus. The rich man was clothed in purple and fine linen and fared sumptuously every day. Lazarus lay at his gate in rags, covered with sores on his body, and desired to eat the crumbs that fell from the rich man's table.

From a human point of view, the rich man was rich and Lazarus was poor. But from a spiritual point of view, the rich man was poor and Lazarus was rich. We see this after their deaths, where the rich man does not have any asset base at all. He does not own even a drop of water. But here is Lazarus sitting in Abraham's bosom possessing all things in the heavens. From the world's point of view, the people in Smyrna were way below the poverty line, but God says they are all billionaires in spiritual wealth.

Jesus not only knew about their works and their tribulation and their poverty and their true spiritual riches; Jesus also knew something else: He knew the identity and the activity of their persecutors. He knew their character and conduct. Notice what He says in the latter part of verse 9: *"I know the blasphemy of them which say they are Jews, and are not, but are the synagogue of Satan."*

From time to time, we have Islamic terror bombings, and the police go on searches and interrogate people to try to find the perpetrators. Jesus does not need to do that. He already knows exactly who did everything. When someone does something to us, He knows who it is and what that person did. He knows his identity and his conduct. He will deal with that person in due time.

Jesus identifies these persecutors as Jews. The Jews who lived in Smyrna were in political confederacy with the Romans in the persecution of Christians. It is a historical fact that Judaism was a recognized and protected religion under Roman rule; and because of that, the Romans did not require the Jews to say, "Caesar is lord," but everybody else had to do it. The Jews saw the Christians leading Jews to Christ and they hated that. Therefore, they became confederates with the Roman government in turning the Christians in to the authorities so they would be imprisoned and martyred. The Jews claimed to be the people of God; but, in fact, they were serving Satan as they informed on the Christians to the Roman authorities, just like they were serving Satan when they informed on Jesus to the Roman authorities and persuaded them to crucify Him.

In Revelation 12:10 it says, *"And I heard a loud voice saying in heaven, Now is come salvation, and strength, and the kingdom of our God, and the power of his Christ: for the accuser of our brethren is cast down, which accused them before our God day and night.*" Satan is the great accuser of the brethren. Therefore, when a Jew accuses the brethren, he is doing the work of Satan. Anyone who attacks and assaults Christians, and anyone who persecutes them or facilitates their persecution is a servant of Satan. That is why Jesus said to the Jews who persecuted Him in John 8:44, that "*Ye are of your father the devil, and the lusts of your father ye will do. He was a murderer from the beginning, and abode not in the truth, because there is no truth in him. When he speaketh a lie, he speaketh of his own: for he is a liar, and the father of it.*"

Persecutors lie about who you are and what you did, and then they kill you based on those lies. That is why these Jews were said to be of the synagogue of Satan; they were doing Satan's work in and through their synagogues in informing on the Christians, lying about them, and then causing them to be murdered.

We see Paul in Acts 26:9–10 describing how he did this. When he is giving his testimony about his past life, he says: "*I verily thought with myself, that I ought to do many things contrary to the name of Jesus of Nazareth.* [10] *. . .and many of the saints did I shut up in prison, having received authority from the chief priests; and when they were put to death, I gave my voice against them.*" Paul lied about the Christians and had them put to death. He was doing the work of Satan. He was of the synagogue of Satan. But then the grace and mercy of God saved him, and he became part of the synagogue of Christ. Wonder of wonders!

Those who reject the Savior and those who persecute believers are no longer the people of God. People think the Jews in the Middle East are the chosen people of God. They are not. They are the discovenanted people of God (Matthew 21:43, 1 Peter 2:9–10); the true Jews are those who are born of the Jew, Jesus Christ, via the new birth, as it says in Galatians 3:29: "*And if ye be Christ's, then are ye Abraham's seed, and heirs according to the promise.*" Who are the descendants of Abraham? Abraham begot Jesus and Jesus begot us through the new birth, and therefore we are the new Judaism. The Christians are the synagogue of Christ, and they are the new nation of Israel.

Romans 2:28–29 says, "*For he is not a Jew, which is one outwardly; neither is that circumcision, which is outward in the flesh:* [29] *But he is a Jew, which is one inwardly; and circumcision is that of the heart, in the spirit, and not in the letter; whose praise is not of men, but of*

God." If you are regenerate and therefore have a circumcised heart, the Bible says you are a Jew; and those who are circumcised in their bodies but not in their hearts are specifically said to not be Jews.

In John 16:2 it says, *"They shall put you out of the synagogues: yea, the time cometh, that whosoever killeth you will think that he doeth God service."* The Jews thought they were serving God. Paul thought he was serving God by casting the Christians out of the synagogue and by putting them to death. The Muslims think they are serving Allah by slaughtering the infidels—that is, anyone who is a non-Muslim. It has always been the case that people in the name of some god they claim to be serving are killing the true people of God.

Jesus knew all about this. He says: "I know their identity, their activity, their character, and their conduct." Our enemies are known to Christ, and He will deal very severely with them in due time. Since they are serving Satan, they will share in Satan's place in the lake of fire under the wrath of God.

His commendation to these people is this: I know your works. I know the service you have done. I know your tribulation. I know the persecutions you have suffered. I know your poverty, and how your finances have been ravaged. I know your enemies, every one of them.

Secondly, notice His warning. Because there is no correction, we are skipping that point. His warning is in verse 10: *"Fear none of those things which thou shalt suffer: behold, the devil shall cast some of you into prison, that ye may be tried; and ye shall have tribulation ten days: be thou faithful unto death, and I will give thee a crown of life."*

The warning in verse 10 is this: Do not be overcome by fear when you are suffering these persecutions as though I have forsaken you or am unwilling to protect and deliver you. We need to understand that no one may harm us without God's permission, but our passage is clear that it is God's permissive will for the wicked to do many terrible things to us. It is God's will that His people suffer affliction and imprisonment and even martyrdom. He allows Satan and his people to do terrible things to us. Why? The middle of verse 10 tells us. It is *"that ye may be tried."* It is for the purpose that you might be put to the test.

Do you know why God allows persecution in our lives and why He allows the wicked to do terrible things to us? Because persecution is the trial that proves the reality of our faith or the lack thereof. Only those with genuine faith will endure persecution rather than deny Christ. Hebrews 12:7 says, *"If ye endure chastening, God dealeth with you as sons."* Endurance under chastening is the proof of sonship.

God has one Son without sin, but He has no sons without suffering. Every one of God's sons suffers because it is through suffering that the reality and the genuineness of our faith is proven. When suffering comes, the thorny-ground hearer and the rocky-ground hearer are choked out and wither up and disappear. But the good-ground hearers continue to grow and serve and follow Christ and keep on bringing forth fruit.

Suffering proves the reality of your faith. When suffering comes, those who do not have genuine faith will abandon Christ rather than endure the suffering. In contrast, those who have genuine faith continue to cling to Christ even though it means enduring suffering. By that endurance, the reality of our salvation and our love for Christ is demonstrated.

It goes on to say in verse 10 that this persecution and suffering is going to last ten days. He says, *"and ye shall have tribulation ten days."* This does not mean ten literal days. "Ten" conveys the concept of perfection.

He is saying that this persecution will neither be too short nor too long; rather, this persecution will last the perfect length of time that is needed to fully prove the character and faith of the believers and to perfectly accomplish the purposes of God in allowing it to come to pass.

Jesus is telling His people: "I know you are suffering. I see it. Recognize that you are going to suffer further, and I am going to allow it."

Jesus' gospel is a gospel of suffering. We get very upset when we suffer. We need to realize suffering is part of the plan, and we suffer the perfect length of time and to the perfect degree of distress in order to perfectly prove the legitimacy of our faith and to perfectly accomplish the purposes of God in allowing it. Suffering is certain, but suffering is limited to the perfect measure, to the perfect degree, and to the perfect length of time.

God says to the people at Smyrna: "Remain faithful, even to the point of death." Notice the last part of verse 10. He says, *"be thou faithful unto death, and I will give thee a crown of life."* "Remain faithful, even if it costs you your life. Do not be faithful until the pain gets to be so much and then cave in and apostatize and abandon

Christ and worship Caesar as lord. Sacrifice your life rather than deny Christ."

The reward for faithfulness to Christ under persecution is the crown of life. This is the crown that was given to the victor in the Olympic Games. It is the victor's crown. The reward for faithfulness to Christ under persecution is the victor's crown, which is resurrection to eternal life.

Jesus said in Matthew 10:39, *"He . . .that loseth his life for my sake shall find it."* This is why the sufferings of this present time are not worthy to be compared with the glory that shall be revealed in us. We have a little suffering, but what do we obtain when we faithfully endure it? We obtain the crown of everlasting life. However, where there is no cross of suffering, there will be no crown of victory. That is why when the crosses come, we take them up daily and carry them. We do not rid ourselves of them by conforming ourselves to the world; we endure them knowing they are temporary, but the crown of life is eternal.

The Conclusion of the Letter

The conclusion of the letter is in verse 11, *"He that hath an ear, let him hear what the Spirit saith unto the churches; He that overcometh shall not be hurt of the second death."*

First of all, notice the exhortation given. It is the same one in every single letter, said in the same way, with the same words. It says, *"He that hath an ear, let him hear what the Spirit saith unto the churches,"* (churches: plural). This letter is not just for those in Smyrna, but for all churches of all time in all places that are experiencing any kind of suffering. It is for them as well. Christ is speaking in this letter to us through the Holy Spirit.

As you read this letter, the Spirit uses this letter to speak to your heart. Listen to it carefully. Reflect on it thoughtfully. Act on it zealously. Do not let what you hear go in one ear and out the other. Spend a lot of time thinking about what you heard, reflecting on what you heard, and applying what you heard to your life. That is the exhortation given.

Secondly, the promise made is in verse 11b, *"He that overcometh shall not be hurt of the second death."* What does overcoming look like? It looks like what Polycarp did when the proconsul said to him:

"I have fire, and I have lions. Deny Christ, worship Caesar, and I will let you go. If you do not, I will throw you to the lions and burn you at the stake." Polycarp said: "Do what you will. Bring it on. I am not denying Christ. I am a Christian." He overcame the proconsul.

Polycarp overcame because he triumphed over the temptation to deny Christ. The proconsul was powerless to triumph over him in getting him to deny Christ. Polycarp was powerful in overcoming the proconsul and maintaining his faith in Christ.

That is what overcoming looks like. Overcomers will not deny Christ, no matter what persecutors do to them. It says to those who do not compromise truth and obedience to escape poverty—who do not deny Christ to escape imprisonment and death, who remain faithful to Christ to the end—that not only will they have a crown of eternal life as verse 10 says, but they will also escape *"the second death"* as verse 11 says.

Revelation tells us what the second death is. Revelation 20:6 says, *"Blessed and holy is he that hath part in the first resurrection: on such the second death hath no power, but they shall be priests of God and of Christ, and shall reign with him a thousand years."* Revelation 20:14 says, *"And death and hell were cast into the lake of fire. This is the second death."* The second death is the lake of fire. Notice verse 15: *"And whosoever was not found written in the book of life was cast into the lake of fire."*

Notice Revelation 21:8. After talking about those who were saved in verse 7, and saying of them, *"I will be his God, and he shall be my son,"* He says in verse 8, *"But the fearful, and unbelieving, and the abominable, and murderers, and whoremongers, and sorcerers, and idolaters, and all liars, shall have their part in the lake which burneth with fire and brimstone: which is the second death."*

Jesus is telling the believers at Smyrna that if they overcome this temptation to apostatize, they will never wind up in the lake of fire. Not only will they have the crown of eternal life, but they will also escape any possibility of ever being in the lake of fire.

The lake of fire is the second death. The first death is when you die physically. We all go through the first death (except Enoch and Elijah and those few who are alive at the second coming of Christ). But the second death is when you die eternally after the final judgment when you are cast into everlasting, conscious torment in the lake of fire.

The first death is not to be feared. It can be overcome by regeneration, by redemption, and by resurrection. Jesus has the keys to hell and death. The point is, the first death is not to be feared; it is remedied by resurrection. But the second death is to be feared above all else because it is irreparable and unchangeable; it is eternal and irreversible; and for it, there is no remedy forever.

This is the reason we read in Hebrews 10:32–39, *"But call to remembrance the former days, in which, after ye were illuminated, ye endured a great fight of afflictions;* [33] *Partly, whilst ye were made a gazingstock both by reproaches and afflictions; and partly, whilst ye became companions of them that were so used.* [34] *For ye had compassion of me in my bonds, and took joyfully the spoiling of your goods knowing in yourselves that ye have in heaven a better and an enduring substance."* In heaven are the real riches, and those are the riches we live for.

Verse 35: *"Cast not away therefore your confidence"* (in Christ) *"which hath great recompence of reward.* [36] *For ye have need of patience, that, after ye have done the will of God, ye might receive the promise"* (the promise of eternal life and deliverance from the second death).

Verse 37: *"For yet a little while, and he that shall come will come, and will not tarry."* Jesus is going to return. How do we live in the meantime? Verse 38: *"Now the just shall live by faith:"* (they will believe the promises and act on them as though they are true) *"but if any man draw back,"* (here is the one who does not overcome, but who is overcome by the persecutors, and therefore denies Christ) *"my soul shall have no pleasure in him,* [39] *But we"* (we real Christians) *"are not of them who draw back"* which leads *"unto perdition;"* (the second death), but we are *"of them that believe to the saving of the soul."*

Both Jesus and the author of the book of Hebrews are saying: "I know your suffering. I know your poverty. I know the pain you are going through because you are being faithful to Me. You keep on being faithful, and in the end, you will have eternal life and you will escape hell. Suffering is temporary, but glory is eternal. Why would you trade a little relief from a little bit of suffering now, to have no relief from infinite suffering forever?"

Paul says in Romans 8:18 *"That the sufferings of this present time are not worthy to be compared with the glory that shall be revealed in us."* The greatest suffering any human has ever had on the face of this earth is nothing compared to the least suffering that any soul has in the lake of fire.

Therefore, do not escape temporal suffering by denying Christ, and thus make yourself liable to eternal suffering. Rather, be faithful to Christ now, knowing this suffering will end. These light afflictions are but for a moment, but they are going to work a far more exceeding and eternal weight of glory. It is that eternal glory for which we live, and by saving faith we know it is true and real, and therefore we endure.

We do what Jesus said to the people of Smyrna: "*Be thou faithful unto death.*" Just be faithful! That is the call. He is not saying you have to do some spectacular thing. "Just keep on believing in Me, no matter how they abuse you, keep on serving me, no matter how they persecute you, and I will reward you beyond your wildest dreams. But do not give up. Keep pressing on." May Christ give us the grace and strength to do so.

14

The Letter to the Church at Pergamos, Revelation 2:12–17

> "12 *And to the angel of the church in Pergamos write; These things saith he which hath the sharp sword with two edges;* 13 *I know thy works, and where thou dwellest, even where Satan's seat is: and thou holdest fast my name, and hast not denied my faith, even in those days wherein Antipas was my faithful martyr, who was slain among you, where Satan dwelleth.* 14 *But I have a few things against thee, because thou hast there them that hold the doctrine of Balaam, who taught Balak to cast a stumblingblock before the children of Israel, to eat things sacrificed unto idols, and to commit fornication.* 15 *So hast thou also them that hold the doctrine of the Nicolaitans, which thing I hate.* 16 *Repent; or else I will come unto thee quickly, and will fight against them with the sword of my mouth.* 17 *He that hath an ear, let him hear what the Spirit saith unto the churches; To him that overcometh will I give to eat of the hidden manna, and will give him a white stone, and in the stone a new name written, which no man knoweth saving he that receiveth it.*"

This is the third letter Christ sent to the churches in what is now modern-day Turkey. These letters express the concern Christ has for His church. Jesus is not indifferent to what goes on in His churches, neither is He ignorant of what happens within them. He is fully aware of all that occurs to them and all they do. In these letters, He addresses their conduct, their needs, and their challenges; and He offers them both direction and comfort in the conduct of their spiritual warfare.

These letters not only express the concern Christ has for His churches; they also show the centrality churches have in the plan of Christ for building His kingdom on earth. Local churches are central in the battle to defeat the kingdom of Satan, and the kingdom of God grows as the number of local churches grows. The kingdom succeeds as local churches are faithful in their witness and worship. The kingdom triumphs as local churches overcome sin and grow in holiness and obedience to Christ.

The point is simply this: The triumph of Christ over Satan is carried out in the world through the local churches. Through them, He defeats the kingdom of darkness and builds the kingdom of light. Therefore, our hearts should be focused where Christ's heart is focused: on the building and blessing and obedience of our own local church. The church is where Christ's concern is focused, and that is where our concern should be focused as well. Let us hear what Christ has to say to the church at Pergamos.

The Introduction to the Letter

The introduction of the letter is contained in verse 12, *"And to the angel of the church in Pergamos write; These things saith he which hath the sharp sword with two edges."* Here in verse 12, we are told who the recipient and the author of the letter is.

First of all, notice the recipient of the letter. The recipient of the letter is the pastor and the church at Pergamos. The angel of the church at Pergamos is the messenger of Christ who is the pastor of that church.

Pergamos was located about fifty-five miles northeast of Smyrna. Ephesus is in the southwest corner of Turkey, Smyrna is about thirty miles above it, and Pergamos is about fifty-five miles north and east, inland from Smyrna.

Pergamos was the capital of the province of Asia, and being fifteen miles inland from the coast, it had no advantages in terms of trade. Its attraction and importance lay in its library. The library at Pergamos contained more than 200,000 parchment scrolls. In fact, our word "parchment" is derived from the name of this city Pergamos. Pergamos was a center of great humanistic scholarship and learning.

Furthermore, it was also the most fanatical in its devotion to emperor worship, and it had a temple in it dedicated to Rome in 29 BC. It even added a second and then a third temple dedicated to Caesar worship. It was the principal center of the imperial cult of Caesar worship in this part of the world.

The city was known for its zeal in the worship of other gods as well. Not only were there temples dedicated to the worship of Zeus and Dionysus and Athena, but this city also placed a special focus on the worship of the god Asclepius. Asclepius was the serpent god, and was considered to be the god of healing. The image of this serpent was displayed throughout the city.

This god was worshiped under the image of a serpent, which, to believers in Christ, is the very image of Satan himself. We know that Satan appeared as a serpent in Genesis 3:1–15 and tempted Eve and Adam into the fall which plunged all of humanity into sin. Indeed, in Revelation 12:9 it speaks of Satan as that *"great dragon. . .that old serpent, called the Devil, and Satan, which deceives the whole world."* In Revelation 20:2, it speaks of the fact that the angel *"laid hold on the dragon, that old serpent, which is the Devil, and Satan, and bound him a thousand years."*

This god Asclepius was a representation of Satan himself. This is what Christ may have been referring to when He said in verse 13, that Pergamos was the place where Satan's throne is. The image of this satanic serpent that represented this false god Asclepius was set up everywhere.

This city of Pergamos was filled with the arrogance of humanistic learning, it was focused on a satanic serpent god, and it was fanatical in its Caesar worship. Because it was the political capital of Asia, it had to keep favor with Rome, and it did so by demanding that all its people offer incense to the image of Caesar and proclaim that Caesar was lord.

Here in this city, Satan had free reign and control over the government and the people. He demanded that his chief ally, Caesar, be worshiped by all, and that his own image of a serpent be displayed throughout the entire city.

We know from our study in the last chapter that there was a synagogue of Satan in Smyrna, but the throne of Satan was in Pergamos. Satan's influence was so powerful in this city that he virtually ruled it. The people did his will and spread his teaching in education, in government, and in its religious life and symbols. The library, the government, and the religion of this city were all satanic. All seven cities referred to in these seven letters in the book of Revelation were pagan, but Pergamos was the worst of them all.

This is the recipient of the letter: It is the pastor and the church at

Pergamos. This tells you the adverse environment in which this church existed and functioned.

Secondly, notice the author of the letter. The author of the letter is Jesus Christ, who here characterizes Himself in verse 12 as He "*which hath the sharp sword with two edges.*"

Once again, this symbolic imagery is taken from chapter 1. In verse 16 when John is describing his vision of Christ he says: "*And he had in his right hand seven stars: and out of his mouth went a sharp twoedged sword: and his countenance was as the sun shineth in his strength.*"

When we looked at the symbolic imagery of the sharp two-edged sword going out of the mouth of Jesus, we saw that this sword represented the power of the Word of God as it is used to do spiritual warfare against the powers of darkness. The powers of darkness are driven by Satan, and the powers of darkness are both outside and inside the church.

Outside the church, Rome is the power of darkness, persecuting and slaughtering believers like Antipas who will not worship Caesar as lord. Inside the church, the false teachers are the power of darkness, who seduce the believers into sinful and immoral behavior like the Nicolaitans did, and like those who had the doctrine of Balaam.

Jesus presents Himself to this church as He who has the sharp sword with two edges because He is going to go to war against the enemies of the church at Pergamos, against those that are outside the church and those that are inside the church.

The Bible tells us something about this sword. In Hebrews 4:12–13 we read, "*For the word of God is quick, and powerful, and sharper than any twoedged sword, piercing even to the dividing asunder of soul and spirit, and of the joints and marrow, and is a discerner of the thoughts and intents of the heart.* [13] *Neither is there any creature that is not manifest in his sight: but all things are naked and opened unto the eyes of him with whom we have to do.*"

Therefore, this sword that proceeds out of the mouth of Jesus is, first of all, a manifestation of His ability to see and discern everything that everyone does, right down to the very core of his innermost thoughts. No one will be able to hide who he is and what he has done from the piercing vision of the Lord Jesus Christ.

Secondly, Revelation 19:15 tells us that this sword is also a sword of judgment. In Revelation 19:15, we have the picture of the returning

Lord Jesus, and it says, *"And out of his mouth goeth a sharp sword, that with it he should smite the nations: and he shall rule them with a rod of iron: and he treadeth the winepress of the fierceness and wrath of Almighty God."*

This sword is not only a sword of discernment that lays open the truth; it is also a sword of judgment to execute God's wrath on the wicked. No one will be able to escape the sentence of judgment Jesus will pronounce against him. Jesus is saying to the church at Pergamos that we do not need to fear the weapons of our enemies, whether those weapons are persecution or seduction. Instead, our enemies need to fear the sword of Christ, because Christ will utterly defeat all who oppose Him and His people. He is saying to the church at Pergamos: "Is Satan fighting against you? I have a sword, and I am going to fight against him. Be of good comfort!"

The Message of the Letter

This message is contained in verses 13 to 16. In verse 13, Jesus opens with this familiar phrase, *"I know."* He introduces His message to every single one of these churches with those two words, *"I know."*

Christ is saying that He pays full attention to each local church. He is fully acquainted with everything that occurs within those churches. He knows their virtues. He knows their struggles. He knows their challenges. He knows every individual within them, and He knows their spiritual condition and conduct. He is intimately acquainted with every detail of the life of every local church, and He cares deeply about what each church does and what goes on in each of them.

Jesus knows what goes on in our own church. He knows our virtues and our vices. He knows our victories and our struggles. He cares about us deeply and He loves us intensely. Jesus could say about every local church that has ever existed: *"I know."*

Notice what He knows about the church at Pergamos.

First of all, we see His commendation in verse 13. He says, *"I know thy works, and where thou dwellest, even where Satan's seat is."* I know that *"thou holdest fast my name, and hast not denied my faith, even in those days wherein Antipas was my faithful martyr, who was slain among you."* I know all those things happened *"where Satan dwelleth."* I know about all of those things.

In His commendation He says, first of all, *"I know thy works."* He is saying: "I know the service you have rendered to Me. I have seen your good works, I have seen your obedience, I have observed your labor, and I have witnessed your sacrifice to bring Me glory and expand My kingdom. Your good works, church of Pergamos, have been fully taken note of."

Secondly, He says, "I know where you dwell," *"even where Satan's seat is."* The word here for "seat" in the original language is the word "throne," and the idea is that these believers are living in an extremely difficult location. They are living in a location where Satan is enthroned. This means that Satan has full sway over the populace of this city. The people are sold out to his evil values and evil conduct, and the culture is saturated with wickedness and false religion.

Living in Pergamos would be like living in the midst of a combination of San Francisco and Mecca. The worst of moral evil and the worst of false religion pervaded this city, and both were designed to corrupt and destroy Christians by the force of the culture and the force of the law. Whether it was the culture or the government, both were designed to destroy Christians and Christianity.

Thirdly, He says even in the face of this, *"I know [that] thou holdest fast my name, and hast not denied my faith."* The believers in the church at Pergamos continued to publicly proclaim their faith in Christ and confess the name of Christ. They remained faithful and loyal to Christ even when pressured to deny Him by the seduction of the world and the persecution of the government. In fact, the persecution by the Roman government at Pergamos was so bad they put one of the Christians named Antipas to death for refusing to deny Christ and for refusing to declare that Caesar is lord. Antipas was faithful unto death, and as we read in the last chapter in Revelation 2:10, Christ would give him a crown of life.

At Smyrna, there was a synagogue of Satan, and Christ said to the church: "You are going to be persecuted. Be faithful to death, and I will give you a crown of life." But persecution had already begun at Pergamos. Jesus is saying to the church at Pergamos, "When you saw one of your own martyred for refusing to deny Me and for continuing to confess his faith in Me, even then, you did not waver."

These are high words of praise Jesus is giving to the believers at Pergamos for their faithfulness to Christ. Even when they saw one of their own killed, they did not back down from confessing the name of Christ or depart from their faith in Christ. They were not intimidated by the martyrdom of one of their own into turning away from Jesus. They remained loyal to Christ, even though it would probably result in their death also. Jesus saw this loyalty and warmly commended them for it.

This shows us that it is possible to live consistently for Christ in the worst of circumstances. You often hear it said that there are so many evil things in our culture that are so easily available, there is so much hostility to Christianity, and it is so hard to stand up for the truth that we cannot be expected to be faithful in such a hostile environment. Yes, you can. You can do it by God's grace and with God's help. The people of the church of Pergamos did it, and you can do it as well.

Even where Satan dwells and even where Satan rules, believers exist, believers remain faithful, and believers triumph over the very worst that Satan can throw at them. God's grace is greater than any challenges that can come against us. Satan may be driving the culture, Satan may be driving the religion, Satan may be driving the educational system, and Satan may be driving the government. But Christ's people shine as lights in the midst of such a perverse and crooked nation and continue to confess Him before people and hold forth the word of life to them without flinching and without backing down.

This is what the believers at Pergamos were doing. They were not any kind of special believers; they were simply genuine believers. We see this in our day and age as well. We have seen the church in China and North Korea and Iran and Saudi Arabia, where the culture and the government and the religion are all designed to crush Christianity, and actively attempt to do so, but they are never successful. The believers will go to jail and they will go to death before they will give up Christ and His proclamation.

Secondly, notice His correction of the church at Pergamos. His correction of the church at Pergamos is in verses 14 to 15. He says that in spite of how wonderful you have been and how faithful you have been; nevertheless, *"I have a few things"* not a lot of things, but a few things "*against thee, because*" and now He tells them what He is very offended by. He says, *"Thou hast there them that hold the doctrine of Balaam, who taught Balak to cast a stumblingblock before the children of Israel, to eat things sacrificed unto idols, and to commit fornication.* [15] *So hast thou also,"* in addition to those folks, *"them that hold the doctrine of the Nicolaitans, which thing I hate."* There are things that God hates. He hates things that are destructive to His people.

Though Jesus is very pleased with how the church is dealing with the seduction and persecution that is coming from outside the church, He has grave concerns about the lack of church discipline within the church. The believers at Pergamos, though they had done a grand job of withstanding the pressure of the world from without, had in fact allowed false teachers and immoral people to remain inside the church and infect it with their pernicious doctrine and their evil practices.

First of all, there were those who held to the doctrine of Balaam. The story of Balaam is a long one, and it is related in Numbers 22–25. These four chapters are all about Balaam, and Numbers 31 gives a retrospective account of what Balaam did. Balaam is also mentioned several times in the New Testament. Balaam is a prominent example of how the people of God can be abused by false ministers of God.

To give a brief summary, Balak, the king of Moab, hired Balaam, who was a prophet of God, to curse Israel because Israel had now come into the land of Moab. The king of Moab summoned the prophet of God and said: "Curse these people. Call God's curse on them so that they cannot fight against us and triumph over us. If you do so Balaam, I will give you a great deal of money."

Balaam the prophet could not curse the people of God because God would not permit him to. Three times he tried to curse them and get the money, but God simply took control of his tongue and mouth and caused him to bless Israel instead.

Therefore, Balaam was in danger of losing the money that Balak had offered him to bring God's curse on Israel. Rather than losing his payment, Balaam told Balak the king how he himself might bring God's curse on Israel. Balaam said: "I cannot do it, but I will tell you how you can do it. You can do it by sending wicked women among them to seduce them into fornication and into engaging in the worship of the false idol god known as Baal."

As long as Israel was serving the Lord and faithful to the Lord and morally upright, God was not going to become upset with them. But Balaam said: "If you can get them to fall into fornication and idolatry, then God will become angry at them and you will achieve your goal. God will curse them." Balak followed Balaam's advice. He sent sinful women into the camp to engage in fornication and to seduce the people of Israel into worshiping Baal. They succeeded, God's curse fell on Israel, and Balaam collected his money. The tactic was successful. Israel fell into immorality and idolatry by means of the seduction of these Moabite women, and Israel came under the wrath of God.

The point is this: Balaam the prophet of God taught Balak the king how to corrupt the people of God so he could collect his fee from Balak for bringing God's curse on Israel. As a result, Balaam has stood forever as an example and metaphor of ministers who corrupt the people of God for personal advantage. Ministers and teachers who hold the doctrine of Balaam are those who are willing to lead the people of God into sin if they can gain personal advantage and profit by doing so.

You can build a big church and obtain a large salary if you tell the people they can worship God however they please and they can live in any way they want and commit any sin they desire. Idolatry is fine; fornication is fine. They may do as they please as long as they fill the offering plate with money. Such mercenary ministers are an abomination to God. They need to be cast out of the church, but the believers at Pergamos had allowed them to remain in the church.

Furthermore, not only did the believers at Pergamos fail to deal with and cast out those who held to the practice and teaching of Balaam, but they also harbored those who adhered to the teaching of the Nicolaitans. Notice verse 15: *"So hast thou also them that hold the doctrine of the Nicolaitans."*

The doctrine of the Nicolaitans was something distinct from those who held to the doctrine of Balaam. Those who held to the doctrine of Balaam were those who were willing to corrupt the people of God for personal advantage. The Nicolaitans were an early Gnostic sect who advocated sinful license in the name of Christian liberty on the basis that sinful self-indulgence would not hinder spiritual maturity and growth. They would be like those today who teach that you can practice homosexuality or fornication and be a true Christian at the same time because what you do with your body really does not affect your spiritual relationship with God.

This dualistic view of the universe in which the material is divorced from the spiritual meant you could do anything you wanted in the flesh and it did not affect what occurred in the realm of the spirit. They taught that what you did with your body had no impact on your soul and that you could be a real Christian while at the same time practice sexual immorality.

God says He hates that teaching and behavior because they are utterly contrary to His will, and they provoke His anger. The church at

Pergamos should have exercised church discipline upon these people, telling them to either repent, or else give up their profession of faith in Christ and leave the church.

False teachers and their corrupting influences are not to be tolerated in the church; and yet, how few churches in our day practice church discipline!

Churches allow corrupt people to engage in openly sinful behavior and teach heresy contrary to the truth of God. This is done under the excuse that they need to be "affirming" and "loving." God says: "I hate that." Tolerance of false teaching and immoral behavior is not a virtue; it is a vice. We should never celebrate that kind of "inclusiveness."

Thirdly, notice the warning given to the church at Pergamos in verse 16. Jesus says, *"Repent; or else I will come unto thee quickly, and will fight against them with the sword of my mouth."* Jesus introduced Himself at the start of this letter as the one who has the sharp sword with two edges.

In verse 16, Jesus is calling on the faithful of the church to repent of their negligence in allowing such teachings and practices to be present in the church. He says: "You need to repent of your inclusiveness and broadmindedness and latitudinarianism and your acceptance of aberrant teaching and corrupt moral behavior." He calls on them to deal with these people in a decisive manner. They must repent or they must be removed. Jesus is saying to the church at Pergamos: "Cut this cancer out of your midst!" If they do not deal properly with these people, Christ Himself will, because He is determined that He will have a pure church.

Notice what He says in verse 16: *"Repent; or else I will come unto thee quickly, and will fight against them"*; that is, Jesus will fight against those who have the doctrine of Balaam, those who have the doctrine of the Nicolaitans, and those who insist on keeping them in the church. Christ utterly condemns those who say: "We should not exercise church discipline; that would be unloving." Jesus said: "I am going to come and fight against such people." You want Jesus fighting for your church; you do not want Jesus fighting against your church. Of these people who hold these aberrant doctrines and practice this deviant behavior, Jesus says: "I am not going to allow this to go on. I am declaring war and I am coming to deal with it." Jesus will use the sword of His mouth; that is, He will use the power of His word to expose them and judge them.

Those who infect the church with deviant teaching and with wicked immorality should not be tolerated by the church; and mark it down, they will not be tolerated by Christ. Those who hold to aberrant doctrine and those who practice deviant behavior are at war with Christ and His people, and Christ and His people must be at war with them. The last thing we should do is allow them to freely function within the assembly of the church. Understand that tolerance of these things is a sin; and that coexistence with open sin is a vice, not a virtue.

The Conclusion of the Letter

The conclusion to the letter is in verse 17: *"He that hath an ear, let him hear what the Spirit saith unto the churches; To him that overcometh will I give to eat of the hidden manna, and will give him a white stone, and in the stone a new name written, which no man knoweth saving he that receiveth it."*

In the conclusion to the letter, notice first of all the exhortation given. The exhortation given is this: *"He that hath an ear, let him hear what the Spirit saith unto the churches."* Notice the plural "churches." What this tells us is that this letter is not just for the church at Pergamos alone; it is for all churches of all time and in all places who face similar situations and circumstances. Churches that live in cities similar to Pergamos have existed through the ages and throughout the world. This letter is to all of these churches.

Christ is speaking to us through His Holy Spirit. He says, *"He that hath an ear, let him hear what the Spirit"* is saying. As the Spirit of God speaks to our hearts through the word of God, we need to listen. We need to listen carefully. We need to meditate thoughtfully. We need to act zealously on what it is that the Spirit is saying to us through the word of Christ.

As the Spirit speaks to us corporately as a church and individually as Christians, we must not grieve Him and quench Him, and let this message go in one ear and out the other. We need to hear it, to think about it, and to ask ourselves: "How does it apply to me, and how does it apply to our church? What do I need to do, and what does our church need to do, in order to respond to what Christ has to say in this letter?" We need to be good stewards of what we have heard.

Secondly, notice the promise made in the latter half of verse 17. It says, *"To him that overcometh will I give. . ."* The promise is made to the overcomer. What does an overcomer look like? What does our text tell us about his characteristics?

- The overcomer is one who holds fast the name of Christ and does not deny the faith of Christ, in spite of fierce persecution from without and within.
- The overcomer is one who rejects the teaching and practice of selfish gain at the expense of the people of God.
- The overcomer is one who rejects the teaching and practice of those who say you can compromise your morality, engage in idolatry, and still be viewed as a Christian.
- The overcomer is one who refuses to be a participant in such practices, and who actively fights against such teachings.
- The overcomer is one who does not give in to persecution from the educational, governmental, and religious systems from without the church.
- The overcomer is one who does not give in to the false teaching and the immoral practices of professing Christians who are within the church.

Promises are made to one who stands with Christ and for Christ. Notice there are two promises. First of all, He says *"To him that overcometh will I give to eat of the hidden manna"*; and secondly, *"and will give him a white stone, and in the stone a new name written, which no man knoweth saving he that receiveth it."*

Of all the verses in the book of Revelation, this one is probably the most controversial in terms of discovering what it means. There are numerous suggestions as to what promise number one and promise number two are referring to, and there is no consensus.

The interpretation we are going to give can be challenged and questioned, and that is fine. But without exception, all of the suggested interpretations recognize that these are wonderful promises that are given to the people of God, and they speak of great blessings that will come. Whatever the hidden manna is, it is wonderful; and whatever the white stone is and the new name written on it is, it is wonderful; whether you take interpretation A, B, C, D, or E.

Here is our best understanding of these phrases.

When it says that *"I will give [them] to eat of the hidden manna,"* what is being promised is that the one who stands firm with Christ and for Christ will have spiritual nourishment and spiritual strength provided by God Himself, which is here called the *"hidden manna."*

In John 4, we have the story of the woman at the well. Jesus is really hungry. He sits down on the well and the disciples go to town to buy food. This woman shows up, He preaches the gospel to her, and she is saved. She runs into town to tell the people about this wonderful Messiah who has come and redeemed her from her sins! While she is gone, the disciples return from town with lunch.

Notice John 4:31–34 says, *"In the mean while his disciples prayed him, saying, Master, eat.* [32] *But he said unto them, I have [food] to eat that ye know not of.* [33] *Therefore said the disciples one to another, Hath any man brought him ought to eat?* [34] *Jesus saith unto them, My [food] is to do the will of him that sent me, and to finish his work."*

In other words, when Jesus was doing the work of God, He received supernatural nourishment and supernatural strength from God that no one else could see. It was hidden. Nevertheless, it so refreshed and strengthened Him that He felt like He had no need to eat at that moment. In essence He was saying, "I have the power of God and the blessing of God and the presence of God working through Me in accomplishing the redemption of this woman's soul, and it so satisfies Me and fills Me with a sense of strength that I am not even interested in eating your lunch."

God fed the people of Israel as they traveled through the wilderness on the way to the Promised Land. He fed them with manna, a physical food for their physical bodies. We, too, are traveling to the Promised Land, and God feeds us with spiritual food that gives us spiritual nourishment and strength for our souls for the journey to our Promised Land, which is the new heavens and the new earth.

Just like God provided manna for Israel in the physical wilderness on the way to her physical Promised Land to give her physical strength, so God provides manna for the New Israel in the spiritual wilderness on the way to her spiritual Promised Land of heaven to give her spiritual strength. This manna is hidden; that is, it cannot be seen by the world. Nevertheless, it is seen and experienced by the believer.

These believers in Pergamos would not partake of the food provided in the worship of the idols. They could not eat the meat offered to idols. Jesus says, in essence, "I have better food to give to you, real manna, that will sustain your souls in a way that this idolatrous food never could or would." That is one interpretation of the hidden manna.

A second interpretation is that the hidden manna is Christ Himself. In John 6:31–35, Jesus talked about the manna that came down from heaven. The Pharisee says, "*Our fathers did eat manna in the desert; as it is written, He gave them bread from heaven to eat.* [32] *Then Jesus said unto them, Verily, verily, I say unto you, Moses gave you not that bread from heaven; but my Father giveth you the true bread from heaven.* [33] *For the bread of God is he which cometh down from heaven, and giveth life unto the world.* [34] *Then said they unto him, Lord, evermore give us this bread.* [35] *And Jesus said unto them, I am the bread of life: he that cometh to me shall never hunger; and he that believeth on me shall never thirst.*"

Jesus identifies Himself as the manna of God that came down from heaven. In that sense, He nourishes us with Himself and with the life He gives us in the salvation He provides. What does it mean that Jesus is hidden? In Matthew 11:27 Jesus said, "*All things are delivered unto me of my Father: and no man knoweth the Son, but the Father; neither knoweth any man the Father, save the Son, and he to whomsoever the Son will reveal him.*"

In this sense, Jesus was the hidden manna. He was hidden from the eyes of the people. Because of their depravity and blindness, they could not see Him for who He was. But He says, "I am the real manna that has come down from heaven, and if you feed on Me—that is, if you believe in Me—then you will have My life given to you. Yes, the world cannot see Me for who I am because I am hidden; and unless the Father reveals Me to them, My true identity cannot be seen." The second interpretation is that Jesus is the hidden manna.

Thirdly, this could be a reference to the food served at the marriage supper of the Lamb. In Revelation 19:9, after the second coming of Christ, the saints are called to the marriage supper of the Lamb. The food we are going to enjoy with Christ in that marriage supper feast is hidden now, but it will be revealed on that day, and it will provide us with eternal nourishment.

These are the three leading interpretations of what the hidden manna is. All of them are wonderful, all of them are biblically true, and all of them convey the idea that the world offers us its nourishment, saying, "Eat the meat offered to the idols!" But Christ says, "No, I have food for your soul, I am the food for your soul, and I will give you food for your soul at the marriage supper of the Lamb."

The second promise is that the overcomer is also promised a white stone, and on this stone a new name is written which is known only by him and the Lord. Notice what it says in verse 17: *"[I] will give him a white stone, and in the stone a new name written, which no man knoweth saving he that receiveth it."* This stone with this new name will be given to the overcomer, apparently at the second coming of Christ.

Once again, it is somewhat uncertain as to exactly what this white stone is or what it symbolizes. We know that in Roman courts when a verdict was rendered, if the accused was guilty, he was handed a black stone. If he was innocent, he was handed a white stone. The white stone was the stone of acquittal of all the accusations and charges laid against the accused. It was white because it was saying that this person is holy and pure and clean in the eyes of the law. So it seems that Jesus is promising that on the day of judgment, the overcomer is going to be declared "Not Guilty" by Christ. He will be given, as it were, the white stone. He will have a pronouncement that he is holy and pure and clean in the eyes of God's law.

We know that the educational system and the governmental system and the religious system at Pergamos heaped horrible accusations on the people of God, even to the point of accusing them of being worthy of death and then actually putting them to death. But Jesus says that on the Day of Judgment, all those accusations are going to be set aside, and this person is going to be declared innocent of all of those slanderous charges that were laid against him. He will be acquitted. Christ will vindicate him.

It goes on to say that not only is the overcomer going to get this white stone, but it is also going to have a name engraved in it, and only the person who gets the stone and the one who gives the stone are going to know what it is. The overcomer is going to be given a new name by Christ—a name that Christ assigns to him, which is a description of what Christ thinks of him for his faithfulness to Him and for his service to Him.

This has Old Testament roots. Speaking of our arrival in heaven, it says in Isaiah 62:2, *"And. . .thou shalt be called by a new name, which the mouth of the LORD shall name."* When we get to heaven, we are not going to be Bill or Joe or John; we are going to be given a new name by Jesus Christ.

This is not without biblical precedent. We often see God renaming people. Saul became Paul. Simon was renamed Peter. Jacob was renamed Israel. There are many examples when people became redeemed and transformed, their old name was no longer suitable, and they were given a new name that was now suitable to their new condition and their new character and their new calling.

Just as Simon was renamed Peter, and just as Jacob was renamed Israel, so each of us will receive a new name that characterizes who we are to Christ and what He thinks of us. We will not lose our individuality in heaven. We will not be absorbed into an undifferentiated mass of faceless humanity in that multitude which no man can number. Rather, Christ will know each of us by name as individuals, and He will give each of us a new name, one that just He and we know, which indicates the intimacy, the closeness, the care, and the concern that Jesus has for each individual saint that comes into His presence in heaven.

The promise is this: We will receive refreshment in this life—the hidden manna; and we will receive honor in the next life—a new name. We will be acquitted of all of our sins, and we will be given a special place of relationship and closeness to Christ through the new name which He gives us. He will know every one of us individually by that name throughout all eternity.

We have manna given to us now that the world cannot see. We will have acquittal and recognition given to us by Christ Himself in that great Day of Judgment and throughout all eternity. That is the promise given to the overcomer.

We are living in an increasingly wicked age. The pressures on us are enormous. We need to be Pergamos Christians who stand fast for Christ, who confess His name, who do not deny His faith, and who continue to stand firm and faithful and loyal to Him even when it costs us up to and including our life.

But there is only one way we are going to be able to do that, and that is if we keep our church pure. That does not mean the church is sinless, but what it does mean is that the church is made up of genuine believers, and they are all sincerely pursuing Christ with integrity. Now in that pursuit, do we fall into sin? Sadly, we do. But instead of justifying it and propagating it and defending it, we repent of it and we seek help for overcoming it.

There is a big difference between a church that is made up of struggling sinners who are seeking righteousness, and a church made up of self-justifying sinners who are defending, proclaiming, and propagating their sin in the church. There is a clear difference between those two groups. The latter, we exercise church discipline against. The former, we support and help in every way we possibly can.

May God help us to hear what the Spirit has to say to this persecuted church and to this compromised church; and may we in our church, seek purity within, and faithfulness without. Let us be the overcomers who receive the hidden manna, the white stone, and the new name.

15

The Letter to the Church at Thyatira, Revelation 2:18–29

> "18 *And unto the angel of the church in Thyatira write; These*
> *things saith the Son of God, who hath his eyes like unto a*
> *flame of fire, and his feet are like fine brass;* 19 *I know thy*
> *works, and charity, and service, and faith, and thy patience,*
> *and thy works; and the last to be more than the first.* 20 *Not-*
> *withstanding I have a few things against thee, because thou*
> *sufferest that woman Jezebel, which calleth herself a prophet-*
> *ess, to teach and to seduce my servants to commit fornication,*
> *and to eat things sacrificed unto idols.* 21 *And I gave her space*
> *to repent of her fornication; and she repented not.* 22 *Behold, I*
> *will cast her into a bed, and them that commit adultery with*
> *her into great tribulation, except they repent of their deeds.*
> 23 *And I will kill her children with death; and all the churches*
> *shall know that I am he which searcheth the reins and hearts:*
> *and I will give unto every one of you according to your works.*
> 24 *But unto you I say, and unto the rest in Thyatira, as many as*
> *have not this doctrine, and which have not known the depths*
> *of Satan, as they speak; I will put upon you none other bur-*
> *den.* 25 *But that which ye have already hold fast till I come.*
> 26 *And he that overcometh, and keepeth my works unto the*
> *end, to him will I give power over the nations:* 27 *And he shall*
> *rule them with a rod of iron; as the vessels of a potter shall*
> *they be broken to shivers: even as I received of my Father.*
> 28 *And I will give him the morning star.* 29 *He that hath an ear,*
> *let him hear what the Spirit saith unto the churches."*

In these letters to the seven churches, we see the heart of Jesus for His church, even though these churches were far from perfect.

I find in these letters the strongest rebuke to those who claim to be Christians but who despise the local church and never attend one even when they are able to do so. Those who claim to be Christians but who despise the church often say, "Well, the church is full of hypocrites." Or, "The people in the church have treated me badly." Or they offer any number of other excuses as to why they do not go to church. Those excuses will not be accepted by Christ.

Christ freely acknowledges in these letters that His churches have problems. Indeed, He makes it clear they have serious problems; and yet, He does not abandon these churches, nor does He tell His people to get out of these churches and start new ones. He does not say that because the church is so corrupt, they are to have church at home with their own family, or they are to go worship God out in nature because everything out there is pure. Instead, Jesus expects that His people will be in church, even in churches that have serious problems. He calls on them to work at fixing the problems in their church, not to abandon the church and just stay at home.

Let us be like Jesus. Let us love the church and participate in the church, recognizing all the problems the church has, but work at fixing the problems in the church instead of running away from them.

If your church has become so apostate as to become a synagogue of Satan, then go find another church to attend, or start a biblical church yourself. But do not, under any circumstances, declare church to be optional or unnecessary for your Christian life. Jesus placed church at the very heart and core of His people's lives and ministry, and it should have that same place in our lives also.

The church in Thyatira was a church that had serious problems, but the solution Christ offered to the people in that church was not to flee the church, but to fix the church. So many churches have descended into apostasy because the good people left the first time they saw something they did not like, instead of staying and fighting for the truth and prevailing against those who were perverting it. Let us do the same. Let us cultivate in our churches the virtues these letters describe so they may become what Christ commends. Let us reject and reform the vices Christ condemns in these letters so we may avoid what displeases Him. Let us work to eliminate the bad that Christ condemns while reinforcing the good that Christ commends so we may be a faithful church.

The Introduction to the Letter

The introduction of the letter to Thyatira is found in verse 18: *"And unto the angel of the church in Thyatira write; These things saith the Son of God, who hath his eyes like unto a flame of fire, and his feet are like fine brass."* The introduction to this letter in verse 18 tells us who the recipient and author of the letter are.

First of all, notice the recipient of the letter. The recipient of the letter is the pastor and the church at Thyatira.

Thyatira is a city that was situated far inland from the coast of Asia. It sat between two major valleys, and was therefore in a good position to be a center of trade as people traveled from one of these heavily inhabited valleys to the other. The city was a significant commercial center, and in particular, it was a commercial center of the trades, and therefore contained a large number of trade guilds.

These trade guilds were associations of craftsmen from various trades. Belonging to the trade guild of your particular trade was essential to your economic survival and success. We know from archaeological research that Thyatira had a very large number of these trade guilds that trafficked in things like wool and linen, garments, pottery, metalworking, leathercraft, the dying of cloth, and a number of other trades. In Acts 16:14 we are introduced to Lydia from Thyatira, who was a seller of purple-dyed garments, who probably belonged to one of these trade guilds.

The problem was that membership in these trade guilds required you to participate in the worship of the particular idol which the guild revered. These were not just commercial organizations; they also had a strong religious dimension. If you were going to have membership in the trade guild, you also had to participate in the worship of the particular idol which the guild revered, and participate in the feasts and the debauchery that went along with the worship of that idol.

This posed an acute problem for Christian craftsmen because it was very difficult for a man to make a living without belonging to the guild that represented his trade, since goods were marketed through the guild. Unless you joined and participated in the guild and the pagan worship and the immoral activity that occurred at its feasts, it was almost impossible to buy and sell in the trade and craft in which you were skilled.

The dilemma the Christians faced was this: To get ahead in the world, you had to belong to a guild, and if you belonged to a guild, you were required to worship its god and participate in its feasts. You were expected to attend the guild festivals, eat the food offered to the god of the guild, and participate in the fornication that followed.

If the Christian quit the trade guild, he lost the ability to buy and sell and participate in the economic activity of his trade. If the Christian stayed in the guild and attended the immoral feasts and ate the things sacrificed to idols, then he denied his Lord. He was in a tough spot. What was he going to do?

In this difficult situation, the prophetess Jezebel declared that one could participate in the worship and fornication of the idol feasts and still remain a Christian in good standing with God. The message offered by this prophetess both pleased the flesh and appeased the conscience, and was the source of Christ's extremely strong reproof to this church.

Secondly, notice the author of the letter. The author of this letter, like all these letters, is Jesus Christ. He identifies Himself by the titles and attributes that were revealed about Him in chapter 1 that are particularly suited to the needs of this individual church. In verse 18, He identifies Himself first as the Son of God. While this exact title is not used in chapter 1, God is called His Father in verse 6, making him the Son of God.

Verse 18 says, *"And unto the angel of the church in Thyatira write; These things saith the Son of God."* This is the only place in the book of Revelation this specific title is ascribed to Jesus. He takes other titles of deity to Himself, such as the Alpha and the Omega, the first and the last, the beginning and the end; but this is the only place He is called the Son of God. This title is used to declare the majesty of His person and the authority He possesses. When He calls Himself the Son of God, He is declaring His divine nature. He is saying: "I am God the Son. I am God's Son."

He also identifies Himself in verse 18 as the one *"who hath his eyes like unto a flame of fire, and his feet are like fine brass."* His eyes of fire and His feet of burning brass symbolize the fiery anger of His wrath against sin. What is the place of eternal damnation, but a place of fire? Therefore, fire is associated with wrath and judgment.

Here Christ is presenting Himself to the church as the divine judge whose flaming eyes penetrate through Jezebel's lies and deceit, and whose burning feet are going to trample and crush her and her followers into eternal damnation.

His eyes burn with indignation, and His feet bring irresistible devastation. Here the Son of God presents Himself as the terrifying judge who will deal harshly with those who try to lead His bride into unfaithfulness to Him like this female prophetess Jezebel was trying to do. If someone were trying to lead your wife into adultery against you, would your eyes flame? This is exactly what was happening here. This woman Jezebel was taking the bride of Christ and trying to involve her in fornication with another god, and Jesus was furiously angry, and was coming as a punishing judge to deal with this person who was attempting to subvert His wife to another god.

The Message of the Letter

First of all, notice His commendation. The commendation Jesus gives the church at Thyatira is in verse 19. He says, *"I know thy works, and charity, and service, and faith, and thy patience, and thy works; and the last to be more than the first."*

Jesus opens His commendation with the words *"I know."* He knows everything there is to know about the church at Thyatira. He knows the virtues the people possess and He knows the works they have done. He knows the challenges and temptations they face. It is a great comfort to realize that Jesus knows everything about us, and therefore understands everything we are going through. No one understands like Jesus, because no one knows us like Jesus.

What does Jesus know about this church? He says first of all, *"I know thy works"*; that is, "I know your acts of obedience to My commands. I know the choices you have made. I know the labor you have expended. I know the deeds you have done out of love to Me and out of submission to Me. You have served My kingdom and sought My glory. I have seen your works, and I am pleased with those works."

The point is simply this: There is nothing you do in service to Christ that He does not take note of. Often when we do things for others, they are either unaware of it or fail to acknowledge it when they are aware of it, but that is never the case with Christ. He sees all we do for Him, and is pleased by it, and remembers every aspect of it. He truly knows our works.

Secondly, He says *"I know thy. . .charity."* The word here for charity is love; *agape* in the original. He is saying: "I know the love you have shown your brothers and sisters in Christ by serving their needs. I know the love you have shown the lost by preaching the gospel and inviting them to come to salvation. I know the love you have shown to Me by keeping My commandments." Unlike the church at Ephesus, which had neglected to maintain its love, Jesus said to the church at Thyatira: "You have been fervent in your love. You have kept it up, and you have expressed it well."

Thirdly, He says *"I know thy. . . service."* He says to them: "You have set aside your own desires and agenda in order to do what I have asked you to do. You have sought first the kingdom of God and what will establish and strengthen it most. When you saw a need, you willingly met it without complaint and with a cheerful heart. You felt it a privilege to be allowed to serve Me and serve My people, and joyfully embraced the opportunity to do so. I have seen how you have acted with a servant's heart and washed the feet of the saints."

Fourthly, He says *"I know thy. . . faith."* It is impossible to keep working for God and loving God and serving God if we do not believe the promises of God are true. The man of faith believes the promises are true even though he does not yet see any indication of their fulfillment. Only those who have genuine faith are able to persevere in the face of every earthly incentive to quit serving God and loving God. Those who have faith live and act as though they have already seen the promises of God brought to pass, even though they have in fact seen no such thing. It says of Moses in Hebrews 11:27 that "*he endured, as seeing Him who is invisible.*"

The man of faith does not grow weary in well-doing. He knows that in due season he will reap if he faints not, because the promises are true. Those without genuine faith soon become apparent because they quickly tire of the sacrifice and self-denial that service to Christ requires. If you do not believe that your work really matters, or that God actually takes note of it and rewards it, then you are going to quit.

The people who have faith are those who continue to serve Christ for a lifetime because they really believe what the Bible says is true; and therefore, it is going to be worth it all in the end. They keep pressing on because they know that the prize of the high calling of God in Christ is awaiting them. They believe it, and they believe it to the point that it motivates them to keep on going. That is the way true faith operates.

Fifthly, He says *"I know thy. . . patience."* Patience is the disposition that bears up under difficulties with a good attitude for as long as it takes to see those difficulties resolved in God's way and in God's time. Anybody can put up with difficulties for a little while. But to put up with them for a really long time, waiting for deliverance from God in His way and in His time, and not making ungodly choices to try to get deliverance from them here and now, requires biblical patience. The patient man is long-suffering under trials, and is long-serving under trials, even when there is little or no visible fruit.

The Christians at Thyatira were not quitters. They exercised obedience in the same direction for a long time, doing the same works, expressing the same love, and carrying out the same service without ever stopping. They were steadfast and unmovable, always abounding in the work of the Lord, because they knew their labor for the Lord was not in vain, even though at times it appeared to be that way. They knew that in the end it would prove not to be in vain, and because they had faith and patience, they kept on following Christ.

Sixthly, He says to them, *"I know. . . thy works; and the last to be more than the first."* As these Christians at Thyatira grew in the Lord, their service to the Lord grew and expanded as well. When they were a new church and when they were young believers, they had a certain level of obedience and service they rendered to God, and it was good.

But over time, that obedience and service grew, both in amount and in degree. It became greater and greater. They did far more for the Lord now than they had ever done in the past. As their knowledge and maturity and experience grew, so did their productivity in serving God more comprehensively and more intensely in their personal lives. They were doing better and better, and they were doing more than they had ever previously done.

Verse 19 paints a picture of genuine, normal Christians. This is who they are, this is how they act, and this is what they look like, and Jesus commends them for it. They work for the Lord, they love the Lord, they serve the Lord, they have faith in the Lord, they have patience with the Lord, and they just keep working harder and harder on behalf of the Lord. That is what real Christians look like.

Secondly, notice the correction of the church at Thyatira. The correction that Jesus gives is in verses 20 and 21. He says, *"Notwithstanding I have a few things against thee, because thou sufferest that woman Jezebel, which calleth herself a prophetess, to teach and to seduce my servants to commit fornication, and to eat things sacrificed unto idols.* [21] *And I gave her space to repent of her fornication; and she repented not."*

Jesus has some very severe criticism for this church at Thyatira because it has tolerated corruption in its leadership in the person of this woman Jezebel. Jezebel is probably not her actual name. But because she was seducing the people of God into idolatry, just like the actual Jezebel of the Old Testament seduced Israel into the idolatry of Baal worship, she is called by the name Jezebel. In her behavior, she acts in the way that Old Testament Jezebel did. Like the actual Jezebel of the Old Testament, she led the people of God away from faithfulness to God and into the worship of a false god, and into all the wickedness which that entailed.

There were several problems with the people at Thyatira allowing this woman to teach in their church. The first problem is the fact that she was a woman. This alone should have disqualified her from any leadership or teaching position in the church. Paul is very clear on the role of women in the church when he says in 2 Timothy 1:12, *"But I suffer not a woman to teach, nor to usurp authority over the man, but to be in silence."*

No woman is ever authorized by God to be a teacher in the church, no matter what. In any church where you have female pastors or female teachers, you always, and without exception, have problems with aberrant teaching. If a woman is going to ignore the part of the truth of the Bible that tells her not to teach or lead, then she will also ignore or twist other teachings of the Bible. God will never bless what He has forbidden, and no female teaching in the church ever conveys the blessing of God to that church, because it is done in direct contradiction to the will of God for that church.

The second problem with this woman teaching in the church is not just that she was a woman, but that she claimed to be a prophetess. Notice, even Jesus says: *"Thou sufferest that woman Jezebel, which calleth herself a prophetess. . ."* She claimed to be more than a teacher. She claimed to receive direct revelation from God. Clearly, her teachings were contrary to the written Word of God, and therefore could not possibly be coming from God. She was teaching that it is perfectly fine to worship idols and commit fornication when God says in the First Commandment: *"I am the Lord thy God, thou shall have no other Gods before me"*; and in the Seventh Commandment:

"Thou shall not commit adultery." How could she be a prophet of God when her teaching directly contradicted the revealed word of God? Her problem was not just that she was a woman, but that she was also a liar. She was no prophetess at all.

The third problem she had is that she was teaching the people of God that it was perfectly fine to commit fornication and to eat things sacrificed to idols. Notice verse 20: *"to teach and to seduce my servants to commit fornication, and to eat things sacrificed unto idols."* The fornication she was teaching them to engage in was both physical and spiritual. It involved participation in the craft guild meetings where physical sexual immorality was practiced as part of the worship of the guild god. This also involved spiritual adultery against God by eating the food offered to the craft guild god as an act of worship to that god. The church is the bride of Christ, and therefore she is supposed to be faithful to Him. When believers worship another god besides Jesus, they are committing idolatry and therefore spiritual adultery against Jesus.

Rather than experience economic loss, and rather than endure public social rejection and ridicule for withdrawing from the wicked association of the craft guilds, this Jezebel-like woman taught the believers that they could commit both physical and spiritual adultery, and that it was acceptable to God. With her teachings, she was seducing them into doing great evil. Just like the serpent seduced Eve into disobeying God in the garden of Eden, this woman was seducing the believers to do great evil against God both in the church and in the society in Thyatira.

What is amazing is the patience and mercy God showed to this woman. Notice verse 21. He says, *"I gave her space to repent of her fornication."* When she first started teaching this heresy, God did not do anything. He gave her time and space to recognize and realize what she was doing was evil and wrong, and turn away from it, but she did not. Verse 21 says, *"she repented not."* She spurned the opportunity to repent and escape the wrath of God, and now that wrath was imminent.

God is very patient with the wicked, and He often withholds His judgment for a long time, and gives them time and space to repent. Eventually, that patience runs out and He lowers the hammer. But until He does, they think, "He must not care because He is not doing anything about my actions." Because judgment against an evil work is not executed speedily, men think evil works are just fine. People stand up and blaspheme God, and nothing happens, so they think God must not care. It must be okay. People commit adultery, and nothing happens. They think, "Well, God must not care, or He must overlook it, or else He does not even see it." This is faulty thinking.

God is provoked, but God is patient. God is merciful. God gives time to repent. Do not take His inactions against your sins as some kind of an indication that He does not care about them or that He is not provoked by them. He is giving you time to repent, and the goodness of God in giving you that time should lead you to repentance.

Thirdly, notice His warning. His warning is in verses 22–25, *"Behold, I will cast her into a bed, and them that commit adultery with her into great tribulation, except they repent of their deeds.* [23] *And I will kill her children with death; and all the churches shall know that I am he which searcheth the reins and hearts: and I will give unto every one of you according to your works.* [24] *But unto you I say, and unto the rest in Thyatira, as many as have not this doctrine, and which have not known the depths of Satan, as they speak; I will put upon you none other burden.* [25] *But that which ye have already hold fast till I come."*

Jesus has been watching the corruption going on in this church, and He has had enough. He has been patient, but now He is ready to act, and He says, in verse 22, *"I will cast her into a bed, and them that commit adultery with her into great tribulation."* A bed for an adulterer is usually a place of great pleasure, but Jesus is saying: I am going to turn that bed into a place of great sickness, great disease, and great sorrow. I will cast her into a bed of sickness from which she will not arise.

But His wrath is not reserved just for her. Those who followed her teachings, and as a result committed spiritual adultery, will be met with great tribulation sent upon them by God Himself. Notice He says not only that He will cast her into a bed of sickness from which she will not arise but also, *"I will cast. . .them that commit adultery with her into great tribulation."*

Verse 22: *". . .except they repent of their deeds."* Christ is going to bring judgment, and the only way to escape it is to repent of their deeds. Immediate repentance is the only means of escape from the wrath of God. As Jesus said, *"Except you repent, you shall all likewise perish."* In the absence of repentance, the only possible outcome is death.

Notice verse 23: *"And I will kill her children with death."* The children of Jezebel are those who follow her teachings. The apostle John said in 1 John 2:1, *"My little children, these things write I unto you."* Those who followed John's teachings were his spiritual children. Therefore, these children threatened with death are Jezebel's spiritual children who are following her teachings and looking up to her as their spiritual leader and parent.

He says, *"I will kill her children with death; and all the churches shall know that I am he which searcheth the reins and hearts: and I will give unto every one of you according to your works."* He is saying, "When I bring judgment on Jezebel and those who follow her teaching, instead of pleasure and prosperity, they will have sickness and death." When all the other churches observe how Christ deals with the people in this church for their spiritual adultery, they will fear the Lord of the churches, and will amend their ways.

We do not have to learn by making our own mistakes. Far better to learn by observing what other people do and what their outcomes are. Do not be so obtuse as to have to learn all your lessons the hard way through your own painful experience. Observe and learn from the bad example of others and modify your behavior accordingly, before you are taken to their unhappy destination.

In verse 18 it says that Christ has eyes like a flame of fire, and He sees all that everyone thinks in their innermost heart and mind. He will reward each person according to his works, whether they are good or evil, and whether they are faithful or adulterous. He says in verse 23, *"I am he which searcheth the reins and the heart,"* or the heart and the mind. The *"reins"* is literally the kidneys, and the kidneys or the intestinal area was considered to be the seat of the emotions, while the heart was considered to be the seat of the thinking. In our present day, we talk about the heart as being the seat of the emotions, and the mind as being the seat of the thinking. The idea Jesus is conveying is that He searches the heart and He searches the mind. He is saying, "I search out what you are feeling and I search out what you are thinking. I know everything that you are inwardly, I know everything you do outwardly, and I will reward you accordingly."

Jesus says, "Be warned! Those who defile My church I will destroy. I will destroy Jezebel and all of her followers." Corrupting the church by false teaching brings the severest censure from Christ and the harshest judgment from Christ. You do not defile Christ's church. You do not defile His bride. If you do, you will have to face the wrath of the husband of the church. Let churches take great care about whom they allow to teach in them.

This was the strength of the church at Ephesus. In Revelation 2:2, Jesus said of the church at Ephesus, *"I know thy works, and thy labour, and thy patience, and how thou canst not bear them which are evil: and thou hast tried them which say they are apostles, and are not, and hast found them liars."* Jezebel would not have lasted thirty seconds in the church at Ephesus, but the love that the church at Thyatira had far exceeded the love that was in the church at Ephesus.

We need to have Ephesian discernment, and we need to have Thyatiran love. The church at Thyatira had tremendous charity. The church at Ephesus had tremendous discernment. Both of those need to be combined in the same church. Jesus said to Ephesus: "Increase your love." He said to the church at Thyatira: "Increase your discernment."

The Conclusion of the Letter

The conclusion to the letter is in verses 24 through 29.

First of all, notice the promise made. In previous letters, we were given the exhortation first and then the promise. But in these subsequent letters this sequence is inverted, and we are given the promise first and the exhortation second.

Understand that not all in the church at Thyatira followed Jezebel's teachings. Notice verse 24: *"But unto you I say, and unto the rest in Thyatira, as many as have not this doctrine, and which have not known the depths of Satan, as they speak; I will put upon you none other burden."*

When there was false teaching in the church, there were people who said, "I am not going along with that. It is immoral, it is unbiblical, and it is dishonoring to God. I am not going to participate in it." Jezebel took the believers to the very depths of Satan's desires and teachings when she took them to the place and practice of idolatry and fornication. Do you want to know what the deep things of Satan are? Look no further than idolatry and adultery done in the worship of a false god.

The people that are mentioned in verse 24 are the same people that are mentioned in verse 19: *"I know thy works, and charity, and service, and faith, and thy patience, and thy works; and the last to be more than the first.*" Verse 24: "*But unto you I say. . .*" Who are the "*you*"? They are the people described in verse 19. "*But unto you I say, and unto the rest in Thyatira,*" as many as did not buy into Jezebel's teaching and did not participate in the satanic instruction she provided; upon you, He says, "*I will put. . .none other burden.*" Jesus is saying to the people of verse 19: "You are doing great! Just keep it up. Keep doing the same things mentioned in verse 19. Keep doing them for a long time, keep doing them to the end, and do not do anything else. Simply keep on being faithful." Verse 25: "*But that which ye have already hold fast till I come.*"

Many people think things like this: For the last fifteen or twenty years, we have been praying and reading the Scriptures and singing hymns and preaching the Bible and practicing the Lord's Supper. Is it not time for a change? Shouldn't we do something different in the future? The answer is: No! Jesus says to them, "Just keep holding fast to what you have been doing. Just keep on doing the same things. Do not innovate; just be faithful in doing the same things over and over again. That which you already have, hold fast until I come."

He gives a promise to these people, and it is this: "[26] *And he that overcometh, and keepeth my works unto the end, to him will I give power over the nations:* [27] *And he shall rule them with a rod of iron; as the vessels of a potter shall they be broken to shivers: even as I received of my Father.* [28] *And I will give him the morning star.*" This promise is made to the overcomer. Who is an overcomer? Someone who "*keepeth my works unto the end.*"

In other words, the overcomer is not some sinless super-saint. The overcomer is someone who keeps on doing the works of verse 19 until the end of his life. The overcomer is someone who works and loves and serves and exercises faith and patience for Jesus all the days of his or her life. This is the overcomer to whom Jesus makes several promises.

First of all, Jesus promises to give him a share of His rule. Notice verses 26 and 27: "*And he that overcometh, and keepeth my works unto the end*" (the works of verse 19), "*to him will I give power over the nations:* [27] *And he shall rule them with a rod of iron; as the vessels of a potter shall they be broken to shivers: even as I received of my Father.*" That is the first promise. Jesus says, "I will give him a share of My rule." Verse 27 is a reference to Psalm 2:9.

This shows that part of the overcomer's reward is going to consist of a share in Christ's rule over the nations. As a reward for His obedience, Christ is given all authority in heaven and in earth, to rule them in the best interests of His people and to the detriment of His enemies. Christ is going to shatter and scatter His enemies like a pottery vessel is shattered and scattered when it is hit with a rod of iron.

Psalm 2 promises all those things to Him as a reward for His obedience. In Matthew 28:18 Jesus says, "All authority is given unto Me in heaven and in earth. I now have what Psalm 2 promised Me, and among those things is power over the nations and the power to shatter them like a pottery vessel struck with a steel rod."

The question is this: How does the believer share in this activity? The answer is in Revelation 3:21, *"To him that overcometh will I grant to sit with me in my throne, even as I also overcame, and am set down with my Father in his throne."* Jesus sat down with His Father in His throne after He died and ascended to heaven. Likewise, we will sit in Christ's throne with Him after we die and go to heaven.

Notice Revelation 20:4. Speaking of this time period between the first and the second coming of Jesus, the time period we are living in right now, He says, *"And I saw thrones, and they sat upon them, and judgment was given unto them: and I saw the souls of them that were beheaded for the witness of Jesus, and for the word of God, and which had not worshipped the beast, neither his image, neither had received his mark upon their foreheads, or in their hands; and they lived and reigned with Christ a thousand years."*

We are in this symbolic thousand-year period right now. It is the perfect length of time for all of Christ's saving work to be completed. During this time period, many believers are being beheaded. They go to heaven, and they are sitting in Christ's throne with Christ, ruling the nations.

Jesus Christ is ruling the nations at this moment, and the saints who have died and gone to heaven are sharing in His rule and, in some way, assisting Him with that rule. As each believer dies and ascends into heaven, he sits with Christ in His throne and exercises kingly rule with Him over the nations of the earth until the second coming.

This is the first promise Jesus makes to overcomers. When they die and go to heaven, they are going to rule with a rod of iron over those who harmed them.

The second promise made to the overcomer is in verse 28. It says, *"And I will give him the morning star."* Not only will Jesus give him a share of His rule, but in verse 28 He promises He will give him a share of Himself. He says, *"I will give him the morning star."* Christ clearly declares in Revelation 22:16 that He Himself is the bright and morning star. Therefore, when Jesus says He will give the overcomer the morning star, Jesus is promising that He will give Himself to the overcomer as his reward for overcoming.

God said to Abraham in Genesis 15:1, *"Fear not, Abram: I am thy shield, and thy exceeding great reward."* "Your reward is Me; not My possessions, but Me." We know of husbands who buy all sorts of material things for their wives, but they are never personally there for them. Are these women satisfied with these nice things? Do they not prefer their husbands over the possessions they receive?

In the same way, when you get to heaven, would you be satisfied with the new heaven and the new earth and all the glory of them if Jesus were off somewhere else? You would not. Christ will not just give the glorified Christian an occupation and possessions in heaven; Christ will give the glorified Christian Himself. While your occupation will be ruling the nations, your fellowship is going to be with Christ.

The overcomer will not just share in Christ's activities; he will also share in Christ's fellowship and friendship and presence. And truly, is not being with Christ what going to heaven is really all about? Everything else is just details. It is not about the streets of gold; it is about being with our beloved Savior.

Secondly, notice the exhortation given in verse 29: *"He that hath an ear, let him hear what the Spirit saith unto the churches."* In other words, let us hear and heed the lesson and message Christ has, not just for this church, but for our church as well. I think there are two things we need to hear very carefully.

Number one: Let us not be weary in well-doing, for in due season we shall reap if we faint not. Jesus says in verses 19 and 25: "Just keep doing those things listed there for the rest of your life, and you will be fine. That is all you need to do." He says in the last phrase of verse 24, *"I will put upon you none other burden."* To paraphrase Jesus' words further, "Just do the things in verse 19, and keep on doing them. No other burden. That is it. Just those things. Carry on. You will be the overcomer. You will have the rule, and you will have the relationship with Me that you long for."

Number two: let us be wary of whom we allow to teach us, that such a person is not teaching us the doctrine of Satan, but the doctrine of Jesus Christ. The great failing of this church is that the people did not vet their teachers properly. They let people into the pulpit who did not belong there.

We need to ask questions such as these: Does this person meet the qualifications for the teaching office? Is he teaching us biblical truth, or is he teaching us the deep things of Satan?

Let us not be weary in well-doing, and let us be very wary of whom we allow to teach us. That is what we need to be hearing, if we have ears to hear it.

When you are selecting a church to attend, what kind of teacher are you going to expose yourself to? Make sure it is someone who is not a Jezebel. Make sure it is someone like the Ephesian elders, who had discernment about who was a legitimate Bible teacher and who was not. What you want are God-called men who are leading the people of God in the narrow way that leads to everlasting life, who build the church on the rock of Jesus Christ and not on their own personality, and who strive to bring glory to God and not to themselves.

16

The Letter to the Church at Sardis, Revelation 3:1–6

> "[1] *And unto the angel of the church in Sardis write; These things saith he that hath the seven Spirits of God, and the seven stars; I know thy works, that thou hast a name that thou livest, and art dead.* [2] *Be watchful, and strengthen the things which remain, that are ready to die: for I have not found thy works perfect before God.* [3] *Remember therefore how thou hast received and heard, and hold fast, and repent. If therefore thou shalt not watch, I will come on thee as a thief, and thou shalt not know what hour I will come upon thee.* [4] *Thou hast a few names even in Sardis which have not defiled their garments; and they shall walk with me in white: for they are worthy.* [5] *He that overcometh, the same shall be clothed in white raiment; and I will not blot out his name out of the book of life, but I will confess his name before my Father, and before his angels.* [6] *He that hath an ear, let him hear what the Spirit saith unto the churches.*"

The church at Sardis is a very sad church because it is a virtually dead church. The deadness of this church was not the result of some dreadful persecution from without that had beaten it down into compromising with the world. Instead, this deadness was an apathy that arose from within, that arose from a failure to place a proper value on the salvation Jesus had provided them with. Familiarity with Christianity had bred boredom and indifference.

This is often the case with second-generation churches. Those who are first saved out of paganism are usually very zealous for Christ because they understand the darkness they were delivered from. They understand the value of redemption from the evil they were in bondage to. But those raised in Christian homes and churches from the time of their birth, who never experience a dramatic deliverance from a wicked and destructive lifestyle like their parents did, often take Christ and Christianity for granted because it is all so familiar to them. They have heard it all, seen it all, and experienced it all from the time they were infants.

Having never experienced the evil of the world, they often think it must have something to offer, and they begin to experiment with it to see what pleasures it can provide. They think like this: "Surely, the world has something more exciting than this boring old Christianity that I have heard about since the time I was born." Church becomes a formality, prayer becomes a performance, and Bible reading becomes a mere mechanical activity.

Worldly entertainments and activities seem so much more exciting, and soon they become immersed in them and defiled by them, and spirituality is replaced with sensuality. Drinking, smoking, dancing, and movies—these things become cutting edge practices and points of discussion among believers, and theological discussions are abstract and intellectual and historical, but never personal and practical. Men get together and discuss the whiskey they are drinking and the cigars they are smoking and the ballroom dancing they are enjoying and the last adventure movie they saw, and then they discuss some obtuse aspect of theology.

Spiritual deadness results, and only the merest shell of religiosity remains. The public reputation of such churches is that they are biblical, but the reality is they are largely dead and devoid of any true spiritual life. This was the condition of the church at Sardis. They knew all about the world, but they knew very little of Christ. It was a church that had a name that it lived, but it was dead.

We need to look at and listen to and learn from this dreadful example at Sardis, and strive to avoid the deadness into which these believers fell.

The Introduction to the Letter

The introduction is found in verse 1a. *"And unto the angel of the church in Sardis write; These things saith he that hath the seven Spirits of God, and the seven stars."* Here we are told who the recipients and author of this letter are.

First of all, notice the recipients of the letter. The recipients of the letter are the pastor and the church in the city of Sardis. Sardis was a city situated on a steep hill, which rendered it nearly invincible to military attack. Because of this, the people of Sardis were confident the city could not be defeated by an invading force. There was only one point of access to this city, which was a very narrow neck of land that could easily be guarded and defended.

However, this city was conquered twice; once in 549 BC by Cyrus, and once again in 218 BC by Antiochus. Because of their carelessness, complacency, and self-confidence, the people had left that one way of access unguarded.

This carelessness, complacency, and self-confidence arose out of the easy wealth and the tremendous prosperity that the city enjoyed. Sardis was situated on major roads of commerce, and it was the capital city of King Croesus, who was legendary for his staggering riches. In fact, it is a proverb to say of someone that he is as rich as Croesus.

The city's easy wealth and self-indulgent lifestyle brought about worldliness and carelessness and indolence that made its inhabitants complacent and overconfident. As a result, they were defeated by their enemies, hardly putting up a fight, because they were not watchful. Sudden destruction came upon them as a thief in the night, while they were asleep and not on guard.

This disposition of a self-satisfied complacency, lack of watchfulness, and unpreparedness for warfare when attacked by the enemy was also reflected in the attitude of the members of the church at Sardis. The church had become formal, careless, complacent, and indolent, to the point that it was failing at spiritual warfare at the most basic level. The church went through the motions of spiritual watchfulness and spiritual worship, but it was empty, formal, and heartless. It was a church that was virtually devoid of spiritual life. Satan was ready to overrun this church, and they were oblivious to it. Their own complacency and empty formalism were preparing them to be utterly defeated and destroyed. One day they would look around and wonder what happened, but then it would be too late.

This church is a church that has a form of godliness but is devoid of its power because its spirituality has diminished to the point that it is nearly dead. This is the state and condition of the recipients of the letter.

Secondly, notice the author of the letter. The author of the letter is Jesus Christ, who identifies Himself in verse 1a as *"he that hath the seven Spirits of God, and the seven stars."*

We were first introduced to this term, *"the seven Spirits of God,"* in Revelation 1:4 which says, *"John to the seven churches which are in Asia: Grace be unto you, and peace, from him which is, and which was, and which is to come; and from the seven Spirits which are before his throne."* Numbers are used symbolically in the book of Revelation, so there are not literally seven different Spirits of God; instead, we saw that the number seven symbolizes completeness.

By using the phrase *"the seven Spirits of God,"* Jesus is saying that the Holy Spirit completely meets every need the church has for salvation, every need the church has for sanctification, and every need the church has for preservation. There is nothing the church needs that the Holy Spirit does not completely supply.

But this church had grieved the Spirit and quenched the Spirit by its coldness, indifference, worldliness, and heartless formalism. This church desperately needed the work of the Holy Spirit to resurrect it and revitalize it and to bring it to repentance. Jesus is said here to be the one who controls and sends the Holy Spirit to do that indispensable work. Jesus will send the Holy Spirit to do this work among them if they will repent and seek the restoration of the work of the Spirit among them once again. Jesus Himself promised in Luke 11:13, *"How much more shall your heavenly Father give the Holy Spirit to them that ask Him?"*

The great gift Christ has to give to His church is the gift of the Spirit, but we as a church need to be praying like this: "Father, send the Spirit through the hand of Your Son to our church, that He may minister in our midst and exercise the spiritual power of salvation and sanctification and preservation among us!" It is only by and through the ministry and work of the Holy Spirit that real spiritual life and genuine spiritual ministry can exist within a church. When the Spirit's work and blessing is absent, then the church winds up merely going through the motions, but it has no real spiritual life. It may appear to have spiritual life. It has all the forms, it has all the documents, and it engages in all the activities. But the reality is that it is spiritually dead because all it does is devoid of the Spirit's work and operation.

Jesus, by declaring He holds the Holy Spirit in His hand, is inviting this church to seek the work and blessing of the Spirit upon them as a gift from Him. He who gave the Holy Spirit on the day of Pentecost gives Him over and over again to each local church, as they beseech Him to give the Spirit to them Lord's Day by Lord's Day.

But not only does Jesus have the Holy Spirit who is perfectly able to perfectly meet all the needs of the church; secondly, notice that in verse 1 Jesus also has *"the seven stars."* In Revelation 1:20 we saw the seven stars are the seven angels or messengers of the churches, whom we identified as the pastors of the churches.

Jesus has the Holy Spirit with all of the perfection of His person and work, and Jesus has His ministers of the gospel. He has both of these things in His possession, ready to dispense upon His churches. Christ not only supplies the churches with the Holy Spirit, but Christ also supplies the churches with pastors who are called and equipped and empowered by Him with both gifts and authority to represent His message to the churches. Ephesians 4:11 says that Christ gave as gifts to His church *"some, apostles; and some, prophets; and some, evangelists; and some, pastors and teachers."*

If any of those individuals exist and rightly occupy those offices, it is because Jesus Christ gave them to His church as gifts. Churches will languish and decay without proper pastoral leadership, and Christ has instructed His people to pray to Him who is the Lord of the harvest to send forth laborers into His harvest. Churches need to pray to the Chief Shepherd to send them His own under-shepherds who will lead the church in the paths of righteousness and in the narrow way that leads to everlasting life. Blessed is the church that has one of the stars in Christ's right hand as its pastor, and cursed is the church that does not.

If this church at Sardis was as dead and formal as Christ says it is, then no small part of the blame for that state can be laid at the feet of the pastor who was leading it. He had led it into formalism, complacency, and worldliness by failing to teach the truth, by failing to call the people to repentance, and by failing to guard the church against compromise.

This church not only needed a new work of the Holy Spirit in its midst, but it also needed new pastoral leadership at its head. It needed a Christ-called, Christ-equipped, Christ-centered preacher ministering within it. Jesus can supply them both. Jesus says He has them both, and the church needs to cry out to Him for both. With a Christ-given Spirit and with a Christ-given pastor, it is possible for this church to recover from its spiritual deadness.

The Message of the Letter

The message of the letter to Sardis is in verses 1b to 4. The message of this letter, unlike all of the letters we have seen up to this point, does not begin with a commendation. To all of the churches in chapter 2, Jesus started with a commendation. But here in chapter 3 with this fifth church, Jesus does not start with a commendation, but with a correction. He immediately begins to rebuke and correct this church because, unlike the previous churches where there was a godly majority and a corrupt minority, here the church is largely corrupt, with only a small minority of godly people within it. Therefore, Jesus starts out with a severe and forceful condemnation.

First of all, notice the condemnation contained in verses 1b to 3. In verse 1b He says, *"I know."* Once again, Jesus opens His address to this church the same way He does with all these churches, with the words *"I know."* The knowledge Jesus has of each of His churches is perfect and complete and absolute; and nothing in any church or in the heart of any person within that church is hidden from His eyes.

This is a great source of comfort to an obedient yet persecuted church like the church at Smyrna. It is a comfort to know that Jesus knows all about our service to Him and our suffering for Him, even when everyone else despises it.

But the opposite side of this knowledge of Christ is that it is a great source of consternation to a hypocritical and compromised church. Jesus sees through the façade of spirituality, sees past the positive public opinion the church has been able to manufacture, and discerns and is displeased with their false godliness and fake spirituality. Jesus is saying to the church at Sardis, "I know your public image and your personal behavior are two different things." This is not good news. This should provoke great concern, and it should provoke immediate repentance.

Notice what Jesus says He knows about this church in verse 1b. He says, *"I know thy works, that thou hast a name that thou livest, and art dead."* He says, in essence, "I know your works, and these works make it clear that though you have a name that you are alive; the reality is, you are a church that is virtually dead."

The public image and reputation of this church was that they had spiritual life and blessing in their midst. But the reality was that they had neither spiritual blessing nor spiritual life that came from God. It was all an illusion created by religious posturing and empty spiritual rhetoric. They may have had people, money, and buildings in abundance, but what they did not have was true biblical spiritual life.

Sardis enjoyed a very good public reputation, but it did not deserve that reputation. There is no indication this church was making an impact on the world around it. We know this to be the case because the believers were not being persecuted by the world since they were really no different from the world. Jesus says of them in verse 4, that there were a few people in the church in Sardis who had not defiled their garments, indicating that the vast majority of those in the church in Sardis had defiled their garments with the sins and the practices of the world.

The result was that neither the Romans nor the Jews were troubled by this church, and therefore, they did not bother to persecute this church because the church was so much like them. It was so worldly that the world did not see any reason to persecute it because it was not a threat to them. The church largely lived like the world lived. The vast majority of the people in the church were defiled by worldliness.

As a result, Sardis was a very peaceful church. But they were peaceful like a cemetery is peaceful. This church was peaceful because it was virtually spiritually dead. There was no confrontation of sin, and there was no correction of behavior. The pastors did not preach the word and reprove and rebuke and exhort with all longsuffering and doctrine. Nobody was offended, everybody was happy, everybody was left in their sin, everybody lived as they pleased, and everybody proclaimed: "Look at the blessing of God on our assembly and its size and its peace and unity!" Jesus said there was barely a spark of spiritual life within them. They were on the verge of spiritual apostasy.

But they have not quite gone over the edge yet, even though they are teetering on the brink. Notice verse 2. He says, *"Be watchful, and strengthen the things which remain, that are ready to die: for I have not found thy works perfect before God."* Jesus looks at this church, and He knows as a church they are about to die. They have not yet died, but they are on the brink of death. They may yet be revived, but if they wait much longer, the opportunity will be gone.

Jesus is saying to this church: "Be alert and be awake to your spiritual danger." Notice verse 2: *"Be watchful, strengthen the things which remain."* His words, in effect, are, "Remember the defeat of the city of Sardis? Be watchful and guard that narrow path! Strengthen your fortifications on the path before the enemy comes in and destroys you. Be alert and awake to your spiritual danger. Strengthen the little spark of spiritual life that you have left. You are largely given over to formalism and sensuality and worldliness, but there is still a small amount of true spirituality in you. Fan that into a flame before it is extinguished. Your lamp is very dim. The candle is almost out. The lampstand will soon be removed if you do not return to being a light to the world, instead of being compromised with the world."

He says in verse 2b, *"for I have not found thy works perfect before God."* What this means is not that God expects us to be perfect people or to do everything perfectly. The idea of perfection is the idea of something being brought to completion. He is saying, "I have not found your works brought to the full expression of obedience. You start to obey, you partially obey, you halfheartedly follow through, but little is actually done in My service and for My glory and in fulfillment of My instructions because you give up before you are half done. You quit when you have barely started."

We see this in churches today. They sing, but they sing songs with shallow lyrics and sensual music. They read Scripture, but they read out of a corrupt Bible version. They pray, but they pray for health and wealth. They preach, but they preach humanistic theology. Yes, there is some truth scattered about in all of these things, but it is overwhelmed by the error and worldly corruption that permeates it all. It is all so tainted with things displeasing to God that these works wind up being an offense to God instead of being acceptable to God, and that is what He means when He says, *"I have not found thy works perfect."*

Jesus is saying in verse 2b that their works fall far short of what they should be and what they could be if they were really attempting to obey Him and please Him with sincerity. The forms of worship are there: the ceremonies are practiced, the religious customs and traditions are carried out, the meetings are held, and the preaching is done. But the substance and the essence, the heart and the spirit, and the faith and the love that God requires are barely present.

These people are disengaged religious formalists who have virtually lost the worship of God in spirit and in truth. They draw near to God with their mouth, they honor Him with their lips, but their heart is far from Him, and in vain do they worship Him, as they teach for doctrines the commandments of men. This is why this severe and strong condemnation is brought to bear on them by Jesus.

Secondly, notice the warning. The warning immediately follows in verse 3. *"Remember therefore how thou hast received and heard, and hold fast, and repent. If therefore thou shalt not watch, I will come on thee as a thief, and thou shalt not know what hour I will come upon thee."*

In this warning, Jesus calls on them to remember how they had first received the gospel and how they had first heard the message when they had initially professed faith in Christ. Back then, they had received the message with excitement and enthusiasm and gratitude and humility. They wanted nothing more than to serve and worship God. They were consumed with living for Him and telling other people about Him. But that was virtually gone now.

They have settled into apathy, complacency, indifference, and yes, even into boredom with the things of God. Jesus is telling them: "Hold fast to who you used to be and what you used to do and the spirituality you used to have. Repent of your departure from your former faith and your former love and zeal for Me."

Therefore, His warning to them in verse 3b is this: "If you continue in your spiritual slumber, if you refuse to awaken to your spiritual danger, if you do not repent and return to spiritual vigilance and spiritual awareness, then I will come suddenly like a thief in the night, and you will receive My judgment and My wrath." Those are sobering words.

Just as the city of Sardis was conquered by surprise because it was too self-confident and too indolent to set a watch and be vigilant, so the church at Sardis will suddenly be judged by Christ if they will not return to spiritual watchfulness and spiritual diligence. This church needs Christ's blessing, not His correction. They need His help, not His chastisement. They have a choice to make. Will they repent? Or will they remain in their catatonic state of spiritual deadness? Do they want Christ to come in blessing? Or do they want Him to come in correction and judgment? They need to make up their mind now. Soon it will be too late.

Will they cry out to Him to give them the work of the Holy Spirit in their midst? Will they cry out to Him to supply them with a Christ-honoring pastor? Or will they be content with the dead formalism they now have, both in the leadership and in the congregation? They have a choice between revival and judgment. What will they choose?

As you see yourself slipping into complacency and indolence in your spiritual life, you too have a choice to make—revival, or moving further toward the judgment and the chastisement of God. Repent before Jesus returns and brings His correction to bear.

Thirdly, notice His commendation in verse 4: *"Thou hast a few names even in Sardis which have not defiled their garments; and they shall walk with me in white: for they are worthy."*

In the midst of His rebuke of the majority of this church, Jesus has not forgotten the minority of faithful believers who have maintained a true spirituality, who have maintained a true separation from the practice of sin, and who have maintained a true pursuit of genuine, heartfelt obedience to Christ. In the midst of all this spiritual declension that characterized the church at Sardis, a few had walked worthy of the high calling of God. A few had not compromised with the culture. A few had not compromised with the worldliness of their fellow church members. As our text says, they had not defiled their garments, as most of them had. They had not gone along with the crowd. They did not float downstream with all the other dead fish. They kept swimming against the current of temptation, their own fallenness, and the pressures of the world, and they kept going after Christ.

It is hard enough when unbelievers are influencing you to sin with their temptations and enticements. It is doubly hard when your fellow church members are doing the same with their compromised lives and examples and encouragements. They say things like, "Relax! You are too strict in following biblical principle in every area of your life. You are being legalistic!"

We expect the world to try to tear us down. We do not expect the people in the church to do so, and it is doubly hard when they do, and try to drag us into their worldliness and mock us when we do not participate. They exclude you from their company because you do not know about the latest movies or celebrity gossip because you have been reading your Bible in the evenings and have no time for worldly entertainment.

We are tempted to say to ourselves things like this: "When all other Christians are spending hours in front of the television and sending their kids to public school and watching all the corrupt movies and participating in all the worldly activity, why should I deny myself? They are good Christians. They do all these things. There is no reason I should not." The reason you should not is that Jesus says they are not good Christians. Jesus says they are spiritually dead.

In spite of all of the horrible influence of their fellow professing believers, those few Christians in Sardis had lived lives worthy of their profession of faith in Christ, and their conduct corresponded with their profession. They were worthy of being declared to be genuine believers in Jesus Christ.

Notice what He says in verse 4. He says, *"They shall walk with me in white: for they are worthy."* They are not "worthy" of having earned their own salvation. They are worthy of being recognized as true Christians because they had lived a life of separation from the world and a life of seeking after Jesus. Their lives had corresponded with their profession of faith in Christ. They are worthy of being declared to be genuine believers in Jesus Christ.

Jesus knows every one of them by name. Verse 4: *"Thou hast a few names even in Sardis."* What an interesting phrase. Jesus knows your name. He knows you individually. He remembers who you are, and He remembers what you have done, and He remembers that you stood against the crowd and you stood with Christ. When all the others were going the way of the world, you went the way of righteousness. Jesus says of them, they will walk with Him clothed in white garments—that is, they will be dressed in a robe of righteousness and walk with Him in heaven. They will enjoy purity of life and the presence of Christ forever.

The Conclusion of the Letter

The conclusion to this letter is in verses 5 and 6. He says, *"He that overcometh, the same shall be clothed in white raiment; and I will not blot out his name out of the book of life, but I will confess his name before my Father, and before his angels. [6] He that hath an ear, let him hear what the Spirit saith unto the churches."*

First of all, notice the promise made. Every time, in every one of these letters, the promise made is always made to the overcomer, and it is made to no one else. Notice verse 5: *"He that overcometh."* The overcomer is the one who overcomes the things Jesus was rebuking the majority of the church of succumbing to. Here is one who does not live a life characterized by defilement with the world. Here is one who does not live as a spiritually dying religious formalist. The overcomer is one who lives a life of holiness and true spirituality. He separates from sin and he seeks after Christ. He is not content to be indistinguishable from the world. He is not content to be devoid of sincere inward heart communion with God. In a word, he lives a life of purity and prayerfulness with a sincere, engaged heart. Such a one, Jesus says, will be clothed in the robes of righteousness.

We are told what these white robes are in Revelation 7:13–14. These robes represent the righteousness which the saints possess in their perfect and purified state in heaven. Jesus is saying that perfect and permanent righteousness will be bestowed on every sincere believer who flees from sin and follows Christ as the evidence of his saving faith. Any faith other than that is a dead faith.

In the book of James, we are told that faith without works is dead. What are the works that show a living faith? They are the works of fleeing from sin and following Christ. It does not mean you are perfect; but it means you follow on to know the Lord, and when you fall into sin, you repent and return to the Lord.

To such a one, Jesus promises negatively in verse 5, *"I will not blot his name out of the book of life."* The book of life is the book that contains the names of all of God's elect. It is a list of all the saved people. Jesus is saying such a one cannot possibly ever run the risk of being unsaved. It will never happen to such a one that his name will not be found in the book of life when he flees from sin and he follows Christ with a genuine, heartfelt, spiritual pursuit.

Then Jesus promises positively, *"I will confess his name before my Father, and before his angels."* Jesus is saying that on the Day of Judgment, He will be the advocate of the overcomer. He will own him as being one of His. He will declare that He has forgiven all of his sins, and will declare that He has given him His own personal righteousness to cover him.

Jesus said in Matthew 10:32, *"Whosoever therefore shall confess me before men, him will I confess also before my Father which is in heaven."* The most wonderful thing that we will ever hear in our entire existence are the words of Christ when He declares us to be His own on the Day of Judgment, and when He confesses our name before the Father, saying that we belong to Him. This is the promise He makes to the overcomer, and no one but the overcomer is the recipient of that promise.

That is the promise made. The spiritually dead do not receive the promise. The spiritually apathetic, the spiritually indifferent, and the spiritually defiled who live their lives on a trajectory of compromise and worldliness until they die are not overcomers. Christians fight the good fight of faith, and by the grace of Christ and the gifts of Christ, they overcome. They triumph. The world does not defile them; they stand separate from the world and call the world out of its defilement and into the holiness of Christian living.

The overcomer does not go through the motions of Christianity while his mind is somewhere else; rather, as he participates in the worship and service of God, his heart and soul and mind are in it. He is more concerned about what Christ thinks about him than he is about what his reputation is in the community. We should rather have people think that our church is dead, and have Christ think it is alive, than for the community to think our church is really a together, going, and growing church, but have Christ think it is dead.

We have to serve and live and work for the eye of Christ and not for our reputation before men. The people of the church at Sardis were so concerned with what the world thought of them that they had become just like the world in order to get the approval of the world. Sadly, many churches consist of an assembly of professing Christians who are really just dead formalists. You can tell them by their fruits.

Secondly, notice the exhortation given in verse 6: *"He that hath an ear, let him hear what the Spirit saith unto the churches."* Let us listen carefully to what the Lord of the church is saying to our church. Jesus is saying to our church that we must constantly seek repentance and renewal and revival so we do not sink into spiritual deadness ourselves.

Every day you have to guard that narrow neck of land by which the devil is coming to conquer you, and you have to fight him back. There are no secrets to the Christian life. It is warfare every day to maintain warmth of heart and love for Christ by plunging yourself into the means of grace that God has given you, and by refusing to walk in the counsel of the ungodly or stand in the way of sinners or sit in the seat of the scornful.

This is why Jesus said the Christian life is a battlefield. We have to fight for spirituality as a church, we have to fight for spirituality as individuals, and there is no place for complacency, self-satisfaction, or coasting.

We have to beware of merely going through the motions of worship. Each time, we need to put our hearts and minds and souls into it. Jesus said they that worship God must worship Him in spirit and in truth, for the Father seeks such to worship Him.

What this means is when you are singing the hymns, participating in the prayer, hearing the Scriptures read, hearing the preaching done, and partaking of the Lord's Supper, do not let your mind be somewhere else. Focus on what you are hearing and singing and praying, and interact with the Lord in your heart as you are doing it.

That is what will save you from religious formalism, because there are two elements to real worship. There is the subjective element that is personal and inward: we have to worship God in spirit. There is the objective element that is external and universal: we have to worship God in and through the truth of the Word of God. It does not do any good to sincerely engage your heart with error. On the other hand, you can have solid truth, but if your heart is disengaged, you have not worshipped.

Think about what you are singing. Think about what is being prayed. Think about what is being read. Think about what is being preached. Think about what is being symbolized in the ordinances. Then lift your heart to God with reference to them and interact in your heart with God regarding them. In this way, you will be worshiping Him in spirit and in truth, and He will be pleased with your worship. He will own it and recognize it as spiritual vitality and life.

In your heart is where your spiritual vitality lives and dies. That is why you have to be a heart Christian, not just an external Christian.

We have to be more concerned with our reputation in the eyes of Christ than we are with our reputation in the eyes of the world. The world may think well of us, or the world may think poorly of us. But the only question is this: What does Christ think of us?

If you find yourself in a formalist church—a dead church like Sardis—you can still be a real Christian in it. There were a few, even in the church at Sardis, who were real believers, sincere believers, separated believers, and believers who sincerely followed the Lord Jesus.

Maybe that is the best you can find, and the best you can attend. Be the best you can within it, and do not let older professing Christians lead you into defiling your garments because they have chosen to do so themselves out of apathy, indifference, and carelessness. You just live for the Lord, and hopefully you will find some other kindred spirits. You can find other folks in those kinds of churches who love Jesus also. Just form your own little circle of fellowship, where you can encourage each other to stand against the deadness and the dullness that comes from the pulpit and that comes from the people who have long since lost their love and zeal for Christ. Keep your zeal up, and keep on going. That is the message. We need to have ears to hear it.

17

The Letter to the Church in Philadelphia, Revelation 3:7–13

> "[7] *And to the angel of the church in Philadelphia write; These things saith he that is holy, he that is true, he that hath the key of David, he that openeth, and no man shutteth; and shutteth, and no man openeth;* [8] *I know thy works: behold, I have set before thee an open door, and no man can shut it: for thou hast a little strength, and hast kept my word, and hast not denied my name.* [9] *Behold, I will make them of the synagogue of Satan, which say they are Jews, and are not, but do lie; behold, I will make them to come and worship before thy feet, and to know that I have loved thee.* [10] *Because thou hast kept the word of my patience, I also will keep thee from the hour of temptation, which shall come upon all the world, to try them that dwell upon the earth.* [11] *Behold, I come quickly: hold that fast which thou hast, that no man take thy crown.* [12] *Him that overcometh will I make a pillar in the temple of my God, and he shall go no more out: and I will write upon him the name of my God, and the name of the city of my God, which is new Jerusalem, which cometh down out of heaven from my God: and I will write upon him my new name.* [13] *He that hath an ear, let him hear what the Spirit saith unto the churches.*"

The church at Philadelphia possesses a distinctive trait that is shared only with the church at Smyrna, and that is that Christ has no criticism or correction to offer to this church. Here is a church that is obedient to Christ in every area of its teaching and its practice. Like the church at Smyrna, it has been faithful in observing all that Christ has commanded them. You often hear people say there is no perfect church. If by that they mean there are no churches with sinless people in them, then they are correct. But if by that they mean there are no churches that do not displease Christ in some way, then they are wrong.

By living according to all the instructions given by Christ both in doctrine and practice, a church may very well be the perfect church—perfect in the sense that there is no defect in doctrine or practice that needs to be corrected. Two out of these seven churches had achieved this status of being perfect churches. They were obeying Christ to the degree that they were blameless before Him. He had no reproof or correction to offer them. His message to them was simply this: "You are doing fine. Stay the course. Keep being faithful. I am with you and I will reward you. Just keep on doing what you have been doing. Do not depart from it."

That is the kind of church we want to be part of, and that is the kind of church we should strive to have. It is the kind of church we can have if both pastor and people fear God and love God and live for God, and if they strive to follow every instruction Christ gives His church in His Word.

Having a blameless church is not hard. It is not a mysterious process. Having a blameless church consists of simply obeying the written word of God and the instructions it contains for what the church teaches and how the church functions.

In 1 Timothy 3:14–15 Paul says to Timothy, the pastor of the church at Ephesus, "*These things write I unto thee, hoping to come unto thee shortly:* [15] *But if I tarry long, that thou mayest know how thou oughtest to behave thyself in the house of God, which is the church of the living God, the pillar and ground of the truth.*" There is a way we ought to behave in the church, both in the doctrine we teach and in the worship and service we practice, and knowing what that is, is as simple as reading the Scriptures and following their instruction without deviation.

The problem is that people want to do church their own way. They want to innovate. They want to try new things. They want to devise new forms of worship, new practices, new teachings, new ministries, and new doctrines. Not satisfied to just keep on doing what Christ has instructed them to do in the Bible, they have to implement what they perceive to be improvements so as to keep the people happy and to keep them coming. This attitude of innovation instead of obedience is the start of every kind of error in practice and every kind of error in teaching.

The good news is that the church at Philadelphia, like the church at Smyrna, did not succumb to the voices that called them to depart from the biblical pattern for how their church should function and what their church should teach. As a result, this was a church that was blameless before Christ. Not only were they blameless before Christ, but they were also warmly commended by Christ and given great encouragement by Him. They were, if you will, the perfect church.

The Introduction to the Letter

The introduction to the letter is in verse 7: *"And to the angel of the church in Philadelphia write; These things saith he that is holy, he that is true, he that hath the key of David, he that openeth, and no man shutteth; and shutteth, and no man openeth."*

The introduction to this letter reveals both the recipient and author of the letter. First of all, notice the recipient of the letter. The recipient of the letter is the pastor and the church in the city of Philadelphia. The city of Philadelphia was located at the crossroads of three major provinces: Mysia, Lydia, and Phrygia. Just as St. Louis in the United States is called the Gateway to the West, Philadelphia was known as the Gateway to the East.

The city was founded by Attalus II, whose renowned loyalty to his brother Eumenes earned him the title "Philadelphos," translated "brother-lover," or "lover of his brother." Since the city was founded by Attalus II Philadelphos, the city derived its name from its founder, and thus it was called Philadelphia, the City of Brotherly Love.

Attalus intended for this city to be a base from which Greek culture, Greek values, and the Greek way of life would be propagated and spread to the rest of the nation. Philadelphia was meant to be a missionary base for the spreading of Hellenistic culture and the Hellenistic way of life.

From the beginning this was supposed to be a missionary city for the spread of Greek culture; and in that respect, it was quite successful in achieving its goals. It is often said that Rome conquered Greece militarily, but Greece conquered Rome culturally. As a result, the New Testament was written in Greek because Greek, not Latin, was the common language of the Roman world.

The church at Philadelphia was apparently quite small, because verse 8 says they had a little strength. However, the smallness and the weakness of the church did not keep them from being obedient to Christ or pleasing to Christ. We must understand this point very clearly.

Notice verse 8. He says, *"I know thy works: behold, I have set before thee an open door, and no man can shut it: for thou hast a little strength."* The fact that they had only a little strength means they were small and poor. They were not a large strong church. They were a small church, a poor church, and thus a weak church. It is not the size of the church but the quality of the church that matters to Christ. Jesus did not say, "You are a small church. You do not have strength and numbers. Shame on you! There must be something wrong with the way you people do church because it is so small and weak." That is how people reason, but that is not how Christ reasons.

Like a diamond, this church was very small in size, but it was highly prized and greatly valued by Christ. It was small and it was poor, but Christ was exceedingly pleased with it and gave it His warmest commendation. In no way did He criticize it for being small and poor. Jesus Himself said in Matthew 18:20, *"For where two or three are gathered together in my name, there am I in the midst of them."* It was not the size of the church; it was the quality of the church that Christ was concerned with. It was not how many people they had, but how faithful they were that mattered to Jesus.

This church had a great deal in common with the church in Smyrna. Like Smyrna, it was blameless in the eyes of Christ. Like Smyrna, its enemies came from outside the church, not from inside the church. And like Smyrna, both churches were persecuted by Jews, who Jesus said served in a synagogue of Satan. The recipient of this letter is a small church, a poor church, but a blameless church—one that is persecuted by the world, but one that is greatly beloved by Christ.

Secondly, notice the author of the letter. The author of the letter is Jesus Christ, who identifies Himself with the most extended description of Himself that is given in any of these seven letters. Notice how lengthy His description of Himself is in verse 7. He says, *"These things saith he that is holy, he that is true, he that hath the key of David, he that openeth, and no man shutteth; and shutteth, and no man openeth."*

First, He identifies Himself as *"he that is holy."* Holiness refers to Christ's spotless purity and His sinless character. The Scripture says in 1 John 3:5, *"He was manifested to take away our sins; and in him is no sin."* But when He identifies Himself as being holy, this not only refers to His spotless purity and His sinless character, it also is a reference to His deity. Jehovah of the Old Testament is called *"the Holy One,"* in Isaiah 40:25 and in Habakkuk 3:3, as well as in numerous other passages in both the Old and New Testament. As it says in Isaiah 6:3, *"Holy, holy, holy, is the LORD of hosts: the whole earth is full of his glory."*

When Jesus says in verse 7, *"These things saith he that is holy,"* He is saying, "Not only do I have spotless purity and sinless character; I am also God. I am taking the title of *'the Holy One'* to myself, a title that belongs to God in the Old Testament."

Secondly, He identifies Himself as *"he that is true."* We have already seen in Revelation 1:5 that Jesus Christ is identified as He *"who is the faithful witness."* There we saw that Jesus was a witness who always told the truth. When Jesus says of Himself that He is the one who is true, He is declaring that His word is completely reliable, wholly accurate, and absolutely trustworthy. When He speaks, there is no doubt that what He says is nothing but the truth. It is always the truth, only the truth, and ever the truth.

It is interesting to note that these two terms "holy" and "true" are used as the title and name of God Himself later in Revelation. Notice Revelation 6:9–10: *"And when he had opened the fifth seal, I saw under the altar the souls of them that were slain for the word of God, and for the testimony which they held:* [10] *And they cried with a loud voice, saying, How long, O Lord, holy and true, dost thou not judge and avenge our blood on them that dwell on the earth?"*

The souls in heaven are saying to the God of heaven, "How long is it going to be before You carry out vengeance on those who slaughtered us?" When they address the God of heaven, they call Him the one who is *"holy and true."* Jesus says about Himself in Revelation 3:7, *"These things saith he that is holy, he that is true."* Once again, it is clear that Jesus is God.

Jesus is not only truthful; Jesus is also the true Messiah. He is the promised Messiah of the Old Testament. He is the true Messiah; not a false one. The Jews said that Jesus was a false messiah, but they were liars. Notice in verse 9 Jesus says of them: They *"do lie."* Jesus is in fact the true One, the true Messiah. He tells the truth, and He is the true Messiah.

Thirdly, He says of Himself that He has *"the key of David."* Keys open locks. David was the king of Israel, and as king he had complete authority over the kingdom to do as he saw fit. Jesus as the Son of David who sits on David's throne in fulfillment of the Davidic covenant has all authority given to Him in heaven and on earth. He is the great antitype whom David foreshadowed.

In this sense, Jesus has the key of David; that is, He has the key of authority to open and close the kingdom to whomever He wills, and the authority to open and close men's minds and hearts and understanding as He sees fit. If Jesus opens someone's eyes and heart to the gospel, no one can close that person's heart and mind to it, no matter how hard they try. And if Jesus closes a person's eyes and heart to the gospel, no one can open them, no matter what efforts they make.

In Job 12:13–14 it says of God: *"With him is wisdom and strength, he hath counsel and understanding.* [14] *Behold, he breaketh down, and it cannot be built again: he shutteth up a man, and there can be no opening."* The kingdom of God is not run by the will of man. Jesus acts and no one can hinder His actions, whether they go in one direction or in the opposite direction. If He opens, no one can shut, and if he shuts, no one can open. People do not run the kingdom; He makes the decisions about what happens and how things turn out. Daniel 4:35 says that "He does according to His will in the army of heaven, and among the inhabitants of the earth: and none can stay His hand, or say unto Him, What doest Thou?"

Christ opens and shuts the hearts of men. Christ opens and shuts the kingdom to men. Christ opens and shuts heaven to men. Christ opens and shuts the New Jerusalem to men. Jesus has the keys to the kingdom, and He opens and He shuts that kingdom as He pleases.

In Revelation 1:18 Jesus said, *"I am he that liveth, and was dead; and, behold, I am alive for evermore, Amen; and have the keys of hell and of death."* Here in 3:7 the keys of hell and death are further expanded, explained, and identified as being the key of David.

Because Jesus has the key of David, we must seek the permission and help of Jesus before we make any attempt to accomplish anything in the lives of people. Jesus alone controls the results, and to try to do the work without His keys is to labor in futility. But if He opens the doors before us, then nothing and no one can defeat our labor for Him. His doors of providence open and close, and we must be sensitive to that, take heed to it, and humbly bow before His choice of the doors He opens and the doors He shuts. Look for the doors Jesus is opening, go through them, and do not chafe against the closed doors and grieve because of them.

Two further passages speak of this opening and shutting. In Matthew 13:10–16, Jesus is speaking to the crowds in parables, "*And the disciples came, and said unto him, Why speakest thou unto them in parables?*" They questioned why He was using this teaching technique. Why not just say it out plain and straight? Verse 11 states: "*He answered and said unto them, Because it is given unto you to know the mysteries of the kingdom of heaven, but to them it is not given.*" He says, in effect, 'I am opening the door of understanding to you, and I am shutting the door of understanding to them." Christ decides who understands His message and who does not.

Verse 12: "*For whosoever hath, to him shall be given, and he shall have more abundance: but whosoever hath not, from him shall be taken away even that he hath.* [13] *Therefore speak I to them in parables: because they seeing see not; and hearing they hear not, neither do they understand.* [14] *And in them is fulfilled the prophecy of Isaiah, which saith, By hearing ye shall hear, and shall not understand; and seeing ye shall see, and shall not perceive:* [15] *For this people's heart is waxed gross, and their ears are dull of hearing, and their eyes they have closed; lest at any time they should see with their eyes, and hear with their ears, and should understand with their heart, and should be converted, and I should heal them.* [16] *But blessed are your eyes, for they see: and your ears, for they hear.*"

Jesus is not acting arbitrarily in shutting people's eyes and ears to the truth of the gospel. Those who have their eyes and their ears shut bear responsibility for it because they have willfully closed their own eyes and ears. Jesus is saying in verse 11, "I have opened and I have shut, and that is why I am teaching the way I am, in order to achieve this goal of opening and shutting."

Notice the second passage, Isaiah 22:20–23. It says: "*And it shall come to pass in that day, that I will call my servant Eliakim the son of Hilkiah:* [21] *And I will clothe him with thy robe, and strengthen him with thy [belt], and I will commit thy government into his hand: and he shall be a father to the inhabitants of Jerusalem, and to the house of Judah,* [22] *And the key of the house of David will I lay upon his shoulder; so he shall open, and none shall shut; and he shall shut, and none shall open.* [23] *And I will fasten him as a nail in a sure place; and he shall be for a glorious throne to his father's house.*"

Verse 22 says of Eliakim what Revelation 3:7 says about the Lord Jesus Christ. Eliakim was the son of Hilkiah the priest, and Eliakim was King Hezekiah's steward over his whole house. As King Hezekiah's steward over his house, Eliakim had the power to either admit or deny entrance into the king's palace. If someone wanted to come into the king's palace, Eliakim had the key of authority to open the door and say, "Come in and see the king," or to shut the door and say, "No, you are not coming in to see the king."

Eliakim is a prophetic type of the Lord Jesus Christ, and in the same way that Eliakim could open and shut Hezekiah's house and control access to King Hezekiah, Jesus can open and shut God's house and control access to God. No one comes to the Father except through Him. Jesus decides who is admitted and who is excluded from the kingdom of God and the new Jerusalem. Jesus has the power to open and close people's eyes and hearts, and Jesus has the power to open and close the kingdom of God and the heaven of God.

This is the author of the letter—One who is holy, One who is true, and One who has the keys of David, who could open and no one can shut, and who can shut, and no one can open.

The Message of the Letter

The message of this letter is in verses 8 through 11. It is an extended commendation and encouragement of this church, followed by a gentle warning of the need to keep up the good behavior they had exhibited up to this point in time.

First of all, notice His commendation. He says to them in Revelation 3:8, *"I know,"* the same thing He says to each of these churches. This awareness that Christ cares enough about each of His churches to know all about every one of them helps us see the value Christ places on His churches.

In life, a man pays attention to that which he cares about. He knows all about that which he sees as valuable and important to him. You have items in your possession. Some of them you know all about in exact detail. Others you have not thought about in perhaps fifteen years. They are out in the shed somewhere covered with cobwebs, and you probably do not even know where they are. Digging through the shed, you may find something and say, "Oh! I had forgotten I had that!" But with another thing, you know exactly where it is, you know exactly what it does, you know what it cost, and you know when you used it last. You know all about it because that item is really important to you.

Christ is telling us that His churches are the special focus of His attention and the special objects of His affection. He sees them as exceedingly valuable and exceedingly important to Him, because He laid down His life for them. He will not neglect that for which He paid so dearly. It reminds us of Psalm 139:1–6 which says: *"O LORD, thou hast searched me, and known me.* [2] *Thou knowest my downsitting and mine uprising, thou understandest my thought afar off.* [3] *Thou compassest my path and my lying down, and art acquainted with all my ways.* [4] *For there is not a word in my tongue, but, lo, O LORD, thou knowest it altogether.* [5] *Thou hast beset me behind and before, and laid thine hand upon me.* [6] *Such knowledge is too wonderful for me; it is high, I cannot attain unto it."*

The psalmist is saying, "God, I am stunned at the degree of knowledge You have of me in the most intimate details and in the most comprehensive fashion of every area of my life, from front to back, from top to bottom, from side to side. I am completely surrounded by the perfection of Your knowledge of who I am. Why would You even pay attention to me to know me to this degree?" It is a declaration of the value that Christ places on His people, that He knows all about them, and that He pays that much attention to them.

It is amazing that Christ would take this kind of interest in us and this kind of notice of us, and yet He does. He says to the church at Philadelphia, *"I know thy works."* His point is this: He knows your faithful obedience over the long haul. He knows the patient perseverance you have exercised in following Him.

Jesus then goes on to say, "I have further work for you to do; I will be with you in that work, and I will ensure the success of that work." He says in verse 8, *"I have set before thee an open door, and no man can shut it."* Christ is going to go ahead of them, and Christ is going to open doors for them so they can accomplish the work He has given them to do.

Paul says in 2 Corinthians 2:12: *"Furthermore, when I came to Troas to preach Christ's gospel, and a door was opened unto me of the Lord."* It is amazing and wonderful that Christ would open up a way before us so we can minister for Him! When Paul was at Philippi and preached the gospel to Lydia the seller of purple, it says of her that she was the one *"whose heart the Lord opened."*

Christ is telling His church at Philadelphia that He is going to open doors of opportunity for the believers to advance the gospel in the lives of the people around them. Jesus has missionary work for them to do, and He says, as it were, "I am going to go ahead of you and open the doors of Providence and the doors of people's hearts because I am opening the doors of heaven for them to come in through the efforts of your ministry. I have the keys to all of those doors."

Christ is going to open the door of people's hearts and minds to be able to understand and receive the gospel they preach. He is going to open the door of the kingdom of God and allow those whom they invite to enter into that kingdom.

In the introduction, we said that the city of Philadelphia was supposed to be a missionary base for the spreading of Greek culture. Jesus says the church at Philadelphia is going to be a missionary base for spreading the gospel. He understands that the church is small and poor. He says in verse 8, *"I know. . . thou hast a little strength."* In other words, this is not a strong church in terms of resources. In themselves, they could never achieve what He has planned for them. But with Jesus going before them, and with Jesus opening doors for them, there is no limit to what they can achieve.

When Paul and Barnabas returned from their first missionary journey in Acts 13–14, they reported on that missionary effort to the church at Antioch which had sent them out. It says in Acts 14:27: *"And when they were come, and had gathered the church together, they rehearsed all that God had done with them, and how he had opened the door of faith unto the Gentiles."* Jesus went before Paul and Barnabas, He opened doors of opportunity, He opened the doors of men's hearts and minds, He opened the doors of the kingdom of God, and the Gentiles they preached the gospel to were brought in.

The reason why Jesus is choosing to use this church in the way in which He is going to use it, even though it is small and poor, is because as verse 8 says, they have *"kept my word, and [have] not denied my name."* They had *"kept my word"*; that is, they faithfully lived by all the commands Jesus had given to the church as to its form, its function, and its message. We want Jesus to walk into our church and say of our church, "You people have kept my word. The form of your church, the function of your church, and the message of your church are all in order and according to all I have instructed you to do."

Jesus then says, "You have *'not denied my name.'*" That is, when the church at Philadelphia was persecuted, the believers did not deny their Savior, they did not deny their faith, and they did not betray their loyalty to Christ. They would rather die than deny that Jesus is Lord. In a word, they had been obedient to Christ, and they had been defiant of the world. They had submitted to Christ, and they had scorned the approval of the ungodly. The result was that they would triumph over the devil through the power and triumph of Christ.

Not only are they going to go out and spoil Satan's kingdom and bring his people into the kingdom of Christ, but notice verse 9: *"Behold, I will make them of the synagogue of Satan, which say they are Jews, and are not, but do lie; behold, I will make them to come and worship before thy feet, and to know that I have loved thee."* Not only does Jesus say He was going to open doors because they kept His word and did not deny His name, but He said He was also going to conquer their enemies because they had kept His word and did not deny His name.

Jesus says in verse 9 that the people in this synagogue say they are Jews. But Jesus says they are not Jews. They are lying. He is not attacking their ethnic, genetic descent. He is not saying that they are not genetically descended from Abraham. They certainly are. He is saying they claim to be the covenant people of God, but they are not. Paul says in Romans 2:28 and 29: *"For he is not a Jew, which is one outwardly; neither is that circumcision, which is outward in the flesh:* [29] *But he is a Jew, which is one inwardly; and circumcision is that of the heart, in the spirit, and not in the letter; whose praise is not of men, but of God."*

Jews are not defined by ethnic descent, and Jews are not defined by circumcision of the body. Jews are now defined by having regenerate hearts. If you are born again of Jesus Christ, you have a circumcised heart; and if you have a circumcised heart, both Jesus and Paul say that you are a true Jew. Galatians 3:29 says, *"And if ye be Christ's, then are ye Abraham's seed, and heirs according to the promise."*

Who are the true Jews? They are these saved Gentiles at Philadelphia. They are the real Jews, and the Jews in the synagogue that are claiming to be Jews are lying about being Jews. They are not Jews any longer. Ethnically and genetically, yes; but spiritually and covenantally, no. The New Israel is made up of those who are in the New Covenant, and all unbelieving Jews became broken-off branches that were cast away, as Romans 11 teaches.

Jesus is saying these servants of Satan who claim to be God's people but are not, who claim to be God's people but who persecute God's true people, will be brought to submission. This synagogue of Satan will be conquered by Christ's sovereign power, and it will be saved by Christ's sovereign grace, and they who are in it will come and submit themselves to those they formerly persecuted, and will realize that those they persecuted were in fact the true people of God whom Christ loves. They will "*. . .come and worship before thy feet, and. . .know that I have loved thee.*"

The illustration of this is the conversion of Saul of Tarsus. He was one who was straight out of the synagogue of Satan and went about persecuting the Christians. On the road to Damascus, Jesus saved him. What did he do? He got up and he found a church and submitted himself to that church and begged to become a member of it, as Acts 9:26–28 records.

Jesus is saying, "I can open the door to these Jews' hearts and I can make them come into your church and sit before your feet, and admit that you are the true people of God, and they are not." Isaiah 60:14 says to the true people of God: "*The sons also of them that afflicted thee shall come bending unto thee; and all they that despised thee shall bow themselves down at the soles of thy feet; and they shall call thee, The city of the* Lord." Jesus is saying this prophecy is going to be fulfilled in the lives of the believers in Philadelphia.

Verse 9 can be interpreted to mean that on the Day of Judgment, those who persecuted the church will bow before those whom Christ owns and acknowledges as the true people of God. But in the context of Christ opening the door and bringing the people into the kingdom, it appears that the right interpretation of verse 9 is that those in this particular synagogue in this town are going to become saved, and are going to come and be part of the church of Philadelphia. The triumph of Christ over the enemies of the people of God will be visible, tangible, and immediate, and the open door will be seen.

He says, "*I will make them to come and worship before thy feet, and to know that I have loved thee.*" The Jews thought God only loved them. They are going to have to admit someday that God loved these Gentile Christians, and bow to them as being the people of God.

Notice verse 10: "*Because thou hast kept the word of my patience, I also will keep thee from the hour of temptation, which shall come upon all the world, to try them that dwell upon the earth."* In verse 10, Jesus gives His church the reassurance that He will protect them in the coming trials that will soon appear. He says in verse 10, *"Because thou hast kept the word of my patience."* That is a very interesting phrase: *"the word of my patience."*

First of all, this is talking about the patience of Jesus Christ Himself. Christ speaks of *"my patience."* The patience of Christ under all trials is well known. His endurance of the most adverse treatment at the hands of His enemies is set forth in Hebrews 12:3, where it says: *"For consider him that endured such contradiction of sinners against himself."* Consider the patience He had; consider the longsuffering He practiced; consider the steadfastness He displayed through it all.

Secondly, this teaching by example that Christ gave of patient endurance under trial was a teaching (a *"word"*) the Philadelphian Christians had kept and followed. Like Christ, they had kept on enduring without flinching, and patiently served under adversity, rejection, and persecution. Jesus says: "Because you kept the teaching of My example in the way I manifested patience, I will keep you also." Notice the parallel in verse 10: "Because you kept, I also will keep. You have been faithful to Me; I am going to be faithful to you. I will keep you," He says in verse 10, *"from the hour of temptation, which shall come upon all the world, to try them that dwell upon the earth."*

This phrase, *"all the world,"* does not necessarily mean the entire globe. Very often, this phrase "all the world" has limited application to a particular region or continent or kingdom. For example, in Luke 2:1 it says, *"there went out a decree from Caesar Augustus, that all the world should be taxed."* Did Caesar tax the folks in South America? No. *"All the world"* just simply meant everyone in Palestine. The tax was on Israel. In Acts 11:28 it says, *"And there stood up one of them named Agabus, and signified by the Spirit that there should be great dearth throughout all the world: which came to pass in the days of Claudius Caesar."* Well, there was a drought in Israel, but there was not a drought in Canada. The point is, this phrase "all the world" refers to perhaps a region or a country, or perhaps even to a locality. It is a term that says, in effect, "Everyone within this region is going to experience this event or circumstance."

It says this *"hour of temptation"* was coming on *"all the world."* This *"hour of temptation"* that was coming on all the world was no doubt the increasing persecution of the Christians that was implemented throughout the Roman Empire by Trajan and his successors beginning in AD 98. From AD 98 through AD 313 when the Edict of Milan was proclaimed, there was a tremendous increase in persecution against the Christians at a level of intensity that had never been known before. It had already started when the book of Revelation was written, but it was going to intensify tremendously in the future. For the next 200 years, the Roman government implemented wave after wave of empire-wide persecution upon the church.

The purpose of this persecution was *"to try them that dwell upon the earth."* Not just the Christians, but all the people in the Roman Empire were put to the test to show what their true nature was in this conflict between the Roman Empire and the Christians.

The point is that conflict reveals character. Do you want to know what somebody is really like? Watch them in the midst of conflict, and then you will find out who they are. Anybody can be nice when everything is going great, and anybody can be loyal when it costs nothing. But when you see someone under conflict, you find out that person's true character. Conflict reveals whether you are on God's side or on Satan's side. All the people who dwelled in the Roman Empire would be proven as to who they were by this conflict that was going on between Caesar and the Christians.

In verse 10, Jesus has a special promise to the believer: *"I also will keep thee from the hour of temptation."* He says: I will keep you *"from." "From"* does not mean, "I will take you out of"; rather it means, "I will protect you through"; that is, "I will keep you from falling or failing in this hour of testing. I will preserve you and I will uphold you." Jesus said in John 17:15 in His high priestly prayer to His Father regarding His people, *"I pray not that thou shouldest take them out of the world, but that thou shouldest keep them from the evil [one.]"* Christ is not praying the Father would take us out of contact with the devil, but that the Father would protect us from falling when he assaults us. We are kept from the outcome Satan is trying to achieve.

Dispensationalists say verse 10 speaks about the rapture. They say that the Philadelphian church represents the church in our day, and Jesus is going to take us off the earth before the great tribulation comes. This interpretation is in error because this passage is not talking about the great tribulation, it is not talking about the entire globe, and it is not talking about removing people from testing. Testing is something that the people of God have always gone through and always will go through. Christ does not say that the last generation of believers is going to get to escape all the troubles that all the previous generations have had to go through. It is a misunderstanding of this passage to teach that it refers to the rapture of the church so believers can escape the great tribulation.

Jesus is saying, "You have kept My word. I will keep your souls. I will keep you from falling or failing in this hour of testing that is coming through the kingdom of Rome, which will not only put you to the test, but will put everybody to the test." In the Day of Judgment, God will be able to say, "Look at your behavior. When the Christians were persecuted, did you stand with them or did you stand against them? That was your test." Jesus is saying to the church at Philadelphia, "I am going to help you pass that test. I am going to ensure that you pass that test. I will keep you from falling or failing in this hour of testing. I will preserve you. You have kept My word, and I will keep your souls. You will pass the test. My power and grace will see to it. I will keep you from the hour of temptation—that is, I will keep you from falling in that hour of temptation."

Notice verse 11a: *"Behold, I come quickly."* This is not talking about the second coming. He is saying, "I will come quickly to help you. When this tribulation comes that is going to put you and others to the test, I will come quickly to your aid. As quickly as the hour of testing comes, that quickly will I come to preserve you in it and through it. I will not leave you by yourself for even a moment." You know that if you are in trouble, and somebody immediately comes to your aid, it is a very good thing to have happen to you. This is what Jesus is saying. "There is coming this hour of temptation that is going to put everyone to the test, and I am going to come quickly to be with you. When the hour of temptation and trial comes, I will come just as quickly as it comes."

People say that they hear about other Christians going through this or that trial of persecution, and they do not think that they themselves could ever endure that. My response to them is this: "Right now you could not, because Christ has not put you there. But at the moment He puts you there, He will also give you the grace and the strength and the ability to deal with it. Because you are not there, you do not have that strength and ability now; therefore, you could not handle it now. But when the trial comes, immediately also comes the grace and strength and presence and power of Christ to help you overcome it. You look back at your life, and you look at the things you have gone through, and you think that you could not go through that now. But if you were called to go through it again, you could, because Jesus would quickly come to help you, just like He did back then. He would not leave you alone for a moment."

This, then, is the commendation and encouragement that Christ gives to the church at Philadelphia.

Secondly, notice His warning to this church in verse 11b. He says, "*. . .hold that fast which thou hast, that no man take thy crown.*" In other words, "Just keep doing what you have been doing. Cling to the pattern of behavior, belief, works, and witness you have practiced up to this point, and change nothing. Stay the course. Maintain your former obedience. If you do so, you will retain your crown of reward and your crown of redemption. I have no correction for you. Keep up the same things you have been doing, so that no man takes your crown." The crown is the crown of reward, and it is the crown of redemption. Notice Revelation 2:10. He says, "*Fear none of those things which thou shalt suffer: behold, the devil shall cast some of you into prison, that ye may be tried; and ye shall have tribulation ten days: be thou faithful unto death and I will give thee a crown of life.*" He says to the people at Philadelphia, "Take heed that no man takes your crown of life from you."

If you are faithful in the future, like you have been in the past, you will have the crown of life. Those who go apostate under persecution lose their claim to eternal life. When they give in to that persecution and they break Christ's word and they deny Christ's name, those who persecuted them have effectively taken their crown of life. Those who go apostate under persecution lose their claim of having eternal life. They show themselves to have never been true believers.

This is the warning. It is a warning not to change. It is a warning not to repent of who they were and what they had done. Jesus says, "Do not change and do not repent of who you are and what you are, in terms of how the church has functioned and what the church has taught." Now individually, as sinners, we always need to repent and change and grow. We can be sinners working on our sanctification, and yet have a church that is obedient to Christ in its form, in its function, and in its message—a church that does not need to change, a church that is not "always reforming." It is where it needs to be, and it simply needs to stay there. That is what He is saying to them: "Do not change, just hold fast to what you have been doing and who you are obeying."

The Conclusion of the Letter

The conclusion of the letter is in verses 12 and 13. Verse 12: *"Him that overcometh will I make a pillar in the temple of my God, and he shall go no more out: and I will write upon him the name of my God, and the name of the city of my God, which is new Jerusalem, which cometh down out of heaven from my God: and I will write upon him my new name."*

First, notice the promise made. The promise is made to the overcomer. In every one of these letters, the promise is only made to the overcomer, and not to the mere professor. The overcomer is someone who keeps the word of Christ and does not deny His name. They are those who follow the example of Jesus of patient endurance under suffering. They are those who keep on being faithful in keeping His word and not denying His name, and who have patient endurance under suffering for a lifetime. They never repent of keeping Christ's word, they never repent of not denying His name, and they never repent of patient endurance under suffering. They just keep on maintaining those things for a lifetime. They are the overcomers, and, to them, Jesus makes two promises.

The first promise is this: *"I [will] make [him] a pillar in the temple of my God, and he shall go no more out."* A pillar is something that never moves. Its place is fixed and permanent; it stays where it is forever. The believer will forever remain in God's temple in heaven, and he will never run the risk of being removed from that temple or put out of that temple once he has entered it. You can take furniture in and out of a building, but not pillars. If you take the pillar out, the building collapses. Once you put pillars in the building, they stay in the building forever. Jesus is saying, "Once I bring you into My heavenly temple, you will be there forever. You will never be moved out."

The overcomer will have a permanent place in the temple of God forever. The desire of David in Psalm 27:4 will be fulfilled for every believer: *"One thing have I desired of the LORD, that will I seek after; that I may dwell in the house of the LORD all the days of my life, to behold the beauty of the LORD, and to enquire in his temple."* David was saying, "I want to go into the temple, and I do not ever want to leave." Jesus is saying that this is exactly what the redeemed are going to have. It will be church every day, all day, for all of eternity. It is very strange that people who do not want to go to church think they want to go to heaven. They would be miserable there. Would they want to be a pillar in the temple, always present, and never leaving? Only those who love Jesus and His worship, and who love His house and His people, are going to love being in heaven.

If you do not love His church here, you are never going to wind up in His church there. After all, where is Jesus' heart? It is with His churches. To whom is He writing these seven letters? To His churches. His heart is in His church, and our heart needs to be in His church as well.

The second promise Jesus makes is that believers will have several names written on them—three of them in fact. Verse 12: number one, *"I will write upon him the name of my God,"* number two, *"and the name of the city of my God, which is new Jerusalem, which cometh down out of heaven from my God."* And number three, *"I will write upon him my new name."* Jesus says the *"name of my God," "the name of the city of my God,"* and *"my [own] new name,"* will all be written on the overcomer.

Names are symbols of ownership and identification. When you bear the name of something or someone, that means you belong to it or them. For example, all my children bear my name. Every one of them is a "Doner." I gave them my name as a symbol that they belong to me and are part of my family. It was a declaration on my part that I would protect them and provide for them and take them as my own forever. We are called by the name "Americans" because we belong to this country and we are citizens of it.

Therefore, when these names are written on us, it is being declared that we belong to God, that we belong to the New Jerusalem, and that we belong to Christ. We are members of the family, we are citizens of the City, and we are joint-heirs with Jesus Christ. All of that is wrapped in us having these three names on us.

This, then, is the promise made. The promise made is that we will be a pillar in the temple of our God and that we will have the names of God and the New Jerusalem and Jesus written on us to show their ownership of us, our identification with them, their protection of us, and our inclusion in their family forever.

Secondly, notice the exhortation given in verse 13: *"He that hath an ear, let him hear what the Spirit saith unto the churches."* What is the Holy Spirit saying to us today? What should we be hearing? There are many things that we could be listening to from this, but I want to emphasize just one of them.

The Spirit is saying to us that we must pray to Him who has the key of David, that He would open the door to people's hearts, so that our gospel witness might enter, and so that they might enter into heaven. This is one of the reasons why we pray for the salvation of people. We are praying to Him who has the key to men's hearts. He has the keys to the kingdom of God. If He opens those hearts and opens that kingdom, then those people will become saved. Without that, there is no hope of their salvation.

Paul requests in Colossians 4:3 of the Colossian church that they would pray for him, *"that God would open unto us a door of utterance, to speak the mystery of Christ, for which I am also in bonds."* Paul says to the Colossians, "Pray that when we go out and preach the mystery of Christ, God will open the doors, so we can speak as we ought, and so the message can enter the minds and hearts of the lost."

When God opens doors, it does not mean it is going to be easy. Open doors are always accompanied by adversaries. In 1 Corinthians 16:9 Paul says, *"For a great door and effectual is opened unto me, and there are many adversaries."* Even when Jesus opens the door, it does not mean we are going to go through that door and gain that victory without a fight.

We must not just mechanically preach the gospel and pass out tracts. We need to pray for those we witness to. We need to pray for those that we have influence over for the gospel. We need to pray after this manner: "Lord Jesus, You have the key of David in Your hand. Open this door, open this heart, open Your kingdom, and admit this one into Your presence. May he become a pillar in the temple of God. Lord Jesus, may you write your name on him. You know that we sought to keep Your word. You know we have not denied Your name. We have been patient under suffering. We are grateful for the way You have protected and preserved us in our tribulations. But we are not content just to be preserved. We want to see the kingdom expanded. Lord Jesus, use Your key. Open a door of utterance for us so that we can say that a great and effectual door was opened by Christ, and many souls were brought into the kingdom."

Now it is up to Him as to how He answers that prayer. But that is how we need to be praying, and this is what the Spirit is saying to us, and this is what we need to be hearing. May the Lord be pleased to grant us listening ears.

18

The Letter to the Church at Laodicea, Revelation 3:14–22

> "14 *And unto the angel of the church of the Laodiceans write; These things saith the Amen, the faithful and true witness, the beginning of the creation of God;* 15 *I know thy works, that thou art neither cold nor hot: I would thou wert cold or hot.* 16 *So then because thou art lukewarm, and neither cold nor hot, I will spew thee out of my mouth.* 17 *Because thou sayest, I am rich, and increased with goods, and have need of nothing; and knowest not that thou art wretched, and miserable, and poor, and blind, and naked:* 18 *I counsel thee to buy of me gold tried in the fire, that thou mayest be rich; and white raiment, that thou mayest be clothed, and that the shame of thy nakedness do not appear; and anoint thine eyes with eyesalve, that thou mayest see.* 19 *As many as I love, I rebuke and chasten: be zealous therefore, and repent.* 20 *Behold, I stand at the door, and knock: if any man hear my voice, and open the door, I will come in to him, and will sup with him, and he with me.* 21 *To him that overcometh will I grant to sit with me in my throne, even as I also overcame, and am set down with my Father in his throne.* 22 *He that hath an ear, let him hear what the Spirit saith unto the churches.*"

This is the seventh and final letter to the seven churches in Asia. It is often the case that people save the best for last, but in this case, the worst was saved for last. Of the seven churches in Asia, the church at Laodicea was the worst; in fact, it was so bad that Jesus does not have a single word of commendation for it.

In the previous six churches, Jesus was able to find something good to say about each of them. But in this church, there is nothing good to say about it. It teeters on the very brink of being disowned by Christ as being one of His churches at all. He says He is about to spew it out of His mouth. This church is about as bad as a church can be and still be called a church of Jesus Christ.

That it actually is a church of Jesus Christ is clear from the fact that it is one of the seven golden candlesticks mentioned in chapter 1, that Jesus calls it a church in verse 14, and that He says in verse 19 that He loves it. But this church at Laodicea is the opposite of the church at Philadelphia. The church at Philadelphia was a blameless church, even though it was small and poor, but the church at Laodicea was a blameworthy church, even though it was large and rich and prosperous.

The point is that Christ does not look at the outward public appearance of the church. He does not look at its size, He does not look at its wealth, and He does not look at its public reputation among men. Instead, He looks at its faithfulness to Him, He looks at its willingness to suffer for Him, and He looks at its faithfulness to His teaching. With reference to those things, Laodicea failed miserably. But the saddest thing about this church is that Christ was outside of it, instead of in the midst of it.

We read in verse 20 that He has to knock on the door of the church to gain admission and have fellowship with these people. The glory has almost departed. It is at the door, and it may very soon go away, and "Ichabod" will be written over the door of the church. The glory will have departed.

This is a very sad church, and we want to learn from its negative example of what we do not want to be. When we looked at the church at Philadelphia, we said this church exemplifies what we want to be like. Now we are looking at the church in Laodicea, and we see that it exemplifies what we do not want to be like. There is much to learn from this negative example.

The Introduction to the Letter

The introduction of the letter to Laodicea is in verse 14: *"And unto the angel of the church of the Laodiceans write; These things saith the Amen, the faithful and true witness, the beginning of the creation of God."*

In this introduction to the letter to the Laodiceans, we are told who the recipient and author of this letter is. First of all, notice the recipient of the letter. The recipient of this letter is the pastor and the church at Laodicea.

Laodicea was a major city situated at the confluence of three major roads. It was one of the richest commercial and banking centers in the world. As a center of finance and banking, Laodicea was a very wealthy city. Here was a church in the midst of an affluent society, and the members of this church shared in that affluence in their personal lives. This was the home of millionaires. This was an upper middle-class, wealthy congregation.

The city of Laodicea was also the home of a famous medical school. This medical school was renowned for the healing eye salve it produced in order to improve the eyesight of those afflicted with various ailments of the eye.

Furthermore, Laodicea was also known for the production of fine garments woven from soft black wool that was produced by a particular variety of sheep they bred. Garments made from this wool were highly prized and very expensive.

The city's water supply originated from hot springs that were six miles away, in the town of Hierapolis. The water that came out of these hot springs was laden with lime. It was brought into Laodicea via an aqueduct; and by the time this water reached Laodicea, it had become lukewarm. Lukewarm, lime-laden water is very distasteful to drink. When you drink cold water, it is refreshing. When you drink hot water, it is therapeutic. But lukewarm water makes you want to spit it out, especially when it is highly mineralized—and this was the nature of the water supply that existed at Laodicea.

This church was apparently founded through the preaching of a man named Epaphras. Epaphras is mentioned repeatedly in the book of Colossians. Colossae was just a few miles away from Laodicea. In Colossians 1:7 Paul says, "*You also learned of Epaphras our dear fellow servant, who is for you a faithful minister of Christ.*" At that point in time, Epaphras was said by Paul to be a minister in the church at Colossae. He was visiting Paul at the time Paul wrote this letter.

Paul says later in Colossians 4:12–13, "*Epaphras, who is one of you, a servant of Christ, saluteth you, always labouring fervently for you in prayers, that ye may stand perfect and complete in all the will of God.* [13] *For I bear him record, that he hath a great zeal for you, and them that are in Laodicea, and them in Hierapolis.*" Hierapolis, Laodicea, and Colossae were three cities that were all within a few miles of each other; and this man Epaphras apparently went from one city to the next to the next, zealously ministering for the Lord among these congregations.

Paul goes on to say in Colossians 4:16 that *"when this epistle,"* (the epistle to the Colossians) *"is read among you, cause that it be read also in the church of the Laodiceans; and that ye likewise read the epistle from Laodicea."* Paul had written a letter to the church at Colossae, which Epaphras took to them; and had also written a letter to the church at Laodicea, which Epaphras also took to them. Paul said that they should be sure to read each other's letters.

We still have the letter that was written to Colossae, but we do not have the letter Paul wrote to the church at Laodicea. It has been lost. God did not see fit to include it in the canon of Scripture; and therefore, God did not see fit to preserve it.

This church at Laodicea was established during the time of Paul's ministry, and it enjoyed apostolic ministry and apostolic communication via letter and through apostolic representatives like this man Epaphras who ministered in the city of Laodicea.

Secondly, notice the author of the letter. The author of the letter is Jesus Christ, who identifies Himself with two descriptive titles. The first title is in verse 14. He says that He is *"the Amen, the faithful and true witness."* The faithfulness of Christ as a witness was spoken of by John in 1:5, where He says that this revelation is *"from Jesus Christ, who is the faithful witness."* Jesus takes up that title from chapter 1 and He applies it to Himself. He says of Himself that He is *"the Amen, the faithful and true witness."*

The word *"Amen"* conveys the idea of truth and faithfulness. When you say "Amen," you are saying that what was just said by another person was a true statement. You are saying that you accept and agree with and endorse what was just said because it is a faithful expression of the truth.

The word "Amen" is used in the Old Testament to describe the faithfulness and truthfulness of God Himself. For example, it says in Isaiah 65:16, *"that he who blesseth himself in the earth shall bless himself in the God of truth; and he that sweareth in the earth shall swear by the God of truth."* What is interesting in the phrase *"the God of truth,"* which occurs twice in Isaiah 65:16, is that it literally reads in the original Hebrew "the God of Amen." When you say "Amen," it is the same as saying, "Truth!"

When Jesus calls Himself "the Amen," He explains the meaning of that title by saying, "I am the faithful and true witness." In other words, faithful and true witness is not something in addition to Amen; it is an explanation of Amen. The word Amen conveys the concept of *"the faithful and true witness."*

Therefore, when Jesus says He is the Amen, He is saying, "I am the faithful and true witness. My word is reliable, My testimony is true, and My statements are trustworthy. When I speak about an issue, My witness is a faithful witness, and when I speak about an issue, I speak the truth about it."

The point that Jesus is making to the Laodiceans when He calls Himself the Amen is that His assessment of their terrible spiritual condition is a true and faithful representation of it. When He says that they are the opposite of who they perceive themselves to be, He is a true and faithful witness. But He is also being a true and faithful witness when He says in verse 19 that He loves them and that He will come and fellowship with them if they open the door to Him.

The true and faithful witness is one whose words need to be taken seriously, whether He is correcting or whether He is comforting. When Jesus speaks, He is the Amen God. He is the truth-speaking God. Therefore, we need to take what He says as absolute truth and take it very seriously.

The second title He applies to Himself in verse 14 is that He is *"the beginning of the creation of God."* This title is taken from 1:8 where Jesus says of Himself, *"I am Alpha and Omega, the beginning and the ending."*

When He says, *"I am the beginning of the creation of God,"* He is saying that creation began with Him. Christ began and Christ completed the creative work of God, and as a result, Christ now rules and reigns over it. In John 1:3 we are told: *"All things were made by him; and without him was not any thing made that was made."*

It says of Him in Colossians 1:16–17, *"For by him were all things created, that are in heaven, and that are in earth, visible and invisible, whether they be thrones, or dominions, or principalities, or powers: all things were created by him, and for him: [17] And he is before all things, and by him all things consist."*

We know the Laodiceans had read the letter to the church at Colossae because Paul told them to read it. He told Epaphras to be sure that the Laodiceans read the letter to the Colossians, and that the Colossians read the letter to the Laodiceans. Therefore, the Laodiceans knew from Colossians 1:16–17 what Jesus meant when He said that He is the beginning of the creation of God. They knew He meant that He is the One who was there at the beginning and He was the source of all that was made. Genesis 1:1 says, *"In the beginning God created the heavens and the earth."* So when Jesus says, "I am the beginning of the creation of God," He is saying that He is the God that was spoken of in Genesis 1:1. He began the creation of God.

The church at Laodicea desperately needed to be restored and renewed back into the image from which it had fallen. It needed to be remade into a living and vibrant church once again. Christ has the power to do that because He who created the first life can restore life into the soul of this church that is teetering on the brink of death. When Jesus says He is the beginning of the creation of God, He is saying He has the power to restore dead churches and deadened Christians back to life because He is the one who created life in the first place.

Jesus' witness regarding the deadness of this church is true, and Jesus' power to restore this church is sufficient. By these titles He gives to Himself He is saying, "I know the truth about this church, and I have the power to change this church."

The Message of the Letter

The message Jesus has for this church is quite an extended message, covering verses 15 to 20. This letter contains no commendation of this church. In this church, there is nothing to commend and there is nothing to praise. There is only something to correct.

First of all, notice the correction in verses 15 to 17. *"I know thy works, that thou art neither cold nor hot: I would thou wert cold or hot. 16 So then because thou art lukewarm, and neither cold nor hot, I will spew thee out of my mouth. 17 Because thou sayest, I am rich, and increased with goods, and have need of nothing; and knowest not that thou art wretched, and miserable, and poor, and blind, and naked."*

Once again, Jesus begins this letter as He has every letter with these words, *"I know."* Jesus knows the true condition of His churches. He sees past the outward image of prosperity and success and public respectability to discern the truth about who they really are. Nothing can be hidden from His eyes. He sees into the heart and into the true spiritual condition of His people, and what He sees in this church appalls Him. As He witnesses the condition of the church at Laodicea, He is sickened.

He says in verses 15 to 16, "I know your works. I see the apathy, the indifference, and the slothfulness with which you do your works. Your efforts at worship and service and witness are weak and half-hearted. Your zeal is tepid. Indolence and listlessness characterize your spiritual activity. In a word, you are lukewarm. I wish you were either cold or hot. Either of these would be preferable to being lukewarm."

It is important that we understand this metaphor of hot, lukewarm, and cold. Most commentators think "hot" symbolizes someone who is on fire for the Lord. "Cold," on the other hand, refers to someone who is openly hostile to the Lord. Lukewarm, then, would be someone who is halfway between a zealous Christian and a hostile unbeliever.

There is a problem with that interpretation. The problem is this: How could Jesus prefer for someone to be cold—that is, openly hostile to Christ and His gospel—over someone who was agreeable to Him and His gospel, even though such a person were not very enthusiastic about it? It seems impossible to me that Jesus would prefer a cold unbeliever to a lukewarm believer and say, "I would rather have you be a cold unbeliever than a lukewarm believer." I do not believe Jesus is ever going to say that. Thus, I think the vast majority of commentators are wrong in the way they handle this metaphor.

I believe the answer to this dilemma lies in a proper understanding of the symbolic language used here. In order to understand that symbolic language, we have to go to the rest of the Bible. In the Bible, "cold" is used in a very positive way in Proverbs 25:25 when it says, *"As cold waters to a thirsty soul, so is good news from a far country."* Matthew 10:42 says, *"And whosoever shall give to drink unto one of these little ones a cup of cold water only in the name of a disciple, verily I say unto you, he shall in no wise lose his reward."* In the context of drinking water, cold is a good thing. Something that is cold is seen as something that is refreshing to drink.

In our introduction, we said that the city of Laodicea had two neighboring cities close by, the city of Hierapolis, and the city of Colossae. Hierapolis had hot springs, which were considered medicinal and therapeutic. On the other hand, Colossae had a cold-water source, which was refreshing and invigorating to drink. However, Laodicea, which was between these two towns, had no good water source, and, as already mentioned, it brought its water in by an aqueduct from the hot springs in Hierapolis six miles away. By the time that hot water got to Laodicea, it was no longer hot. It was now lukewarm. This highly mineralized water tasted fine when it was hot, but when it was lukewarm, it tasted awful, and those who drank it wanted to spit it out because it was repulsive.

Let me ask you a question. Do you like iced tea during the summer? You do. Do you like hot tea during the winter? You do. But do you ever like lukewarm tea? If it sits there and gets lukewarm, either by warming up or cooling down as the case may be, you pour it out and get some hot or cold tea as the occasion may dictate.

Jesus says to the people at Laodicea, "You are like lukewarm water. Nobody wants that. They want it hot or they want it cold, but they do not want it lukewarm. You, the church at Laodicea, are just like your lukewarm mineralized water supply. You are distasteful, you are offensive, and you are undesirable. Nobody likes water in that condition, and I do not like you in your tepid condition."

The Laodiceans' apathetic faith did not make them desirable or pleasing to Christ, and certainly did not make them have much of a witness or an impact on the city. Jesus says in verse 16 that if they remained in this condition, and if they do not repent of their spiritual apathy, he would spit them out of His mouth. The image here is that of drinking water. Drinking cold water? Great. Drinking hot water? Great. Drinking mineralized lukewarm water? Putrid. Spit it out.

Jesus says, "That is what you taste like to Me. If you remain in this condition, if you do not repent of your spiritual apathy, I will spit you out of My mouth, I will disown you as being one of My churches." Therefore, in verse 16 He says, *"Because thou art lukewarm, and neither cold nor hot, I will spew thee out of my mouth."*

Notice verse 17: *"Because thou sayest, I am rich, and increased with goods, and have need of nothing; and knowest not that thou art wretched, and miserable, and poor, and blind, and naked."* The problem with the Laodiceans is that they confused outward physical material prosperity with the approval of God. They thought material blessing was the sign of God's favor. They supposed that gain was godliness. They thought because they had material prosperity, they had need of nothing more. "We are rich! We are full! We have need of nothing!" They had an attitude of self-satisfied complacency.

Jesus shatters this confidence and complacency. He tells them their true spiritual condition, and the report card He gives them is horrendous. He says they are wretched, they are miserable, they are poor, they are blind, and they are naked.

In a word, they thought they were full of blessings, but instead they were full of self-delusion. They had a big church that was full of big people with a big budget. They had all the finest furnishings. They thought like this: "We have it all. Look at us! We are a rich and flourishing church."

Recall the church in Smyrna in 2:9. What did Jesus say about this suffering church? He said to them, *"I know thy works, and tribulation, and poverty, (but thou art rich)."* Everything had been taken away from them materially, but Jesus said it was a rich church! The church at Laodicea had everything materially, and Jesus says, "You are poor. You are destitute. You do not even have any clothing you are so poor. You are naked. I know your material riches, but you are really poor. Even though you have this prosperous banking system, you are poor. Even though you have this famous school of ophthalmology with its eye salve, you are blind. And even though you have a famous textile trade in this soft black wool cloth, you are naked."

This church is on the very brink of apostasy and rejection by Christ. He is about to spew the members out of His mouth, and yet they think they are doing great. They are full. The pews are full. They have need of nothing. They think they are fat with blessing.

Secondly, notice the warning. This is in verses 18 to 20. Jesus is incredibly gracious to this church, and instead of just writing it off, He gives the members wise counsel, and He expresses His wonderful love to them.

First of all, notice His wise counsel in verse 18: *"I counsel thee to buy of me gold tried in the fire, that thou mayest be rich; and white raiment, that thou mayest be clothed, and that the shame of thy nakedness do not appear; and anoint thine eyes with eye salve, that thou mayest see."* His counsel is that they need to acquire spiritual wealth instead of material wealth. They need to acquire spiritual clothing instead of designer clothing. They need to acquire spiritual sight instead of worldly perspective. He says, in effect, "I counsel you to buy from Me. Instead of doing business with the world in order to acquire material things, you need to do business with Me and engage in spiritual transactions with Me in order to acquire spiritual things." They have been buying and selling with the world, but they had not been doing any buying and selling with Christ.

Listen to the words of Jesus regarding His invitation to engage in commercial transactions with Him in Isaiah 55:1–2. *"Ho, every one that thirsteth, come ye to the waters, and he that hath no money; come ye, buy, and eat; yea, come, buy wine and milk without money and without price.* [2] *Wherefore do ye spend money for that which is not bread? and your labour for that which satisfieth not? hearken diligently unto me, and eat ye that which is good, and let your soul delight itself in fatness."*

People will go into the marketplace to buy and sell both labor and goods in order to increase their material wealth, and they give great attention to that. But they never go to the marketplace of Christ, and without money buy and sell with Him in order that they might acquire spiritual riches. Jesus is saying that it is time for them to start doing spiritual transactions with Him instead of with the world.

What spiritual transactions does Christ recommend they engage in? There are three of them. First, He says, *"I counsel thee to buy of me gold tried in the fire, that thou mayest be rich."* The gold Jesus is talking about here is refined gold. He mentions specifically gold purified in fire. Smelting is the means by which impurities are removed from gold. These impurities are removed through heat. The gold is heated, it melts, and all the impurities float to the top. They are skimmed off, and the result is pure gold.

This metaphor of being tried and purified by fire is one that occurs rather often in the Scriptures. For example, 1 Peter 1:6–7 says, *". . .now for a season, if need be, ye are in heaviness through manifold temptations:* [7]*That the trial of your faith, being much more precious than gold that perisheth, though it be tried with fire, might be found unto praise and honour and glory at the appearing of Jesus Christ."* Peter is saying that faith tested in the fires of trials is like gold that is refined in the fire. When believers stop being lukewarm, when they start by faith standing up for Christ, speaking out for Christ, and serving Christ, they are then put through the fires of persecution by the world.

Believers do not seek out persecution, but it automatically comes when they live by faith, and when they live out their faith. When those fires of persecution come, they purify their character as they endure them and exercise faith in God through them. In Job 23:10 it says,

"But he knoweth the way that I take: when he hath tried me, I shall come forth as gold." Trials on earth result in treasure in heaven when endured through faith in Christ and His promises.

He is saying to these people, "Stop being like the world. Live by faith. Start standing up to the world. Speak for Me. Endure the trials and the persecutions that will come through doing that and you will be rewarded as though you had refined gold in your possession." In the Sermon on the Mount Jesus said, "Do not lay up treasure on earth where moth and rust corrupt and thieves break through and steal; but rather, lay up for yourselves treasure in heaven where neither moth nor rust corrupt, and thieves do not break through and steal. For where your treasure is, there will your heart be also" (see Matthew 6:19–21).

We need to gain spiritual wealth from Jesus through faithful service to Him in the midst of trials and persecution, which will come to us when we follow Him instead of the world. That is the gold that He counsels us to buy. When you live for Christ by faith, and as a result of living for Him you suffer for Him, you become rich in rewards from Christ.

Secondly, He says to them in verse 18, *"buy of me. . .white raiment, that thou mayest be clothed."* The Laodiceans made clothing out of soft black wool they produced from their sheep, and they were clothed in these garments. Jesus is saying they needed white garments. White is the symbolic color of purity and holiness. In Revelation 3:4, in the letter to the church at Sardis, Jesus said: *"Thou hast a few names even in Sardis which have not defiled their garments; and they shall walk with me in white: for they are worthy."*

A white garment is an undefiled garment. A defiled garment is symbolic of one who is living in sinful behavior. Jesus is telling the Laodiceans that they need to clean up their moral behavior. They need to live lives of separation and purity and holiness and stop defiling themselves with the sins of the city in which they live. They already have the imputed righteousness of Christ as a result of being saved, but they need to add to it their personal righteousness of good works, not in order to be saved, but precisely because they are saved.

Jesus was saying, as it were, "I look at you and I see naked people; that is, people who are not clothed with personal works of righteousness in your daily behavior. You are compromised with the world, and you are living like the world. Your garments are dark and black. They are defiled. You need some white garments." You need to start living for the Lord so you can have an external testimony of holiness and obedience to Him that people can see. Jesus was telling them that the shame of their sinful compromise, which constituted their nakedness, could be covered with the garment of joyful obedience, which constituted their white robes.

Thirdly, He says to them: Buy of me *"eye salve"* in order to anoint your eyes *"that thou mayest see."* The Laodiceans were blind to the spiritual realities of the spiritual warfare they were in, and needed to have their eyes opened to the truth of the Scriptures as that truth applied to their lives and circumstances. They lacked spiritual perception. They lacked the ability to discern between good and evil. They could not distinguish between right and wrong.

The way they saw it, everything was fine. They were rich and full and had need of nothing. Jesus said, "You are blind, if that is what you see. You need to be able to see as I see. You need to be able to see the spiritual truth and reality about your situation, how the Scriptures apply to it, and what the world around you is really like." It says of Jesus in Luke 24:45, *"Then opened he their understanding,"* (their spiritual eyes) *"that they might understand the scriptures."*

The Laodiceans needed to cry out to Jesus to give them spiritual eye salve that would enable them to see the truth of Scripture, and how the Scripture applied to them and their condition. In the natural realm, we see people who think everything is great, when in fact their life is a total disaster. We shake our heads and wonder how they can be so blind.

If people do this in the natural realm, it is reasonable to think they could be doing this in the spiritual realm too. Sometimes people who are Christians think everything in their life is just wonderful, whereas everything is actually very bad because they do not see their life from a scriptural perspective. They only view their lives from a worldly humanistic perspective. They see themselves as spiritually insightful when they really have a carnal blindness. We need to cry out to Jesus to open our eyes so that we can see like He sees, and have a faithful and true witness as to what things are really like, instead of living in the delusion that so many professing believers live and walk in.

If they repented and sought His help, Christ could enable them to live by faith and obtain treasure in heaven as they endured persecution and trials for His name's sake. Christ could empower them to live holy lives and make their character pure like a clean garment. Christ could open their eyes to be able to see biblical truth and spiritual reality. If He did all these things in them by His creative power, they would cease to be lukewarm. They would begin to have a healthy and refreshing witness for Christ and a healthy and refreshing ministry to Him. No longer would Jesus be disgusted with them. Instead, they would be delightful to Him, like a cup of hot tea or a glass of iced tea. This is the wise counsel He gives them in verse 18.

Secondly, He expresses His wonderful love to them in verses 19 and 20. In verse 19 He says: *"As many as I love, I rebuke and chasten: be zealous therefore, and repent."* What is utterly amazing is that Jesus loved these believers at Laodicea, lukewarm though they were. He was disgusted with them, He was ready to spew them out of His mouth, but He loved them, and He could not do it before He gave them another opportunity to repent.

After giving them this phenomenally severe condemnation and rebuke in verse 18, He says to them, "You know I love you. That is why I say these things to you." He says in verse 19, *"As many as I love, I rebuke and chasten."* It is as if He is saying, "I tell you that you are wretched and miserable and poor and blind and naked, and why am I doing that? Because I want to be mean? No. I am doing that because I love you, and that is why I am rebuking you and correcting you. If I did not care about you, I would just leave you alone and let you go to hell. But I love you too much for that." He says: *"Be zealous therefore, and repent."*

Zeal is the opposite of lukewarmness. Zeal is the opposite of the apathy they had previously been displaying. He is saying in verse 19 that they should put some zeal into their repentance! They should be serious about it. No lukewarm, halfhearted repentance will do. Rather, they should work hard to exercise a full and complete repentance of their spiritual poverty, their spiritual defilement, and their spiritual blindness.

Verse 20: *"Behold, I stand at the door, and knock: if any man hear my voice, and open the door, I will come in to him, and will sup with him, and he with me."* Christ is saying, "I am outside of your church. But I am standing at the door of the church, and at the heart's door of every person in that church, and extending to them individually and collectively this plea: Church at Laodicea, I have been excluded from your corporate and individual lives. You have so filled your lives with the things of this world that there has been no time and no place for Me. You have pushed Me out, and I have withdrawn because of your indifference and self-centeredness and self-sufficiency. You think you are full. You think you have need of nothing, not even Me. But now, if you feel your need of Me, if you have any sense of My love for you, open the door of your hearts and the door of your church once again to Me, so that our fellowship may be renewed and restored and never be lost again!"

Jesus is saying, "If you bring Me back into the center of your lives and the center of your church, our fellowship together around the Word of God and the worship of God and the Lord's Supper will be a feast of good things. It will prefigure that great supper of the Lamb that I will have with you in heaven when I return, when the bride is brought and the groom comes and the marriage supper of the Lamb is enjoyed." (See Revelation 19:7.) "But if you do not repent, all of this will be lost, both in time and in eternity. Church at Laodicea, what will you do? Will you remain lukewarm, or will you become zealous? Those are your options. Choose wisely."

The Conclusion of the Letter

The conclusion of the letter is in verses 21 and 22. First of all, notice the promise made, verse 21. *"To him that overcometh will I grant to sit with me in my throne, even as I also overcame, and am set down with my Father in his throne."*

Notice once again to whom the promise is made. It is made to the overcomer. The overcomer is someone who overcomes an attitude of spiritual apathy and indifference and slothfulness. He is one who overcomes the spiritual lukewarmness that produces this spiritual poverty, nakedness, and blindness.

One who overcomes is one who does so by cultivating and maintaining zeal for Christ. He lives a life of zealous repentance. One who overcomes is one who engages in constant transactions with Jesus Christ in order to obtain spiritual wealth, in order to obtain personal righteousness, and in order to obtain perceptive eyesight in the realm of biblical truth. Such an overcomer, Jesus says, will sit in His throne and share in His rule.

What this includes and how it is expressed is uncertain, but that it is wonderful is beyond dispute. In some way, we will assist Christ in His rule over this world until He returns in glory to make the new heavens and the new earth. That is the promise made.

Secondly, notice the exhortation given in verse 22: *"He that hath an ear, let him hear what the Spirit saith unto the churches."* If you can hear anything, I hope you hear the warning against lukewarmness in your life—lukewarm prayer, lukewarm Bible reading, lukewarm witness, and lukewarm worship. Just settling down for a low level of life support for your Christian walk will lead you to poverty, blindness, and nakedness. It will lead you ultimately to become revolting to Christ, and then He will have to rebuke you and chasten you. You do not want to go there.

My exhortation to you is this: Be zealous for the Lord! Increase your level of spiritual transactions with Jesus Christ daily and on the Lord's Day so that you employ your thoughts and concerns and your cares and affairs around your walk with Jesus Christ, and not around all the material attractions that this world has to offer—money, medicine, and fashion.

We think if we are well dressed, in good physical health, and our bank account is full, we are doing great! But here are the important questions: How is your spiritual bank account? How is your spiritual health? How is your spiritual clothing? This is what you need to be thinking about, and this is what you need to be zealous about.

The second thing that the Spirit is saying to us is that we need to be very careful about pushing Jesus out of our lives and out of our church so He has to knock to get back in. How many churches are full of people, but empty of Christ? How many Christians are full of the world, but Christ is nowhere to be seen or heard about in their lives?

If you have been pushing Jesus out of your life because you are so focused on the things of this world, I urge you to be zealous and repent. Now is the time to say, "Lord Jesus, I want You back in my life. I want You at the center of my life. I want to be fellowshipping with You around Your table in time and in eternity. I want to have a Christ-centered, Christ-focused, Christ-saturated life. The last thing I want is for You to be on the outside knocking to get back on the inside."

Take stock of your life and ask yourself the question: Where is Jesus in my life? Is He outside, or is He inside? Is He on the edge of my life, or is He at the center of my life? Is He out on the porch, or is He in the living room? May the Lord help you to hear what the Spirit is saying to your church collectively, and to you as an individual.

19

The Vision of the Throne in Heaven, Revelation 4:1–6

> *“1 After this I looked, and, behold, a door was opened in heav-*
> *en: and the first voice which I heard was as it were of a trum-*
> *pet talking with me; which said, Come up hither, and I will*
> *shew thee things which must be hereafter. 2 And immediately I*
> *was in the spirit: and, behold, a throne was set in heaven, and*
> *one sat on the throne. 3 And he that sat was to look upon like*
> *a jasper and a sardis stone: and there was a rainbow round*
> *about the throne, in sight like unto an emerald. 4 And round*
> *about the throne were four and twenty seats: and upon the*
> *seats I saw four and twenty elders sitting, clothed in white*
> *raiment; and they had on their heads crowns of gold. 5 And*
> *out of the throne proceeded lightnings and thunderings and*
> *voices: and there were seven lamps of fire burning before the*
> *throne, which are the seven Spirits of God. 6 And before the*
> *throne there was a sea of glass like unto crystal: and in the*
> *midst of the throne, and round about the throne, were four*
> *beasts full of eyes before and behind.”*

In our introduction to Revelation, we saw this book consisted of seven parallel sections. Each of these sections took us on a journey that spanned the time period between the first and second coming of Christ. Each parallel section described from a different perspective the spiritual warfare we will experience during that time.

The first parallel section in chapters 1 through 3 showed us what spiritual warfare would look like in the local churches. The spiritual condition and struggles of these seven churches were not only a reality for them; they also represent the struggles of all the churches that will exist in this age. What happened in these seven churches has been happening in churches for the last 2,000 years, and it will continue to happen until Jesus Christ returns.

When we see what Christ commended in these churches, what He criticized in these churches, the warnings He gave these churches, and the promises He bestowed on these churches, we see these instructions were not just for those seven churches, they were also for our church and every church throughout this age. These seven churches are symbolic and typical of all churches of all time, both in the struggles they have, and in the triumphs they enjoy.

The great questions that faced each of these seven churches were these: Were they being faithful to Christ and the instruction He had given them? Were they being lampstands that shed the light of the gospel on the world around them, or had their light grown dim? Were they preaching the truth of the Scripture, or had they let false teaching enter their church? Were they faithfully confessing Christ before the world, or had they given in to the pressures of persecution? Were they living lives of holiness and righteousness, or had they yielded to the temptation to compromise with the world and its wickedness?

The same questions Jesus set before these seven churches are the questions that have to be answered by every church. We must shine as lights in the midst of a crooked and perverse generation. We must preach the truth of the Scriptures. We must faithfully confess Christ before the world. We must live lives of holiness and righteousness. In a word, we need to be faithful to Jesus Christ and the instructions He has given.

Having completed the first parallel section of Revelation in chapters 1 through 3, we now come to the second parallel section which consists of chapters 4 through 7.

We see the first coming of Christ and His saving work in chapters 4 and 5. As the seals are opened in chapter 6, we see the tribulation and persecution that the wicked cause throughout this age, which then culminates in the second coming. We see the appearance of the saved in heaven in chapter 7. In our last journey through this age, we saw the focus was on the church; but in this journey, the focus is on the world and its wickedness.

Even though we recognize these parallel sections in the book of Revelation, we must not lose sight of the flow of thought that transcends them and unifies them. This book sets forth the spiritual warfare that exists between Christ and His people on the one hand, and Satan and his people on the other hand.

This book opens with a glorious vision of Christ in chapter 1. We see Him there as the glorified, omnipotent God, the Alpha and the Omega, the beginning and the end, the one who has the keys of hell and of death. No one and nothing can stand before Him. All must fall at His feet like John did, in fear and submission and worship.

But this almighty Savior that was revealed to us in chapter 1, before whom the universe trembles, is also the one who stands in the midst of His churches and who holds their pastors in His right hand. This exalted, glorified, and majestic Christ loves His church and sends His church out into the world to invade the kingdom of darkness and to build the kingdom of God.

In chapters 2 and 3, Christ speaks to His church and gives her direction for the conduct of her spiritual warfare. He tells her members how they are doing in the battle. He tells them where they are succeeding and encourages them to continued faithfulness. He tells them where they are failing and exhorts them to change and reform their tactics.

Christ is at the head of the church militant as the church carries out spiritual warfare in this world to advance and build the kingdom of God. But this battle to advance the kingdom of God against the forces of Satan is not merely an earthly battle; it is carried out from the very throne of heaven itself.

Chapters 4 and 5 provide a vision of heaven and the role it plays in this spiritual warfare. We see the Father sitting on the throne of heaven, and from that throne He gives His Son the book containing His decrees. As the Father's decrees are opened and revealed by the Son, the conflict of the church against the world is unveiled. The enthroned God and His Son fight with us and for us and assure our victory in the battle as they direct that battle from the throne room of heaven.

This battle to expand the kingdom of God is not merely an earthly battle that we fight by ourselves. This battle is fought from heaven, and God on His throne has decreed how it will proceed. He has decreed who will win. The Son in heaven carries out the Father's decree contained in the scroll, and in doing so, defeats the devil and delivers the victory to His saints who are fighting the good fight of faith.

In chapters 1 to 5 we have an exalted Christ, we have a warring church, and we have an enthroned God, all working together to defeat Satan and his people. Will we triumph? There can be no doubt. We are and we will be more than conquerors through Him who loved us and saved us and supplied us with everything we need for victory.

We have moved from a vision of the glorified Christ in chapter 1 to a series of letters from Him to His militant church on earth in chapters 2 and 3. Now in chapter 4, we will see the vision of the throne of heaven and the one who sits on that throne, who rules and reigns over all the spiritual warfare on earth, and who leads His church to victory in that battle.

As we begin Revelation 4, there is a dramatic shift in the literary style of the writing. In chapters 2 and 3 the literary style was that of ordinary prose. They contained ordinary letters that were literal in their language and content, with very little symbolic imagery or symbolic language in them. Chapters 2 and 3 were verbally focused and directed to the ear because each of them concludes with the exhortation, *"He that has an ear, let him hear what the Spirit says to the churches."*

But beginning in chapter 4 and continuing to the middle of chapter 22, the emphasis dramatically changes from a verbal focus that is directed to the ear to a visual focus that is directed to the eye. Dozens of times in these subsequent chapters John says, *"I saw," "I looked," "I beheld."* Take special notice: beginning at chapter 4, Revelation becomes a visual picture book, presenting the message God wants to convey to us in highly symbolic visual imagery.

It is important as we shift our focus from ordinary prose to highly symbolic visual imagery that we not get caught up in the details of these symbolic visual images, but that we focus on the primary message these pictures present. We must ask questions such as these as we look at these visual pictures: What is the main message of these images? What is the big picture telling us? We especially need to beware of trying to literalize these symbols or make too much of their details.

Chapter 4 is a vision of God the Father sitting on the throne in heaven. The chapter contains two halves: first, we have the description of God on His throne in verses 1 to 6; and second, we have the worship of God on His throne in verses 7 to 11.

In this chapter, we are going to look at verses 1–6 and see the description of God on His throne. In the next chapter we will look at verses 7–11 and see the worship of God on His throne.

The Introduction to the Vision

The introduction to the vision is in verses 1 through 2a. *"After this I looked, and, behold, a door was opened in heaven: and the first voice which I heard was as it were of a trumpet talking with me; which said, Come up hither, and I will shew thee things which must be hereafter.* [2]*And immediately I was in the spirit. . ."*

Verse 1 opens with the phrase, *"After this I looked, and, behold, a door was opened in heaven."* Apparently, after receiving the letters to the churches, John reverted back to his ordinary state of mind. How long this lasted is uncertain, but subsequent to his vision in chapters 1–3, he had another vision in which he saw a door standing open in heaven. He heard the voice of Christ inviting him to come through that open door and enter into heaven. The reason we know this is the voice of Christ is because it is described as being like a trumpet: *"and the first voice which I heard was as it were of a trumpet talking with me"*

In 1:10 John says, *"I was in the Spirit on the Lord's day, and heard behind me a great voice, as of a trumpet,* [11] *Saying, I am Alpha and Omega. . ."* That voice of the great trumpet was the voice of Jesus. Jesus continues to speak through chapters 1 to 3. When John says in 4:1 that he heard a voice like a trumpet, it is the same voice he heard in chapter 1.

Christ tells John that He is going to reveal what is going to unfold in the future. *"Come up hither, and I will shew thee things which must be hereafter."* He says, in essence, "I have already given you a vision. I am now giving you the next vision, and this vision will reveal future events to you." John is invited by Christ to come into the dwelling place and presence of God—that is, to go through this door into heaven in order to obtain further revelation about the future.

Jesus is inviting John to come up into heaven, and there heavenly realities will be made plain to him. Notice it says in verse 1b, these things "*must be hereafter.*" He is going to show John things which must come to pass.

This book is not a record of what happens to come to pass in the future by random chance; instead, it is a record of what will come to pass in the future by divine decree. These things about to be revealed will certainly come to pass because they are contained in the book of God's decrees, the book that is sealed with seven seals that we are going to be looking at in chapters 5, 6, and 7.

It is a great comfort to believers to know that what occurs in the future will happen because God has decreed that it must come to pass. The spiritual warfare we experience is unfolding according to a plan, and the struggles we face are all under the control of God. History is occurring just as it should, and everything is proceeding according to plan. We know what we face, we know the struggles we are going to have, and we know the outcomes we are going to experience because all these things must come to pass.

John is being called up to heaven to see things from that perspective because it is only from the vantage point of heaven that the things that occur on earth can be properly understood and seen for what they really are. This vision helps us to see the things that occur on earth as God sees them.

We often think thoughts like these: "If I could just understand what God is thinking about this and if I could just see it the way He sees it, that would be so wonderful! Then I could have a proper perspective on it and give a proper response to it." That is exactly what is afforded to John and to us as we are shown into the throne room of God. All things proceed from the throne of God. It is only from the perspective of the throne in heaven that we understand the details that occur on earth. It is a great comfort to know that God in heaven is in control. God has directed what must certainly come to pass, and in that direction is the security, the safety, and the triumph of the saints.

Notice verse 2. It says, *"And immediately I was in the spirit: and, behold, a throne was set in heaven, and one sat on the throne."* Here in verse 2, John declares not that he was transported physically and bodily into heaven itself; but rather, that he was *"in the spirit"*; that is, he went from a state of merely seeing a vision, in which he would still be aware of everything going on around him, to a more profound state, a state of being *"in the Spirit."*

When Stephen was stoned in Acts 7, he looked up and saw God sitting on the throne and Jesus standing at His right hand. Stephen had a vision. But at the same time, Stephen was fully aware of the people around him and the rocks that were landing on him because he was praying: *"Father, forgive them."* He had a vision of heaven, but at the same time he had an awareness of where he was and what was going on around him. In verse 1, this is what is happening to John: *"After this I looked, and, behold. . ."* But in verse 2, something additional happens. It says, *"And immediately I was in the spirit."*

John goes from a state of merely seeing a vision in verse 1 to entering into a prophetic trance in verse 2 in which the reality of the world around him faded into oblivion, and his eyes are opened to see the spiritual world that is ordinarily invisible. The result is that he sees the throne of God, he sees the God who is sitting on the throne, and then with vivid symbolic imagery he begins to describe what he saw. In this spiritual trance, John goes through the door he previously saw in verse 1. He enters into the throne room of God in heaven.

John, as it were, ascends to the throne he sees in his vision, and loses all consciousness of the island of Patmos upon which he physically remains. Having this vision in the spirit makes it as real and vivid in his mind's eye as though he were actually physically there. This is what he means when he says, *"And immediately I was in the spirit."*

The Substance of the Vision

The substance of the vision is in verses 2b to 6. Verse 2b says, *"and, behold, a throne was set in heaven, and one sat on the throne."* Here is the spiritual center of the universe, around which everything revolves. We need to understand the universe is Theocentric. From the throne, God controls everything that occurs in both the physical and spiritual realms.

It is only from the perspective of God's throne that all things can be understood, because of Him, and through Him, and unto Him are all things. The purpose of this vision is to show us that all things are governed by the Lord on the throne, and that includes the spiritual warfare we experience and the trials and tribulations we go through.

The throne of God is in control of all things in heaven and earth. This is why the description of the throne precedes chapters 6 through 20 in which the symbolic descriptions of the trials and tribulations the church must experience are set forth. Chapters 6 through 20 all need to be understood from the perspective of the throne of God. When dealing with any issue or event in our lives, we have to start with the throne, and from that perspective, seek to understand and interpret what happens to us. In chapters 4 and 5 the term "throne" occurs seventeen times. Clearly, God wants us to have our lives and our faith and our focus firmly anchored in the throne. The throne must be our starting point for everything else.

In verses 3 to 6, we have a description of the throne of God that employs symbolic language, and we need to understand those symbols in order to understand the realities they represent. John begins describing God in verse 3, *"And he that sat [on the throne] was to look upon like a jasper and a sardis stone: and there was a rainbow round about the throne, in sight like unto an emerald."*

Whatever John is seeing on this throne is not God Himself, because we read in Exodus 33 and many other passages that no unglorified man can see God and live. Furthermore, this is a vision, not an actual sight of a physical reality. What he does see is the outshining of God's glory, and that glory is like or similar in appearance to three things.

First of all, he says the glory is like or similar in appearance to a jasper. Verse 3: *"And he that sat was to look upon like a jasper."* It was not a jasper, but it was like one. The word in the original language that is translated "jasper" is only used in the book of Revelation, and it is uncertain what this stone actually is. We are told some things about this stone in Revelation 21:11. There John is talking about the New Jerusalem descending out of heaven from God, *"having the glory of God: and her light was like unto a stone most precious, even like a jasper stone, clear as crystal."*

Revelation 21:11 tells us two things about this jasper stone. It tells us that this stone is very precious—that is, it is exceedingly valuable. It also tells us that this stone is as clear as crystal. Therefore, it was something like a diamond. A diamond is a stone that is very valuable, and it is also something that is white and clear. What we have is the flashing brilliance of a valuable diamond that is pure and white, which represents the purity, holiness, and infinite value that God Himself has.

The second thing John sees is that the glory of God is likened to a sardis stone. In the King James Version it says *"sardine,"* but the better spelling is "sardis." In fact, one of the cities in which the seven churches existed was the church of Sardis. This stone is one we know more about. It is a stone that is blood-red in color, like a ruby or a garnet.

Red is the color of wrath and judgment, just like white is the color of purity and holiness. The reason red is the color of wrath and judgment is that red is the color of the blood that is shed for the atonement of sin, representing the wrath of God against that sin. Furthermore, the flames of fire that are in hell are a reddish-orange color. These are all the result of God's wrath against sin.

These two stones by their color represent the holiness of God and the wrath and judgment of God against sin. They represent His purity and His avenging justice.

If this were all that was represented of God, we would be in a terrible condition. But the good news is that there is a third likeness to the glory of God that is set before us. Notice the last part of verse 3: *"and there was a rainbow round about the throne, in sight like unto an emerald."* The rainbow was given to Noah as a sign of the Noahic Covenant that was made after Noah and his family were saved from the wrath of God in the ark in Genesis 9:13. This rainbow is a symbol of God's mercy and God's salvation. It is a sign of God's goodness and God's grace.

Furthermore, this rainbow is said to be like an emerald, which is a green gemstone. Green in the Scripture is the symbol of life. In Psalm 23 it says of God that He makes us lie down in green pastures, and He leads us beside the still waters. Green grass was necessary for the life of animals and people. A green plant is alive. God is a God who gives His people life, and God is a God who saves them from His wrath and judgment in the ark of His safety which is the Lord Jesus Christ.

What we have represented of God on the throne in verse 3 is that He is a God of purity, He is a God of avenging justice, and He is a God of saving mercy and grace who gives eternal life to His people. Purity, justice, and salvation are all conveyed by this visual symbolism.

This brings us to verse 4. *"And round about the throne were four and twenty seats: and upon the seats I saw four and twenty elders sitting, clothed in white raiment; and they had on their heads crowns of gold."* This saving mercy and goodness of God which is manifested in this rainbow that recalls the salvation of Noah and his family is manifested in these twenty-four elders sitting on twenty-four thrones placed around the throne of God. They are all dressed in white robes, and they all have crowns of gold on their heads.

These twenty-four elders represent those whom God has saved of both the Old and the New Testaments. There were twelve tribes of Israel, and there were twelve apostles; added together, they make twenty-four. To demonstrate that this is not speculation, notice Revelation 21:10–14. Here we see the twelve tribes and the twelve apostles together, making up the doors and the foundation of the New Jerusalem.

Revelation 21:10–14: *"And he carried me away in the spirit to a great and high mountain, and shewed me that great city, the holy Jerusalem, descending out of heaven from God,* [11] *Having the glory of God: and her light was like unto a stone most precious, even like a jasper stone, clear as crystal;* [12]*And had a wall great and high, and had twelve gates, and at the gates twelve angels, and names written thereon, which are the names of the twelve tribes of the children of Israel:* [13] *On the east three gates; on the north three gates; on the south three gates; and on the west three gates."*

Israel, the twelve tribes, reached out to the whole world: north, south, east, and west. People from all points of the compass were brought into the kingdom of God through the ministry of the twelve tribes. That is what these gates represent: access into the kingdom of God.

Verse 14: *"And the wall of the city had twelve foundations, and in them the names of the twelve apostles of the Lamb."* The church is built on the foundation of the apostles and the prophets, Jesus Christ Himself being the chief cornerstone. This city is not a literal city but a picture of the church, and the church is made up of those who came in through the twelve tribes and those who came in through the twelve apostles, and together they form its entrance and its foundation.

When we view the twenty-four elders in chapter 4, it seems apparent that they represent the whole body of people saved in the Old Testament and in the New Testament combined together.

It says they are clothed in white raiment, which is their robe of righteousness. It also says they had on their heads crowns of gold. These white robes and these crowns of gold are exactly what Jesus promised to the overcomers in 3:5. *"He that overcometh, the same shall be clothed in white raiment,"* exactly what it says these twenty-four elders have on, *"and I will not blot out his name out of the book of life, but I will confess his name before my Father, and before his angels."*

These elders who have on these white robes have what Jesus promised to His people who overcame. But notice they also have crowns on their heads, which is a sign of authority and rule. Crowns are what kings wear. Notice 3:21: *"To him that overcometh will I grant to sit with me in my throne, even as I also overcame, and am set down with my Father in his throne."*

Jesus promised the overcomers thrones and positions of rulership, which implies crowns. Paul said in 2 Timothy 4:7–8: *"I have fought a good fight, I have finished my course, I have kept the faith:* [8]*Henceforth there is laid up for me a crown of righteousness, which the Lord, the righteous judge, shall give me at that day: and not to me only, but unto all them also that love his appearing."*

It is specifically the crown and the throne, the position of rule and authority, that Jesus has promised to His people. This is what we see these twenty-four elders having and exercising. They have the white robes, they have the crowns, and they follow the pattern of the twelve apostles and the twelve tribes spoken of in chapter 21.

Furthermore, these twenty-four elders are called *"elders."* That is never a designation that is given to any other being than humans. Angels are never called elders anywhere in the Scriptures, but people are frequently called by that title.

Finally, these twenty-four elders confess in 5:8–10 that they have been redeemed by God and made to be kings and priests, things true only of the church, the whole body of God's elect. Notice 5:8–10, *"And when he had taken the book, the four beasts and four and twenty elders fell down before the Lamb, having every one of them* (the twenty-four elders) *harps, and golden vials full of odours, which are the prayers of saints.* [9] *And they sung a new song, saying, Thou art worthy to take the book, and to open the seals thereof: for thou wast slain, and hast redeemed us to God by thy blood out of every kindred, and tongue, and people, and nation;* [10] *And hast made us unto our God kings and priests: and we shall reign on the earth."*

The twenty-four elders are those who are redeemed out of every kindred, tongue, people, and nation, and therefore they must represent all the saved believers of both the Old and New Testament. There is a textual dispute about the true reading of verses 9 and 10. The King James Version is correct in its translation of verses 9 and 10; nevertheless, there is another textual reading that has some support, not much in verse 9, but more so in verse 10. I think that the KJV reading in verse 9 is quite strongly supported. Verse 9 alone would be sufficient to establish that the twenty-four elders are those who are redeemed by the blood of Christ out of every kindred, tongue, people, and nation, and therefore could not be any other than the elect of God from both dispensations. Based on all of the other pieces of data, these twenty-four elders have to represent the redeemed of God. We will explain the textual issue of verses 9 and 10 in chapter 22.

We see that the throne of God is surrounded by the saved of God, who share in God's throne and God's holy character because He has redeemed them and given them the crown and the robe through His saving grace. In this vision, we have God on His throne, and we have the saved people of God sitting on thrones around His, wearing robes of righteousness and crowns of authority and rule on their heads. They represent the collective church of God that surrounds the throne.

Verse 5 says, *"And out of the throne proceeded lightnings and thunderings and voices: and there were seven lamps of fire burning before the throne, which are the seven Spirits of God."* The language of verse 5 causes us to recall the lightning and thunder and the voice that was heard at Mount Sinai when the law was given and the people trembled before the authority and presence of God in Exodus 19 and 20.

These glorified saints around the throne are reminded that although they have escaped the wrath of God, there is still going to be the lightning and the thunder of God's judgment falling upon those who have broken His laws. The thunder and lightning and voices from Mount Sinai were designed to cause the people to tremble before the authority and power and wrath of God, and to cause them to fear breaking His law. Sadly, people have gone ahead and broken His law, and now this thunder and wrath and voices are coming to bring God's wrath upon them.

Furthermore, it says in verse 5 there are *"seven lamps of fire burning before the throne."* This reminds us of the menorah that was in the tabernacle, that seven-armed lamp that was in the Holy Place which had seven flames burning on it to illuminate the tabernacle. We have seen this applied to the Holy Spirit in chapter 1.

Before the throne, there are seven lamps of fire which are declared to represent the seven Spirits of God. As we have seen before, there is only one Spirit, but the number seven is the number of completion. Here we have a representation of the complete perfection of the Holy Spirit in all the fullness of His divine nature and work. He is not just a Holy Spirit; He completely performs the work of God in applying the salvation of God and in revealing and illuminating the Word of God to the saints of God.

We see the Trinity represented quite clearly in this chapter. God the Father, sitting on the throne; the Holy Spirit before the throne represented by these seven lamps; and the Lord Jesus Christ speaking with the voice of the trumpet. In chapter 5 Jesus is even more clearly identified as He appears and receives the scroll out of the hand of the Father.

These seven burning lamps and this lightning and thundering and these voices all manifest the authority of God and the righteous wrath of God that will be poured out upon those who have broken His laws. At Mount Sinai, God thundered out His threats of judgment on those who would defy His authority, and now He is going to carry out those threats against those who have, in fact, defied His authority. Here we see the dreadful power and majesty and authority of God coming in judgment on those who have dared to defy His authority and His law.

Notice verse 6: *"And before the throne there was a sea of glass like unto crystal: and in the midst of the throne, and round about the throne, were four beasts full of eyes before and behind."*

Verse 6 gives us the final descriptive statement of the throne of God, and it says two things. First, it says that *"before the throne there was a sea of glass like unto crystal."*

The meaning of this symbolic imagery is unclear, and many different suggestions have been offered as to what this *"sea of glass like unto crystal"* represents. The best explanation is that this sea of glass represents the peacefulness and the purity that surrounds the throne of God. It is the opposite of what is spoken of in Isaiah 57:20–21 which says: *"But the wicked are like the troubled sea, when it cannot rest, whose waters cast up mire and dirt.* [21] *There is no peace, saith my God, to the wicked."*

Polar opposite to that statement, and in direct contrast with it, here is not a troubled sea, but a perfectly calm sea—not a sea which cannot rest, but one that is perfectly peaceful; not a sea of filthy mire and dirt, but one that is perfectly pure like clear crystal. The turmoil and trouble and the mire and dirt of wickedness are entirely absent from the throne of God, and these things are the opposite of all that characterizes the throne of God. Everything about this sea is pure and peaceful and tranquil and stable. Around the throne of God, there are no ripples of anxiety, no mire of filth, and no restlessness of conscience. None of these things marks the environment around the throne of God. The throne of God is a sea of calmness, peace, and purity.

Secondly, there is the angelic presence around the throne represented by these four creatures full of eyes before and behind. We will explain more about these creatures in the next chapter as we study the worship that takes place around the throne. But suffice it to say for now that there are four of these angelic creatures who are sent to do the will of God in the four corners of the earth: north, south, east, and west. Not only do they do the will of God, but we are also going to see that they lead in the worship of God. They are God's ministers to do His will, they are God's attendants to sing His praise, and they are God's leaders to provoke His worship.

What we have here is a magnificent description of the glory of God. We see His sovereignty as He rules from the throne upon which He sits. We see His purity as He dwells without any sin. We see His power as He executes His wrath upon His enemies. We see His grace as He saves His church and brings His people into His very presence. Above all, we see His glory as He displays His majesty to the world and the saints and the angels.

This is indeed a God to fall down before and worship. This is a God that we can trust and serve, even when in His providence He appoints our sufferings in the execution of the spiritual warfare He assigns to us.

The point is this: in your spiritual warfare and struggles, you have to start with God. You have to start not with the god of modern culture, but with the God of divine Scripture. You have to start with the God who sits on the throne, who is pure, who is an avenging judge, who is a compassionate Savior, who executes His wrath and shows His grace, who displays His majesty, and before whom all the world falls down to worship.

If this God puts you through some trouble in the spiritual warfare that is required to build His kingdom, He is worthy of the worst of your sufferings in order to bring Him the greatest measure of glory possible through your life.

20

The Vision of the Worship in Heaven, Revelation 4:7–11

> "[6] *And before the throne there was a sea of glass like unto crystal: and in the midst of the throne, and round about the throne, were four beasts full of eyes before and behind.* [7] *And the first beast was like a lion, and the second beast like a calf, and the third beast had a face as a man, and the fourth beast was like a flying eagle.* [8] *And the four beasts had each of them six wings about him; and they were full of eyes within: and they rest not day and night, saying, Holy, holy, holy, Lord God Almighty, which was, and is, and is to come.* [9] *And when those beasts give glory and honour and thanks to him that sat on the throne, who liveth for ever and ever,* [10] *The four and twenty elders fall down before him that sat on the throne, and worship him that liveth for ever and ever, and cast their crowns before the throne, saying,* [11] *Thou art worthy, O Lord, to receive glory and honour and power: for thou hast created all things, and for thy pleasure they are and were created.*"

In chapter 1 we saw a glorious vision of the resurrected Christ in all of His exalted majesty, power, and glory. In chapters 2 and 3 we saw the focus of Christ was on His churches and how they were doing in their spiritual warfare.

Now in chapters 4 and 5, we have a vision of heaven opened to us and the role it plays in the spiritual warfare the churches are engaged in. We see this battle to expand the kingdom of God is not merely an earthly battle we fight alone. From His throne, God controls everything that occurs both in the physical and spiritual realms. All things on earth are governed by God in heaven. Therefore, we can be confident that God is managing all our tribulations for our good and His glory, and for the defeat of His enemies and the expansion of His kingdom. In the midst of all of our trials we need to keep our focus on the throne.

In the last chapter, we began to meditate on this description of the throne in heaven on which God the Father is seated. We saw that God's throne is the center of the spiritual universe. As John looked upon the throne, he saw the glory of God was like a jasper stone, which represented His purity and holiness. It was like a sardis stone, which represented His avenging justice. It was like a rainbow, in sight like an emerald, which represented His life-giving salvation. We saw that God upon the throne was a God of purity, a God of avenging justice, and a God of saving mercy who gives eternal life to His people.

Around this throne there were twenty-four elders who represent all of God's elect from the Old and New Testament eras. The thunder and lightning and voices from before the throne manifest the fearfulness of His judgment toward those who would defy His authority and break His laws. The seven lamps of fire represented the Holy Spirit. The sea of glass represented the peacefulness and purity that surrounds the throne of God, and the four living beings around the throne were angels.

Last chapter we saw the description of God on His throne in verses 1 to 6. In this chapter we will consider the worship of God on His throne in verses 7 to 11.

It is important to note that this worship of God naturally followed the revelation of God. God is revealed, and worship immediately follows. Each time we see a manifestation of the person of God to people, they immediately fall on their faces and give Him the honor that is due to His name. We see this occurring in both the Old Testament and in the New Testament. This is what is happening in chapter 4. Whether it is angels or redeemed people, all who are before the throne give glory and honor to the God who sits on the throne. They fall down before Him in worship and praise and thanksgiving—not once, but over and over again. The more we learn of God, the more we are moved to adore and worship Him.

We need to follow the example of worship set before us in the last half of chapter 4 as it is exemplified by both the angels and the redeemed saints.

The Four Angels and Their Worship

The four angels and their worship are spoken of in verses 7 to 9.

"And the first beast was like a lion, and the second beast like a calf, and the third beast had a face as a man, and the fourth beast was like a flying eagle. [8] *And the four beasts had each of them six wings about him; and they were full of eyes within: and they rest not day and night, saying, Holy, holy, holy, Lord God Almighty, which was, and is, and is to come.* [9] *And when those beasts give glory and honour and thanks to him that sat on the throne, who liveth for ever and ever. . ."*

We were introduced to these four living beings in the previous chapter as we looked at verse 6. The last part of verse 6 says, *"and round about the throne, were four beasts full of eyes before and behind."* We now have a further description of these beasts in verses 7 and 8.

We will look first at the identity of these beasts; and then secondly, at the worship of these beasts.

First of all, notice their identity. There are three places in the Old Testament where we have descriptions of similar angelic beings before the throne of God. They are described in Isaiah 6, in Ezekiel 1, and in Ezekiel 10. These chapters are descriptions of God sitting on His throne, and around the throne, angelic creatures are described as giving worship to God.

In Isaiah 6, Isaiah calls them *"seraphim."* They each have six wings. They cry, *"Holy, holy, holy, is the Lord of hosts: the whole earth is full of his glory."* We see in Revelation that these angels have six wings, and they cry, *"Holy, holy, holy, Lord God Almighty."*

In Ezekiel 1 and Ezekiel 10, the angels that are around the throne are called "cherubim," and each one has four faces, and each one has four wings.

The living creatures before the throne in Revelation 4 most closely match the seraphim described in Isaiah 6. Some say they are the cherubim of Ezekiel 1 and 10. But the cherubim only have four wings, while those in Isaiah and Revelation each have six.

In Isaiah 6 we have an Old Testament picture of what is being described in Revelation 4:6–8. We have said that the book of Revelation is to be understood in light of the Old Testament. The strange figures and symbols used in Revelation can all be found in Old Testament passages.

Notice Isaiah 6:1–8: *"In the year that king Uzziah died I saw also the Lord sitting upon a throne, high and lifted up, and his train filled the temple.*" This verse describes Revelation 4:1–6, the first half of our chapter. Verse 2: "*Above it stood the seraphims: each one had six wings; with [two] he covered his face, and with [two] he covered his feet, and with [two] he did fly.* [3] *And one cried unto another, and said, Holy, holy, holy, is the* LORD *of hosts: the whole earth is full of his glory.*" This describes the angels of Revelation 4:6–9. "[4] *And the posts of the door moved at the voice of him that cried, and the house was filled with smoke.*" This is the imagery of the thunders and the lightnings proceeding from the throne in Revelation 4:5.

Isaiah continues: "[5] *Then said I, Woe is me! for I am undone; because I am a man of unclean lips, and I dwell in the midst of a people of unclean lips: for mine eyes have seen the King, the* LORD *of hosts.* [6] *Then flew one of the seraphims unto me, having a live coal in his hand, which he had taken with the tongs from off the altar:* [7] *And he laid it upon my mouth, and said, Lo, this hath touched thy lips; and thine iniquity is taken away, and thy sin purged.* [8] *Also I heard the voice of the Lord, saying, Whom shall I send, and who will go for us? Then said I, Here am I; send me.*"

These angels in Revelation 4 most closely correspond with the seraphim of Isaiah 6. Both have six wings, and both use the threefold description of holiness to God in their worship. However, several details are added to the description of these angels in Revelation 4 that are omitted by Isaiah. It is not that the angels in Isaiah did not have these characteristics; it is just that Isaiah did not happen to mention them. Notice the particular description that John gives of these angels, which John calls "living creatures." In the King James Version they are called "*beasts.*" The New King James has "living creatures," which I think is a better translation. A beast would imply the idea of an animal, but these angels are far more than mere animals.

First of all, notice their location. In Revelation 4:6b it says, "*and in the midst of the throne, and round about the throne, were four beasts full of eyes before and behind.*" These seraphim are in the midst of the throne, and round about the throne. In other words, these angels are right beside the throne. Isaiah 6 says they are hovering above it. In the Holy of Holies, where the ark was, the angels on the ark had their wings touching over the mercy seat, which is where the Shekinah glory of God dwelt. The earthly tabernacle was modeled after the heavenly tabernacle and gives some insight as to what the reality in heaven is like. Just as there were sculptures of seraphim over and around the Shekinah glory of God on the mercy seat in the tabernacle, so there are actual seraphim over and around the throne and glory of God in heaven.

These four angels are next to the throne, and the implication is that they are on the four sides of the throne. Four conveys the concept of the whole world, as described by the four points of the compass: north, south, east, and west. These four angels stand on the four sides of the throne of God, ready to carry out any direction He gives to them to any point on the face of the earth.

Secondly, notice their attributes. It says in verse 6 that they are full of eyes, before and behind. This is a symbolic description of the fact that these angels are ever vigilant. Kids will say: "My mom's got eyes in the back of her head." In other words, they cannot get away with anything with mom, because she sees it all. This is what is being conveyed here. These angels are ever vigilant, nothing escapes their notice, nothing is hidden from them, they overlook nothing, they see everything, and no one sneaks anything past them.

In verse 7 it says, *"The first beast was like a lion, and the second beast like a calf, and the third beast had a face as a man, and the fourth beast was like a flying eagle."* John then tells us these four angels exhibit similarities to these four beasts, and they represent their best characteristics and qualities. He likens them to a lion, a calf (an ox is the idea), a man, and an eagle.

This indicates that these seraphim possess majesty like a lion; strength like an ox; intelligence like a man; and swiftness like an eagle. Majesty, strength, intelligence, and swiftness—those are the characteristics that mark these four seraphim.

The point is this: these angels reflect all that is highest and best in God's created order, whether it is the wild animals, represented by the lion; the domestic animals, represented by the ox; the flying animals, represented by the eagle; or the bearers of God's image, represented by mankind. The angels possess and reflect the best of every order of created beings.

The reason for this is that the angels are the highest of all created beings. We read in Psalm 8:5 that even when man was made, he was made a little lower than the angels. The angels, since they are the highest of all created beings, possess the best attributes that any created beings could have.

Verse 8 says that each of these angels had six wings. Isaiah 6 tells us that with two of those wings he covered his feet, showing that he was not worthy to stand in the presence of God, and with two of those wings he covered his face, showing he was not worthy to look upon God. Here we see the expression of deep humility on the part of these angels. Though they are the highest creation of God, they know they are nothing before God. They are not to be compared with God, and they are not worthy to be in the presence of God even as sinless angels because they are mere creatures.

Isaiah 6 tells us that with two wings he did fly. This shows the seraph's readiness to promptly carry out the commands from the throne, to do whatever duty and go to whatever destination God has appointed him to. The seraphim were sent from the throne to pick up a coal and put it on the lips of Isaiah. These angels with two of their wings are ever ready to go and carry out the will and the command of God, whatever it may be.

Humility and zeal mark these angels in the use of their six wings. Their humility is seen in covering their feet because they are not worthy to stand in the presence of God, and in covering their face because they are not worthy to look upon God. Their zeal is seen in the two wings ready to fly to carry out the command of God to the four corners of the earth, whatever it may be and wherever it is.

It goes on to say in verse 8 that *"they were full of eyes within."* In verse 6, it said they were *"full of eyes before and behind."* The eyes in verse 6 were looking outward: before them and behind them. But now we are told in verse 8 they have eyes within. Just as the eyes that were outward showed they were ever vigilant regarding what was going on around them so that nothing escaped their notice, these eyes within convey the idea that they have acute self-awareness and self-knowledge. They see themselves for who they are in their thoughts and motives. Their self-perception is perfect. They do not deceive themselves about who they are within themselves.

We know our hearts are deceitful. What man really knows himself? Are you not surprised from time to time by the things you say and do? You thought, "I did not think I had the capacity to do that." It may be something good, or it may be something bad. But until then, there is much about ourselves that we do not understand. We fail to see ourselves as we really are. This is not the case with these angels.

This is who the angels are in their person. They are immediately next to the throne of God; they are acutely aware of everything around them and everything inside of them; they possess the highest attributes of all creatures in God's created order; and they are filled with humility and zeal to serve God at the moment He gives them a command.

Secondly, notice the worship of these angels. They worship God by giving *"glory and honour and thanks to him that sat on the throne, who liveth for ever and ever."*

The worship of these angels is continuous. Notice it says in the last part of verse 8, *"And they rest not day and night, saying, Holy, holy, holy, Lord God Almighty, which was, and is, and is to come."*

They have unlimited energy and strength, they never grow tired, they never go to sleep, and they never need a break. They never cease day and night giving praise to God. God's glory is constant, and therefore God's praise must be continuous. There is never a moment when God's glory is shining forth that God's praise should not be coming forth.

This praise to God consists of three things: a declaration of who He is; a declaration of the attributes He possesses; and a declaration of the eternality of His being.

First, notice the declaration of who He is. Three times God is declared to be holy. Who is God? God is holy, holy, holy. First of all, the threefold repetition is a reference to His trinitarian nature: The Father is holy, the Son is holy, and the Spirit is holy. Secondly, the number three also conveys the concept of perfection. Thus, the threefold description of holiness to God is a reference to not only His trinitarian nature; it is also a declaration of the perfection of that holiness.

His purity of character and His separation from sin is absolute, total, complete, and perfect. God will not sin, God cannot sin, God has never sinned, and God will never sin. His actions have been, are now, and always shall be perfect; and His judgments are always and without exception righteous. He is a holy God. It is interesting that His holiness is the perfection that the angels choose to focus on.

Nowhere in the Scriptures do you find angels or people saying of God, "patient, patient, patient" or "loving, loving, loving." The reason is that those things could not and would not exist as they are without His holiness. His holiness informs all of His actions, all of His attitudes, all of His plans, and all of His purposes. God's holiness is His beauty.

Secondly, notice the declaration of the attributes He possesses. They identify these by the names they give Him. They say of Him that He is the *Lord God Almighty*. When they say that He is the Lord God Almighty, it conveys three truths to us about Him. It tells us first of all that He is *"Lord."* This name declares His sovereignty. He is Lord over all things, and He is Lord over all beings. He is sovereign over everything.

It tells us secondly that He is *"God."* This name declares His authority. He is the highest authority in the universe from which there is no appeal. Every person has a god. The identity of anyone's god is the identity of the being to whom he yields the highest authority. Whatever has the highest authority in a person's life is his god. It is the nature of God that He is the highest authority, and there is no authority above Him.

It tells us thirdly that He is *"Almighty."* As the Almighty, there are no limits to His power, with the result that there is nothing He wills to do that He is unable to do. There is nothing too hard for Him. He is omnipotent.

Thirdly, notice the declaration of the eternality of His being. There is a declaration of His eternality in the statement *"which was, and is, and is to come."* He is the God who was, and is, and is to come. He is the one *"who liveth for ever and ever."* He always has been, He now is, and He always will be. He will outlast every enemy the church has: His enemies will die, but He lives forever and ever. He is eternal.

We see from this passage that God is a holy, sovereign, authoritative, almighty God who is eternal and lives forever. Understanding that the God we serve is a God like this is a great comfort to persecuted and embattled believers who must endure spiritual warfare and assaults at the hands of the wicked. God is infinitely greater than the worst of our enemies.

When it says in verse 9, *"And when those beasts give glory and honour and thanks to him that sat on the throne,"* it is telling us what these angels are doing as they utter the phrase, *"Holy, holy, holy, Lord God Almighty, which was, and is, and is to come."* When they say those words, they are giving glory and honor and thanks to the eternal God who sits on the throne. In a word, they are giving God worship.

This then is how God is to be worshiped. We are to speak of His attributes. We are to speak of His identity. We are to speak of His nature. We are to do so with reverence and conviction and enthusiasm, and with all the strength we possess. We are to do so with an attitude of humility and unworthiness. The greater and more perfect your understanding of God, the greater and more powerful is your ability to worship.

We see from the actions and expressions of the seraphim that worship must be intensely theological and exclusively God-centered. It must be a declaration of God as He is revealed in the Bible, and it must be given entirely to God and to Him alone. We cannot worship a god of our own imagination, nor have our worship revolve around ourselves and our importance.

As the seraphim see the greatness of God sitting on the throne in verses 1 to 6, they fall down and worship in verses 7 to 9. A great God leads to great worship, whereas a little god leads to little worship. That is why above all else we have to be theologians—that is, those who study God. The better we know our God, the stronger our worship will be, and the better expressions of worship we will have. As Daniel 11:32 says, *"The people that do know their God shall be strong, and do exploits."*

The Twenty-Four Elders and Their Worship

The worship of the twenty-four elders is described in verses 10 and 11. We are told that upon seeing and hearing the worship the angels were engaging in, *"The four and twenty elders fall down before him that sat on the throne, and worship him that liveth for ever and ever, and cast their crowns before the throne, saying, [11] Thou art worthy, O Lord, to receive glory and honour and power: for thou hast created all things, and for thy pleasure they are and were created."*

First of all, notice their actions of worship. These twenty-four elders represent the redeemed church in heaven. When the angels offer glory and honor and thanksgiving to God who sits on the throne, the saints do not simply sit back and watch. Worship is not a spectator sport, where some worship while others merely observe. If a soul is a redeemed soul, it is always a worshiping soul, and it will not idly sit by while others worship. The Christian will not be busy doing something else while corporate worship is being carried out by others. The saved soul cannot restrain itself. It does not want to restrain itself. It bursts forth with a desire to worship the God it loves, and would rather worship than do anything else.

Therefore, when the angels give glory and thanks and honor to God on the throne, the church immediately joins in. Verse 10: "*The four and twenty elders fall down before him that sat on the throne, and worship him that liveth for ever and ever, and cast their crowns before the throne.*"

The twenty-four elders take a position of humility before the enthroned Father and fall down on their faces before Him. Just as we saw the humility of the angels, covering their feet and covering their faces, we now see the humility of the twenty-four elders. Humility befits any creature before the throne of God.

Humility is always the disposition of the true worshiper. The angels showed humility by covering their feet and faces, and the elders show humility by falling on their faces before God. When we come to worship God, the posture of a bowed and humble heart that recognizes its own unworthiness and the infinite superiority of God over us is the only fitting position for us to be in. The angels see the vast distance between themselves and God because He is infinite and they are finite. He is the Creator, and they are the creature. We not only have those categories, but also the stark contrast between His holiness and our sinfulness. He is holy and we are sinful. Therefore, we have even more reason than the sinless angels to be humble before the throne of God.

When these twenty-four elders fall down to worship Him who lives forever and ever, they cast their crowns before the throne. When we studied verse 4, we saw that these twenty-four elders had crowns of gold on their heads.

A crown is a symbol of rule and authority, and the rule and authority the saints have is given to them. They are given the privilege of sharing in the rule of Christ over the nations as a reward for overcoming the temptations of Satan and remaining loyal to Christ during their pilgrimage on earth.

In Revelation 2:26–27, Jesus says to the church at Thyatira, "*And he that overcometh, and keepeth my works unto the end, to him will I give power,*" (or authority) "*over the nations:* [27] *And he shall rule them with a rod of iron; as the vessels of a potter shall they be broken to shivers: even as I received of my Father.*" In Revelation 3:21, the promise is given to the church at Laodicea: "*To him that overcometh will I grant to sit with me in my throne, even as I also overcame, and am set down with my Father in his throne.*"

When you die and your soul goes to heaven, you are seated on a throne, you are given a crown, and you share in Christ's rule over the earth until He comes again. You are sitting with Christ in His throne participating with Him in running the world.

When they begin to worship, they bow and cast their crowns before the Lord Jesus and God the Father. We are told in Revelation 1:6 that Christ has made them kings and priests unto God, but this does not make them think they are someone great, as the kings of the earth do. They are casting down their crowns before the throne of God in acknowledgment that their authority is derived from God, and that He deserves all of the honor.

There was a police chief who would salute his civilian audience every time he appeared before them. He was asked: "Why are you saluting a civilian audience?" He replied:" Because I derive my authority from them. I am telling them that they are my superior officers."

By casting their crowns before God, the saints are saying to God, "You are my superior, and any authority I have is derived from You. I do not get it from myself or from my worthiness. I received it from You." They are acknowledging that only God has authority; and any other authority in the universe is derived from Him, is dependent upon Him, and owes its allegiance to Him. By casting down their crowns before God, they are openly confessing that God has authority over them, and they are in submission to Him. This is the posture we must take before God: He has authority over me, and I humbly submit myself to Him.

But not only do we see their actions of worship, but we also hear their words of worship. Their actions are that they bow down and cast their crowns before Him. Now we have their words of worship in verse 11: *"Thou art worthy, O Lord, to receive glory and honour and power: for thou hast created all things, and for thy pleasure they are and were created."*

They are saying, "Lord, You are worthy to receive from me and from every other created being an open confession of the glory You have, the honor You deserve, and the power You exercise. You are worthy to receive from me the ascription of glory, the ascription of honor, and the ascription of power. For me to acknowledge that You have glory, You have honor, and You have power is fitting. The glory You have and the honor You deserve and the power You exercise are clearly seen by the creation You made." God's creative work is the reason why they bring this worship. The praise they give is this: God is worthy to be declared to have glory and honor and power because He has created all things. Genesis 1 and 2 are the foundation for worship.

"And for thy pleasure, they are and were created." Creation was conceived and produced by the will of God for the pleasure of God to bring glory to God. Psalm 19:1–3 says: *"The heavens declare the glory of God; and the firmament sheweth his handywork. [2] Day unto day uttereth speech, and night unto night sheweth knowledge. [3] There is no speech nor language, where their voice is not heard."*

The creation declares who God is. These twenty-four elders are saying: "When we look at creation, it moves us to worship You: to ascribe to You glory, to ascribe to You honor, and to ascribe to You power for what You have designed and made. What You have designed and made provokes us to praise and worship You."

You might think that since these twenty-four elders represent the church, they would be praising God for redemption. They will do that in chapter 5. We praise God for both redemption and creation. But here the praise begins with worshiping God for His creation.

To ascribe all that exists in nature to mere natural processes is to rob God of His crowning glory. This is why we will never embrace the fallacy and fantasy of mere natural processes producing the world as we know it. It says in verse 11 that God created all things. The "big bang" did not create them, spontaneous generation did not create them, and evolution did not create them. God created them. Because mankind hates God, people try to come up with other explanations apart from God for what exists. They strive to rob God of His glory for the creation He made.

It is foolish for Christians to buy into even a part of evolutionary theory and say that God produced the building blocks of matter, but used evolution to bring about the present world and its life forms. This concept is known as theistic evolution. What is encouraging is that time is on our side, because as science discovers more about the complexity of life at the cellular level, they are realizing the inadequacy of evolution to explain its origin. Even the simplest cell is so irreducibly complex that it is impossible for it to have been generated through natural processes. The irreducible complexity of the organization and functions of an individual cell demonstrates that life could not have arisen from non-life by natural processes. Furthermore, genetic mutation is entirely inadequate as a mechanism to produce the additional information that is needed in our DNA to produce new organs and limbs.

Evolution would have been abandoned long ago as a scientific theory were it not for the philosophical implications of doing so, because science simply does not support it. As Christians, we are not anti-science; science is on our side. Science is just the discovery of what God has done. Our purpose is not to move into an exposition about the fallacies of evolution, but to notice what the saints are emphasizing about God—that He has created all things. Part of the indispensable essence of our worship is recognizing that in six days, God created the heavens and the earth, and all that is in them, and rested on the seventh day. The doctrine of creation forms the foundation of our worship of God. We must never give it up.

We see the angels worshiping God for who He is in verse 8: The Lord God Almighty, who is holy, holy, holy, who was and who is and who is to come. Then we see the saints worshiping God for what He has done in verse 11: He has created all things.

Therefore, we worship God for who He is like the angels do, and we worship God for what He has done like the saints do. Evil kings and wicked persecutors are going to come and go, but He who lives forever and ever, who is and who was and who is to come, will reign forever.

Notice the emphasis on the eternality of God in this chapter. It says in the latter part of verse 8, *"Holy, holy, holy, Lord God Almighty, which was, and is, and is to come."* Then in the latter part of verse 9, *"who liveth for ever and ever."* Then in the latter part of verse 10, *"worship him that liveth for ever and ever."* In this worship, the eternality of God is repeatedly declared. This is done because this book was written to a persecuted church. The church has continued to be persecuted for the last 2,000 years. But we recognize that while these wicked people who persecute us are going to come and go, God Himself goes on and on. Caesar went away, Stalin went away, and Mao Zedong went away. But who stayed? God. He was there with His church before these people ever showed up, He was there with His church while they were alive, and He is there with His church after they leave. We do not need to worry about persecutors. They are temporary. God is eternal.

Do not fear temporal kings like Domitian, who was alive when this book was written. They will perish, but God will live forever, and He will reign forever. Domitian says: “You are required under penalty of death to burn a pinch of incense and say that Caesar is lord.” Human kings can claim to be lord over us, but there is only one enthroned Lord to whom we are to bow and recognize as Lord. It may seem to us that men are in control of this world, but that is a delusion. God made them all, God is sovereign over them all, and God will defeat them all.

When we begin to tremble under the persecution of men, let us lift our eyes to the throne in heaven, and from that vision draw strength and hope and encouragement for the battle here below. The book of Revelation is saturated with references to the throne because that is the sole comfort a persecuted church has.

But not only is it the sole comfort, it is also a sufficient comfort. When you know that God is in control, even though wicked men are allowed to do their evil, what has been the outcome? God and His people triumphed. They always do. They always will. Job did, and we will, too.

God has not abandoned the world. It is His world. He made all things to serve His will and pleasure and purpose, and they will. Every self-exalting king will cast his crown at the feet of Jesus when He returns, and every knee will bow to Jesus and confess He is Lord to the glory of God the Father. Evil is in the world, but evil is not in control of the world. God is in control of the world. Let us find comfort in that.

21

The Worthiness of Christ to Open the Book, Revelation 5:1–7

"[1] *And I saw in the right hand of him that sat on the throne*
a book written within and on the backside, sealed with sev-
en seals. [2] *And I saw a strong angel proclaiming with a loud*
voice, Who is worthy to open the book, and to loose the seals
thereof? [3] *And no man in heaven, nor in earth, neither under*
the earth, was able to open the book, neither to look thereon.
[4] *And I wept much, because no man was found worthy to open*
and to read the book, neither to look thereon. [5] *And one of*
the elders saith unto me, Weep not: behold, the Lion of the
tribe of Judah, the Root of David, hath prevailed to open the
book, and to loose the seven seals thereof. [6] *And I beheld, and,*
lo, in the midst of the throne and of the four beasts, and in the
midst of the elders, stood a Lamb as it had been slain, having
seven horns and seven eyes, which are the seven Spirits of God
sent forth into all the earth. [7] *And he came and took the book*
out of the right hand of him that sat upon the throne."

Revelation 4 and 5 are amazingly wonderful and overwhelmingly important chapters in this book; indeed, in the entire Scriptures themselves. Revelation 4 and 5 take us into the very heart of heaven and reveal the glory of God in a way that fills us with humility, confidence, courage, joy, and worship.

In our previous studies in Revelation 4, we have been privileged to witness a glorious description of God on His throne in heaven, and the worship given to Him both by the angels and the glorified saints. In chapter 4, the focus is on God the Father and the majesty He possesses and the worship He receives. But now in chapter 5, the focus shifts from God the Father to God the Son. First of all, we see the worthiness of Christ to open the book that is sealed with seven seals in verses 1 to 7. Secondly, we see the worship of Christ for being able to open the book that is sealed with seven seals in verses 8 to 14.

Just as God the Father is revealed and worshiped in chapter 4, God the Son is revealed and worshiped in chapter 5. Both the Father and the Son receive the same kind of worship both from angels and men. In 5:13, both the Father who sits on the throne and the Lamb who is before the throne are worshiped together in the same way, with the same words, as co-equal in glory and in honor.

Notice verse 13: *"And every creature which is in heaven, and on the earth, and under the earth, and such as are in the sea, and all that are in them, heard I saying, Blessing, and honour, and glory, and power, be unto him that sitteth upon the throne,"* (the Father) *"and unto the Lamb for ever and ever,"* (the Son). Verse 13 proves beyond any doubt the full deity of Christ and His full equality with the Father, because they both receive equal worship.

Jehovah says of Himself in Isaiah 42:8, *"I am the LORD: that is my name: and my glory will I not give to another."* We have seen how God has brought severe judgments on His people for giving worship to another god beside Himself; and yet here is Jesus, standing beside the Father, receiving the same worship as the Father. Not only is there not a problem with this, it is embraced and accepted. If Jesus were not God as the Father is God, and if Jesus were not Jehovah as the Father is Jehovah, He would not be receiving the same glory and sharing in the same praise as the Father. The focus throughout the book of Revelation is on Jesus Christ. It is on His glory, His honor, and His power. With Him, God the Father gladly shares His throne, His glory, and His worship.

In this chapter, we will look at the worthiness of Christ to open the book in verses 1 to 7. In the next chapter, we will look at the worship of Christ for opening the book in verses 8 to 14.

The Inability of Men to Open the Book

The inability of men to open the book is seen in verses 1 through 4. Verse 1 says: *"And I saw in the right hand of him that sat on the throne a book written within and on the backside, sealed with seven seals."* Here we are told about a book the Father, who is seated on the throne, holds in His right hand. The "right hand of God" is a term that symbolizes God's power and authority; and the fact that this book is being held in the right hand of God tells us this book and its contents are an expression of God's power, and they proceed from His authority. It is God's book. He produced it and He possesses it by virtue of His power and through the exercise of His authority.

This book is a scroll, a long strip of papyrus that is filled with writing on both sides, rolled up on a rod and then sealed with a wax seal to hold it shut and keep it from unrolling until received by the one to whom it was addressed.

This particular scroll had seven seals—a symbolic number that indicates its contents are complete; that is, it contains the complete decrees of God regarding the remainder of time. Seven is the number of completeness.

The nature of this book is that the seven seals are placed so that the leading edge of the rolled-up book has a seal, and when this first seal is broken, it can be unrolled and read until there is a second seal, which then must be broken to unroll it further so more can be read, and so on.

This scroll represents God's plan and purpose for human history between the first and second coming of Christ, and on into eternity. This is clear from what is revealed as these seven seals are opened. This decree of God about the future of His dealings with the church in the world is a comprehensive decree, which declares all aspects of what spiritual warfare is going to look like, and how it is going to unfold until Christ returns.

This does not mean this book foretells specific future events, like the rise of Constantine, the French Revolution, the establishment of America, World War I, or World War II. It does not contain those kinds of prophecies and predictions regarding the future. But it does foretell the general characteristics of the age to come, the types of blessings that will fall on the believers, and the types of judgments that will fall upon the wicked. It tells us about the struggle between the church and the world and what that will look like. It tells us about the conflict between God and Satan and how that will turn out. It tells us about the second coming of Christ and the eternal state of the saved and the lost.

In short, this book reveals what we might expect to see and experience in the spiritual warfare that will go on until Christ returns, and the outcome His second coming will produce. It tells us about the paradise He will restore to us, and where we will live for all eternity.

This closed and sealed scroll represents God's plan for the remainder of time. But it is a closed book. The plan has not yet been revealed or executed. If this scroll remains sealed, then God's plan and purpose will not be known or carried out. But if the seals are broken, then the plan of God will not only be revealed, but it will also be carried out. It is critical that God's plan regarding the future be revealed and carried out, but it will only be revealed and carried out if someone worthy can be found to break the seals and to open the book.

Notice the question asked in verse 2: *"And I saw a strong angel proclaiming with a loud voice, Who is worthy to open the book, and to loose the seals thereof?"* God's plan regarding the future will only be revealed and carried out if someone worthy is found to open the seals and the book.

This is why a *strong* angel with a *loud* voice calls out to the whole universe in order to find someone who is worthy to open this book. Surely there must be someone somewhere who has the power and the authority not only to reveal God's plan for the future, but also to carry out that plan. Therefore, the angel initiates an aggressive search for the person who could reveal and carry out God's decree regarding the future. Somebody has to open that book.

This leads us to verse 3: *"And no man in heaven, nor in earth, neither under the earth, was able to open the book, neither to look thereon."* The sad reality soon becomes apparent. No one in the entire universe, wherever he might be located, is able or worthy to open the book or even look on it.

No one could look into the mind of God to fathom His decree or to understand His plans, much less did anyone have the power or the authority to carry out that decree and those plans and ensure their execution and accomplishment. No man can penetrate the divine mind. No man can carry out the divine will, because no man has the ability or the power to do so: no man in hell, no man on the face of the earth, and no man in heaven. Why? Because our thoughts are not His thoughts; our ways are not His ways; our authority is not His authority; our strength is not His strength; and our wisdom is not His wisdom.

Therefore, no man is adequate to either comprehend or execute the plan of God. If it were left up to us, the plan of God for the future would never be accomplished. We cannot even accomplish our own plans and our own vision for our own futures. How much less could we accomplish God's? How many start out in life and say, "I am planning to do this thing and achieve these goals"? But when you get to the end of your life and look back, you are compelled to say, "I was not very successful at achieving my plan." If we cannot even accomplish our own plans we have devised, how could we ever accomplish God's plan that He devised? No one had the moral or spiritual or personal fitness to open the book, much less to carry out what it contained.

Verse 4 says: *"And I wept much, because no man was found worthy to open and to read the book, neither to look thereon."* John awaits a response to the angel's call and inquiry, but as he looks for a volunteer to step forward, the silence that meets the angel's call brings him to a crushing awareness that no one is even remotely suited to reveal and execute God's plan for the future. As a result, John begins to weep and sob with heart-crushing grief.

John understands that, when the seals are broken and the scroll is opened, the future of the universe will be governed by God working all things together for the good of His people and the growth of His church and the glory of His kingdom. John understands that if the scroll is opened, then God's redemptive purposes will triumph and paradise will be restored.

But if the scroll is not opened, there will be no victory for God's people; there will be no protection from Satan's ravages; there will be no justice executed upon the wicked; there will be no new heaven and earth; and there will be no paradise restored. This would be cause indeed for the most profound grief and for the loss of all hope.

But the good news is that even though there is no mere man who is able to open the book and carry out the decrees, there is someone who can do so, and that is the God-man, Jesus Christ.

The Suitability of Christ to Open the Book

The suitability of Christ to open the book is found in verses 5 through 7. Notice verse 5: *"And one of the elders saith unto me, Weep not: behold, the Lion of the tribe of Judah, the Root of David, hath prevailed to open the book, and to loose the seven seals thereof."* It is not an angel, but one of the elders who speaks to John. Here is one who had himself experienced the full measure of the saving work of Christ. He is a glorified saint in heaven, and he now has a soul that has been perfected and glorified by Jesus. He brings John a message of unspeakable joy. He says to him, *"Weep not."* John can cease weeping, because Jesus has prevailed to open the book!

The word *"prevailed"* in the original means to conquer. It means to achieve victory. The elder is saying to John that Jesus has prevailed to open the book and the seven seals. Jesus has conquered. Jesus has obtained the victory and therefore He can open the book.

Christ has conquered sin on the cross. Redemption has been purchased. Deliverance from the bondage to Satan has been achieved. Death has been defeated. The works of the devil have been destroyed. The serpent's head has been crushed. As a result, the whole framework for the restoration of paradise has been established.

This is why the story of the defeat of Satan and his people can be unfolded. This is why the story of the victory of Christ and His people can be revealed. This is why the story of our spiritual warfare ending with Paradise restored can be proclaimed. Because Jesus has prevailed in the accomplishment of redemption, He has prevailed to open the book that reveals how that redemption will be applied throughout the centuries and into eternity. Jesus has prevailed to carry out all the book promises to accomplish. He has prevailed!

The reason Jesus has prevailed to open the book and accomplish the decree of God is revealed in the titles given to Jesus. In verse 5 there are two titles given to Him. He is called *"the Lion of the tribe of Judah,"* and He is called *"the Root of David."* Those titles reveal the reason why He has prevailed to open the book.

First of all, He is called *"the Lion of the tribe of Judah."* This title is a reference to Genesis 49:8–10, where Jacob was pronouncing the future blessings that would fall on his twelve sons. When he came to Judah, he said that out of him was going to come the lawgiver; that is, the Messiah, and He was going to be like a lion. Messiah is prophesied to come out of the tribe of Judah; and therefore, Messiah is said to be *"the Lion of the tribe of Judah."*

Obviously, this use of the term *"Lion"* is symbolic speech. The lion is known as the king of beasts, in that he preys on other beasts, but no beast preys on him. He defeats and overcomes all who oppose him, and no one can resist the lion's power and strength. Jesus proves Himself to be the Lion of the tribe of Judah because He defeated Satan, He defeated sin, and He defeated death. None of them could prevail against Him; He prevailed over all of them. Jesus has mastery over all His enemies, and He overcomes them all and defeats them all, and none of them is able to defeat Him.

But Jesus is not only the Lion of the tribe of Judah and all that imagery conveys; He is also *"the Root of David."* This title is derived from Isaiah 11, which is a wonderful prophecy of the coming of the Messiah and the establishment of the new heavens and the new earth, the complete removal of the curse, and the establishment of Paradise restored.

Isaiah 11:1–10 says: *"And there shall come forth a rod,"* (or a shoot) *"out of the stem of Jesse."* The metaphor is that of a main tree trunk, and out of the trunk comes a branch; *"and a Branch shall grow out of his roots."* Jesse was the father of David, and often in the Bible, instead of saying "the son of David" it will say "the son of Jesse," which is saying the same thing as "the son of David." The term "Son of David," and the term "Son of Jesse" are synonymous.

What happens to this *"rod"* or *"Branch,"* who grows out of David's *"roots"*? Verse 2: *"And the spirit of the LORD shall rest upon him"* (the Spirit that came down on Jesus at His baptism), *"the spirit of wisdom and understanding, the spirit of counsel and might, the spirit of knowledge and of the fear of the LORD."*

What is the result of this anointing of the Spirit at the baptism of Jesus? Verse 3: *"And shall make him of quick understanding in the fear of the LORD: and he shall not judge after the sight of his eyes, neither reprove after the hearing of his ears: [4] But with righteousness shall he judge the poor, and reprove with equity for the meek of the earth: and he shall smite the earth with the rod of his mouth, and with the breath of his lips shall he slay the wicked."* We see here a combination of how He spoke and how He judged at His first coming, and also how He will speak and judge at His second coming.

Verse 5: *"And righteousness shall be the girdle of his loins"* (the belt around his waist), *"and faithfulness the girdle of his reins,"* or the belt around His heart. The idea is that righteousness and faithfulness will encompass Him.

Notice the removal of the curse, verse 6: *"The wolf also shall dwell with the lamb, and the leopard shall lie down with the kid; and the calf and the young lion and the fatling together; and a little child shall lead them. [7] And the cow and the bear shall feed; their young ones shall lie down together: and the lion shall eat straw like the ox."* This is how all creatures used to eat before the fall. Before the fall, animals did not attack and eat other animals. There were no carnivores. In the new heaven and the new earth there will be no carnivores either.

Verse 8: *"And the sucking child shall play on the hole of the asp and the weaned child shall put his hand on the cockatrice' den."* There are not going to be any snakes killing people or killing anything else for that matter. This is a description of the new heavens and the new earth, the removal of the curse, and the perfect harmony among all of God's created creatures.

Verse 9: *"They shall not hurt nor destroy in all my holy mountain: for the earth shall be full of the knowledge of the* Lord, *as the waters cover the sea."* That day is coming. It is not here yet, but it is coming, and it will be realized in the new heavens and the new earth. The earth being filled with the knowledge of the Lord is realized in a sense now, in that the gospel is spread over the whole world. There are Christians in every country and every land, and there is no corner of the earth where the gospel has not gone. But in that day, everyone in the new earth will have embraced the gospel.

Verse 10: *"And in that day there shall be a root of Jesse, which shall stand for an ensign of the people; to it [Him] shall the Gentiles seek: and his rest shall be glorious."* This root of Jesse is the Son of David, who is Jesus Christ.

When Revelation 5:5 says that Jesus is the Root of David, this is what it is referring to. The fact that Jesus is the one who came to provide redemption, and who did provide it—who came to remove the curse, and who will remove it—is the reason why He can open the book and carry out the decree that is in the book.

Only someone who can do all of these things and who is the one described in Isaiah 11 is worthy to open the book, because the book contains a description of what Isaiah 11 says is going to be accomplished. Jesus is this Son of David who will sit on the throne of David ruling the kingdom of God forever, and He will bring in all the blessings described in Isaiah 11.

In Luke 1, the angel appeared to Mary and announced that she was to be the mother of the Messiah. Luke 1:30–33 states: "*And the angel said unto her, Fear not, Mary: for thou hast found favour with God.* [31] *And, behold, thou shalt conceive in thy womb, and bring forth a son, and shalt call his name JESUS.* [32] *He shall be great, and shall be called the Son of the Highest and the Lord God shall give unto him the throne of his father David:* [33] *And he shall reign over the house of Jacob forever; and of his kingdom there shall be no end.*"

When the Bible talks about Jesus being the Son of David, or the one who is growing out of the Root of David, it is talking about one who is going to sit on David's throne and rule the kingdom of God forever, defeating all of His enemies and blessing all of His people.

The picture here in Revelation 5:5 is that of a triumphant victor over all people and all things, who would be able to defend His kingdom against every attack and defeat whatever would be brought against it. Jesus is the King who prevails over all kings and over all kingdoms, especially over Satan and his kingdom of darkness. This is why the Bible tells us that Jesus is the King of kings and the Lord of lords. Jesus, sitting on the throne of David, rules over all the kings and kingdoms of this world, including Satan and his kingdom of darkness.

These titles of the Lion of the tribe of Judah and the Root of David speak of Christ as the one who is victorious and powerful; who has defeated and conquered sin and Satan and death; and therefore, who has the right and the ability to open the book and carry out the plan for the future it contains.

After the elder speaks to John and tells him to cease from weeping in verse 5, and identifies the one who has prevailed to open the book as The Lion of the tribe of Judah and The Root of David, John seems to turn and look at the person the elder identifies by these two titles. But what does he see? We would expect him to see a conquering king, with all the majesty and power of a lion. But that is not what he sees.

Notice verse 6: *"And I beheld, and, lo, in the midst of the throne and of the four beasts, and in the midst of the elders, stood a Lamb as it had been slain, having seven horns and seven eyes, which are the seven Spirits of God sent forth into all the earth."* Verse 6 tells us that he sees *"a Lamb as it had been slain."* Here Christ is seen as a sacrificial lamb, which is the whole basis for Christ's authority, power, and triumph as a King who is the son of David, and as a Lion who is of the tribe of Judah.

It was precisely because Jesus died on the cross as the Lamb of God who took away the sins of the world that He could have the authority of a king, and as a result have the triumph of a lion. It was through His work on the cross that He obtained both the crown and the mastery over Satan.

This Lamb was foreshadowed in the Passover lamb spoken of in Exodus 12, and this Lamb was the lamb that is prophesied of in Isaiah 53. This is the Lamb who takes away the sins of the world. Had

He not been humbled as a suffering Savior, He could have never been exalted as a conquering King. The Lamb and the King are complementary, and we could never have one without the other.

It says in Philippians 2:5–11: *"Let this mind be in you, which was also in Christ Jesus:* [6] *Who, being in the form of God, thought it not robbery to be equal with God."* He was not stealing glory that did not belong to Him when He recognized Himself as equal to the Father, "[7] *But made himself of no reputation, and took upon him the form of a servant, and was made in the likeness of men:* [8] *And being found in fashion as a man, he humbled himself, and became obedient unto death, even the death of the cross."* This is the Lamb who was slain.

Notice the next verse: "[9] *Wherefore"* (in light of the fact that He was the Lamb that was slain by His death on the cross) *"God also hath highly exalted him, and given him a name which is above every name:* [10] *That at the name of Jesus every knee should bow, of things in heaven, and things in earth, and things under the earth;* [11] *And that every tongue should confess that Jesus Christ is Lord, to the glory of God the Father."* Here we see how the Lamb that is slain in verse 8 is now the King on the throne in verse 9–11. Because He was the crucified Lamb, He became the conquering King.

In other words, Revelation 5:5 is not possible without Revelation 5:6. The Lamb that was slain is the one who was then able to have the throne of David and have the mastery of the Lion of the tribe of Judah over all His enemies.

Revelation 5:6 further describes this Lamb that had been slain as *"having seven horns and seven eyes, which are the seven Spirits of God sent forth into all the earth."* This is symbolic language. There is not really a lamb physically there with seven horns protruding from His head and seven eyes distributed across His face. This symbolic terminology is used to indicate the attributes Jesus possesses and the work that Jesus accomplishes.

He has seven horns. Seven is the number of completeness. Horns are used throughout the Scripture as a symbol of strength and power. A bull has horns through which all the strength and power of his body are expressed. Therefore, these seven horns speak of the complete power that Jesus possesses and exercises.

He has seven eyes. These seven eyes are the *"seven Spirits of God sent forth into all the earth."* The fact that He has seven eyes, which are called the seven Spirits, means that He has the completeness or the totality of the Spirit of God in Him.

Christians have the indwelling Spirit, and that is wonderful. But it says of Jesus in John 3:34, *"God giveth not the Spirit by measure unto him."* In other words, you and I have some of the operations of the Spirit of God in our life, but He had the complete operation of the Spirit of God in His life. The Spirit does some things through us; the Spirit did everything that the Spirit was capable of doing through Jesus Christ. He had all of the Spirit and all of the Spirit's operations in their totality. As a man on the earth, He was completely filled with the Spirit of God; and as a man in heaven, He is completely filled with the Spirit as well.

This term *"seven eyes"* is a reference to the omniscience that the indwelling Spirit gives Jesus Christ as a man. Elsewhere in this book, the Spirit is called seven flames and seven candlesticks. Here, the Spirit is seven eyes. The reason the word *"eyes"* is used is that eyes are the organs of sight. The idea is that in His humanity Jesus is all-seeing—that is, He is omniscient. In other words, the indwelling Spirit gives Him the power to see everything in heaven and earth, and to miss nothing that occurs there.

Notice Zechariah 4:1–10. *"And the angel that talked with me came again, and waked me, as a man that is wakened out of his sleep, [2] And said unto me, What seest thou? And I said, I have looked, and behold a candlestick all of gold, with a bowl upon the top of it, and his seven lamps thereon, and seven pipes to the seven lamps, which are upon the top thereof."* This is a vision of the candelabra, also called the menorah, which has seven lamps and is in the Holy Place in the tabernacle. *"[3] And two olive trees by it, one upon the right side of the bowl, and the other upon the left side thereof. [4] So I answered and spake to the angel that talked with me, saying, What are these, my lord?"* That is, "What do these symbolize? What is the significance of me seeing these objects?"

Verse 5: *"Then the angel that talked with me answered and said unto me, Knowest thou not what these be? And I said, No, my lord. [6] Then he answered and spake unto me, saying, This is the word of the* LORD *unto Zerubbabel, saying, Not by might, nor by power, but by my spirit, saith the* LORD *of hosts."*

Zerubbabel was trying to get the temple built during the return from the captivity. There was a lot of opposition at various times to building the temple because of the enmity that was stirred up against the Jews by evil men who dwelled in the land. But the power of the Spirit of the Lord would prevail and it would be built, even though the might and power of men was insufficient to accomplish it.

The question is asked in verse 7: *"Who art thou, O great mountain?"* (speaking of the size and strength of the opposition to building the temple) *"before Zerubbabel"* (the Jew leading Israel in rebuilding the temple), *"thou shalt become a plain."* The mountain of opposition is going to be leveled by God's power. *"And he shall bring forth the headstone"* (the final capstone of the temple, the sign the building was finished) *"thereof with shoutings, crying Grace, grace unto it."* The temple was built by the grace of God, and the temple was a manifestation of God's grace in providing a way of redemption, and the people were going to shout that message upon its completion.

Verse 8: *"Moreover the word of the* Lord *came unto me, saying,*
9 *The hands of Zerubbabel have laid the foundation of this house"* (the temple they are trying to rebuild that is being opposed); *"his hands shall also finish it; and thou shalt know that the* Lord *of hosts hath sent me unto you."* Zechariah is saying: "Even though the construction of the temple has been stopped, it is going to be started again, and the same man who started it is going to finish it." It is going to happen in his lifetime.

Verse 10: *"For who hath despised the day of small things?"* Remember, just a very small group has gone back, and they are building a small temple that is not nearly as glorious as Solomon's temple that had been destroyed. *"For they shall rejoice, and shall see the plummet in the hand of Zerubbabel. . ."* A plummet is a plumb bob used to build buildings. Zerubbabel is going to be holding this plumb bob, meaning that he is going to finish building the temple.

Now here is the point of all of this. Notice the end of verse 10. It says, *". . .and shall see the plummet in the hand of Zerubbabel with those seven;"* What seven? Remember the seven lamps in verse 2? He says, *"they" (those seven lamps) "are the eyes of the* Lord, *which run to and fro through the whole earth."*

In other words, these seven lamps were representative of the omniscience of the Spirit of God. He said in verse 6, *"Not by might, nor by power, but by my spirit, saith the* Lord *of hosts."* The menorah represents the Spirit of God, and those seven lamps represent the seven eyes of the Spirit of God, which see all over the whole earth. Here is the point: Jesus has those seven eyes. He has the Spirit of God given to Him not by measure. The Man Christ Jesus in heaven is given omniscience by the operation of the Spirit of God.

The conclusion we draw from this metaphor that Jesus has the seven horns and the seven eyes is this: Jesus is supremely powerful, and Jesus is all-seeing and all-knowing.

We have a declaration of the divine Trinity in this text. We have God the Father sitting on the throne; we have God the Son taking the scroll out of His hand, and we have God the Spirit represented in these seven eyes. All three of them received the worship of the elders and the angels around them.

Verse 7 says, *"And he"* (Jesus) *"came and took the book out of the right hand of him that sat upon the throne."* The momentous importance of that act cannot be overstated. The Lamb came and took the scroll out of the hand of the Father who was seated on the throne; and by that act, Jesus was receiving the authority and power to reveal and execute God's decrees regarding the future of the world that were contained in the scroll.

Jesus, because of His redemptive work on the cross, is given all authority in heaven and earth to reveal and execute the decree of God in applying His work up to and including Paradise restored. All things are now under His control and rule, and He is now going to work all things together for the good of His people, for the growth of His kingdom, and for the glory of His person. He is going to work all things together for the defeat and destruction of Satan and all his works. This is what is going to be accomplished because He now has the scroll in His hand.

As a reward for His redemptive work as the Lamb of God, Jesus received a kingdom to rule that would never end and that cannot be defeated. By the passing of this scroll from the hand of the Father to the hand of the Son, Jesus was invested with the office of King over the universe. That is why He said in Matthew 28:18, "All authority has been given to Me in heaven and in earth." He received all authority in heaven and in earth when He took the scroll.

In Ephesians 1:17–23 Paul is praying for the Ephesians, and he prays *"That the God of our Lord Jesus Christ, the Father of glory, may give unto you the spirit of wisdom and revelation in the knowledge of him:* [18] *The eyes of your understanding being enlightened; that ye may know what is the hope of his calling, and what [are] the riches of the glory of his inheritance in the saints,* [19] *And what is the exceeding greatness of his power to us-ward who believe, according to the working of his mighty power,"* Here are the verses to focus on: "[20] *Which he,"* (God the Father), *"wrought in Christ, when he raised him from the dead, and set him at his own right hand in the heavenly places,* [21] *Far above all principality, and power, and might, and dominion, and every name that is named, not only in this world, but also in that which is to come:* [22] *And hath put all things under his feet, and gave him to be the head over all things to the church,* [23] *Which is his body, the fullness of him that filleth all in all."*

Verses 20–23 are talking about the coronation of the Lord Jesus Christ that took place when the scroll was handed to Him in heaven. He was given authority over all principalities and powers; that is, over all angelic hosts, both fallen and unfallen, and over all people; both the saved and the lost. He now has unlimited authority to rule at the right hand of the Father to carry out the decrees in the scroll.

This is the explanation of Revelation 5:1–7. No person could secure our redemption, no person could execute the plan of God, and no person could bring us out of our fallenness and into Paradise except Jesus Christ. He is able to do that because He defeated death and sin and Satan on the cross. He is the Lion of the tribe of Judah, and He is the Son of David, sitting on the throne of David, executing God's decree for the saving of His people, for the subduing of His enemies, and for the establishment of His everlasting kingdom.

All of these glorious transactions are taking place after the death and resurrection of Jesus when He ascended to heaven at the beginning of this age. We will see, as He opens these seals, that God's decree for this age begins to be unfolded and accomplished. This book that Jesus receives contains everything that is going to happen from His ascension to the establishment of the new heaven and the new earth.

This is a wonderful scene. It is unspeakably glorious. It gives us the assurance that all that Jesus set out to do He will achieve, and that all that is contained in God's decree will be accomplished.

22

The Worship of Christ for Opening the Book, Revelation 5:8–14

> "8 *And when he had taken the book, the four beasts and four and twenty elders fell down before the Lamb, having every one of them harps, and golden vials full of odours, which are the prayers of saints.* 9 *And they sang a new song, saying, Thou art worthy to take the book, and to open the seals thereof: for thou wast slain, and hast redeemed us to God by thy blood out of every kindred, and tongue, and people, and nation;* 10 *And hast made us unto our God kings and priests: and we shall reign on the earth.* 11 *And I beheld, and I heard the voice of many angels round about the throne and the beasts and the elders: and the number of them was ten thousand times ten thousand, and thousands of thousands;* 12 *Saying with a loud voice, Worthy is the Lamb that was slain to receive power, and riches, and wisdom, and strength, and honour, and glory, and blessing.* 13 *And every creature which is in heaven, and on the earth, and under the earth, and such as are in the sea, and all that are in them, heard I saying, Blessing, and honour, and glory, and power, be unto him that sitteth upon the throne, and unto the Lamb for ever and ever.* 14 *And the four beasts said, Amen. And the four and twenty elders fell down and worshipped him that liveth for ever and ever.*"

Revelation 4 and 5 take us into the throne room of God. They tell us that the entire universe is governed by the One who sits on the throne.

In chapter 4, the focus was on God the Father who is seated on the throne. We saw the majesty and glory He possesses, and we saw the worship He receives. We saw His holiness, His sovereignty, His authority, His power, and His eternality. We saw that it is He who created the heavens and the earth and all they contain. As a result of this revelation of the glory of God, all the angels and redeemed saints fell before God in humility, praise, and worship. The Father is worthy to receive our worship and praise for His glory, honor, and power.

But as we moved into chapter 5, we saw that the focus shifted from God the Father to God the Son. Just as God the Father is revealed and then worshiped in chapter 4, God the Son is revealed and then worshiped in chapter 5. Chapter 5 opens with God the Father holding a scroll in His right hand, which contains His purpose, plan, and decree for human history from the first coming of Christ on into eternity. This scroll is sealed shut with seven seals. This closed and sealed scroll represents God's plan for the future, but it is a plan still unrevealed and unexecuted. If this scroll remains sealed, then God's plan and purposes will not be revealed and carried out. But if the seals are broken, then the plan of God from John's time into eternity will not only be revealed, but also carried out.

It is critical that God's plan regarding the future be revealed and carried out, but it will only be done if someone worthy could be found to break the seals and open the book. The good news of our passage is that even though no man is worthy or able to reveal and execute God's decree and plan regarding the future, Jesus Christ the God-man is worthy.

As a result of His worthiness, Jesus is given the book and takes it out of the right hand of the Father in verse 7. It says in verse 7, "*And he came and took the book out of the right hand of him that sat upon the throne.*" By this act, Jesus was given the authority and power to rule the world according to God's decree contained in the book. It was at this point that Jesus was recognized as King of the universe, was crowned with glory and honor, and all authority in heaven and earth was given to Him.

When Jesus entered heaven after His resurrection, He sat down at the right hand of the Father, and all things were placed under His dominion. All of this was involved in the book being given to Christ. The Lamb now reigns. The Lion of the tribe of Judah has the mastery. The Son of David rules the kingdom of God forever.

Because the Lamb rules all things, controls all events, and has authority over all people, believers do not need to fear times of tribulation, persecution, and difficulty as the future unfolds. Jesus is in control of it all, working it all together for our good and His glory and for the establishment of His kingdom. The recognition of this should fill us with joy and confidence and worship, and we see this is the response those in heaven give in the last half of this chapter.

In our last chapter, we saw the worthiness of Christ to open the book sealed with seven seals in verses 1 to 7. Now we want to look at the worship given to Christ because He is able to take the book, open the seals, and execute the plan it contains. The Lamb that was revealed in verses 1 to 7 is now the Lamb that is worshiped in verses 8 through 14.

The Provocation of Praise to the Lamb

The provocation of praise to the Lamb is in verses 8 to 10. Here we see why the Lamb is being praised. Notice verse 8: *"And when he had taken the book."* Stop there for a minute. Consider that phrase: *"And when he had taken the book."* There is the key phrase. This is the pivotal statement out of which flows everything that follows, not only in the remainder of the chapter, but in the remainder of the book. The rest of the book of Revelation is an unfolding of this event of Him taking the book.

When Jesus takes this scroll, He takes to Himself the authority and power of God to rule the universe for the remainder of time. This act of taking the scroll is His enthronement at the right hand of the Father. When He takes the book, we have the fulfillment of Psalm 2. Let us observe that psalm in relationship to this phrase, *"And when he had taken the book."*

Psalm 2 opens with an examination of the attitude of humanity toward God: "[1] *Why do the heathen rage, and the people imagine a vain thing?* [2] *The kings of the earth set themselves, and the rulers take counsel together, against the* Lord, *and against his anointed, saying,* [3] *Let us break their bands asunder, and cast away their cords from us."*

We see the defiance and rebellion of human depravity manifested in the nations of the earth and the kings that rule them in setting themselves against God and saying "Let us cast off God's authority over us. We will cast off his laws and determine for ourselves how we are going to rule. Any suggestion that God has authority over us and we have accountability to Him will not be tolerated. We will persecute anyone who would suggest such a thing."

Therefore, when Jesus comes to earth and says, "God has authority over you, God has laws that bind you, you are accountable to

God, and you must be reconciled to God," the kings of the earth rage against those demands. They vainly imagine they can do away with God and never have any accountability to Him.

How does God respond to this expression of human defiance and rebellion? It says in verse 4, *"He that sitteth in the heavens shall laugh: the LORD shall have them in derision."* Their rebellion against God is like an ant defying an elephant.

Verse 5: *"Then shall he speak unto them in his wrath, and vex them in his sore displeasure."* It is laughable that humanity—mere humans—would think in their collective arrogance that they could do away with God and His authority over them and their accountability to Him. It is insanity for them to think they could escape His judgment for their defiance of Him. God is angry, and God expresses His wrath on them in His sore displeasure. They come under the displeasure of God for defying His laws and declaring themselves not bound by them in any way. God says to them, in effect, "I will execute My wrath on you and I will condemn you to hell for your defiance of My authority over you."

Notice verse 6. God is speaking here: *"Yet have I set my king upon my holy hill of Zion."* We have the kings of the earth in verse 2 setting themselves up, but God says, "No, I have a King, and I am going to set Him up, and He is going to rule over all these kings who think they rule." This act of God setting His King on His holy hill of Zion happened when Jesus was given the book. In other words, Psalm 2:6 occurred at Revelation 5:8.

When God sets Jesus upon the throne of heaven and gives Him the book, Jesus speaks in verse 7: *"I will declare the decree: the LORD hath said unto me, Thou art my Son; this day have I begotten thee. [8] Ask of me, and I shall give thee the heathen for thine inheritance, and the uttermost parts of the earth for thy possession."* Jesus is reporting in verses 7 and 8 what God said to Him upon giving Him the book when He was enthroned in heaven.

Jesus is now enthroned and God the Father has said to Him, "The end result of Your incarnation, of Me begetting you as my Son, is Your enthronement over all people and all things." Notice verse 7: *"the LORD hath said unto me, Thou art my Son; this day have I begotten thee."* This seems to be a reference to the incarnation when Jesus was begotten in the womb of the Virgin Mary. What was the outcome and end and conclusion of that begetting? It was, verse 8, *"I shall give thee the heathen for thine inheritance, and the uttermost parts of the earth for thy possession."* The incarnation of Christ leads to the enthronement of Christ.

In Luke 1:31–33 at the annunciation, the angel said to Mary, "You are going to have a child conceived of the Holy Ghost." This is the incarnation. The angel then says, "This child will sit on the throne of David forever and ever." This is the enthronement. Both the incarnation and the enthronement are spoken of together to Mary as inseparable acts of God, and this is what we see in Psalm 2—the begetting and the enthronement tied together. They are both involved in what God is doing through the Son when He established Him as His King on His holy hill.

Having been enthroned in heaven, having been given all authority in heaven and in earth, and having authority over all the heathen in every part of the earth, Jesus is told in verse 9, *"Thou shalt break them with a rod of iron; thou shalt dash them in pieces like a potter's vessel."*

This is what is going to happen to the heathen and the kings of the earth who rage against the Lord and take counsel against the Lord and the King He has set upon His holy hill. With the rod of power and authority that Jesus has as the enthroned King of the universe, He is going to crush these defiant and rebellious people under the wrath of God. Their rule is going to be shattered by the rule of Christ. Their kingdoms are going to be broken and destroyed by Jesus.

Jesus will be the King of kings and the Lord of lords, and any king or any lord that rebels against Him will have his power and authority completely destroyed. It happened to Rome when it set itself against the kingdom of God, and Caesar said, "You must worship me. I am lord!" The Roman kingdom was shattered with a rod of iron, and so the Roman Empire is no more. This has ever been the case down through history. Every kingdom that defied the Lord Jesus is destroyed by the Lord Jesus.

Notice the counsel in verse 10: *"Be wise now therefore, O ye kings: be instructed, ye judges of the earth,"* those of you in verses 1–3 that are rebelling, hear My counsel: "[11] *Serve the Lord with fear, and rejoice with trembling.* [12] *Kiss the Son"* (the idea is to bow down and kiss His feet in humility and submission), *"lest he be angry, and ye perish from the way, when his wrath is kindled but a little."* (Imagine if it was kindled a lot!) *"Blessed are all they that put their trust in him."*

Here are the two options we have toward the enthroned Jesus with the book in His hand: We can bow in humility, recognize His authority, submit to His will, and be blessed; or we can rebel, and suffer His anger and His shattering wrath. This little phrase in Revelation 5:8, *"And when he had taken the book,"* is expanded and explained as to its meaning in Psalm 2.

When it says that Jesus is made the king on the holy hill of Zion, this does not mean that God the Father has left His throne. What it does mean is that Christ is seated upon the throne with His Father, so that from this moment in Revelation 5:8 forward, this throne, as it says in Revelation 22:1, is *". . .the throne of God and of the Lamb."* No longer is the throne just the throne of God; it is now the throne of God and the Lamb. At this point Hebrews 1:3 tells us, *"He sat down on the right hand of the majesty on high."*

This enthronement of Christ begins a new era in heaven and on earth, in which Christ the Mediator assumes the throne of David, and the glorified saints begin to share in that rule as crowned kings who serve with and under the Son of David, King Jesus. In Revelation 3:21 the promise to the overcomer says, *"To him that overcometh will I grant to sit with me in my throne, even as I also overcame, and am set down with my Father in his throne."*

In Psalm 2, we see Christ being established by the Father as the King, who from that point forward will rule the nations to bring about the final victory of the kingdom of God and the final destruction and ruin of all who rebel against it.

Saints and angels see Christ ascend to His eternal throne when He takes the book from the hand of the Father, and this is the provocation for the outpouring of praise that follows in verse 8b to verse 14. *"And when he had taken the book."* Everything to follow flows out of that act and the monumental event it represents in the enthronement of Christ over the universe.

"And when he had taken the book," things started to happen. Notice: *"The four beasts and four and twenty elders fell down before the Lamb, having every one of them harps, and golden vials, full of odours, which are the prayers of saints."* Notice how both the seraphim, represented by these four beasts, and the glorified saints, represented by the twenty-four elders, fall down before the Lamb. This is the act of those who wish to declare their submission and allegiance to the enthroned King.

In Psalm 2, we are counseled to *"Kiss the Son"*—that is, to bow down and kiss His feet in humility and submission and allegiance. This is what is going on here. They fall down before the Lamb as an act of declaration of their allegiance to the enthroned King. To bow at the feet of the King is to declare one's submission to the King.

It says of the glorified saints represented by these twenty-four elders that they all have harps and golden bowls full of incense, which represent the prayers of the saints. These images have Old Testament roots. For example, in Psalm 33:2 it says, *"Praise the Lord with harp: sing unto him with. . .an instrument of ten strings."* The harp is a very common instrument that was used in the praise of God in the Old Testament.

In Psalm 141:1–2, David prays, *". . .give ear unto my voice, when I cry unto thee. [2] Let my prayer be set forth before thee as incense."* When we pray, our prayers go up to heaven to God. When incense is burned, the smoke of the incense rises upward, and the burning of incense on the altar symbolically represents our prayers going up to God. This is why they burned incense in the Old Testament temple, because it symbolically represented the prayers of the priests ascending to God on behalf of the people.

The harps are instruments of joyful music that are played in praise and honor of the King. The incense represents the petitions that are brought before the King in recognition of His power and authority to grant the requests of those over whom He rules. The offering of praise to the King and the offering of petition to the King are both done out of a recognition of the majesty and honor and authority He possesses.

This brings us to Revelation 5:9–10: *"And they sang a new song, saying, Thou art worthy to take the book, and to open the seals thereof: for thou wast slain, and hast redeemed us to God by thy blood out of every kindred, and tongue, and people, and nation; [10] And hast made us unto our God kings and priests: and we shall reign on the earth."*

It says, *"And they sang a new song."* This song is new in that it contains new content about God's saving works—saving works that had just been accomplished. Therefore, these songs contain content that could not have been sung before, because these saving works had never been accomplished before.

So a new work had been accomplished—namely, the redemption

of sinners by Jesus on the cross; and a new song was being sung about that new work that had just been achieved. This new song is the response of the redeemed saints in heaven to the new saving work and the new covenant He had just established. Since there is a new saving work and a new covenant, there needs to be a new song that would incorporate those new acts in a new expression of worship.

The old song of Moses in Exodus 15 is a response to God saving Israel out of Egypt. He saves them out of Egypt through the ten plagues; He brings them through the Red Sea; and He drowns Pharaoh. How do the people of God respond to this salvation out of the bondage of Egypt? They sing the song of Moses in Exodus 15. The old song of Moses in Exodus 15 is a response to God saving Israel out of Egypt. This new song of Revelation 5 is a response to God saving His people from their sins—saving them not out of Egypt, but out of the kingdom of Satan.

Notice Revelation 15:1–4, *"And I saw another sign in heaven, great and marvellous, seven angels having the seven last plagues; for in them is filled up the wrath of God.* [2] *And I saw as it were a sea of glass mingled with fire"* (this is the sea of glass before the throne in Revelation 4:6) *"and them that had gotten the victory over the beast, and over his image, and over his mark, and over the number of his name"* (those are the twenty-four elders, the saved people in heaven, the glorified saints) *"stand on the sea of glass having the harps of God."*

Verse 3, *"And they sing the song of Moses the servant of God, and the song of the Lamb, saying, Great and marvellous are thy works, Lord God Almighty; just and true are thy ways, thou King of saints.* [4] *Who shall not fear thee, O Lord, and glorify thy name? for thou only art holy: for all nations shall come and worship before thee; for thy judgments are made manifest."*

The song of Moses is the old song; the song of the Lamb is the new song. They are singing about all of God's great redemptive works—His redemptive works under the Old Covenant, and His redemptive works under the New Covenant. These are great and marvelous works that should cause every person to fear before the Lord and to worship the Lord and glorify His name. It is through these works that all nations will come and worship Him.

In Revelation 5, we want to notice the content of this new song, and the marvelous expression it contains of all that Jesus as the Lamb of God accomplished for His people. Notice verses 9–10: *"And they sang a new song, saying,"* (here is the content of the song) *"Thou art worthy to take the book, and to open the seals thereof: for thou wast slain, and hast redeemed us to God by thy blood out of every kindred, and tongue, and people, and nation;* [10] *And hast made us unto our God kings and priests: and we shall reign on the earth."*

"You, Lord Jesus, are worthy to reveal and execute the decrees contained in the scroll of God because You were *"slain"*; that is, You died a sacrificial substitutionary death on the cross to atone for the sins of those for whom You died." They go on to say, *"and hast redeemed us to God by thy blood."* These twenty-four elders are saying, "The reason why we are here is because You redeemed us. There is no other explanation for our presence before Your throne."

There are textual issues at controversy in verses 9 and 10. The personal pronoun "us" in verse 9 has very strong textual evidence for its inclusion; and therefore in verse 9 "us" definitely should be there, even though other modern critical text translations omit it. Even Metzger admits that the omission of it stands on weak evidence[5]. However, in verse 10, the personal pronoun "us" is also included, and there is very weak evidence for its inclusion. It should probably be omitted.

Let us return to the exposition of the text. In verse 9 he says, *"Thou. . .hast redeemed us to God by thy blood."* That is: "You have set us free by the payment of the ransom of Your blood. Your blood was the ransom paid to set us free from the curse of the law and bondage to Satan and the wrath of God. You paid the penalty for our sins that God's law and God's justice required. It says in Ephesians 1:7, *"We have redemption through his blood, the forgiveness of sins, according to the riches of his grace."*

In verse 8 Jesus is taking the book, and the four beasts and the twenty-four elders are falling down before the Lamb. Grammatically, it is the twenty-four elders who have the harps, who offer the prayers, and who sing the new song. The angels are fallen down, but the elders are leading the worship. They are saying to the enthroned Christ, "You were slain. You died a sacrificial substitutionary death on the cross. You have redeemed us to God by Your blood. You have set us free by the payment of the ransom."

In verse 9 they go on to say that You have *"redeemed us to God by thy blood out of every kindred, and tongue, and people, and nation."*

---

5 Bruce Metzger, *A Textual Commentary on the Greek New Testament*, United Bible Societies, London and New York, 1975, 736

This redemption that Jesus accomplished is one of redeeming a people (*"us"*) to God that is drawn *"out of every kindred, and tongue, and people, and nation."* The passage clearly indicates that Jesus did not redeem all men without exception, but He redeemed some men *"out of"* every class and category of people on the earth. The Lamb did not purchase the salvation of every single individual who has ever lived. He paid the ransom for His elect, who are chosen out from among all the various categories of people that have ever lived.

There is nothing narrow or limited about the redemption Christ provided. It is worldwide in its scope and it embraces every ethnic group—that is, every kindred; it embraces every linguistic group—that is, every tongue; it embraces every social group—that is, every people; and it embraces every political group—that is, every nation.

This redemption that Christ provided for some out of every kindred, tongue, people, and nation is not only worldwide in its scope, but it is also overwhelmingly large in its number and size. It says in Revelation 7:9 that John beheld those who were before the throne of God, and he said it was *"a great multitude, which no man could number, of all nations, and kindreds, and people, and tongues, [who] stood before the throne, and before the Lamb, clothed with white robes, and palms in their hands."*

What do we see Jesus doing? We see Him redeeming a people to God out of every class and category of people who have ever lived on the face of the earth. The number of them is such a massive multitude as they stand before the throne of God that John says it is hopeless to even try to count them. There is a breadth and depth and generosity in the redeeming work of Jesus for His elect that is incomprehensible in its size and dimensions. It is so overwhelming that it renders us speechless to try to quantify it with any kind of description or adjective.

Verse 10: *"and hast made us unto our God kings and priests,"* or it could be read (and probably should be read) "and You have made them (the nations, kindreds, people and tongues) unto our God kings and priests: and we shall reign on the earth." Not only has Christ redeemed a multitude which no man can number out of every kindred, tongue, people, and nation; verse 10 tells us He has also made them both kings and priests who will reign with Him as kings, and who will minister before Him as priests, both in heaven now, and later on the new earth when He returns.

Notice the future focus of verse 10. He *"hast made us unto our God kings and priests: and we shall reign [with Him] on the [new] earth."* It is true that we are presently kings and priests on this earth right now, as 1:6 says; but the primary emphasis in Revelation is on the eschatological exercise of those roles. The emphasis is on our being kings and priests in heaven and in eternity.

So the provocation to praise is that Christ is worthy to take the book and open it, that He is carrying out His redemptive work in bringing an uncountable multitude into reconciliation with His Father, and that He is bringing His reconciled people into the privilege of being kings and priests in the New Earth.

The Proclamation of Praise to the Lamb

The proclamation of praise to the Lamb is in verses 11 to 14.

When the created beings of heaven and earth behold the redeeming work of the Lamb of God in saving His people from their sins, and when they behold the honor the Lamb places upon His people in making them kings and priests, and when they behold the authority He possesses sitting in the throne with the Father, they cannot restrain their praise for a moment longer. They begin to zealously and loudly express their worship of the Lamb.

First of all, the praise begins with the angels, the seraphim, and the elders. Verse 11 says: *"And I beheld, and I heard the voice of many angels round about the throne and the beasts and the elders: and the number of them"*; that is, of these angels, which are distinguished from the seraphim (which are also angels), *"was ten thousand times ten thousand, and thousands of thousands."*

We know how many seraphim there are: there are four. We know how many elders there are: there are twenty-four. But when it comes to the angels, there are *"ten thousand times ten thousand, and thousands of thousands."* In other words, there are not just a few angels here. Ten thousand times ten thousand equals one hundred million. On top of that, thousands and thousands more—that is, uncountable thousands more. Ten is a symbolic number that conveys the concept of perfection. The multiplication of numbers is an intensification of the meaning of those numbers. The idea here is perfection times perfection and perfection on top of perfection.

The point is, there is the perfect number of all of the angels in heaven participating in the worship of God, however many angels that may be. However many there are, they are all perfectly participating in the worship of God, and are perfectly represented down to the very last one of them. None is absent; none fails to appear and offer worship. All of them are engaged in the praise of Almighty God. All of the seraphim and all of the elders join in as well. Every being in heaven participates in the worship of the Lamb.

Verse 12 tells us what this worship is, in terms of its expression and content. They were *"Saying with a loud voice, Worthy is the Lamb that was slain to receive power, and riches, and wisdom, and strength, and honour, and glory, and blessing."* They praised the Lamb *"with a loud voice,"* showing the fervency and enthusiasm of their wholehearted worship. He is worthy of nothing less than the highest intensity of worship and praise!

The angels and the seraphim and the elders ascribe to the Lamb who was slain, and precisely because He was slain, seven expressions of praise. Seven is the number of completeness. They completely praised the Lord, and they praised the Lord with completeness.

The Lamb who was slain is worthy to receive praise for having power—that is, the ability to accomplish any task. He is worthy to receive praise for having riches—that is, the resources to meet any need. He is worthy to receive praise for having wisdom—that is, the understanding to solve any problem. He is worthy to receive praise for having strength—that is, the might necessary to overcome any obstacle. He is worthy to receive praise for having honor—that is, the preeminence over all other beings. He is worthy to receive praise for having glory—that is, the majesty that flows out His perfection. He is worthy to receive praise for having blessing—that is, the worship of every creature.

Here is one who has the ability to accomplish any task, the resources to meet any need, the understanding to solve any problem, the power to overcome any obstacle, the preeminence over every creature, the majesty of total perfection, and the right to receive worship. This is the one they are offering their praise to.

This praise begins with the angels and the seraphim and the elders, as they behold the attributes of the Lamb of God who is now enthroned with the book in His hand, who has provided redemption for His people, and who has elevated them into being kings and priests. They are saying, "These are the attributes that enabled Him to accomplish those marvelous works and be in that exalted position. Let us praise Him for what He possesses, and for who He is, and for what He has done." That is what worship is: praise for what God possesses, praise for who God is, and praise for what God has done.

This praise not only proceeds from the angels and the seraphim and the elders; secondly, this praise is now expressed by all of the creatures of the earth. Notice verse 13: *"And every creature which is in heaven"* (the sky or atmosphere), *"and on the earth, and under the earth, and such as are in the sea, and all that are in them, heard I saying, Blessing, and honour, and glory, and power, be unto him that sitteth upon the throne, and unto the Lamb for ever and ever."*

Verse 13 is telling us there is no creature, wherever it may be found and whatever its capacity, that does not recognize the worth of the Lamb of God. Jesus was the one who created them all. All things were made by Him, and without Him was not anything made that was made. All of these creatures of the earth, though they are not redeemed from sin, are the recipients of redemption from the curse which fell on them in Genesis 3. They look to Jesus for redemption from the curse so that one day the lion will be able to lie down with the lamb and no longer be under the curse of being a carnivore. All the creatures are subject to death and pain and disease. Many of them are harmful in their functions. The rose brings forth thorns. All of these manifestations of the curse on the natural creation will be completely removed by the Lamb of God.

Whether the higher creation or the lower creation, whether they dwell in the sky or whether they dwell on the earth, whether they live on the land or whether they live in the ocean, whether they are on the surface or under the surface; all of them, whatever creature it is and wherever it may be located, recognizes and declares the worthiness of God and of Christ to receive ascriptions of blessing and honor and glory and power, because the lower creation knows it will be redeemed from the curse by Christ.

Romans 8:20–22 declares that the creation groans, waiting for the redemption. In the new heaven and the new earth, the animals are going to be there: the birds, the fish, the mammals, and all other creatures we have now, and they will all be delivered from the curse. They praise the Lamb on the throne for the deliverance He wrought for them on the cross, because Jesus did not just redeem us from our sins; He also redeemed the creation from the curse that sin brought on it.

Here is an exuberant repetition and echo of the previous praise offered by the angels and saints, reemphasizing the exalted attributes and magnificent characteristics which God the Son and God the Father share. There are four descriptions of praise here: blessing, honor, glory, and power. There are not seven as before, because four is the number of the earth. The idea is that the whole earth is going to praise God. They take up and echo the praise and worship of the higher creation: the angels, the seraphim, and the redeemed saints. All the creatures of the earth echo that praise.

Notice that this praise is equally given to the Son and the Father. Revelation 5:13, *"And every creature which is in heaven, and on the earth, and under the earth, and such as are in the sea, and all that are in them, heard I saying, Blessing, and honour, and glory, and power, be unto him that sitteth upon the throne"* (God the Father), *"and unto the Lamb"* (God the Son) *"for ever and ever."* This equality of their praise declares the equality of their persons, making it clear that each person possesses all of the divine essence. Everything that is said of the one can equally be said of the other.

Verse 14, *"And the four beasts said, Amen. And the four and twenty elders fell down and worshipped him that liveth for ever and ever."* The four seraphim give their hearty *"Amen"* to the praise given by the creatures of the earth. They endorse and approve and affirm all that the creatures of the earth ascribe to God as true and valid and certain. Then the elders give their "Amen," not verbally but physically, by bowing their faces to the ground in humility and reverence and adoration before the enthroned Lamb of God.

The Father is praised for creation in chapter 4, and the Son is praised for redemption in chapter 5. God made us, chapter 4, and God redeemed us, chapter 5. And for that, we should offer Him endless, exuberant, and loud praise and worship. These two chapters proclaim with absolute clarity that the world's destiny and future are not under the control of some blind fate. We are in the hands of the God who made us and the Son who died for us, and therefore we have nothing to fear from Satan who opposes us. God has crushed and defeated him, and his last efforts to work his will and wreak his havoc are doomed to failure. We see that failure played out in the rest of the book of Revelation. Revelation is a book of the glorious triumph of Christ, and a book of the abysmal failure of Satan. Our persecutors never have the last word. The Lamb on the throne does, and in that is our comfort and our confidence.

As we look at the rest of the book, we must always look at it from the perspective of the throne of God. When you look at your life and the things that happen to you, you must look at them from the perspective of the enthroned Lamb who has the book, and who is executing the decrees of God with respect to your individual life and all the particular details in it. He is working them all together for the defeat of Satan and for the redemption of your soul and for the effectiveness of your work as a king and priest.

When you recognize that, you can live in a spirit of joy and triumph, even though Satan is doing everything he can to try to pull you back and pull you down and pull you away. He is defeated and shall be defeated, not just in general, but in your life in particular. Recognize that, rejoice in that, praise the Lamb, bow before Him, and proclaim Him. We triumph in Him.

23

The Four Horsemen of the Apocalypse, Revelation 6:1–8

> "1 *And I saw when the Lamb opened one of the seals, and I heard, as it were the noise of thunder, one of the four beasts saying, Come and see.* 2 *And I saw, and behold a white horse: and he that sat on him had a bow; and a crown was given unto him: and he went forth conquering, and to conquer.* 3 *And when he had opened the second seal, I heard the second beast say, Come and see.* 4 *And there went out another horse that was red: and power was given to him that sat thereon to take peace from the earth, and that they should kill one another: and there was given unto him a great sword.* 5 *And when he had opened the third seal, I heard the third beast say, Come and see. And I beheld, and lo a black horse; and he that sat on him had a pair of balances in his hand.* 6 *And I heard a voice in the midst of the four beasts say, A measure of wheat for a penny, and three measures of barley for a penny; and see thou hurt not the oil and the wine.* 7 *And when he had opened the fourth seal, I heard the voice of the fourth beast say, Come and see.* 8 *And I looked, and behold a pale horse: and his name that sat on him was Death, and Hell followed with him. And power was given unto them over the fourth part of the earth, to kill with sword, and with hunger, and with death, and with the beasts of the earth.*"

Revelation 5 is the most important chapter in the book of Revelation because it provides the basis for everything else contained in the book. That basis is the victorious enthronement of Christ when He took the scroll from the hand of the Father.

By taking the scroll, Jesus received full authority from His Father to rule over all the kingdoms of the earth. Jesus became the Prince of the kings of the earth. He is now seated in His Father's throne at the right hand of the Father, to reveal and execute the decrees contained in the sealed scroll. Everything else contained in the book of Revelation flows out of this momentous event.

As the seals are opened and the rest of the book unfolds, we see how the authority of Christ extends even over the suffering of the saints. This suffering has a twofold purpose: one is to purify the saints, and the other is to punish the wicked. This book helps us to see that suffering on the part of the saints is not an indication of the absence of God or the indifference of God; instead, it is part of the plan and purpose of God to preserve us and prepare us for heaven.

Some Christians may have wondered if Christ was really sovereign over the horrible persecutions perpetrated on them by the Roman Caesars. The remainder of this book is intended to show that Christ rules over all events, and that suffering does not occur indiscriminately or by chance. Revelation reveals that destructive events are brought about by Christ for both redemptive and judicial purposes, to bring salvation and sanctification to His people, and to bring wrath and punishment on the rebellious.

As soon as Christ takes His position of power and authority at the right hand of the Father, He immediately begins to open the seals so that the events contained in the scroll begin to take place at once, and continue to take place until the Lord returns. The opening of the seals begins the actual revelation and execution of the contents of the scroll spoken of in chapter 5. This makes sense out of the exhortations in the seven letters to the churches to persevere in the face of suffering, because the suffering unleashed by the seals had already begun to take place in the life of these seven churches.

Jesus had ascended to heaven at least sixty years earlier, and the seals began to be opened then. Sixty years later in AD 95 when this book was written, these seven churches were already experiencing the kind of events spoken of in the scroll, just as all the churches throughout this age are going to experience them.

Christ opens each seal in the heavenly throne room and issues the command for the contents of each one to be carried out. As each of the first four seals is opened in verses 1 to 8, a horse and its rider appear, representing conquest and war and famine and death. The opening of the fifth seal in verses 9 to 11 brings into view the souls of the martyrs waiting for the day of vindication. The opening of the sixth seal in verses 12 to 17 brings dreadful calamities that manifest Christ's righteous wrath upon the wicked at His second coming. Chapter 6 gives us a sweeping survey of the major characteristics of the church age and the outcomes it will have for the righteous and the wicked.

We want to consider these first four seals and what occurs as each of them is opened. Here we have the four horsemen of the Apocalypse, and a declaration of what each of them symbolizes.

The Old Testament Background to the Four Horsemen

There is precedent for God using the symbolic imagery of horses of various colors to convey His message in the Old Testament, especially in the book of Zechariah, in which are two instances of God using colored horses as a symbolic image. These are found in Zechariah 1 and 6.

Notice first Zechariah 1:8–13. Zechariah has a vision beginning in verse 8: "*I saw by night, and behold a man riding upon a red horse, and he stood among the myrtle trees that were in the bottom; and behind him were there red horses, speckled, and white.* [9] *Then said I, O my lord, what are these? And the angel that talked with me said unto me, I will shew thee what these be.* [10] *And the man that stood among the myrtle trees answered and said, These are they whom the* LORD *hath sent to walk to and fro through the earth.* [11] *And they answered the angel of the* LORD *that stood among the myrtle trees, and said, We have walked to and fro through the earth, and, behold, all the earth sitteth still, and is at rest.*"

Here the horsemen represent the Lord's knowledge and full awareness of the condition of the whole earth. But that is not all. Notice verse 12. "*Then the angel of the* LORD *answered and said, O* LORD *of hosts, how long wilt thou not have mercy on Jerusalem and on the cities of Judah, against which thou hast had indignation these threescore and ten years*" (these seventy years)? "[13] *And the* LORD *answered the angel that talked with me with good words and comfortable words.*"

Here we have four horsemen. In this case, we have two red horses, a speckled horse, and a white horse. The horsemen here represent the Lord's knowledge and full awareness of the condition of the whole earth, and the condition of His covenant people. What is the report of these four horsemen? The report is: The nations of the earth are at rest, verse 11; but Israel is in a desperate condition, verse 12.

These horsemen are representing the Lord's awareness of the condition of the earth, both the condition of the nations and also the condition of His covenant community. The nations are at rest. The covenant community is in distress.

In Zechariah 6, we have a second record of horsemen and horses of various colors. Notice Zechariah 6:1–8: *"And I turned, and lifted up mine eyes, and looked, and, behold, there came four chariots out from between two mountains; and the mountains were mountains of brass. 2 In the first chariot were red horses; and in the second chariot black horses; 3 And in the third chariot white horses; and in the fourth chariot grisled and bay horses. 4 Then I answered and said unto the angel that talked with me, What are these, my lord? 5 And the angel answered and said unto me, These are the four spirits of the heavens, which go forth from standing before the* L*ORD* *of all the earth. 6 The black horses which are therein go forth into the north country; and the white go forth after them; and the grisled go forth toward the south country. 7 And the bay went forth, and sought to go that they might walk to and fro through the earth: and he said, Get you hence, walk to and fro through the earth. So they walked to and fro through the earth. 8 Then cried he upon me, and spake unto me, saying, Behold, these that go toward the north country have quieted my spirit in the north country."*

Here the four chariots with their colored horses represent the execution of God's wrath upon Babylon to the north, where two chariots and their colored horses are sent; the execution of God's wrath upon Egypt to the south, where one chariot and its colored horses are sent; and God's control of all the nations throughout the whole earth wherever they may be, where the last chariot and its colored horses walk to and fro throughout the earth.

We will make two observations from these two passages, both of which foreshadow our passage in Revelation chapter 6. Here is the first observation: In Zechariah 1, though the horses were of various colors, the horses were all of the same quality and type, in that they all represented the same idea—that of obtaining knowledge. They all served one purpose—that was providing information to God about the status of the nations and the status of His people. All four horses of Zechariah 1 provided the same thing—that is, information to the Lord.

In Zechariah chapter 6, though the horses were of various colors there as well, once again the horses were all of the same quality and type in that they all represented the same idea—that of judgment. Horses went to the north, bringing judgment; horses went to the south, bringing judgment; horses went to and fro throughout the earth, bringing judgment.

The point is this: The horses were homogeneous in nature in each passage as to their mission. One horseman was not radically different from the other horsemen. All four horsemen in Zechariah 1 are doing the same thing: bringing information. All of the horses in Zechariah 6 are doing the same thing: bringing judgment.

A second observation is that the horses of Zechariah chapter 1 represented a different idea than the horses of Zechariah chapter 6.

In Zechariah 1, the horses represented the knowledge of God—His omniscience of all nations. In Zechariah 6, the horses represented the judgment of God—His wrath against the enemies of His people. The point is, the meaning of the horses was different in each case, and the meaning of the horses in each case had to be derived from the passage in which those horses were presented to us.

The symbolic meaning of the horses varies, based on the passage in which the horses are mentioned, and based on how they are used in those passages. You cannot say that the horses in Zechariah 1 mean the same thing as the horses in Zechariah 6. They do not. They mean two different things.

How does this help us in our interpretation of Revelation 6? The horses in Zechariah and their usage there have established two principles that must guide us. The first one is this: These four horses in Revelation 6, though they are different in color, are all of the same quality and type, in that they all represent the same idea. The white horse cannot represent a radically different idea than the red horse, the black horse, and the pale horse.

The meaning of these four horses, just like in Zechariah, is homogeneous. They all represent the same thing. They all represent something bad. They all represent evil things that are going to occur on the earth during the Church Age that will characterize that entire period. They represent oppression and destruction and deprivation and death. Thus, the four horses are homogeneous in nature, just like they were in Zechariah 1, and just like they were in Zechariah 6.

The second principle is this: the meaning of these four horses in

Revelation 6 must be derived from the passage in which they occur, and not from some other passage. The horses meant one thing in Zechariah 1, but the horses meant an entirely different thing in Zechariah 6. Context is controlling in determining the meaning of any passage, and certainly that is the case here. The symbolic meaning of these horses in Revelation 6 must be derived from Revelation 6, and not from Revelation 19, where we find many white horses and many people riding them.

Revelation 6 will interpret itself as to what the meaning of its horses is, and Revelation 19 will interpret itself as to what the meaning of its horses is. The meaning of the horses in Revelation 6 does not determine the meaning of the horses in Revelation 19, and the meaning of the horses in Revelation 19 does not determine the meaning of the horses in Revelation 6. Likewise, the meaning of the horses in Zechariah 1 did not determine the meaning of the horses in Zechariah 6, nor vice versa.

Just as we found in Zechariah, these four horsemen in Revelation 6 all represent a single idea, and that idea which these four horsemen represent is to be derived from the passage itself, and not from another passage in Revelation where horses also appear.

The New Testament Meaning of the Four Horsemen

The meaning of the four horsemen is found in Revelation 6:1–8. Notice verse 1: "*And I saw when the Lamb opened one of the seals, and I heard, as it were the noise of thunder, one of the four beasts saying, Come and see.*" "[2]*And I saw. . . .*" Now we have the unveiling of these four horses and horsemen that bring terrible things to the earth.

It is clearly God's will to give His enemies and His people's enemies a very significant degree of liberty within which to operate and exercise their evil. We see this in the life of Job. God gave Satan a long leash to ravage Job, even though God held the end of that leash. God allowed Satan to ravage Job economically, domestically, socially, and personally, even though God loved him intensely, and had the highest regard for his character and his conduct.

What God allowed to happen to Job personally, God allows to happen to His people corporately. Though Satan is a defeated foe and under the control of God, nevertheless it is God's purpose to allow him room to do a great deal of evil throughout the centuries and across the globe. We see this satanic evil being carried out under the symbolic visual imagery of these four horsemen of the Apocalypse. As Jesus opens each of these seals, He reveals the kind of evil and the category of evil that He allows Satan to accomplish. Here we have a revelation of what Satan will do between the first and the second coming of Christ, and the categories of evil he will carry out in this age.

Therefore, when these categories of events occur, we should not be surprised or dismayed as though somehow the forces of evil are winning. They are not. Sin is always self-defeating, and sin is always self-destructive, and no movement based on sin can ever succeed. Furthermore, Satan is under the control of Christ, and Christ allows him to do evil in order to bring judgment on the wicked through that evil, and in order to purify and sanctify His saints by means of that evil. Any evil that does not serve those two goals is restrained and prohibited from occurring.

First of all, notice the white horse in verse 2. It says, *"And I saw, and behold a white horse: and he that sat on him had a bow; and a crown was given unto him: and he went forth conquering, and to conquer."*

Some have said that the white horse and his rider represents Christ, based on the fact that Christ sits on a white horse in Revelation 19; but in reality, the only similarity between the white horse of Revelation 6:2 and the white horse in Revelation 19 is that they are both white and someone is sitting on them. We did see some similarities between the horses in Zechariah 1 and Zechariah 6. In Zechariah 1, there were red horses. In Zechariah 6, there were red horses. But we saw that though the horses had the same color, the horses meant different things based on the context in which they were found.

In Revelation 6 there is a white horse, and in Revelation 19 there is a white horse. But they do not represent the same thing at all. While the similarities are very small, the differences between the white horse and rider of Revelation 6 and the white horse and rider of Revelation 19 are remarkable.

Each of them has a different weapon. One holds a bow, but the other has a sword proceeding out of his mouth.

Each of them has a different crown. The one in Revelation 6 has a single crown on his head, which is the victor's crown called the "*stephanos*" in Greek; but the one in Revelation 19 has multiple crowns, which are royal crowns called the "*diádēma*" in Greek.

Each of them has a different company. The one in Revelation 6 is all by himself, while the horse in Revelation 19 is accompanied by an army of people who are also all on white horses.

Each of them has a different purpose. The one in Revelation 6 is going out to achieve conquest, while the one in Revelation 19 is going out to execute judgment and wrath.

Finally, each of them has a different context. The white horse in Revelation 6 has the context of the other three horses, and that context is one of war and famine and death, which proceed from the red, the black, and the pale horse. The white horse in Revelation 19 has the context of the marriage supper of the Lamb and the final judgment.

These differences between the white horse of Revelation 6 and the white horse of Revelation 19, coupled with the homogeneous meaning of the four horses of Zechariah 1 and Zechariah 6, lead us to believe that these four horses and their riders in Revelation 6 also have a homogeneous meaning. All four of them mean the same thing, just like all four of the horses in Zechariah 1 meant the same thing, and all four of the horses in Zechariah 6 meant the same thing. All four of the horses in Revelation 6 are all harbingers of evil. They are all bringing wicked purposes to pass. Therefore, the white horse and his rider in this passage cannot represent Christ.

This first horse along with its rider represents the twisting and perversion of the dominion mandate given to humanity by God in the garden of Eden. Men were supposed to exercise dominion over the earth under the authority of God and rule it for the glory of God and the good of their fellow creatures. But because of their fallenness and depravity, men now want to exercise a wicked and sinful dominion over other men. They want to oppress and tyrannize them and subject them to enslavement and servitude.

This white horse represents the spirit of conquest and the desire for dominion that the kings of the earth have exercised and will continue to exercise over people and nations until Christ returns. This king goes forth with a bow, he has a crown on his head, and he goes out conquering and to conquer. This desire of fallen, depraved men to conquer and rule over other men is something that is pervasive during the time period between the first and second coming of Christ. Out of this wicked desire for a tyrannical dominion over other men flow the next three horsemen: war and famine and death.

The white horse represents conquest. It represents sinful economic conquest, sinful political conquest, sinful military conquest, and the sinful spiritual conquest that depraved men under the control of Satan seek to exercise over the people of the earth, and which arises out of their perverted desire for dominion. Men want to rule other men economically, politically, militarily, and spiritually, and subjugate them to themselves.

Between the first and second coming of Christ, there have been, there are now, and there always will be men who seek to rise up and rule the world and establish by conquest a kingdom that stands in opposition to the kingdom of Jesus Christ. This is why we struggle right now under corrupt and tyrannical leaders. They are the men who go forth conquering and to conquer by using weapons of intimidation and power, represented by the bow, in order to subjugate people under them. In Ephesians 6:16, Satan is pictured as using a bow to shoot his fiery arrows at God's people.

We see sinful economic conquest exercised by the international financial and banking institutions and those who run them. Wealthy men would rule the world. We see sinful political conquest exercised by presidents, prime ministers, ayatollahs, and kings. We see sinful military conquest exercised by the armies of the world and their generals. We see sinful spiritual conquest exercised by the Pope, by corrupt denominational leaders, and by cults like Islam.

Everywhere we look, somebody is trying to conquer someone in some way for some evil purpose. Conquest by evil men for evil purposes in every area of life characterizes the age between the first and the second coming of Christ. Oppression and tyranny and enslavement of people by those who seek to conquer them is going to continue until the second coming. What do you see men doing in the last 2,000 years, but rising up and grasping for power and seeking to conquer and subjugate other people under them, either economically, politically, militarily, or spiritually?

Secondly, notice the red horse in verses 3 to 4: *"And when he had opened the second seal, I heard the second beast say, Come and see.*
4 *And there went out another horse that was red: and power was given to him that sat thereon to take peace from the earth, and that they should kill one another: and there was given unto him a great sword."*

The meaning of the red horse is clear. The red horse and its rider represent war and the slaughter it produces and the destruction of peace it causes. War has characterized the earth since the time of Christ, and wars will continue to characterize the earth until Christ returns. Jesus said in Matthew 24:6, *"And ye shall hear of wars and rumours of wars: see that ye be not troubled: for all these things must come to pass, but the end is not yet."*

The point is, peace will be taken from the earth. Nation will rise against nation, and kingdom against kingdom; one political nation will attack another political nation, and the kingdom of darkness will attack the kingdom of light. The result is that there will be disorder and turmoil, and many will be slaughtered. Jesus said in Matthew 10:34, *"Think not that I am come to send peace on earth: I came not to send peace, but a sword."* The idea that somehow world peace will be achieved before the second coming of Christ is a delusion. Men will beat their swords into plowshares and beat their spears into pruning hooks and they will not learn war anymore only after Jesus returns to the earth. The post-millennial idea of a golden age of peace before Christ returns is clearly false. There will be wars and rumors of wars and nations rising against nations until Jesus returns. War is a great evil, and Satan does all he can to stir up the evil of warfare.

Thirdly, notice the black horse in verses 5 and 6: *"And when he had opened the third seal, I heard the third beast say, Come and see. And I beheld, and lo a black horse; and he that sat on him had a pair of balances in his hand.* [6] *And I heard a voice in the midst of the four beasts say, A measure of wheat for a penny, and three measures of barley for a penny; and see thou hurt not the oil and the wine."*

The black horse symbolizes famine. In verse 5, the rider carries a set of scales. Scales were used to weigh out food for sale, but this was something that was done only when food was very scarce. When food was scarce, it was sold by exact weight because every grain of wheat was precious and valuable. Under ordinary times, it was just sold by volume. People would buy a sack of wheat. But now they are weighing it out carefully in a balance so you are not given one more grain than you paid for.

For example, when God threatened Israel for her disobedience, He said to her in Leviticus 26:26, *"And when I have broken the staff of your bread, ten women shall bake your bread in one oven, and they shall deliver you your bread again by weight: and ye shall eat, and not be satisfied."* When you pass food around the table, you do not weigh out each person's portion because there is plenty, and each can take what he pleases. Imagine if bread was so scarce that you weighed each piece and gave each person an equal weight of bread because you wanted to be sure it was fairly distributed.

Notice verse 6. It says, *"And I heard a voice in the midst of the four beasts say, A measure of wheat for a penny, and three measures of barley for a penny; and see thou hurt not the oil and the wine."* A measure of wheat, as it is spoken of in our passage, was a day's ration for an adult. If you need 1,500 calories a day to sustain yourself, a measure of wheat was 1,500 calories. He says, *"for a penny."* A penny in the original language is a denarius, and a denarius was a full day's wages for a worker.

Verse 6 is saying that one day's worth of wheat costs one day's worth of labor for one man who worked a whole day. You go out and work a whole day and you get one denarius. That one denarius will only buy one day's worth of wheat for an individual. But if you have a wife and a child that also need to eat, you cannot afford wheat. You have to purchase barley, a coarser, lesser grain, because a day's wages would purchase a day's ration of barley for three people.

The point is that people are barely able to buy enough to sustain their lives. Food is scarce. Therefore, the price is high, and bare subsistence is the condition of the people. However, oil and wine are not affected by this condition of scarcity. The meaning of this seems to be that there are plenty of expensive goods available for the wealthy to eat well, even when the masses are barely subsisting. The rich oppressor always has the finest food in abundance, but the downtrodden believers who will not participate in the idol-worshiping trade guilds or who will not violate the sanctity of the Lord's Day struggle to find the means to sustain themselves and their families.

Therefore, we should not be surprised that between the first and second coming of Christ, economic hardship and lack of material possessions should be the condition of the masses of people in general, and the condition of Christians in particular. America is a true anomaly in the history of the world with the relative abundance we have enjoyed in the last seventy years or so of our history. This may very well not last, given the direction of our nation.

Severely limited resources to meet basic survival needs has been the characteristic of the age, as the oppressors grind the faces of the poor, and create economic, political, and social structures that favor the tyrants and make it very difficult for the poor and oppressed to meet the basic needs of life. We see it going on in Venezuela right now. We see it going on in African nations where there are repeated famines. Human depravity, coupled with natural disasters and oppressive rulers, has kept most people struggling just to live. This is how it has been and this is how it will continue to be until the end of the age. Satan begrudges the people of the earth barely enough food to live so he can oppress them further. You wonder why you struggle all your life with economic hardship. Here is the reason: the black horse.

Fourthly, notice the pale horse in verses 7 to 8. *"And when he had opened the fourth seal, I heard the voice of the fourth beast say, Come and see.* [8] *And I looked, and behold a pale horse: and his name that sat on him was Death, and Hell followed with him. And power was given unto them over the fourth part of the earth, to kill with sword, and with hunger, and with death, and with the beasts of the earth."*

The pale horse represents death and hell. This is the destiny of every unsaved person, and unsaved people comprise the vast majority of people throughout the age. They die and then they go to hell. This death occurs by various means, some of which are listed.

In verse 8 it talks about killing *"with [the] sword."* That is death by violence of whatever kind. It talks about death by *"hunger."* That is famine which we just discussed. Then it says, *"and with death."* The idea is that of death by natural causes like heart attacks, cancer, strokes, and similar things. Then it speaks of death by *"the beasts of the earth."* This would be things like plagues brought by animals, such as the Bubonic Plague, actual animal attacks, poisonous snakes, spiders, bacteria, viruses, and all of the harm and death that comes to people through the animal creation, from the lowest to the highest forms. All these, and more, are the means whereby death comes to men. And after death, comes damnation and hell.

Believers are not exempt from death by these causes as well. But hell is not their destiny. They go to heaven when they die. We will see this as we study the fifth seal, and also chapter 7. For the believer, though we too experience death, hell does not follow. Heaven follows. To us, death is victory. But to the wicked, death is defeat.

When it says that power was given to Death and Hell over the fourth part of the earth, this means that at any point in time, only part of humanity will be dying, while the rest will live on. In other words, humanity will not be wiped off the face of the earth by death all at one time. Death can only take a portion of humanity at any point in history. There will not be a global catastrophic event that will kill off the entire human race. There will not be a nuclear war or an asteroid impact or some kind of an uncontrollable biological plague, either natural or man-made, that will take out humanity.

However, death will occur at a furious rate. On average over 150,000 people die around the globe every single day. Medical science will not be able to solve the problem of death. People will not bring an end to mortality in this age through the advancement of medical science. The pale horse will not be turned back by medical research. He will continue to ride until the end of the age. Hell will be the destiny for those who defy the Lord Jesus Christ. Heaven will be the destiny of those who obey Him.

In light of the great evil these four horsemen perpetrate, we must be careful not to participate in these evils ourselves. Instead, we must work at resisting them and fighting against them. We can fight against tyranny by seeking to promote economic and political liberty; we can fight against war by seeking to promote peace and by being peacemakers; we can fight against famine by seeking to provide food for ourselves and for others; we can fight against death by promoting good health and medical practices; and we can fight against hell as a destiny by preaching the gospel and holding out the hope of heaven.

Notice three points by way of summary. The first point is this: These four horsemen all exist in parallel with each other at the same time. In other words, it is not like the white horse appears, and then after that the red horse, and after that the black horse, and after that the pale horse. These horses are all riding together, simultaneously, all carrying out their mission at the same time. Conquest, war, famine, and death will characterize the age in which we live, and we will not escape them.

When you look at the condition of humanity from the first coming of Christ until now, these things have always characterized the age. It has been an age of evil conquest, horrible wars, terrible famine, and comprehensive death. Therefore, do not expect that somehow things are going to get better and better. They are not. These things will always characterize the world in which we live, not only in our time but into the future until Christ returns.

The second point is that Christ will use these evil works of Satan to execute His purposes in this age, and those purposes are two: First, to bring judgment on the wicked. This conquest, war, famine, and death take a terrible toll on unsaved people. In fact, unsaved people are the vast majority of the objects of the operation of these four horsemen. Secondly, Christ will use these evil works of Satan to execute His purpose in this age to save and sanctify His people and to build His kingdom.

The Bible tells us in Acts 14:22 that *"we must through much tribulation enter into the kingdom of God,"* but it is precisely by means of that tribulation that we do enter the kingdom of God. When you think about how you became saved and why you became saved, was it not in a context of trouble—and because you had troubles, you sought the Lord, and the Lord used that trouble to draw you to Himself? Thank God for the horsemen, when Christ overrules their evil intent and uses them as instruments to save and sanctify His people.

These four horsemen have a judicial purpose and a redemptive purpose. They are loosed for the sake of judgment and they are loosed for the sake of purification. What the four horsemen do to the wicked in terms of their temporal and ultimate outcomes is different than what they do to the righteous in terms of their temporal and ultimate outcomes.

For example, Rome tyrannized the world and conquered it through terrible wars. As a result, they established a kingdom and a system of roads and a universal language that paved the way for the gospel to rapidly spread throughout the whole world. Roman roads and Greek language allowed the gospel to spread. While Satan was sending forth his people conquering and to conquer and wicked Caesars arose, it also provided an environment for the gospel to explode and grow exponentially across the empire.

The third point is that each of these four horsemen is explicitly under the control of Christ. All of them are given the ability to do what they accomplish, but they are limited in their ability to achieve all they want. It says of the white horseman, he was *"given"* a crown by Jesus; the red horse went out and power was *"given"* to him; the black horse went out, but was limited in what he could do: It was a case of "Do not let things get any worse than this, in terms of the food distribution." The pale horse was sent out and was told, "Only a fourth of the earth and no more!"

Every one of these horses is explicitly under the control of Jesus Christ. Jesus gives them the ability to do what they achieve, but they are limited by Jesus in their ability to achieve all that their wicked hearts desire. Christ gives them power, but Christ limits the power they can exercise. He uses them as His agents to do His will. Just as in Genesis 50:20, these four horsemen mean it for evil, but Jesus means it for good. He is working all things together for the good of His people, even though, as it says in Romans 8:36, they are *"killed all the day long."* Nothing will separate them from the love of Christ.

So here we are. We feel the heel of oppression on our neck. We live under a government that is increasingly crushing our liberties. We are involved in endless wars. We just get done with one and another one starts up.

How many of you have fat checkbooks? Is there not economic oppression? You struggle to make a living. If you did not have to pay all the money the government demands from you in taxes, you would have double what you have now.

Then there is death. Believers die. Sweet, wonderful believers die. The wicked also die. We see the slaughter and murder in our streets. As you look at the chaos that is going on because of conquest and war and economic struggle and the death that occurs from all the diseases and accidents and animals and famine, you ask yourself if the world has gone mad. What is going on in this age? The answer is this: Exactly what is supposed to be going on.

Do not think that somehow evil is out of control, Christ is gone, and the wicked are winning. The four horsemen are riding, but they are doing precisely what Jesus allows them to do, and no more. He puts evil on a leash. He says, "You may do this, but you may do no more. Through you, I will punish the wicked and cast them into hell; and through you, I will save and sanctify My people and bring them to heaven." In the very next seal, where do we see those who died under the reign of the four horsemen? We see them sitting in heaven, conversing with the Lord Jesus.

Everything is going exactly the way it is supposed to be going. As you look around you, and as you read the news, you say, "There go the four horsemen, but I see a leash on every one of them held by Jesus Christ. I see that this has always been the case, and it always will be the case until He comes back, so I am not going to chafe and think that if we just elect this guy, it will all get fixed." It does not matter whom you elect; the four horsemen ride, and they will always ride.

That is not to say we should not try to mitigate oppression and war and famine and death. Certainly, as Christians we fight against all of those things, and well we should. But let us not be deluded that somehow we are going to eradicate them. Let us not grieve over the fact that we are subject to them, but let us patiently and meekly bow before the will of Christ in unleashing these things, and recognize that He is going to work them together for His redemptive purposes, for our salvation and sanctification, and for our good. Seek to live with a spirit of contentment and peace and joy under it, knowing that the end of it will be glorious.

This is the patience and faith of the saints. This is the disposition and the attitude of the overcomer, who will sit with Christ in His throne one day.

24

The Fifth and Sixth Seal, Revelation 6:9–17

> "9 *And when he had opened the fifth seal, I saw under the altar the souls of them that were slain for the word of God, and for the testimony which they held:* 10 *And they cried with a loud voice, saying, How long, O Lord, holy and true, dost thou not judge and avenge our blood on them that dwell on the earth?* 11 *And white robes were given unto every one of them; and it was said unto them, that they should rest yet for a little season, until their fellow servants also and their brethren, that should be killed as they were, should be fulfilled.* 12 *And I beheld when he had opened the sixth seal, and, lo, there was a great earthquake; and the sun became black as sackcloth of hair, and the moon became as blood;* 13 *And the stars of heaven fell unto the earth, even as a fig tree casteth her untimely figs, when she is shaken of a mighty wind.* 14 *And the heaven departed as a scroll when it is rolled together; and every mountain and island were moved out of their places.* 15 *And the kings of the earth, and the great men, and the rich men, and the chief captains, and the mighty men, and every bondman, and every free man, hid themselves in the dens and in the rocks of the mountains;* 16 *And said to the mountains and rocks, Fall on us, and hide us from the face of him that sitteth on the throne, and from the wrath of the Lamb:* 17 *For the great day of his wrath is come; and who shall be able to stand?*"

Chapter 5 revealed that Jesus Christ has received all authority in heaven and in earth. He sits with His Father in the Father's throne, and He is now revealing and executing the decrees of God contained in the scroll that is sealed with seven seals.

Immediately upon His ascension and His enthronement, Jesus began to open the seals of the book of God's decrees. As He opened the first four seals, the four horsemen of the Apocalypse were revealed in Revelation 6:1–8. These four horsemen of the Apocalypse represent the evil that is going to occur on the earth during the current age in which we live.

Satan and his human agents who carry out his will are going to set up a kingdom in opposition to Christ's kingdom. These four horsemen represent the kind of evil Christ allows Satan and his people to carry out in this age. Even though Satan means his work for evil, Christ will use it for good. Christ will use what He allows Satan to do to bring punishment on the wicked and bring salvation and sanctification to His elect. Satan will be restrained from doing anything that does not serve those ends.

The white horse represents the wicked desire that evil men have to conquer other men, economically, politically, militarily, and spiritually. Evil men seek to rise up and rule the world and establish through conquest a kingdom that stands in opposition to the kingdom of the Lord Jesus Christ. Evil men go forth conquering and to conquer through the use of any means they can in order to subjugate people underneath them. Everywhere we look, down through the centuries and across the globe, somebody is trying to conquer someone in some way for some evil purpose. Christians, especially, have been tyrannized and oppressed by the wicked from the time of Christ, and will continue to be persecuted until the time that Christ returns.

The red horse represented war and the slaughter it produces. Conquest is often achieved by means of war, and war has characterized the earth since the time of Christ, and will continue to characterize it until He returns. Men will continue to kill one another until the second coming, and it is only when the Prince of Peace returns that world peace is ever going to be achieved. The thief comes not but for to kill and steal and destroy, and war is the primary means through which this destructive work of Satan is carried out.

The black horse represented famine. This present age is one marked by scarcity, and most people have lived at a subsistence level in which the basic needs of life have barely been met. Economic hardship and lack of material security have been the condition of the vast majority of people in general, and of Christians in particular in this age. Scarcity will always be our condition until Christ returns. The oppression of conquerors and the ravages of war have left most people with severely limited resources. Universal abundance will only exist after Jesus Christ returns to this earth.

The pale horse represented death and hell. Death is the universal outcome for every person as a result of Satan's work in the garden of Eden, and hell is the destiny of all those who reject Jesus Christ. Satan has a whole array of methods for taking the lives of men: war and famine and disease and the beasts of the earth. The pale horse is always riding to reap his prey and fill the graveyards of the earth.

These are the four evil elements that characterize the age between the first and second coming of Christ. This age is going to be characterized by conquest, war, famine, and death, which is followed by hell. This is the aggressive active work of Satan that is being carried out in the world in opposition to Jesus Christ and His people.

Satan would use these four evil elements to destroy believers from the face of the earth if he could, but he cannot. Christ will not permit it. Not only have Christ's people survived under these four evil horsemen of the Apocalypse, but they have also multiplied and spread over the entire globe, and they have penetrated into every single nation on the earth.

These first four seals that we explored in the last chapter leads us to the last two seals mentioned in this chapter, the fifth and sixth seals, in verses 9 to 17.

The Fifth Seal Opened

The fifth seal is recorded in verses 9 to 11. *"And when he had opened the fifth seal, I saw under the altar the souls of them that were slain for the word of God, and for the testimony which they held:* [10] *And they cried with a loud voice, saying, How long, O Lord, holy and true, dost thou not judge and avenge our blood on them that dwell on the earth?* [11] *And white robes were given unto every one of them; and it was said unto them, that they should rest yet for a little season, until their fellow servants also and their brethren, that should be killed as they were, should be fulfilled."*

The first four seals set before us the decrees of God regarding what He will allow Satan to do, how the people who serve Satan will act, and the impact these actions will have upon humanity in general. But now, with the fifth seal, we see how these four horsemen have affected the believers in particular. This fifth seal tells us that in this age the work of the four horsemen has been one of persecution against Christians.

We read in verse 9 that these souls in heaven have been slain. They did not just die, they were slain. They were slain because of the hatred the four horsemen have for Christianity. Notice verse 9 says, *"And when he had opened the fifth seal, I saw under the altar the souls of them that were slain for the word of God, and for the testimony which they held."*

These Christians, who were slain through the activity of the four horsemen, were slain for the word of God; that is, they were slain for preaching the word of God and explaining its message to the world. The world hates the preaching of the truth because it hates being told there is a God to whom they must submit.

They were also slain for the testimony they held. As they told how God had saved them from their sins and transformed them by His grace, and as they lived that testimony out by personal submission to Christ, the world saw their lives, heard their personal testimonies, and hated them for it. The testimony of their lives was a reproach to the wickedness of the world. As they shined as lights in the midst of a crooked and perverse nation, the wicked sought to do all they could to extinguish that light.

Revelation 1:9 states, *"I John, who also am your brother, and companion in tribulation, and in the kingdom and patience of Jesus Christ, was in the isle that is called Patmos, for the word of God, and for the testimony of Jesus Christ."* Caesar sought to extinguish the light that John was shedding by exiling him to the isle of Patmos. Caesar hated John's preaching of the word of God and his witness to Christ's saving work in his life.

All throughout this age, Christians have been slain for preaching the word of God and for giving their personal testimony of Christ's saving work in their lives.

This age has been one of martyrdom. Vast numbers of Christians have been killed for what they taught and for how they lived. Christians have experienced what Christ experienced, which is murder at the hands of wicked men, simply because they served and followed Christ and urged other people to do so as well. They were slain for the word of God and for the testimony which they held.

When you preach the word of God with your lips and when you live out the will of God in your life, expect to be hated, and be prepared for martyrdom. This martyrdom that these Christians experienced was not meaningless. Ironically for these four horsemen, their persecution of the believers only served to spread and expand the kingdom of God. The murder of Jesus forms the whole basis for the kingdom, as Revelation 5:9–10 stated: *"Thou art worthy to take the book, and to open the seals thereof: for thou wast slain, and hast redeemed us to God by thy blood out of every kindred, and tongue, and people, and nation;* [10] *And hast made us unto our God kings and priests: and we shall reign on the earth."*

The redemption and rule of Christ and the spread of Christianity throughout the whole world were established and brought to pass by people who were acting like these four horsemen. They murdered Jesus and thereby initiated the kingdom of God; but not having learned their lesson, they then proceeded to murder Christians and thereby expanded the kingdom of God.

The martyrdom of Stephen in Acts 7 illustrates how his murder resulted in the spread of the gospel throughout all of Asia. Acts 8:4 tells us that as a result of the persecution, the believers were scattered abroad, and went everywhere preaching the word. Martyrdom only served to spread the light of the word of God and the testimony of His saving grace.

Furthermore, this martyrdom did not destroy those who were martyred. It merely promoted them to heaven, where they wait for reunion with their resurrected bodies at the second coming. These souls are fully conscious and aware of what has occurred to them on earth. Though they are in heaven, they know they were unrighteously murdered on the earth. They also know that God is a God of justice, and though their murderers did not receive punishment for their wicked deeds on earth, they know they will receive it eventually.

But the question is this: How long will it be until the wicked who persecuted the martyred Christians are brought to justice? God promised in Romans 12:19, "*Vengeance is mine; I will repay, saith the Lord.*" If that is the case, and it certainly is the case, the question then arises: When is that vengeance going to be accomplished? When are those who have been wickedly murdered going to be vindicated, and their murderers properly punished?

Unexecuted justice is a trial to the soul and grief to the spirit, and we chafe when we see the wicked go unpunished for their wicked deeds, decade after decade. It sorely tries our patience and tempts us to want to avenge ourselves for the evil done to us. Every saved soul has a keen interest in justice being carried out and in wrongs being made right. Therefore, the souls in heaven ask the Father, "How long is it going to be before justice is served?" Notice verse 10: *"And they cried with a loud voice, saying, How long, O Lord, holy and true, dost thou not judge and avenge our blood on them that dwell on the earth?"*

Notice the titles they give to God in their appeal to Him. They call Him *"holy."* This is an appeal to His sinless character, which cannot tolerate sin in His universe, and therefore must destroy all evil out of that universe.

They call Him *"true."* This is an appeal to the truthfulness of His character that requires Him to keep His promises, because He cannot lie. He has promised to repay every sin with vengeance and with justice, and His truthfulness will not let Him fail to keep that promise.

These souls in heaven remind God of His holiness and His truthfulness, and they ask God how long it will be before He will exercise His justice and keep His promise to the saints who have suffered for His name's sake. They are calling upon God to vindicate His holiness and His truth and His people by reversing the sentence of condemnation and rejection that was passed on them by the four horsemen.

God replies to this cry for justice and the vindication of His people in verse 11. *"And white robes were given unto every one of them; and it was said unto them, that they should rest yet for a little season, until their fellow servants also and their brethren, that should be killed as they were, should be fulfilled."*

The first thing He does in reply to their plea for justice is express His recognition and reassurance of their personal righteousness by giving each of them a white robe. By this act, Jesus is telling them He has already passed judgment as to their righteousness; and by implication, the wickedness of those who harmed and persecuted them. The white robe is the pledge of God that they will be vindicated when the matter is finally dealt with in the court of God's justice.

But He also tells them that the time for their public vindication is not yet. They must be patient a little longer, and rest in the fact that the outcome has already been determined, though the accomplishment has not yet been achieved. The reason they must wait is because there are many martyrs yet to come, and many saints who must be unjustly killed just as they were. It is when the full number of persecuted and martyred saints are gathered in that the final judgment will come. Then justice will be done, the saints will be vindicated before the whole world, and the wicked will be utterly condemned.

What God is telling both them and us in verse 11 is shocking. Notice verse 11: *"And white robes were given unto every one of them; and it was said unto them, that they should rest yet for a little season,"* (now notice) *"until their fellow servants also and their brethren, that should be killed as they were, should be fulfilled."*

God says to these saints in heaven in the plainest of terms that He knows that the wicked are killing His people. He knows they will continue to kill a lot more of His people in the future, and He does not intend to intervene to stop that killing. He intends to allow the wicked to continue killing believers without interference, just as He allowed these souls in heaven to be killed without interfering.

We often wonder at the inaction of God regarding the suffering and the slaughter of His people around the world in places like North Korea and China and in all of the Islamic countries. We ask why God does not do something to stop the slaughter of His people that we read about every week. Shockingly, verse 11 tells us that God has no intention of stopping it. Certainly, God is not causing the death of these people, but He is permitting it. He is allowing the four horsemen to run roughshod over His people.

Therefore, when we suffer persecution, we need to understand that God knew it would happen; God determined to permit it; and therefore, it is no indication that He does not know or that He does not care or that He does not love us when He allows it to occur. The purpose of this fifth seal is to show suffering saints the safety, security, and comfort the martyrs enjoy in heaven. It is to show them that permitting martyrdom is part of the plan of God, and that the punishment of those who martyr them is the promise of God. But that promise will be fulfilled not now, but later.

All of this is designed to help us be meek and patient under the unjust suffering at the hands of the wicked. We can be meek and patient because we know that God is allowing it, we know that our destiny is in heaven, we know that our vindication is certain, and we know that our sufferings will be avenged by God. He will avenge us when the time comes for the final judgment, but not until then. Understanding all of this helps us bear up under the martyrdom and suffering we are having now, which is known by God and allowed by God for purposes that are pleasing to Him. This is why the early saints could face martyrdom with peace and joy and confidence, and this is why we can do so today. The fifth seal makes us bold and confident in the face of persecution.

Jesus said to the church in Smyrna in Revelation 2:10, *"Fear none of those things which thou shalt suffer: behold, the devil shall cast some of you into prison, that ye may be tried; and ye shall have tribulation ten days: be thou faithful unto death, and I will give thee a crown of life."*

God says to His church, "My purpose in allowing the four horsemen to ride roughshod over you is so that you will be put to the test for the purpose of proving your faithfulness. When you are faithful to death, you will be given a crown of life. All the world will see that you were genuine Christians, and will see that your death is meaningless in light of the eternal life that I give you. Your suffering was only for a moment, but you have the far more eternal and exceeding weight of glory of eternal life without end."

God's purpose is to allow the four horsemen to ride the whole time between the first and the second coming of Jesus. During that whole time, Christians will be martyred. When they are martyred, the result is that the gospel is spread through the world. These martyred saints are brought to heaven where they are told by having robes given to them that they will be vindicated and their persecutors will be punished. But they need to be patient until the full number has come in and the final judgment arrives. Then they will have what they desire, which is the vindication of the holiness of God for not allowing evil to go unpunished. Then they will have the vindication of the truthfulness of God in the keeping of His promises that He would exercise vengeance against the wicked. Then they will see God reverse the condemnation that was placed on them, and vindicate them before the whole world.

This destroys the "health and wealth" gospel—the theology that says God intends for your life to be one of health, peace, and prosperity here on earth. We have to endure hardness as good soldiers of Christ now. Our peace and prosperity are in heaven. If you expect anything other than the four horsemen riding roughshod over you, you are doomed to disappointment. We need to understand that Christ did not come to send peace on earth but a sword, and we will be hated of all nations for His name's sake. We must through much tribulation enter into the kingdom of God.

Understand that though you treat the world with kindness and generosity and love, you will get back a great deal of ugliness and hostility and persecution. Instead of thinking, "I must be doing something wrong," or "God does not love me," or "Why doesn't God fix this?", understand that this is exactly what is supposed to be happening. It is part of God's plan and purpose; and, in the end, we will see the resolution of all of these issues, and the vindication of God and all of His dealings with us and with the wicked.

We have to be patient until then, and not start finding fault with God, or start throwing our theology away because it is not producing health and wealth. The health and wealth gospel is not the gospel of Christ. Christ does not promise that His people will be either healthy or wealthy in this life. Thank God for the degree of health and wealth He does give us now because it is substantial. But it is not what we live for, and it is not what we expect. What we expect is the fifth seal. This is what is going to happen to us in this age.

The Sixth Seal Opened

The sixth seal is described in verses 12 to 17. *"And I beheld when he had opened the sixth seal, and, lo, there was a great earthquake; and the sun became black as sackcloth of hair, and the moon became as blood;* 13 *And the stars of heaven fell unto the earth, even as a fig tree casteth her untimely figs, when she is shaken of a mighty wind.* 14 *And the heaven departed as a scroll when it is rolled together; and every mountain and island were moved out of their places.* 15 *And the kings of the earth, and the great men, and the rich men, and the chief captains, and the mighty men, and every bondman, and every free man, hid themselves in the dens and in the rocks of the mountains;* 16 *And said to the mountains and rocks, Fall on us, and hide us from the face of him that sitteth on the throne, and from the wrath of the Lamb:* 17 *For the great day of his wrath is come; and who shall be able to stand?"*

When the four horsemen have ridden roughshod over the people of God and have done their worst in their rebellion against God throughout this age, the sixth seal describes their outcome at the end of the age when Jesus returns to the earth.

For Christians, their outcome will be glorious when Jesus returns, as we have already partially seen in the fifth seal, and will see more extensively in chapter 7.

But for the wicked, their outcome will be dreadful when Jesus returns, as this sixth seal makes clear. The scene that is described in verses 12 to 17 is one of utter terror. Everything the wicked looked to for stability and security and all that they trusted in and worshiped is completely shattered.

First of all, he describes the destruction of the natural creation in verses 12 to 14. *"And I beheld when he had opened the sixth seal, and, lo, there was a great earthquake; and the sun became black as sackcloth of hair, and the moon became as blood;* [13] *And the stars of heaven fell unto the earth, even as a fig tree casteth her untimely figs, when she is shaken of a mighty wind.* [14] *And the heaven departed as a scroll when it is rolled together; and every mountain and island were moved out of their places."*

This description of the destruction of the natural creation is foreshadowed and spoken of in many Old Testament passages in the same kind of language. For example, in Joel 2:10, 30–31, 3:15–16; Isaiah 50:3; and Habakkuk 3:6–11 we find this same kind of language. These and many more passages speak of the end of the world involving the destruction of the natural creation.

For one example, notice Isaiah 34:1–4. The context is that of God's wrath being poured out on all the nations of the whole earth. *"Come near, ye nations, to hear; and hearken, ye people: let the earth hear, and all that is therein; the world, and all things that come forth of it.* [2] *For the indignation of the* Lord *is upon all nations, and his fury upon all their armies: he hath utterly destroyed them, he hath delivered them to the slaughter.* [3] *Their slain also shall be cast out, and their stink shall come up out of their carcasses, and the mountains shall be melted with their blood.* [4]*And all the host of heaven shall be dissolved, and the heavens shall be rolled together as a scroll: and all their host shall fall down, as the leaf falleth off from the vine, and as a falling fig from the fig tree."* Verse 4 contains the same language John uses in Revelation 6:12–14.

Furthermore, it is not just the Old Testament that speaks in this kind of language about the end of the world. In 2 Peter 3, we have a description of the end of the world when Jesus comes back, and the language is very similar. It is the language of the destruction of the physical universe.

Notice 2 Peter 3:10–12: *"But the day of the Lord will come as a thief in the night; in the which the heavens shall pass away with a great noise, and the elements shall melt with fervent heat, the earth also and the works that are therein shall be burned up.* [11] *Seeing then that all these things shall be dissolved, what manner of persons ought ye to be in all holy conversation and godliness,* [12] *Looking for and hasting unto the coming of the day of God, wherein the heavens being on fire shall be dissolved, and the elements shall melt with fervent heat?"* Here we have language of the destruction of the physical universe similar to that which we find in Revelation 6.

While vivid symbolic imagery is used in Revelation 6 to describe the destruction of the physical universe, this imagery speaks of a very real physical catastrophe that will occur at the second coming in which the physical universe will be destabilized, deconstructed, and devastated to the point that men will be brought to an acute awareness that the present material universe is coming to an end, and the judgment is about to begin.

What is the chief idol of humanity? Is it not the natural creation? It says in Romans 1:25 that they *"worshipped and served the [creation] more than the Creator."* The unsaved worship the earth and the universe as their god. They think life arose out of the natural creation. They think the material world supplies their needs and sustains them through its ecosystems and its resources. They think the physical laws of nature give their lives predictability and stability. They think the stars give them fixed points of reference to determine time and speed and direction.

In short, the material universe is their god, their stability, their security, and their savior. They think they will be saved through science discovering the natural universe and all it contains. So what does God do? He smashes their idol. He destroys their object of worship and their object of trust. "Gaia" or "Mother Earth" was not a god after all.

All they trusted in is utterly devastated and destroyed, and all that they worshiped is smashed and ruined. They looked to science as their savior, but where is their science when the world on which it is based is gone and the laws which described it become void and meaningless? The foundation on which they stood in defiance against God has literally been pulled out from beneath their feet. He that sits in the heavens laughs.

Secondly, He describes the despair of the wicked. Notice the impact the destruction of the natural creation has on the wicked in verses 15 to 17: *"And the kings of the earth, and the great men, and the rich men, and the chief captains, and the mighty men, and every bondman, and every free man, hid themselves in the dens and in the rocks of the mountains;* [16] *And said to the mountains and rocks, Fall on us, and hide us from the face of him that sitteth on the throne, and from the wrath of the Lamb:* [17] *For the great day of his wrath is come; and who shall be able to stand?"*

The effect the upheaval of creation has on them will be one of total terror. Every category of person will be filled with fear, and neither position or power nor possessions or poverty will exempt the wicked from the wrath of God. They all, like Adam and Eve, want to hide from the presence of God when He comes and escape an accounting to Him for what they have done. Adam and Eve tried to cover themselves with fig leaves and hide in the garden, and these want to cover themselves with rocks and hide in the caves of the earth.

They are fully aware that the God they denied is now going to become their judge, the evil they have done is now going to be brought to account and punished, and the wrath of God which they had scorned will now fall upon them. They never thought God's threats were real or that His punishment would be executed, but now it is too late and they see their imminent doom. The great day of God's wrath has come, and there is no place to hide and no ability to stand. They say: *"Who shall be able to stand?"*

The world they worshiped cannot protect them, and the God they scorned will not deliver them. They are doomed to suffer the wrath of God forever. Here is the justice of God and the vengeance of God which He promised to the martyrs under the fifth seal. The day of His wrath, though long delayed, has finally come and the blood of the martyrs will now be avenged.

The counsel of Hebrews 12:25–29 is very relevant to us: *"See that ye refuse not him that speaketh. For if they escaped not who refused him that spake on earth, much more shall not we escape, if we turn away from him that speaketh from heaven:* [26] *Whose voice then shook the earth: but now he hath promised, saying, Yet once more I shake not the earth only, but also heaven.* [27] *And this word, Yet once more, signifieth the removing of those things that are shaken, as of things that are made, that those things which cannot be shaken may remain.* [28] *Wherefore we receiving a kingdom which cannot be moved, let us have grace, whereby we may serve God acceptably with reverence and godly fear:* [29] *For our God is a consuming fire."*

People want to play games and make jokes about God all the time, but they need to realize the day is coming when all those jokes will die in their throats and all of those games will seem so stupid to have been played. The heavens and the earth will be shaken to pieces and the only thing that will remain is the kingdom of God. You need to be in that unshakable kingdom. Bow before Jesus Christ and embrace Him as your Lord and Savior so that, when He returns, you will be given a white robe and be vindicated, rather than crying out for the rocks of the earth to fall on you and hide you from the wrath to come.

This book is given as a warning of the Day of Judgment that is coming for the four horsemen and all those who follow them and ride with them. It tells us of the blessed escape from the wrath of God that those who receive Christ as their Savior will enjoy, and the vindication they will have. Do not refuse the God who is telling you to repent and be delivered from the wrath to come.

God is not willing that any should perish. God invites all who hear His warnings to come to repentance. Flee the perishing of the sixth seal. Through repentance enjoy the promises of the fifth seal, and thereby be prepared for the Day of Judgment. Repent of your sins, believe in Christ as your Lord and Savior, follow Him with all of your heart, and you will be saved from all that is in the sixth seal.

25

The Church Sealed, Revelation 7:1–8

> "1 *And after these things I saw four angels standing on the four corners of the earth, holding the four winds of the earth, that the wind should not blow on the earth, nor on the sea, nor on any tree.* 2 *And I saw another angel ascending from the east, having the seal of the living God: and he cried with a loud voice to the four angels, to whom it was given to hurt the earth and the sea,* 3 *Saying, Hurt not the earth, neither the sea, nor the trees, till we have sealed the servants of our God in their foreheads.* 4 *And I heard the number of them which were sealed: and there were sealed an hundred and forty and four thousand of all the tribes of the children of Israel.* 5 *Of the tribe of Judah were sealed twelve thousand. Of the tribe of Reuben were sealed twelve thousand. Of the tribe of Gad were sealed twelve thousand.* 6 *Of the tribe of Asher were sealed twelve thousand. Of the tribe of Nepthali were sealed twelve thousand. Of the tribe of Manasseh were sealed twelve thousand.* 7 *Of the tribe of Simeon were sealed twelve thousand. Of the tribe of Levi were sealed twelve thousand. Of the tribe of Issachar were sealed twelve thousand.* 8 *Of the tribe of Zabulon were sealed twelve thousand. Of the tribe of Joseph were sealed twelve thousand. Of the tribe of Benjamin were sealed twelve thousand.*"

In our last chapter, Jesus opened the first six seals of the book of God's decrees which reveal the things that characterize the age between the first and second coming of Christ.

The first four seals reveal the work Satan and his people will carry out during this age under the imagery and symbolism of the four horsemen. As the godless servants of Satan defy God and His laws and persecute Christians for their faith, they will pursue conquest, symbolized by the white horse; they will initiate wars, symbolized by the red horse; they will provoke famine, symbolized by the black horse; and they will facilitate death, symbolized by the pale horse. Conquest and war and famine and death will characterize the age between the first and second coming of Christ.

The fifth seal tells us the destiny of believers who are faithful to Christ to the point of death. When faithful believers die, their souls are immediately taken to heaven. There they consciously enjoy the presence of God and personally engage in fellowship with God. In giving them white robes, God declares them to be righteous and promises them full vindication before the whole world when the end finally comes.

God makes it very clear that persecution and martyrdom will be the experience of believers throughout this age. We should never expect that the world at large will ever be anything other than hostile to Christians. We are told that martyrdom and persecution are going to be the norm for Christians throughout this age, and they will have their vindication, not in this age, but at the end of the age when the Lord Jesus returns and initiates the final judgment.

The sixth seal reveals the outcome of those who identified with and participated in the work of the four horsemen. At the end of the world, when the material universe is deconstructed and destroyed, they will realize too late that God's wrath is real, His judgment is imminent, and His punishment is inescapable. Christ is returning, and they will not be able to stand up against Him, nor will they be able to stand up before Him. They are utterly terrified, and they cry out in fearful dread these awful words: "*The great day of his wrath is come; and who shall be able to stand?*"

The good news is that there are some who will be able to stand without fear before God, and those people are revealed in chapter 7. Notice verse 9 says, "*After this I beheld, and, lo, a great multitude, which no man could number, of all nations, and kindreds, and people, and tongues, stood before the throne, and before the Lamb, clothed with white robes, and palms in their hands.*" The people in 6:17 ask, "*And who shall be able to stand?*" The reply of 7:9 is: These are the people who are able to stand before the Lamb.

What makes the difference between the people of the sixth seal, who are crying out for the rocks and the hills to fall on them to deliver them from the wrath of the Lamb before whom they cannot stand,

and those who are clearly standing before the Father and the Son with joy on their faces and no fear in their hearts? What makes the difference is the seal of God. Who are these people standing before the throne in 7:9? They are those who have been sealed with the seal of God that is described in 7:1–8.

Chapter 7 is the answer to the fearful cry and question of chapter 6. The fearful question of chapter 6 is this: Who will be able to stand before God on the final Day of Judgment? It will not be those who did the work of the four horsemen. It will be those who loved and served the Lord Jesus Christ and who have been cleansed from their sins in His blood, as 7:14 states. The answer to the question "*Who shall be able to stand?*" is this: Those who have the seal of God in their foreheads.

Chapter 7 sets before us a glorious picture of the church of God, the church of all those who have been saved from the wrath to come. As we proceed into chapter 7, we move into a very encouraging chapter. Chapter 6 was one that described great evil: the four horsemen, the martyrdom of the saints, and the wrath of God falling on the earth. But in chapter 7, we have a wonderful interlude of delight and encouragement. Here we are able to pause and rest beside the still waters and lie down in green pastures.

Chapter 7 can be divided into two parts. First of all, we have the church sealed in verses 1 to 8. Secondly, we have the church glorified in verses 9 to 17. In this chapter, we will look at the church sealed, and in the next chapter we will look at the church glorified.

The Restraint of the Four Winds

The restraint of the four winds is found in verses 1 through 3. Verse 1 says, "*And after these things I saw four angels standing on the four corners of the earth, holding the four winds of the earth, that the wind should not blow on the earth, nor on the sea, nor on any tree.*" Here we have the restraint of the four winds by four angels.

In the first phrase of verse 1, John says, "*And after these things I saw.*" This phrase tells us this was the next vision John had in the sequence of visions. He is not saying the things described in chapter 7 follow the things described in chapter 6 in a chronological sequence. He is simply saying: I had this vision, and next, I had this vision.

In verse 1 we have the repeated use of the number four. There are four angels, four corners of the earth, and four winds of the earth.

Three times in one verse John uses the number four. The number four symbolically represents the entire world or the whole earth.

Whatever is happening in verse 1 is something that concerns the entire world. The four corners of the earth are a reference to the four cardinal points of the compass: north, south, east, and west. He is not saying the earth is a square. He is stating the four directions one may go as one travels the earth. The idea is that whatever direction you go, the event spoken of in verse 1 will exist and occur.

The four angels are not identified. There is no indication they are the same as the four seraphim that are around the throne. They are just four angels. Though they are not identified, what they are doing is extremely important. It says that they are holding back the four winds from blowing on the earth, or on the sea, or on any tree. The symbolic meaning of the wind as it is used here is very important. Wind is a symbol of God's judgment.

Notice Jeremiah 49:34–37. The Lord here is talking about the province of Elam. Elam is a geographical area. *"The word of the* L*ORD that came to Jeremiah the prophet against Elam in the beginning of the reign of Zedekiah king of Judah, saying,* [35] *Thus saith the* L*ORD of hosts; Behold, I will break the bow of Elam, the chief of their might."* Now here it is, verse 36: *"And upon Elam will I bring the four winds from the four quarters of heaven, and will scatter them toward all those winds; and there shall be no nation whither the outcasts of Elam shall not come.* [37] *For I will cause Elam to be dismayed before their enemies, and before them that seek their life: and I will bring evil upon them, even my fierce anger, saith the* L*ORD; and I will send the sword after them, till I have consumed them."*

It is apparent that the four winds from the four quarters of the earth are a sign and symbol of God's wrath against the province of Elam. The four winds from the four corners of the earth in Revelation 7:1 will also bring God's wrath and destruction on the earth and its people.

Notice what it says in Revelation 7:2–3a: *"And I saw another angel ascending from the east, having the seal of the living God: and he cried with a loud voice to the four angels"* (the four angels that are holding the four winds from the four quarters of the earth), *"to whom it was given to hurt the earth and the sea,* [3] *Saying, Hurt not the earth, neither the sea, nor the trees,"* until we have done our work of sealing God's people.

These four winds, which these four angels are holding back from the four quarters of the earth, have the power to hurt. The four winds symbolize God's judgments on the earth that will hurt the earth. These judgments will affect the earth and the sea and the trees—and, by implication, those who dwell on the earth and who are dependent on the earth, the sea, and the trees for life.

It is very interesting that in chapter 8, when the seventh seal is opened, there are seven trumpets revealed. How does a trumpet make its noise? It makes it with wind. The trumpet player blows into it and wind comes out the bell.

Notice the first two trumpets, Revelation 8:6–9: *"And the seven angels which had the seven trumpets prepared themselves to sound.*
[7] *The first angel sounded, and there followed hail and fire mingled with blood, and they were cast upon the earth: and the third part of trees was burnt up, and all green grass was burnt up."* In Revelation 8:7, when the wind comes out of the trumpet, the earth and the trees are destroyed. That is exactly what is being said these winds should not do in 7:1–3. It says these winds should not blow on *"the earth"*, or on *"any tree"*.

Notice the next trumpet, Revelation 8:8: *"And the second angel sounded, and as it were a great mountain burning with fire was cast into the sea: and the third part of the sea became blood;* [9] *And the third part of the creatures which were in the sea, and had life, died; and the third part of the ships were destroyed."* Here, the wind from the trumpet brings judgment on the sea. It says in 7:1–3 that these winds should not blow on *"the sea."*

In 7:1–3, God is holding back the winds, which represent His judgment on the earth and the sea and the trees. Then in chapter 8, we have His judgments falling on the earth and the trees and the sea from these trumpets. This idea of wind being the blast of God's wrath falling on the earth is clearly established, not only from Jeremiah 49:34–37, but also from Revelation 7:1–3, and then confirmed by Revelation 8:6–9.

Notice Revelation 7:2–3: "*And I saw another angel ascending from the east, having the seal of the living God: and he cried with a loud voice to the four angels, to whom it was given to hurt the earth and the sea,* [3] *Saying, Hurt not the earth,*" etc. In verse 1, we are introduced to four angels who are holding these four winds in the four quarters of the earth so they do not hurt the earth. Then in verse 2, we are introduced to a fifth angel. This fifth angel comes from the east and he addresses the four angels that are holding back the four winds.

It is significant that this angel arises out of the east. In the Scriptures, the east is the place from which redemption and salvation come. The sun rises in the east. The sun brings us light and blessing. This angel arises to bring great blessing to the people of God in the form of a seal in his hand, which is the seal of the living God.

Malachi 4:1–3 is a wonderful promise God gives to His people. It says in verse 1: *"For, behold, the day cometh, that shall burn as an oven; and all the proud, yea, and all that do wickedly, shall be stubble: and the day that cometh shall burn them up, saith the LORD of hosts, that it shall leave them neither root nor branch."* This "burning" is similar to what is spoken of in Revelation 8:7–8 with the first two trumpets bringing fire falling from heaven that burns, and a burning fiery mountain falling from heaven.

Now notice Malachi 4:2–3: *"But unto you that fear my name shall the Sun of righteousness arise with healing in his wings; and ye shall go forth, and grow up as calves of the stall.* [3] *And ye shall tread down the wicked; for they shall be ashes under the soles of your feet in the day that I shall do this saith the LORD of hosts."*

The Sun of righteousness is clearly a reference to the Messiah, the Lord Jesus. He is called the Sun, and the idea is that the sun rises in the east. The Bible repeatedly uses this metaphor of the sun rising, of redemption coming, of salvation coming, and Messiah coming. The wise men came from the east to find the Lord Jesus. The glory of God entered Ezekiel's temple from the east, Ezekiel 43:1–5. This metaphor of the east is a very positive thing that conveys the idea of blessing and redemption coming to the people of God.

Notice Revelation 7:2. He says, *"I saw another angel ascending from the east."* He is bringing a seal, and it specifically says that it is *"the seal of the living God."* The use of seals in biblical times was very common, and they were also very important. There is a great deal of information in the Bible about seals.

A seal signified three things when it was placed on something. First of all, it signified authentication. When something is authentic, that means it is real and genuine, as opposed to being false and fraudulent. A king would seal his letters with a unique seal that belonged to him alone, so the recipient would know that the letters he received were genuinely from the king and not forgeries from someone else.

In John 6:27, Jesus Himself says, *"Labour not for the meat which perisheth, but for that meat which endureth unto everlasting life, which the Son of man shall give unto you: for him hath God the Father sealed."* Jesus is saying, "God the Father has put His stamp of authentication on Me, that I am the true manna that comes from heaven, and that I am not a false Messiah." At His baptism, God the Father declared Jesus to be the authentic Messiah—and not an imposter—by the descent of the Spirit in the form of a dove upon Him, and by God speaking of Him from heaven. When the Spirit visibly descended on Jesus at His baptism and when God spoke from heaven saying, *"This is my beloved Son in whom I am well pleased,"* this was God's stamp of authentication that He placed on Jesus, proving He is the real, genuine, authentic Messiah. When Jesus says, "I have been sealed," He is saying, "I have been stamped 'authentic'."

The seal not only signifies authentication in the Scriptures; secondly, it also signifies ownership. The seal was the stamp of ownership and made the statement that the item sealed belonged to the one who placed the seal on it. For example, a load of lumber would come in on a ship, the seller would make a deal with the buyer, and the money would be paid. A seal of ownership would be put on the bundle of lumber, the buyer would leave, and later send his servant to get the bundle that had his seal on it. We find cattlemen doing this with cattle when they put their brand (a stamp of ownership) on the cow. By branding the cow, they are saying, "This one is mine."

Second Timothy 2:19 says, *"Nevertheless the foundation of God standeth sure, having this seal, The Lord knoweth them that are his."* When God puts His seal on someone, He is saying, "This belongs to Me. I have authority over it. It is mine. I will take responsibility for it and I will take care of it."

The seal not only signifies authentication and ownership; thirdly, it also signifies security. That which is sealed is secure. In Matthew 27:66, the tomb of Jesus had a seal set on the door in order to make it secure so that it would not be disturbed.

Ephesians 4:30 says: *"And grieve not the holy Spirit of God, whereby ye are sealed unto the day of redemption."* The implication is that the seal of God secures us and preserves us until the day when Jesus returns to finish and fully apply His redemption to us. We cannot fall away. We are safely kept until Jesus comes again because His seal secures us.

In Ephesians 1:12–14, we see the clearest and most extensive passage anywhere in the New Testament on the subject of sealing in relationship to the believer. *"That we should be to the praise of his glory, who first trusted in Christ.* [13] *In whom ye also trusted, after that ye heard the word of truth, the gospel of your salvation: in whom also after that ye believed, ye were sealed with that holy Spirit of promise,* [14] *Which is the earnest of our inheritance until the redemption of the purchased possession, unto the praise of his glory."*

There is a great deal in that passage, but I want to emphasize this: the Holy Spirit Himself is the seal that is given to us, and the seal that is given to us is *"the earnest of our inheritance."*

Every believer has the seal of the Holy Spirit given to him at the moment of salvation. At the moment you believed, you were sealed with the Holy Spirit. Every believer has the seal of God.

If you have bought a house you have put down earnest money. The earnest money is the promise that you are going to complete the transaction in the future. If you do not complete the transaction, the earnest money is forfeited. The earnest money is a promise. It is a promise of future fulfillment. You are giving security that you are going to fulfill your promise to pay the full amount for the house.

What is amazing is that the Holy Spirit is given to us as the security (the earnest money) that God is going to complete His purchase of us by fully applying to us all He has promised us in redemption.

It is interesting that this Greek word *arrabón* translated *"earnest,"* is also the same word that is used for an engagement ring. When a man asks a woman to marry him, the man gives the woman an engagement ring, an *arrabón*. It is his promise that on a specified day in the future he is going to marry her. When that day comes, he fulfills that promise. He marries her in fulfillment of the *arrabón*, the earnest that he gave her when he put the engagement ring on her finger.

Do you know what God's engagement ring to us is? It is the Holy Spirit. He has said, "I am engaged to you. Here is My engagement ring. It is the seal of the Spirit. One of these days, we will have the marriage supper of the Lamb. I will bring you into the relationship and the blessings I promised you in salvation."

In Revelation 7:3, this fifth angel says to these four angels, *"Hurt not the earth, neither the sea, nor the trees, till we have sealed the servants of our God in their foreheads."* It is interesting that these servants of God are sealed in their foreheads.

The seal is said to be in their foreheads for two reasons. First of all, the believer's faith is at the forefront of his mind, and it informs all of his thinking. Your head is what you think with. The forehead represents the forefront of your thinking. Secondly, the believer's faith has the highest place of prominence in his life. When you adorn yourself with jewelry, the higher the ornament is on your body, the more prominent and important it is. An anklet is not as important as a necklace, and a necklace is not as important as a crown. The highest place you can put something is on the forehead. In the Old Testament, the priest that went into the temple had a plate of engraved metal on his forehead that said, *"Holiness to the Lord."* The holiness of God was given the highest place of prominence and importance in the priest's dress.

The point is, Jesus Christ and His saving work has the highest place of prominence and importance in our life. It informs all of our thinking. It is at the forefront of our mind that we are Christians, that God has saved us, and that He is taking us to heaven. It is the matter that is of the highest importance, and nothing is more significant in our lives.

There is not anything literally tattooed onto our foreheads. The seal in the forehead is a metaphor for the idea that the Holy Spirit with the salvation that He conveys is at the forefront of our mind and it has the highest place of prominence in our lives. It is what we lead with.

Negatively, it says in the Old Testament regarding Israel that she had a whore's forehead, meaning that spiritual adultery was at the forefront of Israel's mind and had the highest place of importance in Israel's life.

The forehead is used symbolically of that which is the most important, the most prominent, the most descriptive, and the most characteristic of what you are. This seal is not similar to an implanted computer chip or a barcode tattooed into your forehead; and in the same way, the mark of the beast is not some computer chip or barcode placed into the forehead or hand. It is important to note that the people of God have their mark, and the people of Satan have their mark.

The mark of the beast is not something that is going to occur in the future in the tribulation when Antichrist arises. The mark of the beast is present right now in the life of every person who is unsaved. Every one of them has the mark of the beast. They think like Satan. Satan has the highest place of prominence in their lives. All of his wickedness is at the forefront of their minds. In the same way, every believer has the mark of God, which is the seal of God. Believers think like Christ. The Lord Jesus has the highest place of prominence in their lives. His example and His teaching are at the forefront of their minds.

You are marked in this life either with the seal of God or with the mark of the beast. And just as this seal of God is not physical, the mark of the beast is not physical either.

What we have in 7:1–3 is a restraint upon the execution of God's judgments on the earth until God's people are clearly identified, so that none of those judgments will be brought against them. The angel places God's seal upon these people: he places on them His mark of authentication, declaring that these are the genuine people of God; he places upon them His mark of ownership, declaring that they belong to Him; and he places on them His mark of security, declaring that they are not to be harmed, but protected when God's wrath falls on the earth and all of its inhabitants. This is the significance of the seal on the saints. The intention of God in sealing His people is that they would escape the wrath that is going to fall on the wicked. He says to these four angels, "Do not release the wrath of God until we have identified the people of God, so that this wrath will not fall on them."

We see this foreshadowed in the Passover in Egypt. (Indeed, as we look at the seven trumpets and the seven vials, we are going to see the judgments that fall on the earth are very parallel to the judgments that fell in Egypt.) As the ten plagues fell on Egypt, the Jews in the land of Goshen were spared from those judgments, especially in the tenth plague of the death of the firstborn. The firstborn of the Jews were spared by having the blood of the Passover lamb placed on the doorposts, and the blood was like the seal of God. When the death angel went to kill the firstborn and he saw the blood, he did not execute God's wrath upon those under the protection of this seal—that is, under the protection of the blood of the Passover lamb. If you had the seal of the blood on your door, the judgment did not fall on you; it passed over you.

And so it is, that as God pours out His judgments upon this earth in this age, those sealed with the seal of God will escape the destructive effects of those judgments and not be subject to the wrath they are sent to convey upon the wicked.

This is not to say that those sealed with the seal of God will not experience hardship as God pours out His judgment on the wicked of this age. But it is to say that as believers experience the fallout from God's wrath being poured out on the wicked in this age, the effect it will have on them is that it will be working for their good. Believers will be preserved and sanctified and glorified through the judgments that are sent on the wicked to punish them and destroy them and damn them.

We see this in the life of Daniel. God sent terrible judgments on the people of Israel because of their wickedness. Did Daniel experience some of the fallout from those judgments? Yes he did, but how did God work it together for him? He preserved him, He sanctified him, He brought him to a place of prominence and ministry; and ultimately, He took him to heaven. The same thing that was meant for wrath for the wicked was used to sanctify and bless Daniel, though he did experience suffering as the fallout from God's wrath on the wicked. What works together for evil to the wicked will work together for good for the righteous who are sealed with the seal of God. God's judgments on the wicked will never hurt the saints, though they may create some suffering for the saints.

But oftentimes, the righteous escape the effect of the judgment of God on the wicked altogether because they live lives that are separated from the persons of the wicked, the works of the wicked, and the behaviors of the wicked. As a result, they are separated from the outcomes of the troubles that are sent upon them from God. When you look at all the terrible things that happen to the wicked, a lot of those things happen because of the choices they make to defy the laws of God and to live in disobedience to them. They experience things we never do because we do not do the things they do, and therefore we do not have the consequences they experience.

Notice an Old Testament passage that speaks of the protection from God's judgment that the seal in the forehead affords. Notice Ezekiel 9:1–11: "*He cried also in mine ears with a loud voice, saying, Cause them that have charge over the city to draw near, even every man with his destroying weapon in his hand.* [2] *And, behold, six men came from the way of the higher gate, which lieth toward the north, and every man a slaughter weapon in his hand; and one man among them was clothed with linen, with a writer's inkhorn by his side: and they went in, and stood beside the brazen altar.* [3] *And the glory of the God of Israel was gone up from the cherub, whereupon he was, to the threshold of the house. And he called to the man clothed with linen, which had the writer's inkhorn by his side;* [4] *And the* Lord *said unto him, Go through the midst of the city, through the midst of Jerusalem, and set a mark upon the foreheads of the men that sigh and that cry for all the abominations that be done in the midst thereof."*

He says, "Here are men who are mourning over the sins and the wickedness of their city. Go through and put a mark on their foreheads. That is what your inkhorn is for." He goes through first and marks the righteous people who are grieved with the sins of the age, and then says in verse 5: "*And to the others he said in mine hearing, Go ye after him through the city, and smite: let not your eye spare, neither have ye pity:* [6] *Slay utterly old and young, both maids, and little children, and women: but come not near any man upon whom is the mark; and begin at my sanctuary. Then they began at the ancient men which were before the house.* [7] *And he said unto them, Defile the house, and fill the courts with the slain: go ye forth. And they went forth, and slew in the city.* [8] *And it came to pass, while they were slaying them, and I was left, that I fell upon my face, and cried, and said, Ah Lord* GOD! *wilt thou destroy all the residue of Israel in thy pouring out of thy fury upon Jerusalem?"* (It seemed like there was hardly anybody marked with the mark!) "[9] *Then said he unto me, The iniquity of the house of Israel and Judah is exceeding great, and the land is full of blood, and the city full of perverseness: for they say, The* LORD *hath forsaken the earth, and the* LORD *seeth not.* [10] *And as for me also, mine eye shall not spare, neither will I have pity, but I will recompense their way upon their head.* [11] *And, behold, the man clothed with linen, which had the inkhorn by his side, reported the matter, saying, I have done as thou hast commanded me."*

Ezekiel is saying, "Lord, there were not very many spared; in fact, so few it seemed like You are going to wipe them all out." But no, there were some. When you look at the world today, how many genuine Christians are there? Just a tiny minority. Let us throw out a number and say 5 percent are genuine Christians, which means 95 percent of the world are subject to the wrath of God and bear the mark of the beast. I know a lot more than 5 percent profess faith in Christ, but how many genuine believers are there?

We see from Ezekiel 9 that God's people are always sealed before God's judgment falls. They are identified and protected from those judgments. This is exactly what we see in Revelation 7. Once again, we find repeatedly that the key to understanding Revelation is provided in the Old Testament.

The Sealing of the 144,000

The sealing of the 144,000 is in verses 4–8. Notice verse 4: *"And I heard the number of them which were sealed: and there were sealed an hundred and forty and four thousand of all the tribes of the children of Israel."* He then lists the tribes and says there are twelve thousand sealed out of each of those tribes.

The number used to describe those sealed is clearly a symbolic number. We have previously seen the repeated use of symbolic numbers in the book of Revelation; and indeed, all the numbers in this book are to be taken symbolically unless there is a compelling reason to take them literally. We have seen that the number twelve conveys the concept of the chosen people of God. There are twelve tribes of Israel; there are twelve apostles. These make up the church, as Revelation 21:9–14 makes clear.

We noted in our study of numerology that when numbers are multiplied together, it represents an intensification of the symbolic idea that they represent. Twelve times twelve, which equals 144, is an intensification of the concept of the chosen people of God; therefore, the number 144 fully represents the whole people of God. The number 144 is then multiplied by a thousand, which is ten times ten times ten—ten being the number of perfection.

We have twelve squared and ten cubed, and the multiplication of these symbolic numbers conveys the idea that 144,000 is a perfect representation of the whole number of the saved people of God.

To gain further insight into the meaning of the 144,000, notice Revelation 14. These 144,000 mentioned here are the whole body of people that are redeemed out of the earth. Notice Revelation 14:1–5: *"And I looked, and, lo, a Lamb stood on the mount Sion, and with him an hundred forty and four thousand, having his Father's name written in their foreheads."* There is the seal. It is called the *"Father's name,"* but notice where it is written: in their foreheads.

"[2] *And I heard a voice from heaven, as the voice of many waters, and as the voice of a great thunder: and I heard the voice of harpers harping with their harps:* [3] *And they sung as it were a new song before the throne, and before the four beasts, and the elders: and no man could learn that song but the hundred and forty and four thousand, which were redeemed from the earth.* [4] *These are they which were not defiled with women; for they are virgins"* (that is, they did not commit spiritual adultery by going after other gods). "*These are they which follow the Lamb whithersoever he goeth. These were redeemed from among men, being the firstfruits unto God and to the Lamb.* [5] *And in their mouth was found no guile: for they are without fault before the throne of God.*"

In chapter 14, this 144,000 represents the whole body of the people of God that are redeemed from the earth, who have the seal of God in their foreheads, and who are now standing perfected and glorified before the throne of God. The number 144,000 cannot be literal, because it represents the whole number of the redeemed from the earth who stand before the throne of God, and there are far more than 144,000 people who are saved.

The folly of literalizing this number of 144,000 in chapter 7 is that this same body of people represented by the number 144,000 in 7:4, is represented in 7:9 as being a great multitude which no man can number.

Revelation 7:9: "*After this I beheld, and, lo, a great multitude, which no man could number, of all nations, and kindreds, and people, and tongues, stood before the throne, and before the Lamb, clothed with white robes, and palms in their hands.*" This is the same group that is spoken of in Revelation 14. But now, they are said to be a multitude which no man can number. Anybody can count to 144,000, so it seems plain that this 144,000 is a symbolic number and not a literal number, because it refers to a group of people which "*no man can number*" who are all the redeemed from the face of the earth.

If we literalize these numbers, are we prepared to say that we have exactly 12,000, not 11,999, or 12,001 taken out of each tribe? Does God save a perfectly equal literal number of people out of each literal tribe of Israel? It would be ridiculous to think so. Clearly, these are symbolic numbers.

But the question is, why does our passage refer to these people as being sealed out of these tribes of the children of Israel? The standard teaching of the Dispensationalists is that these 144,000 people are some literal number of ethnic Jews that become saved during some phase of the current age in which we are now living, usually after the rapture and before the second coming. But this can hardly be the case. For one thing, not once in the book of Revelation does John ever draw any distinction between Jewish Christians and Gentile Christians. The Bible makes it clear that, under the New Covenant, there is no difference between the Jew and the Gentile, but we are all one in Christ.

Furthermore, John's list of these twelve tribes does not agree with any biblical list of the twelve tribes found anywhere else in the Bible. For example, the tribe of Dan is omitted from this list. The tribe of Ephraim is omitted from this list. The tribe of Joseph is mentioned, but there was no such tribe in Israel. Joseph had two sons, Ephraim and Manasseh, and those were the tribes that proceeded from Joseph. The tribe of Levi is included when it is ordinarily omitted since it is the thirteenth tribe.

Jacob had twelve sons. But because Joseph became two tribes, Ephraim and Manasseh, the Levites were the thirteenth tribe. If you are going to have twelve tribes, Levi has to be omitted from the list. Levi would be the thirteenth tribe, just like Paul was the thirteenth apostle. The Levites served God as the priestly tribe. They were given no inheritance in the land. The Levites had a special status that was distinct from the twelve tribes, though they were a tribe, just like Paul has a special status distinct from the twelve apostles, though he was an apostle. Levi was a tribe, but distinct from the twelve tribes; and therefore, Levi is ordinarily left out of the list of the tribes.

Furthermore, the order of the tribes is all askew because it starts with the tribe of Judah rather than with the tribe of Reuben who is the firstborn. Jesus came out of the tribe of Judah, and this is why Judah is put in first place—emphasizing the issue of redemption rather than the issue of tribal order by birth.

This very irregular list seems to indicate that John is speaking of spiritual Israel, not ethnic Israel. In other words, he is speaking of New Covenant Israel, which is the church, rather than Old Covenant Israel. James does the same thing in James 1:1, when He describes the church as *"the twelve tribes which are scattered abroad."* Besides, at this point in history, ten of the twelve tribes were lost. You could not even identify them. They were taken into captivity in 722 BC by the Assyrians into the north, integrated into the population, and disappeared through intermarriage. Only Judah and Benjamin came back after the captivity in Babylon and were established in the land of Israel once again; and among the returnees, there were also some Levites.

The church of believers is the true spiritual Israel. The Bible makes this very clear in Galatians 3:6–9, 29. It says: *"Even as Abraham believed God, and it was accounted to him for righteousness. [7] Know ye therefore that they which are of faith"* (those who have faith in Christ), *"the same are the children of Abraham."* If you have faith in Jesus Christ, you are a child of Abraham; thus, you are a spiritual Jew.

Notice verse 8: *"And the scripture, foreseeing that God would justify the heathen"* (that is, the Gentiles) *"through faith, preached before the gospel unto Abraham, saying, In thee shall all nations be blessed.*
9 So then they which be of faith are blessed with faithful Abraham."
Notice that 3:29 says, *"And if ye be Christ's, then are ye Abraham's seed, and heirs according to the promise."*

Those who have the faith of Abraham are the children of Abraham. Christ was the seed of Abraham; believers are the seed of Christ through the new birth. Therefore, all believers are now considered the seed of Abraham. They are spiritual Israel. Believers are the true Jews who are sealed out of all the peoples of the earth and declared to be the real Israel of God.

Notice further Romans 2:28–29: *"For he is not a Jew, which is one outwardly; neither is that circumcision, which is outward in the flesh:*
29 But he is a Jew, which is one inwardly; and circumcision is that of the heart, in the spirit, and not in the letter; whose praise is not of men, but of God." Paul is saying that just because you might be an ethnic Jew, and just because you are circumcised, it does not mean you are a true Jew. The true Jews are those who are circumcised in heart; that is, they have regenerated hearts, they are Jews *"inwardly"* as a result of salvation and faith in Jesus Christ. Christians are the true Jews. Regeneration, whether someone is ethnically Jewish or Gentile, is what defines the true Israel and the true Jew.

Paul says in Philippians 3:3, *"For we are the circumcision, which worship God in the spirit, and rejoice in Christ Jesus, and have no confidence in the flesh."* Paul says that we, Jew and Gentile, are the real Jews because we are those who rejoice in Christ Jesus, not because of some mark in our flesh. We have no concern with genetic descent anymore. We are concerned only and exclusively about regeneration of the heart.

The conclusion is inescapable: It is those who are saved by faith in Jesus Christ who are the true Israel of God and the true children and seed of Abraham.

We see in Revelation 7 that God has chosen people out of various tribes. Each tribe was a distinct people group, and each tribe was in a different geographical location. This conveys the idea that God has chosen the perfect number of people (12,000) out of the various people groups and out of the various geographical locations across the world.

We see that God has chosen people out of various tribes, but out of some tribes, He chose none. There are no Ephraimites there, and there are no Danites there. We see that across the world there are some periods in history in some nations where God chose no people. There was no gospel in some nations, in some periods of time, because there were no elect people in those places at that time in history.

God chose some out of some people groups, and out of some geographical locations, at certain times in history, and He did not choose some out of certain people groups and geographical locations at other times in history. It is His prerogative whom He chooses to elect and save. But what He did choose was the perfect number of people out of the places where He did choose them, and out of the people groups that He chose them from.

We have here a variety of tribes—twelve to be exact. The variety of tribes He has chosen people out of, represent the chosen people of God in various locations and in various identity groups who are saved across the world and down through the ages. It is a multitude that no man can number.

The point of these twelve tribes being mentioned is this: God's electing choices are widely distributed across the broad cross section of humanity, and all across the geography of earth, without universally including every people group and every geographical place at every time in history. This is congruent with what we see in the rest of the Scriptures and what we see in human history.

The central message of our passage is this: When God pours out His wrath against a society that is rebellious and hardened against Him, those who are believers may experience some suffering as a result, but what they experience is not God's judgment, because Romans 8:1 says there is no condemnation for those who are in Christ Jesus. What suffering they experience will only be worked together for their good and not for their harm; for their preservation and not for their destruction; for their sanctification and not for their apostasy; and for their glorification and not for their damnation.

But the wicked who do not have the seal of God will experience the full force of the fury of God against them and all the terror that represents, and they will not be delivered. If the seal of God is not found in the forehead of a person, the angel with the slaughter weapon will destroy them.

The question I have to ask you is this: Are you protected from the wrath of God with the seal of God? Or are you exposed to the wrath of God because the seal of God is absent in your life? How do you know if you have the seal? The seal is the Holy Spirit, as we have seen. If you have the Holy Spirit, then you are going to be bearing the fruit of the Spirit—*love, joy, peace, longsuffering, gentleness, goodness, faith, meekness, and temperance*—all the things listed in Galatians 5:22–23.

Furthermore, He is the *Holy* Spirit, and there will be a heart cry after holiness. Who did the scribe with the inkhorn by his side mark in the forehead? Did he mark the perfect people? No. He marked the people who mourned over the sins they committed and their society committed. They were grieved with sin and they longed for holiness. In a word, they hungered and thirsted after righteousness.

Those that have the seal of God in their forehead are not perfect people, but they are people who love holiness and hate iniquity. They are grieved with their sin and are seeking deliverance from it through Christ and through the pursuit of the means of grace. On them, though sufferings may fall, injury will never occur. Whatever sufferings come will never hurt them but will only sanctify them, preserve them, and prepare them for heaven.

We see the blessed status of the chosen people of God who, upon salvation, are given the seal of God. They are protected from the wrath God is pouring out on the wicked throughout this age, which will find its final expression on the Day of Judgment.

Thank God we are not viewed by God in the same class and category as the unsaved; and therefore, God deals differently with us than He does with them, because we have the seal of God, and they have the mark of the beast.

Choose this day whose mark will be upon you. Go to Christ. Cry out to Him to forgive you, to save you, to redeem you, and to put His mark upon you. Jesus says, *"Him that cometh to me I will in no wise cast out."* Come to Him today. He will receive you and He will protect you.

26

The Church Glorified, Revelation 7:9–17

"[9] After this I beheld, and, lo, a great multitude, which no
man could number, of all nations, and kindreds, and people,
and tongues, stood before the throne, and before the Lamb,
clothed with white robes, and palms in their hands; [10] And
cried with a loud voice, saying, Salvation to our God which
sitteth upon the throne, and unto the Lamb. [11] And all the
angels stood round about the throne, and about the elders
and the four beasts, and fell before the throne on their fac-
es, and worshipped God, [12] Saying, Amen: Blessing, and glory,
and wisdom, and thanksgiving, and honour, and power, and
might, be unto our God for ever and ever. Amen. [13] And one
of the elders answered, saying unto me, What are these which
are arrayed in white robes? and whence came they? [14] And I
said unto him, Sir, thou knowest. And he said to me, These are
they which came out of great tribulation, and have washed
their robes, and made them white in the blood of the Lamb.
[15] Therefore are they before the throne of God, and serve him
day and night in his temple: and he that sitteth on the throne
shall dwell among them. [16] They shall hunger no more, neither
thirst any more; neither shall the sun light on them, nor any
heat. [17] For the Lamb which is in the midst of the throne shall
feed them, and shall lead them unto living fountains of wa-
ters: and God shall wipe away all tears from their eyes."

As we concluded our study of Revelation 6, we looked at the sixth seal in which God is pouring out His wrath on the wicked at the end of the age. We see the wicked who assisted in the work of the four horsemen crying out in terror as they see the wrath of God descending upon them.

The great day of His wrath has come, and who shall be able to stand? They will certainly not be able to stand up to the wrath of the Lamb nor stand before the presence of the Lamb. When Jesus returns, they will fall before Him and be smitten by Him with His rod of iron, and they will be cast into hell forever.

But the good news is that there will be some who will be able to stand before God without fear. They are revealed in 7:9: *"After this I beheld, and, lo, a great multitude, which no man could number, of all nations, and kindreds, and people, and tongues, stood before the throne, and before the Lamb. . ."* Chapter 6 closes with this terrifying cry, *"Who shall be able to stand?"* Chapter 7 answers: "These shall be able to stand."

Who are these people who can stand, and how do they differ from those of Revelation 6:17 who have no chance of standing before the throne? They are those described in 7:1–8, which we looked at in the last chapter. They have the seal of God in their foreheads.

We saw that God restrains the execution of His judgments on the earth until God's people are clearly identified so that none of His judgments will fall upon them. Believers receive the seal of God which is a mark of authentication, ownership, and security. God's people are thus identified and thereby protected from the wrath which He pours out on the ungodly during this age.

This is not to say that God's people do not experience some suffering in this age, but it is to say that whatever suffering they do experience is meant for their good. It is meant to sanctify them and preserve them. Our suffering in this age is not in any way an expression of God's wrath against us because there is no condemnation for those who are in Christ.

When God pours out His wrath against a society that is rebellious and hardened against Him, believers in that society may experience some suffering as a result, but what they are experiencing is not God's judgment. As God's judgment falls on those around them, what falls on believers and falls out in their lives is God working all things together for their good and their godliness. No suffering of any saint who is sealed by God ever results in his spiritual destruction; it only helps him to be more like Jesus, to be matured in the faith, and to be preserved from apostasy.

In the last chapter, we considered the number of the people who were sealed, and we observed that they were chosen from various tribes of the nation of Israel. There were 144,000 sealed—12,000 from each tribe. These numbers are symbolic and were used to convey the idea that the entire body of God's elect, represented by this perfect number 144,000, makes up the true Israel of God. These are the genuine Israelites who are children of Abraham through faith in Jesus Christ. The symbolism of 7:4–8 teaches us that God has chosen the perfect number of people out of various people groups and from various geographical locations.

Verse 9 tells us there are some that are taken from every nation and kindred and people and tongue. Israel is no longer defined by ethnic descent as it was in the Old Testament. It is now defined by divine sovereign election, and it is revealed by the presence of the seal of the Holy Spirit in the lives of these people. As they bring forth the fruit of the Spirit, it is proof they have the seal of the Spirit. Just as Old Covenant Israel was identified by the external mark of circumcision, so New Covenant Israel is identified by the internal mark of circumcision of heart and the sealing of the Spirit, which is then manifested in the behavior of those who bring forth the fruits of regeneration and the indwelling Spirit of God.

What we have in these first eight verses is a symbolic picture of the church as the true Israel of God and the protection she receives from the wrath of God poured out on those who are in rebellion against Him.

As we move into a consideration of verses 9 to 17, we have a revelation of the actual dimension and size of the church and the blessedness she enjoys in the presence of God after she is faithful unto death.

We have the symbolic number 144,000 which speaks of the complete perfection of the full number of the people of God. There is none of God's elect that is not sealed by God. Next, we have an actual description of the number of God's elect in verse 9. How large is the actual number of God's elect? Is it 144,000? It is not. It is a multitude that no man can number.

We have seen the church sealed in verses 1 to 8. Now we want to look at the church glorified in verses 9 to 17.

Revelation 7:9–17 is one of the most precious passages in all of the Scripture because in it we see in great detail the destiny and blessedness of the believer in Jesus Christ. The book of Revelation is sprinkled with passages like the last half of chapter 7. The purpose of this constant reminder of the destiny of the suffering saints is to encourage them in their spiritual warfare and sufferings for the name and the gospel of Jesus Christ. The encouragement offered to saints in the midst of spiritual warfare is this: though you may be suffering now, here is your destiny, and this destiny makes the suffering experienced in getting there all worthwhile.

The purpose of passages like this second half of Revelation 7 is to tell us that our afflictions are temporary, but our joy is eternal. It is to tell us that the sufferings of this present time are not worthy to be compared with the glory that shall be revealed in us. As Christians, we go through much hardship and we endure many sufferings in serving the Lord Jesus Christ on this earth. We have to deny ourselves, we have to take up our cross daily, and we have to follow Him. We have to lose our lives.

Sometimes we ask ourselves: Is it worth it? The pain and suffering and rejection and scorn and shame we endure for following Christ—is it really worth it? This passage in Revelation 7 and many more just like it answers that question and declares in no uncertain terms: It is worth it indeed!

This passage is a balm to the wounds of the suffering saints. It says to them, "These light afflictions that are but for a moment are going to work for you a far more exceeding and eternal weight of glory. Do not look on these things which are seen, but on the things which are unseen. Do not dwell on the present sufferings, but on the future glory. Recognize that this short time of suffering is nothing compared to the eternity of joy you will have in the presence of Christ."

Remember this: if you suffer with Him, you will also reign with Him. Here is what that reign looks like. Keep your eye focused on the prize, endure the cross, despise the shame, and run the race with patience. Soon you will cross the finish line and enter into the glorious winner's circle. Here is what that winner's circle looks like. Just because your side aches and your muscles groan and your joints hurt as you run the race in this life, do not quit, do not stop, and do not turn aside. Press on toward the prize of the high calling of God in Christ.

Here is what that prize looks like.

Let us consider this eternal reward that those who faithfully persevere through tribulation and persecution obtain when they reach the end of their lives. Let us consider the glory of heaven.

Heaven Is a Place That is Well Populated

Notice verse 9. *"After this I beheld, and, lo, a great multitude, which no man could number, of all nations, and kindreds, and people, and tongues, stood before the throne, and before the Lamb, clothed with white robes, and palms in their hands."*

John sets before us an unforgettable picture of the vast crowd of people from every nation on earth who are now experiencing the indescribable joy of heaven. This vast crowd is innumerable. It is too large to be counted. John could not even begin to start counting. He recognized it was a hopeless endeavor.

The definite symbolic number of 144,000 in 7:4 symbolized the perfect completion of the church. None was missing. But the great throng described in verse 9 shows the impossibility of counting the vast number of redeemed symbolically represented by the number 144,000. Who are these people before the throne, this vast uncountable multitude? They are both Jews and Gentiles. We are told that they come from *"all nations and kindreds and people and tongues."* No sector of humanity is excluded from heaven.

These are the same categories of people that are spoken of in Revelation 5:9. It says, *"And they sang a new song, saying, Thou art worthy to take the book, and to open the seals thereof: for thou wast slain, and hast redeemed us to God by thy blood out of every kindred, and tongue, and people, and nation."*

In chapter 5, Jesus was seen as having just ascended to heaven from His work on the cross, and that work was declared to have redeemed a people—a people out of every kindred and tongue and people and nation. Now in chapter 7, we see the application of that redemption to the perfect and complete body of God's elect. We see that the people Jesus purchased have been brought into heaven, and this body of saved people comes from every nation and kindred and people and tongue.

In heaven, every national group, every ethnic group, every social group, and every linguistic group is represented. No one is excluded from heaven but those who exclude themselves. Only by rebellious unbelief can you stay out of heaven. The vastness of this multitude tells us of the vast generosity of God's electing love. It is neither small nor narrow. It is immense and boundless, stretching across all ages and all categories of people.

The vastness of this multitude tells us of the tremendous success of the evangelistic efforts of the people of God through the ages. Often when we witness, we ask ourselves if anybody is going to be saved. It seems we see so little by way of results! Our passage is clear: a multitude which no man can number is going to be saved through the witness of the people of God. Be encouraged. God has an uncountable number of people to be led to Christ, and when you preach the gospel to the lost, you are going to be involved in leading some of them to Him.

Indeed, what we have in verse 9 is the fulfillment of the promise made repeatedly to Abraham in Genesis 13:16, 15:5, and 22:17, when God said to him that his seed would be like the dust of the earth, his seed would be like the stars of heaven, and his seed would be like the sand of the sea. If you can count the dust of the earth, the stars in the universe, and all the grains of sand on the seashores, then you can count this multitude before the throne.

They are standing before the throne and before the Lamb. They are serene, they are confident, and they are certain of their approval by God and their acceptance with God. They are not in the condition of those in Revelation 6:15–17. There is also a great multitude represented in that passage, too: *"And the kings of the earth, and the great men, and the rich men, and the chief captains, and the mighty men, and every bondman, and every free man,"*(that covers every category of people) *"hid themselves in the dens and in the rocks of the mountains;* [16] *And said to the mountains and rocks, Fall on us, and hide us from the face of him that sitteth on the throne, and from the wrath of the Lamb:* [17] *For the great day of his wrath is come; and who shall be able to stand?"* We see the terror, the fear, and the dread in the people of the sixth seal.

But here we see the serenity, confidence, and joy of those whom God has sealed. Colossians 1:22 says of the people that stand before the throne in Revelation 7:9 that they are "*holy and unblameable and unreproveable in His sight.*" God has not one negative thing to say about them. As Jude 1:24 promised, they are "*faultless*" before the presence of God. As Hebrews 10:19 says, they have "*boldness to enter into the holiest*" dwelling place of God Himself.

Why can they stand before God when others cringe in the presence of God? Because verse 9 tells us that they are "*clothed with white robes*," and these white robes are symbolic of their having been cleansed from their sin and adorned in the righteousness of Jesus Christ. They do not have on the filthy rags of those of Revelation 6:17; they have on the glorious wedding garment of Christ. Through the saving work of Jesus Christ, they have been made as morally pure as God Himself. They are holy as He is holy. Therefore, they can stand unafraid in His presence. Not only can they stand unafraid; they can stand with confidence and boldness.

The good news of the gospel is that you will not cringe before God on the Day of Judgment. Instead, you will be confident before God on the Day of Judgment. You will be able to humbly hold up your head and behold His face and not have to cast your eyes down in any kind of shame or fear. That is what Jesus Christ has done for you in His cleansing, saving work, and in the lovely robe of righteousness He has provided for you. Knowing that Jesus has brought you from crying and cringing before God, to being confident and cheerful in the presence of God, is what will move you to eternal worship and praise of God for all eternity. Heaven is a place that is well populated with those who possess a perfect righteousness and are therefore able to stand in the presence of God.

Heaven Is a Place That Is Full of Praise

Our text says in verse 9 that they stood before the throne and before the Lamb, clothed in white robes and with *"palms in their hands;*
[10] *And cried with a loud voice, saying, Salvation to our God which sitteth upon the throne, and unto the Lamb."*

The last phrase of verse 9 tells us that these people before the throne had palm branches in their hands. Palm branches were used during the Feast of Tabernacles for the purpose of building booths to temporarily live in. The Feast of Tabernacles, in which palm branches figured so prominently, was a celebration of God's protection of Israel during her pilgrimage from Egypt to the Promised Land.

When Moses led Israel out of Egypt, it took them forty years to get to the Promised Land, and they lived in tents along the way. The Feast of Tabernacles, in which they would build small tentlike structures out of palm branches and live in them for a week, was designed to remind them that they were sojourners during those forty years, and how God protected them and watched over them during that time. It was a time of tremendous joy and rejoicing as they built their little shelters and praised and worshiped God as they reflected on His goodness in preserving and providing for Israel on her journey from Egypt to the Promised Land.

Likewise, in heaven we will be celebrating God's preservation and protection of us during our pilgrimage through this life as we journeyed to heaven through the wilderness of a God-hating and Christ-rejecting world. There was nothing in the wilderness that was friendly to the Jews as they traveled through it. There is nothing in this world that is friendly to us as we travel through it either. Galatians 1:4 says this present world is an evil world. John the Baptist himself said, regarding his identity and ministry, *"I am the voice of one crying in the wilderness."*

That is what we live in: a wilderness. We are on a pilgrimage through this life, dwelling in tents, and looking for the city whose builder and maker is God. When we finally get to that city, we are going to look back on that journey and pilgrimage, and we are going to say, "Jesus led me all the way. Jesus protected me every step." The palm branches are reminiscent of that rejoicing in the protection and provision that God made for us during that pilgrimage.

In verse 10, we see the praise of these saints who stand before the throne. It says that they *"cried with a loud voice, saying, Salvation to our God which sitteth upon the throne, and unto the Lamb."* This phrase, *"Salvation to our God which sitteth upon the throne, and unto the Lamb,"* is a declaration of the saints that both the Father and the Son are the cause of their salvation. One of them did the electing and the other did the redeeming. One chose the 144,000 and the other washed them in His blood.

The saints recognize that both the Father and the Son are the cause of their salvation, and both the Father and the Son are to be praised for their salvation. They recognize they could never stand before the throne and before the Lamb without the salvation provided by the Father and the Son. For that priceless gift they give endless praise to them both, and they say, "We are here because They saved us. Our salvation is ascribed entirely to the One who sits on the throne, and to the Lamb."

But not only do the redeemed saints praise the Father and the Son for the salvation They provided to God's elect, but the angels praise the Father and the Son as well. Notice verses 11 and 12: *"And all the angels stood round about the throne, and about the elders and the four beasts, and fell before the throne on their faces, and worshipped*

God, [12] *Saying, Amen: Blessing, and glory, and wisdom, and thanksgiving, and honour, and power, and might, be unto our God for ever and ever. Amen."*

The angels are righteous before God. They have not received salvation. They have no need of salvation. Instead, they worship God for who He is. Once again, these angels set forth the sevenfold ascription of praise they offered in 5:11–12. It says: *"And I beheld, and I heard the voice of many angels round about the throne,* [12] *Saying with a loud voice, Worthy is the Lamb that was slain to receive power, and riches, and wisdom, and strength, and honour, and glory, and blessing."* There was a sevenfold ascription of praise in 5:12, and now in 7:12, they offer that same sevenfold description of praise, with one change. "Riches" is removed and "thanksgiving" is put in its place, but the other six are the same.

The angels declare that the Father and the Son are worthy to receive praise and worship for the blessings They bestow. They are worthy to receive praise and worship for the glory They possess. They are worthy to receive praise and worship for the wisdom They display. They are worthy to receive praise and worship for the thanksgiving They are owed. They are worthy to receive praise and worship for the honor They deserve. They are worthy to receive praise and worship for the power They exercise. Finally, They are worthy to receive praise and worship for the might They exert.

All the Father and the Son did in providing salvation for the saints not only provokes the saints to worship and praise God, but it also provokes the angels to worship and praise God for what He did for those saints. The angels have seen all of the attributes of God displayed in the salvation of the redeemed saints standing before the throne, and they cannot contain themselves. As they hear the saints praise the Father and the Son, they have to add their voices and praise the Father and Son as well, and join in that thunderous expression of praise to God on the throne and to the Lamb.

In heaven, there will be perfect harmony between the praise of the saints and the praise of the angels before the throne. If you wonder what your loved ones in heaven are doing right now, this is what they are doing. They are standing up there saying, *"Salvation to our God which sitteth upon the throne, and unto the Lamb."* Then they listen to the angels as they give the sevenfold ascription of praise, and then they all say in unison, *"Amen!"*

Heaven Is a Place That Is Free from Tribulation

Notice verses 13 and 14: *"And one of the elders answered, saying unto me, What are these which are arrayed in white robes? and whence came they?* [14] *And I said unto him, Sir, thou knowest. And he said to me, These are they which came out of great tribulation."*

In verse 13, the elder asked John this question, not because the elder does not know the answer or needs information, but in order to focus John's attention on the reason these saints are able to be in heaven, and why they are not cringing like the people in Revelation 6. So he asks: "Where did these people come from? What is their history? What have they passed through? How did they get here? What makes them both able and worthy to stand before the throne of God?"

John says very respectfully, "Sir, you tell me. You know the answer better than I do. I am a student at your feet, ready to learn from your instruction." The elder supplies the answer to him. He tells John, "If you stand before the throne of God in heaven, you are among those who have passed through and endured great tribulation." Notice he says in verse 14, *"These are they which came out of great tribulation."* He speaks about their history, and their history is that they came out of great tribulation. Notice: They came *"out"* of great tribulation. They are no longer in it. They are freed from it. They will never experience it again. It is behind them.

This great tribulation referred to here is not that short period between the loosing of Satan and the return of Christ, which is often referred to by theologians as "The Great Tribulation." It is fitting to use that terminology. Jesus spoke of *"great tribulation"* in Matthew 24:21 which describes that short period. This period between the loosing of Satan and the second coming of Christ is called "The Great Tribulation" due to the extreme intensity of the trans-national persecution of Christians that occurs under the reign of Antichrist. We are going to see this as we proceed through the book of Revelation. It is that symbolic short three-and-a-half-day period, as opposed to the symbolic long three-and-a-half-year period that describes the New Covenant era.

However, the great tribulation referred to here in Revelation 7:14 is the tribulation which began at the ascension of Christ into heaven when Satan was cast out of heaven and down to the earth. It will continue until the second coming of Christ, with a tremendous intensification of it right at the very end.

Where was Satan before the ascension of Christ into heaven? We read in Job 1–2 that Satan had access to God in heaven. God asked, "Where did you come from?" Satan said, "I was walking back and forth in the earth, and going to and fro in it." This conversation took place in heaven. From the time of the fall of man until the ascension of Christ, Satan had direct access to the throne and the person of God. That is not to say he was not fallen or that he was not evil, but it is to say that he was able to be in heaven. However, at the ascension of Christ, something happened. There was war in heaven between Michael and his angels and Satan and his angels, and Satan was cast out of heaven and down to earth, as we read in Revelation 12. When that happened, all hell broke loose on earth.

Notice Revelation 12. The entire birth, life, death, resurrection, and ascension of Christ are included in verse 5. *"And she brought forth a man child, who was to rule all nations with a rod of iron; and her child was caught up to God, and to his throne."*

Notice what follows Christ's ascension to heaven in verse 6–11: *"And the woman fled into the wilderness"* (that is, the church fled into the wilderness), *"where she hath a place prepared of God, that they should feed her there a thousand two hundred and threescore days"* (three and a half years). "[7] *And there was war in heaven: Michael and his angels fought against the dragon; and the dragon fought and his angels,* [8] *And prevailed not; neither was their place found any more in heaven.* [9] *And the great dragon was cast out, that old serpent, called the Devil, and Satan, which deceiveth the whole world: he was cast out into the earth, and his angels were cast out with him.* [10] *And I heard a loud voice saying in heaven, Now is come salvation, and strength, and the kingdom of our God, and the power of his Christ: for the accuser of our brethren is cast down, which accused them before our God day and night.* [11] *And they overcame him by the blood of the Lamb, and by the word of their testimony; and they loved not their lives unto the death."* Now heaven no longer has Satan in it. He has been kicked out.

Notice the outcome for both heaven and earth in verse 12: *"Therefore rejoice, ye heavens, and ye that dwell in them."* You are never going to have to be in the presence of Satan ever again. That is a cause for rejoicing. But look at the next phrase: *"Woe to the inhabiters of the earth and of the sea! for the devil is come down unto you, having great wrath, because he knoweth that he hath but a short time."* Now

Satan is dwelling on the earth, he is furious, his doom has been sealed, and he knows he only has until all of the elect are gathered and then he is finished. Therefore, he is going to do all the damage he can in the time he has left.

Verse 13: "*And when the dragon saw that he was cast unto the earth, he persecuted the woman*" (the true Israel of God, the church) "*which brought forth the man child*" (who is Jesus). "[14] *And to the woman were given two wings of a great eagle, that she might fly into the wilderness, into her place, where she is nourished for a time, and times, and half a time*" (three-and-a-half years, the entire church age), "*from the face of the serpent.*"

"[15] *And the serpent cast out of his mouth water as a flood*" (a flood of persecution) "*after the woman, that he might cause her to be carried away of the flood.*" The flood of persecution that wicked people bring against the church is enormous. "[16] *And the earth helped the woman, and the earth opened her mouth, and swallowed up the flood which the dragon cast out of his mouth.*"

We have been protected by God in this age from annihilation, which is what Satan sought to accomplish as he brought persecution upon us through one government or another. Verse 17: "*And the dragon was wroth with the woman, and went to make war with the remnant of her seed*" (all who have been born of her), "*which keep the commandments of God, and have the testimony of Jesus Christ.*"

The point of this passage, especially verses 12 and 17, is that when the ascension happened, great tribulation began on the earth because Satan was cast down to the earth. The persecution of the people of God was carried on and carried out at a scale that the world had never previously experienced. To support this assertion, notice in Daniel 12 that an interesting individual is mentioned, and an interesting event is described.

Notice Daniel 12:1: "*And at that time shall Michael stand up, the great prince which standeth for the children of thy people.*" We just read about Michael in Revelation 12. He was the angel who stood up and led the battle against Satan and cast Satan and his angels out of heaven. Daniel 12:1 is talking about that event that took place at the ascension of Christ. It goes on to say, "*and there shall be a time of trouble, such as never was since there was a nation even to that same time: and at that time thy people shall be delivered, every one that shall be found written in the book.*" Those written in the book are those who have the seal of God. And what is the next event? Notice verse 2: *"And many of them that sleep in the dust of the earth shall awake, some to everlasting life, and some to shame and everlasting contempt."*

Daniel 12:1–2 covers the time period from Michael standing up and casting Satan out of heaven until the return of Christ, when the resurrection happens and the sheep and the goats are divided. The time frame between Michael standing up and the final resurrection occurring is called a *"time of trouble,"* such as never was since the first nation was formed on the face of the earth. The point is that we are living in the great tribulation right now. It began when Satan was cast to the earth. It will end when Jesus returns, and at the end of this time there will be a massive intensification of it when Satan is loosed. But right now, we are in the time of great tribulation.

John himself spoke of presently being in this time of *"[the] tribulation"* in Revelation 1:9. That is why he was on the isle of Patmos. It says, *"I John, who also am your brother, and companion in [the] tribulation"* (the article "the" is there in the original language) *"and in the kingdom and patience of Jesus Christ, was in the isle that is called Patmos, for the word of God, and for the testimony of Jesus Christ."* John is preaching the word of God, he is giving testimony of his salvation by Jesus Christ and he is experiencing great tribulation, he is being persecuted, he is exiled to Patmos, and he is saying, I am in *"the tribulation."*

Notice Revelation 2. This is the suffering church, the church at Smyrna. Reading from verse 8: *"And unto the angel of the church in Smyrna write; These things saith the first and the last, which was dead, and is alive;* [9] *I know thy works, and [the] tribulation and poverty, (but thou art rich) and I know the blasphemy of them which say they are Jews, and are not, but are the synagogue of Satan.* [10] *Fear none of those things which thou shalt suffer: behold, the devil"* (the person that was cast down to the earth and is now actively persecuting the church in a way he never did before) *"shall cast some of you into prison, that ye may be tried; and ye shall have tribulation ten days"* (the number ten is symbolic—it is the number of perfection), *"be thou faithful unto death, and I will give thee a crown of life."*

He says that you are going to be martyred. There have been far more martyrs for the name of Christ in the New Covenant era than there were in the previous 4,000 years. Jesus promised us that our life would be a life of tribulation. He said in John 16:33, *"In the world ye shall have tribulation: but be of good cheer; I have overcome the world."* In Acts 14:21–22, it says that Paul went about preaching the gospel, strengthening the churches, and telling them that they *"must through much tribulation enter into the kingdom of God."*

All of these passages combined together tell us that the period between the first and second coming of Christ is a period of extraordinarily great tribulation for the followers of Christ. Because Satan is now cast down to the earth, the persecution is greater than the Old Testament saints ever knew or experienced. Old Testament saints certainly experienced much tribulation, but now there is a greatly elevated level of tribulation. It is to the one who overcomes this tribulation by remaining faithful to Christ through it that all that the promises of entering heaven are made. The saints prove the genuineness of their faith by persevering through great tribulations for His name and for His truth without turning back or turning away.

The point is this: All true believers go through great tribulation and none who get to heaven escape it. Who are these people in heaven? It says specifically in verse 9 that they are *"a great multitude, which no man could number of all nations, and kindreds, and people, and tongues."* There are a lot of things that differentiate them: nations, people, kindreds, and tongues. But there is one thing they universally possess—and that is, they all, without exception, suffered great tribulation.

This great tribulation cannot be referring to just the saints that live between the loosing of Satan and the second coming. This is a picture of all the saints, all 144,000, the complete and total number of the elect of God, a multitude which no man can number. Every one of them comes out of the great tribulation. All true believers go through great tribulation and no one who gets to heaven escapes it. This great tribulation that all of us go through takes many forms and it varies in its expression from believer to believer, but all experience it in one way or another.

Christian, if you have great tribulation in your life that has tempted you to turn away from Christ, understand that what you are going through is nothing unusual. Every single saint before you has gone through it, and every single saint after you will go through it, because there is no saint in heaven who has not gone through it. Inflicting great tribulation on the saints is the work of Satan in this age, and no one escapes his assaults. God has no children who do not come out of a life of great tribulation.

You may think that your tribulation is not as great as someone else's, but the word "great" is a relative term. A mouse is great in size compared to an ant, but it is not great in size compared to an elephant. Great tribulation might look entirely different to you than it looks to someone else based on your capacities, your resources, your gifts and graces, and on the amount of the presence and power of Christ given to you. But every person in his particular situation, with his particular abilities and degree of grace, experiences what is, for him, great tribulation.

Maybe you were not burned at the stake and the other believer was. But you have gone through things that are just as bad in comparison to what the other person went through in light of your capacity for handling difficulty. Christ provides great grace to those in great tribulation, and less grace to those in less tribulation. God promises in 2 Corinthians 12:9: *"My grace is sufficient for thee, for my strength is made perfect in weakness."* Those who were burned at the stake had great grace—far greater than those who do not face a trial of that magnitude. The greatness of the tribulation is directly related to the capacity for suffering you are given in your particular life circumstances. Every believer, in light of his individual life circumstances, goes through great tribulation. Jesus said that if they have persecuted Him, they will persecute you. If you are not persecuted for the sake of Christ, then you have to ask yourself: "Am I really a disciple of Christ at all? Am I really living for Him and am I living in defiance of Satan and his helpers?"

Heaven Is a Place That Is Completely Pure

Notice verses 13 and 14: *"And one of the elders answered, saying unto me, What are these which are arrayed in white robes? and whence came they?* [14] *And I said unto him, Sir, thou knowest. And he said to me, These are they which came out of great tribulation, and have washed their robes, and made them white in the blood of the Lamb."*

Those who stand before the throne are *"clothed in white robes."* They have washed their robes and made them white in the blood of the Lamb. Notice 7:14 says: *"These are they which. . .have washed their robes, and made them white in the blood of the Lamb."*

Washing their robes and making them white in the blood of the Lamb is a metaphor which speaks of the purity they obtained through the washing away of their sins by the substitutionary, saving work of Jesus Christ. He shed His blood on the cross to provide an atonement to cleanse them from their sins.

Isaiah 1:18 says, *"Come now, and let us reason together, saith the* L*ORD: though your sins be as scarlet, they shall be as white as snow; though they be red like crimson, they shall be as wool."* The only time you can take red sins and wash them in red blood and obtain a white garment is through the saving work of Jesus Christ. It says in Ephesians 1:7, "*We have redemption through his blood, the forgiveness of sins, according to the riches of his grace.*"

This is why they are able to stand before the throne. It is not only because they proved the genuineness of their faith by their faithfulness through great tribulation, but because their only object of faith was the Lord Jesus Christ and His saving work for the forgiveness of their sins.

For those in heaven, the battle with sin is over. It is over forever. They have no sin on their record and they have no sin in their persons, and this is why they are pictured as clothed in white robes. On earth they hungered and thirsted after righteousness, and in heaven they are filled with righteousness. They are perfectly pure, with no blemish, no spot, and no wrinkle on their character. They are holy as God is holy, and their character is as pure as His. Heaven is a place that is perfectly pure, and it is perfectly pure people who are washed in the blood of the Lamb who are present there.

You can be washed from all of your sins by the blood of Jesus Christ, no matter how terrible they are, by repenting of those sins and by believing in Jesus as your Savior. First John 1:7 says, "*. . .the blood of Jesus Christ his Son cleanseth us from all sin.*"

It says in 1 Corinthians 6:9–11: *"Be not deceived: neither fornicators, nor idolaters, nor adulterers, nor [cross-dressers, nor homosexuals],* [10] *Nor thieves, nor covetous, nor drunkards, nor revilers, nor extortioners, shall inherit the kingdom of God."* People who do such things and practice them cannot inherit the kingdom of God. If we appear before God with any of those sins on our record and in our character, we are doomed. He says, "[11] *And such were some of you: but ye are washed, but ye are sanctified, but ye are justified in the name of the Lord Jesus, and by the Spirit of God.*"

There is no one who cannot be washed in the blood of the Lamb. There is no one who cannot make his character white by going to the fountain for sin and uncleanness and plunging himself into the grace and mercy of Jesus Christ, and saying to Him, "Lord Jesus, wash me and cleanse me from my sins."

Heaven is a place that is completely pure, and only pure people will be there. You ask, "How can I become pure so I can be there?" Answer: You can be washed in the saving sacrifice of Jesus Christ by repenting of your sins and asking the Lord Jesus to save you and cleanse you from them. If we confess our sins, He is faithful and just to forgive us our sins, and to cleanse us from all unrighteousness.

Heaven Is a Place That Is Totally Peaceful

Notice verses 15 to 17. It says, "*Therefore,*" because they believed in Christ for the cleansing of their sin, and because they proved the genuineness of their faith in Christ by persevering through great tribulation, they "*are. . . before the throne of God, and serve him day and night in his temple: and he that sitteth on the throne shall dwell among them.* [16] *They shall hunger no more, neither thirst any more; neither shall the sun light on them, nor any heat.* [17] *For the Lamb which is in the midst of the throne shall feed them, and shall lead them unto living fountains of waters: and God shall wipe away all tears from their eyes.*"

Verse 15 says: "*Therefore are they before the throne of God, and serve him day and night in his temple.*" We love to serve the Lord Jesus Christ, but our flesh resists serving Him. We really struggle to serve the Lord as much as we would like to. But in heaven, the struggle to serve Christ will be gone. Service to Him will be all that we want to do, and the resistance of the flesh against that desire will vanish.

Heaven will be a place of activity. There will be much work and service to be done, and we will never tire of doing it. It says we will serve Him day and night. We will have zeal and energy that enable us to never have to sleep again. We can just go on serving and serving without intermission because we will have the strength and the zeal and the desire to do it. We will find our greatest joy in serving God in His temple without rest or remission because we will have unwearied strength to do so, we will have unlimited zeal to do so, and we will derive endless satisfaction and pleasure from doing so.

But it will not be some distant and detached deity that we will be serving. It says in verse 15 that we are before the throne of God, and He that sits on the throne will *"dwell among"* us. The meaning of this language is that He will spread His tabernacle over us. The idea is that He will bring us into His dwelling place—into His very home. He will live in our midst. Our fellowship with Him will be perfect and continuous. It will be all we could ever want in a relationship with God. We will serve Him, He will live with us, we will live with Him, and there will be an intimate fellowship of service and love flowing back and forth between Him and us for eternity.

Notice verse 16: *"They shall hunger no more, neither thirst any more; neither shall the sun light on them, nor any heat."* That is, there will be nothing we desire that we do not have, and all of our needs will be fully met. Verse 16 is based on Isaiah 49:10. This passage speaks prophetically of what Messiah will do; and in Revelation 7:16, we see Him as having done it. Isaiah 49:10 says prophetically: *"They shall not hunger nor thirst; neither shall the heat nor sun smite them: for he that hath mercy on them shall lead them, even by the springs of water shall he guide them."*

What was promised in the Old Testament is provided in the New Testament. There will be no unmet needs in heaven like there are on earth. Heaven will be a place of full provision and full protection.

We must understand that the Holy Land was a place of burning sun and scorching heat that assaulted the health and well-being of the people. In Israel, the sun was not your friend. People constantly sought protection from the damage it could do to them. Did you ever wonder why in those incredibly hot climates people are wearing full-body robes? You wonder whether those clothes do not make them sweat. But they would not survive long if their skin were exposed to such brutal solar intensity. Therefore, the sun's scorching heat became a metaphor for any kind of harmful assault upon the people of God.

But in heaven, nothing and no one will assault us: nothing in nature, nothing in humanity, nothing in angels, and nothing in God. We will never be hungry, and we will never be harmed. Those in heaven are full and they are safe.

Verse 17: *"For the Lamb which is in the midst of the throne shall feed them, and shall lead them unto living fountains of waters: and God shall wipe away all tears from their eyes."* Verse 17 says we will be fed physically. The garden of Eden will be restored and we shall have all we need to eat and drink. The black horse of famine and scarcity will never ride in heaven.

We will not only be fed physically, but we will also be fed spiritually. Never again will we have to hunger and thirst after righteousness. We will be filled. The Bread of Life will be there to satisfy our spiritual hunger, and the Water of Life will be there to quench our spiritual thirst. In a word, Christ will feed our bodies and Christ will feed our souls; and furthermore, Christ will comfort our hearts.

Notice the last phrase of verse 17: *"and God shall wipe away all tears from their eyes."* There are many things on this earth that cause many tears: disappointment, rejection, loss, pain, and failure. But every cause for sorrow will be removed, and every means of happiness will be supplied. Just as life without tears is impossible on earth, life with tears will be impossible in heaven, because every cause of tears will be completely and permanently removed.

We will have unlimited and uninterrupted happiness in heaven. Psalm 16:11 says, *"In thy presence is fullness of joy; at thy right hand there are pleasures for evermore."* There, "fullness" and "forever" describes the happiness of people in heaven. How could you ever have tears when you are full of happiness forever and there is nothing else?

Heaven is a place that is totally peaceful. There is no anxiety about what we are going to do—we are going to serve the Lord; no anxiety about God's attitude toward us—He dwells with us; no anxiety about what I am going to eat or drink—He will feed us; no anxiety about whether I might suffer some kind of disappointment or rejection or loss or failure—none of that will be there. All conflict will be gone forever.

This is what enables us to persevere through the great tribulation that every one of us lives in right now. We endure because we understand that if we persevere through this tribulation, we will enjoy a future of infinite blessedness in heaven—a place that is well populated, where all our beloved brethren will be; a place that is full of praise, where the Father and the Son will be glorified for the salvation They provided and the protection They gave as we traveled through the wilderness of this world; a place that is free from tribulation caused by Satan and his helpers; a place that is completely pure, where there will be no sin; and a place that is totally peaceful, where there will be nothing to disturb our joy and happiness forever.

Now if that is your destiny, but you have to go through the humility of confessing yourself a sinner and believing in Christ as your Savior; and you have to go through tribulation and struggle in this life to get there; is it not worth it? If you can get to a place that is full of people you love, that is full of praise to God, that is free from all tribulation, that is completely pure from all sin, and that is totally peaceful in every respect, is not the humility of saying you are a sinner and you want Jesus to save you worth it? Is not the difficulty of persevering through the worst kind of tribulations worth it?

This book was written to encourage suffering saints by giving them a vision of the outcome and the end of their suffering for Christ. When you start getting really troubled about the Christian life and all the tribulation and hardship and struggle you have, read this chapter and tell yourself that this is where it is all leading. When you do, you will be able to hang on for one more day, and one more day, and one more day, until finally one day you pass into the presence of God. Keep that vision before you, and the great tribulation you are presently going through will be endurable.

27

The Seventh Seal Opened, Revelation 8:1–6

"1 And when he had opened the seventh seal, there was silence in heaven about the space of half an hour. 2 And I saw the seven angels which stood before God; and to them were given seven trumpets. 3 And another angel came and stood at the altar, having a golden censer; and there was given unto him much incense, that he should offer it with the prayers of all saints upon the golden altar which was before the throne. 4 And the smoke of the incense, which came with the prayers of the saints, ascended up before God out of the angel's hand. 5 And the angel took the censer, and filled it with fire of the altar, and cast it into the earth: and there were voices, and thunderings, and lightnings, and an earthquake. 6 And the seven angels which had the seven trumpets prepared themselves to sound."

The transition from Revelation chapter 7 to chapter 8 brings us to the third parallel section of this book.

When we introduced the book of Revelation, we said it was not written in a linear fashion; instead, it was written in a cyclic fashion in which it repeatedly takes us on a journey through the time period between the first and second coming of Christ.

There are seven of these parallel journeys, each of which emphasizes different aspects of that time period. We have been through two of these parallel sections of this book already, and now we enter the third.

The first parallel section was in chapters 1 to 3, which opened with a vision of the resurrected and glorified Christ addressing the seven churches. These seven churches represent and illustrate the challenges and triumphs that churches will face and experience between the first and second coming of Christ. That section closed with an allusion to the great marriage supper of the Lamb that will occur at the second coming when we will sit with the Lord Jesus Christ in His throne. This first parallel section took us from the resurrection to the second coming, and it focused on the spiritual warfare the churches will face during that time frame.

The second parallel section was in chapters 4 through 7. It opened with a vision of the resurrected Christ being given all authority in heaven and in earth when He was given the scroll that was sealed with seven seals. As each seal was opened it told us how evil men would behave between the first and second coming of Christ. We looked at the metaphor of the four horsemen and saw that evil men will carry out their evil work of pursuing conquest and instigating wars and causing famine and bringing about death. We also saw that evil men will hate and persecute and martyr Christians during this age. All of this was disclosed in the first five seals. But we saw in the sixth seal that at the end of the age when Jesus returns, His wrath will fall on the wicked, while the righteous saints will be protected from that wrath and will be brought into the glories of heaven to be in the presence of Christ forever.

So the first parallel section told us what the churches would experience between the first and second coming of Christ. The second parallel section told us how evil men would conduct themselves in the world and toward Christ and Christians between the first and second coming of Christ.

We now begin the third parallel section, which spans chapters 8 through 11. In this third parallel section, the seven trumpets are sounded. We saw seven churches in the first parallel section; we saw seven seals in the second parallel section; and now in the third parallel section we are going to see seven trumpets.

These trumpets indicate various kinds of judgments that God is going to pour out upon the wicked during the time between the first and second coming of Christ. The work of the four horsemen and their persecution of the Christians will not go unanswered by God. At the same time that the seals are revealing the works of evil men, God is sending forth His trumpets of judgment upon them.

These trumpets, just like the seals, do not represent a chronological series of events; rather, they are events that characterize the period between the first and the second coming. The seals and the trumpets occur throughout this age, they occur around the world, and they occur over and over through the generations. The four horsemen ride in every century and around the world. Christians are persecuted and martyred in every century and around the world. Likewise, the trumpet judgments occur in every century and around the world. The only chronological aspect of the seals and the trumpets is when they speak of the execution of the final judgment at the end of this age, which we saw in the sixth seal, and which we will see in the seventh trumpet.

The purpose of these trumpets is to bring temporal physical and spiritual judgments on the wicked for the evil that they have done and to call them to repentance. The trumpets are a sample of God's wrath to come. They are warnings to flee from the far greater wrath that is to come in the future.

Trumpets sound warnings of impending doom. Notice Ezekiel 33:1–4: *"Again the word of the* L*ORD came unto me, saying,* [2] *Son of man, speak to the children of thy people, and say unto them, When I bring the sword upon a land, if the people of the land take a man of their coasts, and set him for their watchman:* [3] *If when he seeth the sword come upon the land, he blow the trumpet, and warn the people;* [4] *Then whosoever heareth the sound of the trumpet, and taketh not warning; if the sword come, and take him away, his blood shall be upon his own head."*

The watchman is on the wall. He sees the enemy approach, and he blows the trumpet of warning that the sword is coming. If the people do not believe it, and the sword comes and they die, it is their own fault because they did not listen to the trumpet of warning.

These seven trumpets God is sounding in chapters 8 through 11 are trumpets of warning. They are saying to the wicked that God's wrath is coming and the sword is on its way. However, these trumpets do not just give out a sound, but they also give a sample of what God's judgment is going to be like. They are making the point that if a sample of God's judgment is this bad in this life, what must it be like in the next? Therefore, hear the sound, heed the warning, and flee from the wrath to come. If you are greatly disturbed by all the negative things you experience in this life that are just samples of God's wrath for your wickedness, how much more are you going to be plunged into utter despair when the real judgment finally comes?

The wicked are going to experience much judgment from God in this age for the evil things they do, and the trumpets tell us what those judgments will look like. These judgments are designed to call them to prepare for the Day of Judgment through repentance and faith in Christ. Sadly, we will see as we proceed through the trumpet judgments that, in spite of how bad they are, people are going to harden their hearts and not repent of their wicked deeds.

These trumpet judgments are expressed in language that reflects the ten great plagues that God poured out upon Egypt. What God did to Pharaoh foreshadows what God will do to the wicked in this age who resist the voice of the prophet of God. In Pharaoh's day, the prophet of God was Moses. Pharaoh refused to hear Moses' voice, even though many warning plagues were brought to bring him to repentance. He continued to harden his heart. He was destroyed in the Red Sea.

The prophet in our day is the Lord Jesus Christ, and Christ is bringing plagues upon the world, calling the world to repent. The world is going to harden its heart, just like Pharaoh did, and the world is going to be destroyed in the sea of God's wrath in the end. They are going to be destroyed, not in the Red Sea, but in the lake of fire. The parallels are compelling and clear.

As we look at these trumpet judgments, we see things like hail and darkness and locusts and blood and death imposed on the wicked. All of these things are intensifications of the kinds of plagues that came upon Egypt. They are intensifications of these plagues because they occur over the entire earth, and they occur in every generation. These things do not harm believers, but they bring great harm to unbelievers. This is not to say these things will not cause some suffering to believers, but they do not bring any harm to them. They are only worked together for their good. However, they bring not only suffering to the unbeliever, but great harm to them as well. They will be worked together for their misery.

As we look at the opening of the seventh seal, we see that out of it not only do the seven trumpets flow, but the entire rest of the book as well. Remember, when God the Father gave God the Son the book in chapter 5, it was a book with just seven seals, and six of them have already been opened. When the seventh one is opened, it contains everything else in the remainder of Revelation.

The Opening of the Seventh Seal

The opening of the seventh seal is in verse 1. Notice: *"And when he had opened the seventh seal, there was silence in heaven about the space of half an hour."*

The reaction to the opening of the seventh seal is somewhat surprising to us. It was one of complete and utter silence in heaven, and it was not a momentary silence, either. It says that it lasted about the space of half an hour—a full thirty minutes. You have probably been dumbstruck from time to time by something that has happened. You have been rendered speechless for a few moments, but pretty quickly you recover your wits and start chattering away about what it was that you saw. But have you ever been dumbstruck for half an hour? That is a long time to be dumbstruck.

Why was there the reaction of this profound and extended silence in heaven? We have to look at the Old Testament to understand the significance of silence in the presence of God, and what we find is that silence is commanded in the presence of God's impending judgment.

Notice Zephaniah 1:1–18: "*The word of the* Lord *which came*
unto Zephaniah the son of Cushi, the son of Gedaliah, the son of
Amariah, the son of Hizkiah, in the days of Josiah the son of Amon,
king of Judah. [2] *I will utterly consume all things from off the land,*
saith the Lord." This phrase tells us of God's impending judgment.
"[3] *I will consume man and beast; I will consume the fowls of the*
heaven, and the fishes of the sea, and the stumblingblocks with the
wicked; and I will cut off man from off the land, saith the Lord. [4] *I*
will also stretch out mine hand upon Judah, and upon all the inhab-
itants of Jerusalem; and I will cut off the remnant of Baal from this
place, and the name of the Chemarims with the priests; [5] *And them*
that worship the host of heaven upon the housetops; and them that
worship and that swear by the Lord, *and that swear by Malcham;*
[6] *And them that are turned back from the* Lord; *and those that have*
not sought the Lord, *nor enquired for him.*" Now here it is: "[7] *Hold*
thy peace at the presence of the Lord God: *for the day of the* Lord
is at hand: for the Lord *hath prepared a sacrifice, he hath bid his*
guests. [8] *And it shall come to pass in the day of the* Lord's *sacrifice,*
that I will punish the princes, and the king's children, and all such as
are clothed with strange apparel. [9] *In the same day also will I punish*
all those that leap on the threshold, which fill their masters' houses

with violence and deceit. [10] *And it shall come to pass in that day, saith the* L*ORD*, *that there shall be the noise of a cry from the fish gate, and an howling from the second, and a great crashing from the hills.* [11] *Howl, ye inhabitants of Maktesh, for all the merchant people are cut down; all they that bear silver are cut off.* [12] *And it shall come to pass at that time, that I will search Jerusalem with candles, and punish the men that are settled on their lees: that say in their heart, The* L*ORD* *will not do good, neither will he do evil.* [13] *Therefore their goods shall become a booty, and their houses a desolation: they shall also build houses, but not inhabit them; and they shall plant vineyards, but not drink the wine thereof.* [14] *The great day of the* L*ORD* *is near, it is near, and hasteth greatly, even the voice of the day of the* L*ORD*: *the mighty man shall cry there bitterly.* [15] *That day is a day of wrath, a day of trouble and distress, a day of wasteness and desolation, a day of darkness and gloominess, a day of clouds and thick darkness,* [16] *A day of the trumpet and alarm against the fenced cities, and against the high towers.* [17] *And I will bring distress upon men, that they shall walk like blind men, because they have sinned against the* L*ORD*: *and their blood shall be poured out as dust, and their flesh as the dung.* [18] *Neither their silver nor their gold shall be able to deliver them in the day of the* L*ORD's wrath; but the whole land shall be devoured by the fire of his jealousy: for he shall make even a speedy riddance of all them that dwell in the land."*

What we observe in this declaration of this horrible judgment to come are both silence and trumpets. Verse 7: "*Hold thy peace at the presence of the Lord* G*OD*." Verse 16: "*A day of the trumpet and alarm against the fenced cities.*" This helps us to understand what the silence and the trumpets mean in Revelation 8.

Revelation 8:1 says, "*And when he had opened the seventh seal, there was silence in heaven about the space of half an hour.*" In other words, when that seal was opened, those in heaven saw the judgments that were coming, and they went silent.

It is not just in Zephaniah that we have this principle of silence in the face of God's impending wrath. In Zechariah 2:13 it says, "*Be silent, O all flesh, before the* L*ORD*: *for he is raised up out of his holy habitation.*" God is getting up to execute His judgment, therefore: "*Be silent.*" In Habakkuk 2:20 it says, "*But the* L*ORD* *is in his holy temple: let all the earth keep silence before him.*" It says in Psalm 46:10, "*Be still, and know that I am God: I will be exalted* *among the heathen, I will be exalted in the earth."*

Every time God is ready to exercise judgment, He commands silence. The point is that the judgment of God is so terrible that all those in heaven fall silent as they contemplate its imminent outpouring. Something so terrible is about to happen that the people are rendered speechless. So fearful and awful is this retribution that is going to be inflicted upon the wicked, that the inhabitants of heaven stand dumbfounded in silent amazement at the dreadfulness of it all.

What do they see as the seventh seal is opened? What strikes them silent and speechless? What they see is the revelation of the seven trumpets of God's judgment.

The Revelation of the Seven Trumpets

The revelation of the seven trumpets is in verses 2 to 6. Notice verse 2: *"And I saw the seven angels which stood before God; and to them were given seven trumpets."*

When this seventh seal is opened, there is a revelation of seven angels standing before the throne of God with seven trumpets. Seven is the number that symbolizes completeness. These seven angels with these seven trumpets represent the idea that God will be complete in the judgment He brings upon the wicked in this age. He will not fail to bring retribution against every wicked person, and none will escape His wrath. His wrath will be complete. There will be no places or people that are missed in its execution.

Our passage says that these seven angels had seven trumpets. As we have seen, trumpets were used in the Old Testament to announce God's judgment. That is how they are being used here. Trumpets were used for other things too, but they were certainly used to announce God's judgment. It is important to understand why these judgments from God are being sent upon the wicked. These next four verses tell us that one of the reasons God is pouring out His wrath against the wicked is in response to the prayers of the people of God.

Notice verses 3 and 4: *"And another angel came and stood at the altar, having a golden censer; and there was given unto him much incense, that he should offer it with the prayers of all saints upon the golden altar which was before the throne. [4] And the smoke of the incense, which came with the prayers of the saints, ascended up before God out of the angel's hand."*

The Old Testament high priest would go into the tabernacle with hot coals from the brazen altar that was outside the tabernacle and put them on the golden altar of incense. Then he would sprinkle incense on the coals, and the smoke of the burning incense would rise up. This smoke was a symbolic picture of the rising up of the prayers of the people of God to the throne of God. Burning incense is a metaphor for the rising up of our prayers to God.

When the fifth seal was opened in Revelation 6:9–11 it states: "*And when he had opened the fifth seal, I saw under the altar*" (this is the altar in heaven, the same altar incense is being burned on in 8:3) "*the souls of them that were slain for the word of God, and for the testimony which they held.*" These souls were unjustly murdered. They were not slain for some evil they had done. They were slain for bearing witness to the gospel.

Verse 10: "*And they cried with a loud voice, saying, How long, O Lord, holy and true, dost thou not judge and avenge our blood on them that dwell on the earth?*" That is the prayer: "Lord, when are You going to avenge our blood on the earth?" God says to them in verse 11 that the final vengeance for their blood upon the earth is not going to take place until their fellow servants and brethren are killed as they have been. But that does not mean God is doing nothing between their martyrdom and the final judgment. What He is doing between their martyrdom and the final judgment is executing the wrath of the seven trumpets.

What were the saints in heaven asking for? They were asking for justice and vengeance against their persecutors. In this eighth chapter, we see God's answer to their prayers in the sounding of the seven trumpets. While these seven trumpets are not the full or final expression of God's vengeance against those who have persecuted and martyred His people, they are the beginning of it and they are the earnest of it. They are the down payment of the full vengeance that will come at the end of the age.

Revelation 8:3–4 is God's recognition of the prayers of His saints, not only in heaven but also on earth. It says in verse 3, "*the prayers of all saints.*" It is saints in heaven in Revelation 6:10 and saints alive on earth who together are crying out to God against their persecutors. It says God recognizes the prayers of His saints, not only in heaven but also on earth. He hears their prayers for Him to exercise His justice and to bring vengeance upon their persecutors.

What does God do with this prayer? Verses 5 and 6 tell us. *"And the angel took the censer, and filled it with fire of the altar, and cast it into the earth: and there were voices, and thunderings, and lightnings, and an earthquake.* [6] *And the seven angels which had the seven trumpets prepared themselves to sound."* Verses 5 and 6 are God's answer to the prayers of the saints that are offered before Him in verses 3 and 4. He hears their cries for justice. He sees the evil their persecutors have done. He takes action in response to their prayers for justice to be carried out, and begins His retribution by the sounding of the trumpets.

God has heard the prayers of the saints, and the judgments on the earth are His answers to those prayers. He begins even in this life to punish the wicked for the evil they have done, and, unless they repent, they will obtain the full measure of that punishment on the final Day of Judgment. The point is that God hears the cries of His persecuted people, and He will avenge them. Our prayers for justice in every generation set God's judgment in motion in every generation.

Jesus said in Luke 18:7–8a, *"And shall not God avenge his own elect, which cry day and night unto him, though he bear long with them?* [8] *I tell you that he will avenge them speedily."* We are told that prayers for vengeance are somehow unchristian, and yet we see Jesus saying, "Your prayers for vengeance are totally legitimate, and I am going to answer them, and I am going to exercise that vengeance." When the saints in heaven in Revelation 6:11 cry for vengeance, God does not say, "Oh, how unchristian of you! Why are you not praying for these people's conversion?"

This is not to say we should not pray for the conversion of people like Saul of Tarsus and for all other persecutors of Christians. But a prayer for their salvation and a prayer for God's justice to be done are not mutually contradictory, because if you are praying for their salvation, you are praying for God's vengeance against their sins to fall on Christ instead of on them. It is still a prayer for vengeance; it is just that the object of the vengeance is their Substitute instead of they themselves. Never think that prayer for vengeance is somehow ungodly, because God always gets vengeance for sin, either in our Savior or in us. Thank God that the vengeance did not fall on us, but instead, it fell on Christ in our place.

The point is that the wicked do not get away with their wickedness. The suffering that God inflicts on them will be far greater than the suffering they inflict on us. It is a fearful thing to fall into the hands of the living God, and that is exactly where these wicked have fallen. Those who ride with the four horsemen and those who facilitate the persecutions of Christians will have the Christians cry out to God for justice against them. God says, "I will begin to bring justice. I will cast My lightning and My thunder and My earthquakes into the earth and these seven trumpets are what that will look like."

These voices and thundering and lightning and earthquakes spoken of in verse 5 are God's answer and assurance that He is in the process of pouring out His wrath on the wicked. That wrath is expressed in these seven trumpets, which we will look at in the next chapter.

The point is this: God is well aware of the work of the wicked in this age. God is well aware of the pain and the prayers of His people. God is moving even now in answer to our prayers to bring judgment upon the wicked in this age with increasing intensity until it is fully poured out on the Day of Judgment at the second coming of Christ.

We have the trumpets sounding; we have the vials being poured out; and by them, God is bringing judgment, then increasing judgment, and then even more intense judgment, until there is the final judgment. All along, He is saying to these rebellious people that they should bow and repent! But these people continue their defiance and rebellion against God and their persecution of God's people. This book, as we have said, is a book of spiritual warfare. It is about the four horsemen riding, and the saints crying out, and God blowing His trumpets of judgment and pouring out His vials of wrath.

God sends out His trumpets of wrath against them, oftentimes not totally destroying them, but severely punishing them. We read in the news all the time of the calamities that happen to the wicked. These are the messengers of God saying to them, "Stop persecuting My people! Repent of your rebellion against Me!" And yet, do they hear? They think it was just a natural event or it was just a chance circumstance. When God sends His messengers, they reject them as being from God. The world blindly goes on in stupid defiance against God, even until the final Day of Judgment.

Recognize that even now God is acting to bring many temporal and limited judgments upon the world to punish it for its hatred of Christ and for its hatred and persecution of Christ's people. When terrible things happen and we suggest that these things are God's judgment, people say, "Who are you to say what God is doing? Do you have God's mind?" Our answer must be that what we have is God's word.

When we read about the kinds of things He says He is doing through His trumpets and His vials, we can say that when those things happen on the earth, it was the hand of God that brought it to pass.

Think about it: does anything in this world happen without the hand of God? Did the AIDS/HIV crisis arise from pure naturalism? No. It is the wrath of God upon sexual promiscuity, and it is saying, "Repent! Obey God in the area of sexual conduct. If you do not, death awaits you."

We can say the same thing about wars and plagues and earthquakes and tornados and tsunamis that occur—events that wipe out (in the case of the 2004 tsunami) 200,000 people in one day. That is the voice of God. It is God blowing His trumpets. When calamity and disaster and death and disease happen on this earth, what is that? It is God blowing His trumpets. The people need to listen because there is nothing that happens on this earth that does not happen according to the decree of Almighty God. While evil agents may bring evil events to pass, God is in control and God uses those things as expressions of His trumpets.

It should encourage you that God is actively responding to your prayers for deliverance from persecutors and persecution, and He is actively persecuting your persecutors. Therefore, when you face persecution from people as you speak for Jesus Christ, and you cry out to God for either their salvation or their judgment, God hears, and God will act in this age in response to your prayers. He will bring vengeance.

The point of this passage is that the prayers of the people of God set in motion the judgments of God. They pray, and God casts out His thundering and His lightning; they pray, and God sends out His trumpets. God wants us to know that our prayers have a large part in the execution of His judgments on this earth.

Therefore, we do not wait for all of God's judgment to happen at the end of the age. A lot of judgment is beginning to happen now, and will be perfected and completed at the end of the age—just like a lot of your salvation is happening now, but it is going to be perfected and completed at the end of the age. God deals judgment to the wicked progressively just like He bestows salvation progressively. The vast bulk of salvation will be realized in the end; and in the same way, the vast bulk of judgment is reserved for the end as well.

28

The First Four Trumpets, Revelation 8:7–13

> “7 *The first angel sounded, and there followed hail and fire mingled with blood, and they were cast upon the earth: and the third part of trees was burnt up, and all green grass was burnt up.* 8 *And the second angel sounded, and as it were a great mountain burning with fire was cast into the sea: and the third part of the sea became blood;* 9 *And the third part of the creatures which were in the sea, and had life, died; and the third part of the ships were destroyed.* 10 *And the third angel sounded, and there fell a great star from heaven, burning as it were a lamp, and it fell upon the third part of the rivers, and upon the fountains of waters;* 11 *And the name of the star is called Wormwood: and the third part of the waters became wormwood; and many men died of the waters, because they were made bitter.* 12 *And the fourth angel sounded, and the third part of the sun was smitten, and the third part of the moon, and the third part of the stars; so as the third part of them was darkened, and the day shone not for a third part of it, and the night likewise.* 13 *And I beheld, and heard an angel flying through the midst of heaven, saying with a loud voice, Woe, woe, woe, to the inhabiters of the earth by reason of the other voices of the trumpet of the three angels, which are yet to sound!*”

As we move into chapter 8, we have entered the third parallel section of this book. This third parallel section in chapters 8 through 11 contains the seven trumpets of judgment. The seven trumpets make it clear that the assaults of the wicked against Christ and His people in this present age will be punished by God in this present age.

During this present age, these trumpet judgments are God’s answer to the prayers of His saints for His vengeance and justice to be executed against their persecutors. We saw the Christians were praying in 6:10 for God to exercise vengeance upon their persecutors. We saw these prayers offered once again in 8:3–4. The saints are crying out to God in this age against their persecutors, and God's response to those prayers in this age is the seven trumpets.

The purpose of the trumpets is to bring temporal physical and spiritual judgments on the wicked as partial retribution for the evil they have done and are currently doing to the saints. These seven trumpets are not only a partial retribution for the evil they have done to the saints, but they are also a powerful incentive for these wicked men to repent of that evil, and to turn to God in humility and faith before the final wrath of God falls upon them. The trumpets are a sample in this age of the final and far greater wrath that is going to fall on them at the end of the age.

The point is that the wicked are going to experience much judgment from God in this age for the evil they do. The trumpets tell us what those judgments will look like.

These trumpet judgments are neither the full nor the final expression of God's vengeance against those who have persecuted and martyred His people. Instead, they are a promise of the wrath to come if these people do not repent. God is well aware of the work of the wicked in this age, and God is well aware of the pain of His people and the prayers they have offered regarding that pain. God is moving right now in this age in answer to our prayers to bring judgment on the wicked.

As we consider these trumpet judgments, we recognize they are not individual judgments that occur one time and then are over. Instead, they represent categories of judgments that occur in every generation, all around the globe, among all people and in all nations.

These first four trumpets in this chapter speak about the calamities of nature that God brings on the wicked for their evil works. Such calamities in the realm of nature occur in every generation and around the world. They occur in every century, and they will continue to occur in every century until Jesus returns again. They cannot be escaped. The reason they cannot be escaped is that they arise out of every realm of nature, and they occur in every place in the world.

In the first trumpet, we see calamities that occur on the land; in the second trumpet, we see calamities that occur in the sea; in the third trumpet, we see calamities that occur with reference to the inland fresh waters; and in the fourth trumpet, we see the calamities that occur in the atmosphere and the heavenly bodies.

There is no place and no people that can escape the avenging hand of God as He acts in the realm of nature to execute His wrath upon them, irrespective of the realm of nature they might happen to be in. People might think, "If there are problems in the land, I will get in a boat and go out in the sea. If there are problems on the sea, I will go onto a lake. If there are problems there, I will get in an airplane and fly up into the sky." There is no place you can go in nature in this world to escape the wrath of God.

People talk about the so-called "natural disasters" that occur in this world. When there is a tidal wave or a tornado or a hurricane, people say that those are "natural disasters." When people use this kind of language, they are assuming that nature acts independently of God, and that God is not in control of nature. They think what occurs is just the outcome of impersonal forces and the laws of nature at work. Understand this: There are no natural disasters. There are only acts of God in the realm of nature.

God is either in control of everything or else God is in control of nothing. If, as Ephesians 1:11 says, *"[He] worketh all things after the counsel of His own will,"* this has to include all the disasters that occur in the realm of nature. Every disaster in the realm of nature is the judgment of God against the wicked, and it is the voice of God calling the wicked to repentance. "Acts of nature" are acts of God, and they need to be seen and understood as messages from God, either to convey His blessing or to convey His wrath.

Some acts of God in the realm of nature convey His blessings: the food we enjoy, the air we breathe, the water we drink, and the animals we interact with. All of these things are gifts of God and show the goodness of God to us. But in the case of these first four trumpets of judgment, some acts of God in the realm of nature convey His wrath against the wicked and are intended as punishment for sin. God makes His wrath known in the disasters of nature, and these first four trumpets tell us what these disasters of nature look like.

As we said in our previous chapter, these trumpet judgments occur during the same time period and in parallel with the opening of the seals. We saw the seals began to be opened with the first coming of

Christ and they ended with the second coming. In the same way, the trumpets began with the first coming and end with the second coming.

While the four horsemen are riding and doing their wicked work of conquest and war and famine and death and persecution, at the same time, the trumpets are sounding judgments of God's wrath against them, warning them to stop that behavior and to repent of it lest they experience the greater wrath to come.

The seals show the evil work of evil men and the trials believers must endure at their hands, but the trumpets show the avenging work of a wrathful God and the judgments the wicked must endure at God's hands. These two themes are playing out through the time period between the first and second coming of Christ, and both can be seen operating in parallel during that time.

The First Trumpet

The first trumpet is in verse 7. It says, "*The first angel sounded, and there followed hail and fire mingled with blood, and they were cast upon the earth: and the third part of trees was burnt up, and all green grass was burnt up.*"

These trumpet judgments are patterned after the plagues of Exodus. Just like the Exodus plagues, they are designed to punish the persecutors of the people of God for the evil they have done and for the hardness of their hearts. Just like the plagues of Egypt finally resulted in Israel being liberated from her persecutors and being brought into the Promised Land, so the trumpets of this age will finally result in God's new Israel being liberated from her persecutors and being brought into the promised land of the new heaven and the new earth. This is where these seven trumpets are leading us.

This first trumpet corresponds to the plague of hail and fire that fell on Egypt in Exodus 9:22–25. Notice it says in verse 7, the trumpet "*sounded, and there followed hail and fire mingled with blood.*" This is actually an intensification of the Egyptian plague. In the Egyptian plague there was hail and fire, but here the additional element of "*blood*" is mentioned, and the blood is mixed in with the hail and the fire.

Furthermore, this first trumpet plague is not directed at a single nation like Egypt; rather, it falls upon the entire earth—that is, upon all the land where trees and grass grow. God is causing these disasters; He is the one causing this hail and fire and blood to be "*cast upon the earth."* As a result, a third part of the trees are burned up, and all of the green grass.

When we introduced the book of Revelation, we said that it uses highly symbolic visual imagery and language. The symbolic language used here indicates that God will afflict the persecutors of the church with various disasters that will take place on the land. This would include things like earthquakes, volcanoes, lightning, tornadoes, forest fires, epidemic diseases, droughts, crop failures, hurricanes, and other damaging events that affect the land and those that live upon it.

Under the symbolic imagery of hail and fire and blood falling on the earth, which then burns up a third of the trees and all of the green grass, is conveyed the reality of all of the disasters that occur in the realm of nature that affect the land. These are all acts of God of judgment and wrath on the wicked of the earth. The hail and the fire and the blood symbolize any kind of destruction which at any time damages the land on which men live, and damages the men who live on that land. That it destroys only one third of the trees shows the limited nature of these judgments that God sends upon the earth. The number "one third" is used to indicate that these are partial judgments, not total judgments.

When we studied numerology, we saw that the division of primary numbers represented a diminished level of the meaning of the symbolic significance of those numbers. We saw that "three" is the number of perfection, completion, and finality. By employing a division of that number, "one-third," God is telling us that these judgments are imperfect, incomplete, and temporal manifestations of the final judgment and justice of God. Though great destructions will afflict the earth, the earth will not be destroyed. Though distresses will afflict mankind, the majority of mankind will survive. These are partial judgments, not perfect judgments; they are incomplete judgments, but not final judgments.

The Second Trumpet

The second trumpet is mentioned in verses 8 through 9. It says in verse 8: *"And the second angel sounded, and as it were a great mountain burning with fire was cast into the sea: and the third part of the sea became blood;* [9] *And the third part of the creatures which were in the sea, and had life, died; and the third part of the ships were destroyed."*

We saw that the first trumpet affected the land, where the trees and the grass grow. This second trumpet affects the sea—that is, the ocean. Here a great object (it does not say it is a mountain; it says *"as it were"* a mountain) burning with fire is cast into the sea. The results are dramatic. A third part of the sea becomes blood, a third part of the sea creatures die, and a third part of the ships are destroyed. Once again, this number "one third" speaks of a partial judgment and not a total judgment; an incomplete judgment and not a perfect judgment.

This second trumpet corresponds once again to one of the Egyptian plagues. It corresponds to the plague of Exodus 7:20–21 by which the waters were turned to blood and the fish in the waters died. This blazing object that is cast into the sea symbolizes the terror of God's judgment on the sea.

God has brought many disasters upon the seas of this world, and many people have perished on the ocean as a result of them. For example, the great tidal wave of 2004 in the Indian Ocean killed over 200,000 people in one day. There have been many more major earthquakes in the sea since 2004, generating great tidal waves, and causing tens of thousands of more people to die. The list of tidal waves in history is gigantic; as far as human history goes back there is a record of massive tidal waves destroying massive numbers of people. Due to storms and high waves, hundreds of thousands if not millions of ships have perished on the oceans, with the loss of innumerable lives. The sea affords no refuge from God's wrath, as Jonah found out to his dismay. Great storms and cyclones in the ocean have destroyed countless mariners.

If the loss of lives and property in all the sea disasters through all the centuries since Christ came could be calculated, it would be seen that God's wrath has been expressed in a massive way upon those who dwell on, take shipping across, or dwell next to the oceans of the world.

The Third Trumpet

Notice the third trumpet in verses 10 to 11. *And the third angel sounded, and there fell a great star from heaven, burning as it were a lamp, and it fell upon the third part of the rivers, and upon the fountains of waters;* [11] *And the name of the star is called Wormwood: and the third part of the waters became wormwood; and many men died of the waters, because they were made bitter."*

The first trumpet affected the land, the second trumpet affected the sea, and now the third trumpet of God's judgment affects the inland waters—that is, the springs and wells and rivers and lakes. All fresh water on land is comprehended by this trumpet.

Here we have the symbolic imagery of a burning star falling from heaven and impacting and affecting all the fresh water supplies on the earth. The star is called "*Wormwood.*" Wormwood is a plant that grows in the Middle East which has a strong and very bitter taste. It is frequently used in the Scripture as a symbol for bitterness and sorrow and calamity.

The result of this burning Wormwood star falling on the rivers and the springs is dramatic. One third of the inland fresh water supply, so necessary for sustaining human life, is made bitter so that men die when they drink it. Polluted waters and waterborne and water-related diseases have killed millions of people during this age through diseases like malaria and cholera and typhoid and hepatitis A.

There are about twenty waterborne diseases that occur because of bad water, or because the water has become polluted or defiled in some fashion or other. Waterborne diseases have resulted in massive numbers of deaths in the last 2,000 years across the world.

Then there are droughts from which the lack of water has caused crop failures and starvation and death by dehydration. Great storms and floods have killed millions more as floodwaters and mudslides have overflowed towns and villages, and massive snow avalanches have killed many.

The point is, that which is so essential to sustaining life, which man cannot do without for any more than just a couple of days, can be and has been used by God to bring His judgments on wicked men. Once again, these are partial judgments, because only a third part of the waters are affected; but even so, many people have died due to God's judgment on the waters on the earth.

Just as God made the fresh water in Egypt undrinkable by turning it into blood, as Psalm 78:44 says, here God makes the waters across the earth undrinkable as well. Jeremiah 9:15 says, "*thus saith the . . . God of Israel; Behold, I will feed them, even this people, with wormwood, and give them water of gall to drink.*"

It is interesting to note that fire, which symbolizes God's wrath, has been mentioned in all three of these trumpets. But that wrath has been restrained to only a partial and incomplete expression. This is why we have the constant repetition of "*one third*" of this and "*one third*" of that. What is being said here is that God has not poured out all the wrath He could have. In this age, He has graciously only carried out partial judgments upon humanity for the wickedness they have done to His people and to His name.

The Fourth Trumpet

The fourth trumpet is found in verses 12 and 13. "*And the fourth angel sounded, and the third part of the sun was smitten, and the third part of the moon, and the third part of the stars; so as the third part of them was darkened, and the day shone not for a third part of it, and the night likewise.* [13] *And I beheld, and heard an angel flying through the midst of heaven, saying with a loud voice, Woe, woe, woe, to the inhabiters of the earth by reason of the other voices of the trumpet of the three angels, which are yet to sound!*"

The first trumpet affected the land, the second trumpet affected the sea, the third trumpet affected the inland fresh waters. The fourth trumpet affects the heavens above, all the bodies it contains, and all the effects it produces. The passage says the third part of the sun, the third part of the moon, and the third part of the stars were smitten so that the third part of them was darkened, and the day and the night were reduced by a third as well. Once again, "*one third*" signifies that these are partial judgments, not perfect judgments.

The effect of the stellar heavens upon human life is profound. Any abnormality in the heavens can have a dramatic effect on the life on the earth. We saw this in the Exodus plagues in Exodus 10:21–23, in which thick darkness covered the land for three days. The people could not do anything; they had to feel their way around. There was no ambient light.

The actions that occur in the heavens have a profound effect on the earth. Things like giant solar flares, falling meteorites, electrical storms, volcanic ash obscuring the sun for days on end, giant asteroid impacts—all of these have produced negative effects on humanity. And while there are not as many of those as there are disasters on the land or in the sea or in the inland waters, there have been some, and it may be that many more will occur in the future as the age continues to unfold.

All evils that are due to the abnormal functioning of the heavenly bodies throughout this entire age are comprehended in this trumpet. We will not be able to get into a spaceship and go to Mars or some other planet and escape the temporal judgments of God. This intermittent disorder in the heavens is but a sample of the ultimate destruction of the universe on the final Day of Judgment. We looked previously at the sixth seal in Revelation 6:12–14 which says: *"And I beheld when he had opened the sixth seal, and, lo, there was a great earthquake; and the sun became black as sackcloth of hair, and the moon became as blood;* [13] *And the stars of heaven fell unto the earth, even as a fig tree casteth her untimely figs, when she is shaken of a mighty wind.* [14] *And the heaven departed as a scroll when it is rolled together; and every mountain and island were moved out of their places."*

We saw that at the end of this age, God is going to destroy the present heavens and earth. The sun, moon, stars, and heavens are all going to be displaced and disrupted. Any abnormalities in the stellar heavens now are a foretaste and foreshadow of the cataclysmic destruction that is going to take place in the end.

Notice Isaiah 13. The Lord is threatening His wrath and judgment, and in verses 6 to 11 He says, *"Howl ye; for the day of the* LORD *is at hand; it shall come as a destruction from the Almighty.* [7] *Therefore shall all hands be faint, and every man's heart shall melt:* [8] *And they shall be afraid: pangs and sorrows shall take hold of them; they shall be in pain as a woman that travaileth: they shall be amazed one at another; their faces shall be as flames.* [9] *Behold, the day of the* LORD *cometh, cruel both with wrath and fierce anger, to lay the land desolate: and he shall destroy the sinners thereof out of it.* [10] *For"* (here it is) *"the stars of heaven and the constellations thereof shall not give their light: the sun shall be darkened in his going forth, and the moon shall not cause her light to shine.* [11] *And I will punish the world for their evil, and the wicked for their iniquity; and I will cause the arrogancy of the proud to cease, and will lay low the haughtiness of the terrible."*

This is how it will be at the end. The heavens will be shaken to their very foundations.

Historical records have chronicled many anomalies in the heavens. Back in the 1800s, a tremendous solar flare struck the earth in the eastern United States that actually lit the telegraph lines on fire. It was called the "Carrington event" and occurred in 1859. There was the "Tunguska event" in 1908, in which a tremendous asteroid struck the Siberian wilderness in Russia, and the evidence showed that it devastated hundreds of square miles of forest.

While these events do not occur often, they are very devastating when they do occur. Alfred Plummer says in The Pulpit Commentary:

> God can turn even the benign influences of the sun and the planets into means for the destruction of man. In the countless evils which have their origin in the excesses or the defect of the power of the sun, we may see the fulfillment of this judgment.[6]

Sometimes there is too much sun, and people die from sunstroke and dehydration in the excessive heat, and sometimes there is too little sun, and people die from freezing in the excessive cold.

These four judgments symbolically portray the partial retribution of God in the physical realm against the wicked in the physical world that has literally been taking place for the last 2,000 years, and will continue to take place until Jesus returns again. God uses every part of the natural world to bring His judgments on unsaved humanity. There is no part of the world and there is no part of the universe to which men may go to escape the retribution of God. When people experience so-called "natural disasters" of any kind in any realm of nature, they need to understand that these are not "natural disasters." These are acts of God in which He is speaking to rebellious humanity, punishing people for their sins, and calling them to repentance.

To say that God has nothing to do with disasters in the realm of nature is to deny the sovereignty of God over all things. It is to deny that He is managing the very world which He Himself created. This is nothing less than practical atheism. Yet this is what the godless world would have us believe. Godless people want us to believe that God does not act in nature because really, as they would say, there is no God at all. It is all just the laws of nature at work, it is all just happenstance and chance, and it does not mean a thing.

When Hurricane Katrina destroyed New Orleans, they said it was just a natural event and meant nothing! No, that was the wrath of

6 Spence and Excell. *The Pulpit Commentary*, Vol. 22, *Revelation*, Grand Rapids: Wm. B. Eerdmans Publishing Company, 235.

God against a wicked city and against a wicked nation. The people of God understood what it was, and the wicked needed to understand what it was. It was a partial outpouring of God's wrath on them for the evil they had done.

If God has the power to generate the kind of destruction a hurricane produces, how much more does He have the power to destroy the entire earth? Here is just a sample of the power He possesses.

Flee from the wrath to come, because as bad as these judgments in the realm of nature are, they are nothing compared to what will come when the next three trumpets sound. Revelation 8:13 says: *"And I beheld, and heard an angel flying through the midst of heaven, saying with a loud voice, Woe, woe, woe, to the inhabiters of the earth by reason of the other voices of the trumpet of the three angels, which are yet to sound."*

As we have read about these four trumpets, we recognize that these are terrible things; and yet it is going to get worse, because when the fifth and the sixth and the seventh trumpets open, it will make the first four seem like child's play. We are going to look at these three woes in future chapters. The point is that we need to listen to the voice of God when He speaks in judgment as He brings to pass in the realm of nature things that harm and injure and kill people.

God speaks in His management of nature, and we need to listen. When God so manages nature that we wind up having food on our plates, we thank God. And when God manages nature in such a way as to bring tremendous destruction and loss, we fear God. We need to respond to God as He acts in nature, both by way of bringing blessing and by way of bringing His partial judgments.

For Christians, the disastrous events God sends on the earth should deepen our faith and increase our thankfulness that these things are not meant to punish us. Instead, God will use them to develop our character, to increase our maturity, and ultimately, to bring us to heaven.

For the wicked, when these natural disasters occur, they say, "Let us hide in the caves! Mountains and rocks fall on us! Hide us from the wrath to come! Who can stand?" But how do Christians respond when those things happen? In Psalm 46:1–3, notice what David says about natural disasters:

"God is our refuge and strength, a very present help in trouble.
2 *Therefore will not we fear, though the earth be removed, and though*

the mountains be carried into the midst of the sea; [3] *Though the waters thereof roar and be troubled, though the mountains shake with the swelling thereof.*"

David is saying that when God brings natural disasters upon the world (which he describes in symbolic language) he will not be afraid because in those natural disasters, God is his refuge and strength. God is present to help him; therefore, he will not fear.

The wicked have every reason to fear. But while God is working all these things together for their harm, the believer recognizes that God is working all these things together for his good. For the wicked, these disasters are meant to increase their fear and dread of the hand of God being against them and move them to repentance before the final judgment falls. But when they deny that God has any part in the disasters of nature, they rob themselves of the very lesson they are meant to learn. They harden themselves against the warnings of the wrath to come and ensure their entrance into the greatest of all disasters of nature, which is the lake of fire.

Remember trumpet one spoke of fire falling; trumpet two spoke of fire falling; trumpet three spoke of fire falling; and trumpet four, describing the anomalies of the sun, certainly alluded to fire falling. Why? To warn the ungodly against the ultimate place of fire, which is the lake of fire itself.

When these natural disasters occur, Christians recognize that they may cause us suffering, but they will never cause us harm. They may cause us pain, but that will be worked together for our good, for our godliness, for our preservation, for our growth, for our testimony and witness, and ultimately for our deliverance into heaven. Therefore, the same judgments that are meant to hurt the wicked are meant to help and bless the righteous. We have no reason to be afraid when these things happen. But when they do happen, we need to say to the ungodly, "This is a sample of the wrath of God. Flee from the wrath to come."

These first four trumpets teach us how to understand and interpret and react to the disasters of nature that have been occurring for the last 2,000 years and will continue to occur until Jesus returns again. May we have spiritual eyes to see that there are no acts of nature; there are just acts of God. While God uses instruments to accomplish His act, they are, nevertheless, His acts. When the tornado took out Job's children by destroying the house they were in, that was no act of nature. Job looked on that and said, "The Lord gave and the Lord took away. Blessed be the name of the Lord." Job traced the event in nature back to the One who controlled nature and worshiped Him for it. May we always do the same.

29

The Fifth Trumpet, Revelation 9:1–11

> *"1 And the fifth angel sounded, and I saw a star fall from heaven unto the earth: and to him was given the key of the bottomless pit. 2 And he opened the bottomless pit; and there arose a smoke out of the pit, as the smoke of a great furnace; and the sun and the air were darkened by reason of the smoke of the pit. 3 And there came out of the smoke locusts upon the earth: and unto them was given power, as the scorpions of the earth have power. 4 And it was commanded them that they should not hurt the grass of the earth, neither any green thing, neither any tree; but only those men which have not the seal of God in their foreheads. 5 And to them it was given that they should not kill them, but that they should be tormented five months: and their torment was as the torment of a scorpion, when he striketh a man. 6 And in those days shall men seek death, and shall not find it; and shall desire to die, and death shall flee from them. 7 And the shapes of the locusts were like unto horses prepared unto battle; and on their heads were as it were crowns like gold, and their faces were as the faces of men. 8 And they had hair as the hair of women, and their teeth were as the teeth of lions. 9 And they had breastplates, as it were breastplates of iron; and the sound of their wings was as the sound of chariots of many horses running to battle. 10 And they had tails like unto scorpions, and there were stings in their tails: and their power was to hurt men five months. 11 And they had a king over them, which is the angel of the bottomless pit, whose name in the Hebrew tongue is Abaddon, but in the Greek tongue hath his name Apollyon."*

The seven trumpets represent the judgments of God. They are God's retribution against the wicked in this age. As the wicked carry out their evil actions against God, against one another, and against Christians, God responds with these trumpet judgments to punish them for their sins and to call them to repentance.

These judgments are present in every generation, and they exist all around the world. Human sins call for divine judgment; and those who defy and rebel against God cannot escape His wrath, either in this life or in the next.

These trumpet judgments are only a partial and incomplete expression of God's wrath against sin. They are designed to be a warning to the wicked to flee from the wrath to come that will be revealed at the last judgment. God's wrath at the end of this age will be far greater and far more severe than any of these trumpet judgments.

It is a great encouragement to persecuted saints to know that the wicked are not going to go unpunished for their wickedness against God and His people. They are being partially punished now in these trumpet judgments, and they will be fully punished later in the lake of fire if they do not repent.

In the previous chapter, we looked at the first four trumpet judgments. We saw these judgments consisted of calamities of nature which God brings to pass on the land, on the sea, on the inland waters, and on the heavens above. These disasters that occur in these four realms of nature are acts of God by which He expresses His wrath on all those who defy Him. There is no place people may go to escape the retribution of God.

Every disaster in the realm of nature is God's messenger to sinful humanity to repent, and it is a sample of the wrath to come if people do not. Every kind of natural calamity—forest fires, earthquakes, tidal waves, hurricanes, volcanoes, epidemic diseases, drought, floods, solar flares, and asteroid impacts on the earth—all of them are brought to pass on sinful men by the hand of God to punish them for their sins. They are designed to call them to repentance, lest they experience even greater wrath in the Day of Judgment. But as bad as these physical disasters in the realm of nature are, they are not nearly as bad as the three remaining trumpet judgments which have yet to be described.

As we proceed through chapters 9, 10, and 11, we are going to see three additional trumpet judgments that are far worse than these first four we looked at in the last chapter. In these first four trumpet judgments, we had natural calamities; but in the next three trumpets we are going to have spiritual calamity, man-made calamities, and the final calamity of the last judgment. The spiritual calamity, which we will be looking at in this chapter, is that of satanic activity and oppression unleashed on the wicked in the fifth trumpet. Then we will see in the sixth trumpet at the end of chapter 9 the man-made calamity that consists of the great wars which men incite across the globe and through the ages, and through which hundreds of millions of people suffer and die.

The last trumpet in chapter 11 contains the final calamity, which is the day of God's wrath, in which the final destruction of the wicked occurs, and the vindication and reward of the righteous is declared. For the wicked, the seventh trumpet will be the greatest horror that could possibly be imagined; but for the righteous, the seventh trumpet will be the greatest honor that could ever be conceived.

These are the three woes that are yet to come spoken of in 8:13: *"And I beheld, and heard an angel flying through the midst of heaven, saying with a loud voice, Woe, woe, woe, to the inhabiters of the earth by reason of the other voices of the trumpet of the three angels, which are yet to sound."* Those three woes are the spiritual calamity, the man-made calamity, and the final calamity which will be the day of God's ultimate wrath.

In this chapter, we will examine the fifth trumpet, which is the first woe that is spoken of in 8:13. This judgment of the fifth trumpet involves God permitting Satan to unleash the deceptions of hell and the demons of hell on all those who reject the gospel.

When people fail to respond to God's gracious gospel invitations and set themselves against Christ and His people, God gives them over to demonic forces. They suffer the consequence of rejecting Christ as Lord, and the consequence is that they have Satan as lord. Satan is an abusive lord and treats those who follow him with deadly deceptions and with cruel torments. In this fifth trumpet judgment, we see God's retribution against the wicked for their wicked deeds by giving them over to Satan—who then viciously abuses them and gives them a foretaste in this life of the hell they are going to suffer in the next life. The way of the transgressor is hard, and part of the pain that transgressors endure for their defiant transgressions is revealed in this fifth seal.

The purpose for allowing Satan to abuse the rebellious and the wicked is certainly to begin to punish them for their sins in this life. But the purpose is also to show them that it is a painful and wretched life when they are exposed to satanic abuse, and therefore they need to repent so they might be released from the cruelties of Satan. If they are tormented by Satan in this life and are miserable because of it, how much more will they be tormented by Satan in hell and be infinitely more miserable? Recall what the rich man said when he was in hell. He said, *"I am tormented in this flame."* If serving Satan is so bitter for people now in this life, how will they bear the horrors of hell later?

Therefore, there is mercy even in this trumpet blast of God's temporal judgment in unleashing part of Satan's evil upon Satan's people in this life. By giving them a foretaste of what Satan's torment will be like in the future, God is giving them an immense incentive to repent and turn away from serving Satan. He provides them with powerful motives to repent and serve the Lord Jesus Christ. Thus, they are given a foretaste of hell in this life so they might repent and not experience the full horrors of hell in the next life.

Let us examine this fifth trumpet judgment, and consider what it is like to be on the receiving end of God's judgment in this life; and in particular, what it is like when He unleashes Satan on unsaved people.

The Opening of the Pit

The opening of the pit is in verses 1 through 2a. *"And the fifth angel sounded, and I saw a star fall from heaven unto the earth: and to him was given the key of the bottomless pit.* [2] *And he opened the bottomless pit."*

When the fifth angel sounded, John saw a star fall from heaven to earth. This star is a symbolic visual image representing Satan himself who is a fallen angel, and an angel who has been cast out of heaven and down to the earth. Angels are often referred to as "stars" in the Scriptures. For example, we saw in Revelation 1:20 the seven stars in the hand of Jesus are the angels of the seven churches. Furthermore, speaking of the time of the creation of the earth, Job 38:7 calls the angels *"the morning stars [who] sang together"* for joy over the creation God had made.

Revelation 9:11 identifies this angel of this bottomless pit by the name "destroyer," in both Hebrew and in Greek.

Jesus identifies this destroyer as Satan himself in John 10:10 when he says, *"The thief cometh not, but for to steal, and to kill, and to destroy."* Notice verse 11 of our chapter: *"And they had a king over them, which is the angel of the bottomless pit, whose name in the Hebrew tongue is Abaddon, but in the Greek tongue hath his name Apollyon."* Abaddon means destruction, and Apollyon means destroyer.

In John 10:10, Jesus says the thief comes not but for to kill and steal and destroy. Jesus says, in contrast to that thief, *"I am come that they might have life, and that they might have it more abundantly."* So whoever the thief is, he is doing the opposite of the work of Jesus Christ. Clearly, the thief is Satan, who opposes Christ and His work.

The verb "destroy" in John 10:10 is a translation of the same Greek word that is translated Apollyon in Revelation 9:11. The Apollyon of Revelation 9:11 is the thief who comes to steal and kill and destroy in John 10:10.

This star that falls from heaven to earth is Satan, and Jesus refers to this event of him falling from heaven to earth prophetically when He says in Luke 10:18, *"I beheld Satan as lightning fall from heaven."* The context of that statement is when Jesus sent out the seventy to preach the gospel, and they returned and said, *"Lord, even the devils are subject unto us through thy name."* Then Jesus said, "I saw Satan fall as lightning from heaven." When did this fall spoken of in Revelation 9:1 actually occur? It occurred at the ascension of the Lord Jesus.

Revelation 12:1–12 says: *"And there appeared a great wonder in heaven; a woman clothed with the sun, and the moon under her feet, and upon her head a crown of twelve stars"* (the woman is Israel, the old covenant community of the people of God): *"[2] And she being with child cried, travailing in birth, and pained to be delivered. [3] And there appeared another wonder in heaven; and behold a great red dragon, having seven heads and ten horns, and seven crowns upon his heads. [4] And his tail drew the third part of the stars of heaven, and did cast them to the earth: and the dragon stood before the woman which was ready to be delivered, for to devour her child as soon as it was born."* Herod wanted to destroy Jesus as soon as He was born. Verse 5: *"And she brought forth a man child"* (Jesus), *"who was to rule all nations with a rod of iron"* (He was going to inherit the throne of David), *"and her child was caught up unto God, and to his throne."* Here is the birth, death, burial, resurrection, and ascension of our Lord Jesus Christ.

"[6] And the woman" (the new covenant community of the people of God, the new Israel), *"fled into the wilderness, where she hath a place prepared of God, that they should feed her there a thousand two hun-*

dred and threescore days. [7] *And there was war in heaven: Michael and his angels fought against the dragon; and the dragon fought and his angels,* [8] *And prevailed not; neither was their place found any more in heaven."* Notice verse 9: *"And the great dragon was cast out, that old serpent, called the Devil, and Satan, which deceiveth the whole world: he was cast out into the earth, and his angels were cast out with him.* [10] *And I heard a loud voice saying in heaven, Now is come salvation, and strength, and the kingdom of our God, and the power of his Christ: for the accuser of our brethren is cast down, which accused them before our God day and night.* [11] *And they overcame him by the blood of the Lamb, and by the word of their testimony; and they loved not their lives unto the death."*

Here are the results of Satan being cast out of heaven by the newly ascended Christ, verse 12: *"Therefore rejoice, ye heavens, and ye that dwell in them. Woe to the inhabiters of the earth and of the sea! for the devil is come down unto you, having great wrath, because he knoweth that he hath but a short time."*

When Jesus ascended to heaven and presented His work before the Father of having redeemed His elect, Satan the accuser of the brethren was defeated. He was cast out of heaven, and down onto the earth. He was that star that fell from heaven to earth, and what happened when he hit the earth is that he opened the bottomless pit. This is comprehended in verse 12: *"Woe to the inhabiters of the earth and of the sea! for the devil is come down unto you, having great wrath, because he knoweth that he hath but a short time."*

When the New Covenant era ends and Jesus returns, the devil's time is up. The inhabitants of the earth and the sea (all of humanity) are in a terrible state of woe now because Satan is now dwelling, not in heaven, but on the earth. Heaven is a better place now because Satan has been cast out. Verse 12: *"Rejoice, ye heavens, and ye that dwell in them."* Earth is far worse off now because Satan has moved his residence, and he is now resident on the earth. *"Woe to the inhabiters of the earth."*

What happened when Satan fell to the earth? He unleashed his lies and his demonic hordes in order to persecute the people of the earth. When Christ ascended to heaven, Satan was cast out of heaven and down to the earth, and to him was *"given"* the key to the bottomless pit.

Revelation 9:1: *"And the fifth angel sounded, and I saw a star fall from heaven unto the earth: and to him was given the key of the bot-*

tomless pit." Notice the key *"was given"* to him. He does not possess it, and he does not control it. It was given to him. Who controls the key? Jesus does, because we read in Revelation 1:18, Jesus says that *"I. . .have the keys of hell and of death."*

The point is that Satan can do nothing without the permission of God, and the only thing he is able to do is what Jesus allows him to do. He is a defeated foe, and we are going to see this increasingly as we move through the rest of the book of Revelation. We are going to have an ever-expanding awareness and understanding of the degree of the sovereignty and control that Jesus has over Satan and over the wicked.

Jesus is not involved in some desperate battle in which it is uncertain whether He is going to win or lose. He has already won the battle, and He is now executing His victory. He has complete and total domination over His enemies. We begin to see this as Jesus hands him the key to the bottomless pit. Jesus is going to allow him to do some limited things that will serve the purposes of Christ. Satan will think he is achieving his goals, but Christ will use even Satan's worst actions against him to accomplish Christ's purposes.

Satan was given permission by Christ to employ his lies and his demons, here called *"locusts,"* in order to torment and deceive the people of the earth and to bring upon them misery and darkness.

This bottomless pit is the prison of the demons where they are contained until the final judgment. In Luke 8:31, when Jesus was casting the demons out of the man of Gadara, they besought him that He would not command them to go out into the abyss; that is, into the pit. This is the same word that is used here of the bottomless pit.

We read about this abyss, this bottomless pit, this place where the demons are contained, in Revelation 11:7, in Revelation 17:8, and in Revelation 20:1, 3. What we see is this abyss or pit is the place out of which all evil on the earth arises. It is the place out of which Satan sends forth his minions to accomplish his work here on earth.

In Jude 1:6, it says of the fallen angels, *"And the angels which kept not their first estate, but left their own habitation, he hath reserved in everlasting chains under darkness unto the judgment of the great day."* This is why the demons did not want to be sent back to the abyss. They liked being free on the earth to torment people, and they did not want to be sent back where they could not do that work. This abyss is the holding tank of all of Satan's demons and all of Satan's evil.

The Contents of the Pit

The contents of the pit are described in verses 2b to 11: *"And he opened the bottomless pit; and there arose a smoke out of the pit, as the smoke of a great furnace; and the sun and the air were darkened by reason of the smoke of the pit. 3 And there came out of the smoke locusts upon the earth: and unto them was given power, as the scorpions of the earth have power. 4 And it was commanded them that they should not hurt the grass of the earth, neither any green thing, neither any tree; but only those men which have not the seal of God in their foreheads. 5 And to them it was given that they should not kill them, but that they should be tormented five months: and their torment was as the torment of a scorpion, when he striketh a man. 6 And in those days shall men seek death, and shall not find it; and shall desire to die, and death shall flee from them. 7 And the shapes of the locusts were like unto horses prepared unto battle; and on their heads were as it were crowns like gold, and their faces were as the faces of men. 8 And they had hair as the hair of women, and their teeth were as the teeth of lions. 9 And they had breastplates, as it were breastplates of iron; and the sound of their wings was as the sound of chariots of many horses running to battle. 10 And they had tails like unto scorpions, and there were stings in their tails: and their power was to hurt men five months. 11 And they had a king over them, which is the angel of the bottomless pit, whose name in the Hebrew tongue is Abaddon, but in the Greek tongue hath his name Apollyon."*

Out of this bottomless pit that Satan opened there arose two things. First of all, a thick black smoke that obscured the sun; and secondly, a great horde of locusts that tormented men. This is reminiscent of the plague of locusts that Moses brought upon Egypt in Exodus 10:12–20. The result of this plague of locusts was that they covered the face of the earth, the land was darkened because of them, and they consumed every green plant.

This trumpet judgment, while using language that echoes the Egyptian plague, speaks of something far worse than a literal plague of locusts. The darkness this trumpet judgment produces and the locusts it brings forth are a symbolic visual image of something far greater than the plague of Egypt.

First of all, consider the smoke out of the pit described in verse 2. Notice it says, *"And he opened the bottomless pit; and there arose a smoke out of the pit, as the smoke of a great furnace; and the sun and the air were darkened by reason of the smoke of the pit."* What we see is a thick black smoke rising out of this bottomless pit that obscures the light of the sun and any illumination that might come from the sky.

Light is used in the Scriptures as a metaphor for truth, and for purity or holiness.

It is used as a metaphor for truth in many places, for example, Isaiah 8:20: *"To the law and to the testimony: if they speak not according to this word, it is because there is no light in them";* that is, because there is no truth in them. If you do not speak according to the Scriptures, there is no truth in you; in other words, there is no light in you because light is a metaphor for truth. Psalm 119:130: *"The entrance of thy words giveth light; it giveth understanding unto the simple."* Light is equated with understanding and truth.

Light is also a metaphor for purity or holiness. In 1 John 1:5 it says, *"God is light, and in him is no darkness at all."* In Isaiah 10:17 the *"light of Israel"* is also called the *"Holy One"* of Israel. These are names of God; God is named the Light of Israel, and He is also named the Holy One of Israel, light being a metaphor for holiness or purity.

Therefore, this smoke that obscures the light of the sun and darkens the sky is simply the opposite of truth and purity. The smoke represents the deception and lies of Satan that obscure and hide the truth, and the moral defilement he promotes that corrupts purity and holiness. Satan produces spiritual darkness out of the pit; and by it, he obscures the light of truth. Satan produces spiritual defilement out of the pit; and by it, he obscures the light of purity and holiness. Satan produces both lies and immorality.

This smoke is the false religions of the world and the false teachings and heresies in the church that obscure the light of the gospel. This smoke is the assault on biblical morality that teaches that the murder of unborn children is fine, adultery and fornication are acceptable, and lying and stealing are justified. Satan floods the world with the darkness of lies and immorality; and by employing them, blinds men to the truth and brings them into the practice of evil.

When the mass of people believe lies and practice wickedness, horrible outcomes are the result. Lives are destroyed, marriages are destroyed, churches are destroyed, cultures are destroyed, and nations are destroyed. As verse 11 says, Satan is a destroyer, and he destroys the unsaved by plunging them into lies and immorality. He clouds the minds of the lost and darkens their understanding, and he drives them into corrupt moral practices.

Our culture we are living in right now is a culture of smoke from the pit. What comes out of the entertainment industry? The smoke from the pit. What comes out of our universities and colleges? The smoke from the pit. What comes out of our public schools? The smoke from the pit. What comes out of the mouths of our politicians and our courts? The smoke from the pit. What do you see and hear on TV and radio and on the Internet? The smoke from the pit. In every one of those institutions and activities, you see the lies of Satan belching forth, and you see the immorality of Satan being powerfully promoted.

When you hear the lies and hear and see the promotion of immorality, you need to say to yourself that it is the smoke from the pit. And what is that smoke doing? It is obscuring the light of the gospel. It is obscuring the light of purity. Satan is working throughout this world to becloud the minds of people with lies and with immorality, lest the light of the glorious gospel should shine in unto them, and they should be saved.

This is the plague that Christ allows Satan to bring upon the ungodly. He clouds their minds with lies, he clouds their lives with wickedness, and as a result of the lies they believe and the wickedness they practice, they have terrible outcomes. They have miserable lives. The way of the transgressor becomes very, very hard.

Secondly, notice the locusts of the pit. The locusts of the pit are described at length in verses 3 to 11. John's vision of these locusts recalls two passages in which they appear—that of the Exodus plague, which we have already mentioned in Exodus 10:12–20, and also the terrible plague of locusts that were sent as God's judgment on Israel mentioned in the book of Joel. In Joel 1 the plague of locusts is described, and the destruction of the land and the people is declared. In Joel 2, an intensification of the plague of locusts is promised unless the people repent and return to the Lord. The locust plague of Egypt and the locust plague of Joel 1 and 2 form the backdrop and provide the meaning for the plague of locusts in Revelation 9.

Notice Revelation 9:3: *"And there came out of the smoke locusts upon the earth: and unto them was given power."* These two great locust plagues, the one in Egypt and the other in Israel, the one in Exodus and the other in Joel, both foreshadow the plague of locusts in Revelation 9. They convey the message of God's wrath being poured out on Egypt in Exodus and on Israel in Joel for their defiance of God and their rebellion against Him.

When Pharaoh in Egypt defied God, rebelled against God, and persecuted God's people, God sent locusts. When Jews in Israel rebelled against God, defied God, and persecuted God's prophets, God sent locusts. Here we have the ungodly people of the world defying God, rebelling against God, and persecuting the people of God—and God says, "I will send My locusts."

But the locusts described in Revelation 9 are not literal locusts. These locusts in Revelation 9 do not attack the plant life of the earth. Notice verse 4a: *"And it was commanded them that they should not hurt the grass of the earth, neither any green thing, neither any tree."* These are not ordinary locusts because locusts are herbivores, and these locusts do not eat any plants of any kind. Instead, we see that they attack people, and they attack only a select group of people. It says in verse 4b, *"only those men which have not the seal of God in their foreheads."* It says in verse 4, that they are not to hurt the vegetation, but to hurt those men who do not have the seal of God in their foreheads.

We explained this seal of God that is on believers at length in chapter 25. The point is that these locusts attack and harm only the unsaved people of the earth. They do not harm the believers. They are forbidden to harm the believers. If you have the seal of God in your forehead, these locusts cannot touch you. But if you do not, they are all over you.

As we look at the description of these locusts, we see two things about them. First of all, they are terrible in both their appearance and their abilities. First, they have the power of scorpions. Three times we are told they have the power of scorpions. In verse 3 it says, *"unto them was given power, as the scorpions of the earth have power."* In verse 5, *"their torment was as the torment of a scorpion, when he striketh a man."* And in verse 10, *"And they had tails like unto scorpions, and there were stings in their tails."*

The sting of a scorpion is terrible. It is like being lit on fire, far worse than any bee sting. Depending upon the species of scorpion such a sting can even be fatal, though most of the time they are not.

They cause tremendous pain to those they sting. Our text emphasizes repeatedly that these locusts have the power of scorpions.

Second, they have strength like battle horses, verse 7a: *"And the shapes of the locusts were like unto horses prepared unto battle."* This is a strong, virile stallion that is eager to go into battle and to create mayhem and terror.

Third, they have authority like kings, verse 7b: *"And on their heads were as it were crowns like gold."*

Fourth, they had the intelligence of men, verse 7c: *"And their faces were as the faces of men."*

Fifth, they have the seductive power of women, verse 8: *"They had hair as the hair of women."*

Sixth, they have the fierceness and the cruelty of lions, verse 8b: *"And their teeth were as the teeth of lions."*

Seventh, verse 9 says they have the invincibility of armored troops. *"They had breastplates, as it were breastplates of iron."*

Eighth, they have overwhelming numbers, verse 9b: *"And the sound of their wings was as the sound of chariots of many horses running to battle."*

All of these are metaphors. This is all symbolic visual imagery to convey that these locusts are superbly equipped to inflict tremendous damage on all they assault. They have the power of scorpions, the strength of battle horses, the authority of kings, the intelligence of men, the seductive power of women, the fierceness and cruelty of lions, the invincibility of armored troops, and overwhelming numbers. They are superbly equipped to inflict tremendous damage on all they assault. These locusts represent nothing other than Satan's demons who have capabilities no literal locust could ever possess, and who seek to harm that which no literal locust would ever attack.

But these locusts are not only terrible in their appearance and their abilities; secondly, these locusts are also terrible in their activity and their effect. In particular, their whole purpose is to hurt and torment men and to drive them to despair and self-destruction. It is to drive them to a state of anguish and grief and sorrow by filling their lives with misery and pain. Notice verse 4. It says, *"And it was commanded them that they should not hurt" [any plant life, but they should hurt] "only those men which have not the seal of God in their foreheads."*

The purpose of these demons that Satan unleashes is to hurt men, but a particular group of men—men who do not have the seal of God, men who are unsaved. They are going to damage and harm the lost. Verse 5 says, "*To them it was given that they should not kill them, but that they should be tormented five months: and their torment was as the torment of a scorpion, when he striketh a man.*"

Not only are these demons unleashed on the unsaved to hurt them and harm them, but they are also unleashed to torment them. They will torture the lost with painful afflictions, like the sting of a scorpion. They will be tormented with physical, emotional, and mental pain and anguish. Notice verse 6: "*And in those days shall men seek death, and shall not find it; and shall desire to die, and death shall flee from them.*"

Not only will they hurt the unsaved and torment them, but they will also drive them to despair and depression and hopelessness so that it seems to the unsaved they are better off dead than alive. They will bring them to despondency and despair and the brink of suicide. They will wish they could die, but they cannot bring themselves to kill themselves, so they go on in the misery of a living death.

Twice we are told this torment and this driving to despair that these demons will accomplish on the unsaved will last for five months. Notice verse 5: "*And to them it was given that they should not kill them, but that they should be tormented five months.*" And verse 10: "*And they had tails like unto scorpions, and there were stings in their tails: and their power was to hurt men five months.*"

When we studied numerology, we saw that ten conveys the concept of perfection. Therefore five, which is a division and a diminution of the number ten, conveys the idea of that which is imperfect and incomplete—a partial torment as opposed to a perfect torment. It represents something less than the worst possible suffering which the number ten would represent. The number five represents a partial suffering. Notice, this partial suffering is for 100 percent of the people; not a third of them, but all of them.

All of the unsaved without exception will have torment in this life from Satan's demons. They will have something less than perfect suffering or the worst possible suffering; they will have a partial suffering, which is a foretaste of the total suffering they will have and the perfect suffering they will experience in the lake of fire.

The hurt and driving to despair these demons inflict is the trumpet judgment God unleashes on the wicked for their defiance and rebellion against Him, and for their persecution of His people. Even though the people who are being tormented are the people of Satan, Satan does not care for the well-being of his people. He is pleased when they experience pain and despair.

Here is a description of how Satan treats his people, and this is the misery his demons inflict on them. God punishes the unsaved for their persecution of His people by giving Satan liberty to abuse them. Even though they serve Satan and his purposes, Satan views them with contempt. He views them as mere useful idiots, and he torments them for his pleasure as they diligently serve him.

Notice verse 11: *"And they"* —that is, these demons—*"had a king over them, which is the angel of the bottomless pit, whose name in the Hebrew tongue is Abaddon, but in the Greek tongue hath his name Apollyon."* The king over these demons is Satan himself, the star that fell in verse 1.

Here he is called by two titles that describe who he is and what he does. The first title given to him in Hebrew is Abaddon, which means destruction. His second title in Greek is Apollyon, which means destroyer. Therefore, his name is Destruction and Destroyer. Satan is a destroyer who works destruction, and that disposition also inhabits the demons he directs to do his will.

John 10:10 says: *"The thief comes not, but for to steal, and to kill, and to destroy,"* and that is what Satan does to all the people he is given liberty to act upon. Thank God Satan is not given liberty to act on us. This is not to say that Satan does not act on us at all, but Satan's broad charter of liberty given to him by God for acting on the wicked is something entirely different than the limited and restricted degree of liberty Satan is given to act on us.

God uses Satan's action against the wicked to punish and destroy them, and He largely gives Satan a free hand. But God uses Satan's actions against us to save us and sanctify us and preserve us, in spite of Satan's desires and efforts to the contrary. We see this in the book of Job. God forbids Satan to exercise a destroying influence on those who are sealed with the seal of God. We are protected from the trumpet judgments, just like the Israelites were protected from the ten plagues of Egypt.

In order to demonstrate this, Luke 10:1 says, *"After these things the Lord appointed other seventy also, and sent them two and two before his face into every city and place, whither he himself would come."* He then gives them instructions for this ministry, and they carry them out.

Notice verse 17: *"And the seventy returned again with joy, saying"* (now notice), *"Lord, even the demons are subject unto us through thy name."* In other words, the demons did not have their way with the believers; the believers had their way with the demons. When Jesus says in response to the report of the seventy in verse 18, *"I beheld Satan as lightning fall from heaven,"* He is prophetically declaring the event of Revelation 9:1 and Revelation 12:12.

Jesus is speaking prophetically about what will occur at his ascension. Jesus is saying that implicit in your subduing of the demons now is a guarantee of the casting out of Satan in the near future. It is so certain to occur, that it can be seen as already having occurred. In fact, it did occur in just a year or two at His ascension into heaven.

Jesus said in verse 18, *"I beheld Satan as lightning fall from heaven."* Notice the next verse, verse 19: *"Behold, I give unto you power to tread on serpents and scorpions."* We have just read about scorpions in Revelation 9. Jesus is not referring to real snakes and real scorpions like the snake-handling cults think. When He says He gives them power to tread on serpents and scorpions, He is telling them He gives them power to tread on Satan and his demons. Satan is the serpent referred to here, and his demons are the scorpions. Jesus then goes on to say: *"and over all the power of the enemy: and nothing shall by any means hurt you."* Notice: nothing shall by any means hurt you.

This fifth trumpet judgment will not hurt you. The fact that Satan has demons in this world, and they have been released out of the pit, and are going about stinging and hurting and tormenting people, making their lives miserable and driving them to the point of suicide, is something that is not going to happen to you. Those demons and the commission they have been given in the fifth trumpet cannot touch you. You have the seal of God. The message is this: These demons are forbidden to hurt you.

Jesus has triumphed over the Evil One. He has triumphed over principalities and powers and over the forces of darkness. We have the armor of God, and with it, we can quench Satan's fiery darts and defeat and push back Satan and his demons. He throws his fiery darts, but we have the shield of faith. The ungodly have no shield. Every fiery dart strikes them with its full force.

Woe unto those who have no such protection from God. To be given over to Satan's will is the worst of all judgments. Do you wonder why the way of the transgressor is hard? Do you wonder why the ungodly have so much pain and misery and depression in their lives? Wonder no more. When people live in the darkness of lies and in the darkness of sin, and when they are tormented by evil spirits, it is no wonder why they act out self-destructive behaviors.

We observe drug addiction, criminal behavior, promiscuity, alcoholism, divorce, and many other self-destructive behaviors on the part of the unsaved. We look at people and think, "Why are they doing these things? Do they not realize how these things are going to destroy their lives?" This passage explains why they are doing those self-destructive things. It is because the demons are at work, clouding their minds, tormenting their souls, and driving them to seek pleasure in sin. But ultimately, they find those very pleasures are the things that destroy them.

Jesus has offered them terms of reconciliation, but if they will not receive them, they shall receive the just recompense of their defiance and rebellion and rejection of Christ in this life. They shall have the sorrow and misery and pain that Satan brings them, with no comfort of promises, no strength for deliverance, and no good shepherd to lead them by the still waters and into the green pastures.

You wonder why nations go on suicidal courses of action like so many are doing right now. This is why. It is the smoke of the pit. It is the work of Satan and his demons. This is the payback God gives them for persecuting us. They are the ones to be pitied. All this slaughter and mayhem and murder in the Middle East—where does that come from? It comes from the thief who comes to steal and kill and destroy. This is the essence of Islam: killing and stealing and destroying. And yet, Western countries gladly welcome this smoke from the pit because they, too, reject Christ and persecute His people.

I want to say to any of my readers who are yet unsaved: you need to flee from Satan. You need to flee from his demons. There is only one place you can run in order to get away from them, and that is to Jesus Christ. Flee to Christ for protection from Satan. Come out of his kingdom of darkness. All of these lies that deny the truth of the Scripture, all of this wicked behavior that is in defiance of God's law—repent of it. Turn away from it. Say, "I am done with Satan, I am done with his lies, I am done practicing his wickedness, I am done with the torment that his demons have brought into my life emotionally, physically, and mentally. I want deliverance. Lord Jesus, save me! Save me from the Evil One. Save me from my sins." Do you know what Jesus will do? He will crush the one who is trying to crush you. That is what is promised in Genesis 3:15. It says that He will crush the head of the serpent.

You cannot crush Satan. When you look at the description of these demons, are you going to be able to fight them? They are far more powerful than you are, far more clever than you are, and they have far more weapons than you possess. You need a Savior—a Savior who will deliver you from the Evil One, and who will give you the seal of God so Satan cannot touch you.

There is a lot of phony demonology being taught in the name of Christianity that says believers can be possessed by demons or that people can cast demons into you. Recognize this: it says in Revelation 9:4 that they cannot hurt those who have the seal of God in their foreheads. You do not have to worry about Satan and the demons somehow getting some horrible hold on you and destroying your life. They are forbidden to do that.

Yes, Satan walks about as a roaring lion seeking whom he may devour, and we need to resist him steadfast in the faith—no question about that. But what happens when we resist the devil? He flees from us. We drive him away. He does not control us, he does not run our lives, and he does not determine our outcomes.

Rejoice in the fact that you have been translated out of the kingdom of darkness and into the kingdom of His dear Son. You have been delivered from Satan and his demons, and you need to fear him and them no more. When he comes and whispers in your ear and tells you to follow him, he has no power to compel you to do that, and you can tell him to depart from you—and he will. You can go on serving the Lord Jesus. Do not buy into the false demonology which says that Christians have something to fear from Satan. We have nothing to fear from him. He is a defeated, deposed snake, and Christ has crushed him under His heel on the cross.

Jesus prepares a table before us in the presence of our enemies, and all the demons are compelled to stand back while we feast, with the result that goodness and mercy will follow us all the days of our life, and we will dwell in the house of the Lord forever.

30

The Sixth Trumpet, Revelation 9:12–21

> "12 *One woe is past; and, behold, there come two woes more hereafter.* 13 *And the sixth angel sounded, and I heard a voice from the four horns of the golden altar which is before God,* 14 *Saying to the sixth angel which had the trumpet, Loose the four angels which are bound in the great river Euphrates.* 15 *And the four angels were loosed, which were prepared for an hour, and a day, and a month, and a year, for to slay the third part of men.* 16 *And the number of the army of the horsemen were two hundred thousand thousand: and I heard the number of them.* 17 *And thus I saw the horses in the vision, and them that sat on them, having breastplates of fire, and of jacinth, and brimstone: and the heads of the horses were as the heads of lions; and out of their mouths issued fire and smoke and brimstone.* 18 *By these three was the third part of men killed, by the fire, and by the smoke, and by the brimstone, which issued out of their mouths.* 19 *For their power is in their mouth, and in their tails: for their tails were like unto serpents, and had heads, and with them they do hurt.* 20 *And the rest of the men which were not killed by these plagues yet repented not of the works of their hands, that they should not worship devils, and idols of gold, and silver, and brass, and stone, and of wood: which neither can see, nor hear, nor walk:* 21 *Neither repented they of their murders, nor of their sorceries, nor of their fornication, nor of their thefts."*

The trumpet judgments are God's punishment on the wicked in this age for the evil they have committed against God and His people. The trumpet judgments are the answer of God to the prayers of persecuted saints for vengeance to be wrought on those who have persecuted them. We saw these prayers in 6:10 when the martyrs in heaven *"cried with a loud voice, saying, How long, O Lord, holy and true, dost thou not judge and avenge our blood on them that dwell on the earth?"*

We saw these prayers for vengeance also being offered in 8:3–5 where it says: "*And another angel came and stood at the altar, having a golden censer; and there was given unto him much incense, that he should offer it with the prayers of all saints upon the golden altar which was before the throne.* [4] *And the smoke of the incense, which came with the prayers of the saints, ascended up before God out of the angel's hand.* [5] *And the angel took the censer, and filled it with fire of the altar, and cast it into the earth: and there were voices, and thunderings, and lightnings, and an earthquake.*"

These seven trumpet judgments are God's answer to the prayers of the saints in heaven and earth for vengeance on their persecutors. God is executing vengeance in this age on those who persecute His people. These trumpet judgments describe what this vengeance consists of and what it looks like.

We saw God's vengeance against the wicked is executed through disasters in the realm of nature in the first four trumpets. These were physical punishments executed in the physical realm of nature.

But the fifth trumpet revealed that God's judgments against the wicked not only take place in the physical realm, they also take place in the spiritual realm. In Revelation 9:1–11, we saw that after Satan was cast out of heaven, he came down to the earth and unleashed his lies and deceptions in order to obscure the light of the gospel and promote immorality and wickedness. This was the smoke that went up out of the pit.

Furthermore, we saw that Satan unleashed his demons to torment and oppress the wicked, and these were symbolized by the locusts that came out of the pit. Through the work of his demons, Satan brings extreme mental, emotional, and spiritual anguish upon the unsaved. The demons torment the unsaved with pain in their souls that is likened to the sting of a scorpion. Because of demonic activity, hopelessness and depression and despair characterize the lost. They go on in the misery of a living death—afraid to die, but too miserable to be alive.

The wicked are like the troubled sea when it cannot rest, whose waters cast up mire and dirt. "*There is no peace, saith my God, to the wicked.*" This lack of peace is due to the demonic torment described in the fifth seal. Satan is a destroyer, and he produces destruction in the souls of his followers through his lies and deceptions, and through his demons that he unleashes on his own people.

God not only uses nature to bring His judgments on the ungodly through physical punishments, as we saw in the first four trumpets, but He also uses Satan to bring His judgment upon the ungodly through spiritual punishments, as we saw in the fifth trumpet.

This brings us to the sixth trumpet judgment. The fifth trumpet judgment unleashed deception and misery, but the sixth trumpet judgment unleashes slaughter and death. In this sixth trumpet judgment, the judgment of God against the wicked is greatly intensified. Instead of locusts, there is now a huge army of horsemen mounted on powerful and frightening horses; and instead of the torment of the scorpion sting, there is now death and slaughter.

The intensity and the awfulness of this sixth trumpet is not only designed to punish the wicked, but it is also designed to call them to repentance. But they do not repent, no matter how severe the judgment brought upon them because of the hardness and depravity of their hearts. This tells us we should not expect the world to repent, even if we supply people with compelling reasons for doing so, and put enormous pressure on them to do it.

No matter how severe God's judgments, the world goes on in its rebellion and defiance, because depraved people would rather destroy themselves than submit to God. They would rather be consumed with wars than bow before the Prince of Peace. In a word, they would rather be slaughtered than saved. They would rather have war than worship the true and living God. When people rebel against God, they do not triumph over God; they are simply destroyed by God, and the sixth trumpet describes this destruction.

The destruction described in this sixth trumpet is that of satanically inspired and satanically driven war in which hundreds of millions of people have been killed throughout this age. When nations wage war with one another, and when kings provoke conflicts and pursue conquest, this appears on the surface to be a man-made disaster of epic proportions—and indeed it is. But behind those men who declare and wage these wars is a satanic inspiration, a satanic motivation, and a satanic energy that moves them to engage in the holocaust of war.

The sixth trumpet of judgment represents all the wars that occur between the first and second coming of Christ, all of which are satanically driven and satanically inspired, and which are instigated and carried out by evil men seeking to conquer and control and oppress other peoples and nations. War is a man-made disaster of epic proportions, inspired by Satan and used by God as a judgment on the wicked in this age. This is the nature of the sixth trumpet, and we want to consider it together in more detail.

The Origin of the Judgment of War

The origin of the judgment of war is found in verses 12 to 14: "*One woe is past; and, behold, there come two woes more hereafter.* [13] *And the sixth angel sounded, and I heard a voice from the four horns of the golden altar which is before God,* [14] *Saying to the sixth angel which had the trumpet, Loose the four angels which are bound in the great river Euphrates.*"

From the time of Christ to this present day, wars have been fought in every nation and all around the world and in every generation. There has been no century—indeed, there has been no decade—that has been free from war. War is a terrible thing. The sorrow it causes, the destruction it brings to pass, and the cost to humanity it incurs cannot be calculated. War is the worst thing that people can inflict on one another, and it is the most terrible thing that people can do to each other. War is a terrible scourge on humanity, and the question is: if it is so awful, then why does it occur so much? This passage tells us why.

The first reason war occurs is because war is a judgment of God. Notice verses 13 and 14: "*And the sixth angel sounded, and I heard a voice from the four horns of the golden altar which is before God,* [14] *Saying to the sixth angel which had the trumpet, Loose the four angels which are bound in the great river Euphrates.*"

As the sixth angel sounds the trumpet of God's judgment, a voice from the golden altar in heaven speaks. This golden altar is the same altar spoken of in Revelation 6:9–10, where we see the souls of the saints in heaven beneath the altar crying out, "How long, O Lord, will it be before You exercise vengeance on those who killed us?" This is the same altar spoken of in 8:3–5, where the prayers of all saints are offered before God for vengeance, and God casts out His lightnings and thunderings, and the seven angels with their seven trumpets assemble and begin to sound. This golden altar spoken of in 9:13 is the same altar where saints are offering their prayers to God for vengeance upon their persecutors.

This altar is said to be *"before God,"* and God now speaks in response to the prayers of the people of God and directs the sixth angel who had the trumpet to release the four angels who are bound in the great river Euphrates. The result of this act of God in directing the release of these four angels is that terrible war breaks out upon the earth.

The point is simply this: God is in control of the wars that occur among the nations. God is in control of wars as to when they occur, who is involved, and the length of time they go on. God inflicts war on the world as a judgment on the world for her persecution of Christians and for her rebellion against God. He inflicts this war by directing these angels to be released.

Perhaps you have heard the quote from General Sherman of the Northern Army during the American Civil War when he said, "War is hell." And indeed, war is a foretaste of hell, with all of the misery and sorrow and torment it causes. The grief and anguish of war, and the weeping and wailing and gnashing of teeth that the pain of war brings to pass, is a foretaste of what hell will be like.

God sends this lesser hell of war onto the earth to give wicked men a taste of what the real hell will be like, and to move them to flee from the wrath to come by repenting of their rebellion against God. War is a judgment of God sent by God as a punishment upon the wicked, and as a warning of the greater wrath that is yet to come.

The second reason war occurs is because war is a work of Satan. While it is true there can be no war without the act of God in permitting it and speaking from before the golden altar that it shall begin to occur, it is also true that when God does permit it, it is satanic demons who bring it to pass and who cause it to actually be carried out.

Notice verse 14 again. God says *"to the sixth angel which had the trumpet, Loose the four angels which are bound in the great river Euphrates."* These four angels are evil angels because it says of them that they are *"bound."* The fact that they are bound shows that they are not good angels. Good angels are never bound. They are free and they freely do God's will. But these angels are in chains. They are evil beings who have to be restrained from doing the evil they want to do and actually will do when their restraints are taken away. These are evil angels who cannot act until God releases them to act and do what they desire to do.

It says of these four evil angels that they are bound in the great river Euphrates. It was from across the river Euphrates that the enemies of Israel came. Both the Assyrians that attacked the Northern Kingdom and the Babylonians that attacked the Southern Kingdom came across the river Euphrates to wage war against Israel and execute the judgment of God on Israel. Historically, war arrived from the Euphrates River, and the Euphrates River is used here as a symbol of the coming of war, and as the symbol of God's judgment on wicked people.

The fact that there are four angels tells us that war will occur over all of the earth—in the north, the south, the east, and the west—since the number four symbolizes the whole earth. The point regarding these four angels is this: once they are released by God, these evil demons become the driving force behind all wars. These evil demons inspire, motivate, and empower wicked men to go forth conquering and to conquer, to take peace from the earth, and to cause men to kill one another. We saw them doing this in the first and second seals in chapter 6.

Wars are not merely the idea of men. Wars are driven by demons inspiring men to engage in it, motivating men to pursue it, and empowering men to be able to carry it out. As William Hendriksen said: "In times of war, wicked men seem to become incarnate demons."[7] When you see the horrible things people do in war, you ask, "How can people commit those kinds of atrocities? How can they deny their own humanity to do the horrible things they do?" This is how and this is why: because they are being driven by demons. Satan loves to steal and kill and destroy, and there are no better means for him to carry those activities out than to provoke war between nations.

What is the origin of the judgment of war that is visited on the earth? War is a judgment of God, and war is a work of Satan. When God releases the demons of war, those demons then move wicked men to instigate war and thereby cause great numbers of death and great amounts of destruction on the earth. This sixth trumpet describes the origin of war, and not just the origin of one war, but the origin of all wars, past, present, and future that occur in the time frame between the first and second coming of Jesus Christ.

---

7 William Hendriksen. *More Than Conquerors: An Interpretation of the Book of Revelation*. Grand Rapids: Baker, 1962. 122.

The Execution of the Judgment of War

The execution of the judgment of war is contained in verses 15 to 19. Once God has released the demons of war, they employ the instrumentality of human agents to carry it out. Remember the account of Job? God released Satan to go to war against Job. How did Satan execute that war? He employed human agents to accomplish it. Satan employed the Sabeans and the Chaldeans to actually carry out his evil plans against Job. Human agents were the instruments to kill Job's servants and steal Job's herds. So it is here. The demons of war incite men to carry out the carnage of war. Demonic desires are carried out through human instruments.

Let us consider several points regarding the execution of the judgment of war.

First, we see that the time of war is appointed. Verse 15 says, *"And the four angels were loosed, which were prepared for an hour, and a day, and a month, and a year, for to slay the third part of men."* The timing of the loosing of the demons of war by God is not haphazard. War is precisely timed in the decrees of God. God determines the year, the month, the day, and the hour in which these wars begin.

God's judgments are always precise in their timing. He does not bring His judgments on the wicked too soon, nor does He bring them too late. When the wickedness of men builds up to a certain point, and when the iniquity of a nation is finally full, then God brings the temporal judgment of war upon them. War occurs according to God's sovereign timetable. Just like every event in history is under the ultimate authority of God, war between the nations is under His authority as well. He determines its beginning, its duration, and its end.

Second, we see that the scale of war is massive. Notice verse 16. It says, *"And the number of the army of the horsemen were two hundred thousand thousand: and I heard the number of them."* Here John is told the number of the army of the horsemen involved, and the number is two hundred million. This number is symbolic. It stands for a vast army that is so large it cannot be counted. John must be told the number of this army because it would be impossible for him to arrive at the number by counting himself.

Indeed, countless millions of people have made up the armies of the nations throughout this present age. In the last 2,000 years, the number of soldiers that have been enlisted in armies and all the people involved in supporting the work of those soldiers and armies is beyond calculation. Only God knows the number of them. The point is, war has been a huge part of God's judgment on the earth, and Satan and his demons have enlisted vast numbers of people to carry out his evil work of stealing and killing and destroying through the instrument of war.

This satanic work of assembling vast armies to wage war will find its culmination at the end of this age in the final battle of Armageddon, in which Satan will gather together a vast transnational coalition army to destroy the people of God from the face of the earth. The number of the army in our text is two hundred million. Two is the number of interdependence. Therefore, we have all of the people of the earth interdependently cooperating together to attempt to bring about the eradication of Christianity from the earth in that final assembly at the battle of Armageddon.

When Satan is loosed and gathers the armies of the earth together against the saints, Jesus will return and destroy both Satan and that wicked army and will deliver His people from them, as we are told in 20:7–10. So we see that the time of war is appointed, and the scale of war is massive all throughout this age, but especially massive in that final war at the end of the age.

Third, we see that the destruction of war is terrible. This is found in verses 17 to 19:

"And thus I saw the horses in the vision, and them that sat on them, having breastplates of fire, and of jacinth, and brimstone: and the heads of the horses were as the heads of lions; and out of their mouths issued fire and smoke and brimstone. 18 *By these three was the third part of men killed, by the fire, and by the smoke, and by the brimstone, which issued out of their mouths.* 19 *For their power is in their mouth, and in their tails: for their tails were like unto serpents, and had heads, and with them they do hurt."*

Horses are extensively referred to in this passage in verses 17 to 19 because horses are an established symbol of warfare in the Bible. Time and again, horses are used in a symbolic fashion to refer to the power of armies in war. For example, in Psalm 20:7 it says, "*Some trust in chariots, and some in horses: but we will remember the name of the LORD our God.*" Chariots and horses are symbolic of military strength and power.

However, these horses in this passage are clearly not ordinary horses. Nothing about these horses is to be taken literally. These horses are symbolic visual images of the terrible destructive power of warfare, and the terror and fear it provokes, and the slaughter and death it produces. These horses, from their head to their tail, are equipped and empowered to terrify and destroy.

These horses represent all the horrors of battle. Fire and smoke and brimstone are repeatedly mentioned in verses 17 to 19. Fire and smoke and brimstone are symbols of God's judgment. We see them falling on Sodom and Gomorrah. Furthermore, fire and smoke and brimstone are elements of hell, and war is a foretaste of hell. The fear, the destruction, and the death that war produces are all a sample of what hell is going to be like.

The result of this hellish warfare that occurs between the first and the second coming of Christ is that a third of mankind is killed. This is mentioned in verse 15, and it is mentioned again in verse 18. The number three symbolizes perfection and completion and finality. Therefore, one third represents an imperfect, partial, and temporal measure of what is being considered. Not all of humanity is killed in these repeated judgments of war, but a large number of them have been.

In the twentieth century alone, it is estimated that 100 to 150 million people died in wars across the world. This is not calculating all the people that died from famine and disease and the other things that occurred as a result of war. If all of those deaths occurred just in one century, only God knows how many died as a result of war in the previous nineteen centuries since Christ came the first time.

War produces immense suffering and destruction around the world and through the centuries. It is an expression of the judgment of God on wicked men, and it is an expression of the malevolence of Satan toward wicked men. It is only when Jesus returns and eradicates sin that men will beat their swords into plowshares and their spears into pruning hooks.

The Effect of the Judgment of War

The effect of the judgment of war is set forth in verses 20 to 21. One of the effects of the temporal judgments of God represented in these six trumpets is that people should be moved to repent, lest a worse thing come upon them. But sadly, human depravity is so great and human pride is so strong that men would rather suffer God's wrath than worship before God's throne. The effect of the judgment of war is that men do not repent before God. Men do not repent of their sins.

First of all, notice they do not repent of their false worship, verse 20. *"And the rest of the men which were not killed by these plagues yet repented not of the works of their hands, that they should not worship devils, and idols of gold, and silver, and brass, and stone, and of wood: which neither can see, nor hear, nor walk."*

Notice that these men who are not Christians are also not atheists. There is no such thing as a true atheist. There are only Christians and idolaters. There are only those who worship Christ or who worship false gods. Those are the categories of people that are mentioned here. There are the believers who worship Christ; and then there are those left alive after the carnage of war who continue to worship devils and idols of gold, the very things that brought the judgment of war on them in the first place.

So-called atheists worship at the altar of science and human reason. In a word, they worship men rather than God. The lost look to anything other than God as their ultimate source of authority, and whatever they look to as their ultimate source of authority becomes their god. Whether it is an actual demon they worship, or a physical idol made of wood or stone, or another man, or even themselves, all of them are powerless to save them from either the temporal or eternal wrath of God.

Not only do men refuse to repent of their false worship, but they also refuse to repent of their awful sins. Notice verse 21. It says, *"Neither repented they of their murders, nor of their sorceries, nor of their fornication, nor of their thefts."* No matter how much suffering their sins cause them, no matter how much they experience the temporal wrath of God for those sins, they continue doing them. The classic example of this is Pharaoh in Egypt. It did not matter how many judgments God brought on Pharaoh; he kept on defying God and rebelling against God until the time he was destroyed by God in the Red Sea. Temporal judgments never brought him to repentance.

In the same way, the temporal judgments that fall on this world in the form of these trumpet judgments do not bring men to repentance either. Unless God regenerates the heart, no number of external incentives, no matter how powerful or compelling, will bring men to saving faith in Jesus Christ. It says in Jeremiah 5:3, *"O Lord. . .thou hast stricken them, but they have not grieved; thou hast consumed them, but they have refused to receive correction: they have made their faces harder than a rock; they have refused to return."*

In spite of these temporal judgments that God has been bringing on mankind during the entire time between the first and the second coming of Christ, men have not repented of breaking the first table of the law; they continue to worship idols. Nor have they repented of breaking the second table of the law; they continue in their murders and fornications and thefts. Therefore, the only thing that is left to them is final judgment in hell for all eternity, which will be brought at the seventh trumpet described in chapter 11.

Here, then, is the source of war. It is a judgment of God, it is a work of Satan, it is a foretaste of hell, and it is a warning to repent. The good news is that when the Prince of Peace returns, war will cease forever. You can see in this battle between God and Satan and between God and wicked men, Satan and wicked men always lose, and God always wins.

If as you read this you are at war with God in your heart, I urge you to surrender now. Stop fighting with God. You cannot win that battle. Surrender now before it is too late. You can see from the negative example of these people experiencing the sixth trumpet that even though God brought tremendous incentives upon them to repent of their rebellion and defiance against God, and even though He showed them the evil that Satan brings to pass in this world, yet still they continue to serve Satan and defy the One calling them to repentance and salvation.

When it says the rest of the men did not repent, the clear implication is if they had repented, they would have had forgiveness, they would have had mercy, they would have been reconciled to God, and they would have been delivered from the scourge of His wrath and from the scourge of being under the lash of Satan.

If you are at war with God, surrender now. Repent now. Turn away from your rebellion in worshiping any gods other than the true God. Turn away from committing sins that are in defiance of the laws that God has given you to follow. Believe in Jesus as your Savior and submit to Him as your Lord.

I want to say to you if you are a believer, recognize that when God says, "*Vengeance is mine; I will repay, saith the Lord,*" this is one of the ways in which He has been repaying. The wicked do not escape the wrath of God, either in this age or in the next. They experience it partially now and they will experience it fully then. Recognize that they are not getting away with their persecution and martyrdom of believers in Christ.

You can afford to be patient and wait on God to bring His vengeance to bear. He will bring it through these trumpet judgments in time, and He will bring it in the damnation of hell for eternity. Understanding this allows you to let go of the injustices that have been done to you by the wicked. You can let those things go into the hands of God, knowing that He will deal righteously with them, and He will vindicate you.

I also want to say to you if you are a believer: do not be surprised when the wicked do not repent when you witness to them. If they will not repent when God goes to war against them and brings this kind of horror to bear on them, how much less will they repent when you only verbally describe the horrors of hell to them! Is it any wonder they laugh you off when the realities of the horrors of hell in the warfare that takes place in this age do not move them to repent? Humanity claims to want peace. The United Nations was established to achieve it. We have more war now than we have ever had because people will not go to the One who truly has control over war and peace—and that is the Lord Jesus Christ. If people do not repent at the present hell of war, do not be surprised if they are not moved to repentance by a verbal description of future hell in the lake of fire.

This is a dreadful passage, and yet it is a passage that tells us how God's wrath ratchets up higher and higher, until finally those who insist on continuing to rebel against it are destroyed by it. May we not be among that company. May we be those who flee from the wrath to come by fleeing to the Lord Jesus for the forgiveness of our sins and for deliverance from the wrath of God.

31

The Angel and the Book, Revelation 10:1–11

“1 *And I saw another mighty angel come down from heaven,
clothed with a cloud: and a rainbow was upon his head, and
his face was as it were the sun, and his feet as pillars of fire:*
2 *And he had in his hand a little book open: and he set his
right foot upon the sea, and his left foot on the earth,* 3 *And
cried with a loud voice, as when a lion roareth: and when he
had cried, seven thunders uttered their voices.* 4 *And when the
seven thunders had uttered their voices, I was about to write:
and I heard a voice from heaven saying unto me, Seal up those
things which the seven thunders uttered, and write them not.*
5 *And the angel which I saw stand upon the sea and upon the
earth lifted up his hand to heaven,* 6 *And swore by him that
liveth for ever and ever, who created heaven, and the things
that therein are, and the earth, and the things that therein
are, and the sea, and the things which are therein, that there
should be time no longer:* 7 *But in the days of the voice of the
seventh angel, when he shall begin to sound, the mystery of
God should be finished, as he hath declared to his servants the
prophets.* 8 *And the voice which I heard from heaven spoke
unto me again, and said, Go and take the little book which
is open in the hand of the angel which standeth upon the sea
and upon the earth.* 9 *And I went unto the angel, and said unto
him, Give me the little book. And he said unto me, Take it,
and eat it up; and it shall make thy belly bitter, but it shall be
in thy mouth sweet as honey.* 10 *And I took the little book out
of the angel's hand, and ate it up; and it was in my mouth
sweet as honey: and as soon as I had eaten it, my belly was bit-
ter.* 11 *And he said unto me, Thou must prophesy again before
many peoples, and nations, and tongues, and kings.*”

When we studied the seven seals, we saw that between the sixth and the seventh seal there was an interlude. In Revelation 6, six seals were opened, but the seventh seal was not opened until chapter 8. Chapter 7 was an interlude between the sixth and seventh seal. We have the same structure with the seven trumpets. As we proceed through the seven trumpets, we see an interlude between the sixth and the seventh trumpet that extends from 10:1–11:14. In 11:15 the seventh trumpet finally sounds.

Therefore, we pause from the progression of the trumpet judgments to consider this interlude which consists of a description of the gift of the gospel, the preaching of the gospel, and the response to the gospel.

Reflect for a moment on what we have seen in the previous chapters. There are the seven churches of chapters 2 and 3, which represent all the churches that will exist between the first and the second coming of Christ. There are the seven seals, which represent the evil conduct that the ungodly will engage in between the first and the second coming of Christ. Then there are the seven trumpets, which are God's limited and temporal judgments against the wicked for their evil conduct in this age.

But also, between the first and second coming of Christ, there is the preaching of the gospel to the whole world, which is the subject of chapters 10 and 11. The seven churches, the seven seals, and the seven trumpets all run parallel with each other. They all run in the timeframe between the first and second coming of Jesus. But right alongside the seven churches and the seven seals and the seven trumpets, the preaching of the gospel also takes place. All of these things occur in parallel at the same time.

As we looked at the first six trumpet judgments in chapters 8 and 9, we saw that even though God brought His wrath to bear against the wicked in this age, they did not repent of their evil.

In 9:20–21 at the conclusion of the six trumpets, which were God's retaliation against their behavior that is described in the seals, it says, "*And the rest of the men which were not killed by these plagues yet repented not of the works of their hands, that they should not worship devils, and idols of gold, and silver, and brass, and stone, and of wood: which neither can see, nor hear, nor walk:* [21] *Neither repented they of their murders, nor of their sorceries, nor of their fornication, nor of their thefts.*"

But it is not just that the wicked refuse to repent at the message of God's trumpets of judgment against their sin; they also refuse to repent at the preaching of the gospel, which was going on at the same time the trumpet judgments were being sounded.

The wicked in this age are given a double incentive to repent. Negatively, they have the temporal judgments of God that have occurred all throughout this age, represented by these first six trumpets. These are a foretaste and sample of the wrath to come if they do not repent. Positively, they have the gracious preaching of the gospel in which forgiveness of sins, eternal life, reconciliation with God, and entrance into heaven is freely offered to them on the basis of the saving work of Jesus Christ.

And yet in spite of this double incentive, they refuse to repent. As a result, all that is left for them is judgment. Judgment is what comes in 11:15 when the seventh trumpet sounds.

This section between the sixth and the seventh trumpet is not something that occurs chronologically between the sixth and the seventh trumpet; instead, it runs parallel with the first six trumpets and gives us additional information about what is occurring as they sound over and over again during this age. It tells us how Christians persevere in their witness in the face of hostile opposition, and it tells the destiny of those who provide that hostile opposition to the gospel.

The Declaration of God's Judgment on the Impenitent

The declaration of God's judgment on the impenitent is found in 10:1–7. "*And I saw another mighty angel come down from heaven, clothed with a cloud: and a rainbow was upon his head, and his face was as it were the sun, and his feet as pillars of fire:*
2 And he had in his hand a little book open: and he set his right foot upon the sea, and his left foot on the earth,
3 And cried with a loud voice, as when a lion roareth: and when he had cried, seven thunders uttered their voices.
4 And when the seven thunders had uttered their voices, I was about to write: and I heard a voice from heaven saying unto me, Seal up those things which the seven thunders uttered, and write them not.
5 And the angel which I saw stand upon the sea and upon the earth lifted up his hand to heaven,
6 And swore by him that liveth for ever and ever, who created heaven, and the things that therein are, and the earth,

and the things that therein are, and the sea, and the things which are therein, that there should be time no longer: [7] *But in the days of the voice of the seventh angel, when he shall begin to sound"* (this is the seventh trumpet that is going to sound in Revelation 11:15), "*the mystery of God should be finished, as he hath declared to his servants the prophets."* The seventh trumpet is the announcement of the end of this age.

As we saw in 9:20–21, in spite of thousands of years of enduring the judgments of God in the form of the six trumpet judgments which occurred over and over again, wicked mankind still refuses to bow before the person and law of God. The result of this intransigence and rebellion is that God is going to pronounce His final judgment on the wicked in the form of the seventh trumpet, which brings to pass the second coming of Christ and the last judgment. God sends a mighty angel to pronounce this final judgment and the conclusion of God's work on earth.

Notice two things about this angel.

First of all, notice in verses 1 to 4, the angel's appearance. "*And I saw another mighty angel come down from heaven,*" verse 3, "*and cried with a loud voice.*" This is not the first appearance of a mighty angel in the book of Revelation.

We saw this previously in 5:2. "*And I saw a strong angel*" (a mighty angel: the same Greek word is used) "*proclaiming with a loud voice, Who is worthy to open the book. . . ?*" and Jesus appears and opens the book. The angel is not Jesus; he is just a mighty angel with a loud voice. Notice 8:3: "*And another angel came and stood at the altar.*" These angels appear in the narrative as it unfolds, and now in 10:1 we have another one of them: "*And I saw another mighty angel.*" We have a succession of angels appearing who are saying and doing various things.

This angel in chapter 10 is one that is highly important because of his appearance and his pronouncements. His appearance reflects many of the characteristics of God which shows his closeness to God and the degree to which he represents God.

It says in verse 1, "*And I saw another mighty angel come down from heaven,*" (now notice) "*clothed with a cloud: and a rainbow was upon his head, and his face was as it were the sun, and his feet as pillars of fire.*"

God's judgment is reflected in the cloud with which the angel was clothed. In the Old Testament, clouds are symbolic of God's judgment and are accompanied by lightning and thunder to show the coming storm of God's wrath.

God's covenant faithfulness to His promises is reflected in the rainbow that is over the head of this angel. The rainbow reminds us of the Noahic Covenant and the promises God has made and God has kept. God will keep His promises to bring vengeance upon the wicked as well, and His covenant faithfulness ensures that He shall.

God's holiness is reflected in the angel's face that shines like the sun. When Moses came down from Mount Sinai after receiving the Ten Commandments, his face shined like the sun. That did not mean he was God, but it meant he was in the presence of God and was reflecting the glory of God in his visage.

God's triumph over His enemies is reflected in this angel's feet being like pillars of fire. The idea here is that God will trample His enemies under His feet, and that they will not escape His terrible wrath or the fiery heat of His anger.

In this angel, God's judgment is reflected in the clouds with which he is clothed; God's faithfulness is reflected in the rainbow over his head; God's holiness is reflected in his shining face; and God's triumph over His enemies is reflected in these fiery feet.

Because he has all of these characteristics of God reflected in his person, some commentators say this angel is actually Jesus Christ. But Christ is never called an angel in the book of Revelation, and much less is He ever called "another" angel—that is, one of many, as though He were just one in a series of beings just like Himself.

Furthermore, when John is in the presence of this angel, he does not fall down and worship him. When he was in the presence of Christ in chapter 1, he was instantly on his face. But here, John does not fall on his face. What we have in 10:1 is God's glory being reflected in His messenger whom He sends to represent His glorious person and His authoritative message.

Finally, this angel in verse 6 swears by God, and therefore cannot be God, because God only swears by Himself. This angel is swearing by someone other than himself. Therefore, this angel cannot be a manifestation of the Lord Jesus Christ.

Notice verse 2 says, "*and he had in his hand a little book open: and he set his right foot upon the sea, and his left foot on the earth.*" This mighty angel has an open book in his hand which contains the word of God.

The angel also stands astride the whole earth, indicating that this book and its message have authority over the whole earth. This angel sets his right foot on the sea and his left foot on the earth, showing his mastery over them both. His message is a universal message that applies to all people, wherever they may be on the globe.

The book he holds is open which indicates his message is open, available, and intended to be known. Its instructions are meant to be obeyed by all of humanity wherever they may live on the globe. The gigantic size of this angel indicates the importance of the word of God he is holding in his hand, and the towering significance it has over humanity. The message of that book will span the globe, the message is exalted far above anything else on earth in terms of its significance and its importance, and that message is open and available to the whole world.

This symbolic visual image conveys the message that God's word is supremely important, it towers over all the affairs of men, and it is universally applicable to all peoples wherever they live on the earth.

In verse 3, it says this angel *"cried with a loud voice, as when a lion roareth: and when he had cried, seven thunders uttered their voices."* This angel now cries out with a loud voice, and it sounds like the roar of a lion. The volume of his voice makes it clear that his message concerns the whole earth and needs to be heard by all people. This is not a quiet whisper. This is an overwhelming demand for attention that cannot be ignored.

His cry causes the seven thunders to utter their voices as well. It is interesting that God's voice is frequently likened to thunder in the Old Testament. Psalm 29 speaks of the seven thunders that are spoken of in Revelation 10.

Psalm 29:1–11: *"Give unto the LORD, O ye mighty, give unto the LORD glory and strength. [2] Give unto the LORD the glory due unto his name; worship the LORD in the beauty of holiness."* Now here it is, verse 3: *"The voice of the LORD is upon the waters: the God of glory thundereth: the LORD is upon many waters. [4] The voice of the Lord is powerful; the voice of the LORD is full of majesty. [5] The voice of the LORD breaketh the cedars; yea, the LORD breaketh the cedars of Lebanon. [6] He maketh them also to skip like a calf; Lebanon and Sirion like a young unicorn. [7] The voice of the LORD divideth the flames of fire. [8] The voice of the LORD shaketh the wilderness; the LORD shaketh the wilderness of Kadesh. [9] The voice of the LORD maketh the hinds to calve, and discovereth the forests: and in his temple doth every one speak of his glory.* [10] *The* LORD *sitteth upon the flood; yea, the* LORD *sitteth King for ever.* [11] *The* LORD *will give strength unto his people; the* LORD *will bless his people with peace."*

Seven times it says, "*The voice of the* LORD," "*The voice of the* LORD," "*The voice of the* LORD. . .." Furthermore, it says "*The voice of the* LORD*. . . thundereth.*"

In Revelation 10:3 when it says the "*seven thunders uttered their voices,*" this is a reference to the voice of the Lord speaking seven times, seven being the number of completion. The idea being conveyed is that God speaks completely and God speaks powerfully. The seven thunders are the voice of God in all of the fullness of His power, His majesty, and His authority. God speaks fully, powerfully, authoritatively, and majestically with these seven thunderous voices.

Notice verse 4: "*And when the seven thunders had uttered their voices, I was about to write: and I heard a voice from heaven saying unto me, Seal up those things which the seven thunders uttered, and write them not.*" The voice of these seven thunders was clearly intelligible to John. He understood exactly what was being said and he started to write down the words just like he had written down so many words that had been spoken before. But he was ordered to stop writing down the words of the seven thunder voices. He was forbidden to record what they said.

We need to understand the importance of this. What matters here is not what the seven voices uttered. We cannot know what they said, we are not allowed to know what they said, and it is vain and useless and even presumptuous to speculate about what they said. What matters here is that we are made aware that there are some facts about the work of God among men that are intentionally concealed from men. There are some things we are not supposed to know, there are some things we cannot know, and there are things we will never know—not at least in this life. There are things we are not allowed to know about what God has to say and about what God intends to do. We need to be content with that, and not chafe against the fact that we do not have all of the information and all the facts about what God is doing in this world.

Deuteronomy 29:29 says, "*The secret things belong unto the* LORD *our God: but those things which are revealed belong unto us and to our children for ever, that we may do all the words of this law.*" This should cause us to have a degree of humility and modesty regarding how the future will unfold, especially regarding things like setting dates for the second coming. God wants to make it clear to us that we do not have all the information, and that He has intentionally withheld some information from us. Therefore, let us not be presumptuous in thinking we can have a complete understanding regarding all prophetic events from a study of the book of Revelation. We simply do not. There are some things we just do not know, and this text is designed to teach us that lesson.

We know enough to understand all we need to know for the job God has given us to do, and with that we need to be content. He has kept some things secret from us, but He has revealed other things to us, and those things are sufficient and adequate to be able to accomplish everything God wants us to do, and to understand everything God wants us to know. With reference to those other things, we must not lean on our own understanding. We need to simply trust in the Lord with all of our hearts that He is managing all things well. We have to conclude there are some things we simply do not know the answer to.

Having seen the angel's appearance in verses 1 to 4, notice secondly, the angel's oath in verses 5 to 7. In verse 5 it says, *"And the angel which I saw stand upon the sea and upon the earth lifted up his hand to heaven,* [6] *And swore by him that liveth for ever and ever, who created heaven, and the things that therein are, and the earth, and the things that therein are, and the sea, and the things which are therein, that there should be time no longer:* [7] *But in the days of the voice of the seventh angel, when he shall begin to sound, the mystery of God should be finished, as he hath declared to his servants the prophets."*

This angel has been revealed to pronounce God's judgment on the wicked. In verses 1 to 4 we have this incredible being showing up and a description of him is supplied, and now in verses 5 to 7 we have the message of this incredible being and what he has to say. What he has to say is that God's hammer is going to fall because God is all done with rebellious humanity.

We have seen that even though God brought many temporal judgments on the wicked, they still refused to repent and submit themselves to the Lord. Therefore, the angel now lifts up his hand and swears an oath in the name of God that the time for repentance has ended and the opportunity for repentance is over. Notice verses 5 and

6: *"And the angel which I saw stand upon the sea and upon the earth lifted up his hand to heaven,* [6] *And swore by him that liveth for ever and ever, . . .that there should be time no longer."*

The lifting up of the hand is a common gesture in the swearing of an oath. We do the same thing in our own courts of law. We first see this raising of the hand to swear an oath in Genesis 14:22 when Abraham swears an oath, and it is used in other Old Testament passages as well.

This oath the angel swears makes an extended descriptive statement about the God he is swearing by. He speaks of God's eternal existence. He swears *"by him that lives for ever and ever,"* and then he speaks of God's creative power, *"who created"* the heavens, the earth, and the sea, and everything in them. The reason he gives this description of the God he is swearing by is to remind both us and all those he is pronouncing judgment on that God is sovereign over time—He lives forever and ever; and that God is sovereign over creation—He made the heaven and the earth and the sea.

His authority and power are without limit as to their duration, and His authority and power are without limit as to their extent. He knows the exact time that He has allotted to this world and the people in it, and He has perfect control over all the people He has made and all the circumstances in which they find themselves. The angel swears regarding God's timetable that there comes a time when there should be time no longer.

When he says in the latter part of verse 6 *"that there should be time no longer,"* this does not mean that chronology will end and we will enter some timeless state of an eternal present with no past and no future. What it means is that there will be time no longer for repentance and salvation. There will be no further delay in the coming of God's judgment. Now is the day of salvation, but the time for salvation will come to an end. There will no longer be time to be saved.

The course of this world will come to a halt, and the very next verse tells us what he meant in verse 6 when he said: *"time will be no longer."* Verse 7: *"But"* (here is the explanation of time being no longer) *"in the days of the voice of the seventh angel,"* (when the seventh trumpet sounds in 11:15) *"when he shall begin to sound, the mystery of God should be finished, as he hath declared to his servants the prophets."*

When the seventh trumpet sounds, Christ returns, the final judgment occurs, and as 11:15 says, *"the kingdoms of this world become the kingdoms of our Lord, and of His Christ; and he shall reign for ever and ever."* The seventh trumpet announces the second coming and the end.

This mystery of God which he refers to in verse 7, *". . .the mystery of God should be finished,"* is simply the hidden plan of God to save His people and destroy the works of the devil that have been in operation since the foundation of the world. It has been largely hidden from human eyes because it is primarily worked out in the spiritual realm.

Romans 16:25–27 tells us what this mystery of God is. It says, *"Now to him that is of power to establish you according to my gospel, and the preaching of Jesus Christ,"* (now here it is) *"according to the revelation of the mystery, which was kept secret since the world began,* [26] *But now is made manifest, and by the scriptures of the prophets, according to the commandment of the everlasting God, made known to all nations for the obedience of faith:* [27] *To God only wise, be glory through Jesus."*

This whole plan of salvation, from beginning to end, God refers to as a *"mystery."* It is a mystery because it would have never been known had God not revealed it. Who would have ever thought that God would send His own Son to die in the place of His elect in order that they might be forgiven on the basis of grace? No one would have ever conceived of it. It was a mystery.

This mystery of God's saving work is not fully revealed until the New Testament is given. What Paul is saying in Romans 16 is this mystery of the gospel and the preaching of Jesus Christ was foretold in the prophets of the Old Testament and is now fully revealed in the New Testament.

This mystery of God's saving work was not fully revealed until the New Testament was given. But when it was, it was *"made known to all nations for the obedience of faith."* But this saving work will finally be finished and come to a conclusion and close. We are told about this in the Old Testament prophets, and the angel reaffirms it with his oath.

When God's saving purposes are finished and when all of His elect are saved, then the seventh trumpet will blow, and for those who have refused to repent it will be too late. The time to be saved will be no longer. It will be gone forever.

John wants his readers to understand something. These mighty world forces and governments that seem so powerful, and under whose oppression they suffered, are all going to be decisively overthrown. They will not triumph; Christ and His people will triumph. The mystery of God will be accomplished and finished. God's patience with the wicked will end, and then the end will come.

We have seen in Revelation 10:1–7 the declaration of God's judgment on the impenitent. God sends this angel clothed with His own authority, reflecting His own power and covenant faithfulness, and the angel makes this declaration to these impenitent people: "Your time is up. You are done. There is no higher appeal. I swear it in the name of God. It is settled, it is fixed, and it is finished." When the seventh trumpet sounds, the day of salvation is over forever. It will never come back.

The Delivery of God's Gospel to the Church

The delivery of God's gospel to the church is symbolized by the angel handing John the little book in verses 8 through 11.

"And the voice which I heard from heaven spake unto me again, and said, Go and take the little book which is open in the hand of the angel which standeth upon the sea and upon the earth. [9] *And I went unto the angel, and said unto him, Give me the little book. And he said unto me, Take it, and eat it up; and it shall make thy belly bitter, but it shall be in thy mouth sweet as honey.* [10] *And I took the little book out of the angel's hand, and ate it up; and it was in my mouth sweet as honey: and as soon as I had eaten it, my belly was bitter.* [11] *And he said unto me, Thou must prophesy again before many peoples, and nations, and tongues, and kings."*

After reading verses 1–7 and the angel saying the time is up and the mystery is finished, we would have expected verse 8 to be the sounding of the seventh trumpet. We would expect that because in verse 7 he says, *"in the days of the voice of the seventh angel, when he shall begin to sound, the mystery of God should be finished, as he hath declared to his servants the prophets,"* that the next verse would say: "and I heard the seventh angel sound. . ."

However, that is not what we get. The seventh angel does not sound until 11:15. Something intervenes; and what that is, will be the subject of 10:8 to 11:14.

What we have in this section is first John, and then the two witnesses of chapter 11, being given the gospel message to preach to the world. In other words, they are given the word of God, the little book, and out of it they are to preach God's message to the world.

It is interesting that the same voice in verse 4 that told John to conceal the message of the seven thunders is exactly the same voice that tells him in verse 8 to take the open book out of the hand of the angel so he might preach it. God says, "You cannot know this one truth, but this other truth is to be proclaimed to the world."

Everything we have to proclaim to the world is in the book. We do not need anything else to know the message of God and to convey it to others. The message of God is not the voices in your head. The voice of God is the book, and it is the book that John is given to preach.

Notice that this book is an open book. It stresses it again. It said in verse 2, "*and he had in his hand a little book open,*" and then in verse 8, "*take the little book which is open in the hand of the angel.*" This is an open book, not a closed book. This book is meant to be read, it is meant to be studied, and it is meant to be understood. God has hidden some things from us, but thankfully He has not hidden the gospel from us. He has revealed the gospel in His book, and He gives that book to His messengers to consume for themselves first, and then to proclaim to others. Notice John eats the book in verse 10: "*and I took the little book out of the angel's hand, and ate it up,*" and it is because of this message in this book that he consumes, that he now has a message to "[11]. . .*prophesy. . .before many peoples, and nations, and tongues, and kings.*"

Notice that John is an active participant in this process. He has to go to the angel, he has to ask the angel for the book, he has to take the book out of his hand, and then he has to eat it. This is what he is instructed to do in verses 8 and 9; and in fact, this is exactly what he does. He is not told to just passively sit and wait for somebody to put it into his mind. He is actively involved in seeking the book and taking the book and consuming the book. We, too, must be actively involved in seeking out, learning, and internalizing the message of the Bible.

He is told in verse 9 what will occur when he consumes the book. It will be sweet in his mouth, but, having been swallowed, it will be bitter in his stomach. This, in fact, is what he experienced. "[10] *And I took the little book out of the angel's hand, and ate it up; and it was in my mouth sweet as honey: and as soon as I had eaten it, my belly was bitter."* Eating the book is a symbolic visual image of taking the gospel into our hearts and our minds, of receiving and believing the gospel ourselves, and making its message our own through belief and study and the application of it in our lives. This is what it means to eat the book: Something that is outside of you becomes internalized to you by reading it and studying it and understanding it and applying it in your life.

The psalmist, using the same metaphorical language, says in Psalm 119:103, *"How sweet are thy words unto my taste! yea, sweeter than honey to my mouth!"* In Psalm 19:10, the psalmist says of the Scriptures that they are *"sweeter also than honey and the honeycomb."* Perhaps the clearest illustration in the Old Testament of this metaphor of the eating of the book is in Ezekiel 3:1–4. Ezekiel is having a vision of God. Let us start with Ezekiel 2:9.

Ezekiel 2:9 says, *"And when I looked, behold, a hand was sent unto me; and, lo, a roll of a book was therein;* [10] *And he spread it before me,"* as he opened it up, *"and it was written within and without: and there was written therein lamentations, and mourning, and woe."* Chapter 3 verse 1: *"Moreover he said unto me, Son of man, eat that thou findest; eat this roll, and go speak unto the house of Israel.* [2] *So I opened my mouth, and he caused me to eat that roll.* [3] *And he said unto me, Son of man, cause thy belly to eat, and fill thy bowels with this roll that I give thee. Then did I eat it; and it was in my mouth as honey for sweetness.* [4] *And he said unto me, Son of man, go, get thee unto the house of Israel, and speak with my words unto them."*

This is parallel to what the angel tells John to do. We see John consuming the message of the word of God so that he might proclaim it to others, just like God metaphorically gave Ezekiel His word under this symbolic visual imagery of eating so that it would fill his mouth, and, with his mouth filled with God's message, Ezekiel would then go and preach to the people.

John is consuming the message of the word of God so he might proclaim it to others. Revelation 10:11 makes this clear: *"And he said unto me, Thou must prophesy again before many peoples, and nations, and tongues, and kings"*—that is, to all of mankind. John consumes the message of the gospel, not only so that he might be saved by it himself, but also to proclaim it to others.

But what occurs when John does proclaim this message to others? They despise the message and reject it. They refuse to repent, and thereby condemn themselves to hell. They hate and persecute the messenger. We are going to see this expanded in 11:1–14 when we look at that passage in subsequent chapters.

When you preach, the word is sweet in your mouth, and you want to tell others about the sweetness of the gospel. But what happens when you preach that message, and they despise it, reject it, and refuse to repent? What happens as you watch them condemn themselves to hell by their blasphemy against the word of God? What happens when you preach the gospel to the lost and they heap shame and scorn and rejection and persecution on you? What happens is that it makes you sick in the pit of your stomach.

Have you ever engaged in any spiritual warfare with haters of the gospel? Does the thought of that conflict and the experience of it make you sick inside? In a word, does it make your belly bitter? It does mine. When I was a child on the schoolyard, at times kids would get into fistfights with other kids, and just the thought of getting into a fistfight made me sick to my stomach.

In the same way, here we are in the field of spiritual warfare, and we are going out with this wonderful gospel; but we know we will also receive terrible hatred and rejection and scorn and reviling when we preach it.

God is saying to John that when he preaches the gospel, it is going to be sweet in his mouth, but he is going to be repaid with persecution and rejection and hostility that will make him sick in his stomach. It makes me sick in my stomach to do spiritual warfare and have spiritual conflict with people, and I hate that feeling. It is the price you pay to prophesy—that is, preach—before many peoples and nations and tongues and kings.

We are going to read a lot more about this stomach-churning spiritual warfare in 11:1–14. But this is the Christian life in the world today, it has been since the first coming of Christ, and it will be until He returns. We love the gospel, and it is so sweet to us because we have been saved by it, but when we preach the gospel, we get persecution back, and the thought of that conflict makes our stomach churn and our belly bitter.

On the one hand, the gospel is sweet. We experience the sweetness of the forgiveness of sin, and freedom from guilt, and deliverance from judgment and hell. We experience the sweetness of reconciliation with God and fellowship with God and having the smile of God. We experience the sweetness of having God's strength and God's protection and God's provision. We experience the sweetness of possessing eternal life and the comfort of the Holy Spirit and the inheritance of heaven. We experience the sweetness of spiritual sight and spiritual illumination and spiritual understanding. We experience the sweetness of the promises of the Scripture and the wisdom they provide and the security they afford to us.

We experience the sweetness of having the family of God and the brothers and sisters and fathers and mothers in Christ who love us and who pray with us and who minister to us. We experience the sweetness of prayer before the throne of grace, adoption into the family of God, and the hope of the resurrection from the grave. We would not trade any of that for anything.

But the Christian life is not all just sweetness, is it? There is some bitterness that comes as we experience hostility from the wicked. But know this: The bitterness in your belly is temporary; the sweetness in your mouth is eternal. The sufferings of this present time, the bitterness of the belly we have now as we engage in spiritual conflict and warfare, is not worthy to be compared with the glory that shall be revealed in us.

So the gospel is glorious and sweet, but its proclamation is always followed by bitter persecution. In the next chapter, when the two witnesses go out and preach the gospel, everybody does not respond by saying things like, "We are so glad you preached this message to us! We have wanted to be saved for so long, and we are so glad that you have told us how!" They do not get that reaction. They get massive persecution, and the persecutors push back hard to the point that they finally triumph over them and kill them, and rejoice over their dead bodies in the street. That is the spiritual warfare we engage in. That is a stomach-churning experience. But we cannot therefore say that because we do not want that bitterness in our belly, we are not going to talk about the sweetness that is in our mouths. We must speak in spite of persecution.

Sweetness and suffering: this is the nature of the Christian life between the first and second coming of Christ. We have to expect it and we have to embrace it. We have to speak to ourselves in words like these: "Rejection and hostility is coming, it is going to happen, and it is going to make me sick—I know that. But I am going to triumph over it, and preach the word in spite of it."

The Christian life is spiritual warfare, but we have to do it. The good news is that when we do it, God's elect are going to be saved. Thank God that there is some sweetness in proclaiming the gospel to the lost when an elect person responds positively. The work of ministry is not all bitterness in the belly. But the majority of the time we will experience the bitterness of the reprobate rejecting us and persecuting us. But in the end, Christ is coming back, the seventh trumpet will sound, all our sorrows will end, and all of our sweetness will be intensified and become permanent for all of eternity.

As John writes this book to persecuted believers at the end of the first century, he is saying to them, "Yes, I know Rome is pushing back hard, but this is our message, and this is our mission." We have an open book, so let us preach that book. God will deal with them. Their time is going to run out. Our time will go on forever.

May this encourage us to keep on preaching the sweet message of the gospel, in spite of the sick feeling in our stomachs, and to stand against the world and to proclaim the gospel to them. God's elect are among them. For the elect's sake, let us endure persecution and persevere in preaching the sweet message of the gospel.

32

The Temple and the Courtyard, Revelation 11:1–2

> "[1] *And there was given me a reed like unto a rod: and the angel stood, saying, Rise, and measure the temple of God, and the altar, and them that worship therein.* [2] *But the court which is without the temple leave out, and measure it not; for it is given unto the Gentiles: and the holy city shall they tread under foot forty and two months.*"

Revelation 11 is a very complex chapter that contains highly detailed symbolism which will require extended investigation and explanation. As a result, we will focus on only the first two verses of this chapter.

In the last chapter, we observed that 10:1 through 11:14 was an interlude between the sixth and the seventh trumpet judgments. In this interlude, we are told that the gospel is being preached to the wicked. But just like they do not repent when God brings His trumpet judgments to bear on them, neither do they repent when the gospel invitations and promises are extended to them.

The whole time between the first and second coming of Christ, the gospel is preached to a rebellious world, but the world despises the message and persecutes the messengers. Only the elect embrace the gospel, but they are a small minority in every generation. The world as a whole rejects both the message and the messengers of the gospel, and this compounds both their guilt and the wrath of God that is finally brought to bear on them. They do not listen to the trumpet judgments, and they do not listen to the gospel.

In 10:8–11, the gospel was given to John the apostle who was ministering at the very beginning of the time between the first and second coming of Christ. John was given an open book to consume, which represents the Bible and its gospel message. Having taken the gospel into his heart and soul, having received and believed the message of salvation, he finds it sweet to his taste as he personally experiences all the blessings of the gospel.

But as he begins to preach that message to the peoples and nations and tongues and kings mentioned in 10:11, he experiences the bitter persecution that always follows the proclamation of the gospel. We see in 1:9 that he himself is now exiled on the island of Patmos. He is experiencing the bitterness of spiritual warfare that arises when the sweetness of the gospel is preached to a defiant and rebellious world.

John experienced both the sweetness and the suffering that believing and proclaiming the gospel always brings. The gospel is sweet as we experience the forgiveness of our sins and reconciliation with God and the possession of eternal life. But the gospel is bitter as we experience great suffering at the hands of Satan and his people who treat us with hostility and contempt as we preach it, and who persecute us to the point of death.

As we move into chapter 11, we see that the sweetness and the suffering the gospel brings are things not only John and the first-century Christians experienced; they are things that believers in every generation experience. Chapter 11 reveals the two witnesses, who represent believers who preach the gospel to every generation throughout this age, and they receive the same treatment John did.

We have John preaching at the beginning of the gospel era, and we have the two witnesses preaching up to the very end. We have a sweet message to preach, but we do not get a sweet response in return; instead, we receive a bitter response. We see that theme expanded in Revelation 11. The two witnesses preach the gospel, and they get persecuted and killed for doing so.

Make no mistake. Preaching the gospel is spiritual warfare, and we should not be surprised when we receive hostility from the enemy. But the message of chapter 11 is clear: In the end, Christ and His message and His people will prevail over those who oppose them. Even though we may be killed for preaching the gospel, as these two witnesses were, we will not lose, and we will not be defeated. Like them, we will ultimately triumph.

The triumphing of the wicked is short. Revelation 11:9 says it is symbolically only three and a half days. This is compared to the symbolic three and a half years that the two witnesses had been preaching. The triumphing of the wicked is short, but their defeat is eternal. Those who are martyred for Christ will be resurrected by Christ to eternal life, as we see in verses 11 and 12, whereas the wrath of God will fall on their persecutors and they will be cast into hell, as we see in verse 18.

The point we need to understand is that much conflict is going to result from preaching the gospel in this age, but we must preach it nonetheless. We will be assaulted. We will fight back with spiritual weapons, and the war will rage. Finally, though the church will almost be extinguished from the earth, Christ will return, resurrect His people, rescue His few living saints, destroy the wicked, the kingdoms of this world will become the kingdoms of our Lord and of His Christ, and He will reign forever and ever.

What should we expect in this age? We should expect that as we preach the gospel, all of God's elect will be saved, the church will be persecuted by the world, and, at the end, the world will temporarily prevail over the church. But then Christ will return, and the church will triumph over the world for all eternity. That is the message and the promise of Revelation 11.

The Measurement of the Temple

The measurement of the temple is in verse 1: *"And there was given me a reed like unto a rod: and the angel stood, saying, Rise, and measure the temple of God, and the altar, and them that worship therein."*

John is told to measure the temple of God, the altar, and all the people who worship inside that temple and at that altar. The question arises: What temple is he referring to? He cannot be referring to the Jewish temple that was in Jerusalem. The Jewish temple in Jerusalem was destroyed in AD 70 by the Romans, and the book of Revelation was written about twenty-five years after that event. Therefore, the temple being referred to must be some other temple.

This temple is the one that replaced the old Jewish temple. It is the New Covenant temple—namely, the church. The church is the new temple of God here on earth which replaces the old Jewish temple that was destroyed in AD 70. The New Testament provides abundant evidence that the church is the temple of God on earth.

Three passages establish this fact. The first passage is Ephesians 2:19–22: "*Now therefore ye are no more strangers and foreigners, but fellow citizens with the saints, and of the household of God;* [20] *And are built upon the foundation of the apostles and prophets, Jesus*

Christ himself being the chief corner stone; [21] *In whom all the building fitly framed together groweth unto an holy temple in the Lord:* [22] *In whom ye also are builded together for an habitation of God through the Spirit."*

Where was the habitation of God under the Old Covenant? It was the temple. The Shekinah glory of God dwelt in the Holy of Holies. Where is the habitation of God through the Spirit under the New Covenant? It is the New Testament church. The church collectively and universally is a *"holy temple."* Christ is the chief cornerstone, the apostles are the foundation, and believers are the superstructure. Each individual local church is a visible manifestation of that temple and is a habitation of God.

In the Davidic Covenant, God promised David that his son would build God a house. The proximate fulfillment of that promise occurred when Solomon built the Old Testament temple. But the ultimate fulfillment of that promise occurred when the ultimate Son of David, Jesus Christ, builds the New Covenant temple, called the house of God in 1 Timothy 3:15, which is made up of the saved people of God.

The second passage that shows the church is the new temple of God is 1 Corinthians 3:16–17. Paul is speaking to this local church collectively, and he says to them, *"Know ye,"* referring to them collectively. *"Ye"* is plural. It is not "thou" individually, but *"ye"* collectively, speaking to the church as a whole. He says: *"Know ye not that ye are the temple of God, and that the Spirit of God dwelleth in you?* [17] *If any man defile the temple of God, him shall God destroy; for the temple of God is holy, which temple ye are."*

He says to the church at Corinth that they collectively make up a temple of God. If someone came in and defiled the Old Testament temple, he was put to death. If someone comes in and defiles the New Covenant temple, he is put to death as well—that is, he is excommunicated from the church. He is destroyed from being among the people of God.

Paul is teaching the Corinthians that the church needs to be pure. Its members cannot allow defiling elements into the church. In particular, the church at Corinth had an individual living in sin with his father's wife. Paul is saying, "Cast that person out! Do not defile the temple of God with such wicked things."

The third passage that shows the church is the new temple of God is 1 Peter 2:5: "*Ye also, as [living] stones, are built up a spiritual house, a holy priesthood, to offer up spiritual sacrifices, acceptable to God by Jesus Christ.*"

The local church is the temple, the spiritual house where spiritual sacrifices to God are offered by New Covenant priests, who are all the believers in any biblically constituted local church.

The indisputable teaching of these three passages is that when the local church gathers, it gathers based on the foundation of Jesus Christ and the teaching of the apostles. Each person is a living stone, which collectively make up a house of God, within which spiritual sacrifices are offered to God by New Covenant priests. Therefore, the New Testament church is the new temple of God. It is a spiritual temple made up of people, rather than a physical temple made up of stones. It offers spiritual sacrifices of worship and praise, rather than physical sacrifices of animals. Rather than a special class of priests, all believers are priests of God.

Therefore, the temple referred to in Revelation 11:1 is the church. That is what John is measuring. There is also an altar at which they worship. "*And there was given me a reed like unto a rod: and the angel stood, saying, Rise, and measure the temple of God, and the altar, and them that worship therein.*"

When the believers gather, they comprise the New Covenant Temple, and they have an altar at which they worship. Just like the Old Covenant tabernacle had an altar; we have an altar, and the altar at which we worship is the cross on which Jesus died, and the atonement He provided upon that altar. The sacrifice of Christ on the cross is at the very center of New Covenant Temple worship. The sacrifice of Christ on the cross is the altar at which we worship.

The book of Hebrews is written in order to demonstrate the superiority of New Covenant Christianity over Old Covenant Judaism. The author of the book of Hebrews makes numerous comparisons: Here is what the Old Covenant Jews have, but here is what the New Covenant Christians have, which is so much better. We have a better covenant, we have a better temple, we have a better sacrifice, and we have a better priesthood, etc.

Notice what is said in Hebrews 13:10: "*We have an altar, whereof they have no right to eat which serve the tabernacle.*" The priests of the Old Covenant tabernacle would eat of the sacrifices of the tabernacle. We, too, have an altar, and we eat of the sacrifice of our altar.

Notice it says further in verses 11–13: *"For the bodies of those beasts, whose blood is brought into the sanctuary by the high priest for sin, are burned without the camp.* [12] *Wherefore Jesus also, that he might sanctify the people with his own blood, suffered without the gate.* [13] *Let us go forth therefore unto him without the camp, bearing his reproach."*

He is saying they have an altar and a sacrifice, and we have an altar and a sacrifice. They do not have a place at our altar. They have no participation in our sacrifice. All they have is a brazen altar and a dead bull. We have the cross of Jesus and we have the Son of God as the sacrifice upon it, and that is the altar at which we worship.

This is why the central ordinance of the church is the Lord's Supper in which we remember the sacrifice that was made upon that altar. It is in the merit and worth of that sacrifice on that altar that we New Covenant Christians, in our New Covenant temple, with our New Covenant spiritual sacrifices of praise and worship, approach God in the confidence that He will receive us with favor.

This temple John is measuring is clearly the church. Now the question arises: Why is he told to measure it, and what does that mean? What is the significance of this measurement? We have to look once again at the Old Testament in order to discover the significance of measuring, and what we find is very interesting. The reason John is told to measure the church is in order to mark it out for protection and preservation. The metaphor of measuring has nothing to do with the actual dimensions of the object being measured. Things were often measured in order to identify them to be specially marked out, either for destruction or for preservation.

Notice 2 Samuel 8:1–2. *"And after this it came to pass, that David smote the Philistines, and subdued them: and David took Metheg-ammah out of the hand of the Philistines."* David has gone to war, and he is conquering people and places. Notice verse 2: *"And he smote Moab, and measured them with a line, casting them down to the ground; even with two lines measured he to put to death, and with one full line to keep alive. And so the Moabites became David's servants, and brought gifts."*

Verse 2 tells us David has come and conquered the Moabites, and he has a number of prisoners. He tells them to lie down in a row on the ground. They all lie down in a row on the ground. He has a fixed length of rope. Let us say, for the sake of argument, that it is ten feet long. Here the Moabites are lying on the ground, and he takes this ten-foot rope and he lays it down once, and then he moves it and lays it down a second time. So he marks out twenty feet worth of people lying on the ground. He says regarding them, "Kill them all." Then he lays out the rope a third time, which is another ten feet, and he says, "Save them alive." This is repeated until all the captives are dealt with.

So he is measuring out twenty feet worth of people to put to death, and then the next ten feet of people to save them alive. That is what is described in verse 2. Those measured out by the first two lengths of rope were put to death. Those measured out by the third length of that rope were allowed to live. By this measurement, two thirds were killed and one third were preserved, and that one third who were preserved became the servants of David.

Symbolically, to measure something was to have authority over it, and thereby determine its fate, either for destruction or for preservation, depending upon the context and the circumstance. In effect, God is saying to John, "Measure the church and all within it; both its worship and its people, and I will mark it out for preservation. I will save it from destruction."

This does not mean that some of the saints will not be martyred, and it does not mean that the church will not go through suffering. But what it does mean is that the church, which is the New Covenant temple of God, will not be destroyed; instead, it will be protected. It is marked out by God for protection.

The Giving Over of the Court

The giving over of the court is in verse 2. *"But the court which is without"* (or outside) *"the temple leave out, and measure it not; for it is given unto the Gentiles: and the holy city shall they tread under foot forty and two months."*

While John is told to measure the temple of God, and thereby mark it out for protection, he is forbidden to measure the court that is outside the temple. In the Old Covenant, there was the temple, and there was a courtyard outside of it. Outside the temple was the court of the Gentiles. Only the priests were allowed to go into the temple. The gentiles had to stay out of the temple. In the same way, in the New Covenant temple, only true priests are allowed into the church—that is, into the membership of the church, to minister within the church. Outside of the church is the world.

In verse 2, the outer court is not to be measured because it will receive no protection from God. He measures the temple out for protection, but He does not measure out the court because He has no intention of protecting it. It is not marked out by God as being under His preserving care or to receive His benevolent protection. This outer court is not part of the temple of God; that is, it is not part of the church. It is called *"the court which is without"*; that is, outside the temple which is the church.

This court that is outside the temple is the whole world that exists outside the church. In the Bible, we have the church and the world. This court represents the world. This court is the totality of the kingdom of darkness that stands outside of the kingdom of light. This court is *"given"* to the Gentiles by God, indicating that God is in control of the courtyard, not the Gentiles. The Gentiles only have the court by permission. They only have it because God has allowed them to have it. He has given it to them, or else they would not have it at all. Notice verse 2: *"for it is given unto the Gentiles."*

Who are these Gentiles? The Gentiles referred to here are the whole body of the unsaved. The collective body of unsaved people in the world is called *"Gentiles"* because the true Israel of God, the true Jews, are the Christians. Christians, whatever their ethnic descent, are no longer considered Gentiles in the Bible. They are spiritual Jews because they are born of Christ and because they are circumcised in their hearts.

I want us to look at three passages together. The first is Galatians 3:6–9, 29. Speaking about Abraham in verse 6, Paul says, *"Even as Abraham believed God, and it was accounted to him for righteousness."* Abraham was saved by faith. Verse 7: *"Know ye therefore that they which are of faith, the same are the children of Abraham."*

Do you have faith in Jesus Christ? Then verse 7 says you are a child of Abraham. And if you are a child of Abraham, what does that make you? It makes you a Jew. Abraham both began and defined the Jewish nation. If you are a descendant of Abraham, then you are a Jew. But how did you descend from Abraham? Abraham through the generations produced Christ who was the Seed promised to Abraham, and then Christ produced you through the new birth. You have been born of Christ, who was born of Abraham, which makes you a spiritual descendant of Abraham, which makes you a spiritual Jew.

Notice verse 8: *"And the scripture, foreseeing that God would justify the heathen"* (us former Gentiles) *"through faith, preached before the gospel unto Abraham, saying, In thee shall all nations be blessed."* Now here is the conclusion, verse 9: *"So then they which be of faith"* (the Christians) *"are blessed with faithful Abraham."* We went from being heathen to being those who share the blessings and faith of Abraham.

Galatians 3:29 says, *"And if ye be Christ's, then are ye Abraham's seed, and heirs according to the promise."* If you are born of Christ, then you are Abraham's seed—and therefore, you are a Jew. Abraham's seed are Jews. Abraham has two seeds. He has a physical seed, which may or may not be saved as stated in Romans 9:6: *"They are not all Israel which are Israel."* He also has a spiritual seed, all of whom are saved, some of whom are ethnic Jews, and some of whom are ethnic Gentiles, but all of whom are spiritual Jews, because all of them have Abraham as their father, as described in Romans 4:11–12, 16–18.

The second passage is Romans 2. Notice how being a Jew is defined under the New Covenant. Romans 2:28 says, *"For he is not a Jew, which is one outwardly; neither is that circumcision, which is outward in the flesh."* Jews are no longer defined by genetic descent, and Jews are no longer defined by physical circumcision. Notice how Jews are now defined. Verse 29: *"but he is a Jew, which is one inwardly; and circumcision is that of the heart, in the spirit, and not in the letter; whose praise is not of men, but of God."*

Under the New Covenant, Judaism is not defined by physical external circumcision of the body or by genetic descent. Judaism is now defined by internal circumcision of the heart, which is equivalent to regeneration, irrespective of genetic descent. Every regenerate person, regardless of genetic descent, is now classified as a Jew.

The third passage is Philippians 3:2–3. It is interesting that Paul now calls the Jews "mutilators of the flesh." What had been physical circumcision he now calls the mutilation. *"Beware of dogs, beware of evil workers, beware of the concision [the mutilation]. [3] For we are the circumcision, which worship God in the spirit, and rejoice in Christ Jesus, and have no confidence in the flesh."* Under the New Covenant, circumcision did not go away; it just changed from a mark on the outer part of the body to a transformation of the inner part of the body. Circumcision went from being in the body to being in the soul.

The New Covenant worshipers who worship God in the spirit, and who trust in the work of Christ rather than the works of the flesh for salvation, are the true Jews and the true circumcision.

These three passages make it clear that the true Jews are the Christians. They are those who are Christ's. They are those who are circumcised in heart. They are those who worship God in the spirit and rejoice in Christ Jesus. In a word, the true children of Abraham, the true Jews, the true seed of Abraham, are now the Christians who believe in Christ as their Savior, and who have had their hearts circumcised by the Spirit in the work of regeneration.

Humanity is now separated into two groups. There are the spiritual Jews, also called Christians, who are made up of ethnic Jews and non-Jews, who believe in Jesus as their Savior from sin, and who have their hearts regenerated by the Spirit of God. The second group humanity is separated into is the spiritual Gentiles, who are also called "the lost." Spiritual Gentiles are made up of ethnic Jews and non-Jews who reject Jesus as their Savior from sin.

Ethnicity no longer matters in determining the category someone is in. An unsaved Jew is a Gentile, just like an unsaved Gentile is a Gentile; and a saved Jew is a Jew, and a saved Gentile is a Jew, because Judaism is now defined by being regenerate and a believer in Christ, irrespective of ethnicity. Spiritually, you are a Jew if you are saved; and spiritually, you are a Gentile if you are lost. That is the bottom line. If you are saved, you are a Jew; if you are lost, you are a Gentile. That is what the New Covenant teaches us. Ethnicity is irrelevant.

Notice once again Revelation 11:2: *"But the court which is without the temple leave out, and measure it not; for it is given unto the Gentiles: and the holy city shall they tread under foot forty and two months."* The whole body of the lost, who are called *"the Gentiles"* in verse 2, are going to tread the holy city under their feet for forty-two months. Now we have two questions: What is the holy city, and what are the forty-two months?

First of all, what is the holy city? The holy city is the church. Just as the church is called a temple in verse 1, in the same way the church is called the holy city in verse 2. The holy city was a term that referred to the literal city of Jerusalem in the past, but now this term *"holy city"* refers to the New Jerusalem, which is the church. We are not only the temple of God; we are also the city of God.

Revelation 20:7–8 says, *"And when the thousand years are expired,*

Satan shall be loosed out of his prison, and shall go out and deceive the nations which are in the four quarters of the earth, [8] *Gog and Magog, to gather them together to battle: the number of whom is as the sand of the sea."* This describes the transnational coalition that is going to be assembled after Satan is loosed, the three-and-a-half-day period that is spoken of in Revelation 11:7–12, who are going to come against the people of God.

Notice verse 9: *"And they went up on the breadth of the earth, and compassed [surrounded] the camp of the saints about, and the beloved city."* The camp of the saints and the beloved city are the same thing. *"And fire came down from God out of heaven, and devoured them."* So the camp of the saints is a group of people gathered together in a location. The metaphor here is that this camp of the saints is the beloved city. The saints collectively are referred to as a city that is loved.

We have an even clearer indication of this in Revelation 21. Notice verses 1 and 2: *"And I saw a new heaven and a new earth: for the first heaven and the first earth were passed away; and there was no more sea.* [2] *And I John saw the holy city,"* (Remember Revelation 11:2: *"and the holy city shall they tread under foot."* Here we are not called *"the beloved city,"* but called exactly the same term as 11:2, *"the holy city."*) Verse 2: *"And I John saw the holy city, new Jerusalem, coming down from God out of heaven, prepared as a bride adorned for her husband."* Immediately, we observe that this city is not a literal city. It is a bride. The church is the Bride of Christ.

We have further illumination in Revelation 21:9–10. *"And there came unto me one of the seven angels which had the seven vials full of the seven last plagues, and talked with me, saying, Come hither, I will shew thee the bride, the Lamb's wife."* So we are going to see the bride, the Lamb's wife. What does she look like? Verse 10: *"And he carried me away in the spirit to a great and high mountain, and shewed me that great city, the holy Jerusalem, descending out of heaven from God."* The city is the bride. Clearly, the city is not literal. The city is the church.

The holy city is the bride of Christ, and the bride of Christ is the church, as Ephesians 5 says when it speaks of the church being Christ's bride, and as Revelation 19 says when it speaks of the marriage supper of the Lamb, when His bride, the church, comes to the feast and is brought to heaven. Therefore, what is the holy city of Revelation

11:2? It is the same as the temple in Revelation 11:1. It is the collective people of God—namely, the church.

In Revelation 11:2 we see the unsaved, here called the Gentiles, trampling the church, here called the holy city, under their feet. Verse 2: "*But the court which is without the temple leave out, and measure it not; for it is given unto the Gentiles:*" (the unsaved) "*and the holy city*" (the believers) "*shall they*" (the Gentiles, the unsaved) "*tread under foot forty and two months.*"

Just like the Babylonians came and trampled Old Jerusalem under their feet, so the unsaved will trample the New Jerusalem under their feet also. The unsaved will treat the church like dirt under their feet. They will treat the church with scorn, contempt, and disdain, and will spit on the church like people spit on the ground. In the eyes of the Gentiles—that is, the unsaved—the church is unworthy of any respect or any regard, so they will persecute the church as much as they are able, and will seek to stamp it out with their feet.

So, then, to trample the church is to persecute the church. The question is. How long will this persecution go on? Verse 2 tells us it will last forty-two months. Forty-two months is exactly three and a half years according to the Jewish calendar, which has twelve months of thirty days each. The Jewish year is 360 days long.

Notice 11:3: "*And I will give power unto my two witnesses, and they shall prophesy a thousand two hundred and threescore days, clothed in sackcloth.*" What is interesting is that a thousand two hundred and sixty days is also exactly forty-two months; it is also exactly three and a half years. These three time measurements are all equivalent to each other.

Notice 12:6 says, "*And the woman fled into the wilderness, where she hath a place prepared of God, that they should feed her there a thousand two hundred and threescore days,*" which is the same length of time—one thousand two hundred sixty days.

Notice 12:14: "*And to the woman were given two wings of a great eagle, that she might fly into the wilderness, into her place, where she is nourished for a time, and times and half a time, from the face of the serpent.*" Here, "*a time*" is one year, "*and times*" is two years, and "*a half a time*" is one-half year, for a total of three and a half years.

That this is the meaning of time, times, and half a time is clear from the parallel nature of 12:6 and 12:14. In both passages, terminology about the woman being protected and nourished in her place in the wilderness is parallel, and therefore the time statements are parallel as well. "Three and a half times" is numerically equal to one thousand two hundred and sixty days. We will see this further explained in Chapters 38 and 40.

Forty-two months, three and a half years, and twelve hundred and sixty days are all referring to an identical length of time. This time period of three and a half years, or forty-two months, or one thousand two hundred and sixty days, occurs repeatedly in the book of Revelation.

When we studied numerology as we introduced the book of Revelation, we saw that seven was the number that symbolized completeness. God completed the creation of the world in seven days. Therefore, seven also symbolizes the complete scope of human history. We also saw that the complete scope of human history, symbolized by the number seven, is divided into two halves: the time from the creation to Christ, and the time from Christ to the consummation.

So the complete period of human history symbolized by the number seven has a dividing point, and that is the coming of Christ. Everything that occurred from the creation to Christ is the first half; everything that occurred from Christ to the consummation is the second half. So if human history is then divided into two halves, the number three and a half would symbolize the first half of history, and the number three and a half would symbolize the second half of history; that is, the time between the first and the second coming of Christ.

Three and a half years, forty-two months, and twelve hundred and sixty days are all symbolic numbers that represent the time period between the first and the second coming of Christ, which is the second half of human history. These symbolic numbers represent the entire church age. How long is forty-two months? It is the time between the first and second coming of Christ. How long is twelve hundred and sixty days? It is the time between the first and second coming of Christ. How long is three and a half years, a time and times and half a time? It is the time between the first and the second coming of Christ. This will become abundantly clear as we study Revelation 12.

How long do the two witnesses in verse 3 witness on the face of the earth? The entire time between the first and the second coming of Christ. That is how long the gospel witness goes on: forty-two months, or twelve hundred and sixty days, symbolically speaking.

During this entire time between the first and second coming of Christ, the unsaved are going to trample the church under their feet. They are given space and time to do so by God. He gives them their space when He gives them the court—that is, the world—in which to function; and He gives them their time when He gives them forty-two months—that is, the time between the first and second coming of Christ.

This explains what we have seen for the last two thousand years. The unsaved have everything outside of the church. They have the whole world in which to function. The unsaved have dominated the globe for the last two thousand years, and they have trampled the church under their feet for the last two thousand years; and yet, the church has been protected by God and the church has been preserved by God. Though the church has been small, it has been safe from all efforts to stamp it out. The kingdom of God has never been defeated or destroyed.

On the other hand, the kingdoms of this world are not under the protection of God. They were not measured. Therefore, the kingdoms of this world have been destroyed countless times and will continue to be destroyed. The kingdoms of men come and go. The kingdoms of men rise and fall. The kingdoms of men are transient and passing because they are all the kingdoms of the unsaved, and they are not under the protection of God.

But the kingdom of God has continued for two thousand years without being extinguished, and it will continue to go on until Christ returns. At the very last, when the Gentiles are almost on the brink of extinguishing it, Christ will return and destroy them and deliver His people.

We are told of the ultimate defeat of the Gentiles and our ultimate triumph when the seventh trumpet sounds and *"the kingdoms of this world become the kingdoms of our Lord, and of his Christ; and he shall reign for ever and ever,"* in 11:15. The church will finally own the courtyard that is currently outside the church, and the whole earth will become ours. The third Beatitude says, *"Blessed are the meek, for they shall inherit the earth."* Someday, the temple is going to own the courtyard, and the Gentiles are all going to be cast into hell. No longer will they trample us under their feet. Then they will be under Christ's feet and under the feet of His people, and we shall reign forever and ever.

What do we expect in this age? The church will be persecuted by the world, and the church will be protected by God. God has marked out the church for Himself, and He will preserve it until the end of the age.

We have looked at the identity of the church, we have looked at the protection of the church, and we have looked at the temporary permission that the world has to trample on the church. In the next chapter, we are going to look at the witness of the church and see the reaction the world has to that witness, as we look at the two witnesses who are also called the two olive trees and the two candlesticks.

Who are we? We are the temple of God. At what altar do we worship? Christ on the cross. Who is inside the temple? Jews. What is outside the temple? The world. Who is in the world? The Gentiles. What are they doing? Trampling on the people of God. For how long? Between the first and the second coming of Christ. Therefore, do not be surprised if the church is persecuted; but remember, the church is also protected.

Have you ever wondered how the church has lasted this long? It is because we have been measured and marked out for the protection of God. It does not mean we will not be martyred, and it does not mean we will not suffer, but it does mean the kingdom of Christ will not be destroyed. Where is Babylon? Where is Medo-Persia? Where is the Roman empire? They have all been destroyed. No kingdom of this world ever lasts, because none of them is marked out for protection by God. But the kingdom of God is marked out for protection, and it will last. This is our comfort and confidence and optimism regarding the future.

33

The Two Witnesses, Revelation 11:3–6

> "[3] *And I will give power unto my two witnesses, and they shall prophesy a thousand two hundred and threescore days, clothed in sackcloth.* [4] *These are the two olive trees, and the two candlesticks standing before the God of the earth.* [5] *And if any man will hurt them, fire proceedeth out of their mouth, and devoureth their enemies: and if any man will hurt them, he must in this manner be killed.* [6] *These have power to shut heaven, that it rain not in the days of their prophecy: and have power over waters to turn them to blood, and to smite the earth with all plagues, as often as they will.*"

In a previous chapter, we saw that Revelation 10:8–11:14 describes the preaching of the gospel between the first and the second coming of Christ. This gospel preaching will go on during the time of the seven churches, the seven seals, and the seven trumpets. All of these run parallel with each other and all of them occur throughout the church age.

We see how the gospel is going to be received in this age, and how the preachers of the gospel are going to be treated. While the gospel is sweet to those who believe it and proclaim it, the world reacts viciously to the preaching of the gospel. The elect receive and believe the gospel, but the vast majority of humanity despise the gospel and persecute those who preach it.

It is a painful and difficult thing to preach the gospel to a hostile and hateful world. It makes us sick in our stomach to enter into conflict and spiritual warfare, to endure the rejection and scorn of others, and to experience the bitter hatred they express toward us. In spite of their hatred, out of a love for Christ and a desire to see His name and glory proclaimed, we preach the gospel anyway. Out of a love for the lost and out of a desire to see them saved, we preach the gospel faithfully. Out of a love for the truth and a delight in the truth, we preach the gospel boldly. This is what believers have always done, and this is what believers will always do in spite of the bitter opposition they receive when they do it.

This passage enables us to understand what the spiritual warfare of preaching the gospel to the lost is like, and what we should expect when we preach it to a hostile world. Some may ask, "Why preach the gospel at all if this is the reaction we are going to get? People try to hurt us. We have bitter conflict with them, and eventually, they destroy us. Why should we preach the gospel at all?"

We preach the gospel because this is how God calls out His elect from among the lost. We preach the gospel because this is how you yourself got saved. Somebody was willing to take the risk of receiving a hostile response from you as he had from so many people before; and yet out of love to you, he preached the gospel to you anyway, and you must do the same for others.

As you preach the gospel, you are looking for God's elect among the sea of humanity to whom you speak, and you will know them by the response they give both to you and to the message of salvation from sin. The response of God's elect to the preaching of the gospel will be different from the vast majority of the responses you have gotten. They will be receptive and will want to hear more. This is the response you live for, you long for, and you look for. This is the response that fills you with joy.

This is why you put up with the bitter conflict and the hostile reaction you get from the vast majority of people. You are looking among them for the person God is drawing to Himself and whom He will bring to saving faith in Jesus Christ. As for all those hostile responses, you simply endure them and fight the good fight of faith against them. This is the nature of the warfare between the kingdom of light and the kingdom of darkness all throughout this age and in every generation until Jesus returns.

Let us then examine the spiritual warfare of preaching the gospel that we are commissioned to engage in.

The Description of the Witnesses

The description of the witnesses is found in verses 3 and 4. Notice God says, *"And I will give power unto my two witnesses, and they shall prophesy a thousand two hundred and threescore days, clothed in sackcloth.* [4] *These are the two olive trees, and the two candlesticks standing before the God of the earth."*

In the last chapter we looked at verses 1 and 2, and we saw the conflict between the church and the world that will occur throughout the time between the first and second coming of Christ. We saw the church described as a temple in verse 1, and we were told that it is under the protection of God. We saw in verse 2 that the world, also called the Gentiles, tramples the church under its feet. But this trampling of the church by the world does not destroy this holy city, because the church has the protection of God.

Furthermore, this trampling of the church by the world does not silence the church. The church continues to bear bold and public witness before the world, and this bold and public witness is represented by the symbolism of these two witnesses described in verse 3. Verse 3 says, *"And I will give power unto my two witnesses, and they shall prophesy a thousand two hundred and threescore days, clothed in sackcloth."*

There are several reasons why these two witnesses are not two literal men, but rather are symbolic visual representations of the witness of believers throughout the church age.

First of all, these two witnesses prophesy for the entire church age. Verse 3 states they prophesy for one thousand two hundred and sixty days. In the previous chapter we saw that this is a symbolic number that represents the entire period between the first and the second coming of Christ, a time period that has now lasted over 2,000 years. No literal man has lived that long.

Secondly, these two men symbolize the witness of the church and the believers because two witnesses were necessary to give competent legal testimony in a court of law. Deuteronomy 19:15 says that at the mouth of two witnesses a matter would be established as being true. The truthfulness of the facts of the gospel and the truthfulness of the message of the gospel are therefore symbolized by these two witnesses as they bear testimony to the world. Jesus said in John 8:17, *"It is also written in your law, that the testimony of two men is true."* There is a sense in which these two witnesses are bringing testimony in the court of God against the world for their wickedness, bearing witness to that wickedness, and calling them to repentance.

Thirdly, when Jesus first came and commissioned His disciples to go out and bear witness of His message and coming, He sent them out two by two, a pattern we see repeated over and over again in the

New Testament. In Luke 10:1, it says, ". . .*the Lord appointed other seventy also, and sent them two and two before his face into every city and place, whither he himself would come.*"

Before Jesus came to a city or place, He sent two witnesses before Him to announce His coming. The witnesses to Christ preceded the coming of Christ.

This pattern of sending witnesses before His coming to announce His coming is replicated here. Jesus is coming a second time to this earth, so He is sending out His disciples to go before Him into the entire world, proclaiming His gospel and declaring that He is coming along behind them. They declare He will personally appear and bring His judgment or His salvation, based upon how people respond to the witness that believers bring.

Fourthly, since the temple and the city of 11:1–2 are symbolic representations of the church, then it stands to reason that the two witnesses in verse 3 are a symbolic representation of the church as well.

Fifthly, in verse 4 these two witnesses are also said to be two olive trees and two candlesticks, which are clearly symbolic designations. We have symbolic images of the church in verses 1–2, and we have symbolic images in verse 4, so it stands to reason that verse 3 is a symbolic image as well.

Therefore, we conclude that the two witnesses represent the church on earth, bearing witness to Christ and His coming through the gospel preaching of pastors, missionaries, and ordinary Christians. Day by day, every day, for all the days between the first and second coming, God's people bear witness to God's message to a hostile world. Every day of the symbolic one thousand two hundred and sixty days, the church is going to preach the gospel to the world.

We are told in verse 3 that these two witnesses, who represent the church on earth bearing witness to the gospel through the preaching of Christians, are clothed in sackcloth. Sackcloth is a symbol of mourning and sorrow. It was a biblical custom when anyone was grief-stricken that he would put off his clothes and dress in sackcloth. The church, as it witnesses to the world, is in a condition of grief and mourning. The church mourns and sorrows over the blindness of the world to the free offer of the gospel. The church weeps over the multitudes that go to hell who could have gone to heaven had they just humbled themselves and repented and believed. It brings grief to a witnessing believer to see so many going to hell.

How many times has your heart been broken and tears been brought to your eyes as you have seen loved ones die in defiance of the gospel and you know, every day, they are burning in hell? Believers reflect the heart of Jesus Christ who wept over Jerusalem when He cried out with tears, "*O Jerusalem, Jerusalem, thou that killest the prophets, and stonest them which are sent unto her, how often would I have gathered thy children together, even as a hen gathereth her chicks under her wings, and you would not! Behold, your house is left to you desolate.*"

The representation of Christianity which says that we ought to go through life with a euphoric happiness as though this constitutes normal Christian joy is not even remotely biblical. It is true we have the fruit of the Spirit which is joy. But we also have the sorrow of Christ which is grief over the lostness of the people of the world and their defiance of God and their damnation in hell. If you can think about people going to hell and not be heartbroken over that, I have to wonder if you are a Christian at all. All through this age, we mourn over the lostness of the world and the damnation that is coming to it because of its defiance against God. We are clothed in sackcloth.

This work of witnessing for God is a work that could never be done out of mere human strength, and it is a work that could never be accomplished with a merely human message.

Verse 3 tells us that God "*will give power unto my two witnesses.*" The church has strength from God to carry out her work, and in that power and strength she is able to accomplish her task.

Jesus told the apostles in Acts 1:8 to stay in Jerusalem because they would receive power after the Holy Ghost came upon them, and they would then be witnesses of Jesus in Jerusalem and Judea and Samaria and to the uttermost parts of the earth. Jesus recognized the disciples could not accomplish the work of being witnesses of Him without power being given to them. Verse 3 tells us that we do not have to do this work in human strength. God will give us divine power to be witnesses to Him, and He will do it through the gift of the Holy Spirit.

Verse 3 also tells us that the church has a divinely given message; that is, they will speak the prophecy of God. Notice verse 3: "*And I will give power unto my two witnesses, and they shall prophesy.*" Our message is not merely a human message that arises out of the human imagination. Our message is one of proclaiming divine revelation, and only divine revelation. This is the prophecy that comes from God contained in the little book that was given to John to eat and swallow and speak before many peoples and nations and tongues and kings.

Paul told Timothy in 2 Timothy 4:2–5 to preach the word, whether it was popular or not. He told him to patiently exhort and reprove and rebuke those he preached to. He told him the time would come when people would not endure gospel preaching, and they would seek out teachers who would tell them what they wanted to hear. He told Timothy he would endure afflictions as a result, but he was to stick to the message, to keep doing the work of an evangelist, and trust the message to do its work in the lives of God's elect. He was to speak the prophecy of God contained in the word of God—nothing more, nothing less, and nothing else. The little book given to John in chapter 10 is all we need. It is the prophecy that we speak.

The church has the power of God and the message of God to give them both the strength and the content they need in order to be faithful witnesses of God.

But that is not all. Notice verse 4: *"These are the two olive trees, and the two candlesticks standing before the God of the earth."* In the description of these witnesses, we have further information given to us. Here are two more symbolic visual images used to describe the witnesses of the gospel—that of two olive trees and two candlesticks. This imagery is taken out of Zechariah 4, which we have looked at a couple of times previously.

In Zechariah 4 there is a candlestick, a candelabra with seven lamps like the menorah in the Holy place. Above this candlestick is a bowl from which seven pipes go to these seven lamps that burn oil. There are two olive trees, and these two olive trees pour oil into the bowl; and from the bowl, the oil goes through the pipes to the seven oil lamps on the candelabra. The olive trees produce the oil that feeds that candlestick so the light the candlestick contains never goes out. In Zechariah 4, the olive tree and the oil it produces are representative of the Holy Spirit. The candlestick and the light it produces are representative of the church and the light of the gospel that it preaches into a darkened world.

Jesus uses the symbolic visual image of candlesticks to represent the seven churches in Revelation 1. As He speaks to these churches, He says, "Be faithful, or I will take your candlestick away—that is, the light you are supposed to shed on the world will be extinguished." Furthermore, Jesus says in the Sermon on the Mount that believers are the light of the world, and He goes on to describe them as candles set on a candlestick that gives light to all that are in the house. Since the candlestick represents the seven churches, this is one more reason these two witnesses represent the church and are not individuals.

It is because the church is constantly supplied with the oil of the Spirit that the lamp of the church's witness is not quenched by the opposition of evil men. We have the Spirit of God pouring out the oil of God so that the lamps remain lit, shedding the light of the gospel into the world. The Holy Spirit continually ignites the light of gospel witness in the lives of the believers. This is what verse 4 is telling us. The work of God is done *"not by might, nor by power, but by my Spirit, saith the LORD"* as it says in Zechariah 4:6, where this imagery is set forth. Notice that the last phrase of Revelation 11:4 says that these two witnesses stand before the God of the earth. This is virtually a quote from Zechariah 4:14.

These two witnesses, who as olive trees and candlesticks have the power of the Spirit to be able to shed the light of the gospel, are *"standing before the God of the earth."*

First of all, this phrase conveys the idea that God has commissioned them to carry out their work, and He will empower and enable them to do it. They are standing before Him; and He, as it were, sends them forth.

Secondly, it conveys the idea that they do their work for God with their eyes on God seeking the approval of God. They are standing before Him and as they are doing their work, they are under His eye, He is in their eye, and it is in the light of that perspective that they do their work.

Thirdly, it conveys the idea that they fear no man upon the earth because God is the God of the earth, and God exercises power and dominion over every unsaved person upon it.

Just as Joshua the priest and Zerubbabel the prince were able to complete the Old Covenant temple through the power of the Holy Spirit despite all the opposition of the enemies that were all around them, in the same way, these two witnesses will be able to complete the New Covenant temple—the church—through the power of the Spirit despite all the opposition that is all around them. This imagery from Zechariah 4 is brought forward to describe the work of the church in its witness to the world in Revelation 11.

The Power of the Witnesses

The power of the witnesses is found in verses 5 to 6. It says, *"And if any man will hurt them, fire proceedeth out of their mouth, and devoureth their enemies: and if any man will hurt them, he must in this manner be killed.* [6] *These have power to shut heaven, that it rain not in the days of their prophecy: and have power over waters to turn them to blood, and to smite the earth with all plagues, as often as they will."*

Even though these two witnesses are proclaiming the sweet message of the gospel, the good news of salvation, and the free grace of God, they receive anything but a warm welcome from the world. Twice it says in verse 5 that men will attempt to hurt them. Notice verse 5: *"And if any man will hurt them,"* and verse 5 again, *"and if any man will hurt them."* Incredibly, men will attempt to hurt them in response to their gospel preaching. People will try to injure and harm them when they preach the gospel to them.

When you preach the gospel to people, why do they want to hurt you in return? It is because the gospel is a direct affront to the pride of men, the self-will of men, and the self-righteousness of men. The gospel requires men to submit themselves to the sovereignty of God, to confess their sinfulness to God, and to humble themselves before God. All these things are an affront to fallen man who wants to serve only himself and who wants to answer to no one but himself. Therefore, when you tell men they have to serve God and answer to God, they take that as a direct assault on their personal sovereignty, self-will, and self-righteousness.

Feeling assaulted, he assaults us in return, and, as verse 5 says, seeks to hurt and harm us. This spiritual warfare leveled against us is something we must expect to occur. This is a war we have to engage in with the spiritual weapons that God has left at our disposal. We must fight back against those who seek to silence our gospel witness, and these verses tell us how it is to be accomplished.

Notice the language of verses 5 and 6. It says, *"And if any man will hurt them, fire proceedeth out of their mouth, and devoureth their enemies: and if any man will hurt them, he must in this manner be killed.* [6] *These have power to shut heaven, that it rain not in the days of their prophecy: and have power over waters to turn them to blood, and to smite the earth with all plagues, as often as they will."* Here is a description of the church fighting back against the world that is trying to hurt them.

This passage reminds us of the ministry of Elijah. In 2 Kings 1:1–17 Ahab sent out fifty men with a captain to capture Elijah and drag him back to the palace. Elijah called down fire from heaven and it consumed that captain and those fifty men. Ahab sent out another group, and Elijah called down fire from heaven and burned up that captain and his fifty men. Twice Elijah called down fire from heaven to consume the captain and the 50 soldiers who came to arrest and harm him. This was an act of physical warfare.

But under the New Covenant, we have acts of spiritual warfare. Notice the fire in verse 5 does not come down from heaven. It comes out of the mouth of the two witnesses. This means that the enemies of the gospel are killed by the power of the word of God that proceeds out of the mouth of the people of God as they preach the gospel. God says to Jeremiah the prophet in Jeremiah 5:14, "*. . .behold, I will make my words in thy mouth fire, and this people wood, and it shall devour them.*"

Never once did Jeremiah call down fire from heaven, but Jeremiah spoke with his mouth, and God said, "Your words are going to be like fire, and they are going to burn up all of these people." This occurred during the captivity of Israel by Babylon. When the judgments of God fell upon Israel, the Babylonian king came, leveled the place, burned it to the ground, slaughtered the people, and hauled the remnant off to captivity for seventy years. The pronouncements of God's wrath and judgment that proceeded out of the mouth of Jeremiah burned up the people. It brought God's judgment down on them.

In this record of God's work through Jeremiah, we have an indication of the meaning of Revelation 11:5 when it says, "*fire proceeds out of their mouth and devours their enemies.*" When we pronounce the judgments of God contained in the word of God against the wicked, those are not empty words. God honors the threats against the haters of His person and His people which He makes in the Scriptures. When we pronounce those threats against those who persecute us, God honors those threats and brings destruction upon them.

The wicked may scorn us and our message of God's coming judgment upon them, but the words we speak are not empty words, and they will be performed by the Lord who gave them. The point is, no one can harm God's witnesses before their mission has been accomplished; and when they try, the judgment of God we pronounce against them destroys them. Jesus said in Luke 10:19, *"Behold, I give unto you power to tread on serpents and scorpions"* (those represent the satanic opposition that is raised against us) *"and over all the power of the enemy: and nothing shall by any means hurt you."* Those who try to hurt the believers only succeed in bringing destruction upon themselves. The kingdoms that have persecuted the church have all fallen, and the church goes on unharmed, continually expanding across the globe and continually growing in numbers. After all, where is the Roman Empire? Where is the Ottoman Empire? Where is Hitler's Third Reich? They and many other kingdoms are gone, but the church goes on.

We use the sword of the Spirit, which is the word of God, to smite those who smite us with their literal swords; and it is a historical fact that the sword of the Spirit has prevailed over the sword of the kingdoms of men in the last 2,000 years, and it will continue to prevail. A gun is a poor weapon to use against the word of God. The kingdom of God has never been extinguished, but the kingdoms of men too numerous to list which persecuted Christianity have disappeared into oblivion. They have, in the words of verse 5, been devoured and killed.

Notice verse 6: *"These have power to shut heaven, that it rain not in the days of their prophecy: and have power over waters to turn them to blood, and to smite the earth with all plagues, as often as they will."* In verse 6, the power of the two witnesses—that is, the power of the church throughout this age—is further described. The work of Elijah in 1 Kings 17:1 in withholding the rain for years in Israel, and the work of Moses in turning the water to blood and smiting the earth with all kinds of plagues, are both further indications of the spiritual weapons which the church possesses.

While the power of verse 5 was directed against men themselves, the power of verse 6 is directed against nature—that is, against that which supports and sustains men. Disasters in the realm of nature, as we saw in the first four trumpet judgments in chapter 8, have smitten the persecutors of the people of God, and are God's punishment for their persecution of the people of God all throughout this age. As we pray, God brings trumpet judgments in the realm of nature on our persecutors for the harm they do to us.

The point of verses 5 and 6 is that the wicked world will not be able to prevail against the church to any significant degree or to stop the church from fulfilling her mission. The world fights against the church, and the church fights back against the world. But she does so with spiritual weapons of faith and prayer and blameless lives, calling upon God to protect her and vindicate her, and to punish the wicked both directly and in their support structures. God answers those prayers, gives His people the victory, and defeats the kingdoms of the world. The church prevails in the battle. You remember that Ahab did not prevail against Elijah, and Pharaoh did not prevail against Moses. The kingdoms of this world will not prevail against the church until the work of the church is done.

The point is this: Our prayers set in motion the judgments of God against the wicked in this age. When we cry out to the Lord for deliverance and for vengeance, He hears us and acts on our behalf. We have already seen that in the fifth seal. When the saints under the altar cry out to the Lord for vengeance in 6:9–10, and when the saints in 8:1–5 cry out to the Lord at the altar of incense, the seven trumpet judgments follow. When we cry out to the Lord for deliverance and vengeance, He hears us and He acts. The wicked should fear to harm the church, lest the God of the church smite them with the trumpets of His judgments.

Christ is telling us we have the resources and power Elijah and Moses had when they fought their spiritual warfare, because we worship and serve the same God they did. And while their help was in the realm of the physical and our help is in the realm of the spiritual, it is no less powerful and it is no less impressive. Therefore, we need to press on with confidence as we evangelize the world. We are not only marked out for protection by God, as verse 1 made clear to us, but we are also given God's power and God's Spirit and God's authority to call down His judgments upon our persecutors who try to hurt us.

The church cannot be stopped, and the church cannot be defeated. The church will prevail over the world, and the church will accomplish the work that God has given to her to do.

We are the two witnesses with the power of God and the message of God, standing in the presence of God with grief and sorrow and sackcloth, mourning over the lostness of the world, having the power of the Holy Spirit to make our lamps of witness burn brightly as we preach the gospel into the darkness. And as the darkness retaliates, we have the power and the resources of God to fight back against it and defeat it.

Revelation 17:14 says that they overcame him (the accuser of the brethren) by the blood of the Lamb and by the word of their testimony, and they loved not their lives to the death. We march forward, we march on, and we roll over the top of the kingdom of darkness, and spread the gospel to the whole world so that all of God's elect are saved. Nothing the wicked do can ever stop it or keep it from being completed.

Evangelism is not a walk in the park. It is warfare. We have to fight, but we have been given the whole armor of God. Jesus said to Peter, "I am giving you the keys to the kingdom, and what you bind on earth will be bound in heaven, and what you loose on earth will be loosed in heaven." Whatever that meant, it meant at least this: Heaven recognizes the prayers of the people of God on earth, and heaven cooperates with those prayers. Mark 16:20 says, regarding the work of the disciples, that the Lord went with them and worked with them, *"confirming the word with signs following."* They went everywhere preaching the word, and the Lord worked with them. That is what happened with Moses and Elijah and Jeremiah: God worked with them. God is going to work with us as well.

Recognize that people are going to try to hurt you just because you live like a Christian and you preach the truth. But recognize also that God will fight against them, and He will fight for you and with you, and they will not defeat you. Therefore we can sing: "Onward, Christian soldiers, marching as to war, with the cross of Jesus, going on before." We will triumph. Second Corinthians 2:14 promises it: *"Now thanks be unto God, which always causeth us to triumph in Christ."*

34

The Rise and Ruin of Antichrist, Revelation 11:7–14

> “7 *And when they shall have finished their testimony, the beast that ascendeth out of the bottomless pit shall make war against them, and shall overcome them, and kill them.* 8 *And their dead bodies shall lie in the street of the great city, which spiritually is called Sodom and Egypt, where also our Lord was crucified.* 9 *And they of the people and kindreds and tongues and nations shall see their dead bodies three days and an half, and shall not suffer their dead bodies to be put in graves.* 10 *And they that dwell upon the earth shall rejoice over them, and make merry, and shall send gifts one to another; because these two prophets tormented them that dwelt on the earth.* 11 *And after three days and an half the Spirit of life from God entered into them, and they stood upon their feet; and great fear fell upon them which saw them.* 12 *And they heard a great voice from heaven saying unto them, Come up hither. And they ascended up to heaven in a cloud; and their enemies beheld them.* 13 *And the same hour was there a great earthquake, and the tenth part of the city fell, and in the earthquake were slain of men seven thousand: and the remnant were affrighted, and gave glory to the God of heaven.* 14 *The second woe is past; and, behold, the third woe cometh quickly.*”

Revelation 10:8 to 11:14 describes how the gospel is going to be received in this present age and how the preachers of the gospel are going to be treated by the world.

God’s elect will repent and receive and believe the gospel, but the vast majority of humanity is going to hate and despise the gospel and will persecute those who preach it. Preaching the gospel is an act of spiritual warfare, in which we call on the world—unsaved sinners—to repent of their pride and self-will and self-righteousness, and submit themselves to Jesus Christ as Lord and Savior. The world is deeply offended by such a message because unsaved men want to serve themselves and answer to no one but themselves. Unsaved men view the gospel not as good news, but as an assault on their personal sovereignty and as an affront to their pride and self-righteousness.

As a result, the unsaved attack believers and seek to harm and hurt them. We saw in 11:1 that the believers are under the protection of God, and therefore the unbelievers cannot prevail over the church and silence it, no matter how harshly they attack us and no matter how long they try. Until the work of calling God's elect out of the world is completed, God frustrates the efforts of the wicked to destroy us, and He frustrates their efforts with His trumpet judgments.

The church is invincible against the world as long as God is saving His people. We saw in verses 5 and 6 that if anyone tries to hurt them, they are able to resist that effort. They have the same God protecting them that Elijah and Moses had; and just as Elijah prevailed over Ahab, and Moses prevailed over Pharaoh, the church is going to prevail over the world.

But there will come a day when all of God's elect have been saved, and there is none left whom God intends to save. The church will have finished her testimony to the world, as verse 7 says: *"And when they shall have finished their testimony."* When the church has finished her testimony to the world at some point in the future, verses 7 to 14 tell us what will happen next.

At the end of the age, after all of God's elect have been called and saved, the Antichrist will appear, and he will go to war against the church. The church will be largely wiped out, and it will appear for a short period of time that Satan and the forces of evil will have triumphed because the public visibility of the church and the public testimony of the church will be gone. But just when the wicked are celebrating the elimination of the church from the world as a visible public voice and presence, Christ will return for the small remnant of believers who are left alive. They will be instantly glorified, He will raise the dead believers from their graves to that same glorification, and both will be caught up together to meet the Lord in the air. Then He will destroy the wicked.

This is the overview of the passage before us. Let us consider it in further detail as we proceed through it verse by verse.

The Martyrdom of the Witnesses

The martyrdom of the witnesses is in verses 7 to 10. "*And when they shall have finished their testimony, the beast that ascendeth out of the bottomless pit shall make war against them, and shall overcome them, and kill them.* [8] *And their dead bodies shall lie in the street of the great city, which spiritually is called Sodom and Egypt, where also our Lord was crucified.* [9] *And they of the people and kindreds and tongues and nations shall see their dead bodies three days and an half, and shall not suffer their dead bodies to be put in graves.* [10] *And they that dwell upon the earth shall rejoice over them, and make merry, and shall send gifts one to another; because these two prophets tormented them that dwelt on the earth.*"

Notice verse 7 says, "*And when they shall have finished their testimony.*" Since Christ first came to the earth, the church, represented by these two witnesses, has been bearing testimony to the gospel of Christ. As long as there were some of God's elect who have yet to be saved, the testimony of the church to Christ and His gospel is going to go on, and the church will be invincible.

But there will come a day when all of God's elect have been saved, and therefore the need for the church to bear testimony to the gospel will be finished. The church will have finished her work of evangelizing the lost. Until then, the church was invincible, and the world stood defeated before the church in its efforts to silence her testimony. But when the church has completed her task of evangelism and proclamation of the gospel, God will allow the enemies of the church to overcome the church and virtually destroy its presence from the face of the earth. Notice it says in verse 7, "*And when they shall have finished their testimony, the beast that ascendeth out of the bottomless pit shall make war against them, and shall overcome them, and kill them.*"

Up to this point in time they could not overcome them. Verse 5 says, "*And if any man will hurt them, fire proceedeth out of their mouth, and devoureth their enemies: and if any man will hurt them, he must in this manner be killed.*" Prior to this point in time, when someone tried to destroy the church, they wound up being destroyed.

But now when this beast that ascends out of the bottomless pit attempts to destroy the church, he succeeds, but only after their testimony is finished, and not until. The world never stops the church from completing the purposes that God has for His church. But in the end, there is a beast that ascends out of the bottomless pit who achieves the destruction of the church.

This beast that ascends out of this bottomless pit, who will accomplish this near annihilation of the people of God from the face of the earth, is one of three beasts we are introduced to in the book of Revelation. There is the beast that ascends out of the bottomless pit here in 11:7. There is the beast that ascends out of the sea in 13:1. There is the beast that ascends out of the earth in 13:11.

These three beasts, the beast that ascends out of the abyss, the beast that ascends out of the sea, and the beast that ascends out of the earth, represent three separate concepts, which we will see as we come to each of them. What we see is that each of these three beasts is Satan's agent and instrument to carry out his agenda. They are Satan's helpers.

This first beast that ascends out of the abyss is the Antichrist, also known as the man of sin. The Antichrist arises out of the bottomless pit in the sense that he is indwelt and inspired by Satan, and therefore possesses the character and conduct of the inhabitants of the bottomless pit. He exhibits all the evil of those who dwell there. Spiritually, he arises out of the bottomless pit. But physically, he arises out of the sea of humanity, just like any other human would.

Notice two passages. The first passage is 2 Thessalonians 2. Verse 1 says: *"Now we beseech you, brethren, by the coming of our Lord Jesus Christ, and by our gathering together unto him."* This describes the second coming of Jesus back to the earth. He comes back, and we are going to be gathered together with Him by the resurrection and the rapture. Verse 2, *"That ye be not soon shaken in mind, or be troubled, neither by spirit, nor by word, nor by letter as [if] from us, as that the day of Christ is at hand."*

Paul is saying the Thessalonians have been misled and deceived because somebody has claimed to have a prophetic spirit or some word from God; they even presented a letter that was supposedly from Paul. The message of this false information was that Christ's coming was imminent—that is, it could happen at any moment. Paul says, "I do not want you to be troubled in your mind and think that Christ's coming is imminent or that it could happen at any moment. The day of Christ's coming is not at hand."

Here is the truth. Verse 3: *"Let no man deceive you by any means:*

for that day shall not come"; that is, the second coming of Christ spoken of in verse 1, when He comes and gathers us to be with Himself. That day will not come except there come first, *"a falling away"*; that is, a great apostasy among professing believers; and second, *"and that man of sin be revealed, the son of perdition; [4] Who opposeth and exalteth himself above all that is called God, or that is worshipped; so that he as God sitteth in the temple of God, showing himself that he is God."*

When Christ comes and gathers us together to be with Himself, that day is not going to occur until two things happen first. First, there is going to be a tremendous falling away. There is going to be a great apostasy among professing Christians. Second, this man of sin, who presents himself to the world as being God on earth, is going to appear, sit in some kind of a temple, declare he is God, demand that people worship him, and exalt himself above everything that has previously been called God. Christ is not going to return until this great apostasy occurs, and this appearance of the man of sin occurs.

Could Jesus come back today? No. Jesus cannot come back today because at this time we have not seen the worldwide apostasy of the church, and we have not seen the appearance of this man of sin. The teaching that Jesus could come back at any moment is not true. Jesus said there are going to be certain signs, and when these signs occur, then you know that the second coming is close. But until these signs occur, it is not close.

Now of this individual who comes, it says in verse 8, *"then shall that Wicked [one] be revealed"* (this man of sin), *"whom the Lord shall consume with the spirit of his mouth, and shall destroy with the brightness of his coming: [9] Even him"* (this man of sin), *"whose coming is after the working of Satan with all power and signs and lying wonders, [10] And with all deceivableness of unrighteousness in them that perish; because they received not the love of the truth, that they might be saved. [11] And for this cause God shall send them strong delusion, that they should believe a lie: [12] That they all might be damned who believed not the truth, but had pleasure in unrighteousness."* Whoever this man of sin is, it says in verse 9 that he is driven and empowered by Satan and is given tremendous ability by Satan to deceive people into thinking that he is God on earth.

The second passage is 1 John 2:18. *"Little children, it is the last time." "The last time"* refers to the time between the first and second coming of Christ. We have been in the last time for 2,000 years. It is the last time because it is the last covenantal arrangement God will ever make before He brings the consummation. We are in the last covenantal arrangement. There will be no more covenants after this. Therefore, we are in *"the last time."*

Verse 18 says, *"and as ye have heard that Antichrist shall come."* Antichrist will come. An individual who is opposed to Christ and who substitutes himself as being Christ will come. He is the man of sin spoken of in 2 Thessalonians 2:3–4. He is the beast that arises out of the abyss in Revelation 11:7. John states in verse 18: *"Little children, it is the last time: and as ye have heard that Antichrist shall come, even now are there many Antichrists; whereby we know that it is the last time."*

Throughout the age between the first and the second coming of Christ, many people are going to rise up who oppose Christ, or who claim they are Christ. The many antichrists John speaks of certainly include the popes who have occupied the Vatican in Rome, who have said they are Christ on earth, and are to be worshiped as the representative of Christ on earth. There are many antichrists, but there is the Antichrist, who is going to appear at the end of this age, who is going to fulfill the description of the man of sin given in 2 Thessalonians 2:3–4, and who is this beast that arises out of the abyss in Revelation 11:7.

At the end of this age, when the church has finished the proclamation of the gospel because all of God's elect for whom Christ died are now saved, it says in 11:7 that the beast that ascends out of the bottomless pit is going to make war against the church *"and shall overcome them, and kill them."* The reason it says he *"ascendeth out of the bottomless pit"* is that the bottomless pit is where he derives his power from—that is, from Satan. We saw in 2 Thessalonians 2:9–10 that his working is *"after the working of Satan with all power and signs and lying wonders, and with all deceivableness."*

This Antichrist is a human being, but he is indwelled and empowered by Satan, and he is the one who will be successful in doing what no one before him ever was, which is overcoming and destroying the church from the earth as a visible presence and as a public voice. This Antichrist that arises builds a transnational coalition of all of the nations of the earth who submit their sovereignty to him, so that all the nations under his authority will cooperatively persecute the church and successfully destroy it.

Notice two passages. The first is Matthew 24:9–14. In Matthew 24, Jesus is talking about how the age is going to unfold, and how the age is going to end.

Here is how the age is going to unfold, starting in Matthew 24:4: *"And Jesus answered and said unto them, Take heed that no man deceive you. [5] For many shall come in my name, saying, I am Christ; and shall deceive many."* There will be great religious deception. We can think of the popes of Rome. We can think of all of the false teachers who have risen and said they are Christ on earth. Verse 6: *"And ye shall hear of wars and rumours of wars. . . [7] For nation shall rise against nation, and kingdom against kingdom."* There will be great national conflicts and wars. Notice a third characteristic of this age, verse 7: *"and there shall be famines, and pestilences, and earthquakes, in divers places."* There will be great natural disasters such as famines, diseases, and earthquakes.

This age is going to be characterized by great religious deceptions, tremendous wars between nations, and catastrophic natural disasters. These things have been going on for the last 2,000 years. But when all those things happen, it is not a sign of the end. "[6]. . .*See that ye be not troubled: for all these things must come to pass, but the end is not yet.*" "[8]*All of these are the beginning of sorrows.*"

There will be religious deception, constant wars, and natural disasters that will characterize this age. These are a foreshadowing of the sorrow that is going to come, but they are not signs of the end.

But a big change is indicated in verse 9 when it says, "*Then.*" Then, when the end of the age comes, *"Then shall they deliver you up to be afflicted, and shall kill you: and ye shall be hated of all nations for my name's sake."* All the nations are going to come together to afflict the church, attack the church, and virtually destroy the church.

Here is the great apostasy, verse 10: *"And then shall many be offended, and shall betray one another, and shall hate one another."* There is going to be a vast falling away of people from the church. They will be offended that they have to lay down their lives for Christ. The false Christians will betray the true Christians to the Antichrist. Notice verse 11: *"And many false prophets shall rise, and shall deceive many."* We will see the work of the third beast, the beast that arises out of the earth, greatly intensified. This is the false prophet and all of his servants who will powerfully deceive the nations to a degree they have never been deceived before. Verse 12: *"And because iniquity shall abound, the love of many shall wax cold."* This will also feed into the great apostasy. People's love for the Christians and love for God will disappear. They will plunge into the iniquity that the Antichrist is going to promote, as we read in 2 Thessalonians 2:8–12. They loved iniquity, and therefore they would not receive the love of the truth.

Verse 13: *"But he that shall endure unto the end, the same shall be saved."* That is, those who endure this transnational persecution—those who endure this apostasy and the betrayal and the hatred that arise out of their formerly professing Christian brethren—will be saved in the end by the second coming of Christ. Notice verse 14: *"And this gospel of the kingdom shall be preached in all the world for a witness unto all nations; and then shall the end come."* When they finish their testimony to the whole world, then the end will come.

Matthew 24:9–14 is a description of what is going to occur during the rise of this beast out of the abyss, this Antichrist. There is going to be a transnational coalition of nations that are going to persecute and kill the Christians. There is going to be a great apostasy and a great love for iniquity. The preaching of the gospel is going to be completely and finally finished. Then, the end will come. (This interpretation is much more fully explained and proven in Appendix 1.)

The second passage explaining how the age is going to unfold and end is Revelation 20. Verse 1: *"And I saw an angel come down from heaven, having the key of the bottomless pit and a great chain in his hand.* [2] *And he laid hold on the dragon, that old serpent, which is the Devil, and Satan, and bound him a thousand years,* [3] *And cast him into the bottomless pit, and shut him up, and set a seal upon him, that he should deceive the nations no more, till the thousand years should be fulfilled: and after that he must be loosed a little season."*

When Jesus died on the cross and rose again, He bound Satan, as described in Matthew 12:22–30. He entered the strong man's house and bound him, and Satan has been bound ever since. This symbolic thousand-year period describes the church age. Satan is bound with reference to one particular activity. He is bound with reference to his capacity to deceive the nations—that is, to get all the nations to cooperate together to attack the church.

The church age is described from the perspective of heaven in verses 4 to 6, and then we have the end of the church age, verse 7: *"And when the thousand years are expired, Satan shall be loosed out of his prison,* [8] *And shall go out to deceive the nations."* Deceiving the nations is what he was bound with reference to. That is why the world has never been able to agree together to destroy Christianity. Though individual nations have tried, there have not been enough of them in a coalition together to achieve that goal.

"[7] *And when the thousand years are expired, Satan shall be loosed out of his prison,* [8] *And shall go out to deceive the nations which are in the four quarters of the earth"* (north, south, east, and west), "*Gog and Magog* (Antichrist and his nations), "*to gather them together to battle: the number of whom is as the sand of the sea.*" All the nations will be unified to go to war. But who are they going to war with? Verse 9: "*And they went up on the breadth of the earth, and compassed [surrounded] the camp of the saints about, and the beloved city.*" They are going to attempt to destroy the church. "*And fire came down from God out of heaven, and devoured them.* [10] *And the devil that deceived them was cast into the lake of fire and brimstone, where the beast and the false prophet are, and shall be tormented day and night for ever and ever.*"

At the last minute, Jesus is going to come and prevent the total annihilation of the church. Though it will be largely destroyed from off the face of the earth, there will be a remnant who endure to the end. They will be saved. (This is much more fully explained and proven in Chapters 57–59.)

Jesus Himself said, "*Except those days should be shortened, there should no flesh be saved: but for the elect's sake those days shall be shortened.*" We will presently see just how short this period really is.

Matthew 24:14 says, "*And this gospel of the kingdom shall be preached in all the world for a witness unto all nations; and then shall the end come.*" Revelation 11:7 says: "*And when they shall have finished their testimony,*" then the end comes. Matthew 24:14 and Revelation 11:7 are saying the same thing and are referring to the same event. The gospel is finished being preached, Antichrist arises, the great apostasy occurs, and the transnational persecution begins.

The result of the rise of Antichrist and the coalition of nations that will cooperate with him is that they will make war with the church, represented by the two witnesses, and they will overcome the church, and they will kill the church. Revelation 11:7 tells us that for all intents and purposes, the church will be destroyed from the face of the earth. The voice of the church in the world will be silenced. Only a small remnant will remain, who are scattered and powerless and voiceless.

Here is another reason, in addition to the five I listed previously, why these two witnesses cannot be two literal individuals: a transnational coalition would not be necessary to defeat two human beings. But notice it says in verse 7, *"And when they shall have finished their testimony, the beast that ascendeth out of the bottomless pit shall make war against them."* You do not need to mount a transnational coalition of nations to wage war against two individual human beings. Once again, we see that they represent the church.

Notice it says in verse 8, *"And their dead [body],"* singular, *"shall lie in the street."* The King James has *"bodies,"* plural, but the noun is singular in the original. The church is just one body. The body of the church, the body of Christ, is going to lie dead in the streets. A transnational coalition would not be necessary to defeat two humans. But to do a worldwide takedown of the entire visible church across the entire globe would require a transnational coalition headed up by the Antichrist to achieve that feat, and that is what happens in verse 7.

Notice Revelation 11:8: *"And their dead [body] shall lie in the street of the great city, which spiritually is called Sodom and Egypt, where also our Lord was crucified."* This chapter speaks of two cities. In verse 2 we read about the *"holy city"* which we saw represented the church. In verse 8 it talks about the *"great city"* which represents the world. We have the city of God and the city of man. We have a city that represents the church and a city that represents the world.

This great city spoken of in verse 8 is called Sodom, which represents the immorality of the world. It is called Egypt, which represents the bondage of the world. Finally, it is called Jerusalem, the city where our Lord was crucified, representing the apostasy of the world. This is the city over which Antichrist rules. It is a city of sexual immorality, a city of slavery to civil government, and a city of religious apostates who hate Christ and His people.

In Sodom, the people were immoral. In Egypt, the people were in bondage and enslaved to civil government. In Jerusalem, the people were apostate and viciously attacked God in the person of Jesus Christ. This world of impurity and oppression and ungodliness is the world over which Antichrist rules, and this is the world that makes war on the Christian.

Immorality, enslavement, and apostasy will characterize the kingdom of Antichrist that goes to war against the church.

This kingdom of Antichrist slaughters the Christians at the end of this age, and their dead bodies lie in the streets. Not only is there no sorrow for the multitude of slaughtered believers, but there is only contempt for them and rejoicing over their elimination.

Notice verses 9 and 10: *"And they of the people and kindreds and tongues and nations shall see their dead bodies three days and an half, and shall not suffer their dead bodies to be put in graves.* [10] *And they that dwell upon the earth shall rejoice over them, and make merry, and shall send gifts one to another; because these two prophets tormented them that dwelt on the earth."*

Notice verse 9 says, *"And they of the people and kindreds and tongues and nations."* Here is the transnational worldwide coalition of nations and people who are united in their persecution and slaughter of the church. When they see the defeat and destruction of the church, they only have contempt and hatred for the church, and this is shown by this symbolism of refusing to give the two witnesses a decent burial.

The world sees the defeated and destroyed church as having no worth or value; and therefore, there is no reason to mourn them or memorialize their loss. Because they see the church as having no worth or value, the corpse of the church is worthy only to be kicked into the gutter and left there to rot. This is the contempt they have for the church of God.

Furthermore, this wicked world over which Antichrist rules not only views the church with utter contempt, but it is thrilled to the point of total delight that the Christians' public witness and message has been silenced. The people of this wicked world celebrate the demise of the church and rejoice that their consciences will no longer be tormented by the message that they need to repent and submit themselves to Christ and the gospel. We see them partying and sending gifts to each other and rejoicing that the church is finally silenced. They do this because the message of the gospel is a torment to their conscience, and that is why they hate those who preach it, and why they are glad when they are freed from their presence.

Notice it says in verse 10, *"And they that dwell upon the earth shall rejoice over them, and make merry, and shall send gifts one to another because these two prophets tormented them that dwelt on the earth."* If we are not tormenting the consciences of the lost when we preach the gospel, then we are not preaching the gospel. The Christian church in America today is largely not persecuted because it is telling people they can live any way they want and still go to heaven. Ahab said to Elijah in 1 Kings 18:17: *"Art thou he that troubleth Israel?"* Ahab recognized that Elijah's message was one that disturbed the self-satisfied, self-righteous, self-determination of the apostate people of the nation of Israel, and he said, "You are stirring up trouble in Israel by preaching the truth."

When you preach the truth and say that homosexuality and abortion and fornication are abominations to God, people get furious with you because you are troubling their consciences about the evil they are doing or defending. This is why the Jews hated Jesus. He tormented their consciences with His teaching and example. Jesus said in John 7:7, *"The world cannot hate you; but me it hateth, because I testify of it, that the works thereof are evil."* You, too, will be hated when you tell the lost that their works are evil and they need to repent of them.

The world will rejoice when those they hate are destroyed by the Antichrist. This triumph of Antichrist and his kingdom will last for three and a half days according to verse 9: *"And they of the people and kindreds and tongues and nations shall see their dead bodies three days and an half."* It also says in verse 11, *"And after three days and an half."*

This three and a half days stands in contrast to the three and a half years that the gospel witness continues on earth between the first and second coming of Christ mentioned in Revelation 11:3: *"And I will give power unto my two witnesses, and they shall prophesy a thousand two hundred and threescore days."* The witness of the church will go on for the length of this symbolic number of one thousand two hundred and sixty days, which is three and a half years.

The gospel age is symbolically represented by one thousand two hundred and sixty days, and the reign of Antichrist is symbolically represented by three and a half days. Three and a half days is less than one third of one percent of one thousand two hundred and sixty days. The gospel age has so far lasted two thousand years. One-third of one percent of two thousand years is six years. If you assume the gospel age lasts two thousand years, and all the elect are now saved, then the reign of Antichrist will last six years if the proportion indicated by these numbers is maintained. The point is that the reign of Antichrist is a very short period of time in proportion to the length of the gospel age.

The reign and rule of Antichrist at the end of this age and the defeat and destruction of the Christian church will be an extremely short period of time compared to the time the church age has lasted, during which the gospel message has been powerfully proclaimed over the whole world. The triumphing of the wicked is short, and the joy of the hypocrite is just for a moment. Think of Jesus' ministry: there were three years of preaching the gospel, and three days in the grave. The time of His ministry and triumph was large; the time of His apparent defeat was very short. So it will be at the end of this age.

Matthew 24:22 says, *"And except those days should be shortened, there should no flesh be saved"*—that is, saved physically alive. No believers would be left alive if these three and a half days were extended to a longer period. *"But for the elect's sake those days shall be shortened,"* because Christ will not allow the total defeat of His church and the complete eradication of believers from the earth. He will allow His enemies to have a significant victory, but not a total one. There will be a remnant left alive.

The Resurrection of the Witnesses

The resurrection of the witnesses is in verses 11 to 14. Verse 11 says, *"And after three days and an half the Spirit of life from God entered into them, and they stood upon their feet; and great fear fell upon them which saw them.* [12] *And they heard a great voice from heaven saying unto them, Come up hither. And they ascended up to heaven in a cloud; and their enemies beheld them.* [13] *And the same hour was there a great earthquake, and the tenth part of the city fell, and in the earthquake were slain of men seven thousand: and the remnant were affrighted, and gave glory to the God of heaven.* [14] *The second woe is past; and, behold, the third woe cometh quickly."*

The triumph of the Antichrist and his kingdom over the visible church and its message will not only be short, but it will also come to a very shocking end. That shocking end is described in verses 11 and 12. These verses describe the resurrection and the rapture of the saints that will occur when Christ returns. The language that is used in verses 11 and 12, when it says that *"the Spirit of life from God entered into them, and they stood upon their feet,"* is taken directly out of Ezekiel 37:1–10 where we have the vision of the valley of dry bones. Ezekiel sees a valley full of dry bones, and God says to Ezekiel, "Can these bones live?" Ezekiel says, in essence, "Lord, You know whether they can or not." God then commands Ezekiel to speak to them, and in verses 4–10 Ezekiel speaks to these dry bones and they are resurrected back to wholeness, the Spirit of life from God enters into them, and they stand up on their feet alive. This is a picture of the resurrection at the end of the age, and John imports this same language into our passage.

What is being said in verses 11–12 regarding this resurrection and being caught up into the heavens is expanded and explained in 1 Thessalonians 4:13–17. *"But I would not have you to be ignorant, brethren, concerning them which are asleep, that ye sorrow not, even as others which have no hope.* [14] *For if we believe that Jesus died and rose again, even so them also which sleep in Jesus"* (those who have already died), *"will God bring with him."* Their bodies are in the grave, but they are in heaven, and they are coming back with Jesus. "[15] *For this we say unto you by the word of the Lord, that we which are alive and remain unto the coming of the Lord. . ."* How many people will that be? A very, very small number. I have heard a lot of people say that they hope they are alive when Jesus returns. If you are alive when Jesus returns, that means you have gone through the world's most horrible persecution and tribulation ever, and you are one of the tiny remnant that is left alive after Antichrist is done destroying the church. How many of the believers are going to be left alive when Jesus returns? If He let the persecution go on any longer, there would be none; but He cuts it short, so there will be a few. How few? Will it be a thousand, ten thousand, or a hundred thousand? We do not know, but a far smaller number than what comprised the church before the persecution.

Verse 15: *"For this we say unto you by the word of the Lord, that we which are alive and remain unto the coming of the Lord shall not prevent [precede, or go ahead or in front of] them which are asleep.* [16] *For the Lord himself shall descend from heaven with a shout, with the voice of the archangel, and with the trump of God:"* (here is the description of the same event contained in Revelation 11:11–12) *"and the dead in Christ shall rise first,* [17] *Then we which are alive and remain shall be caught up together with them in the clouds, to meet the Lord in the air: and so shall we ever be with the Lord."*

In Revelation 11:11–12, the resurrection and the rapture are set forth in that order. All these dead bodies come back to life and then there is a voice from heaven that says, *"Come up hither,"* and they all go up. That is exactly the order being described in 1 Thessalonians 4:16–17.

Notice 1 Thessalonians 5:1, *"But of the times and the seasons, brethren, ye have no need that I write unto you."* The question is: When is all this going to occur? He says, "You do not need for me to write to you as to when it will occur. You already know the answer." Here is the answer: "[2] *For yourselves know perfectly"* (you know perfectly well the answer) *"that the day of the Lord so cometh as a thief in the night."* Here is the answer, verse 3: *"For when they shall say, Peace and safety; then sudden destruction cometh upon them, as travail upon a woman with child; and they shall not escape."* First Thessalonians 5:3 is Revelation 11:9–13. In Revelation 11:9–10, all the dead bodies are in the street, and the wicked are saying, "Finally, we have gotten rid of the Christians! Now we will have peace and safety!" They think that now that the Christians are all gone, the world will now be a place of peace and safety and tranquility and happiness. They are saying, "We have finally reached our humanistic paradise! We have finally wiped the Christian religion off the face of the earth!" But what happens when they finally achieve what they think they want? Sudden destruction comes, and they will not escape.

When is Jesus going to return? Not until Antichrist arises, not until the great apostasy occurs, not until the church is virtually wiped off the face of the earth, not until the world is saying, "We finally achieved the eradication of the Christians!" Then Jesus will return. Is the second coming of Christ imminent? It is not. It cannot and will not occur until all these things occur first.

In Revelation 11, we saw that the church has been decimated, and the people are now rejoicing and relaxing. They are now saying, "Peace and safety! Everything is just the way it is supposed to be!" At that moment the resurrection occurs, the rapture occurs, and Jesus comes in flaming fire taking vengeance on them that do not know God and on them that do not obey the gospel of our Lord Jesus Christ, and they will all be destroyed with everlasting destruction from the presence of the Lord.

The wicked world will behold the resurrection of the saints, they will behold the transformation of those few saints that are still alive, and they will see them caught up to meet Christ in the air. Notice verse 12: *"And they heard a great voice from heaven saying unto them, Come up hither. And they ascended up to heaven in a cloud; and their enemies beheld them."* This is not going to be some secret rapture, in which people are just walking down the street, and suddenly they just disappear and nobody sees anything. The whole idea of a secret rapture is not even remotely biblical. It says in verse 12 that they will see it: *"and their enemies beheld them."* The church will be restored to life, the church will be restored to honor, the church will be restored to power, the church will then be caught up to be with Christ in the air, and the world will see it happen.

Notice verse 13: *"And the same hour was there a great earthquake, and the tenth part of the city fell, and in the earthquake were slain of men seven thousand: and the remnant were affrighted, and gave glory to the God of heaven."* In verse 13, the destruction of the world begins and the slaughter of the wicked by Christ starts. We read about this in Revelation 20:9 when they surround the camp of the saints, and God comes back and totally destroys them. Verse 13 is describing that destruction.

The Lamb opens the seals in chapter 6; and we have the four horsemen of the apocalypse which describe the activity of the unsaved during this age: the white horse, the red horse, the black horse, and the pale horse. The fifth seal reveals the persecution of believers and the martyrdom of believers.

Then comes the sixth seal—notice Revelation 6:12–17: *"And I beheld when he had opened the sixth seal, and, lo, there was a great earthquake;"* (just as in Revelation 11:13) *"and the sun became black as sackcloth of hair, and the moon became as blood;* [13] *And the stars of heaven fell unto the earth, even as a fig tree casteth her untimely figs, when she is shaken of a mighty wind.* [14] *And the heaven departed as a scroll when it is rolled together; and every mountain and island were moved out of their places.* [15] *And the kings of the earth, and the great men, and the rich men, and the chief captains, and the mighty men, and every bondman, and every free man, hid themselves in the dens and in the rocks of the mountains;* [16] *And said to the mountains and rocks, Fall on us, and hide us from the face of him that sitteth on the throne, and from the wrath of the Lamb:* [17] *For the great day of his wrath is come; and who shall be able to stand?"* This is an extended description of Revelation 11:13.

Notice what it says in 11:13: *"And the same hour was there a great earthquake, and the tenth part of the city fell."* This is the same city we read about in verse 8. *"And their dead bodies shall lie in the street of the great city, which spiritually is called Sodom and Egypt, where also our Lord was crucified."*

The city is the kingdom of Antichrist. It is the world over which Antichrist rules. Verse 13 is saying that one tenth of his kingdom is immediately destroyed. It says, *"And the same hour was there a great earthquake, and the tenth part of the city"* (the kingdom of Antichrist) *"fell."* Ten is the number of perfection. So one tenth is therefore a partial as opposed to a perfect destruction due to this worldwide earthquake. When Christ returns, part of the world in terms of its physical infrastructure is destroyed by this great earthquake. It also says there were seven thousand men killed in the same earthquake.

Seven is the number of completion and ten is the number of perfection. When you multiply completion by perfection, you have totality. You have ten times ten times ten which is a thousand, and then you have seven times a thousand which is seven thousand. Whenever we multiply primary numbers together, it results in an intensification of the symbolic meaning of that number, just as when we divide them it results in a diminishing of the idea conveyed by that number.

When it says there were seven thousand killed, it is saying that the people in the kingdom of Antichrist were virtually all completely killed. They were not totally killed, but what we have is a proportionate response by Christ. What did Antichrist and his kingdom do to the Christians? They killed all of them except for a very small remnant. So what does Jesus do to the kingdom of Antichrist when He returns? He kills all of them except for a very small remnant. That remnant is spoken of in verse 13. It says there *"were slain of men seven thousand: and the remnant were affrighted"* (note that there is just a remnant) *"and gave glory to the God of heaven."* Just like there is a remnant of Christians left alive as a result of the work of Antichrist, there is just a remnant of the wicked left alive as a result of the coming of Christ. They are the ones crying out in 6:15–17.

This small remnant of the wicked recognizes that God was God after all and Antichrist was not God. They recognize God as God, and they are terrified. This is like the terror felt by the guards who were watching over the tomb of Jesus. Here is the scene: He is in the grave, and they think He is dead. It is as if they are saying, "We now have peace and safety, and we can relax." Then suddenly, Jesus comes out of the tomb, and what happens to the guards? They are prostrate with terror. After the destruction of the visible Christian church on earth, the world is thinking, "We now have peace and safety. The Christians are all gone. We finally eliminated Christianity and the Christian God. We can relax." But then the Christian God shows up, and all the dead Christians rise up; and just like the guards at the tomb, they are terrified.

When it says they are giving glory to God, it means they are acknowledging that God exists and that they are in trouble. It is the same acknowledgment that is expressed in the last verse of Revelation 6 which says, "[17] *for the great day of his wrath is come; and who shall be able to stand?*" They are giving glory to God by acknowledging that He exists and that His judgment is coming. They are recognizing who He is and what is about to happen to them, and they are filled with terror. These people are not saved; they are simply acknowledging what they had previously denied, which is the existence of God and His coming judgment and wrath. Revelation 19:21 tells us that they are all then slain by Christ. None is left alive.

Notice verse 14. It says, "*The second woe is past;*" (we just read about it) "*and, behold, the third woe cometh quickly.* [15] *And the seventh angel sounded. . . .*" There is the short-term reign of Antichrist, the resurrection of the believers, and then the seventh trumpet immediately sounds. There is no delay or lapse of time between the resurrection and the sounding of the seventh trumpet. It "*cometh quickly.*"

We will look at the seventh trumpet in a subsequent chapter. But we need to understand two things from this passage. First of all, Christ will triumph over the wicked. Every knee is going to bow, and every tongue is going to confess that Jesus Christ is Lord, to the glory of God the Father. We see this happening in verse 13. We Christians voluntarily bowed our knee and confessed to salvation. But the wicked are going to bow their knee and confess in abject terror their recognition of their immediate condemnation and damnation in hell.

The second thing this passage tells us is that we also have hope in the midst of martyrdom. Although we see the church being slaughtered wholesale and virtually eliminated from the face of the earth, we see Jesus fixing that problem upon His return. The believers are killed by Antichrist, but they are not defeated by him. Because the resurrection is coming, death is a solvable problem. This is why God allows His people to be martyred; He can fix that problem!

It is like when a child spills milk on the floor it is not a big deal. Mom can fix it. She just gets a rag and wipes it up, and it is like it never happened. It is not a problem. For God, for us to be killed is no big deal, because He can fix that. He resurrects us right out of the grave, and we go on living for all eternity. It will be as though nothing happened.

When we see our brethren being martyred today, and if we live into this final time period and we are martyred or else all of our loved ones are, it is not a problem. They will be raised from the dead, and we will be with them forever.

In the next two chapters, we are going to look at Daniel 2 and Daniel 7. We are going to see that they run parallel to this passage in Revelation 11:1–14. We will find that what Daniel says is an expansion and clarification of Revelation 11. Therefore, we want to tie these two books together, especially those two chapters.

We are going to see that Revelation 11:7 is explicitly spoken of in Daniel 7:21. We are going to see that this three-and-a-half-day period is explicitly spoken of in Daniel 7:25. We are going to see the little horn (Antichrist) that rises up and subdues the three kings, and how all the kings come under the authority of Antichrist. Three is the number of perfection and completion. Therefore, he is going to perfectly and completely dominate the whole world. It is amazing how Daniel so clearly declared exactly what Revelation 11 sets forth. When we finish Daniel 2 and 7, we will come back and deal with the seventh trumpet.

35

The Image and the Future, Daniel 2:14–45

The time has come in our exposition of Revelation to go to the book of Daniel, and see how it illuminates and expands the teaching of the book of Revelation. In this chapter, we will expound Daniel 2:14–45 in relationship to Revelation 11:7–13.

Daniel lived while Israel was in captivity in Babylon from about 608 BC until 538 BC. During those seventy years, Daniel received a number of important revelations from God. We will look at two of them in particular.

The first is in Daniel 2 and the second in Daniel 7. These two chapters are parallel with each other. They are teaching on the same subject, but they use different imagery to illuminate that subject and they each provide details the other does not.

Daniel 2 and Daniel 7 are like the four Gospels, which have parallel narratives of the life of the Lord Jesus, but each one provides additional details and supplemental instruction regarding His life the other does not. In the same way, Daniel 2 and Daniel 7 are teaching about the same subject, but from different perspectives and with additional details supplied in each of them.

Both of these chapters in Daniel set forth a road map for all subsequent human history from Daniel's time until the second coming of Jesus Christ. This has particular relevance to us at this point in our study in the book of Revelation because of the dramatic parallels between Daniel 2 and 7 and Revelation 11:7–13.

Daniel is the book that contains much of the Old Testament material that is referenced in the book of Revelation both by way of symbolic imagery and through the teaching it provides. As you read about beasts and horns and other symbolic images in Revelation, you wonder where those symbols come from. They come from the book of Daniel. Therefore, any study of the book of Revelation must take into account the teaching of the book of Daniel.

In this chapter, we will examine the dream of King Nebuchadnezzar in Daniel 2. Nebuchadnezzar had a very troubling dream, but when he awoke he could not remember its content. He called all the wise men of Babylon to tell him what the dream was, and what the dream meant. The wise men were unable to do so, but God enabled Daniel to reveal to the king both the dream and its interpretation.

The Revelation of the Dream to Daniel

The revelation of the dream to Daniel is in Daniel 2:19–30: "*Then was the secret revealed unto Daniel in a night vision. Then Daniel blessed the God of heaven.*" In verse 19, God has revealed Nebuchadnezzar's dream to Daniel. Daniel responds with a profound expression of gratitude and praise to God.

Verse 20: "*Daniel answered and said, Blessed be the name of God for ever and ever: for wisdom and might are his.*" This dream and its message are a glorious display of God's transcendent wisdom and power. Wisdom is God's; He has the understanding to control all events in the world to achieve His purposes. Might is God's; He has the power to control all the events in the world to achieve His purposes.

Verse 21–22: "*And he,*" (God) "*changeth the times and the seasons: he removeth kings, and setteth up kings: he giveth wisdom unto the wise, and knowledge to them that know understanding: [22] He revealeth the deep and secret things: he knoweth what is in the darkness, and the light dwelleth with him.*"

God controls the "*times and the seasons*"—that is, the timing of events as to when they begin, how long they last, and when they conclude. He controls the rise and the fall of every empire, nation, and civil government by removing kings and establishing kings. He gives "*wisdom... and knowledge,*" He reveals "*the deep and secret things*"; in other words, He controls what men discover and know and understand. Nothing can be known apart from Him, and all that we know comes from Him.

God is in control of history. God knows how history is going to unfold because He is the one who predestinated it. God is revealing to Daniel the previously unknown future of human history. He is telling Daniel what the future will consist of until the end of time.

Notice verse 23: "*I thank thee, and praise thee, O thou God of my fathers, who hast given me wisdom and might, and hast made known unto me now what we desired of thee: for thou hast now made known unto us the king's matter.*" As Daniel reflects on this revelation of what God is like, he breaks forth into praise and worship and thanksgiving. Daniel now knows the king's dream; and more importantly, Daniel now knows how human history is going to unfold until the end of time; and for this, Daniel gives profound worship and praise and thanks to God.

Notice verses 24 to 30: "*Therefore Daniel went in unto Arioch, whom the king had ordained to destroy the wise men of Babylon: he went and said thus unto him; Destroy not the wise men of Babylon: bring me in before the king, and I will shew unto the king the interpretation.*
25 Then Arioch brought in Daniel before the king in haste, and said thus unto him, I have found a man of the captives of Judah, that will make known unto the king the interpretation.
26 The king answered and said to Daniel, whose name was Belteshazzar, Art thou able to make known unto me the dream which I have seen, and the interpretation thereof?
27 Daniel answered in the presence of the king, and said, The secret which the king hath demanded cannot the wise men, the astrologers, the magicians, the soothsayers, shew unto the king;
28 But there is a God in heaven that revealeth secrets, and maketh known to the king Nebuchadnezzar what shall be in the latter days. Thy dream, and the visions of thy head upon thy bed, are these;
29 As for thee, O king, thy thoughts came into thy mind upon thy bed, what should come to pass hereafter: and he that revealeth secrets maketh known to thee what shall come to pass."

This dream describes what is going to come to pass hereafter in the latter days. Verse 30: "*But as for me, this secret is not revealed to me for any wisdom that I have more than any living, but for their sakes that shall make known the interpretation to the king, and that thou mightest know the thoughts of thy heart.*"

In verses 24 to 30, Daniel does two things. First of all, he gives glory to God and points the king to God as the one who should receive the praise and honor for revealing the king's dream. Daniel wants no credit for himself. God is the great revealer of truth regarding the future. We know nothing about the future unless God reveals it to us.

Second, Daniel emphasizes that the content of the dream is a revelation from God as to what is going to take place in the future.

God knows the future because He controls the future. God is making known what will happen in time to come as His plans and His purposes unfold because God controls all that occurs. Here is a prophecy and a prediction of what the history of the world is going to look like from this point forward. Nebuchadnezzar is going to get to see the future before it actually unfolds.

The Explanation of the Dream to Nebuchadnezzar

The explanation of the dream to Nebuchadnezzar is in verses 31 to 35. *"Thou, O king, sawest, and behold a great image. This great image, whose brightness was excellent, stood before thee; and the form thereof was terrible.* [32] *This image's head was of fine gold, his breast and his arms of silver, his belly and his thighs of brass,* [33] *His legs of iron, his feet part of iron and part of clay.* [34] *Thou sawest till that a stone was cut out without hands, which smote the image upon his feet that were of iron and clay, and brake them to pieces.* [35] *Then was the iron, the clay, the brass, the silver, and the gold, broken to pieces together, and became like the chaff of the summer threshing floors; and the wind carried them away, that no place was found for them: and the stone that smote the image became a great mountain, and filled the whole earth."*

Here is the revelation of the dream Nebuchadnezzar had. Nebuchadnezzar saw a gigantic statue that was immense in its size. It was extraordinary in its splendor and its impressiveness, and it was intimidating and terrifying in its appearance. It had four distinct sections: the head was of gold, the chest and arms were of silver, the belly and thighs were of bronze, and the legs were of iron with the feet partly iron and partly clay.

Then a mighty stone was observed breaking loose from the side of a mountain without any human agency, rolling down the mountain until it struck the feet of the statue, causing the entire statue to collapse, be destroyed, and vanish away. The stone then expanded and grew in size until it filled the entire earth.

The vision begins with a great statue, verse 31; and the vision ends with a great mountain taking its place, verse 35. The result is that the statue is no more—not even a particle of it remains. The wind comes and blows every speck of the crushed statue away like chaff is blown away from the threshing floor. All that remains is the mighty stone that fills the earth.

The Interpretation of the Dream

The interpretation of the dream is in verses 36 to 45. Notice verse 36. *"This is the dream; and we will tell the interpretation thereof before the king."* What we discover as we proceed through this interpretation is that this great statue represents the rise of these kingdoms, the order in which they appear, and their ultimate fall in the course of human history.

Notice verses 37 and 38. *"Thou, O king, art a king of kings: for the God of heaven hath given thee a kingdom, power, and strength, and glory.* [38] *And wheresoever the children of men dwell, the beasts of the field and the fowls of the heaven hath he given into thine hand, and hath made thee ruler over them all. Thou art this head of gold."* Daniel says that the head of gold on this statue represents the kingdom of Babylon, along with her king.

Verse 39: *"And after thee shall arise another kingdom inferior to thee."* This is the chest and arms of silver, which represent a second kingdom that will arise after Babylon falls. We know from Ezra and Nehemiah and Esther that this second kingdom that defeated the Babylonian Empire was the Medo-Persian Empire. It lasted a much shorter period of time than the Babylonian Empire lasted, and, in that sense, it was inferior to the Babylonian Empire.

Notice verse 39b: *"and another third kingdom of brass, which shall bear rule over all the earth."* The belly and the thighs of brass or bronze represent the third world kingdom of Greece. This was the Greek Empire of Alexander the Great. He ruled the entire known world until his death when his kingdom was then divided between his four generals. This is all spoken of by name and predicted in Daniel 8:21–22, where it specifically says that the Grecian Empire was going to conquer the Medo-Persian Empire. Then the Grecian Empire was going to be broken into four heads, and this is what happened after Alexander the Great died. He had four generals, and his empire was divided up into four pieces, and there was tremendous warfare between the kingdom that was centered in Syria and the kingdom that was centered in Egypt. There was warfare back and forth between them which is predicted in detail in Daniel 11 and which is chronicled in the extrabiblical book of 1 Maccabees during the intertestamental period when the Seleucids and the Ptolemy's fought back and forth.

This was all predicted in the Bible. We are not using secular history and reading it into the Bible. The Bible itself talks about the Persian Empire that took the place of the Babylonian Empire, and the Bible itself talks about the Grecian Empire that took the place of the Persian Empire, and that the Grecian Empire was broken up into four parts. Secular history simply confirms what is contained and predicted in the Bible itself.

That brings us to verses 40 to 43: *"And the fourth kingdom shall be strong as iron: forasmuch as iron breaketh in pieces and subdueth all things: and as iron that breaketh all these, shall it break in pieces and bruise.* [41] *And whereas thou sawest the feet and toes, part of potters' clay, and part of iron, the kingdom shall be divided; but there shall be in it of the strength of the iron, forasmuch as thou sawest the iron mixed with miry clay.* [42] *And as the toes of the feet were part of iron, and part of clay, so the kingdom shall be partly strong, and partly broken.* [43] *And whereas thou sawest iron mixed with miry clay, they shall mingle themselves with the seed of men: but they shall not cleave one to another, even as iron is not mixed with clay."*

This fourth kingdom represents the Roman Empire, and receives quite extensive treatment, because it covers the greatest span of time, and takes us clear to the end of the world. This kingdom symbolized by the legs of iron with feet of part iron and part clay began to conquer and consume the four parts of the old Greek Empire. The Roman Empire had the strength of iron, and we are told of its destructive power in verse 40: *"And the fourth kingdom shall be strong as iron: forasmuch as iron breaketh in pieces and subdueth all things: and as iron that breaketh all these, shall it break in pieces and bruise."* Iron is stronger than gold, stronger than silver, and stronger than brass.

This fourth kingdom is going to be a kingdom that crushes and destroys all things under its iron heel. The Roman legions were well-known for their ability to crush all of their enemies under their iron heel and with their iron weapons. But as time went on, the kingdom began to fragment and lose its cohesion. Notice verse 41 and 42: *"And whereas thou sawest the feet and toes, part of potters' clay, and part of iron, the kingdom shall be divided; but there shall be in it of the strength of the iron, forasmuch as thou sawest the iron mixed with miry clay.* [42] *And as the toes of the feet were part of iron, and part of clay, so the kingdom shall be partly strong, and partly broken."*

As our gaze proceeds down the statue, we are also proceeding down the column of time. As we are proceeding in time through history, we have come to the legs of iron which represent the Roman Empire. But as we proceed further forward in time, we see this kingdom begin to fragment and lose its cohesion. This is represented by the feet made up partly of iron and partly of clay.

Iron and clay do not fuse together. There is no strength or binding chemistry between them. Something of the firmness of iron remains, but something of the brittleness of clay is present, so it is an easily broken conglomeration. There is no blending of the iron and the clay. This division and lack of unity is especially seen in the ten separate toes of the statue, which are made of clay and iron. The number ten is not specifically mentioned here; it will be mentioned in Daniel 7 which we will look at in the next chapter. Nevertheless, this is clearly a statue of a man, and a man has ten toes, and the toes are separate from each other. This division and lack of unity is especially seen in the ten separate toes that are also made of clay and iron.

The point is this: As time goes on, the Roman Empire loses cohesion. It becomes brittle and divided, and separate nations like separate toes are formed, and there is only the loosest of loyalties and connections between them as the centuries unfold. The kingdom is partly strong and partly broken, as time and history unfold and as the centuries go by. There are some alliances and treaties between nations to bring them together, thereby making them partly strong. But there are also some divisions and enmities between nations to divide them apart, thereby making them partly broken, as described in verse 42.

Though there are intermarriages between rulers and peoples of various nations, even this will not produce another unified world kingdom of the kind that Babylon was, Medo-Persia was, Greece was, and Rome was in the days of its glory. Notice verse 43: *"And whereas thou sawest iron mixed with miry clay, they shall mingle themselves with the seed of men."* The idea is that intermarriages between kings to create alliances, or intermarriages among various ethnic groups to try to make a melting pot, still will not fuse them together into a unified worldwide kingdom. Even though they will try to mingle themselves into a one-world power in this fashion, it says in verse 43 that they *"shall not cleave one to another, even as iron is not mixed with clay."* To this very day, there has never again been a one-world power.

This fourth and final kingdom will start out being very powerful and strong, as represented by the legs of iron, but it will evolve into a multitude of nations with shifting alliances who lack cohesion among themselves. The ten toes represent and symbolize the perfect total of all the nations that will descend out of the old Roman world empire, because ten is the number that symbolizes totality and perfection. The ten toes of the image are symbolic of the totality of all of the nations that will follow after the Roman Empire until the end of time. We are going to see the ten horns in Daniel 7 just as we have seen the ten toes here. These are parallel ideas.

This brings us to verses 44 and 45, which describe the meaning of the stone that breaks this great image into pieces and grows to fill the whole earth. Notice verse 44: *"And in the days of these kings shall the God of heaven set up a kingdom, which shall never be destroyed: and the kingdom shall not be left to other people, but it shall break in pieces and consume all these kingdoms, and it shall stand for ever.*
45 *Forasmuch as thou sawest that the stone was cut out of the mountain without hands, and that it brake in pieces the iron, the brass, the clay, the silver, and the gold; the great God hath made known to the king what shall come to pass hereafter: and the dream is certain, and the interpretation thereof sure."*

We are told in verse 44 this great stone represents the kingdom of God: *"And in the days of these kings shall the God of heaven set up a kingdom."* This stone that appears is the kingdom of God. This kingdom of God was established by Jesus Christ at His first coming, during the time of the legs of iron at the time of the Roman Empire. This stone, this kingdom of God, is made without hands—that is, it came into existence not by the agency of men, but by the agency of the invisible God. All human kingdoms are made by the hand of men. The Babylonian Kingdom, the Medo-Persian Kingdom, the Greek Kingdom, the Roman Kingdom, and indeed, all earthly kingdoms that follow thereafter were all made by men. But the kingdom of God is made by God Himself. Human agency is not its source, and human agency is not its cause.

Invisible forces are at work in the creation of Christ's kingdom. The kingdom grows and triumphs over all the kingdoms of the world, and every kingdom that ever rose against it has fallen before it—and yet no one can see how or why that triumph is achieved. In the days of these kings that arose in this fourth empire, Christ came and began His kingdom on earth, a kingdom unlike all earthly kingdoms that have been destroyed and that will be destroyed. Christ's kingdom is not of this world.

Verse 44 tells us that Christ's kingdom can never be destroyed; instead, the kingdom of God will grow until it destroys all other kingdoms and fills the whole earth. This has been going on for the last 2,000 years and will continue to go on until the seventh trumpet sounds, the end comes, and the kingdoms of this world become the kingdoms of our Lord and of His Christ, and he shall reign forever and ever over the new heavens and the new earth.

Unlike earthly kingdoms that pass from one group of people to another, the kingdom of God will never be taken over by someone else or by other people. It will never change hands. It will never be transferred to others. Verse 44 says, "*which shall never be destroyed: and the kingdom shall not be left to other people.*" The Babylonians left their kingdom to other people; the Persians left their kingdom to other people; and the Greeks left their kingdom to other people. Christ's kingdom will never be left to others. Instead, it will break in pieces all other kingdoms, it will completely consume them, it will stand forever; and in the end, it will be the only kingdom there is, and there will not be a trace of any earthly kingdom left. Other kingdoms will be like chaff driven by the wind that just disappears into nothingness.

In the eternal state, there will be no presence of the Babylonian Kingdom, or the Persian Kingdom, or any other kingdom. They will be utterly destroyed by the kingdom of God. What we saw in history was a succession of kingdoms, one kingdom being conquered by another which was conquered by another. But that cycle and process is going to come to an end. A new power comes into the world in the person of Christ the King, and He will end this cycle of endless replacement of one kingdom after another. He will establish the final kingdom and the everlasting kingdom, after which there will be no other kingdom, because it will remain forever.

This is what will occur in the unfolding of human history, and this is what God wanted Nebuchadnezzar to know, and this is what God wants us to know as well. On this victorious note, the interpretation of the dream ends. Daniel asserts in verse 45 that it is an accurate interpretation, and it will certainly come to pass, just as Daniel stated it. He says, "*God hath made known to the king what shall come to pass hereafter, and the dream is certain, and the interpretation thereof sure.*"

To this very day, men have been trying to establish a world empire, and they have failed. Hitler was going to have his Third Reich, the emperor of Japan was going to take over the whole world, and the Muslims thought they would have in their Ottoman Empire a worldwide caliphate. To this day, men have been trying to establish a world empire, and they have failed because it is just iron and clay. They can never put it all together. It always winds up falling apart.

Christ's kingdom outlasts them all, outgrows them all, and crushes them all. It does so with a stone that grows into a mighty mountain, which smashes and overwhelms and crushes them into utter oblivion. Even Antichrist's short-term, one-world kingdom that appears to defeat the kingdom of God on earth right at the end of time will be destroyed by the Rock of our salvation when He returns in all of His glory.

Here is the story that is played out in Revelation 11:1–14 that we have been looking at. In Revelation 11, Christ's kingdom—the temple and the Holy City of verses 1 and 2—appears to be trampled underfoot by the Gentile kingdoms of this world. But they cannot stop the witness of the church, represented by the two witnesses. The kingdoms of this world are defeated by the church as they strive to destroy the church; and in fact, the church grows, and, as it grows, the Gentile kingdoms fall before it. The kingdom of Jesus Christ never falls apart because it has as its cohesive principle the person of Jesus who holds it together into one temple and one city. The kingdom of Christ is not partly weak and partly strong, because we are all joined together by one Spirit into one kingdom. The kingdom of God is as strong as a rock.

Right at the very end, Antichrist (the beast that rises out of the abyss), seems to somehow have bound all the iron and the clay together for a moment in time to form a one-world government of all the nations to defeat the kingdom of God; and it seems like he has succeeded. But he has succeeded for only a symbolic three and a half days. His apparent success is a very short-term illusion. Christ returns to resurrect and rapture His church and to destroy the kingdom of Antichrist and the kingdoms of the world forever. The seventh trumpet sounds, and the kingdoms of this world become the kingdoms of our Lord and of His Christ, and He shall reign forever and ever.

Daniel 2 is parallel with Revelation 11. We will see even more striking parallels when we expound Daniel 7 in the next chapter.

36

The Beasts and the Future, Daniel 7:1–28

In Revelation 11:1–13 we have seen the church symbolized as a temple, a holy city, and as two witnesses.

We have seen that the church is invincible in its gospel witness to the world, and every kingdom that arises against it falls before it until the testimony of the church to the world is completed. But when the last elect person has been saved out of the kingdom of Satan and brought into the kingdom of Christ, then the Antichrist arises, puts together a coalition of all the nations of the earth, and makes war against the church.

The result is that the visible presence of the church disappears, the voice of the church is silenced, and the vast majority of the church is killed during the reign of Antichrist. The coalition of nations under the leadership of Antichrist rejoices. They are thrilled to finally rid the planet of all visible manifestations of Christianity. The victory over the church is complete except for a small, scattered, and hidden remnant of believers who are left.

But this victory of Antichrist and his coalition of nations only lasts for a small period of time, symbolically spoken of in Revelation 11 as three and a half days. Christ returns before the church is totally exterminated and eradicated from the earth. Christ resurrects all the dead believers; He transforms the few remaining living believers, and He raptures them all up together to meet Him in the air. He then returns with them to the earth in judgment. He judges the Antichrist and his followers and casts them into the lake of fire, as described in Revelation 20:7–10.

This section in Revelation 11:7–13 that speaks of the rise of Antichrist, the near extermination of the church on earth, and the return of Jesus Christ in judgment is also spoken of in Daniel 7.

In the last chapter, we looked at Daniel 2 and we saw the vision of a giant human figure which symbolically represented the entire sweep of human history from Daniel's day until the end of time. In Daniel 7, we see this same sweep of history from Daniel's day until the end of time, except this time this sweep of history is symbolized not by a human figure, but by a succession of four terrible beasts.

These four terrible beasts speak to us of the cruel and wicked nature of the kingdoms of this world. Governments are not kind. Nations are like predatory animals as they go forth conquering and to conquer, and thereby inflict war and famine and death upon the world as represented by the four horsemen in Revelation 6.

Both Daniel 2 and 7 present the remainder of all of human history, and they do so with a repetitive use of the number four. They use the number four because it signifies the world. Four empires are represented by the four-part human figure of chapter 2, and the same four empires are represented by four beasts in chapter 7.

These four empires represent the sum total of the powers that the world produces in the course of its history from Daniel's day until the second coming. Daniel 2 was more general and less detailed in introducing us to the remainder of all of human history. Daniel 7 is far more specific and gives a more detailed view of all of human history and how it is going to unfold, especially at its end.

The Gospel of Mark is very brief, compact, and limited in the amount of information it reveals, though it does give a complete picture of the life and ministry of Jesus. The Gospel of Luke is much larger and more detailed and provides much more information about the life and ministry of Jesus Christ. In the same way, Daniel 2 is more general and less specific, whereas Daniel 7 is more detailed and much more specific regarding its description of subsequent human history.

Let us examine this parallel but much more detailed description of what we saw in the last chapter in Daniel 2.

Daniel's Vision Revealed

Daniel's vision is revealed in verses 1 through 14. Notice verse 1 says, *"In the first year of Belshazzar king of Babylon Daniel had a dream and visions of his head upon his bed: then he wrote the dream, and told the sum of the matters."* We are told the time of Daniel's vision, that it occurred just before Babylon fell to the Medo-Persians during the reign of Belshazzar.

Notice verses 2 and 3: *"Daniel spake and said, I saw in my vision by night, and, behold, the four winds of the heaven strove upon the great sea.* [3] *And four great beasts came up from the sea, diverse one from another."* Here we have a description of powerful winds whipping up the sea into a maelstrom. There are four winds from the four quarters of the earth—north, south, east, and west—all colliding and churning up the sea like it would in a great storm. This restless sea represents the churning mass of unsaved humanity as described in Isaiah 57:20, *"But the wicked are like the troubled sea, when it cannot rest, whose waters cast up mire and dirt."* Sin always produces tremendous turmoil, whether it is in the life of an individual, a society, or a nation. Daniel shows us this tumultuous churning turmoil of the mass of unsaved humanity in the world.

Now out of this troubled sea—that is, out of this churning mass of unsaved humanity—four great beasts arise in order, one after the other, and each one different from the other. These four beasts are four successive world empires that follow after each other, each of which has distinctive traits and characteristics.

Daniel 7:17 says, *"These great beasts, which are four, are four kings, which shall arise out of the earth."* It says in verse 3 that they arose out of the sea; in verse 17, it says they arose out of the earth. This is not a contradiction. The idea is they arose out of the world, and most of the world is covered by the sea. Astronauts out in space look down and they may say, "There is planet Earth." They are talking about the land and the sea together as being "earth." Therefore, there is no contradiction here. These four beasts are four kings and kingdoms that have arisen from beneath, from out of the earth, from out of the churning mass of humanity, which is symbolized by the sea.

These four beasts, these four world empires that arise in succession, are like rapacious beasts of great strength and cruelty. The reason God uses the metaphor of beasts to describe these kingdoms is that these kingdoms are beastlike in their character. In Daniel 7, the character of each of these kingdoms is indicated by the predatory symbol that is used to describe them.

Notice verse 4: *"The first [beast that arose out of the sea] was like a lion, and had eagle's wings: I beheld till the wings thereof were plucked, and it was lifted up from the earth, and made stand upon the feet as a man, and a man's heart was given to it."* This lion with the wings of an eagle on his back represents the Babylonian Empire, just as the head of gold represented the Babylonian Empire in Daniel 2. Both the lion and the eagle are recognized as being the dominant predators in their respective realms—either of the earth, in the case of the lion, or of the air, in the case of the eagle. In fact, sculptures of winged lions that guarded the gates of the royal palaces in Babylon have been discovered by archaeologists.

Babylon was swift and fierce in its conquest of other nations, and it devoured all competing kingdoms. But as Daniel kept on looking at this winged lion, its wings were torn out and it assumed an upright posture like a man. Furthermore, it received a new heart, a man's heart, to replace its animal heart.

This is a reference to the experience of Nebuchadnezzar, King of Babylon, recorded in Daniel 4:30–37. There he expressed pride and arrogance. God humbled him so he became like an animal eating the grass of the field, and then God restored him. God saved and regenerated him and gave him a new heart, and he started praising and worshiping and following the God of heaven. This is an allusion to that event.

Nebuchadnezzar was given a new nature. He became a worshiper of Daniel's God. When Nebuchadnezzar became saved, Babylon lost its cruel vicious predatory nature and became a kingdom of humanity and decency, rather than one of pillage and conquest. It is the nature of Christian kings and kingdoms that they do not function in the way pagan kings and pagan nations do.

Verse 5 says, *"And behold another beast [which arose out of the sea], a second, like to a bear, and it raised up itself on one side, and it had three ribs in the mouth of it between the teeth of it: and they said thus unto it, Arise, devour much flesh."* This bear with three ribs in its mouth represents the Medo-Persian Empire, just as the arms and the chest of silver were representative of the Medo-Persian Empire in Daniel 2.

The bear is a powerful and rapacious creature. He is more cumbersome than the lion, and he is pictured here as raised up on his side, so his head and shoulders are up off of the ground, while his hindquarters remain down on the ground. This seems to represent the two halves of the Medo-Persian Empire. The Medes as a people were more passive and inclined to inaction, while the Persians were more aggressive and inclined to conquest. It was the nature of this combined kingdom that the Persians carried the Medes along and led them to greatness.

This bear had three ribs in his mouth held between his teeth. Three is the number that represents perfection and completion and finality when it is used symbolically, as it is here. These three ribs represent the complete and final conquest that the Medo-Persian Empire will achieve as it arises and devours the remainder of the nations that oppose it.

Notice verse 6. It says, *"After this I beheld, and lo another [beast which arose out of the sea], like a leopard, which had upon the back of it four wings of a fowl; the beast had also four heads; and dominion was given to it."* This third beast is said to be like a leopard. This leopard has four wings on its back, and it has four heads. This leopard represents the Greek Empire, just as the belly and thighs of brass were representative of the Greek Empire in Daniel 2. The four wings and the four heads represent the division of the kingdom after the death of Alexander the Great among his four generals. When Alexander the Great died, his kingdom was divided up into four pieces, and his four generals each ruled a piece. Daniel 8:21–22 predicts this division.

The leopard is fierce, swift, and agile in its predatory behavior. Alexander the Great and his four generals swiftly advanced their conquest of the nations of the world. God gave Alexander the Great and his four generals the ability to achieve world dominion with the amazing rapidity of a running and flying leopard. In just ten years Alexander the Great conquered the entire known world.

In these first three beasts, the lion, the bear, and the leopard, we have the Babylonian Empire, the Medo-Persian Empire, and the Greek Empire represented.

Now we come to the fourth and most important empire, the empire that takes us from the end of the Greek Empire to the end of time, and that is the Roman Empire and the subsequent kingdoms that follow it.

Notice verses 7 and 8: *"After this I saw in the night visions, and behold a fourth beast [which arose out of the sea], dreadful and terrible, and strong exceedingly; and it had great iron teeth: it devoured and brake in pieces, and stamped the residue with the feet of it: and it was diverse from all the beasts that were before it; and it had ten horns."*

This fourth beast is not identified with any beast of the earth. It is not identified, but instead it is described because it is not like any known animal, and it outranks in fierceness all the animals of the earth put together. It is fiercer than a lion or a bear or a leopard. No other creature on earth is as fierce as this beast. He is not to be compared with any creature on earth.

This fourth beast is described as being dreadful and terrible and exceptionally strong, having great iron teeth. This fourth beast with the iron teeth represents the Roman Empire, just as the legs of iron represented the Roman Empire in Daniel 2. The violence of this fourth beast, this Roman Empire, is especially taken note of just as it was in Daniel 2:40. It says in the last half of verse 7 that it had great iron teeth and *"it devoured and brake in pieces, and stamped the residue with the feet of it."*

This was a devouring, breaking, crushing kingdom. Rome was exceedingly violent and cruel and crushed all nations under its iron heel. Rome could never get enough of conquest, and it ruthlessly broke and crushed and ground into the dirt all the nations and kingdoms it conquered and defeated. But as we shall see, this Roman kingdom takes us to the end of time, when the kings of this world are destroyed and the final judgment by God is carried out.

In Daniel 2, we saw that the Roman Empire, which was symbolized by the legs of iron, was further described as having feet and toes made of iron and clay. We saw this Roman Empire took us all the way to the end of time when the stone that was cut out without hands destroyed the image. In the same way, this iron beast also takes us to the end of time.

We saw that the feet and ten toes of iron mixed with clay followed chronologically after the iron legs of the Roman Empire. In Daniel 2, we saw that this fourth kingdom, the Roman Empire, started out as very strong and very powerful, but eventually, the empire broke up into a multitude of nations as time went on. Ten is a symbolic number that represents totality and perfection, and the ten toes of the image of Daniel 2 represented and symbolized the perfect total of all the nations that follow after the Roman Empire all the way to the end of time.

Having seen that the statue of Daniel 2 had ten toes that followed the Roman Empire, what do we find with this fourth beast in Daniel 7? We find that he has ten horns. In 7:7 it says, *"After this I saw in the night visions, and behold a fourth beast, dreadful and terrible, and strong exceedingly; and it had great iron teeth: it devoured and brake in pieces, and stamped the residue with the feet of it: and it was diverse from all the beasts that were before it; and it had ten horns."*

These ten horns correspond to the ten toes of the image in Daniel 2. In the Bible, horns are symbolic of strength and power and rule and authority. These horns represent nations that exercise power and rule and authority. These ten horns represent the perfect total of all the nations that follow after the Roman Empire to the end of time, just like the feet and the ten toes of iron and clay represented the perfect total of all the nations that followed after the Roman Empire to the end of time.

As the chronology proceeds, we have Babylon, Medo-Persia, Greece, Rome, and then all of the individual nations and kingdoms that followed after, represented by the ten toes and by the ten horns. This takes us to the end of time when the final judgment occurs.

Verse 8 gives us some additional information about these nations that follow after the Roman Empire, information that was not supplied in Daniel 2. Notice verse 8: *"I considered the horns, and, behold, there came up among them another little horn, before whom there were three of the first horns plucked up by the roots: and, behold, in this horn were eyes like the eyes of man, and a mouth speaking great things."*

As Daniel considers these ten horns, he sees an additional eleventh horn come up. It is called in verse 8 a *"little horn."* But this horn is not little either in its power or arrogance. It is only *"little"* in terms of the time it is allowed to rule; a symbolic three and a half days, as we shall see. This little horn subdues three horns, and this little horn has the eyes of a man. It has the mouth of a man that speaks great blasphemies. This little horn represents the Antichrist that appears at the end of time.

We have previously said that horns represent kingdoms, but this horn is unique. This horn has eyes and it has a mouth; therefore, it represents an individual. This individual subdues all kingdoms currently in existence under him as he displaces these three horns. Three is the number that conveys the idea of perfection and completion and finality, just as it did with the three ribs in the mouth of the bear. To subdue three kings is to subdue the complete number of kingdoms that exist on the earth when Antichrist arises. His dominion over all the kings of the earth will be perfect and final, and he will rule a one-world government. But his rule is going to be very short-lived.

Notice verses 9 and 10: *"I beheld till the thrones were cast down, and the Ancient of days did sit, whose garment was white as snow, and the hair of his head like the pure wool: his throne was like the fiery flame, and his wheels as burning fire.* [10] *A fiery stream issued and came forth from before him: thousand thousands ministered unto him, and ten thousand times ten thousand stood before him: the judgment was set, and the books were opened."*

We see that this fourth beast takes us to the end of time with his ten horns and the appearance of Antichrist right at the last. At the end of time, God will come in judgment and wrath and will cast down all the thrones and kingdoms that have set themselves against the Lord and against His Anointed and joined themselves to the Antichrist.

If you have a different Bible version, verse 9 might say, "I beheld till the thrones were set," as though somebody went in and arranged a number of thrones, and then God came down and chose one of them and sat on it. The King James Version is correct in its translation. The thrones were cast down. The idea is that when God exercises His authority from His throne, all other thrones are destroyed and cast down. The thrones that are cast down represent these kingdoms symbolized by these ten horns, and these last three in particular, who submit themselves to Antichrist and who form this transnational coalition that persecutes and makes war against the church.

The language used here to describe God the Father and the glory of His person, His throne, and His attendants reflects the language used by Ezekiel in chapters 1 and 10 when Ezekiel is describing his vision of the throne room of God. The whole description is glorious and breathtaking in the picture it presents of the majesty of God and the fearful awesomeness of His judgment: the fire that proceeds out of the throne, the myriad of innumerable attendants around the throne, and the exalted glory and majesty of the one who is sitting on the throne, who is called the Ancient of Days.

What does the Ancient of Days do? Notice verse 11: Once the judgment is set and the books are opened, verse 11 says, "*I beheld then because of the voice of the great words which the horn spake.*" This horn is the Antichrist, with his mouth of blasphemies. "*I beheld even till the beast was slain, and his body destroyed, and given to the burning flame.*" Antichrist and his beastly kingdom are going to be destroyed and cast into the lake of fire.

This coming of God, this capturing of Antichrist and His beastly kingdom, and their being judged and cast into hell is spoken of in Revelation 11:13–15. From this point forward, we are going to be going back and forth between Daniel 7 and Revelation 11.

Notice Revelation 11:7–12. It says, *"And when they,"* (the church, represented by the two witnesses) *"shall have finished their testimony, the beast that ascendeth out of the bottomless pit"* (the little horn of Daniel with the mouth and the eyes) *"shall make war against them, and shall overcome them, and kill them.* [8] *And their dead bodies shall lie in the street of the great city, which spiritually is called Sodom and Egypt, where also our Lord was crucified.* [9] *And they of the people and kindreds and tongues and nations"* (the coalition of these symbolic three kings that submitted themselves to Antichrist, which are all the kingdoms of the earth), it says they *"shall see their dead bodies three days and an half, and shall not suffer their dead bodies to be put in graves.* [10] *And they that dwell upon the earth shall rejoice over them, and make merry, and shall send gifts one to another; because these two prophets tormented them that dwelt on the earth."* Here is the pinnacle of Antichrist's triumph, but it quickly comes to an end, verse 11. *"And after three days and an half the Spirit of life from God entered into them, and they stood upon their feet; and great fear fell upon them which saw them.* [12] *And they heard a great voice from heaven saying unto them, Come up hither. And they ascended up to heaven in a cloud; and their enemies beheld them."*

Revelation 11:13 is equivalent to Daniel 7:11. Daniel 7:11 is now played out in Revelation 11:13: *"And the same hour was there a great earthquake, and the tenth part of the city fell, and in the earthquake were slain of men seven thousand: and the remnant were affrighted, and gave glory to the God of heaven."* Notice further verse 15: *"And the seventh angel sounded; and there were great voices in heaven, saying, The kingdoms of this world are become the kingdoms of our Lord, and of his Christ; and he shall reign for ever and ever."*

Revelation 11:13 and 15 is a description of what the Ancient of Days is doing. When He comes, He opens the book, He sets the judgment, and the first thing He does is seize Antichrist and his kingdom and sends them to hell, and the kingdoms of this world become the kingdoms of the Ancient of Days and of His Christ, and they shall reign forever and ever.

This judgment is also spoken of in Revelation 19:19–20. Jesus is returning, and it says in verse 19, *"And I saw the beast"* (the beast that ascended out of the bottomless pit, the Antichrist, the little horn), *"and the kings of the earth and their armies"* (his transnational coalition, the symbolic three kingdoms that submitted themselves to him), *"gathered together to make war against him that sat on the horse, and against his army."*

They have already attacked the church and destroyed it, and now Jesus has come and they say, "Now we are going to make war against Jesus and His returning army." Verse 20: *"And the beast was taken, and with him the false prophet that wrought miracles before him, with which he deceived them that had received the mark of the beast, and them that worshipped his image. These both were cast alive into a lake of fire burning with brimstone.* [21] *And the remnant were slain with the sword of him that sat upon the horse, which sword proceeded out of his mouth: and all the fowls were filled with their flesh."*

This is the same event that is spoken of in Revelation 20:7–10. *"And when the thousand years are expired, Satan shall be loosed out of his prison"* (when he is loosed, he raises up Antichrist, the little horn), *"*[8] *And shall go out to deceive the nations which are in the four quarters of the earth, Gog and Magog,"* (Antichrist and his transnational coalition army) *"to gather them together to battle: the number of whom is as the sand of the sea.* [9] *And they went up on the breadth of the earth, and compassed [surrounded] the camp of the saints about, and the beloved city: and fire came down from God out of heaven, and devoured them.* [10] *And the devil that deceived them was cast into the lake of fire and brimstone, where the beast and the false prophet are, and shall be tormented day and night for ever and ever."*

We will see the beast and the false prophet on the earth because they are physical beings leading a physical body of people. Satan is the indwelling and energizing force behind them, therefore not only are the beast and the false prophet cast into the lake of fire along with the kingdom they rule (the one-world government), but Satan who is behind it all is also cast into the lake of fire. This is the final judgment in Daniel 7:9–11 being carried out.

In Daniel 7, when the Ancient of Days, who is God the Father, returns and begins to execute this judgment, He judges Antichrist and kills all of his people and casts them all into hell. Notice verse 12: *"As concerning the rest of the beasts"* (the winged lion, the bear with three ribs in his mouth, the leopard with the four heads and the four wings), *"they had their dominion taken away."* As each successive kingdom came, the previous kingdom lost its dominion. *"Yet their lives were prolonged for a season and time."* The people who were in one defeated kingdom lived and passed into the subsequent kingdom.

The end of the fourth kingdom and the Antichrist who is its final ruler is different from the ending of these three previous kingdoms. The preceding three kingdoms lost their dominion, as verse 12 says, but those who populated those kingdoms did not all die, and they did not cease to remain on the earth. They continued to live though conquered; "*their lives were prolonged for a season and time.*" They remained on the earth for a time in the next kingdom until they eventually died.

Though that is how these first three kingdoms ended, that is not the case with the fourth kingdom and how it ends. When it is destroyed, all of those who populate it are destroyed as well, because the end of the fourth kingdom is the end of the lives of all of its citizens without exception; whereas, with the end of the other kingdoms, most of the citizens lived. But this is not the case with the end of the fourth kingdom. When Jesus returns, He will slay all of the citizens of the kingdom of Antichrist, and none of their lives will be prolonged past the end of that kingdom, as Revelation 19:21 states.

Notice verses 13 and 14 where Christ is explicitly brought up and mentioned. Verse 13: "*I saw in the night visions, and, behold, one like the Son of man came with the clouds of heaven, and came to the Ancient of days, and they brought him near before him.* [14] *And there was given him dominion, and glory, and a kingdom, that all people, nations, and languages, should serve him: his dominion is an everlasting dominion, which shall not pass away, and his kingdom that which shall not be destroyed.*"

In verses 13 and 14, God the Father, the Ancient of Days, gives the kingdom to Jesus Christ, His Son. In verses 13 and 14 is the climax and the goal of the vision. The kingdom of Christ is the fifth and final kingdom, after which there will never be another. It says here that Jesus comes, in verse 13, "*with the clouds of heaven.*" To come with the clouds of heaven is a metaphor that often speaks of God coming in wrath and judgment—so to come with the clouds is to come with wrath and judgment. We explored that concept in detail in our study in Revelation 1:7–8 in Chapter 9.

It is not just the Ancient of Days but also the Son of man who comes to execute judgment upon the earth. We see Him doing this in Matthew 25:31–46 as He separates the sheep from the goats. But the focus here is on the eternal, universal, and absolute dominion that Christ shall have and exercise in His kingdom over all people and nations and languages. In contrast to the kingdoms of this world, all of which have fallen and ended, Christ's kingdom is an everlasting kingdom which will not pass away and will never be destroyed. It is given to Him by His Father as a reward for His work of redemption, and Jesus will rule the redeemed saints in the new heavens and the new earth for eternity without end.

Christ will have a kingdom that is the opposite of these cruel, animalistic kingdoms that devour people. His kingdom will be one of unmitigated goodness, happiness, holiness, and delight—one that will serve not only the glory of the King but also the good of the people. This is Daniel's vision revealed.

Daniel's Vision Explained

Daniel's vision is explained in verses 15 to 28. I have used a lot of material out of this section to interpret the first section because what follows is the inspired explanation as to what the first section of this chapter means.

Notice verses 15 and 16. It says, *"I Daniel was grieved in my spirit in the midst of my body, and the visions of my head troubled me.* [16] *I came near unto one of them that stood by, and asked him the truth of all this. So he told me, and made me know the interpretation of the things."*

Daniel is grieved and troubled by all he has seen and all that it meant, so he spoke to one of the angels mentioned in verse 10 and asked for an explanation. Verses 17–18 tell us the explanation: *"These great beasts, which are four, are four kings, which shall arise out of the earth.* [18] *But the saints of the most High shall take the kingdom, and possess the kingdom for ever, even for ever and ever."*

In verses 17 to 18 we have a brief but complete summary of the meaning of the entire vision. The four beasts are four kings and kingdoms which will arise out of this world; that is, they will arise by human means and through human agency out of the churning troubled mass of humanity. These kings and kingdoms will arise out of the seething sinful cauldron of lost humanity, but their kingdoms will not last. Believers in Christ shall achieve by the grace of God what the wicked could never achieve by mere human and military and political effort.

The saints will inherit the kingdom of Christ, they will possess it, and they will retain it forever. In a word, the church will triumph over the world. The kingdom of God will defeat and overcome and destroy all worldly kingdoms. The world will lose all of its kingdoms, but the church shall have the kingdom of Christ forever and ever.

But this little two-verse summary in verses 17 and 18 of the interpretation of this vision does not satisfy Daniel. There is an extremely important detail that Daniel feels he has to understand better, and that is the meaning and identity and activity of the little horn. He wants to understand in more detail the work of this final and last king on the earth, otherwise known as Antichrist.

Notice verses 19 to 20: *"Then I would know the truth of the fourth beast, which was diverse from all the others, exceeding dreadful, whose teeth were of iron, and his nails of brass; which devoured, brake in pieces, and stamped the residue with his feet;* [20] *And of the ten horns that were in his head, and of the other which came up, and before whom three fell; even of that horn that had eyes, and a mouth that spake very great things, whose look was more stout than his fellows."* In verses 19 and 20, Daniel asks about the fourth beast and the horns; and in reply, the angel grants him further visions of the activity of that eleventh horn in verses 21 and 22.

Here is the further vision: *"I beheld, and the same horn"* (the eleventh horn), *"made war with the saints, and prevailed against them;* [22] *Until the Ancient of days came, and judgment was given to the saints of the most High; and the time came that the saints possessed the kingdom."* Notice how clearly verse 21 describes the work of Antichrist in Revelation 11:7.

Daniel 7:21: *"I beheld, and the same horn made war with the saints, and prevailed against them."* Now Revelation 11:7: *"And when they shall have finished their testimony, the beast that ascendeth out of the bottomless pit shall make war against them, and shall overcome them, and kill them."* These are parallel passages. The eleventh horn is the beast that came out of the bottomless pit. He is that last king that appears at the very end of history who puts together his transnational coalition and destroys the church. The eleventh horn is the Antichrist.

This making war with the saints spoken of in Daniel 7:21 and his prevailing against them does not last long. Notice verse 22. It says it happens *"until the Ancient of days came, and judgment was given to the saints of the most High; and the time came that the saints possessed the kingdom."* In verse 22, it says that upon Antichrist's defeat of the church on earth, God comes in judgment, He rules in favor of the saints and against Antichrist, and He grants to the saints the possession of the kingdom of Christ.

But the angel is not done. The angel now gives further information to Daniel and explains the remainder of the matter in verses 23 to 27. Notice first of all verses 23 to 24: "*Thus he*" (the angel that explained to him the summary meaning in verses 17 and 18) "*said, The fourth beast shall be the fourth kingdom upon earth, which shall be diverse from all kingdoms, and shall devour the whole earth, and shall tread it down, and break it in pieces.*" This is a reference to the Roman Empire in its brutal conquering of the then-known world. Verse 24: "*And the ten horns out of this kingdom are ten kings that shall arise: and another shall rise after them; and he shall be diverse from the first, and he shall subdue three kings.*"

In verse 23, we have a description of the Roman Empire and its unique nature. It is unique in the degree of its cruelty, and it is unique in the extent of its dominion. It will rule the whole earth and it will tread it down and devour it and break it. The Roman Empire was greater in cruelty and greater in extent than any of the previous three kingdoms. It devoured the whole earth, it trod down the whole earth under its feet, and it broke in pieces every nation it conquered.

But verse 24 now speaks of all the remaining nations that flowed out of and followed chronologically from the Roman Empire, represented by these ten horns. Horns are symbols of power and strength and rule and authority. Horns are representative of kings and kingdoms. So all remaining nations flowed out of the Roman Empire and followed it, and are represented by the ten horns, until the last nation and king arose, represented by the little horn that subdued the three surrounding horns. This is the kingdom of Antichrist, who will subdue with perfection and completeness and finality the kingdoms that exist when he arises.

These symbolic three kings who fall into submission to the one-world rule of the Antichrist represent the coalition of nations which gather together through the deception of Satan to attack the church on earth. Three is the symbolic number of perfection, completeness, and finality. He perfectly, completely, and finally brings all the kingdoms of the world under his rule, and then he makes war on the saints, and he overcomes them and kills them.

Notice verse 25: *"And he"* (Antichrist, the eleventh horn), *"shall speak great words against the most High, and shall wear out the saints of the most High, and think to change times and laws: and they"* (the saints) *"shall be given into his hand until a time and times and the dividing of time."* What does Antichrist and his coalition of nations do? They are going to commit great blasphemy against the most High God. Second Thessalonians 2:3–4 says: *"that man of sin [will] be revealed, the son of perdition;* [4] *Who opposeth and exalteth himself above all that is called God, or that is worshipped; so that he as God sitteth in the temple of God, shewing himself that he is God."*

That is blasphemy. Antichrist appears and says, "Forget all your other gods; I am god. Worship me." That is the blasphemy that he speaks. The real Christians are not going to worship him. Therefore, he is going to slaughter them. Just like the early Christians would not say that Caesar is lord, and were thrown into the Coliseum to be eaten by the lions, that is an illustration of what Antichrist will do. When Antichrist comes and demands worship from the whole world, Christians will not give it to him, so Christians will be slaughtered.

He will horribly oppress the saints of the most High God. He makes unremitting war on them because they are the only ones on earth who will not worship him as god on earth. He will attempt to change times and laws—that is, to overthrow every established and permanent principle of human activity and human morality. An example of this took place during the French Revolution when a ten-day week was instituted and sexual anarchy was promoted. They sought to change times and they sought to change laws.

Now for a brief time, as verse 25 says, Antichrist will appear to be victorious in changing times and laws. He will be victorious for a very limited period of time. Verse 25 says, *"until a time and times and the dividing of time"*; that is, a three-and-a-half-time period. What three-and-a-half-time period is this? It is the three and a half days of Revelation 11:9–10. It is the three and a half days when Antichrist wins and defeats the church and the dead bodies of the saints lie in the street and the whole world is rejoicing. The end of verse 25 is talking about those same three and a half days. Antichrist will triumph over the saints, and the saints will be given into his hand for that very short period of time, symbolized by three and a half days: this *"time, and times, and the dividing of time."*

But it will not last. Verse 26: *"But the judgment shall sit."* This is the judgment spoken of in Daniel 7:9–10. *"But the judgment shall sit, and they shall take away his dominion"* (Antichrist's dominion), *"to consume and to destroy it unto the end,"* spoken of in Daniel 7:11.

The kingdom of Antichrist and his apparent triumph over the church will not last. Judgment will come, the Antichrist and his kingdom will be destroyed, and his dominion will be taken away by the Ancient of Days and His Son when they come in judgment. That is what we are going to see as we look at the seventh trumpet in Revelation 11:11–19. When the Ancient of Days and His Son come, that is the end of Antichrist's little three-and-a-half-day triumph.

Notice verses 27–28, *"And the kingdom and dominion, and the greatness of the kingdom under the whole heaven, shall be given to the people of the saints of the most High, whose kingdom is an everlasting kingdom, and all dominions shall serve and obey him.* [28] *Hitherto is the end of the matter."*

Verse 27 tells us the conclusion of the matter. Christ will be enthroned as King of the world, and the saints will possess the kingdom, nevermore to be trodden under the foot of the Gentiles. The saints, once oppressed and slaughtered, are now victorious and possess eternal life. The Antichrist, once briefly victorious and triumphant as the ruler of the whole world and worshiped as God, is now utterly defeated, stripped of his authority and rule, disgraced as a fraud, and cast into the lake of fire.

The point of Daniel 7 and Revelation 11 is that the days of the kingdoms and rulers of this planet are limited. History has a definite predestinated end. What we are experiencing now is not going to go on forever. The clock is running out for the kings and kingdoms of this earth. We are in the time of the fourth beast, we are past the Roman Empire, we are into the feet of clay mixed with iron, and we are into the time of the ten horns. What we have not seen yet is the rise of the little horn.

The rise of the little horn will occur when Satan is loosed. When will that occur? No one knows. It could be tomorrow, or it could be a thousand years from tomorrow, but that will be the triggering event. Satan will be loosed, Antichrist will arise, the transnational coalition will form against the church, the great apostasy will occur, and the church will be wiped off the earth with the exception of a small remnant. This will last for a short period of time. Jesus will return, He will resurrect His dead martyrs, He will rapture His living saints, His wrath will be poured out on Antichrist and his kingdom, they will all be cast into hell. The kingdom of Christ will be established, and we will possess it forever, and it will never end. That is biblical eschatology.

This is why the wicked rulers of this world will not win. They have power for a short time. What happens to every one of them? They fall. What happens to their kingdoms? They are destroyed. What replaces them? The everlasting kingdom of Christ.

The wicked rulers of this world have power for a little time, they can persecute the people of God for a while, but their time is limited, and then they will be cast into hell. The kingdom will be ours forever and our King will be Christ for all eternity. We will suffer for a time, but we will triumph forever.

The optimistic eschatology that the Scripture sets before us is that the kingdoms of this world are all going to fall, but the kingdom of Christ is going to stand forever. It will be the final kingdom, after which there will be no more kingdoms.

Do you struggle with living under the kingdoms of this world? Take heart. The Ancient of Days is coming, the Son of man is coming, and the Stone is going to smash and crush the kingdoms of this world. Recognize that your present state is temporary and you will be delivered from it. Whatever persecutions you are under will be remedied and rectified, and you will be restored to everlasting life and happiness in the kingdom of Christ forever and ever without end. That is the good news of the eschatology of the world and of the church. The Prince of Peace is coming.

37

The Seventh Trumpet, Revelation 11:15–19

> *"[15] And the seventh angel sounded; and there were great voices in heaven, saying, The kingdoms of this world are become the kingdoms of our Lord, and of his Christ; and he shall reign for ever and ever. [16] And the four and twenty elders, which sat before God on their seats, fell upon their faces, and worshipped God, [17] Saying, We give thee thanks, O Lord God Almighty, which art, and wast, and art to come; because thou hast taken to thee thy great power, and hast reigned. [18] And the nations were angry, and thy wrath is come, and the time of the dead, that they should be judged, and that thou shouldest give reward unto thy servants the prophets, and to the saints, and them that fear thy name, small and great; and shouldest destroy them which destroy the earth. [19] And the temple of God was opened in heaven, and there was seen in his temple the ark of his testament: and there were lightnings, and voices, and thunderings, and an earthquake, and great hail."*

After spending two chapters looking at Daniel 2 and 7, we return to our exposition of Revelation 11. To recap where we have been, we have been looking at the third parallel section in the book of Revelation. The first parallel section consisted of the letters to the seven churches in chapters 1 to 3. The second parallel section consisted of the seven seals in chapters 4 to 7. The third parallel section we are currently in consists of the seven trumpets in chapters 8 through 11.

Each of these parallel sections describes the things that will characterize the age between the first and second coming of Christ. Each of these parallel sections takes up a theme and explains the circumstances that will characterize the age regarding that theme. The seven churches tell us the challenges the churches will face and the spiritual warfare they will experience between the first and second coming of Christ. The seven seals tell us how the unsaved will behave and the wickedness they will accomplish between the first and second coming of Christ. The seven trumpets tell us the temporal judgments God will bring on the unsaved between the first and second coming of Christ for their wicked behavior described by the seven seals.

As we have looked at the seven churches and the seven seals and the seven trumpets, we have seen that each of them not only tells us what will characterize this age between the first and second coming, but each of them also brings us to the end of the age, and describes what will happen when Christ returns.

The believers in the churches will be called to the marriage supper of the Lamb, as described in Revelation 3:20–21. The wicked will see the destruction of the material world and will call out for the rocks and the mountains to fall upon them and hide them from the final wrath of God, as described in Revelation 6:12–17. God will bring His final judgment on the wicked when Christ returns to resurrect and rapture the saints, to slay the wicked and destroy all of their kingdoms, and to establish the eternal kingdom of Christ, as described in Revelation 11:11–19.

As we look at the sounding of the seventh trumpet, we see there is no longer time for repentance. The day of salvation has ended. The mystery of God is finished. Revelation 10:6 says that the angel *"swore by him that liveth for ever and ever, who created heaven, and the things that therein are, and the earth, and the things that therein are, and the sea, and the things which are therein, that there should be time no longer"*; that is, the time for salvation has ended. There will no longer be time, space, or opportunity for salvation. The day of salvation has concluded. Revelation 10:7 says, *"But in the days of the voice of the seventh angel when he shall begin to sound, the mystery of God should be finished, as he hath declared to his servants the prophets."*

God's plan of salvation, which is a mystery to the world, has now been completely fulfilled. The full number of the elect has been saved, the testimony of the church is finished, and all that is left is the judgment of the wicked, the destruction of Antichrist and his kingdom, and the establishment of the kingdom of Christ and His people in the new heavens and the new earth. This is what we find in the sounding of the seventh trumpet.

At the end of the sounding of the sixth trumpet, Christ has resurrected and raptured His saints, and He has slain the wicked and the Antichrist, as we saw in 11:11–13. Now we come to the seventh trumpet, and here we have the final judgment and the establishment of Christ's eternal kingdom.

As we progress through each of these parallel sections (there will be seven of them), the declaration of the nature of the final judgment becomes clearer and it is described in more detail. In the seventh trumpet, we find more detail than we found in the sixth seal, which had more detail than we found in the seventh church.

When the Seventh Trumpet Sounds, Voices from Heaven Are Heard

When the seventh trumpet sounds, immediately John begins to hear voices from heaven, and he hears two sets of voices. First of all, he hears the voices of angels speaking. Notice verse 15: *"And the seventh angel sounded, and there were great voices in heaven, saying, The kingdoms of this world are become the kingdoms of our Lord, and of his Christ; and he shall reign for ever and ever."* These voices are great voices. They are loud voices. They are a multitude of voices. They are millions of voices of angels, all speaking in unison in heaven. They make a declaration about the defeat of the Antichrist and his worldwide kingdom, and they make a declaration about the triumph of Christ and His eternal kingdom.

This glorious swelling tidal wave of praise in verse 15 is a result of seeing the conclusion of the plan of God and the victory of the Son of God over the greatest opposition mankind has ever raised or could raise against God. All the kingdoms of this world have been united against Christ. But all the kingdoms of this world have fallen and have been defeated by Jesus Christ. We saw that defeat at the end of the sixth seal in 6:12–17.

Christ's return ends the dominion and rule of Antichrist and his one-world government of all the nations. In the place of this kingdom that Christ has defeated, God the Father and God the Son have established an everlasting kingdom that shall never fall, and a King who will never change or pass away.

It is certainly true that God has always ruled the world in the sense that He is in ultimate control of all events. He is sovereign over all things, and He has been since the beginning of time. But His rule and authority were challenged by Satan, and He allowed Satan to fall. His rule and authority were challenged again in the garden of Eden, and He allowed mankind to fall.

Ever since that time, Satan and fallen humanity have raged against the Lord and against His Son, they have conspired together to cast off His rule and authority, and they have sought to live autonomously and independently from God. God has allowed Satan and fallen humanity time and space to do their worst, and the result is that it has seemed that God has been dethroned and Satan and his people have ruled supreme over the earth without fetter or limit.

Never will this appear to be more the case than when Satan enables Antichrist to subdue all the nations of the earth under his authority, when he causes all men to worship the Antichrist as God on earth, and when Antichrist successfully destroys the visible presence of the church from the earth. But once the Day of Judgment arrives, Christ returns in wrath and vengeance, and then God's will shall be done on earth as it is in heaven.

When the seventh trumpet sounds, the full visible rule of God will be openly manifested and revealed on earth, all opposition will be abolished, the kingdoms of this world will visibly become the kingdom of our Lord and of His Christ, and His reign and rule will be plain for all to see and experience.

It is then that Psalm 2 will be fulfilled. "[1]*Why do the heathen rage, and the people imagine a vain thing?* [2]*The kings of the earth set themselves. . .against the* Lord*, and against his anointed, saying,* [3]*Let us break their bands asunder, and cast away their cords from us.*" This is what the world has been doing since the garden of Eden, and this is what the world will continue to do until the seventh trumpet sounds.

God gives His Son a rod of iron, and as a pottery vessel is shattered in pieces when struck with an iron rod, so the kingdoms of this world will be shattered and destroyed when Christ returns. He will crush them under His wrath. He will bring His judgment to bear on them and He will rule on the throne of David over the whole world forever.

When the seventh trumpet sounds, not only will Psalm 2 be fulfilled, but Daniel 7:13–14, 26–27 will also be fulfilled, which says: "*I saw in the night visions, and, behold, one like the Son of man came with the clouds of heaven, and came to the Ancient of days, and they brought him near before him.* [14] *And there was given him dominion, and glory, and a kingdom, that all people, nations, and languages, should serve him: his dominion is an everlasting dominion, which shall not pass away, and his kingdom that which shall not be destroyed. . .* [26] *But the judgment shall sit, and they shall take away his [Antichrist's] dominion, to consume and to destroy it unto the end.* [27] *And the kingdom and dominion, and the greatness of the kingdom under the whole heaven, shall be given to the people of the saints of the most High, whose kingdom is an everlasting kingdom, and all dominions shall serve and obey him."*

When this seventh trumpet sounds, Luke 1:31–33 will also be fulfilled. The angel appears to Mary and announces that she is going to be the mother of the Messiah. The angel says: *"And, behold, thou shalt conceive in thy womb, and bring forth a son, and shalt call his name Jesus.* [32] *He shall be great, and shall be called the Son of the Highest: and the Lord God shall give unto him the throne of his father David:* [33] *And he shall reign over the house of Jacob for ever; and of his kingdom there shall be no end."*

In Psalm 2, in Daniel 7, and in Luke 1 it was prophesied that even though the kingdoms of this world are going to fight viciously against the kingdom of God, the kingdom of God is going to triumph, it is going to destroy the kingdoms of this world, and the rule of Christ will prevail over the entire planet. All opposition to that rule will be completely eliminated.

Imagine a perfect kingdom, with perfect citizens, with perfect laws, with a perfect King, on a perfect planet, all of which will never change for all eternity. All of that is coming to pass when the seventh trumpet sounds. Satan has been behind all the political kingdoms that have persecuted believers all throughout history, but these satanic political kingdoms will never exist again.

Handel's *Messiah* and the "Hallelujah Chorus" that is at the end of it say over and over again, "And He shall reign forever and ever. And He shall reign, and He shall reign. . ." Those words are taken directly out of Revelation 11:15. This passage was Handel's inspiration. If you have never listened to Handel's *Messiah*, I would urge you to do so. It is pure worship of Christ and His glorious kingdom and His triumph over all the wicked.

But the voices of the angels are not the only voices from heaven that are heard when the seventh trumpet sounds. Secondly, the twenty-four elders speak. Notice verse 16–18: *"And the four and twenty elders, which sat before God on their seats, fell upon their faces, and worshipped God,* [17] *Saying, We give thee thanks, O Lord God Almighty, which art, and wast, and art to come; because thou hast taken to thee thy great power, and hast reigned.* [18] *And the nations were angry, and thy wrath is come, and the time of the dead, that they should be judged, and that thou shouldest give reward unto thy servants the prophets, and to the saints, and them that fear thy name, small and great; and shouldest destroy them which destroy the earth."*

The twenty-four elders symbolically represent the redeemed church in heaven. They represent the totality of those who are saved by Christ. What do the redeemed saints in heaven have to say when the seventh trumpet blows? First of all, they fall on their faces and worship. Notice verse 16 says, *"And the four and twenty elders, which sat before God on their seats, fell upon their faces, and worshipped God."* These redeemed saints have been sitting in heaven, and they have been watching. Now they have seen it all.

They have seen the entire sweep of the plan and purpose of God carried out on earth. They have seen the church saved, the church persecuted, and the church preserved. They have seen the church complete her task of witness against all opposition that tried to silence it. They have seen the church destroyed under the reign of Antichrist. They have seen the church resurrected and glorified in the second coming of Christ. They have seen Satan, his nations and kingdoms, his Antichrist, and all of his people destroyed. They have witnessed the kingdoms of this world become the kingdoms of their Lord and of His Christ, and they are filled with wonder and love and praise for the triumph of Christ and the victory He achieved and the deliverance He provided for all His people from the hatred and persecution of Satan.

They see all of these works of God in all of their grand sweep and scope, and what is their response? They fall on their faces and worship God. But they do not just fall on their faces and worship. Secondly, they declare the reason for their worship in verses 17 and 18. They see all God has done for His people and for His glory, and they give thanks for it all.

Notice verse 17: "*We give thee thanks,*" and then they recite the summary and essence of who God is and what God has done in His work of destroying His enemies and in redeeming and vindicating His people. This describes once again the essence of worship. What is the essence of worship? It is a declaration of who God is, coupled with a declaration of what God has done.

First of all, notice what they say about who God is. Verse 17a: "*We give thee thanks, O Lord God Almighty, which art, and wast, and art to come.*" He is the "*Lord God Almighty,*" and this name tells us a great deal about the Person that we worship.

This name declares His sovereignty. He is the "*Lord.*" He is Lord over all things, and over all beings. He has universal sovereignty. Furthermore, this name declares His authority. He is the Lord "*God.*" He is God, the highest authority in the universe, from whom there is no appeal. He has ultimate and final authority. Finally, this name declares His power. He is the Lord God "*Almighty.*" He is the one who can do all things, and the one for whom nothing is too hard to do.

Furthermore, this sovereign, authoritative, powerful God is also the eternal God. The elders say of Him that He is the one "*which art, and wast, and art to come.*" That is, He is the one who exists now—He is; He is the one who has always existed from eternity past—He was; and He is the one who will exist forever into eternity future—He is to come. The point is, God always has been, is now, and always will be, because He is the eternally self-existent God. He did not derive His existence from someone else. His existence does not depend on anything outside of Himself.

Who is this God that we worship? The God we worship is a sovereign, powerful, eternal God, who possesses ultimate and final authority over all things and all people, and who is in control of all things that ever have or ever will occur on the earth. This is the source of endless comfort and security for the saints of God, and it is an endless motivation for the worship of God.

Knowing these things about God fills us with gratitude, confidence, praise, and worship. When you know that God is sovereign, powerful, eternal, and authoritative, you know you have a God who is worthy of worship. You know you have a God who can take care of you. You know you have a God who will keep His promises. You know you have a God who is able to save to the uttermost those who come to Him through Christ.

But having seen what the twenty-four elders say about who God is, notice secondly what they say about what God has done. Verse 17b and verse 18: "*thou hast taken to thee thy great power, and hast reigned.* [18] *And the nations were angry, and thy wrath is come, and the time of the dead, that they should be judged, and that thou shouldest give reward unto thy servants the prophets, and to the saints, and them that fear thy name, small and great; and shouldest destroy them which destroy the earth."* God does not just possess power and He is not just the Lord God Almighty; He also exercises that almighty power in the execution of His sovereign will. It says in verse 17b that God uses His great power to carry out His reign and rule over the whole earth.

Verse 18 says, *"the nations were angry."* They hated God's authority, and they hated God's law, and the nations raged against it. They were angered by it. They sought to cast off the constraints of God's authority and God's law. They set themselves against the Lord and against His anointed—that is, against His Son. But they did not prevail in their rage against God. God's wrath instead was manifested not only in His temporal judgments against them as we saw in the first six trumpets, but also in His final judgment on them as we see in the seventh trumpet. The wicked do not escape the wrath of God, nor do they escape the judgment of God.

Verse 18 says that the time will come when both the wicked dead and the righteous dead will be resurrected. *"And the nations were angry, and thy wrath is come, and the time of the dead."* This phrase *"the time of the dead"* is speaking of the resurrection, when all of the dead are resurrected. The time will come when both the righteous dead and the wicked dead will stand before God. It says, *". . .the time of the dead, that they should be judged, and that thou shouldest give reward unto thy servants the prophets, and to the saints, and them that fear thy name, small and great; and shouldest destroy them which destroy the earth."*

As for the righteous who repented of their sins and received Christ as their Savior and who were faithful to God in their witness and lives, they will be given a reward. They will inherit eternal life. They will inherit the earth. They will inherit the kingdom of God forever and ever. That is their reward. Those who receive Christ as Lord and Savior—whether they were prophets or whether they were saints, whether they were small or whether they were great, if they feared the name of the Lord, if they bowed in submission and reverence and faith before the Lord God Almighty so they became obedient to the gospel and its message—to them, God will give the reward of eternal life.

But there is another class and category who are at this judgment, and that is the wicked. It says not only will God give a reward to His servants, but He will *"destroy them which destroy the earth."* The wicked who destroyed the earth and those upon it with their sin and evil, God will destroy in the lake of fire. God created and provided humanity with a pristine world, and the wicked destroyed the world with the fall, which affected not only all humanity but all the natural creation as well.

There was a physical destruction and a spiritual destruction wrought by the wicked, and therefore the wicked will themselves be destroyed. They will receive the reward of their rebellion, just as the righteous will receive the reward of their faith and obedience. As it says in Matthew 25:46, *"And these shall go away into everlasting punishment: but the righteous into life eternal."*

Revelation 11:18 makes it clear there will be a Day of Judgment. The question is, what will be your outcome on that day? Will you go away into everlasting punishment, or will you go away into everlasting life? Let me ask you another question that will help you answer the one I just asked: Are you among the company of the two witnesses who proclaimed Christ and His gospel by life and word to a hostile world? Or are you among the company of those who persecute the two witnesses, and rejoice when the voice of the gospel is silenced so you do not have to be tormented with its demands any longer?

Your response to the gospel and its messengers determines your destiny and your reward. Therefore, you need to choose wisely. There are no second opportunities. On the Day of Judgment, what will it be for you? Will it be reward or will it be retribution? The choice is yours. It will be determined by whether you follow Christ, or whether you follow Antichrist. There are only two choices in this world. You either follow along with those who are for Christ, or you follow along with those who are against Christ.

When the Seventh Trumpet Sounds, Visions of Heaven Are Revealed

We have heard voices in verse 15: "*And the seventh angel sounded; and there were great voices.*" Now notice verse 19: *"And the temple of God was opened in heaven, and there was seen. . ."* We go from hearing things to seeing things.

In verse 19 there is a revelation of the temple of God in heaven.

"And the temple of God was opened in heaven, and there was seen in his temple the ark of his testament"; that is, the ark of His covenant. The word *"testament"* is the word "covenant" in the Greek, and it should therefore read "the ark of his covenant." Furthermore, *"there were lightnings, and voices, and thunderings, and an earthquake, and great hail."*

This temple and the ark of God's covenant in heaven are the substance of which the earthly tabernacle and the earthly ark Moses built were but the shadow. The things on earth were just a pattern of the things that actually existed in heaven.

At this point in eschatological history, after the final judgment is completed and the rewards are given to the wicked and to the just, the vision presented here is one in which the sanctuary of God is now wide open. There is now no veil, there are now no walls, there is now nothing hidden or concealed. Verse 19 states: *"And the temple of God was opened in heaven, and there was seen. . ."*

The Old Testament temple was all closed up. People were not allowed to see anything within it, or what was going on in it. Only the high priest could enter the holy of holies once a year with blood, and just for a moment. But now the walls are gone, the veil is gone, and only the ark is there, all out in the open. That is the picture.

The Ark of the Covenant, which symbolizes the most intimate contact and fellowship with God, is now completely unveiled. The Ark of the Covenant is the symbol of intimate, real, deep, and perfect fellowship with God. The point is, no longer are the people separated from fellowship with God by a veil.

In Exodus 25:22, regarding the Ark of the Covenant, God said, *"And there I will meet with thee, and I will commune with thee from above the mercy seat. . ."* God Himself declared that the ark was the place of communion with Him. Therefore, when the ark is fully revealed and when access to the ark is completely opened, we understand this to mean that the believers are now able to have unfettered fellowship and communion with God, and are able to fully enter into that fellowship and communion without limit or restriction. Now every believer can enter into the presence of God, into His most intimate personal presence, and commune with Him. This is what it means for the ark to be wide open.

John is communicating by this vision that all barriers between God and man have been permanently and finally removed. In the words of Hebrews 10:19–22, we now have boldness to enter into the holiest presence of God and are able to draw near to Him with a full assurance that He will gladly receive us, because of the cleansing and reconciling blood of Jesus that presents us faultless before His presence.

For us, the way into the holiest presence of God is now opened through the blood of Christ, and that was the symbolic significance of the tearing open of the veil in the temple from top to bottom when Jesus died on the cross. This rending of the veil when Jesus died was saying that the day is going to come when all of this is going to be removed and there are going to be no barriers between people and God. Instead, there will be perfect communion and fellowship and intimacy between them. This is what happens after the final judgment and the believers are given their reward.

God said to Abraham in Genesis 15:1, "Abraham, I am your exceeding great reward." What is the reward in heaven for believers? It is God Himself. He gives Himself openly, freely, and transparently to His people, and invites them to come and to find in Him the satisfaction of all of their desires and the meeting of their deepest needs for everything they ever wanted, and for everything they were created to enjoy.

For us, the way into the holiest presence of God is made both possible and joyful. But for the wicked, the vision of the presence of God is one of abject terror. For them, the open presence of God depicted in verse 19 is not one of sweet fellowship, but one of lightnings and thunders and voices and hail and a great earthquake. Notice the second part of verse 19: *"there was seen in his temple the ark of his testament: and there were lightnings, and voices, and thunderings, and an earthquake, and great hail."*

Those things recall the judgments of Egypt and the ten plagues. This is what the wicked are going to experience when they stand exposed before the presence of God. Right now, the wicked can, in a way, hide from God. He is "up there" and they are "down here," and they do not have to be around Him. They do not have to show up to church, they do not have to read the Bible, and they can stay away from Christians. They can pretty much stay away from God and avoid being in His presence.

But in heaven, they are not going to be able to get away from God, and it is going to be horrible for them. It is going to be the worst thing possible for them, even as it is the most wonderful thing conceivable for us. For us, there is the Ark of the Covenant. It is a vision of delight and a place of sweet fellowship with God. But for them, there is lightning and thunder and hail and a vision of wrath and judgment.

People naively say that hell is a place without God. It is precisely the presence of God that makes hell to be hell for them. They cannot get away from His wrath, they cannot get away from His judgment, and they cannot get away from His presence. They cannot run around saying, "I do not believe in God. I am an atheist. Therefore, I do not have to have anything to do with God." They are going to have to have something to do with God for every second of their lives for all eternity as they burn in the lake of fire, because it says of God in Hebrews 12:29 that *"our God is a consuming fire."*

The worst torment in hell will be for them to live under the eye of the God they rejected while they were here on earth. It says regarding the wicked in Revelation 14:10–11 that they *"shall be tormented with fire and brimstone in the presence of the holy angels, and in the presence of the Lamb:* [11] *And the smoke of their torment ascendeth up for ever and ever: and they have no rest day nor night."* They will have to live under that eye for all eternity—that unblinking, wrathful eye of judgment. In heaven, it will be a privilege to see God; in hell, it will be a terror to see God. For us, it will be wonderful; for them, it will be dreadful.

This is how it is all going to end. What a blessed hope we have. We know that even though the wicked seem so successful today, this is their end. And even though we seem so downtrodden and scorned and mocked and persecuted and martyred, this is our end. Therefore, we can afford to be patient, because God always has the last word, and His word is all that matters when it is all said and done.

Let us persevere until we are gathered around the presence of God, and there enjoy His smile and fellowship forever and ever. This is the promise of the seventh trumpet. Let us reflect on that promise and find comfort in that promise as we do spiritual battle against the many antichrists that exist now. Let us be faithful until the day when the Antichrist finally arises and the climactic battle between good and evil is carried out, and Christ triumphs, and His people triumph through Him.